# Sport Public Relations

## Managing Stakeholder Communication

### SECOND EDITION

**G. Clayton Stoldt, EdD**
Wichita State University

**Stephen W. Dittmore, PhD**
University of Arkansas

**Scott E. Branvold, EdD**
Robert Morris University

Human Kinetics

**Library of Congress Cataloging-in-Publication Data**

Stoldt, G. Clayton, 1962-
  Sport public relations : managing stakeholder communication / G. Clayton Stoldt,
Stephen W. Dittmore, Scott E. Branvold. -- 2nd ed.
      p. cm.
  Includes bibliographical references and index.
  ISBN 978-0-7360-9038-4 (hard cover) -- ISBN 0-7360-9038-X (hard cover)  1.
Sports--Public relations. 2.  Mass media and sports. 3.  Communication in
organizations.  I. Dittmore, Stephen W., 1968- II. Branvold, Scott E., 1949- III.
Title.
  GV714.S77 2012
  659.2'9796--dc23
                                        2011046526

ISBN-10: 0-7360-9038-X
ISBN-13: 978-0-7360-9038-4

The web addresses cited in this text were current as of October 2011, unless otherwise noted.

**Acquisitions Editor:** Myles Schrag; **Developmental Editor:** Kevin Matz; **Assistant Editors:** Steven Calderwood, Derek Campbell, and Brendan Shea; **Copyeditor:** Bob Replinger; **Indexer:** Betty Frizzéll; **Permissions Manager:** Dalene Reeder; **Graphic Designer:** Nancy Rasmus; **Graphic Artists:** Nancy Rasmus, Dawn Sills, and Denise Lowry; **Cover Designer:** Keith Blomberg; **Photographer (cover):** © Maksim Yarbinen/Epsilon/Getty Images, © Human Kinetics, and © Jason Allen; **Photographs (interior):** © Human Kinetics unless otherwise noted; **Photo Asset Manager:** Laura Fitch; **Visual Production Assistant:** Joyce Brumfield; **Photo Production Manager:** Jason Allen; **Art Manager:** Kelly Hendren; **Associate Art Manager:** Alan L. Wilborn; **Illustrations:** © Human Kinetics; **Printer:** Sheridan Books

Printed in the United States of America      10  9  8  7  6  5  4  3  2  1

The paper in this book is certified under a sustainable forestry program.

**Human Kinetics**
Website: www.HumanKinetics.com

*United States:* Human Kinetics, P.O. Box 5076, Champaign, IL 61825-5076
800-747-4457
e-mail: humank@hkusa.com

*Canada:* Human Kinetics, 475 Devonshire Road Unit 100, Windsor, ON N8Y 2L5
800-465-7301 (in Canada only)
e-mail: info@hkcanada.com

*Europe:* Human Kinetics, 107 Bradford Road, Stanningley, Leeds LS28 6AT, United Kingdom
+44 (0) 113 255 5665
e-mail: hk@hkeurope.com

*Australia:* Human Kinetics, 57A Price Avenue, Lower Mitcham, South Australia 5062
08 8372 0999
e-mail: info@hkaustralia.com

*New Zealand:* Human Kinetics, P.O. Box 80, Torrens Park, South Australia 5062
0800 222 062
e-mail: info@hknewzealand.com

E5066

# contents

# preface

**Public relations may** be more important in sport than it is in almost any other field. Given intense public and media interest in sport, issues that might be problematic in other industries are full-blown crises in sport. One need look no further than the case of Tiger Woods for an illuminating example. In fall 2009 Woods was widely recognized as the greatest golfer in the world. He was earning nearly $100 million annually in endorsements and was rated in public opinion research as one of America's favorite athletes, second only to Michael Jordan. Then in late 2009 Woods was involved in a series of events that included a mysterious car crash, news reports of multiple extramarital affairs, and public statements from many women who claimed to have been involved in Woods' infidelity. Woods ultimately took a break from the golf tour, entered therapy, and later publicly apologized for his behavior. Months later Woods returned to golf, but he had suffered a significant loss in public support and been dropped by several sponsors, including Gatorade and AT&T. Throughout the crisis, Woods was criticized both for his actions that led to the scandal and for his reluctance to be more forthcoming with the public.

Sport public relations professionals serve individuals and organizations in the field by proactively seeking to build and maintain mutually beneficial relationships with key publics. They may provide counsel regarding how to avoid actions that would harm those relationships, and when mistakes are made, they prescribe actions designed to minimize and repair the damage done.

Anyone who watches ESPN's *SportsCenter* or visits a sports news website will find an array of public relations topics under discussion. Whether the setting is a college athletics program dealing with student–athlete complaints, a professional sport organization advocating the public funding of a new sport facility, a public school system considering a reduction in sport programs, or a coalition of sport organizations promoting better health for the local community, public relations concerns are ubiquitous in sport.

Public relations does not focus exclusively on such concerns. Many sport organizations use public relations as a tool to establish brand awareness and identity and to promote their products or services. Others use public relations to demonstrate social responsibility. Still others design public relations programs to communicate with employees, customers, and investors. Because of these multiple functions, public relations expertise is particularly important for sport management professionals.

This book is written for upper-level undergraduate and graduate students studying sport management or public relations. It will likely also be valuable to practicing sport managers who wish to expand their knowledge of public relations. Although the book briefly discusses the foundations of communication, it assumes that readers already have an understanding of effective written and oral communication. It also assumes that readers understand the scope of the sport industry and have studied fundamental marketing concepts.

The text begins with a chapter on the basics of public relations, including distinctions between public relations and marketing. Chapters 2 and 3 examine the linkages between sport public relations and strategic management. Specifically, they discuss the importance of integrating public relations considerations into managerial decision making and the effects that those decisions can have on the reputation, or more accurately the reputations, of the sport organization. The chapters also address the management of public relations and the way in which campaigns may be planned to maximize effectiveness.

Chapters 4 and 5 pertain to organizational communication. The former chapter considers the many facets of web public relations, and the latter chapter deals with more traditional forms of organizational media. The web public relations chapter includes discussion of both organizational websites and the many forms of social media that have transformed the field in the last five years.

Chapters 6 through 10 examine media relations. Chapter 6 considers the unique relationship between sport and the mass media and related benefits and consequences. Chapter 7 addresses how sport entities can effectively manage their relationships with members of the mass media. Chapter 8 deals with information services such as news releases. Chapter 9 discusses managing the media at events such as news conferences. Chapter 10 focuses on crisis communications, including how to plan for a crisis and select strategies when managing a crisis.

Chapters 11 and 12 focus on the broader community. Chapter 11 deals with unmediated forms of communication, such as public speeches and open houses. Chapter 12 addresses social responsibility and describes how public relations professionals can be involved in managing social responsibility initiatives.

Chapters 13 and 14 examine other key publics. Chapter 13 is devoted to employee and investor relations, and chapter 14 discusses customer, donor, and government or regulator relations.

The 15th and final chapter of the book addresses key legal and ethical considerations in sport public relations. Its subject matter relates in one way or another to all the chapters that precede it.

Within each of these chapters, readers will find a number of elements to assist them in applying the concepts presented. Chapters include Insights From a Professional sidebars written by practitioners that describe what they do and how they do it. Readers will find examples of public relations materials such as a news release and an employee newsletter. They will also find lists of key terms to look for in the chapters and activities for further learning about public relations in sport.

Just as the subject matter of the text is diverse, the purposes of the book are also multiple. Its purposes include helping readers to understand the following:

- The nature of sport public relations, its relationship to sport marketing, and its benefits to sport organizations

- Reputation management in sport and the ways in which sport organizations can use public relations programs to foster desirable relationships with key publics and design campaigns to attain specific public relations objectives

- Organizational media, including traditional and web-based platforms, designed to facilitate communication with key publics

- The unique relationship between sport and the mass media, and related benefits and consequences

- The foundations for effective media relations in sport, including providing appropriate information services to members of the media, staging media events such as news conferences, and offering necessary services to members of the media at events

- The critical nature of crisis communications plans, including crisis planning and crisis management considerations

- The importance and varied nature of community relations, including direct contact with members of key publics through unmediated communication tactics and the development of social responsibility initiatives to benefit both the sport organization and its community

- The purposes and benefits of internal public relations programs directed at employees and investors and external programs designed for customers, donors, and regulators

- The legal and ethical considerations relevant to sport public relations

The text is designed to provide both the theoretical basis for sport public relations as well as guidance on how to apply those concepts. For example, readers will learn about the importance of two-way public relations practices. They will also learn how to gather information from publics using methods such as focus groups and written surveys so that they are prepared to practice two-way public relations.

The authors of the book possess significant professional experience in sport public relations and strongly advocate public relations in their teaching and research. They recognize that other textbooks have made important contributions in the effort to educate students in sport public relations. But they also believe that there is a need for a more comprehensive treatment of the subject. Public relations has traditionally been thought of as publicity that supports the marketing function and media relations that leverage the media's interest in sport organizations. Although these functions are critical, sport public relations includes much more than just promotion and media services. Furthermore, such notions tend to compartmentalize the public relations function rather than present it as a key consideration in strategic management and as an orientation that permeates the sport organization.

The authors hope that this text addresses the need for a more comprehensive treatment in several ways. First, the text addresses media relations as well as other areas such as community relations, employee relations, and government relations. Second, it addresses the links between public relations and managerial concerns such as reputation management. Third, it offers numerous perspectives from sport management experts, practicing public relations professionals, and their constituents regarding how the effects of public relations may be maximized. Guest authors Dr. Anastasios Kaburakis and Dr. Galen Clavio wrote the chapter on legal and ethical considerations. Dr. Kaburakis is an attorney and an assistant professor of management and sports business at Saint Louis University. Dr. Clavio is an assistant professor in the kinesiology department at Indiana University at Bloomington. Other experts have contributed to the Insights From a Professional sidebars found in each chapter.

Readers will find general public relations theory woven into the text, but they may also expect sport-specific applications. Many of the concepts advocated by James Grunig, Larissa Grunig, and David Dozier, authors of the landmark Excellence Study funded by the International Association of Business Communicators, are discussed. The authors are indebted to these scholars and other public relations and sport management experts who have made valuable contributions to the field.

Students who want to break into the field can expect to find enough how-to information in this text to help them write their first news release or plan a community outreach event for a sport organization. Future sport managers can expect to encounter ideas that will prompt them to become proactive in their approach to public relations rather than reactive. And ultimately, professionals in the public relations field can expect this book to help them and their organizations become more progressive in their public relations practices,

resulting in better relationships between sport organizations and their key publics.

## Instructor Resources

New for this edition are the following instructor ancillaries:

- The **instructor guide** includes a summary of each book chapter, sample lecture outlines, student assignments and activities with suggestions regarding how instructors may utilize those activities, selected readings that will enable instructors and students to expand their examination of topics addressed in each chapter, and tips for presenting selected key topics for each chapter. The instructor guide also contains a sample syllabus and a semester-long group project.
- The **test package** includes more than 200 questions, including multiple choice and short answer/essay questions.
- The **presentation package** includes approximately 250 slides of text, artwork, and tables from the book that instructors can use for class discussion and presentation. The slides in the presentation package can be used directly within PowerPoint or printed to make transparencies or handouts for distribution to students. Instructors can easily add, modify, and rearrange the order of the slides.

All instructor ancillaries are offered through the text's website located at **www.HumanKinetics.com/ SportPublicRelations**.

# acknowledgments

**A number of** gracious and skilled people contributed to the development of this text. The authors offer them all a word of sincere appreciation.

Special thanks go to Dr. Anastasios Kaburakis, assistant professor of management and sports business at Saint Louis University, and Dr. Galen Clavio, assistant professor of sport management at Indiana University, for coauthoring the chapter on legal and ethical considerations.

Grateful appreciation also goes to the many writers of the Insights From a Professional sections.

- Chandra Andrews, Wichita State University
- Ted Ayres, Wichita State University
- George Babish, consultant, Y of the USA
- Chris Branvold, Sewickley Heights Golf Club
- Bob Condron, U.S. Olympic Committee
- Murray Evans, Oklahoma Christian University
- Mitch Germann, Edelman
- John Halpin, consultant, sport public relations
- Kathleen Hessert, Sports Media Challenge and BuzzManager
- Tom Kelly, U.S. Ski and Snowboard Association
- John Koluder, Real Salt Lake
- Janae Melvin, MGM Resorts International
- Aprile Pritchet, D.C. United
- Ron Ratner, Northeast Conference
- Dr. Bill Smith, Northwestern State University
- Chris Wyche, Sporting Kansas City
- Frank Zang, Boise State University

Dr. Mark Vermillion, assistant professor of sport management at Wichita State University (WSU), and Mike Ross, sport management educator at WSU, contributed additional sidebars. Ashley Byers, graduate research assistant at Wichita State, compiled the data on media guides displayed in table 5.1 and took several photos that appear in the text. Dr. Kathy Babiak, associate professor of sport management at the University of Michigan, provided valuable information in support of the text examination of corporate social responsibility.

The authors thank Kenny Mossman, senior associate athletic director, communications, at the University of Oklahoma, and Jared Thompson, associate director, communications, at the University of Oklahoma, for their assistance in providing the pages from the Oklahoma 2010–11 Women's Basketball Team Guide found in appendix A.

Several people made important contributions to the sample crisis management plan in appendix B. They include Larry Rankin, assistant athletic director for media relations at Wichita State University; Mike Ross, sports management educator at WSU; and the students of KSS 726, Communication in Sport, from the spring 2003 semester.

The sample community relations plan in appendix C was developed by Kristin Lynch, now with Edward Jones Investments of St. Louis, and Steve Shaad, now with BG Products in Wichita, Kansas. Both are former staff members with the now-defunct Wichita Wranglers baseball franchise.

A number of individuals were of particular assistance in aiding the authors as they sought permission to reprint copyrighted material. They include Dr. Richard Lapchick, endowed chair and director of the DeVos Sport Business Management Program at the University of Central Florida; Geoff McQueen, manager, sales and service, with the Tampa Bay Rays; and Dr. Eric Sexton, athletic director at Wichita State University.

Dr. Scott Branvold expresses gratitude to his colleagues at Robert Morris University—Dr. Artemis Apostolopoulou, Dr. John Clark, and Dr. David Synowka—for their support throughout the process of writing this text. Dr. Steve Dittmore thanks two of his doctoral students at the University of Arkansas—Gi-Yong Koo and Shannon McCarthy—for their assistance in the development of ancillary materials. And Dr. Clay Stoldt offers appreciation to his faculty colleagues at Wichita State University—Dr. Mark Vermillion, Dr. Jeff Noble, and Mike Ross—as well as administrative specialist Mary Myers and graduate assistant Ashley Byers.

Sincere appreciation goes to Myles Schrag, acquisitions editor at Human Kinetics, Kevin Matz, developmental editor, and the rest of the staff at Human Kinetics for partnering with the authors in the development of this text.

Finally, the authors would like to offer a special word of thanks to their families for the sacrifices that they made while the text was being written. Clay thanks his wife, Sally, and son, Ryan; Steve thanks his wife, Andrea, and son, Andrew; and Scott thanks his wife, Lynda, and son, Christopher and family.

# Introducing Sport Public Relations

**After reading this chapter, students should be able to**

- define public relations in sport and distinguish it from related concepts such as marketing, promotion, and publicity;
- understand the basic skills that sport public relations professionals need to perform their job;
- identify common forms of public relations practice in sport; and
- recognize the benefits that the public relations function brings to sport organizations.

**Key terms discussed in this chapter include**

- sport public relations,
- publics,
- sport marketing,
- promotion,
- publicity,
- media relations,
- community relations, and
- brand.

**Promotion, hype, spin.** These are just a few of the ways that people commonly think of public relations. Consider the following examples.

- Promotion: "I'm really exciting. I smile a lot. I win a lot, and I'm really sexy."

  *Serena Williams, professional tennis player*

- Hype: "You're talking about the transformation of a society. This project can actually bind the nation."

  *Danny Jordan, CEO of the World Cup Organizing Committee, as quoted in Sports Illustrated about South Africa's preparing to host the 2010 event*

- Spin: "During the times I gambled as a manager, I never took an unfair advantage. . . . I never allowed my wagers to influence my baseball decisions. So in my mind, I wasn't corrupt."

  *Pete Rose, former baseball manager, admitting that he bet on baseball but arguing that it did not compromise the integrity of the game.*

But are these examples truly indicative of public relations in sport?

In the best tradition of academic writing, the answer to that question is both yes and no. Yes, those are examples of public relations in action, although at least one is not necessarily the best example of effective public relations practice. And no, they do not come close to representing the whole of what public relations is within sport.

Therefore, it seems appropriate to begin this book with an examination of the nature of public relations, its relationship with marketing, and the ways in which it may be distinguished from promotion and publicity. This chapter also describes the basic skills that sport public relations professionals must possess to perform effectively. The chapter also discusses the most common forms of public relations practice in sport. These forms include, but are not limited to, media relations, community relations, employee relations, and customer relations. Finally, it addresses the benefits that public relations brings to the sport organization.

## Definition of Sport Public Relations

Disagreement exists regarding the definition of public relations in general and sport public relations in particular (Hall, Nichols, Moynahan, & Taylor, 2007). Most of the writing on the subject within the realm of sport management has focused on public relations as a marketing tool (Stoldt, Dittmore, & Branvold, 2003). But sport public relations has also been discussed from a broader perspective (see, for example, McGowan & Bouris, 2005; Pedersen, Miloch, & Laucella, 2007; Stier, 2003). For the purpose of this text, the authors blend elements of three definitions that skew toward the latter, broader approach. The first definition is from Broom (2009), who defined public relations as "the management function that identifies, establishes, and maintains mutually beneficial relationships between an organization and the various publics on whom its success or failure depends" (p. 7). The second is similar, coming from Stoldt, Pratt, and Dittmore (2007), who described sport public relations as the "organizational function that fosters the development of positive relationships between the organization and its most important publics" (p. 243). The third comes from the scholars behind the Excellence Study (Grunig, 1992), a comprehensive study of public relations practice in varied settings. They described public relations as the management of communication between an organization and its publics.

The resultant combination of those three approaches follows and serves as the working definition for this text.

> **Sport public relations** is a managerial communication-based function designed to identify a sport organization's key publics, evaluate its relationships with those publics, and foster desirable relationships between the sport organization and those publics.

Several aspects of this definition warrant explanation. First, sport public relations is a management function. It is as critical to the organization's effectiveness as other managerial activities such as human resource management and marketing. In fact, public relations overlaps with both of those and other managerial activities. This overlap is discussed in detail later, but the critical point for the moment is that public relations cannot be effective unless it is integrated into the organization's managerial function (Dozier, Grunig, & Grunig, 1995).

Second, sport public relations is a communication-based practice. Although not exclusively composed of communication activities, it is certainly predicated on them. Relationship experts ranging from Dr. Phil to public relations scholars will attest to the reality that healthy relationships are characterized by effective communication between the parties involved. Communication is so critical to public relations that some scholars use the two terms interchangeably (Dozier et al., 1995). Of course, communication is much more than public relations. The sidebar titled Conceptualizing Communication in Sport describes a model that portrays the broad and diverse nature of sport communication.

Third, sport public relations must be a systematic practice if its effectiveness is to be maximized. It begins with the identification of the sport organization's key publics. **Publics** may be thought of as groups of people who relate to the sport organization in similar ways. They may include members of the mass media, members of the sport organization's community, as well as its employees, customers, donors, and investors. But it is simplistic to assume that everyone within a general stakeholder group holds similar perspectives and attitudes (Grunig & Repper, 1992). Sport organizations must often target public relations activities at specific publics within broader stakeholder groups. For example, neighbors and nearby businesses may be a stakeholder group for a professional sport franchise, but a select group of those nearby residents who complain about the noise and trash associated with home events are a specific public who warrant organizational attention. Parent (2008), in an analysis of the 1999 Pan American Games in Winnipeg, Canada, noted this distinction by observing that although members of stakeholder groups appeared to hold common interests, they sometimes differed in regard to the specific issue categories that concerned them. For instance, the members of the media stakeholder group shared general interests such as access to the information that they needed to succeed in their work, but the specific issue categories varied among print, radio, and television representatives. These findings demonstrated the "need to analyze stakeholder issues at a sub-stakeholder-group level" (Parent, 2008, p. 155).

After those important substakeholder groups or publics have been identified, the sport organization must evaluate the nature of its relationships with those publics, the relative strengths of those relationships, and the issues that will likely influence those relationships in the future. Such an assessment is critical before the sport organization can develop public relations programs and campaigns.

Finally, if effectively practiced, sport public relations results in desirable relationships. The nature of these relationships varies by public, and many will be addressed in subsequent chapters. One such outcome might be that the sport organization is treated well by members of the mass media. Another might be that members of the community view the organization as socially responsible. Still another might be that the organization's stockholders value their investment and are satisfied with the organization's financial performance. Whoever the public may be, the management team of the organization can define a realistically desirable relationship that might exist between the two parties. The function of public relations is to facilitate achievement of that desired outcome.

# Characteristics of Sport Public Relations

Public relations is often confused with marketing, but the two are distinct yet complementary functions within the sport organization. The relationship between the two functions involves promotion and publicity—two other terms often used synonymously with public relations. The sections that follow distinguish public relations from marketing, promotion, and publicity.

## Public Relations and Marketing

Like public relations, marketing in sport has been defined in several ways. One commonly accepted definition comes from Mullin, Hardy, and Sutton (2007), who wrote the following:

> Sport marketing consists of all activities designed to meet the needs and wants of sport consumers through exchange processes. Sport marketing has developed two major thrusts: the marketing of sport products and services directly to consumers of sport, and the marketing of other consumer and industrial products or services through the use of sport promotions. (p. 11)

**Sport marketing** is the organizational function that focuses on consumers, identifies how the sport organization may meet the consumers' desires, and structures marketing programs accordingly. As a result, certain exchanges take place. The sport organization provides its consumers with something of value—entertainment, recreation, fitness, or some other commodity. In exchange, consumers provide the sport organization with something of value—commonly money, but sometimes things such as their time, energy, or attention.

3

# Conceptualizing Communication in Sport

In their book *Strategic Sport Communication*, authors Pedersen, Miloch, and Laucella (2007) presented the strategic sport communication model (SSCM, see figure 1.1). The model conceptualizes the nature of sport communication, the types of communication, and the various settings in which communication occurs within sport. Although it is recommended that students read this important book in its entirety, this sidebar includes a summary of the model's central elements.

The sport communication process is portrayed as the model's upper and lower elements and rightfully so. Pedersen et al. recognized what many other communication scholars (i.e., Lasswell, 1948; Shannon & Weaver, 1949) have concluded—that communication is a multifaceted and dynamic process. For a message to be communicated, it must have a sender who encodes it in some form and sends it by some communication channel to a receiver who decodes the message within a particular environment that may be subject to message interference. Other factors may influence the process of the communication as well, so the process that permeates sport communication is in itself quite complex.

The first component in the middle of the SSCM features the types of communication that occur at the personal and organizational levels. Intrapersonal communication relates to the internal communication that occurs within people as they think and experience life. Interpersonal communication takes place between two people, and small group communication occurs when the participants number three or more. Organizationally, communication happens on an intraorganizational, or internal, basis and interorganizational, or external, basis. These concepts relate directly to the various forms of public relations described in this

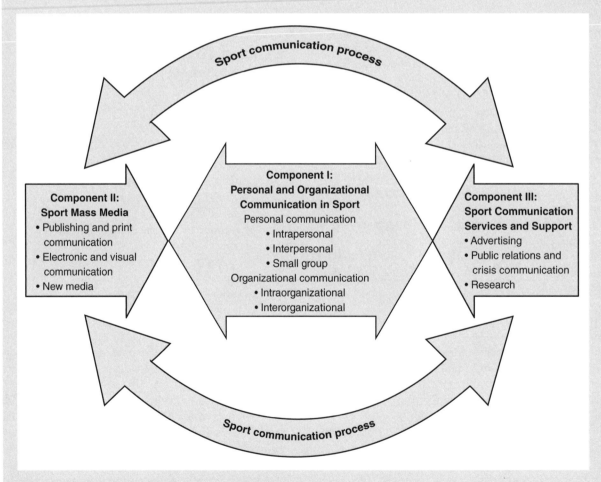

**Figure 1.1**  Strategic sport communication model.

Reprinted, by permission, from P.M. Pedersen, K.S. Jiloch, and P.C. Laucella, 2007, *Strategic sport communication* (Champaign, IL: Human Kinetics), 85.

text—intraorganizational including employee relations and interorganizational including media relations and other forms of public relations.

The second component among the middle elements of the SSCM represents one of the major settings for sport communication, the sport mass media. This setting includes professionals working in print media settings such as newspapers and magazines, electronic media settings such as television or radio stations, and new media settings such as sport websites. A significant portion of this textbook is devoted to media relations in sport, so the sport mass media will be discussed in detail later in the book.

The third component among the middle elements of the SSCM depicts the organizational units commonly tasked with executing the communication services and providing communication support. Advertising is one such unit, a function that will be described in more detail later in this chapter. Public relations, the subject of this text, is also included in this component, as is research. The research function is critical to the effective use of advertising and public relations, and research will be addressed in subsequent chapters.

Sport marketing varies from sport public relations in at least two fundamental ways. First, marketing focuses on consumers, but public relations focuses on more diverse groups of publics (Broom, 2009). Consumers are a stakeholder group critical to both functions, but the scope of public relations activity extends well beyond consumers.

Figure 1.2 illustrates this notion. It is an admittedly simplistic portrayal of the interactions between a sport organization and some, but not all, of its most important publics, both internal and external. The figure illustrates several important points. First, the sport organization's public relations programs may relate to numerous publics as indicated by the solid arrows extending from the organization to and from the various publics. The marketing programs, however, are directed only toward the target markets within the organization's population of consumers (or even potential consumers) as indicated by the dashed arrow extending to and from the organization and its customers. Second, public relations programs may be directed at both broad stakeholder groups and specific publics within larger stakeholder groups. The large boxes represent stakeholder groups such as the local community, although a number of specific publics may exist

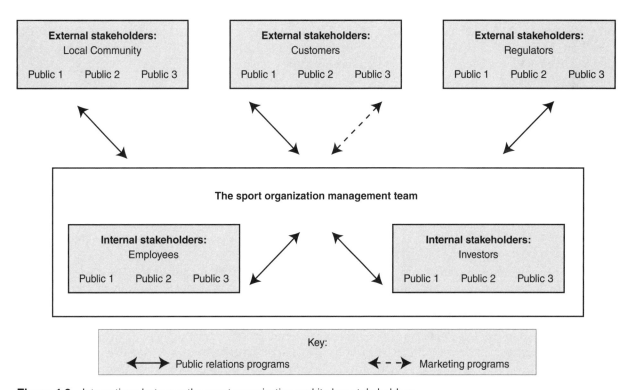

**Figure 1.2** Interactions between the sport organization and its key stakeholders.

within each of those groups. For instance, within the local community are specific publics such as neighbors, charitable groups, and complementary businesses who may have vested interests in the sport organization. The issues of interest, again, vary from one public to another. Third, public relations programs may be directed at external stakeholders such as members of the community and regulators (e.g., governmental entities) as well as internal stakeholders (e.g., employees). Fourth, public relations programs should involve two-way communication between the sport organizations and its publics, as the two-way arrows indicate.

Such discussion is not meant to minimize the importance of marketing. The exchanges that marketing facilitates are critical to the existence of most sport organizations. But by definition the marketing function does not address publics outside the organization's target markets. These publics may include employees, investors, regulators, the local community, and more. Public relations, on the other hand, does engage such publics.

Another difference between the two functions is that the goal of marketing differs somewhat from the goal of public relations. As noted, exchanges are at the heart of marketing activities (Broom, 2009; Milne & McDonald, 1999; Shilbury, 2009). Public relations, however, focuses on the broader concept of relationships. The two concepts are related but not synonymous. Scholars differentiate between exchange relationships and communal relationships (Clark & Mills, 1979). Exchange relationships are based on the sharing of benefits between the parties involved. One provides benefits and expects to receive benefits in return. Communal relationships, however, are predicated on concern for the other party. One provides benefits to the other but does not expect to receive anything in return except seeing the other party benefit. A 2008 newspaper report told the story of how University of Oklahoma football coach Bob Stoops had spent the last eight years visiting kids in an area children's hospital (Helsley, 2008). Few knew of his charitable work before that time. As stated by one of Stoops' former players, "It's not a publicity thing. It's him being who he is" (Gutierrez quoted in Helsley, 2008). Such activity by Stoops and the many other sport figures who maintain low profiles while engaging in charitable work stand as evidence of communal relationships in sport.

Some similarities do exist between public relations and marketing. For example, the two functions are both concerned with identifying specific groups of people (i.e., publics, target markets), learning about those people, and then systematically interacting with them (Hallahan, 1992). Public relations and marketing are similar in another way. Sport organizations not only market their own products and services but also may serve as platforms for other organizations, such as corporate sponsors, to market their products and services. Similarly, sport organizations not only engage in their own public relations programs but also may serve as vehicles for nonsport organizations to execute their own public relations programs. One such example of this is detailed in chapter 12, which describes how sport and nonsport businesses may engage in partnerships that leverage both parties' community relations efforts.

## Public Relations, Promotion, and Publicity

Sport marketers seek to develop a marketing mix that will meet the needs and wants of their consumers. The marketing mix is made up of the four Ps—product, price, place, and promotion (McCarthy, 1960). The product component focuses on developing goods or services customized to consumers' needs. The price component specifies the costs that consumers will incur in exchange for the product. The place component relates to distribution decisions, physically linking the consumer and the product. And **promotion** relates to communicating messages to the consumer regarding the product and attempting to motivate the consumer to make the exchange.

Sport marketers often think of public relations as a promotional tactic. Four elements make up the promotional mix—advertising, personal selling, sales promotions, and publicity. Advertising may be described as commercial messages regarding the product carried by mass media. In personal sales a representative of the sport organization interacts with consumers in an effort to motivate them to buy. Sales promotions vary, but they frequently include additional incentives to the consumer such as premium giveaways, discounts, or other attempts to add value to the core product. Finally, **publicity** refers to information regarding the product or sport organization conveyed through the mass media for free.

Figure 1.3 portrays the marketing and promotional mixes as traditionally described. Some sport marketing experts, recognizing the increased importance of public relations to effective marketing, have added public relations as a fifth P to the marketing

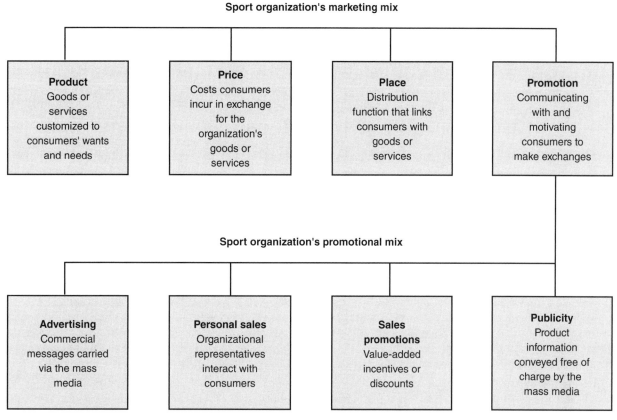

**Figure 1.3** The sport marketing and promotional mixes.

mix (Mullin et al., 2007). Their rationale is that some sport businesses (e.g., professional sport, collegiate sport) experience such high levels of media visibility that public relations warrants consideration as a distinct aspect of the marketing mix.

Still another approach to conceptualizing the promotional mix lists both publicity and community relations alongside advertising, incentives, personal contact, atmospherics (e.g., interior design, sensory elements), licensing, and sponsorship (Irwin, Sutton, & McCarthy, 2008). Community relations is included because of its potential to enhance the reputation of the sport organization, because the organization's reputation affects its ability to market its products and services. Community relations also has the power to generate positive publicity.

Given the distinctions among public relations, promotion, and publicity, it is erroneous to refer to the three terms interchangeably. Public relations frequently generates publicity. This publicity can be effective in informing people about the sport organization's product and motivating them to consume. Public relations thus may rightfully be considered as directly relating to promotion, but promotion is not the only function of public relations within the

sport organization. In addition, the publicity that frequently results from public relations activity is only one of many possible positive results that public relations can generate. Informed sport managers both think and speak of these concepts distinctively.

# Sport Public Relations in Practice

Although the practice of public relations is diverse within sport, practitioners must possess certain basic skill sets. The sidebar titled Basic Skills Underlying the Practice of Public Relations in Sport lists these skills and offers some ideas regarding potential resources for developing them.

The two most prominent ways in which public relations is practiced in sport are media relations and community relations (Mullin et al., 2007; Stoldt et al., 2007). Subsequent sections address those two forms of public relations as well as other types of public relations such as employee relations, investor relations, customer relations, donor relations, and government relations.

# Basic Skills Underlying the Practice of Public Relations in Sport

Sport public relations is predicated on the employment of basic skills. These skills are the foundation on which the more advanced skills described in this text are based. Readers likely already possess some competency in these areas. Following are a summary of underlying skill sets and recommendations regarding how students may further develop their capabilities in these areas.

## Writing Skills

Professionals working in a variety of sport industry sectors cite the preeminent importance of writing skills (Britten, 2001; Laubscher, 2001). Although the channels through which information is carried vary from news releases to publications to blogs, the core competency remains constant—being able to write effectively. Writing skills cannot be developed simply by accessing educational resources. They must be honed through practice. Students interested in sport public relations or even those who anticipate using such skills in jobs that are not public relations specific should look for any opportunity to develop such skills. Writing for campus publications can provide invaluable experience, as can volunteer work alongside sport public relations professionals. Newspapers often hire "stringers" who write small stories (e.g., high school sports reporting) on a part-time basis. Students should also consider taking writing-intensive college courses, such as those offered in many mass communication programs. The key element in each of these settings is that professionals or educators critique the students' writing and offer suggestions for improvement. Students looking to develop their writing skills can also access a variety of resources that provide insights on writing effectiveness. One commonly recommended resource is *The Elements of Style* (Strunk & White, 2008), a handbook that addresses basic grammatical and syntax issues that writers commonly encounter.

## Public Presentation Competencies

Although public relations professionals may not be called on to give speeches as often as high-profile coaches and managers are, they frequently moderate news conferences and other special events and serve as organizational spokespersons. Furthermore, they may be called on to coach other members of the organization such as senior managers, coaches, and athletes as they seek to develop their own public presentation abilities. Like writing, this skill requires practice. Communication courses that focus on public speaking can offer invaluable experience, and the professional literature includes many books on the topic. The National Speakers Association offers student memberships that include both networking and professional development benefits.

## Desktop Publishing Capabilities

Many sport public relations professionals produce printed materials such as news releases, brochures, flyers, media guides, game programs, and posters. Layout and design skills are required to produce such publications. Many colleges and universities offer desktop publishing courses that prospective sport public relations professionals should definitely take. Most of the software applications for producing these materials provide user's guides, and books specific to applications such as InDesign, PageMaker, and Photoshop are available. As noted, reading the book is an important step, but practicing the development of the skill is critical.

## Internet-Related Competencies

A set of skills that is taking on even greater importance involves Internet-related competencies. All prospective sport managers, whether public relations is specific to their position or not, need to have basic competencies in areas such as using e-mail and navigating the Internet. Public relations professionals often need to take those skills to the next level by being able to create and update web pages and generate content in multiple settings. They are frequently expected to possess graphic arts and design skills specific to website development. Further, public relations professionals are increasingly using social networking platforms such as Facebook and Twitter, and they are interacting with members of their key publics by blogging. College courses pertaining to Internet-related skill are now common. Books such as *Groundswell: Winning in a World Transformed by Social Technologies* (Li & Bernoff, 2008) and *The New Rules of Marketing and*

*PR: How to Use News Releases, Blogs, Podcasting, Viral Marketing, and Online Media to Reach Buyers Directly* (Scott, 2008) are also excellent resources.

## Interpersonal Skills

A final set of skills critical to the profession is interpersonal competencies (Britten, 2001; Douglas, 2001; Laubscher, 2001; McGowan & Bouris, 2005). People who are highly skilled in the technical aspects of the job but do not possess strong interpersonal skills will be less successful in the field. Some people possess a personality that lends itself to success in this area. They enjoy interacting with others, can multitask without becoming stressed, and can remain calm in adversarial situations. Others may need to cultivate these qualities. Courses in leadership or team building are often beneficial in building interpersonal skills. Many colleges have counseling centers that offer interpersonal skill assessments and services that may assist in the development of these critical qualities.

# Media Relations in Sport

The most common form of public relations program in sport is media relations. More sport management jobs are likely available in this public relations specialization than in any other. Accordingly, this text devotes considerable attention to media relations and introduces its readers to a number of practitioners working in sport media relations. Mitch Germann is one such professional, and the sidebar titled Building a Career in Sport Public Relations describes his career in media relations and other forms of public relations.

## Goals of Sport Media Relations

As the term implies, **media relations** aims to foster desirable relationships with members of the mass media. Media relations programs are designed to generate favorable publicity and minimize unfavorable publicity. Publicity may be thought of as information regarding the sport product or organization conveyed free through the mass media. It is an extremely credible form of communication because the information comes from a mass media outlet, not the sport organization (Ries & Ries, 2002). For example, sports fans might expect their local minor league hockey team to tout the importance of its next game, but they are likely to perceive a similar, noncommercial message received through their local newspaper or television station as more credible. The greater the quantity of favorable publicity that the organization receives, the more likely it is that the organization and its products or services will be held in high regard by consumers and other key publics.

Most sport organizations seek favorable publicity of some kind or another. Professional sport leagues, teams, and events seek to maintain a significant presence on sports pages, broadcasts, and websites frequented by audiences on a local and regional level, if not a national level. Intercollegiate athletics programs seek similar levels of visibility. For-profit and nonprofit fitness centers seek publicity to introduce new services to the public or to showcase new facilities. Sporting goods manufacturers cultivate publicity for new products or for the achievements of high-visibility coaches or athletes who use their products. Specialized sport service providers such as agents and marketing representatives also look for publicity to enhance their clients' reputations and ultimately make them more valuable to their team and affiliated sponsors.

Two models commonly describe the practice of sport media relations. The first is a press agentry and publicity model (Grunig & Hunt, 1984). Practitioners employing this model seek to cultivate as much publicity as possible for their organizations. Some even violate the boundaries of what many people consider acceptable behavior to receive that publicity. "There's no such thing as bad publicity," they rationalize, and their tactics are often successful in gaining media coverage. Former Major League Baseball player Jose Canseco has frequently sought media attention as he has confessed his own use of performing-enhancing drugs, accused other players of similar cheating, and disparaged franchise managers and league officials. Although Canseco is rarely portrayed as a sympathetic figure, he did benefit from the coverage because his books have made him possibly the most successful athlete author of all time (Rovell, 2008). The press agentry and publicity model is also often used in ethical fashion. For example, many professional and college teams hold media days at some point during their preseasons. One of the primary purposes of media days is to generate favorable publicity in advance of the new season. Perhaps the largest (and, in some instances,

# Building a Career in Sport Public Relations

## Mitch Germann

Photo courtesy of Mitch Germann.

By today's standards, I got a late start to my career in sports public relations. It wasn't until near the end of my undergrad days at the University of Kansas (KU) that I realized I wanted to pursue that career path.

Once I knew I wanted to focus on sports public relations, I went to work on gaining experience. I was fortunate during the summer before my final year at KU to secure an internship with the Wichita Advantage, a team in the World Team Tennis league. The experience of being involved in every aspect of operations for a small pro team helped pave the way for what was yet to come.

Two significant things happened the following spring—I was accepted into the sports administration master's program at Wichita State University (WSU), and I was chosen to work on a press information team for the 1996 Olympic Games. Both were key factors in advancing my career.

Fresh upon graduation from the University of Kansas and coming off my experience at the '96 Olympics, I started grad school at WSU in the fall of 1996. Although public relations was my passion, I wasn't able to secure a graduate assistant position in the athletics media relations office. Instead, I was placed in the development department, where I worked on projects for the Shocker booster program. But the athletics department staff at WSU let me volunteer for as many events as possible doing media relations work. They knew my goal was to work in sports public relations, and they allowed me to gain some much-needed experience at the collegiate level.

After completing my year of class work and getting good experience in the WSU athletics department, I landed an internship back at my alma mater in the KU athletics media relations office. I spent that season learning the ins and outs of the office, assisting with football and men's and women's basketball, and serving as the primary media contact for the softball team.

Following that season, I was offered the position of assistant media relations director to replace the primary media contact for volleyball and baseball. My goal at the time was to become the primary media contact for a Division I men's basketball team, so I spent every free minute I had outside my duties with volleyball and baseball chipping in with all the men's basketball work I could handle.

I spent two seasons in that role before being given an opportunity I never expected. When our primary men's basketball contact left, I was promoted to director of media relations to be the primary media contact for the KU men's basketball team. Despite receiving resumes from all over the country from people who were much more qualified than I was, Doug Vance, Richard Konzem, Coach Williams, and the late Dr. Bob Frederick took a chance and promoted me from within. I'll never be able to thank them enough for that opportunity.

What followed were four of the most memorable years of my career. Working with the Jayhawks men's basketball team, I was able to experience two Final Fours and work with All-American players like Nick Collison, Drew Gooden, and Kirk Hinrich. I also had the pleasure of working with and learning from a Hall of Fame coach in Coach Williams for three years and one of the best young coaches in the country in Coach Self for one season. To top it off, I was lucky enough to work closely with an amazing group of local, regional, and national media members who covered college basketball.

Then, just after the 2003–04 season, I made one of the most difficult decisions of my career.

Despite my love for KU and all the amazing experiences I had working for my alma mater, I decided I needed to broaden my experience. All my experience in public relations to that point had been reactive—I never had to work to place a story in my life. In fact, I probably spent more time saying no to reporters than saying yes. I believed that to advance my career and be in a position to take on more responsibility, I would need to see public relations from the other side.

> I needed to understand the process behind working proactively to get coverage, meshing public relations with marketing efforts, and driving results to increase revenue.

I needed to understand the process behind working proactively to get coverage, meshing public relations with marketing efforts, and driving results to increase revenue.

Enter Fleishman-Hillard (FH). As the world's largest public relations firm, FH has offices everywhere and already had a portfolio of sports-related clients. I landed a position in the Kansas City office working with such clients as Hallmark, the National Collegiate Athletic Association (NCAA), and country music singer Clay Walker. That job gave me two years of invaluable experience and a crash course in proactive public relations work.

Although my time at FH was crucial to advancing my career, I was mindful that if you stay out of sport for too long, you will likely have a tough time getting back in. That said, I was intrigued when I received a call one day from the Professional Bowlers Association (PBA). One of my former coworkers at KU worked there and recommended me for the position of director of public relations.

The PBA was purchased by three of the original employees of Microsoft, who moved it to Seattle and hired some of the best sport marketing minds in the country, many from Nike, to boost its exposure. I was offered a position to head up public relations for the league, and I ended up overseeing marketing and community relations as well. This was a great opportunity to combine my experience at KU with what I learned at FH and try to help the league get more exposure and drive results.

What I didn't know at the time was the PBA would provide me with additional experience that drove getting me where I am today. Because of our Microsoft connections and having a cutting-edge young staff, we were ahead of the game in terms of using social media platforms to help drive marketing and public relations results. In my two-plus years with the PBA, we were deep into relationship marketing. Using targeted e-mail outreach, we launched bowling's first-ever online social network, a mobile platform, and an on-demand online video channel.

Then another surprise came my way when I received a call from a recruiting firm about a job with Maloof Sports & Entertainment, working for the Sacramento Kings and Monarchs. I was immediately interested. Basketball has always been my passion, Sacramento has an excellent reputation for supporting its teams, and I heard great things about the Maloof family.

After a long and educational interview process, I was offered the position of vice president of business communications in December 2007. I was excited, knowing that this was the exact role I had in mind when I made the decision to leave KU in 2004. Overseeing new media, public relations, and community service for an NBA and WNBA franchise seemed like just the right fit, and it certainly has been so far.

*Mitch Germann is the former vice president of business communications for Maloof Sports & Entertainment. In 2011 he accepted a new position as vice president, digital for Edelman in Seattle.*

the zaniest) media day is the one staged by the NFL each year before the Super Bowl. An estimated 5,000 media representatives—some from traditional sport media outlets, others from non-sport-related entertainment properties—participated in media day activities before the 2011 Super Bowl (Horn, 2011). Additional information pertaining to media days is presented in chapter 9.

The second model is a public information model that focuses on providing effective service to members of the mass media who are already inclined to cover the sport organization (Grunig & Hunt, 1984). Professionals using this model do not want to risk embarrassing their organization by using questionable methods to seek attention. They may not even actively solicit media coverage, but they do nurture the coverage that they receive by effectively meeting the informational needs of the media. For instance, they may accommodate a newspaper reporter who contacts them in the hope of arranging an interview with a player or coach, or they may produce a media guide that members of the press can use as a reference tool throughout a particular sport's season.

Grunig and Hunt (1984) argued that sport is one of the most common settings in which the press agentry model is employed. Sport media relations professionals with minor league sport teams, athletics programs that are not NCAA Division I, sport service providers, and sporting goods manufacturers are among those who operate as press agents, proactively seeking publicity for their organizations. Those working at the highest levels of professional and college sport are much more likely to be able to operate from a public information model and still secure substantial media presence for their organizations. Sometimes media relations professionals within a single organization use both proactive and reactive models depending on the season or time of year. For example, public relations staff members at the Maryland Jockey Club function as press agents for most of the year, proactively seeking attention in the mass media. But they shift to a public information model each spring as their marquee event, the Preakness (the second leg of horse racing's Triple Crown), approaches (Henniger, 2003).

Favorable publicity is an asset that sport organizations covet, but unfavorable publicity is a liability that they cannot afford. Results of an experiment regarding how audiences responded to positive and negative news relating to a Major League Baseball team indicated that the publicity affected readers' feelings and beliefs about the organization, and these effects were particularly pronounced among some segments of the audience (Funk & Pritchard, 2006). Specifically, audience members who were not predisposed to a high level of commitment to the team were particularly affected by the publicity. The researchers observed that "negative publicity can pose a very real threat to a sport organization's market base and affect revenue beyond the turnstile" (Funk & Pritchard, 2006, p. 619). Arguably, the potential for damage resulting from negative publicity is even greater in today's communications environment that features real-time communication on social media platforms, much of which comes from individuals who are not necessarily concerned with traditional journalistic values such as accuracy and fairness. For instance, when NFL Chicago Bears quarterback Jay Cutler left a 2011 playoff game with a knee injury, several other NFL players immediately posted tweets (i.e., Twitter account messages), accusing him of lacking toughness (Trotter, 2011). Those tweets were then repeated by others and subsequently reported in mainstream media channels, resulting in a major storyline relating to the Bears' loss to the Packers.

Media relations professionals can sometimes negate unfavorable publicity by advising members of their organizations how to avoid public relations mistakes. They can choose to withhold embarrassing or damaging facts from members of the media. They can even lead their organization in successfully weathering a crisis when embarrassing or damaging facts about the organization have been publicized. But it is inappropriate for media relations professionals or other sport organization employees to ask members of the mass media not to report such information after it has been discovered.

## Jobs in Sport Media Relations

Sport media relations professionals work in a variety of settings, including professional sport teams and leagues, college athletics programs and their conference offices, and national governing bodies. Media relations responsibilities may be among those assumed by marketing and promotions directors at fitness centers or by the corporate communications staff in sporting goods companies. When it comes to full-time jobs in media relations, however, the two most common job settings are professional sport, where job titles usually include the term *media relations*, and intercollegiate sport, where job titles often include the terms *sports information* or *athletic communications*.

Professional teams and leagues at the highest levels may employ multiple employees in their media relations departments. On the other end of the continuum are minor league teams, which are more likely to have just one full- or part-time media relations employee. Major League Baseball's Arizona Diamondbacks employ nine staff members in their communications department, a unit that includes media relations but not community relations (MLB Advanced Media, n.d.). One of their minor league affiliates, the Lancaster (California) JetHawks, assigns media relations responsibilities to its radio play-by-play broadcaster (Lancaster JetHawks, n.d.).

The college media relations setting is similar to professional sport in that the size of the staff varies according to the size of the organization. Within the National Collegiate Athletic Association (NCAA), some of the larger programs have more than 20 people working in their media relations departments. Athletics programs at the NCAA Division II or III level and within the National Association of Intercollegiate Athletics (NAIA) and the National Junior College Athletic Association (NJCAA) usually have a full-time or part-time media relations employee, or they may assign media relations to a coach or university public relations employee. Ohio State University, a NCAA Football Bowl Subdivision program, employs 12 full-time media relations staff members along with an intern and 10 students who work on a part-time basis. Friends University, a NAIA Division II program in Wichita, Kansas, has no one assigned to media relations on a full-time basis. Its athletic director also serves as its sports information director.

A modest amount of research has been devoted to sport public relations in general, and a handful of studies have addressed college athletic communications work in particular. Table 1.1 summarizes

## Table 1.1 Four Studies of Sports Information Professionals

| Variable | Neupauer (1999) | Stoldt (2000) | Hardin and McClung (2002) | Miloch and Pedersen (2006) |
|---|---|---|---|---|
| Sample | 61 sports information staff members at varied competitive levels | 187 CoSIDA members at NCAA I-A level | 86 sports information directors at NCAA I-A and I-AA levels | 15 sports information directors in a NCAA I mid-level conference |
| Age—range | NA | 24–57 years | 23–60 years | 92.9% were 25–49 |
| Age—mean or median | NA | 34.9 years | 35.4 years | NA |
| Gender breakdown | 11.5% female 88.5% male | 29.9% female 70.1% male | 10.8% female 89.2% male | 7.1% female 92.9% male |
| Education breakdown (highest degree attained) | 82.0% bachelor's 18.0% master's | 0.5% high school 63.1% bachelor's 36.4% master's | NA | 53.3% bachelor's 33% master's 13.7% other |
| Area of undergraduate study | NA | NA | 38% journalism or public relations 24% communications 15% business 10% sport management 13% other | All had either bachelor's in journalism or master's in sport management |
| Years of professional experience—range | NA | 2–32 years | 3–36 years | 69% 5 years or fewer 23.9% 6–15 years 7.1% 16–20 years |
| Years of professional experience—mean or median | NA | 11.7 years | 16.8 years | NA |
| Salary—range | NA | $16,000–$69,700 | NA | NA |
| Salary—mean or median | NA | $35,633 | NA | NA |
| Salary breakdown | 62.3% $38,000 or less 37.7% more than $38,000 | NA | 18.1% less than $35,000 21.7% $35,000–$44,999 33.7% $45,000–$54,999 18.1% $55,000–$64,999 8.4% more than $65,000 | "Highest percentage" $45,000–$54,900 14.2% less than $35,000 14.2% more than $55,000 |
| Staff size—range | NA | 1–14 people* | 5–29 people** | NA |
| Staff size—mean | NA | 4.62 people | 13.21 people | NA |

NA = Not available.

*Defined as full-time staff members.

**Defined as full-time staff members, interns, undergraduate students, and graduate students.

13

some of the descriptive statistics that those studies generated. Although the makeup of the samples varied, some trends are evident. The average age of athletic communications professionals is the mid-30s. Males dominate the profession. Most athletic communications professionals possess bachelor's degrees, and a smaller number possess master's degrees. The sidebar Research on College Athletics Media Relations addresses other facets of the aforementioned studies and introduces key findings from a few others.

Media relations professionals in professional and collegiate sport assume a similar set of primary responsibilities. These responsibilities include

## Research on College Athletics Media Relations

A number of studies conducted in recent years have shed light on the nature of college athletics media relations work. Hardin and McClung (2002) reported that sports information professionals at the Division I-A (now known as the Football Bowl Subdivision) level have more professional experience and receive higher salaries for non-entry-level positions than do their counterparts at I-AA (now know as the Football Championship Subdivision) institutions. Division I-A sports information staffs were also larger than I-AA staffs in terms of both full-time staff members and total staff members, including students and interns.

Miloch and Pedersen (2006) surveyed sports information directors in a mid-level NCAA Division I conference regarding their relationships with members of the media. Respondents indicated their relationships with media professionals were highly important, positive, and mutually beneficial. They also reported those positive relationships directly impacted the type of coverage their sports programs received and that coverage impacted the marketability of those programs. The study's authors concluded "...relationship building in sports information is a key aspect of the SID's professional obligations" (Miloch & Pedersen, 2006, p. 101).

Stoldt (2000) reported that there are two professional roles for sports information practitioners—manager and technician. Managers assume responsibility for public relations, counsel athletics management regarding how to address public relations concerns, and facilitate communication between the organization and its publics. Technicians employ specific communication crafts such as writing news releases, maintaining media contacts, and producing sports information materials. Most sports information professionals in the 2000 study functioned primarily as technicians.

In a related study, Stoldt and Narasimhan (2005) examined how college athletics media relations professionals rated their skills in a variety of public relations tasks and how important those tasks were to the organizations they served. Results indicated that practitioners believed that they were more skilled in executing the technical tasks than the managerial, and they believed that those technical tasks were more important to their organizations than managerial tasks. But professionals who were serving in primarily managerial roles rated managerial tasks as more important than did their colleagues who functioned primarily as technicians.

Gender was the focus of a study conducted by Whisenant and Mullane (2007) to determine whether the gender of the athletic director at an institution related to the gender of the sports information director. They reported that just 12% of the sports information directors were women. Further, they found the gender of the athletic director was related to the gender of the sports information director. Female athletic directors were more likely to have female sports information directors on their staffs, and male athletic directors were less likely to have female sports information directors on their staffs.

Battenfield and Kent (2007) examined the culture of communication within a Division I-A college athletics media relations department. They reported that internal communication diminished because of the physical space separating staff members within the office and a tendency on the part of the staff to avoid interacting with one another. They also observed that the sports information staff was so focused on producing the organizational media for which they were responsible that communication with other constituents suffered.

Finally, Neupauer (1999) found no significant difference between NCAA I-A sports information professionals and those at lower competitive levels in terms of shyness, willingness to communicate, assertiveness, and indicators of compulsive communication (i.e., "talkoholic" tendencies). But Division I-A sports information professionals were found to be more responsive to the demands placed on them by various constituents.

Each of these studies has contributed to our understanding of the profession. Clearly, however, more research is needed to understand and enhance this specialization in which 2,000 sport managers work.

- cultivating publicity,
- managing statistical services,
- managing the media at games and competitions,
- creating publications, and
- generating online content.

### Cultivating Publicity

As noted, publicity is a powerful tool for sport organizations, and soliciting and nurturing it is a critical part of the media relations professional's job (Favorito, 2007; Helitzer, 2000). Practitioners use a variety of techniques to generate publicity. They issue general news and event information releases, a topic addressed in chapter 8. They stage news conferences so that members of the mass media may personally interact with important newsmakers, a subject examined in chapter 9. They also host media days and other special events tailored to the mass media, also described in chapter 9. They may even develop publicity campaigns for players and coaches in contention for various honors. Campaign planning is covered in chapter 3.

### Managing Statistical Services

Tracking, analyzing, and storing statistical information is a major responsibility for many sport media relations professionals (Favorito, 2007; Helitzer, 2000). They track statistics on a game-by-game or event-by-event basis and produce in-depth statistical reports, many of which are detailed enough to offer play-by-play information regarding how the contest unfolded. They also calculate season totals that can be broken down for analysis by category (home versus away games, nonconference versus conference contests). Sport media relations professionals are also archivists in that they maintain past records and update them as subsequent seasons unfold.

### Managing the Media at Games and Competitions

Sport media relations professionals are responsible for much more than tracking statistics at games and events. Managing the media at those events is a critical aspect of their jobs (Favorito, 2007; Helitzer, 2000; Hall et al., 2007). They are responsible for cultivating media attendance at the competitions, administering credential requests, providing media work space and other relevant services, and generating the various forms of information for members of the media. This subject is addressed in detail in chapter 9.

### Creating Publications

Media guides, game programs, posters, and schedule cards are just a few examples of the publications that sport media relations professionals create in the course of their jobs (Favorito, 2007; Helitzer, 2000; Hall et al., 2007). *Media guide* is the term traditionally used to describe the information-rich publications that they create on an annual basis, but those publications serve multiple promotional purposes. Many media relations professionals are also responsible for producing game programs and other print pieces as detailed in chapter 5. Further, some of these "publications" are moving online as sport organizations look to save money on printing costs and to connect with web savvy audiences.

### Generating Online Content

This aspect of the job has probably changed more than any other in the last 10 years. Given that the media relations office is usually the information hub for professional sport franchises and college athletics programs, it is not surprising that many media relations professionals were given responsibility for managing their organization's website. Now, however, the opportunities for audience engagement online extend well beyond organizational websites. Sport media relations are interacting with audiences through blogs (web logs), discussion forums, and social media platforms such as Facebook and Twitter. Generating online content is the subject of chapter 4.

## Community Relations in Sport

The second most common form of public relations in sport is community relations (Mullin et al., 2007; Stoldt et al., 2007). **Community relations** may be defined as organizational activity designed to foster desirable relationships between the sport organization and the communities in which it is either located or has strategic interests. Accordingly, it is related to corporate social responsibility, which is considered to be an organization's discretionary practices that positively affect its community (Freitag, 2008). Community relations programs can be complex given that they encompass a range of activities ranging from managing a speakers' bureau to initiating a charitable program to touting environmental initiatives. Further, some sport organizations wish to cultivate multiple communities. Some sport organizations have offices and manufacturing facilities in a number of communities or sell their products in a multitude of communities. For instance, shoe and apparel manufacturer New Balance has community relations programs in place in five of its primary U.S. facilities (New Balance, n.d.). Other sport organizations may be located in a single place, but their "community" may extend well beyond the physical boundary of the host municipality. For example, the University of Nebraska's football program draws fans from towns and rural areas across the state, not to mention other states and countries. It hardly makes sense for the university to limit its community relations programs to its home community of Lincoln. Location is not the only relevant factor for sport organizations with constituents dispersed over broad areas (Irwin et al., 2008).

Although media relations generally publicizes what happens on the field of competition, community relations communicates what happens off the field (Shani Tate, personal communication, February 13, 2002). That said, the two programs ultimately work in concert to facilitate the attainment of several important goals.

## Goals of Sport Community Relations

Community relations has traditionally been described as a long-term investment in community goodwill (Mullin et al., 2007). For that reason, among others, sport organizations have traditionally devoted more resources to media relations, which is perceived to provide a quicker return on investment through the publicity that it generates. Nonetheless, the value of community relations should not be underestimated. Favorable attitudes among community members may be fostered by positive interactions between representatives of the sport organization and the public and by the charitable contributions, financial and otherwise, that a sport organization makes to its community.

Because of their community relations programs, sport organizations may realize such outcomes as demonstrating social responsibility, building public awareness, generating favor with customers, increasing employee morale, contributing to their community's well-being, and gaining tax advantages. They may also be able to reach publics who are not targeted by the organization's other marketing and public relations activities (Berkhouse & Gabert, 1999).

Community relations may be particularly important for sport organizations that have difficulty attracting positive media attention for being successful in other areas (Irwin et al., 2008). One such example may be a professional franchise or collegiate program that has a losing reputation and limited prospects for improvement in the near future. Such a franchise could receive favorable media coverage if its players and coaches were to serve meals to the homeless. Another example may be a sporting goods manufacturer or an event management group that endures frequent public criticism. By making financial donations to worthy causes like educational programs, these organizations may be portrayed in a positive light by members of the media. In such cases, community relations activities are particularly critical in cultivating more favorable attitudes among key constituents.

## Jobs in Sport Community Relations

Fewer full-time positions exist in sport community relations than in sport media relations, although opportunities are proliferating as more organizations embrace the value of strong community relations programs. Community relations responsibilities are sometimes included in the job responsibilities of sport managers with other titles. For example, the director of media relations for a minor league hockey team may also be responsible for coordinating public appearances by players and coaches. College athletic administrators coordinating student–athlete support services may be called on to involve their student–athletes in community relations initiatives. And marketing personnel in the fitness sector of the industry may collaborate with nonprofit health advocacy groups to promote wellness in their communities.

Most teams and governing bodies at the highest levels of professional sport employ full-time employees in community relations. Maple Leaf Sports and Entertainment, the corporation that owns the NHL's Maple Leafs, NBA's Raptors, MLS' Toronto FC, and the AHL's Marlies, lists more than 20 people on their community partnerships staff (MLSE, 2009). Sporting goods manufacturers also employ community relations personnel, although their job titles may not necessarily include the term *community relations*. For instance, Nike's community relations activities are coordinated by staff members working in both its community and business affairs and Nike Foundation units (Burt, Kelly, Shatek, & Shields, 2002).

Whether the community relations function is executed by someone with full-time responsibilities in the function or not, it generally involves two sets of tasks—coordinating direct contact initiatives and executing charitable programs.

### Personal Contact Programs

Face-to-face contact between representatives of a sport organization and members of the general public can be a powerful public relations tool, especially for professional and collegiate organizations whose coaches and athletes are likely to be both recognizable and respected because of the media attention afforded them. Making players and coaches accessible to members of the public is conducive to desirable outcomes such as building fan identification (Milne & McDonald, 1999).

Representatives from sport organizations make speeches and other public appearances, elite professional teams and college athletics programs stage caravan tours promoting their upcoming seasons, and a variety of professional and college teams host autograph days. Unmediated communication initiatives are also employed by health clubs, golf courses, and tennis centers as they seek opportunities to attract prospective customers by hosting open houses. Chapter 11 addresses this subject in detail.

### Corporate Social Responsibility Programs

Corporate social responsibility (CSR) is one of the dimensions that affect an organization's reputation. Specific considerations include supporting good causes, being environmentally responsible, and treating people well (Value Based Management. net, n.d.). Community relations activates many CSR programs and communicates others. For instance, professional sport teams, sporting good manufacturers, and fitness and recreation service providers frequently make cash and in-kind contributions to charitable causes. Some stage events for the express purpose of making money for charity. Community relations programs may also highlight sport organizations' environmental initiatives. These topics are examined in chapter 12.

# Other Public Relations Program Areas

Although the practices of media relations and community relations may be the most common forms of public relations in sport, they are not the only ones. Sport organizations may also plan public relations activities to cultivate desirable relationships with other key publics such as employees, investors, customers, donors, and governmental parties and other regulators.

## Employee Relations

Although often taken for granted, employees are a critical stakeholder group that deserves specific public relations consideration. Frequent communication between senior management and employees and between employees in various functional units is an important part of the equation, but employee relations extends beyond even that. Some sport organizations design employee relations programs to enhance employee motivation, performance, and job satisfaction.

Employee relations also relates to organizational culture (Pettinger, 1999; Sriramesh, Grunig, & Buffington, 1992). The communication environment fostered within the organization, not to mention the way that the organization addresses diversity within its staff, has important ramifications. Such considerations are particularly important given that each member of the organization is in essence a public relations representative. By cultivating a public relations orientation among employees, an organization is more likely to enjoy positive relationships with other publics such as customers, neighbors, and the community in general. Employee relations is one of the subjects of chapter 13.

## Investor Relations

Some sport organizations are publicly owned. This form of ownership is most common in the sporting goods industry. Manufacturers such as Adidas and Callaway Golf and retailers such as Foot Locker and Dick's Sporting Goods have stockholders who have invested in the company. Some sport facilities, such as Churchill Downs and Lowe's Motor Speedway (owned by Speedway Motorsports), are also publicly held. Publicly owned sport organizations must pay special attention to their investors and related publics such as financial analysts to keep them informed about the company's financial performance and to convince them that investment in the organization continues to be a sound financial strategy. Given the importance of investors to the continuing existence of publicly held sport organizations, this aspect of public relations is critical. This area is also highly regulated, meaning that public relations professionals must know which information is mandated for disclosure and how to present information in ways that do not violate the law (Broom, 2009). Investor relations are discussed in chapter 13.

## Customer Relations

As noted, the sport organization's marketing staff designs programs to facilitate transactions with customers, and public relations plays a key role in the promotional mix. But public relations can make other contributions in fostering desirable customer relations. Some public relations professionals frequently communicate with their organization's customers. For example, they may include customers on their distribution list for news releases, publications, and other forms of communication. The public relations office is a common point of contact for customers who have questions or complaints. Public relations professionals may also communicate with customers through blogs or other forms of online social media. Customer relations is addressed in chapter 14, along with donor and government relations.

### Donor Relations

Given the vast number of sport organizations that operate in nonprofit settings, donor relations is an important sport public relations consideration. Fitness and recreation providers such as the YMCA need donors to support sport programs, particularly those designed for children from economically disadvantaged backgrounds. College and high school athletics programs establish booster clubs, some of which require substantial membership fees, to enhance their programs. Individuals and organizations who donate to such programs must be recognized for their generosity, presented with benefits of value, and groomed for future donations. Frequent communication between the sport organization and its donors is at the center of such processes.

### Government and Regulator Relations

Sport organizations frequently function in relationship to numerous government agencies and other regulatory organizations. Most sport businesses are highly regulated by federal, state, and local laws. Sometimes, sport organizations advocate certain policies that are beneficial to their sustained existence, such as the Sports Broadcasting Act, which allows professional sport leagues to gain antitrust protection in packaging their games for sale to broadcast partners. Sport organizations may also seek public support in the form of tax dollars for facility initiatives. In such situations, sport managers must devote considerable effort to developing relationships with key governmental agencies as well as public constituencies.

Other sport organizations face additional regulation through voluntary affiliation with organizations such as college athletics associations (e.g., NCAA, NAIA), state interscholastic athletics organizations, athletics conferences, national governing bodies, and even professional leagues. These organizations commonly lobby their regulators for the implementation and maintenance of particular policies deemed desirable by the organization.

# The Value of Public Relations

Public relations offers two broad benefits to sport organizations. First, it generates revenue by supporting the marketing of products and services, by providing products that can be sold, and by advancing the sport organization's reputation with key publics. Second, it enables sport organizations to save money by avoiding mistakes that would alienate customers and other important publics.

## Generating Revenue

Public relations generates revenue for sport organizations in several ways. First, it promotes the organization's products and services. Branding has become a key concern for sport managers (Hardy & Sutton, 1999). A **brand** is identified by terms (e.g., Under Armour) and logos or symbols (e.g., the Nike swoosh) that represent the products or services offered by a particular organization. Effectively built, a brand can come to be associated with positive characteristics and benefits in consumers' minds. For example, the Olympic brand, commonly represented by the five interlocking rings, is commonly associated with elite sport competition and community building on a global scale. People seeking the thrill of watching elite performers compete and the inspiration that comes from seeing diverse people join in a common cause are likely to attend Olympic events or at least watch television broadcasts of the Games because they know the brand represents those qualities. Brands possessing value in consumers' minds enjoy significant advantages in a cluttered, competitive marketplace. The sidebar Evaluating the World's Top Sport Brands identifies some of the brands that have been most successful in this regard.

Public relations is an effective brand-building tool because of its ability to generate positive publicity. Because most consumers perceive publicity information as coming from a nonbiased third-party member of the mass media, publicity is a highly credible form of communication. Information from a mass media outlet regarding a fitness center offering a new service or a local sport team enjoying a successful season is more likely to generate a response from consumers than the same information conveyed through an advertisement or other promotional vehicle from the sport organization.

*The Fall of Advertising and the Rise of PR* argues this point persuasively, stating, "To get something going from nothing, you need the validity that only third-party endorsements can bring. The first stage

of any new campaign ought to be public relations" (Ries & Ries, 2002, p. xx). To marketers looking to build brand awareness and identity, they offer a simple formula—public relations first, advertising second. Gatorade, they note, is an excellent example. The Gatorade brand is built largely on the publicity

## Evaluating the World's Top Sport Brands

Tiger Woods, Nike, the Super Bowl, and Manchester United were the top sport brands in their respective categories in 2010 according to *Forbes* magazine (Schwartz, 2010). The magazine published a Forbes Fab 40, the top 10 sport brands in four categories—athlete, business, event, and team. Woods earned top honors among athletes based on his endorsement income relative to the average endorsement income of his peers. Nike placed first among sport businesses given its market value compared with its book value in light of others in the industry. The Super Bowl was selected as the top sport event because of the magazine's revenue per event day calculations. Manchester United was chosen as the top team brand based on the portion of the team's value not derived from its demographic base or from revenues shared among other teams in its league. The magazine noted, "While polls can provides a whimsical take on how someone feels at a particular moment, our brand values quantify the equity built up in a name over many years" (Schwartz, 2010).

**Manchester United was deemed by *Forbes* magazine as being the top sport team brand in the world.**

Rex Features via AP Images

that the product received in the mid-1960s when the University of Florida football team used the product during a highly successful season. Since that time, Gatorade's advertising and endorsement programs have served simply to remind consumers of what their brand offers. The product was initially positioned in consumers' minds through public relations.

A second way that public relations can make money for the sport organization is by producing inventory to be sold. As noted, many public relations professionals in professional and collegiate sport produce publications such as game programs and media guides. Game programs generate revenue through advertising sales, and both forms of publications are commonly sold to members of the public.

In addition, the information that public relations professionals produce for their organization's websites must be considered a revenue producer. The more visitors the site draws, the more value site sponsorships have and the more opportunities the sport organization has to sell products through the site. A direct link exists between site content and revenue. As Migala (2000) stated, "In the Internet world, content is king. In the sports Internet world, content is capital." The potential for generating revenue through online content is growing as sport organizations learn how to monetize social media.

A third way that public relations generates revenue for the sport organization is by enhancing the organization's reputation with various publics. A national opinion study indicated that 65% of Americans indicated it was either extremely or very important to them that they buy products or services from companies with values similar to their own (National Consumers League, 2006). When public relations practitioners facilitate community relations initiatives that demonstrate social responsibility, they increase the likelihood that people will support the organization. Similarly, when public relations practitioners attract favorable publicity, offer customer support services, motivate employees, communicate with and recognize donors, and inform and convince investors, they are benefiting the sport organization's bottom line. The ultimate value of these activities is far more difficult to track than the value from, for instance, sponsorship sales in the marketing department, but the effects are clear.

## Saving Money

Although public relations has plenty to offer in terms of contributing revenue to the sport organization, its other major contribution is helping the sport organization avoid expense. Specifically, public relations professionals should assist their organization in avoiding costly mistakes. In fact, some public relations experts argue that this benefit outweighs public relation's role in generating revenue (Grunig, Grunig, & Dozier, 2002).

The value of public relations in avoiding costly mistakes is illustrated in the following three vignettes:

• Nike made a public relations mistake in the early 1990s when it established the Tonya Harding Defense Fund and contributed $25,000 to that cause because Phil Knight, its chief executive officer, believed her innocent until proven guilty (Carter, 1996). Harding had recently been implicated in an attack on fellow figure skater Nancy Kerrigan, and calls to Nike headquarters regarding the company's support of Harding were overwhelmingly negative. Furthermore, some retailers cancelled orders for Nike products.

• Bud Selig, commissioner of Major League Baseball, arguably made a public relations mistake by deciding to end the 2002 All-Star Game in a tie. Critics argued that the decision was an insult to fans (Caple, 2002). By the time the 2003 All-Star Game rolled around, the stakes had been raised by giving the winning league home-field advantage for the World Series, still another controversial decision.

• The United States Golf Association (USGA) first made a public relations mistake and then attempted to correct it in 2009 when the first day of the U.S. Open was rained out after the lead group had played just 11 holes. More than 40,000 ticket holders were told that they would receive no refunds on their $100 tickets and that the tickets could not be used on other days of the tournament. But after a barrage of complaints and a wave of negative publicity, the USGA reversed course and told ticket holders that they could use their first-round tickets to gain admission to the Monday conclusion of the tournament (Greenstein, 2009).

All organizations, sport and otherwise, make public relations errors. And each of the sport organizations in this list has demonstrated public relations savvy on other occasions. The key point, however, is that by attuning themselves to public relations considerations, sport organizations may minimize the frequency of those errors and reduce the effects of those errors when they occur.

The precise financial value of this benefit is impossible to determine. What was the financial value of the media airtime and space devoted in each of these situations? What was the financial value of

Fans attending the soggy first day of the 2009 U.S. Open were invited to return for the Monday conclusion of the tournament when the USGA reversed course on its ticket policy.

Andy Altenburger/Icon SMI

the future sales, viewership, and donations that the three organizations lost because of their public relations mistakes? As difficult as it may be even to estimate the cost of the errors, it is even more difficult to determine the financial value of a mistake that is avoided thanks to public relations counsel.

## SUMMARY

Sport public relations is a managerial, communication-based function designed to identify a sport organization's key publics, evaluate its relationships with its publics, and foster desirable relationships between the organization and its publics. Although the public relations function often complements the marketing function within sport organizations, it is distinct in that it engages a more diverse group of publics and seeks relational rather than transactional outcomes. Public relations is a powerful promotional tool capable of generating substantial publicity for the sport organization, but promotion and publicity do not represent the whole of public relations.

The practice of public relations within sport is diverse, but its two most common forms are media relations and community relations. Media relations programs focus on building relationships with members of the mass media to maximize positive publicity and minimize negative publicity. Community relations programs are structured to allow members of the sport organization to come in direct contact with their constituents and to allow the sport organization to gain public favor by contributing to charitable initiatives. Other forms of public relations in sport include employee relations, investor relations, customer relations, donor relations, and government relations. Regardless of the nature of the specific public relations activity, effective practice is based on several fundamental skills, including the ability to write well, interact with others, make public presentations, design publications, and exploit Internet-related capability.

Effective public relations offers several benefits to the sport organization. First, it is a powerful marketing tool that can generate brand awareness and brand associations. Second, it generates information that can be effectively marketed as a product extension (e.g., content on websites, game programs). Third, public relations counsel can help sport organizations save money by preventing the occurrence of damaging mistakes in relation to key publics. The precise value of a crisis avoided or at least effectively managed may be difficult to determine, but the costs of public relations mistakes can be significant and long lasting.

## LEARNING ACTIVITIES

1. Conduct a brief personal, telephone, or e-mail interview with a sport public relations professional. Media relations professionals who work with professional teams or collegiate programs may be the easiest to identify. Your community may also include professionals in sport community relations, employee relations, or even investor relations. How does that person describe the public relations function within the organization? How does he or she describe the relationship between public relations and marketing?

2. Find examples of publicity relating to each of the following forms of sport products and services:

   • An upcoming professional or college game

   • A service being offered by a local fitness center

   • A new sporting goods product being introduced to the marketplace

   What is the source of this information? What effect is the information likely to have on audience members?

3. Visit the website of the College Sports Information Directors of America (CoSIDA), www. cosida.com, to learn about the organization, the services it offers, and the nature of its membership.

4. Visit the website of the professional sport team of your choice. Based on the staff directory and any staff profiles that it may provide, describe the way that its public relations responsibilities are assigned. Does it have a public relations staff? If so, how is that staff organized? If not, is there any indication of who is responsible for executing the public relations function?

5. Assess your own competencies in terms of the five basic skills that underlie public relations practice. If you are considering a career in sport public relations, you may benefit by having a trusted faculty member assist you in this evaluation. What skills should you seek to develop further while pursuing your education?

# Integrating Public Relations With Strategic Management

## After reading this chapter, students should be able to

- articulate the role of public relations as a part of the strategic management process,
- discuss the purpose and value of mission and vision statements in public relations efforts,
- specify various strategies for public relations communication,
- describe the importance and challenges of public relations assessment,
- identify key organizational stakeholders and publics,
- detail the connection between issues management and relationship building, and
- outline the components and values of reputation and image.

## Key terms discussed in this chapter include

- strategic management;
- mission, vision, and values statements;
- Grunig's four models of public relations;
- nonpublic and latent, aware, and active publics;
- issues management;
- reputation;
- brand and brand equity; and
- reactive and proactive public relations.

**In chapter 1,** public relations and marketing are described as complementary but distinct organizational functions. Marketing tends to focus on consumers and an exchange of value, whereas public relations is likely to focus on a wider range of targets as well as the building and nurturing of relationships with a wide variety of publics. Mullin, Hardy, and Sutton (2007) defined public relations for the purposes of sport marketing as "an interactive marketing communication strategy" consisting primarily of a combination of media relations and community relations. But they also acknowledged that public relations is a management function that reflects policies set at the top levels of management. Harris (1998) used the term *marketing public relations* to describe aspects of public relations more directly involved in marketing objectives and the term *corporate public relations* to describe public relations activities directed toward broader corporate objectives. This useful distinction emphasizes the point that public relations is a management function that must be addressed in the overall strategic management process rather than used exclusively as a publicity driver or crisis management tool. For Hutton (1996), marketing and public relations were the basic components of integrated marketing communication. The overlap between the two domains represents the marketing role of public relations. Marketing functions such as corporate advertising and certain aspects of media relations and sponsorship differ from other public relations activities such as investor relations, employee communications, charitable affiliations, and government relations.

Lesly (1998) noted that most public relations activities are concerned with the daily execution of techniques, but this daily involvement is driven by narrower groups who are involved with the tactics and strategies that give direction to all public relations activity. As an example, in college athletics the sports information staff executes a variety of public relations tactics (e.g., news releases, website updates) that are supervised by a sports information director (SID) and perhaps a marketing director. The SID and marketing director develop the tactical course that will be taken in promoting an athlete for a national award or implementing a media brochure concept. These individuals in turn are guided by the organizational leadership such as the athletic director and institutional president, who establish philosophy and direction for the athletics program and institution as a whole. This chapter considers public relations at the strategic level, not as activity exclusively reserved for the marketing department but as activity that involves the entire management team (and indeed the entire organization). The chapter includes discussion of how public relations fits into the strategic management process, the need for thorough identification of organizational stakeholders and publics, the strategic advantages of proactive issues management, the significance of organizational reputation and strategies for assessing its value, and the challenge of producing organizational action consistent with the organization's desired image.

# Public Relations as a Strategic Management Tool

Pearce and Robinson (2005) defined **strategic management** as "the set of decisions and actions that result in the formulation and implementation of plans designed to achieve an organization's objectives." It is composed of several critical tasks including the following:

1. Mission formulation
2. SWOT analysis (assessment of internal capabilities and external environment)
3. Identification of desirable options
4. Development of long-term and short-term objectives and strategies
5. Implementation of strategic choices through appropriate resource allocation
6. Evaluation

These high-level managerial functions provide direction for the entire enterprise.

Few of the many strategic management models make any direct mention of public relations. This does not mean, however, that there is no connection between strategic management and public relations. On the contrary, the claim can be made that public relations begins in the early stages of the strategic management process. The idea that public relations is not just a marketing activity and should be viewed as a management tool speaks directly to the contention that public relations should be integrated throughout organizational operations. Integration should begin in the early stages of the strategic planning process and include preparation of organizational mission, development of communication systems and processes, establishment of goals and objectives that serve as the basis for evaluating public relations activity, identification of the significant relationships with key publics, and proactive strategic consideration of desired reputation and relevant issues. Thorough assimilation of public relations into the fabric of an organization requires careful thought in all these areas. Strategic attention to public relations is designed to create an environment in which the desired image is clearly defined, consistently reflected, and systematically assessed across all areas of organizational operation.

Most strategic management models begin with some effort to identify what an organization is and wants to be. This is typically done by developing vision and mission statements and performing a SWOT (strengths, weaknesses, opportunities, threats) analysis. The sidebar titled Conducting a SWOT Analysis describes this process. These steps establish a foundation for organizational direction and for developing goals and objectives and crafting broad organizational strategies. These steps are important because they lay the groundwork for the desired image of the organization and begin the process of positioning the organization in the marketplace. Given the relationship between public relations and image management, early stages of the strategic management process should have clear links to public relations.

## Mission and Vision Statements

Many sport organizations have embraced the use of some combination of mission statements, vision statements, and values statements to provide fundamental assertions of the organization's purpose, goals, operating philosophy, and priorities. **Mission statements** should give insight into what the organization does well (distinguishing attributes), who its stakeholders and publics are, and how it views its responsibilities to those publics. **Vision statements** often furnish a sense of the future direction that an organization sees for itself. These statements of atti-

## Conducting a SWOT Analysis

SWOT (strengths, weaknesses, opportunities, threats) analysis is an important assessment and planning tool that involves evaluating both the internal attributes of an organization (strengths and weaknesses) and the external environment in which it operates (opportunities and threats). Although SWOT analysis can be used in a variety of ways, when used as a strategic management tool the focus is on assessing the primary functions of the organization.

The internal assessment attempts to identify what competencies and capabilities exist within the organization and how effectively they are being employed to achieve organizational goals. This analysis is done by addressing questions related to marketing, finance, personnel, structure, leadership, technology, operations, production, adaptability, efficiency, and so on. The analysis should produce insights into organizational capacities and limitations.

The external assessment attempts to gauge what influences the environment of the organization has on its direction and ultimate success. Addressing questions related to short- and long-term economic developments, technological changes, social changes, industry trends, and the actions of competitors will provide information regarding what opportunities and concerns may present themselves in the future.

The two types of assessment interrelate in that strengths may be the basis for capitalizing on opportunities and weaknesses must be dealt with to fend off potential threats. The SWOT analysis serves as the basis for refining organizational goals and objectives and for developing a strategic plan.

Effective SWOT analysis usually combines input from throughout the organization. For example, an athletics department SWOT analysis might ask each sport and each functional area (i.e., marketing, ticketing, medical services, development, facilities) to assess strengths, weakness, opportunities, and threats from these narrower perspectives. This information is then combined with the insights of upper-level administration to create an overall picture of departmental possibilities and problems. Such an analysis can then be used in planning organizational direction, setting priorities, and supporting priorities with appropriate resource allocation.

Organizations may construct a checklist or create a matrix that is tailored to their specific circumstances as a way of providing focus to the SWOT process. Many templates of varying complexity have been developed that may be useful in getting a SWOT analysis started. One example is a checklist fashioned by Kotler (2000) that includes both a rating scale and a priority scale in the assessment of various functional dimensions.

tude, outlook, and orientation are relatively endur-ing representations of an organization's self-concept and the image that it desires to project (Pearce & Robinson, 2005). Some organizations are now also using **values statements** to describe organizational beliefs that guide actions and behaviors. They tend to be less specific than codes of conduct but can serve as the foundation for such behavioral codes. These statements are fundamental elements of an organization's public relations platform. They serve to communicate with a variety of constituencies (both external and internal) about the basic nature and aspirations of the operation. (One excellent example of these statements can be found on the Columbia University web page: www.gocolumbia lions.com. Follow the Mission Statement link under "Inside Athletics.")

There is no magic formula for developing mission and vision statements. They vary substantially in length, content, style, and terminology. Some are so vague that they might apply to any organization of any type. Others have been criticized as being little more than pages in the employee handbook or puff pieces on a website. In too many cases the mission or vision statement has become a creative-writing exer-cise that is forgotten after it is completed rather than actively used as a tool for organizational guidance (Pentilla, 2002). Meyer (2005) contended that these statements often have little influence on organiza-tional performance or employee behavior because they are too ambiguous and are drafted to include the popular buzz words of the moment. Perhaps one way to assess the relevance of these statements is to see whether employees can articulate any of them, or are even aware of their existence.

Some of the most commonly agreed-upon components of mission statements include target market, products and services offered, geographic scope of the market, concern for growth and prof-itability, organizational philosophy and values, company identity and image, the importance of employees, and distinctive competencies of the firm (David, 1996). These declarations of mission are not to be etched in stone, never to be revisited. A suitable mission statement for a Division II ath-letics program may have some serious shortcom-ings when the school decides to move to Division I. A mission statement well-suited to a fledgling local sporting goods store early in its business life may have little relevance as the store expands to a regional or national presence.

As sport organizations have become more busi-nesslike in their operations, many have seen the advantages of preparing mission statements. As part of its certification process, the National Col-legiate Athletic Association (NCAA) has required Division I members to develop mission statements, disseminate them widely, and ensure that they are consistent with the institutional mission statement. Finding congruence between institutional and athletics department mission statements can be a challenge in some cases. Despite the pervasive presence of athletics on many campuses, the role of athletics programs is often not clearly articulated in the institutional mission.

Figures 2.1 and 2.2 are sample mission and vision statements from two sport organizations.

The trends in mission statement development are to make them more concise and explicit and to expend greater effort in identifying the competen-cies, distinguishing features, and important publics of the organization. The last element is especially important from a public relations standpoint in that it becomes a focal point for identifying the key rela-tionships that the organization is trying to nurture.

# Public Relations Communications

As stated in chapter 1, public relations is commu-nications activity that involves interaction with a wide range of publics, both internal and external. One of the key strategies for consistent public rela-tions efforts is to assure that a communications system is in place that provides the appropriate information to the right people at the right time. Mullin, Hardy, and Sutton (2007) maintained that the establishment, understanding, and monitoring of communication platforms with various publics are key public relations functions. They contended, however, that public relations personnel are often left out of the strategic planning loop and have to live with objectives set by others, leading to a reac-tive approach to public relations.

Although communication must be tailored to the various stakeholders, it must also be communicated in a manner consistent with organizational identity and mission. This undertaking is complex because of (1) the number of people involved in communi-cating with various publics, (2) the wide range of audiences in which communication occurs, and (3) the vast array of communication tools available.

**Grunig's four models of public relations** pro-vide an overview of the nature of public relations communications. Two of the models, press agentry, which involves seeking attention in almost any form, and public information, which seeks to dis-

# National Baseball Hall of Fame and Museum Mission Statement

The National Baseball Hall of Fame and Museum is a not-for-profit educational institution dedicated to fostering an appreciation of the historical development of the game and its impact on our culture by collecting, preserving, exhibiting and interpreting its collections for a global audience, as well as honoring those who have made outstanding contributions to our National Pastime.

Through its mission, the Museum is committed to:

- Collecting, through donation, baseball artifacts, works of art, literature, photographs, memorabilia and related materials which focus on the history of the game over time, its players, and those elected to the Hall of Fame.

- Preserving the collections by adhering to professional museum standards with respect to conservation and maintaining a permanent record of holdings through documentation, study, research, cataloging and publication.

- Exhibiting material in permanent gallery space, organizing on-site changing exhibitions on various themes, with works from the Hall of Fame collections or other sources, working with other individuals or organizations to exhibit loaned material of significance to baseball and providing related research facilities.

- Interpreting artifacts through its exhibition and education programs to enhance awareness, understanding and appreciation of the game for a diverse audience.

- Honoring, by enshrinement, those individuals who had exceptional careers, and recognizing others for their significant achievements.

**Figure 2.1**  National Baseball Hall of Fame and Museum's mission statement.

National Baseball Hall of Fame and Museum.

seminate accurate and favorable information about the organization, are one-way models in which communication is directed toward a public. Press agentry and public information have long been common public relations models in sport. These strategies are still employed, although the evolution of public relations has resulted in other practices that are in better keeping with the more current view of relationship-oriented public relations. Grunig's two-way asymmetrical and two-way symmetrical models place much more emphasis on interaction and dialogue. The asymmetrical model incorporates research in an effort to persuade publics to act in desirable ways. The symmetrical model uses both research and dialogue to produce a dynamic relationship between an organization and its publics, resulting in public relations actions that are mutually beneficial (Grunig & Hunt, 1984). The element of dialogue is crucial to modern public relations because it places much more importance on practitioners as receivers of information rather than merely information disseminators. This aspect is particularly true because technology has altered the communications landscape. Communication and

social networking technology has given everyone a public forum in which to disseminate information quickly and expansively. Sport organizations can sit by passively and observe dialogue taking place, or they can become an active part of the dialogue that shapes public perception.

Grunig (2006) provided additional clarity to the distinctions among these models by suggesting that the one-way models are largely concerned with using public relations in a more interpretive way in which the primary function is to shape public perception while embracing such concepts as reputation and brand. Such an approach reduces public relations to a largely tactical role that emphasizes buffering the organization from its environment. Two-way communication and the symmetrical model take a more strategic view in which public relations serves as a bridging function. This approach places more emphasis on cultivating relationships and collaboration in which publics have a voice that influences organizational behavior and strategic decisions.

Cook (1998) articulated the importance of assimilation, documentation, and presentation of facts as

# Canadian Olympic Committee Statements

## Vision

The Canadian Olympic Committee (COC) envisions a future where:

- Sport is at the centre of our culture
- We promote and support the pursuit of excellence
- We are recognized for quality, innovation, and success; individuals' lives of all ages and abilities are enriched by their experience in sport
- We promote Olympism and sport as an agent of positive social change, uniting through peaceful cooperation and respect
- We are accepted as a leader – earning the trust of those we serve – for the betterment of sport.

## Mission

The Canadian Olympic Committee is dedicated to developing and advancing sport and the Olympic Movement for all Canadians from coast-to-coast-to-coast.

## Core Values

The COC Olympic Values have been established to remind athletes and their supporters that the life skills and experience obtained through athletic preparation, competition and teamwork are far more valuable than any medal ever awarded.

## Excellence

We believe in the right of all people to pursue their personal levels of excellence.

## Fun

We believe in sport being fun.

## Fairness

We believe in fairness on and off the field of play, as characterized by equality, integrity and trust.

## Respect

We believe in free and open communication and respect for the views, role and contribution of all.

## Human Development

We believe that the short and long term physical, social, mental and spiritual well-being of all should be enhanced through appropriate behavior and practices. We also believe that the visual and performing arts complement sport in the development of that well-being.

## Leadership

We believe those who participate in sport have a responsibility to teach and apply the values of the Olympic Movement, involving others in the Olympic experience and inspiring and empowering them to reach their potential.

## Peace

We believe in sport as a vehicle to promote understanding and harmony within and among nations.

**Figure 2.2**   Vision and mission statements from the Canadian Olympic Committee.

Reprinted, by permission, from the Canadian Olympic Committee.

the "bricks and mortar" of public relations, which counters the image of those who view public relations as the practice of distorting, suppressing, or spinning information. The ability of organizations to build trust with their publics is essential to establishing long-term relationships.

Edelman, a private public relations firm, has developed an annual trust barometer that attempts to assess the level of trust that people have for business. This survey suggests that trust is a product of organizational values and actions that are reflected in such factors as product quality, fair and transparent business practices, customer attentiveness, philanthropic activity, innovative business practices, stakeholder dialogue, employee treatment, and visible leadership. The process of establishing trust requires an approach to communications that is transparent and encourages employees to establish credibility with stakeholders. It also requires continuous communication efforts using a credible media mix that may rely more on earned media (publicity) and less on paid media exposure (Edelman, 2010). The growth of the Internet as a platform for all forms of communication provides expanded opportunities for quality interaction but also poses strategic information management challenges. New media and social networking options provide useful channels for this type of communication. Chapter 4 deals more specifically with some aspects of the influence of technology on the nature of public relations communication, and examples of the influence of new media on various public relations practices appear throughout the book.

Public relations communication is designed to inform or influence the target public in some way. Kelly (2001) summarized communications objectives as the desire to create, change, or reinforce cognitions, attitudes, and behaviors. Cognitive awareness may be the easiest to accomplish, whereas communication that alters attitudes and behaviors can prove to be more of a challenge. For example, a small university in a large metropolitan market can probably make people aware that it

has added football to its athletics program, but it is quite another matter to change perceptions about the quality of the program or elicit behavior supporting the program. The effort required to shape attitudes and behaviors implies a long-term and more strategic view of public relations communications. Table 2.1 outlines a simple grid that may be useful in clarifying the desired outcomes for public relations communications as they are directed at particular audiences.

An additional concern and one of the more confounding public relations communication issues that organizations must face is making sure that all employees communicate the desired impression. Although control of official communication of the organization may be a challenge, controlling the unofficial communication that emanates from any organization is a daunting task. What a company employee says about his or her employer at a party and how an athlete acts during a summer away from school are messages that may have important effects but little oversight. In many cases sport organizations confront public relations problems resulting from actions that have little if any direct connection to the primary activities of the organization (e.g., misbehavior or criminal activity outside the scope of employment). Michael Vick's involvement in dog fighting or Ben Roethlisberger's sexual assault charges had nothing to do with football, but the NFL and the players' respective teams each had to deal with the effect of those actions. All people within an organization need to feel a sense of responsibility for the impressions that they make with the organization's various publics. Athletes are often given counseling and advice on how to deal with

## Table 2.1 Establishing Desired Public Relations Communications Outcomes About a NCAA Division II Athletics Program

| Objective | Knowledge | Attitudes | Behaviors |
| --- | --- | --- | --- |
| Create public relations target audience: *local media* | Players with ties to local high schools | Belief that community interest exists for information and coverage | Increased exposure; more expansive stories |
| Change public relations target audience: *prospective student–athletes* | Location of the school; athletics department reputation and successes | Perceptions of the quality and competitiveness of Division II athletics | Visits to the school |
| Reinforce public relations target audience: *student body* | When and where athletics events are scheduled | Value of student attendance at contests | Continued attendance; encouraging classmates and friends to attend games |

the media. Most college athletics programs now have departmental policies regarding how athletes can use social media such as Facebook, MySpace, or Twitter because of embarrassing information that has been published on those social networking sites. These are examples of how teams and athletics programs try to manage impressionable communication. Creating a sense of accountability is a strategic challenge at the heart of managing an organization's relationship with its internal publics.

# Organizational Stakeholders and Constituents

A fundamental activity that establishes the connection between the strategic management process and public relations is the identification of an organization's publics—those groups of people who have some interest or stake in organizational action. Grunig (2006) described public relations as "a strategic management function that uses communication to cultivate relationships with publics that have a stake in the behavior of the organization—either because they benefit from or are harmed by what Dewey called the consequences of that behavior." Several terms have been used, somewhat inconsistently, to describe the various groups with which an organization has or seeks relationships. Such terms as *stakeholder, constituency, target audience,* and *population* are often used either as synonyms for *public* or as a particular type of public. For the purpose of this text, the term *stakeholder* is used to describe large groups of people who hold similar standing in relation to the organization. The term *publics* refers to specific groups of people within stakeholder groups who hold similar attitudes and dispositions toward the organization.

One public relations professional called public relations "the art of earning and leveraging the trust of an organization's stakeholders" (Ries & Ries, 2002). The uninitiated commonly take a narrow view of a sport organization's publics, often taking in no more than clients, customers, and the media.

Although consumers and the media are publics on which most sport organizations would place a high priority, other groups must not be ignored. The number of publics that have a vested interest in or may be influenced by an organization's operations is often expansive, even for small organizations. Lesly (1998) referred to the scope of public relations as the public relations universe. This universe

provides insight into the potential breadth of public relations activity as well as the range of publics with which interaction may exist. Figure 2.3 illustrates this concept.

Developing a thorough inventory of relevant publics serves as the foundation for much of the public relations activity that occurs within any organization. Sport organizations should certainly try to determine what stakeholder relationships exist or are needed and how they might be nurtured. As part of strategic planning, one useful approach would be to begin with broad categories of stakeholders and then narrow the focus to more specific target publics. As an example, many sport organizations place a high priority on media publics. This focus can be narrowed to particular media forms (e.g., print, television, radio, Internet) and refined even further using criteria such as geography, target audience, and distribution data (ratings, circulation) to identify specific target groups within each broad public. See figure 2.4. This approach can be used for many publics and may help establish priority relationships and determine the way in which public relations resources will be allocated. Using a systematic method to identify important publics may also help locate gaps in the public relations effort. Periodically reviewing the results of this process can be useful as an auditing tool.

After extensive review of stakeholder theory, stakeholder management, and public relations, Rawlins (2006) produced a more sophisticated model that prioritizes stakeholders through a four-step process. He suggested first identifying stakeholders according to the type of relationship that they have with the organization. This can be done using the linkage model first developed by Grunig and Hunt (1984). The linkages include functional linkages, normative linkages, enabling linkages, and diffused linkages. Table 2.2 provides a brief description of each linkage and some examples of stakeholders that likely fall in each category.

After stakeholders are identified, prioritization can occur. A variety of categorizations may be used to clarify these priorities including relational attributes, situational factors, and communication strategy. Relational attributes consider such things as the relative power of stakeholders, the legitimacy of the relationship in legal and moral terms, and the urgency of the issues connecting the organization and the stakeholder. As an example, the Major League Baseball Players' Association (MLBPA) is an important stakeholder of Major League Baseball. When looking at relational attributes, the increased power of the MLBPA beginning in the early 1970s

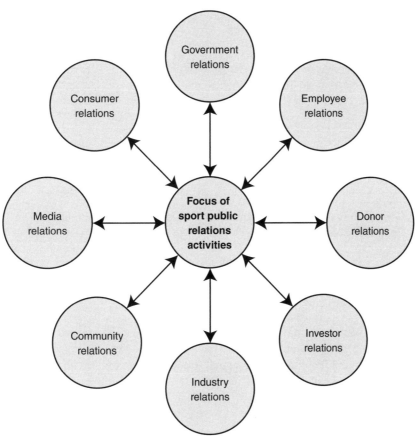

**Figure 2.3** Sport public relations universe.

Adapted from Lesly 1998.

has changed the nature of the relationship. A variety of legal constraints shape the behavior of Major League Baseball as it conducts its business with the MLBPA, particularly in the area of labor

negotiations. The relationship is also influenced periodically by the urgency of the collective bargaining process. Each of these relational attributes influences the priority of the relationship between

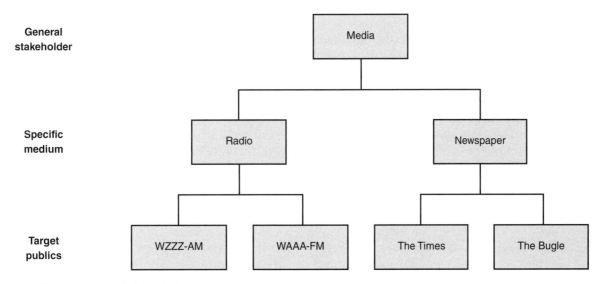

**Figure 2.4** From stakeholders to target publics.

## Table 2.2  Public Relations Linkages and Related Stakeholders

| Linkage type | Description | Example |
|---|---|---|
| Functional | Relationships essential to the function of the organization related to input functions that provide the labor and resources to create products or services | Employees<br>Unions<br>Suppliers |
| | Relationships essential to the function of the organization related to output functions that consume the products or services | Consumers (e.g., fans, members)<br>Retailers<br>Distributors (e.g., media partners) |
| Normative | Groups that share the organization's interests, values, goals, or problems | Competitors<br>Peer institutions<br>Professional associations |
| Enabling | Stakeholders who have some control and authority over the organization, allowing the organization to have resources and autonomy to operate | Board of directors<br>Government regulators<br>Stockholders |
| Diffused | Stakeholders who may not have frequent interaction with the organization but become involved because of the actions of the organization (publics that often arise in times of crisis) | Special interest groups<br>Community activists<br>Media |

Summarized from Grunig and Hunt 1984.

the two parties and demonstrates the dynamic nature of the relationship.

Use of situational factors produces a more refined attempt to establish stakeholder precedence. Dozier and Ehling (1992) developed four classifications for describing the situational nature of publics: nonpublic, latent public, aware public, and active public. A **nonpublic** includes people who have no common interest in or connection to an issue confronting an organization. A **latent public** includes people who have some common interest or link to the organization but fail to recognize it. After recognizing that common interest or connection, they become an **aware public**. When an aware public takes coordinated and focused action to affect the relationship with the organization, they become an **active public**. For example, let's say that a city is considering closing a local community recreation center. People in certain parts of the community may have no interest in this issue (nonpublic). Others may be unaware that the center might close (latent public). Another group may have heard or read about the potential closing (aware public), and yet another group may be lobbying city council or initiating a petition drive to prevent the closing (active public). Although the active public will certainly be the focus of public relations efforts, proactive attention to latent and

aware publics reflects a more encompassing vision of public relations.

Rawlins (2006) refined the situational nature of publics further by considering whether the stakeholders are supportive or nonsupportive and active or inactive. Strategies for communicating with advocate stakeholders (active and supportive) differ from strategies for reaching dormant stakeholders (inactive and supportive). Adversarial stakeholders (active and nonsupportive) are approached differently than apathetic stakeholders (inactive and nonsupportive). These useful differentiations should be clear from the previous illustration. Active publics likely exist on both sides of the issue of closing the recreation center, a circumstance that is true with many issues that confront sport organizations.

Grunig's situational theory (Grunig & Hunt, 1984) captures the dynamic nature of linkages with publics. Grunig and Hunt noted that "publics come and go depending on what an organization does and how people and organizations react to that organizational behavior." Kelly (2001) criticized public relations process models that ignore attention to ongoing relationships. By adding stewardship to the ROPE model (research, objectives, programming, and evaluation) developed by Hendrix (1998), Kelly's ROPES model provides

**The Houston Astros moved quickly to remove scandal-plagued Enron's image from their ballpark and secured a new naming-rights deal with Minute Maid.**

John Korduner / Icon SMI

a comprehensive approach to how relationships with all publics should be managed (table 2.3 summarizes this process). Although most of these steps are common to public relations models, stewardship adds a component that directly addresses fostering associations over the long term. For instance, nurturing relationships with the business community as potential sponsors, suppliers, and consumers is vital to many sport operations. The economic landscape changes constantly, and these fluctuations can provide important new relationship opportunities or threaten long-standing associations. The business environment can undergo changes that have national and international implications, or changes may be confined to a local community that experiences the benefits or suffers the damages when a major employer enters or leaves the economy. The recent economic downturn has affected sport organizations of all types. Sponsorship agreements are harder to establish and maintain, donors are more cautious with contributions, and the media (particularly newspapers) are cutting back on coverage. Golf tours have seen longstanding tournament sponsors drop their sponsorships. The Olympic movement could not fill the 12 corporate slots for its TOP sponsorship program for the 2010 Games; the 2010 Vancouver Games ended up with only 9

TOP sponsors. Currently, the London Games is one sponsor short of filling its 12 slots for TOP sponsors. Some companies have questioned the value of a large sponsorship commitment in tight economic times, including Kodak, which has been a partner since the inception of the TOP program in 1985 (Balfour and Jana, 2008). NASCAR has also been a victim of the economic downturn. Some teams have been forced out of business, and other teams have merged or significantly reduced operations (Fryer, 2010). Another example are sport organizations that have had to seek new naming-rights sponsors after the company that purchased the naming rights to their facility collapsed or merged. A classic example occurred in 2002 when Enron, owner of the naming rights to the Houston Astros' ballpark, collapsed in one of the biggest business scandals in history. More recently, BP Oil Company's affiliation with various sport properties has come into question after the oil spill in the Gulf of Mexico created public outrage.

In addition to relationships with external publics such as the media, consumers, and the community, there is a need to attend to industry-specific relationships as well as relationships with governmental entities, investors, international groups, the financial community, and opinion leaders. Internally, employee relations are important not just from the

## Table 2.3 Application of the ROPES Model

| Public relations process steps | Focus |
|---|---|
| Conducting research | Organization (history, personnel, products, services) <br> Publics (history, nature of relationship, involvement) <br> Issues (viewpoints, urgency, risks, rewards) |
| Setting objectives | Output objectives—measures related to public relations techniques (how many stories, how much direct mail, how much newsletter circulation?) <br> Impact objectives—measures related to awareness, understanding, behavior (what effect did the public relations techniques have?) |
| Programming | Planning—developing activities designed to produce desired outcomes outlined in the objectives <br> Implementation—execution of the planned public relations activities |
| Evaluation | Preparation—pilot testing <br> Process—control mechanisms <br> Program—summative evaluation of results |
| Stewardship | Reciprocity—demonstrating gratitude <br> Responsibility—acting as good citizens <br> Reporting—keeping publics informed <br> Relationship nurturing—treating publics well |

Based on Kelly 2001.

standpoint of morale and productivity but because of the public relations role that all employees play in projecting the image of the organization. Subsequent chapters will discuss these publics in more detail.

Although an organization should consider all important stakeholders in developing its strategic management plan, Neely, Adams, and Crowe (2001) pointed out that the relationships between an organization and its constituencies should be viewed as reciprocal rather than unidirectional. Sport organizations must deliver value to their stakeholders, but they should also recognize the contributions that stakeholders make to the organization. Not all stakeholders are equally vital to organizational success, and resource limitations sometimes necessitate difficult choices that benefit some constituents at the expense of others. A systematic evaluation of the nature and extent of these stakeholder contributions will help managers prioritize organizational efforts and resources as they oversee these stakeholder relationships.

## Public Relations Evaluation

The inherent ambiguity of some aspects of public relations makes evaluation of public relations efforts challenging, but unless an organization is committed to evaluation, the old adage "You can't manage what you don't measure" will come into play. As public relations receives more formal attention in strategic planning, additional effort will be required to measure how it contributes to organizational success.

Hon (1998) suggested that it is useful for public relations planning to occur in a systematic way because the public relations goals are likely to be articulated in more specific terms and tied more directly to the organizational mission. This in turn will produce more accountability and clearer assessment and evaluation. Assessment may have both quantitative and qualitative components. As various public relations strategies are developed, effort should be made to attach clear assessment criteria. For some public relations activities, the goals are relatively short term and quantifiable. For example, a new fitness club that conducts an open house can evaluate the success of the event based on the desired number of attendees or the number of resulting memberships. The club can also collect qualitative information by conducting follow-up surveys to assess visitor attitudes and perceptions.

Grunig (2006) pointed out that many of the metrics used to evaluate public relations tend to focus on tactical activities such as media placements and their effect on sales or consumer preference. Although such tactical measurement is necessary, from a strategic standpoint, evaluating public relations strategies and tactics should be done in terms of how effective they are in cultivating quality relationships. Hon and Grunig (1999) identified six components for evaluating the outcomes of long-term relationships including mutual control, trust, satisfaction, commitment, exchange relationship, and communal relationship. Table 2.4 provides clarifying explanations for each component.

Other public relations activities may have effects that are harder to measure. The college cross-country team that participates in an elementary school program that encourages children to read or the sporting goods store that donates $1,000 of equipment to the local Special Olympics will produce public relations effects that are ambiguous and difficult to evaluate. Poole (2004) acknowledged the often qualitative nature of the contribution that public relations makes to organizational success. This qualitative value involves the vagaries of brand partiality and loyalty that may generate "top-of-mind" brand preferences when employed effectively. Poole cited the success of Home Depot's association with the United States Olympic Committee's (USOC's) Olympic Job Opportunity Program before the 2002 Winter Olympics as an example of how public relations can multiply sponsorship value. These types of public relations initiatives have a broader and more qualitative intent and are usually better assessed collectively over a longer time span. They may be designed to influence broader attributes such as reputation or public engagement rather than focus on narrower marketing goals such as increases in sales or market share. From a strategic perspective, however, whatever public relations plans are developed should be thoughtfully designed with a clear

## Table 2.4 Relationship Components

| Relationship components | Description | Example |
|---|---|---|
| Mutual control | The degree to which parties agree on who has the rightful power to influence one another | Management–union relationship |
| Trust | Each party's level of confidence in and willingness to be open to the other party (three dimensions to trust: integrity, dependability, competence) | Sports information–media relationship |
| Satisfaction | The extent to which each party feels favorably toward the other because positive expectations about the relationship are reinforced | Team–sponsor relationship |
| Commitment | The extent to which each party believes that the relationship is worth the expenditure of energy to maintain and promote (two dimensions of commitment: continuance commitment and affective commitment) | Athletics department–donor relationship |
| Exchange relationship | The sense that one party gives benefits to the other only because the other has provided benefits in the past or is expected to do so in the future | Employee–employer relationship |
| Communal relationship | The willingness of each party to provide benefits to the other because of concern for the welfare of the other, even when receiving nothing in return | Sport team–charity relationship |

Adapted from Hon and Grunig 1999.

connection to organizational mission and a focus on strengthening key relationships.

# Issues Management

Although identifying relevant publics is a fundamental public relations activity, equally important is recognizing the concerns that are likely to create the connection between the sport organization and those publics. **Issues management** is defined by the Public Affairs Council, a nonpartisan association for public affairs professionals, as "the process of prioritizing and proactively addressing public policy and reputation issues that can affect an organization's success" (Pinkham, 2004). Lesly (1998) noted that an issue is a matter of mutual concern where there are differing points of view regarding the appropriate action. Dale (2002) described issues as the product of problems, opportunities, uncertainties, and controversies, and suggested that issues warrant strategic consideration by key organizational decision makers. He proposed a systematic response to issues that begins with issue recognition, which involves a strategic diagnosis of both the internal and external environments. Issue shaping follows and includes prioritizing and screening issues based on effects and likelihood. This step also involves a more refined and precise statement of the issues. The final step is issue resolution, in which real options are developed, evaluated, and implemented.

An example of a situation that would require issues management for various organizations is the construction of a new stadium. Numerous publics will have a wide array of opinions on the issues that arise from such a project, ranging from whether it should be done at all to how it should be funded to where it should be located to what companies should be awarded the work. When the Pittsburgh Pirates and Pittsburgh Steelers attempted to generate support for replacing Three Rivers Stadium with individual facilities for each team, they were met with substantial resistance by some groups. For the teams, one issue was the desire to extract as much public funding as possible for the facilities. They wanted the stadiums and the teams to be viewed as public assets worthy of public support. An initial effort was made to raise the sales tax in the region under a proposal known as the Regional Renaissance Initiative. The taxpayers resoundingly defeated the referendum largely because they saw the proposal as a stadium development plan rather than an economic development plan. Groups opposed to public subsidization of the stadiums effectively positioned the issue as tax support for rich owners, which undermined supporters' efforts to position it as regional economic development. Stadium proponents were also hindered by the fact that the stadium being replaced (Three Rivers Stadium) was not yet paid for and the promise of economic development surrounding Three Rivers had never materialized. Perhaps greater emphasis on how much each team was contributing to its new stadium and how the facilities might be used in other ways to benefit the region would have affected voter attitudes. Firm commitments for surrounding development would also have helped overcome the credibility gap.

Lesly (1998) distinguished among issues, crises, and emergencies. A crisis is a pivotal turning point that will have lasting effect on an organization's future and tends to be much more critical than an emergency, which is an unexpected occurrence that lacks the potential long-range effects of a crisis. In the previous example, the Pirates in particular were confronting a crisis when the taxpayers voted down the sales tax increase. Without a new stadium the Pirates were in all likelihood going to consider relocation as a viable option, which energized efforts to find an alternative strategy for financing the ballpark.

Public relations plays an important role in managing crises and emergencies, and plans must be in place to direct those efforts. From a strategic perspective, issues management provides a foundation for a great deal of public relations activity because issues serve as the connection between organizations and their publics. Effective issues management may prevent or at least minimize the effects of emergencies and crises.

Heath (1997) identified four essential aspects of issues management:

1. Anticipate and analyze issues.
2. Develop organizational positions on the issues.
3. Identify key publics affected by the issues.
4. Identify the desired behavior of those publics.

Organizational action that has a substantive effect on one or more of its publics may qualify as an issue. Anticipating a public's reaction and developing an organizational response are key public relations responsibilities. For instance, the use of Native American nicknames and mascots for sport teams has been prevalent in the United States for many years. Protests have periodically raised awareness of the issue and, on occasion, schools have changed their nicknames. Any school using such a name can reasonably expect that the name will become an issue at some point and should plan accordingly. What is the institutional position on the issue, and what publics are likely to have an interest? What public relations activities will be required to produce acceptance of the organizational position? Will the organizational position need to be modified to align more closely with a public's position? This issue has seen several organizations move away from the existing organizational stance in recent years.

Some issues can pose public relations problems when an organizational action contradicts the organization's stated mission or position. As an example, the NCAA and its members continually stress the student in the term *student–athlete* but, according to some, often make decisions that don't appear to be in the best interest of the student. Schedules become longer, and the financial stakes associated with football and basketball success continue to grow. Approximately one-third of the money that the NCAA distributes to Division I schools hinges on basketball success. In the 2010–11 distribution period, each win in the NCAA tournament was worth nearly $240,000 to the winning school's conference, and the total allocation from the basketball fund was around $180 million. From an economic standpoint the emphasis that schools and the NCAA put on basketball is probably a logical action given that approximately 90% of the NCAA's revenue comes from television rights for the Division I men's basketball tournament (NCAA, 2010a). Certainly, the NCAA is not interested in jeopardizing the popularity of its cash cow, and the economic incentives associated with basketball success have resulted in athletics departments continuing to pump significant resources into their basketball programs. But the economic emphasis on one sport seems at odds with the NCAA's stated purpose, which is in part "to promote and develop educational leadership, physical fitness, athletics excellence, and athletics participation as a *recreational* (emphasis added) pursuit." The basic purpose, according to the NCAA, "is to maintain intercollegiate athletics as an integral part of the educational program and the athlete as an integral part of the student body, and by so doing, retain a clear line of demarcation between intercollegiate athletics and professional sports" (NCAA, 2010b). The conflict between the NCAA's stated purpose and some of its actions has stirred debate surrounding issues related to commercialization and professionalization and is consistently a public relations challenge for the NCAA as it deals with critics (an adversarial public) of college athletics.

An interesting issue confronting the major professional sport leagues (NFL, MLB, NHL, NBA) as well as college sport in the United States is approval in 2009 by Delaware's legislature of legalized sports gambling. These sport organizations have long been publicly opposed to sports gambling, and Delaware's move to legalize sports wagers is certainly a challenge to that stance. The result has been a lawsuit filed by the leagues and the NCAA to stop Delaware from taking bets on their games, contending that such action violates state gambling laws as well as the Professional and Amateur Sports Protection Act (PASPA). The leagues and the NCAA believe that such action challenges the integrity of their games and damages their reputation and goodwill (Millman, 2009). Although the lawsuit appears to be consistent with the sport organizations' long-standing position on the issue, some believe it to be inconsistent with actions that support fantasy sports involvement and willing acceptance of sponsor deals with lotteries and casinos. When NFL pregame shows have the studio panel predicting the outcome of upcoming games against the spread, critics are likely to view the league's stance against gambling to be inconsistent with its actions.

The importance of issues management should not be underestimated. It can serve to clarify, maintain, and even enhance relationships with key publics. How issues are handled is likely to be a primary influence on stakeholder perceptions of reputation. When organizations proactively consider issues and give stakeholders the sense that their views are considered and that dialogue is possible, they may be able to defuse some potentially serious public relations problems.

# Organizational Reputation

Descriptions of public relations often include the management of image or **reputation**. Such a reference may cause some confusion. Reputation management is often narrowly perceived as the protection or repair of reputation during a crisis. This important aspect of public relations is considered in some depth in chapter 10, but it is shortsighted to think that the only time an organization should attend to reputation management is during a crisis. Many decisions made during the strategic management process have great influence on organizational reputation, which brings us to the source of confusion on a conceptual level. What is reputation? How is it different from brand or image? Are the distinctions important, and if so, what are the implications for public relations practice?

Contributing to the uncertainty about the concept of reputation is the interchangeable and inconsistent use of other terms such as brand, identity, and image and the combination of such terms (e.g., brand identity, brand reputation). Many attempts have been made to define reputation and to distinguish reputation from **brand**. Perhaps the most consistent distinction between reputation and brand is the idea that brand is a "consumercentric" term more associated with marketing and marketing communications. Reputation is a "companycentric" term that focuses on credibility and respect among a broader set of constituencies and is more likely to rely on public relations techniques. Branding is the effort to differentiate an organization or product from others, whereas reputation is largely built on attributes to which all organizations aspire such as integrity, reliability, and quality (Ettenson & Knowles, 2008; Macnamara, 2006).

Barnett, Jermier, and Lafferty (2006), after an extensive review of the definitions of "corporate reputation," found no consistent usage but several similarities that centered on reputation as stakeholders' collective perceptions, reputation as stakeholders' judgment and evaluation, and reputation as a valued intangible asset. This investigation led to a model that differentiated corporate reputation from some of the related concepts. The model suggests that corporate identity includes the central features of the organization that make it distinctive. The corporate image involves stakeholder impressions of the organization and is often shaped by marketing and public relations efforts. Corporate reputation is the judgments made by stakeholders about the organization. Although these judgments may stem from identity and image, reputation is often influenced by direct interaction with the organization or some external event (an issue perhaps) that provides some opportunity for evaluation.

Reputation and brand are clearly connected. Damage to one can create problems for the other, and there is surely interest at the strategic level for development of strategies to establish a brand identity and to sustain reputation. Ries and Ries (2002) contend that brand building is the fundamental role of public relations and that other public relations functions will have little effect on organizational success without a great brand. Aaker (1991) described **brand equity** as "a set of assets and liabilities linked to a brand . . . that add to or subtract from the value provided by a product or service."

He suggested that potential assets include loyalty, awareness, and perceptions of quality that can enhance consumer confidence and produce competitive advantages. These assets as they relate to a specific brand are much like the benefits that a good reputation provides for an organization as a whole. Certainly, sport organizations have an interest in developing an identity that is viewed positively and serves the operation well. Colleges and universities often attempt to capitalize on the strength of their athletics brand to support the institutional brand. Consider how effectively ESPN has built its identity over the past 25 years. It has developed a brand name that is virtually synonymous with televised sport and continues to expand its presence with ESPN2, ESPN3, ESPN Classic, ESPN News, and ESPN Deportes among other offerings (Martzke & Cherner, 2004).

Segments of the sport industry that receive extensive publicity are particularly vulnerable to reputational challenges. The exposure received by major professional and college teams and individual sports stars is often outside their control and comes with an intense scrutiny that makes the task of managing reputation extremely demanding. Some organizations and individuals employ consultants to assist them with reputation-related issues. The sidebar titled Working as a Sport Public Relations Consultant, written by Kathleen Hessert of Sports Media Challenge, describes the work of public relations consultants and offers sage advice.

Some sport organizations have improved their strategic focus on reputation in recent years by devoting more attention to mission development and identification of publics. Prominent individual athletes (e.g., Tiger Woods, LeBron James) have some of the same public relations concerns as organizations do and would be well served to take a strategic look at reputation as they position themselves in the marketplace. Unfortunately, many still tend to ignore strategic reputation management and settle for crisis management.

Scandals and misbehavior seem to be a routine part of the sport landscape. The Tour de France and Major League Baseball are among the prominent victims of image problems created by use of performance-enhancing drugs. Some local YMCAs have been challenged for appearing to operate much like commercial health clubs while enjoying tax-exempt status. Various professional teams have been characterized as extortionists for using money from local taxpayers to build new stadiums and arenas. The list of athletes and coaches who have tarnished their own reputations as well as those of

# Working as a Sport Public Relations Consultant

## Kathleen Hessert

Courtesy of Sports Media Challenge / BuzzManager Inc.

Over the past couple of days I've counseled an ousted hoops coach on steps that he will have to take to be reinstated, analyzed a print article about a client and owner of a pro team embroiled in a labor dispute, begun writing a speech for a celebrity athlete, and participated in a Citizenship Through Sports Alliance (CTSA) national advisory board meeting focused on improving sportsmanship and overall conduct in athletics. In this business there's lots of variety and never a dull moment.

Since 1988, when I launched Sports Media Challenge, a division of my company, Communication Concepts, we've provided strategic communication consulting and training throughout sport from amateur to professional ranks, at the collegiate, Olympic, and even high school level. When my children began to excel athletically as early as 10 years old and then be recruited for Division I sports, I started looking for reasonable and cost-effective ways to provide media training, reputation management, and personal brand development where appropriate for kids and their coaches.

Over the years, in speeches and media training sessions for SIDs, athletic directors, and public relations professionals, I've lamented the fact that we provide our athletes with the best possible equipment and conditions in which to compete and then leave them to fend for themselves when their competitive position thrusts them squarely in the glare of public exposure. Frankly, that's unethical. We allow them and in many cases force them to publicly represent themselves, their teams, and their institutions with minimal or no training in public speaking and dealing with the media. They're forced to either hide or answer difficult and often unseemly questions with microphones thrust in their face to capture every word, glaring lights straining their eyes, strangers, even adversaries, scribbling every word, noting every grimace, and capturing on camera every bead of perspiration and angst.

Whether athletes or coaches are competing for outrageous marketing dollars, participating in job interviews at the NFL Combine, or simply representing their team on the local *Athlete of the Week* show, what they say and how they say it, whether right or wrong, bland or outrageous, ripples through their lives. For example, a particular African American track star competing in the Atlanta Olympics typically expressed herself with intelligence and insight. That skill was blatantly obvious and welcomed by journalists, but to the athlete their acknowledgment of her skill was problematic. She complained to me that every story portrayed her as intelligent! A Stanford student, she was obviously bright, but she was offended that the media felt the need to brand her that way. She said, "They wouldn't feel the need to say that about me if I were white." I looked her and her teammates in the eye and explained that if that was the worst they could write about her she was lucky. The biggest stereotype that this talented group and soon-to-be Olympic medalists had to fight was almost universal and very insidious: They had to fight the perception that they were dumb jocks. There's a widespread perception that if you're physically gifted, you don't have much on the intellectual end.

I'm often asked why seasoned and well-publicized athletes like shortstop Derek Jeter, quarterback Peyton Manning, and tennis players Venus and Serena Williams would need a media coach

> We provide our athletes with the best possible equipment and conditions in which to compete and then leave them to fend for themselves when their competitive position thrusts them squarely in the glare of public exposure. Frankly, that's unethical.

*(continued)*

*(continued)*

or image strategist like me after being on the world stage for so long. The reason is exactly the same as the reason they still use athletic coaches: They strive for excellence in all areas of their lives. The best always look for the edge—something to make them even slightly better when measured against their opponents. Their standard of excellence is significantly higher than those of us with much more common talents.

Standout athletes, coaches, and sport administrators of high-profile organizations have an image of their own or others' making. The basis for my training and consulting is founded on the premise that you can let the world define you and your image or you can actively participate in its creation, refinement, and perpetuation. It's your name, so teach them how to spell it! That requires the right measure of thought, effort, and outside guidance.

I tell my clients, "You are your brand, so make it one to be proud of." Whether your exposure is brought on by a crisis or a championship, whether the medium is broadcast, Internet, talk radio, or a speech in a high school gym, consistently sell your brand.

In my book *The Coach's Communication Playbook* (1998), I introduce the concept of the *success pie*. To succeed as a person, product, or business, there are three essential components: performance, image, and exposure. Without equal balance of the three, you're facing serious limitations. It's no longer enough to just be really good at what you do. You've heard the line, "I'll do my talking on the field." A racecar driver who wins on the track but can't articulate his passion for the sport will have limited value to a sponsor who pays to make the car competitive.

I also teach clients three core principles:

1. Never engage in an interview with the thought that you don't need to prepare because you're just going to answer their questions. When you don't prepare, you're handing over all the power to the opponent. Go into every session with a clear, strong agenda of your own both to balance the power and to direct the interview where you want it to go.

2. When in crisis, "Go for the quick hemorrhage, not the slow bleed." Silence tends to create a void that feeds negative speculation.

3. Tell audiences something they can't see or hear for themselves. The most effective interviews draw on the person's senses, providing a unique perspective on the goal, loss, play, putt, and so on. What did you hear when you were skating your very best on the way to a world record and the fans were chanting your name? Silence. That sort of unique perspective adds insight and contrast to the fan's experience.

When athletes can paint an indelible picture in the fans' minds, when they can tug at the heartstrings by giving fans a glimpse of their souls, then they've become not only champion competitors but also champion communicators, and prized members of any team.

*Kathleen Hessert is the president of Sports Media Challenge, a speaking, training, and consulting firm based in Charlotte, North Carolina, and is the founder and CEO of BuzzManager.*

their employers seems to grow almost daily. Few examples of the effect of behavior on reputation have been as spectacular as the recent Tiger Woods fiasco. Tiger's carefully crafted public image quickly crumbled under the scrutiny of all forms of media that not only left Tiger's reputation in tatters but also put the PGA and Woods' endorsement partners in difficult positions. All these problems require **reactive public relations** responses as organizations and individuals seek to repair damaged reputations. Strategic reputation management, however, requires **proactive public relations** that concentrates on building and sustaining the desired reputation. Regrettably (or perhaps appropriately), even the most meticulously constructed reputation plans may fall apart under the weight of scandalous behavior.

## Elements of Reputation

As sport organizations examine the benefits of reputation management, they must first determine the attributes that their publics are likely to find important. This process is more complex than might first be imagined. The first complication is that most organizations have multiple publics. Different publics are likely to have differing opinions about what makes an organization reputable. Duke University receives accolades for its rigorous academic standards and high graduation rates. Would as many dedicated fans camp out for basketball tickets if the team didn't also win plenty of games? Would the faculty be willing to accept lower academic standards if that were necessary to continue to win basketball games? In this case two publics with somewhat different priorities are appeased, and each has its expectations met. In many cases reconciling competing expectations may not be so easy. As an example, an athlete has certain privacy rights that limit how much information can be released to the public. The media might want a great deal more information about a star athlete's academic difficulties than the institution can share or desires to share.

Beyond the complication of multiple publics is the variation within publics. Among long-suffering Pittsburgh Pirates fans (19 straight losing seasons as of the writing of this manuscript) are those who are outraged with the team's continual trading away of

some of the fans' favorite players. Others contend that the most popular players have not been able to prevent losing seasons and that building the system through trades is the way to move the organization forward. A third group of fans want to see a winner but are perfectly willing to follow the team and attend a few games a year in a great ballpark as long as prices remain reasonable. Three sets of fans have three different expectations of the organization. Each of the three publics has the potential to feel betrayed if the strategic choices made by Pirates' management fall short of their expectations. Some of each group will likely feel let down when stories come out about the Pirates' ownership making a profit while the team continues to lose. Reputation is built largely on confidence and trust. When organizations or individuals undermine the faith that their publics hold in them, they jeopardize the relationships that public relations is trying to build.

Fombrun (1996) described reputation as a reconciliation of all the images people have of an organization that convey the relative prestige and status of a company compared with its competitors.

Duke University's men's basketball program has successfully managed to satisfy fans' desire for a perennial winner without compromising Duke's academic reputation.

Jason Moore/Icon SMI

41

Reputation is an intangible corporate asset that can enhance success and temper the damage of crises. Reputation reflects the ability of an organization to meet the expectations of its publics and the strength of the relationship that various stakeholders have with the organization.

As organizations seek to develop, enhance, and preserve their reputations, they must have clearly identified publics and know what those publics value in their relationships. Fombrun, Gardberg, and Sever (1999) developed an instrument that attempts to measure reputation. The Corporate Reputation Quotient of Harris-Fombrun (*Corporate Reputation Quotient*, n.d.) is a multidimensional assessment of reputation that recognizes that various stakeholders have different perspectives and expectations. It is designed to measure corporate reputation by assessing stakeholder perceptions, and it also clarifies what attributes tend to be the most influential determinants of reputation. Although not constructed specifically for sport organizations, it can be applied to a variety of sport settings.

The model identifies six reputation drivers and 20 attributes. The reputation drivers include emotional appeal, products and services, vision and leadership, workplace environment, financial performance, and social responsibility. Each of these drivers has an associated set of attributes, most of which can be applied to any organization. Both the reputation drivers and many of their associated attributes are summarized in table 2.5. Note that this model was designed to include the perceptions of multiple stakeholders, not just consumers or members of the media. This feature enhances its usefulness because it becomes more of a strategic management tool rather than simply another consumer behavior model. It can also serve as a tactical assessment and development tool as organizations attempt to discover how they are perceived by various publics.

## Emotional Appeal

Emotional appeal includes attributes associated with admiration, respect, trust, and positive regard. The spectator sport segment of the industry can readily relate to this aspect of reputation given the zeal with which some fans attach themselves to their teams. Many companies would love to see the same type of emotional attachment that some fans exhibit for their alma mater or hometown team. NASCAR fans are particularly well known for their loyalty, not only to the race-car drivers but also to the sponsors who fund them. Sport organizations

### Table 2.5 Reputation Quotient

| Reputation drivers | Driver attributes |
| --- | --- |
| Emotional appeal | Good feeling<br>Respect<br>Trust |
| Products and services | Stands behind products<br>Innovative<br>High quality and good value |
| Vision and leadership | Excellent leadership<br>Clear vision<br>Opportunistic |
| Workplace environment | Well managed<br>Appealing place to work<br>Good employees |
| Financial performance | Profitable<br>Good investment with bright future<br>Outperforms competition |
| Social responsibility | Supports good causes<br>Environmentally responsible<br>Treats people well |

Adapted from Fombrun, Gardberg, and Sever 1999.

must identify what produces such loyalty and take steps to foster it.

## Products and Services

Products and services incorporate reputation-related attributes such as product quality, innovation, and value. This aspect of reputation addresses many of the positioning issues that most organizations must wrestle with. For example, a sporting goods manufacturer such as a golf-club producer must weigh a variety of options as it positions itself in the marketplace. Quality versus value, high-end versus mainstream, broad distribution versus narrow distribution, skim pricing versus penetration pricing, and cutting-edge innovation versus established technology are all choices that must be made. Larger operations may have the luxury of positioning themselves across a spectrum of positions, but they risk creating confusion about their brand identity. Sponsors and investors are publics that are likely to place a high priority on products and services as well. Sport organizations must be aware of the significance of this facet of reputation in establishing and maintaining relationships with these stakeholder groups.

## Vision and Leadership

Vision and leadership deal with perceptions of who is directing the organization as well as the direction that the organization is taking. Vision and leadership are of particular importance to employee relations. Employee productivity, enthusiasm, and morale are greatly enhanced by effective leadership, but these qualities can be decimated when employees lack a strong belief that leadership knows what they are doing.

Relationships with the financial community and political community are also influenced by the quality of leadership in an organization. The belief that an organization is capable of capitalizing on opportunities and making progress will engender confidence among those publics. As an example, politicians are much more inclined to support requests for stadium funding when they have confidence that the team is well run. When teams are constantly in a rebuilding phase or demonstrate little stability and focus, they do not boost the image that they present to their constituencies. For high-profile sport operations such as professional teams, leadership tends to be highly visible and is likely to have an important effect on external stakeholder perceptions of how competently the organization is managed. Some of these leaders (e.g., George Steinbrenner, Mark Cuban, Jerry Jones) may be controversial and create public relations problems at times.

## Workplace Environment

Workplace environment focuses on attributes of reputation concerned with employees and the conditions under which they work. The quality of the work environment is a primary determinant of how employees feel about their work and their employer. Although the focus of this reputation attribute is directed toward an internal public, it has important external implications. Because all employees are reflections of the organization, they will have an effect on the perception held by the publics with whom they interact. The receptionist who greets club members in a positive and friendly manner and the marketing director who tells colleagues that she is treated well by her employer are simple examples of the image that organizations want to reflect. Attitude and word of mouth are powerful influences in the marketplace. When employees represent the working environment in a positive way, keeping customers, recruiting quality employees,

and portraying the organization as well managed becomes much easier. Many tools are available to assess employee satisfaction and engagement, and companies that ignore how their employees feel are failing to pay attention to an important public relations asset.

## Financial Performance

Financial performance includes profitability, investment potential, and competitiveness. These basic success measures are essential to corporate reputation. Sound financial operations have great appeal for investors and donors and give the impression that the organization is well run. In spectator sport, financial success and on-field success are often closely related, and sponsors desire associations with successful operations. The trappings of financial success are also important to the perception of an organization. For example, sport organizations try to reflect financial success and stability through facilities. College athletics programs are caught up in an arms race of facility development that involves building bigger and better stadiums, practice areas, weight rooms, and support facilities to lure recruits.

## Social Responsibility

Social responsibility consists of supporting causes and community—in essence, corporate citizenship. An organization like the YMCA may enjoy benefits of this image attribute because of their fundamental purpose as a community servant. Other sport organizations must embrace this aspect of reputation more purposefully. The NFL has had a long association with the United Way, and the NBA promotes the Read to Achieve program. A number of sporting events benefit charities such as the PGA tournament in Memphis that benefits St. Jude Children's Research Hospital. Many golf and tennis tournaments as well as some football bowl games and basketball tournaments have charity partners. Individual athletes also support and in some cases initiate fund-raising events for particular causes. For example, the Mario Lemieux Celebrity Invitational golf tournament raised several million dollars for cancer research. Local professional teams often have events to raise money for a variety of social purposes, and the *NCAA News* routinely chronicles college athletics programs involved in community service. Commercial enterprises also engage in such endeavors by affiliating with charitable events and occasionally by developing their own programs (e.g., NikeGo). This "cause marketing" demonstrates organizational interest for important social concerns and enhances stakeholder perceptions about the social contribution that these organizations make. (Chapter 12 discusses this aspect of reputation in more detail.)

Another avenue of social responsibility that has been embraced in recent years is the growing emphasis on "green" operations and sustainability. "Going green" is a familiar concept that addresses primarily environmental concerns such as recycling and energy conservation. Sustainability in its broadest interpretation looks to provide integration and balance of environmental, social, and economic concerns and the tradeoffs that exist among them (Adams, 2006). Many sport organizations have become more attuned to the environmental aspect of sustainability, particularly in the construction and operation of facilities. A few existing sport facilities such as Phillips Arena in Atlanta and American Airlines Arena in Miami have received leadership in energy and environmental design (LEED) certification for their environmental efforts (Environmental Leader, 2009). The Pittsburgh Penguins are seeking gold level certification for their new arena, which would be the first major sport facility in the United States with such a designation ("Penguins' New Arena," 2009). Other sport operations such as golf courses and ski resorts also have become much more aware of their impact on the environment and the value of being perceived as responsible community stewards. The November 10–16, 2008, *SportsBusiness Journal* had a special report on environmental efforts of various organizations and leagues.

## Measuring Reputation Value

The value of reputation, an intangible asset, is difficult to establish in precise and objective terms. What value can be attached to names like the Yankees, Manchester United, and the National Football League? A 2007 report by Ozanian and Schwartz attempted to identify the world's strongest sport brands by using a variety of financial measures while emphasizing that the value built up in the name occurred over years or decades. They ranked the brands across four categories: athlete, business, team, and event. Table 2.6 lists the top brands in each category.

Sport organizations should make an effort to assess what constituencies think about the organization and how that translates into behavior toward the organization. The connection between perceptions and behaviors is an important practical matter. Public relations practitioners may become preoccupied with superficial symbolic activities that alone may have little effect on organizational success. Substantive behavioral relationships must be built with the stakeholders (Grunig, 1993). Although having their organization viewed in a positive light is good, at some point sport managers would like to see some tangible benefit (e.g., more fans, members, sponsors, publicity) from the efforts to build a strong reputation. In some respects the desire is to combine a good reputation (corporate interest) with a strong brand (marketing interest). Aaker (1991) outlined

## Table 2.6 Top Sport Brands

| Athlete | Business | Team | Event |
|---|---|---|---|
| Tiger Woods | ESPN | Manchester United | Super Bowl |
| David Beckham | Nike | Real Madrid | Summer Olympics |
| Phil Mickelson | Adidas | Bayern Munich | FIFA World Cup |
| Roger Federer | Under Armour | New York Yankees | Daytona 500 |
| LeBron James | EA Sports | Arsenal | NCAA Final Four |
| Maria Sharapova | Sky Sports | AC Milan | Winter Olympics |
| Ronaldinho | Reebok | Dallas Cowboys | Rose Bowl |
| Dale Earnhardt Jr. | YES Network | Barcelona | World Series |
| Peyton Manning | IMG | Boston Red Sox | Kentucky Derby |
| Jeff Gordon | MSG Network | Washington Redskins | NBA Finals |

Based on Ozanian and Schwartz 2007.

several approaches that might be used to determine the value of so-called brand equity. In many cases a good reputation helps support premium pricing. Nike may be able to charge more for shoes, Titleist more for golf balls, and Easton more for bats than the competition because of their brand strength in the marketplace. Another approach tries to gauge the effect of the brand name on customer preferences and attitudes. For example, if consumer approval ratings for an athletic shoe improve after the brand name is known, the inference can be made that the brand equity can be quantified by a difference in ratings. Loyalty measures such as satisfaction and repeat consumption may also be useful in assessing reputation. Efforts to assess stakeholder awareness, attitudes, and perceptions about the organization will be useful in judging reputation strengths and weaknesses.

Many facets of reputation contribute to organizational identity. As sport organizations nurture relationships with all their relevant publics, they must make strategic choices about managing reputation. Those decisions must then be translated into behaviors that are consistent with how the organization wants to be perceived in the marketplace. The sidebar titled An Identity Crisis for the LPGA focuses on the LPGA Tour's operational concerns as it tries to position itself in the marketplace and address important issues that affect its brand and reputation.

## An Identity Crisis for the LPGA

The LPGA is one of the oldest and most well-established professional sport organizations for women. From its initial total prize money of $50,000 in 1950, the LPGA increased its prize money to nearly $60 million in 2008. Despite this growth and its established reputation, the LPGA is facing a wide range of issues as it moves forward. From a financial perspective, the economic downturn has created a series of problems for the LPGA, as it has for most sport organizations. The tour has lost 10 events since 2008 and is down to 24 events for 2010, including only 13 in the United States (Newport, 2009). The Corning Classic, a tour staple for over 30 years, is coming to an end, and McDonald's is dropping its sponsorship of the LPGA Championship. This circumstance is only part of the problem, however, as the LPGA struggles to carve out a niche in the landscape of spectator sport.

### What Are the Barriers That the LPGA Faces in Building Its Identity?

One issue is the age-old battle that women's sports have faced to gain attention among sports fans. Despite additional avenues for distribution (e.g., the Golf Channel, regional sport networks, international outlets), women's sports rarely reach into the mainstream of sport consciousness. The LPGA operates in the shadow of the PGA, particularly the dominating presence of Tiger Woods. Tiger is the center of the golf universe, and any golf event without his involvement tends to be viewed as inconsequential by many fans. TV ratings for "Tiger-less" PGA events plunged anywhere from 11% to 61% when Woods left the tour with a knee injury halfway through the 2008 season (DiMeglio, 2010). A second issue deals with the increasingly successful contingent of foreign players, particularly those from Asia. In the 2009 U.S. Open, 20 of the 72 players to make the cut were from South Korea and 5 of them finished in the top 10 (Hunsberger, 2009). The need for an interpreter to conduct postevent interviews presents problems in creating connections between fans and players. At one point former LPGA commissioner Carolyn Bivens attempted to enact an English fluency requirement for LPGA members. This effort created a great deal of negative publicity and was criticized as being at the very least insensitive, and many considered it racist. This issue also extends to the lack of a dominant American star or another transcendent player who can be used as the face of the tour. Much of the tour's operation is in the United States, and the tour relies on support from American fans and sponsors. Lorena Ochoa (Mexico), Annika Sorenstam (Sweden), and Karrie Webb (Australia) all have had a period of dominance on the tour in recent years. Sorenstam, a legitimate sports superstar who was extremely valuable in attracting attention to the sport, retired in 2008, and Ochoa followed suit early in 2010, leaving the game without its two biggest stars of recent years. Some have speculated that Michelle Wie might provide a spark for the tour, but the effect of her regular presence on the tour is still linked at least in part to her performance, which has been somewhat disappointing to this point.

*(continued)*

(continued)

## What Opportunities Exist for Building the LPGA Brand?

The LPGA has attempted to be a fan-friendly, sponsor-friendly operation that allows both fans and sponsors the opportunity to relate on a personal level and create connections with the players. One of the problems with the presence of so many non-American players is that those connections are somewhat difficult to forge. The LPGA has expanded the number of events outside the United States in recent years as one strategy for capitalizing on the international player pool. In fact, the tour only held two events in the United States in the first four months of 2011. The largest single revenue source for the LPGA is rights fees paid by Korean television (Lipsey, 2010). The Solheim Cup, a female version of the Ryder Cup that pits players from the United States and Europe against each other in a team competition, has experienced some success, and another team event featuring Asian players might showcase women's golf to another audience. In addition, some players view the global nature of the game as being helpful in expanding their endorsement opportunities beyond American markets. Dottie Pepper, tour veteran and golf analyst, suggested that a more human touch could help nurture relationships between tournaments and their sponsors and charity partners, especially during turbulent economic times (Pepper, 2009).

## SUMMARY

As sport organizations vie for attention and support in a competitive marketplace, they must strive to accommodate the expectations of their publics. The demand for immediacy can produce impatience on the part of both organizations and publics. This compressed window of opportunity may entice some to disregard the ideals of their vision for more immediate rewards, resulting in an environment in which relationships are viewed as short-term commodities rather than long-term assets. The temptation to take shortcuts often results in action that is inconsistent with the mission statement and creates public relations problems. If public relations is to contribute fully to organizational success, it must be integrated into the strategic planning process. Sport managers must have a clear understanding of what their organization's mission is, who its key publics are, and what issues connect the organization to its publics. With this knowledge, public relations can serve as a key component in managing the reputation of an organization and developing and prioritizing the relationships crucial to the success of virtually all sport organizations.

The real measure of an organization's values is how its managers direct their resources. Many organizations profess a commitment to public relations without allocating the necessary resources to integrate public relations into the fabric of the operation. Without dedicating both human and financial resources to public relations, this commitment lacks substance.

Both the organizational chart and the budget should in some way reflect public relations as an organizational priority. One indication of the level of commitment is whether an autonomous public relations department exists within the organization. Another indicator is the number and placement level of public relations personnel in the organizational structure. The allocation of financial resources also demonstrates the priority of public relations within an organization. When public relations is simply a line item in the marketing or corporate communications budget, it may not carry much weight in the organizational chain of influence.

1. Locate the mission, vision, or values statements for three to five sport organizations (Many of these statements are posted on organizational websites.) Critique them using the guidelines and purposes for mission statements outlined in the chapter. Are they concise? Do they include the fundamental components recommended? Do they identify distinguishing organizational features? Do they identify the publics with which they have connections and relationships?

2. Select a sport organization and identify the publics with which it likely has relationships. How might the organization prioritize those relationships? Do the organization's actions appear to be consistent with those priorities?

3. Choose among the publics mentioned in the previous activity and identify two or three issues that will likely connect the organization and each specific public. What are the benefits of handling the issues well? What are the consequences of handling the issues poorly?

4. Evaluate a selected sport organization's reputation using the six drivers of reputation in the Corporate Reputation Quotient. Which of the six drivers are most and least critical to the organization's reputation?

5. Create a list of sport-related entities with a strong brand identity or reputation. Discuss what makes them brand leaders and what potential threats exist to their images.

# Creating Public Relations Campaigns

**After reading this chapter, students should be able to**

- describe the nature of public relations campaigns and distinguish them from public relations programs,
- understand research methods that campaign planners use,
- detail the steps involved in campaign planning,
- list key considerations in campaigns,
- address methods of assessing the effectiveness of campaigns,
- discuss the use of public relations firms to plan and execute campaigns, and
- comprehend case studies of public relations campaigns from diverse areas of the sport industry.

**Key terms discussed in this chapter include**

- programs,
- campaigns,
- integrated communication,
- impressions, and
- public relations firms.

**Chapter 2 addressed** how public relations may be involved in the strategic decisions of a sport organization's management team and how that involvement can contribute to building, maintaining, and improving the organization's reputation. This chapter examines how public relations initiatives within the sport organization may be approached systematically. Public relations campaigns may be executed in ways that facilitate the achievement of important organizational goals. They are most likely to be effective when thoroughly planned from start to finish.

This chapter examines a variety of topics relating to public relations campaigns. First, it describes both public relations programs and campaigns and distinguishes between the two. Second, it details the campaign planning process, examining each step from precampaign research to postcampaign assessment. Third, it discusses the use of public relations firms that specialize in the design and execution of campaigns. Fourth, it presents examples of successful public relations campaigns in diverse areas of the sport industry.

Campaigns differ from programs in several ways (Smith, 2009):

- They have a specific purpose rather than general goals.
- They address a particular issue rather than the overall relationship with a public.
- They are periodic (have distinct time lines) rather than sustained and ongoing.

Table 3.1 highlights the differences between programs and campaigns.

Campaigns often operate within the framework of public relations programs. For example, the media relations program within a college athletics department may initiate a campaign to gain support for an All-America candidate. The community relations program of a professional sport league may execute a campaign to publicize its charitable donations. Public relations programs may administer several campaigns simultaneously and may even work in consultation with external public relations firms, as discussed later in the chapter.

## Distinguishing Between Programs and Campaigns

Chapter 1 noted that two of the more common forms of public relations within sport are media relations and community relations. These activities are now standardized within many sport organizations, and as such they operate as public relations **programs**. They function continuously in an effort to foster desirable relationships with particular stakeholder groups such as the mass media or employees.

## Planning and Executing Campaigns

As with many professional processes, public relations campaigns have been described in numerous ways. For instance, Kendall (1996) used the acronym *RAISE* to describe a five-step model that includes research, adaptation, implementation, strategy, and evaluation. Hendrix (1998) used a similar approach in advocating ROPE, a four-step model whose primary components were research, objectives, programming, and evaluation. Broom (2009) offered a four-step model that includes the following steps:

### Table 3.1 Public Relations Programs Versus Campaigns

|  | Programs | Campaigns |
|---|---|---|
| **Purpose** | Generally desirable relationships | Specific goals |
| **Focus** | Public | Issue |
| **Duration** | Ongoing, continuous | Short term |
| **Example 1** | Media relations | Heisman Trophy candidate promotion |
| **Example 2** | Employee relations | Fitness program promotion |

Based on Smith 2009.

- Defining problems
- Planning and programming
- Taking action and communicating
- Evaluating

Although they vary conceptually, most of these models incorporate similar ideas such as the centrality of research to the campaign planning process, the necessity of carefully defining publics, and the importance of employing carefully crafted messages.

This chapter uses a four-step model to describe the campaign process. Illustrated in figure 3.1, it is the framework that the Public Relations Society of America uses in evaluating campaigns submitted for the organization's prestigious Silver Anvil Awards, which recognize excellence in public relations. (See the sidebar titled What Is the PRSA? for information about this organization.) Each step in the model—research, planning, execution, and evaluation—includes multiple considerations.

These steps and their related considerations are examined in the following sections.

## Research

Research has been described as the compass that guides the campaign planning process (Matera & Artigue, 2000). The authors of the comprehensive Excellence in Communication study argued that research is so critical to success that two of the five competencies that public relations professionals must have to function well as managers involve research skills (Dozier, Grunig, & Grunig, 1995). The first skill is to use research to identify important publics. The second is to conduct research to evaluate the effectiveness of public relations activities.

Despite the importance of research, some public relations professionals rush headlong into planning campaigns without doing the necessary background work. This approach can be disastrous.

**Figure 3.1** The public relations campaign process.

## What Is the PRSA?

Established in 1947, the Public Relations Society of America (PRSA) is the largest organization of public relations professionals in the world. The organization boasts more than 32,000 members from a wide variety of industries, including sport. According to its strategic plan, the PRSA serves its members by providing the following four services (PRSA, n.d.a):

- Lifelong learning
- Vibrant, diverse, and welcoming professional communities where members can network and develop their professional expertise
- Recognition of capabilities through its credentialing program and accomplishment through its awards program
- Thought leadership and advocacy for ethics and professional excellence

The PRSA's highly touted accreditation program offers certification of public relations expertise to professionals in the field (PRSA, n.d.b). People seeking APR (accredited in public relations) status are required to have five years of professional experience before applying for the examination. Those receiving APR status may maintain it by accruing points for professional development and service on an ongoing basis.

Although many who work in sport public relations are PRSA members and possess APR status, others do not. A study of collegiate sports information professionals in the mid-1990s found that no one in a group of 95 survey respondents was a PRSA member (McCleneghan, 1995). Some within that sector of the industry wonder whether the pursuit of APR status might enhance the level of respect afforded sports information professionals.

For more information about the PRSA accreditation program, visit www.prsa.org.

Austin and Pinkleton (2006) indicated that research can assist public relations professionals in a variety of areas:

- Identifying problems that exist, their histories, and their prevalence
- Defining the magnitude of problems and their effects on various publics
- Suggesting strategies for successfully solving problems
- Testing strategies to determine whether they possess desired effects
- Tracking implementation plans to ensure that design results in execution
- Evaluating the results of the strategies implemented

Research on the publics involved in a particular problem or issue is typically a good starting place in the campaign planning process. Such research may also provide valuable information regarding what they know, how they feel, and how they are acting regarding the issue. For instance, a nonprofit sport service provider may face a problem of low renewal rates among donors to its programs. Before proceeding with a campaign to quell that trend, its public relations staff should carefully examine which donor groups—corporations, individuals, and foundations—are dwindling in their support and why. What issues must the campaign address to have the desired effect? Another example is a professional sport franchise that seeks public tax support for a new facility. Before launching a public relations campaign advocating such support, the organization's staff and any external agencies it retains should attempt to identify the diverse groups that would be affected by such tax support and the way in which they would be affected. What do they know about the proposal thus far? What are their attitudes regarding the franchise, the prospect of a new facility for the franchise, and the notion of public support for such an initiative? Finally, how might they act when presented with the sport franchise's proposal?

Finding answers to such questions usually requires much more than a seat-of-the-pants approach. The following sections address the types of research and specific methods that sport public relations professionals may use to generate information in a systematic manner.

## Types of Research

Research takes numerous forms, including some that many people may not consider research. Research may be categorized along several dimensions—primary and secondary, formal and informal, and qualitative and quantitative.

## Primary and Secondary Research

Sometimes sport public relations professionals engage in research activities to generate new information. When they do so, they are engaged in primary research. Other times they may access research that has been previously conducted either within their own organization or by people outside the organization. This is the nature of secondary research.

Oddly enough, secondary research usually precedes primary activities, because it often reveals information critical to the design of primary research methods (Harris, 1998). The example presented earlier in this chapter of a nonprofit sport service provider illustrates this concept. An organization's analysis of its own development records can identify specific trends that it may want to address if it chooses to survey donor groups. Furthermore, a literature search may reveal studies in academic journals or articles in professional publications that may provide information critical to the definition of additional research activities.

Common sources of secondary information may include not only organizational records but also other information such as directory sources (e.g., a Google search on the Internet) or subscription-based data from information providers (e.g., Sports Business Research Network). Tracking media coverage of particular subjects is also of value. Although the sport public relations professional benefits by having as much information as possible available for analysis, experts caution that the quality of information should be carefully scrutinized (Harris, 1998; Spoelstra, 1997). Invalid data may prove to be misleading and harmful.

## Formal and Informal Research

Informal research may yield significant information of value to the investigator, but it is not data that can be generalized to a larger population (Stacks, 2006). Focus groups are a form of informal research because they often provide perspectives that enable researchers to gain better understanding of how people view an issue or problem. Informal methods provide investigators with in-depth data pertaining to a question. But to generalize, formal research is needed (Stacks, 2006). Formal research generates findings that may be applied to large publics. It is purposeful and systematic, and it typically involves

- articulating specific research questions,
- searching for existing information relative to the research questions,

- defining and executing additional research methods that will address the research questions,
- analyzing the data generated by the research methods employed, and
- interpreting how the data may be applied to the research questions.

## Qualitative and Quantitative Research

Distinctions between qualitative and quantitative research are also important for sport public relations professionals. Quantitative research involves the use of numbers and statistical analysis to measure variables relating to research questions. Qualitative research uses language rather than numbers to convey research findings. An example of quantitative research is a survey sent to customers of a sporting goods manufacturer asking them to rate the manufacturer's products on multiple dimensions using a scale that ranges from 1 to 4. Hard numbers would be used in analyzing the data and generating findings. An example of qualitative research is conducting a series of interviews with a select group of customers and asking them to describe their thoughts about the sporting goods manufacturer's products. Their words would then be analyzed and interpreted to generate findings.

Although numerous differences exist between quantitative and qualitative research, both have significant value for sport public relations professionals. But one important caution applies. Qualitative data are less likely than quantitative data to be appropriate for generalization from one group to another. In addition, just because a study is quantitative does not mean it is appropriate for generalization. Careful attention must be paid to a study's sampling technique, method of inquiry, and form of data analysis before such an assumption may be made.

## *Methods*

The array of specific research methods available to sport public relations professionals is too vast to be addressed comprehensively in this text. Therefore, this section offers limited discussion of three methods commonly used by public relations professionals (Ahles, 2003; Stoldt & Ledbetter, 2005) and frequently encountered in secondary sources of information: interviews and observations, focus groups, and surveys.

## Interviews and Observations

Interviews involve conversations designed to gain information regarding specific questions and issues. Interviews are often one to one but may involve questioning two or more respondents at once. Analysis of award-winning general public relations campaigns indicates that interviews with and observations of key audiences are used in 65% of the campaigns (Ahles, 2003).

Interviews offer several advantages as a public relations research tool. First, they can be highly controlled because the interviewer directs the line of conversation. Second, they can provide a depth of information that may be difficult to obtain through other methods. Interviewers can probe for more details regarding a response by asking follow-up questions. Third, they can result in multiple layers of information because interview subjects respond not only verbally but also through facial expressions, gestures, and body language. All are valuable because research has found that facial cues and tone of voice are more important communication elements than the spoken word (Mehrabian, 1972).

The primary disadvantages of interviews are that they require significant time to conduct and can cost thousands of dollars (Stacks, n.d.). Even relatively brief interviews involving 8 to 10 questions can easily last 30 minutes. In-depth interviews may be an hour at a minimum, not including the time involved in preparing for the interview, making arrangements with the subjects, traveling to the interview site, and transcribing the interview notes. If travel and sophisticated recording equipment are required, costs can be significant, especially given the employee time devoted to interview preparation and execution. Given such costs, sport public relations professionals may choose to use a limited number of interviews with key individuals to suffice or to serve as the foundation for a survey that can be more comprehensive in nature.

Interviews may be conducted in a variety of ways. They may take place either in person, by telephone, or on the Internet. In-person interviews offer the advantage of permitting the subjects to be observed as they respond. Phone and Internet interviews, however, usually save time and money. Such tradeoffs should be weighed carefully.

Whether conducted in-person, by phone, or on the Internet, interviews may be structured in various ways (Gratton & Jones, 2004). They may range from highly structured conversations in which the interviewer sticks closely to a list of carefully structured questions to unstructured interviews in which the interviewer enters the conversation with a general purpose in mind but no particular questions. Many interviews fall between those two extremes. The interviewer may work from a list of questions but choose to pursue new directions as the conversation unfolds.

Assuming that the interview is to have some structure, development of the interview schedule is a critical step toward effectiveness (Gratton & Jones, 2004; Stacks, 2002). The interview schedule is simply the agenda that the interviewer uses to direct the conversation. It should include a purpose statement for the interview, specifics regarding why the respondent should participate and how the responses will be used (e.g., confidentiality and attribution concerns), questions that address the topic of interest, and expressions of gratitude following the conversation. One of the goals of most interviews is to build rapport between the two parties so that the respondent is willing to open up and be forthcoming. Establishing such rapport requires excellent interactive skills on the part of the interviewer and can be difficult even for the most skilled professionals.

Finally, documenting the results is an important aspect of interviews. Again, public relations professionals have choices on this front. Some simply take notes, others choose to record the interview (given the subject's consent) with audiotape or videotape, and still others do both. Notes may be particularly important because recording systems sometimes fail, but note taking can distract the interviewer from the task of building rapport. Recording devices, particularly those that record video, may be valuable in subsequent analysis of tone of voice or body language. But transcribing interviews by hand is time consuming, and word-by-word transcriptions often include material that may not be vital to analysis. Transcription services and software may be a prudent investment, but researchers should consider both costs and confidentiality issues.

## Focus Groups

Focus groups are common in public relations practice. They are usually composed of about 10 people who are led in a discussion by a moderator. Focus groups are like interviews in that they can offer a depth of information and multiple layers of data such as comments, facial expressions, and so on that may be hard to achieve through surveys. An additional advantage is that they allow participants to react to one another and advance the conversation based on previous comments. Like interviews, focus groups are time consuming to plan and execute and can be costly, especially if a professional moderator is employed. Additional costs may be incurred if, as is often recommended, participants are provided with compensation or gifts. An additional disadvantage is that focus groups can be difficult to manage and can easily veer off course in directions that may not be pertinent to the primary issue.

Given such tendencies, the focus group moderator plays a key role. Moderators must walk a fine line. They must keep the discussion on topic, but they must also allow group members to take the discussion in directions that may not be anticipated. They must foster an environment conducive to diverse opinions, and while doing so, they must avoid injecting their own biases on a given issue. They must find ways to draw out more reserved members of the group while reining in more talkative members.

Focus groups can be conducted in a variety of settings: in person, online, and by phone. Public relations professionals may find in-person focus groups to be particularly valuable because they observe the participants' body language, facial expressions, and gestures in addition to hearing their comments. Online or phone meetings are more convenient and less expensive if focus group members are geographically dispersed. Group dynamics will differ based on the forum selected, so the researcher must recognize the particular advantages and disadvantages of each type of focus group.

One general recommendation that applies to most focus groups is that the participants should be relatively homogenous and come from a single public. If a public relations professional is researching an issue that affects diverse publics, multiple focus groups are necessary. For instance, if a large sporting goods manufacturer wants to address employee opinions regarding the company, it should hold different meetings for those employees involved in the manufacturing process and those involved in management functions. Differing opinions may be voiced within each group, but the members of each group will be speaking from similar perspectives.

Several other considerations, some of which are particularly relevant to face-to-face focus groups, include the following:

• Convening at least two focus groups per public is often advisable (Stacks, 2002). If each group offers common themes, then the most important feedback considerations have likely been defined. If not, additional group meetings may be appropriate.

• The standard period for most focus groups is 60 to 90 minutes, but if the issue calls for in-depth feedback, meetings can expand to all-day affairs that include appropriate breaks and meals.

• Multiple recording mechanisms are highly recommended. If one fails, the other can serve as a backup. Videotape, although sometimes intimidating to group members, is particularly valuable in that it allows public relations professionals to identify later which group member is speaking at a given moment.

• Given that the moderator has a full plate in leading the discussion, an assistant commonly plays a crucial role in monitoring the recording equipment and taking notes that may be valuable during data analysis.

• Most moderators work from discussion guides that are semistructured (Gratton & Jones, 2004). Figure 3.2 offers an example of a discussion guide for a focus group that is discussing a proposed tax-supported sport arena. An important aspect of the introduction is some form of icebreaker that allows the group to begin building rapport.

• If the focus group is meeting in person, the meeting room should be conducive to group discussion by being free from distractions (e.g., ringing telephones, people walking by). It should also offer some level of insulation from intimidating factors (e.g., supervisors who may disapprove of critical remarks).

• Transcribing focus group recordings is a long, tedious process that can also be costly, whether performed in house or outsourced to a transcription service.

• Although focus groups often yield results that are useful to public relations professionals, their value may be further enhanced when the findings are used as a foundation for additional research, such as surveys (Smith, 2009).

## Surveys

Surveys, one of the most common methods of research in public relations and sport (Ahles, 2003; Gratton & Jones, 2004; Stoldt & Ledbetter, 2005), can be used to assess attitudes, knowledge, and perceptions (Austin & Pinkleton, 2006). They may be characterized as a set of questions posed to a group of people on an individual basis. Surveys tend to be lengthier and more in-depth than polls, which may be conducted to assess respondents' attitudes or behaviors on a limited array of questions (Stacks, 2006).

Surveys have numerous advantages (Austin & Pinkleton, 2006; Gratton & Jones, 2004). First, they allow researchers to access members of dispersed publics in a systematic fashion. Second, assuming that they are well constructed, they can reduce bias because the questions are delivered in a nonpersonal manner. This may eliminate or reduce subtle messages that may be communicated by the researcher in face-to-face settings. Third, surveys allow participants to respond anonymously, so they may be more forthcoming in voicing opinions. Finally, surveys are excellent tools for measuring changes over time. Surveys conducted before and after a public relations campaign may yield strong indications of the success or failure of the campaign.

Like all research methods, surveys also have limitations (Austin & Pinkleton, 2006; Gratton & Jones, 2004). Written surveys do not allow researchers the opportunity to clarify questions that respondents may not fully understand. They do not allow researchers to spontaneously ask follow-up questions to intriguing responses. Also, low response rates can sometimes compromise the reliability of data generated by surveys.

Surveys are commonly conducted in three different forms. Telephone surveys provide the researcher with at least some certainty regarding who is answering questions, as opposed to mail surveys that could be completed by someone other than the addressee. But telephone surveys are costly in that they consume significant staff time or require additional people to be employed as callers. Traditional mail surveys allow addressees to pick a convenient time to answer the questions, but as noted, they lack the control of being able to verify the respondent's identity. Internet surveys offer similar convenience to respondents and can be relatively inexpensive to conduct, but people outside the defined sample group may respond to online surveys unless security measures are used to control access. These measures may include response codes assigned to individuals within the sample. Internet surveys may also introduce sample bias unless the researcher is highly confident that most of the people within the public have basic computer skills and Internet access.

Numerous other points bear consideration when conducting survey research. They include, but are not limited to, the following:

• *Sampling decisions*: Care must be taken when selecting those who will be surveyed. For a sample to be truly representative of a larger population, random sampling must be conducted in a way that allows every person in the population to have an equal chance of being selected for participation.

• *Sample size*: Typically, the larger the sample is, the lower the margin of error is in generalizing survey results. At some point, however, researchers encounter diminishing returns. For a 5% margin of error, a sample of 217 people will suffice for a population of 500 (Smith, 2009). A sample of 400 will adequately represent an unlimited number. In each instance, the sample size would need to increase if the margin of error is to be reduced.

# Focus Group Discussion Guide

## Introduction, Facilitator Ground Rules

- Moderator will introduce discussion points, traffic responses from guests, and ask follow-up questions
- Athletics representatives will be observing, taking notes, and, if necessary, answering questions

## 2008 Season Details Recap

- Included in guest packet
- Review bullet points

## Introduction of Season Ticket Holders

- Name, number of years as season ticket holder
- General feedback regarding experience as a season ticket holder
  - What do you like the most about attending Shocker Volleyball matches?
  - What do you like the least?
  - Do you feel that Shocker Volleyball provides good entertainment value in relation to the cost of the season ticket?
- Follow-up questions as appropriate

## 2009 Reserved Seating Proposal

- Because of the volume of season tickets sold, expectation for future growth, and as a response to feedback from some season ticket holders, Shocker Athletics is considering a reserved seating plan for 2009 volleyball season tickets.
- How many of you would be interested in purchasing reserved tickets if they were offered in the following sections (proposed seating chart included in guest packet)? Tickets would be $10 more than GA season tickets.
- For those that are not interested, why would you continue to purchase GA tickets?
  - Don't like seat locations? Price difference? Other?
- If parking was only available with a reserved season ticket, would you purchase reserved seats instead?
  - If not, would you continue to purchase GA tickets?
- Are there other factors that would increase the likelihood of you purchasing reserved season tickets instead of general admission season tickets?
- When selecting your reserved seats, would you prefer to indicate a preference when renewing your season tickets?
- Would you like to be given a timeframe to come out to the arena to select seats, etc?
- Follow-up questions as appropriate

## Promotions/Operations Questions

- Season tickets included parking, a season ticket dinner, and two pre-match chalk-talks with Coach Lamb.
  - How many attended the season ticket dinners?
  - Chalk-talks?
  - Please share your thoughts on these add-ons. How much did you like/dislike the events?

**Figure 3.2** Sample semistructured discussion guide.

- Are there other benefits that could be included in season tickets that might help increase sales?
- Please take a look at the promotional giveaways on the 2008 recap sheet.
  - Did any of you receive the promotional items this season?
  - Which did you like/dislike?
  - Are there other promotional items you would be interested in receiving?
- Is there any feedback on arena concessions?
  - Menu items?
  - Pricing?
  - Locations?
  - Service?
- Please share any thoughts you have on the level of customer service in the following areas:
  - Ticket office
  - Souvenir shop
  - Ushers/Ticket-Takers
- Follow-up questions as appropriate

## Conclusion and Thank You

- Does anyone have any final comments or questions before we wrap-up?
- Thank you for your time this evening. Your participation is greatly appreciated.

---

**Figure 3.2** *(continued)*

Reprinted, by permission, from ICAA Wichita State University.

- *Survey construction*: Survey questions may be either closed ended (e.g., agree or disagree, scaled responses) or open ended. Answers to closed-ended questions are usually easier to analyze, but they may not be as revealing because the researcher predefines the array of responses. Regardless of whether an item is closed ended or open ended, it should address just one idea. Multiple ideas require multiple questions.

- *Pretesting*: Before administering a survey to a sample, it is advisable to administer it to a small group of people from within the population to make sure that they fully understand the questions. Poorly designed surveys can result in misleading data.

- *Incentives*: Researchers are advised to do everything possible to enhance response rates. One way to do so is to provide potential respondents with incentives such as monetary rewards or offers to share results. Another way is to remove disincentives, such as asking respondents to pay the cost of the postage necessary to return the survey.

- *Response rates*: Low response rates can be a serious threat to a successful survey. Researchers who initiate multiple and varied contacts with people within their sample are likely to enhance response rates (Dillman, Smyth, & Christian, 2009). Advance notices of forthcoming surveys and reminders regarding survey deadlines are often important components of the survey process.

- *Data analysis*: Responses to closed-ended questions can be analyzed quantitatively with techniques ranging from the simple (e.g., frequencies, mathematical means) to the complex (e.g., measuring relationships between survey responses, establishing patterns of responses within the data). Statistical software may assist in this process, but a general understanding of statistics is still necessary to analyze data accurately.

As evident from the preceding, surveys are an effective mechanism for gaining feedback from key publics. Even so, they should not be considered mandatory elements of a public relations assessment. Specific research questions are what ultimately drive the selection of the research method. More often than not, some combination of methods yields the most reliable data.

# Planning

If research is to be considered the compass that orients sport public relations professionals to the most critical considerations about an issue or opportunity, campaign planning may be thought of as the road map that guides them toward a particular destination (Matera & Artigue, 2000). As stated by Jackson (2000), "The biggest mistake practitioners and their clients or employers make is to plunge into tactical activities without a guiding strategy" (p. 104).

The campaign planning process involves multiple decisions, and sport public relations professionals must carefully coordinate each of those decisions. Specific considerations include goals and objectives, publics, strategies and tactics, messages, channels, and budget.

## Goals and Objectives

The terms *goals* and *objectives* are often used interchangeably. Practically speaking, the choice of terminology does not usually make a difference in the effectiveness of a public relations campaign. But sport public relations students may find it helpful to consider the terms as two distinct concepts that allow practitioners to think through the campaign planning process systematically.

A public relations goal is simply the desired outcome of a campaign. In some cases, public relations goals are stated in a general fashion that does not lend itself to specific measurements. In such cases, a series of related and specific objectives may be useful in assessing progress toward the goal.

The scenario presented earlier in this chapter of a nonprofit sport service provider may illustrate this point. One of the goals of a campaign to increase corporate donor renewals may be "To increase awareness among corporate donation contacts relating to the diverse services offered to the community." This general goal may then be supported by a series of specific objectives:

- To increase awareness regarding youth sport programs to 85% by the end of the calendar year
- To increase awareness regarding after-school child care programs to 80% by the end of the calendar year
- To increase awareness regarding adult fitness programs to 65% by the end of the calendar year

Each of these objectives defines measureable outcomes in direct relationship to the stated goal.

On other occasions, goals themselves may be easily assessed without supporting objectives. For instance, a goal such as "To achieve an awareness of 85% regarding youth sport programs by the end of the calendar year" may be assessed without the use of related objectives. Whichever approach is used, either the broader goals or their accompanying objectives should be written so that they lend themselves to postcampaign assessments of success.

Public relations experts offer four guidelines for writing measurable goals or objectives (Broom, 2009). First, the goal or objective should begin with the word *To* and then be followed by a verb. Second, the goal or objective should define an outcome that is to be reached because of the campaign. Third, the goal or objective must specify the desired magnitude or level of the outcome. Fourth, the goal or objective should define a date by which the outcome is to be attained. Each of the three examples of objectives listed previously meets these requirements.

A common mistake that students and even some professionals make is listing strategies and tactics as objectives. For example, "To use Twitter as a communication platform" is a tactic, not a goal or objective. The Twitter idea may possess considerable merit, but it is an action taken in the hope of achieving a desired outcome—it is not an outcome itself. Goals and objectives typically relate to desired knowledge, attitudes, and behaviors among key publics.

In some cases, goals and objectives specify changes within the sport organization itself. Chapter 2 discussed the various one-way and two-way models that public relations professionals employ. This concept bears additional emphasis here because although many campaign goals focus on persuasion, others mandate negotiated outcomes. Two examples bear out this distinction. Community leaders in Wichita, Kansas, used two-way communication to craft a successful communications campaign for a temporary sales tax to fund a new downtown sport and entertainment facility in 2004 (Stoldt, Ratzlaff, & Ramolet, 2009). Poll numbers indicated that 64% of voters opposed the tax in September, but the campaign changed many people's opinions and the ballot initiative passed with a 54% majority just two months later. The NBA's Orlando Magic had to take another approach (Mitrook, Parish, & Seltzer, 2008). The team began campaigning for a new, publicly funded arena in 2001, but after meeting surprisingly strong resistance from the media and members of the public, the Magic adjusted their strategy. Rather than advocate for a new or even renovated arena, the team accommodated public sentiment and simply appealed to the public for greater attendance at games to keep the franchise viable.

Sport public relations professionals should recognize two other considerations relating to goals and objectives. First, goals and objectives should be linked to the organization's strategic direction. Clear linkages should exist among the sport organization's mission, its strategic priorities, and the goals of any public relations campaign. If a campaign does not relate to an organization's general strategy, it is probably not worth the investment of organizational resources.

Second, campaign planners must consider the degree to which their activities work in concert with other organizational functions, especially marketing. **Integrated communication** is "the use of PR along with advertising, direct marketing, promotion, and other tools to shape public opinion and deliver audience actions" (Mogel, 2002, p. 19). It entails a synergistic approach to communications that allows congruent brand-related messages to be delivered through multiple promotional techniques (Irwin, Sutton, & McCarthy, 2008). The formula advocated by Ries and Ries (2002) in their book *The Fall of Advertising and the Rise of PR* assumes such an approach. Public relations may build the brand, and advertising may defend it, but both tools must advocate the same brand identity.

## Publics

Public relations campaigns are directed at publics who relate to the sport organization in a particular way. As defined in chapter 1, publics are more specific in nature than stakeholders; a stakeholder group is usually composed of multiple publics. Members of the mass media may be considered a stakeholder group, but a specific group of media members would be considered a public. For example, when Miami University planned an information campaign to promote its quarterback Ben Roethlisberger, it targeted the 870 media members who had a Heisman vote (Cuneen, Schneider, Gliatta, & Butler, 2006). Although some campaigns are designed to reach full stakeholder groups, they are more easily planned and executed when designed for specific publics. The more specifically that communicators can define their audience, the more likely they will be to reach them.

Smith (2009) lists five characteristics of publics:

- *Distinguishable*: They possess distinct qualities that set them apart from other groups. Such qualities are often described in terms of demographics (e.g., age, location) or psychographics (e.g., values, attitudes).

- *Homogenous*: They may not know one another, but they possess common qualities in terms of their relationship to the sport organization.

- *Important*: Not every group is important to the sport organization, but some are capable of affecting the attainment of organizational goals. Such groups warrant attention.

- *Large enough to matter*: There is no magic number here. Individuals and small groups usually do not merit public relations campaigns. But if the group has the critical mass necessary to affect the organization, it should be considered a distinct public.

- *Reachable*: The campaign planning process assumes that communication with key publics is somehow possible. Careful identification and research of a particular public often yields insights regarding how it may be most effectively reached.

One common approach is to target opinion leaders within a public. The rationale for such an approach is that if desirable outcomes can be attained with opinion leaders, those influential individuals may affect other people within the public. Sport marketers have advocated such a diffusion theory, noting that organizational communication with opinion leaders is frequently followed by highly credible word-of-mouth communication between the opinion leaders and others in the marketplace (Higgins & Martin, 1996). Further, a study of the influence of the weekly *Scripps Howard/Rocky Mountain News* Heisman poll on overall voting supported the notion that the weekly poll of select Heisman voters may have influenced other voters during the 2001 through 2003 seasons (Seltzer & Mitrook, 2009).

## Strategies and Tactics

Having researched the issue or opportunity, specified the desirable outcomes, and defined the publics involved, the campaign planner is now well equipped to define the strategies to attain campaign goals. Sport public relations professionals can employ a wide range of strategies in the pursuit of campaign goals. Selecting the most effective approaches is at the heart of strategy formulation.

Some strategies are more difficult to formulate than others, often because some goals are harder to attain than others. Grunig and Grunig (2001) listed five audience effects that communicators may seek to achieve:

- *Exposure:* Audience members are exposed to the communicator's message.

- *Retention:* Audience members remember the message.

- *Cognition:* Audience members understand the message.
- *Attitude:* Audience members favorably evaluate the message.
- *Behavior:* Audience members act differently in response to the message.

Each of these seemingly simple outcomes relates to multiple complex concepts. For instance, scholars examining attitude theory link the strength of attitude to other variables—persistence, resistance, cognitive processing, and effects on behavior—and these variables are also multifaceted (Funk, Haugtvedt, & Howard, 2000). The attitudes that a person holds toward a particular sport organization may have been affected by thousands of incidents throughout the person's life.

That said, each effect following exposure is more difficult to achieve than the previous one. Figure 3.3 illustrates this concept. As indicated, successfully exposing an audience to a message is less difficult than securing retention, which is less difficult than gaining understanding, and so forth up the list. Behavioral change is the most difficult outcome to achieve. In fact, some public relations experts argue

that even the most skilled campaign planners may have difficulty persuading people to change behaviors (Dozier & Ehling, 1992).

Ahles (2003) recommended that campaign planners work backward from the behaviors they would like their key publics to display in order to identify the attitudes, knowledge base, and awareness levels that must first be cultivated among those publics. The running example in this chapter of a nonprofit sport service provider takes this approach. The campaign is directed at a behavioral change—increasing renewal rates among donors. Its related goals and objectives, however, dealt with awareness levels. Such awareness may be a necessary foundation if the behavioral changes are ever to occur.

Implicit in this discussion is an underlying mandate that the campaign be tailored for the specified audience. Such considerations are especially critical when defining key messages to be conveyed and communication channels to be used. And those choices are inevitably linked to the campaign budget.

Figure 3.4 displays the relationship among messages, channels, and budgets. As illustrated, campaign planners must select messages and channels either in accordance with an available budget or by building a budget based on the costs of the messages that they produce and the channels that they use to distribute those messages. Similarly, campaign planners must find congruence between messages and channels. When athletic officials at Penn State University built a campaign to promote their star running back Larry Johnson for the 2002 Heisman Trophy, they were faced with cost constraints while desiring to supply voters with dynamic messages such as highlights of Johnson in action (Migala, 2003). Their solution was a permission-based e-mail campaign directed at Heisman voters. The e-mails contained video clips and links to a website that contained Johnson's detailed statistics and portions of interviews that had been conducted with him. With this approach, Penn State realized considerable cost savings in comparison with strategies employed by other institutions (Migala, 2003).

## Messages

Message selection is one of the most challenging aspects of strategy planning. Most people are exposed to hundreds of media messages and commercial exposures daily. Given such clutter, how may messages be crafted that resonate with key publics?

The concepts of selective exposure, selective perception, and selective retention are all relevant to campaign planners (Hyman & Sheatsley, 1947).

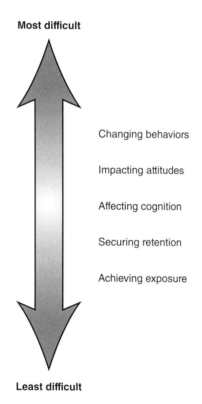

**Most difficult**

Changing behaviors

Impacting attitudes

Affecting cognition

Securing retention

Achieving exposure

**Least difficult**

**Figure 3.3** Degree of difficulty in attaining communication effects.

Based on Grunig and Grunig 2001.

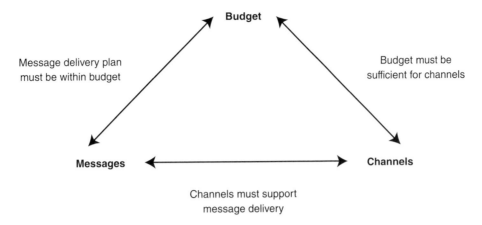

**Figure 3.4** Relationships among strategy elements.

Selective exposure is the notion that people are most likely to pay attention to messages that relate to subject matter of existing interest. Selective perception means that people interpret the messages that they do attend to through the filters of their life experiences, values, and attitudes. Selective retention relates to people's tendency to remember messages that are consistent with their existing attitudes. A related concept, cognitive dissonance, refers to the inclination to avoid or minimize the credibility of information that conflicts with current values and attitudes (Festinger, 1957).

Sport public relations professionals must strive to connect their messages to topics of interest among key publics. They must be intentional in the ways that they choose either to reinforce current beliefs and behaviors or to argue why publics should reevaluate their beliefs or behaviors. Finally, they must craft messages that are relevant enough for members of publics to retain as foundations for future beliefs or behaviors.

Broom (2009) noted that messages contain both denotative meanings and connotative meanings. Denotative meanings are cognitive; they are the commonly understood meaning of a message. Connotative meanings are affective, meaning that they have emotional substance as well. The best messages have both meanings.

Because persuasion is a common goal of public relations campaigns, practitioners must take care not to violate legal or ethical boundaries with hype. As noted by one set of experts, "Creative presentation is okay. Exaggeration, flattery, and puffery are not" (Nichols, Moynahan, Hall, & Taylor, 2002, p. 197). In other words, the selective use of statistics in support of an all-star candidate is generally acceptable; the inflation of those statistics is not.

Other considerations also apply. The *Kasky v. Nike* case set a legal precedent for public relations messages being considered commercial speech, similar to advertising (Collins, Zoch, & McDonald, 2004). Accordingly, they may be subject to legal challenges when perceived as false advertising. "Commercial speech needs to be scrupulously accurate, but noncommercial speech is freer to voice opinion based on fact" (Heath & Coombs, 2005, p. 221).

Sport public relations professionals may also be subject to communication regulations imposed by relevant governing bodies. Returning to the example of Miami University and the Ben Roethlisberger information campaign, NCAA rules limited what the institution could do in directly promoting the player for the Heisman (Cuneen et al., 2006).

Given the critical importance of messages within public relations campaigns, an advisable step is to pretest key messages on a small number of people from the public being addressed. Research indicates, however, that message testing is not particularly common, even among award-winning campaigns (Ahles, 2003; Stoldt & Ledbetter, 2005). Several reasons may be at play here. One is that public relations budgets are usually stretched thin even without costly testing procedures. A second is that aggressive campaign timelines may prevent systematic testing.

## Channels

Just as the key messages within a public relations campaign must be carefully matched to the intended audience, so too must the communication channels be intelligently chosen. Channels are the delivery systems that carry messages. Again, campaign planners have considerable latitude in making these selections. The two primary determinants are the attributes of the intended public and available resources (the budget).

Broadly speaking, campaign planners can choose from two approaches. They may make direct contact with their intended audience, or they may make indirect contact through the mass media. Communication channels making direct contact include

- open houses,
- organizational media,
- organizational websites,
- personal meetings,
- public appearances,
- public speeches,
- social media (e.g., Facebook),
- special events, and
- "town hall" meetings.

Communication channels using indirect contact include

- interviews,
- media advisories,
- media events,
- news conferences,
- news releases, and
- video news releases.

Each of the direct-contact tactics delivers messages directly from the sport organization to its key publics. These tactics include both organizational websites and social media, because although they are impersonal, they deliver organizational messages directly to audience members. The indirect tactics are designed to garner retransmission of intended messages by the mass media to key publics. This form of communication may be credible, but it also leaves the sport organization at the mercy of media gatekeepers who decide whether and how to relay the message to the public. For instance, a sport organization may send a news release to its local media outlets. Editors and producers at those media outlets will review the release and then decide whether to devote space or airtime to the information. If they decide in favor of coverage, they will likely rewrite the information or use only portions of it. Meanwhile, the sport public relations professionals cross their fingers and hope that the key messages survive the editors' review and repackaging.

## Budget

Because all public relations campaigns involve some level of costs, budgets are an important consideration in the planning process. As noted, the authors of the Excellence in Communication study identified five competencies that public relations professionals must possess to execute a managerial role successfully, one of which is the ability to manage budgets (two others deal with research skills, and the other two relate to two-way communication practices described in chapter 2) (Dozier et al., 1995).

Budgeting for campaigns is usually different from budgeting for public relations programs. Because most programs are continuous, standard budgeting techniques in the field are usually used. For instance, programs may be funded using incremental formulae (e.g., the previous year's budget plus 2.5%) or percentage of sales criteria (e.g., 1% of the previous year's gross sales). Given the short-term nature of public relations campaigns, a historical precedent on which to base a budget is not often available. Campaigns are thus funded in one of two ways—by using whatever money is available in the regular budget or by gaining special allocation of funds based on the specific needs of the campaign. The former approach may seriously compromise the success of the campaign if the amount of funding available does not lend itself to a viable campaign plan. The latter approach is clearly preferable, but even then, two concerns may arise. The first is that the amount of money that senior management is willing to approve for campaigns will likely be directly linked to the value of the campaign's goals. Campaigns that can demonstrably earn significant money or prevent future losses for the sport organization will gain more funding than those that do not offer such benefits. Using the chapter's running example, a campaign whose goals result in an additional $100,000 in corporate donations for the nonprofit sport service organization may warrant a $10,000 budget. The second point is that regardless of the potential benefits of the campaign, sport public relations professionals must inject an element of realism in their budget planning. Unrealistic budget requests may doom an important campaign initiative before it is ever launched.

Campaign planners incur two types of costs in any campaign (Matera & Artigue, 2000). The first is the cost of the human resources necessary to plan and execute the campaign. At a minimum, this involves the cost of having current employees devote portions of their employee hours to the campaign.

At the other end of the spectrum, it could involve hiring additional employees to execute a complex campaign or contracting with an external public relations firm. More will be said of public relations firms and their related costs later in this chapter. The second type of expense that campaign planners incur is the hard cost of the campaign itself. Most of the strategies specified in the campaign plan will have associated expenses, which may include the cost of research activities (e.g., focus groups), the cost of communication delivery systems (e.g., news releases, websites), and the cost of assessment techniques. Skilled sport public relations professionals account for these expenses early on while planning campaigns and then monitor the execution of the campaign to ensure that costs stay on track.

# Execution

A well-crafted campaign plan is of little value without careful execution. Thorough plans specify schedules and sequences of events and identify which people are to carry out various tasks. Broom (2009) stated, "Who should do and say it, and when, where, and how?" (p. 268).

Sport public relations professionals who manage campaigns should monitor the execution of the campaign plan to ensure that the strategies and tactics are being implemented as planned and to assess whether new developments should prompt revisions in the campaign plan. The latter point is illustrated in the example of Upper Deck, a sport memorabilia company that planned to launch a Pen-Cam product, a video camera within a pen that can document the authenticity of athlete autographs on Upper Deck memorabilia, in fall 2001 (Henninger, 2002). The designated launch date was September 11, and the news releases regarding the introduction of the product were distributed just as a series of terrorist attacks was launched against New York and Washington, D.C. Campaign managers, knowing that their launch would be completely lost amid the day's crisis, decided to act as if the product introduction never happened, and they started over in November of that year. The campaign was then executed as planned.

# Evaluation

After the campaign has been executed, the final step in the campaign process is to evaluate its effectiveness. Just as public relations professionals have numerous options in the planning process, they also have numerous methods of assessing campaign suc-

cess. One common method is the seat-of-the-pants approach whereby effectiveness is assessed without supporting research (Brody & Stone, 1989; Dozier, 1981). This approach is not recommended because it offers no foundation for the resulting evaluation. Because such assessments are often made by the people who planned the campaign, personal biases are a major problem.

Systematic evaluation can take place at many levels. In fact, one author set forth a model containing 33 types of evaluation (Kendall, 1996). This chapter offers three general areas in which the relative success of a campaign can be assessed: evaluation of execution, evaluation of media coverage, and evaluation of impact.

## Evaluation of Execution

One level at which the campaign can be assessed is the execution. This assessment simply tracks the degree to which the plan was followed and the number of outputs that it generated. These measurements may include but are not limited to

- the number of news releases distributed and the number of media outlets receiving them,
- the number of news conferences held and the number of media members attending,
- the number of public service announcements distributed,
- the number of campaign events held and the number of audience members attending, and
- the amount of organizational media produced in support of the campaign.

These concerns are all relevant to campaign managers, because if the campaign is not well executed, it will likely be ineffective. That said, evaluation of execution is only the first phase of the assessment process.

## Evaluation of Media Coverage

A more sophisticated level of evaluation is assessment of media placement. This level recognizes that tactics such as news releases and news conferences are of little value if they do not prompt some sort of media coverage. Media coverage of a campaign can be an important indicator of its relative success. Evaluating media coverage can occur in a variety of ways:

- *Placement rates*: Rate at which news releases were picked up by the media outlets to which they were sent.

- *Number of stories*: Total number of stories appearing in the mass media because of the campaign's publicity efforts.

- *Impressions*: **Impressions** are the total number of people (e.g., readers, viewers, listeners) who potentially received information from the campaign through the mass media. These numbers are based on the number of stories appearing in each media outlet and the size of the estimated audience for each story using circulation figures or broadcast ratings.

- *Space or airtime*: The number of column inches in the print media and the amount of airtime in the broadcast media devoted to the campaign.

- *Value of exposure*: The estimated value of the print space or airtime devoted to a campaign based on the advertising rates of the media outlets in which the publicity appears.

- *Content analysis*: The tone of related media coverage, including the degree to which it is favorable or includes key words such as brand names or themes (i.e., key messages).

Table 3.2 features a typical media tracking chart that might be used by a regional tennis association. Note that the table displays the event that resulted in the coverage, the media outlet providing the coverage and its audience number, the value of the media coverage, and a brief description of the value of the content.

Placement data may document the effectiveness of a campaign in gaining media coverage, but such data are not the ultimate measure of the success of a campaign. Marker (1977) offered a story about evaluation that has now become legendary within the field. He told how he had been asked to make a presentation to his boss regarding the value of his company's public relations efforts. Marker carefully documented the vast amount of publicity that had resulted from the company's public relations programs and felt quite comfortable in his defense of the expenditures. "And then it came," he recounted,

## Table 3.2 Media Tracking Chart

| Event | Outlet | Circulation | Date | Ad rate × space or airtime | Value | Content |
|---|---|---|---|---|---|---|
| Local Paralympic player wins another major | *Kansas City News* | 252,000 | February 11, 2010 | $550 × 2 inches (5 cm) | $1,100 | Short blurb on results of recent tournament |
| Local player wins national event | *Tulsa Dispatch* | 118,000 | May 19, 2010 | $115 × 2 inches (5 cm) | $230 | Item in "Sports Update" about local player winning first national tournament of her career |
| Tennis Block Party | KZAA, Tulsa, Oklahoma | NA | May 23, 2010 | $300 per 30 seconds × 3:30 | $2,100 | Morning news show report about Tennis Block Party promotion showing reporters learning the game |
| Lincoln, Nebraska, tournament | *Lincoln Post* | 77,000 | June 15, 2010 | $75 × 12 inches (30 cm) | $900 | Story focusing on local players participating in this year's tournament |
| National tournament | *Springfield World* | 59,000 | July 6, 2010 | $110 × 11 inches (27.5 cm) | $1,210 | Story about national tournament and local player who is defending champion |

"the question no one had asked before: 'But what's all this worth to us?'" (p. 52). The answer to that question requires a measurement of impact.

### Evaluation of Impact

The highest order of campaign evaluation is impact (Broom, 2009; Dozier & Repper, 1992). This form of measurement attempts to assess the effect of campaign strategies and related media coverage on the designated public. It may consider a number of variables, including awareness, knowledge, attitudes, and behaviors. The variables are, of course, interrelated, but behavioral change within the audience is the ultimate effect.

The best way to assess campaign impact is to go back to the goals and objectives specified in the campaign plan and evaluate the degree to which they were met. Keep in mind that the best goals and objectives are specific and measurable, so they may often be assessed by using the same research techniques used when planning for the campaign. The example of the nonprofit sport service provider may illustrate this point. As mentioned, one of the goals of the campaign to improve low renewal rates among donors was "to increase awareness levels among corporate donation contacts relating to the diverse services offered to the community." One of the specific objectives in support of this goal was "to increase awareness levels regarding youth sport programs to 85% by the end of the calendar year." A postcampaign survey of the organization's corporate donors may measure that awareness level and offer strong evidence regarding the success of the campaign. Similar techniques may be used to measure knowledge or attitudes, and behaviors may be assessed in numerous ways including, but not limited to, purchases, donations, attendance, votes, volunteerism, trial samples, and conduct standards.

# Working With Public Relations Firms

Sometimes the scope of a public relations campaign exceeds the expertise and resources of a sport organization. In such cases, sport managers may seek the services of **public relations firms**. These firms offer a variety of services ranging from campaign planning and execution to media training to crisis communications counsel. They vary in size from one person consulting within a single market to international firms with hundreds of employees. Practitioners in many of these firms indicate that

their sport public relations acumen has evolved to the point that they are highly credible with both clients and members of the mass media (Roberts, 2002).

The primary advantage of working with public relations firms is that they likely offer expertise and services at levels beyond what a small public relations department within a sport organization possesses. In fact, the most common reasons why organizations hire public relations firms are (Council of Public Relations Firms, 2005) because they

- provide "additional arms and legs" (i.e., larger staff),
- "complement our own internal capabilities,"
- provide "strategic market insight and experience," and
- offer an "objective point of view."

Of course, all these advantages come with a price tag. Public relations firms commonly charge their clients a monthly retainer fee for a specified level of service. In other situations, fees may be based on the number of personnel hours devoted to a particular campaign or the expenses anticipated in the planning and execution of a specific project (Smith, 2009).

Searching for a public relations firm that is the best fit for the sport organization can be time consuming, and businesses may hire consultants to assist with the search process. The Council of Public Relations Firms (n.d.) offers three general guidelines that should be considered during the selection process:

- *Credentials*: The firm has the resources and expertise to get the job done.
- *Chemistry*: The personalities and work ethic of people working on both sides of the account should mesh to create a productive partnership.
- *Strategic insight and counseling capabilities*: The firm has the strategic counseling ability to help the business achieve its objectives.

The Council of Public Relations Firms (n.d.) also offers an assessment tool that should be regularly used to evaluate the service offered by public relations firms. The criteria are as follows:

- Responsiveness
- Ability to meet deadlines
- Quality of writing
- Strategic counsel

- Creativity
- Media placement
- Chemistry
- Enthusiasm for what they do
- Commitment to excellence in client service
- Initiative
- Approach to financial account management; budget management
- Measurement protocols
- Ability to meet all needs
- Accessibility
- Willingness to take instruction

Firms that score well on these measures are likely providing effective service to their clients. The sidebar titled Working With Public Relations Agencies is written by Janae Melvin, who has worked both in sport-specific public relations positions and with a public relations agency. Her article addresses how public relations firms and sport organizations can work together effectively.

# Learning From Case Studies

The public relations campaign model discussed in this chapter is frequently used within the sport industry. This section offers three case studies that illustrate how diverse organizations have successfully used the model. The PRSA has recognized each campaign profiled as a Silver Anvil Award winner.

## Case 1: U.S. Figure Skating Championships

As the 2008 U.S. Figure Skating Championships approached, the local organizing committee in St. Paul, Minnesota, recognized that it was facing a variety of challenges (PRSA, 2008a). The 2007 championships in Spokane, Washington, had been a resounding success, so expectations were higher than ever. But the sport lacked star power among its current competitors, and the U.S. Figure Skating Association had switched broadcast partners, ending a long relationship with ABC and ESPN and partnering with NBC. A two-person public relations team was appointed to develop a plan to enable the event to resonate in a market accustomed to major sport events.

## Research

Both primary and secondary research were conducted (PRSA, 2008a). The organizers attended the 2006 and 2007 championships, gathered attendance information, and debriefed past organizers. They performed a media audit of coverage pertaining to past championships and events leading up to the 2008 championships. They also conducted a focus group with local women aged 25 through 54 and interviewed some of the sport's most avid fans. Secondary research focused on analyzing national media coverage of past events and securing biographical information on the 2008 competitors.

## Planning

Armed with a significant amount of information because of their advance research, the public relations team crafted the following plan (PRSA, 2008a).

- *Goals and objectives*: The campaign had three goals. The first was to generate interest in the community. The second was to secure attendance of at least 100,000 during the eight-day event. The third was to realize a local economic impact of $25 to $30 million as had previous championships.

- *Audiences*: The campaign was directed toward three audiences. The first was local skating fans, primarily middle-aged women and gay men. The second was visitors, especially avid fans who followed the sport. The third was target media at both the local and national levels.

- *Strategies*: The campaign employed a variety of strategies to achieve its goals. Planners leveraged athletes with local ties and the state's figure-skating history to create an emotional connection with their key audiences. They communicated the significance of the event by securing live advance coverage from NBC's *Today* show and by employing former figure skating stars Kristi Yamaguchi and Nancy Kerrigan. They linked the event to the St. Paul Winter Carnival to realize a brand association with fun. And they minimized barriers to consumption by educating the public on the sport and making athletes highly accessible to the media. The campaign budget was $30,000.

## Execution

Execution of the campaign hinged on successfully engaging the media in numerous ways, including pitching ideas that enabled reporters to cover the event creatively (PRSA, 2008a). Planners also connected with their public audiences by posting

Photo courtesy of Janae Melvin.

## Working With Public Relations Agencies

### Janae Melvin

It's not a surprise that athletics departments and sport programs benefit from public relations programs. Anyone who works within the sport industry is familiar with the success that comes with a hard-working media relations or sports information department. I spent three years working for two different sports information departments and deployed my fair share of press releases, pregame notes, game program stories, and media guides. The growth that motor sports saw during the five years I worked within the industry was incredible, moving from small-market, dedicated fans to mainstream recognition. For most sports enthusiasts a last name is not needed when referring to Dale, Jeff, or Jimmie. Even in Las Vegas, where lights, glitter, and gambling run the town, the yearly NASCAR race weekend is a virtual sell-out.

While working public relations for both groups rarely was I challenged to think outside the box or look for new and different ways to promote these sport organizations to the general public. In the athletics world we have our little bubble we operate within and focus on what we know and are comfortable with—it works, so don't mess with it.

Inevitably, though, the time comes when the boss or athletic director wants more—more widespread awareness to help raise funds or a campaign to assist with the school's top point guard being named an All-American. The question then becomes whether there is enough time or staff to tackle these new projects.

The thought of going outside the department for assistance in reaching the nonsporting audience was something I never thought was an option. Money is already budgeted within the organization for salaries and personnel, and why would I, a sports information graduate assistant, have a job if someone else could do it better, and possibly cheaper? Plus, why would a public relations firm want to work with my athletics department and what could a sporting organization gain by utilizing the services offered by a firm?

It wasn't long after I joined The Firm Public Relations & Marketing that I realized just how valuable working with a public relations firm can be for all areas of business, regardless of your target market. A public relations firm has a broader outlook on promotions and publicity and can help sport-minded individuals and organizations reach beyond their comfort zone and introduce themselves to an entirely new audience. I quickly saw the tools I could have used within my previous employment that could have helped me reach my goals within the organization. Sure, I could get my message out to the sportscasters on television, the sports talk radio guys, and the sports page editors. But how could I get my message across to the mother of five who works all day, takes care of her family at night, and doesn't even know that my school has a rowing team? And why would I even want her to know?

A public relations firm provides many services that can benefit an athletics organization. Whether it's the creation of a public relations plan for the department, a social media strategy, or story pitches to specific media members, a firm can successfully integrate itself within a sport organization and work alongside the director, president, and others to fulfill specific goals put forth by the organization. On the surface, paying yet another individual or group to handle public relations when you already have a department in place can seem like a crazy idea, but once you

> **Inevitably, though, the time comes when the boss or athletic director wants more—more widespread awareness to help raise funds or a campaign to assist with the school's top point guard being named an All-American.**

*(continued)*

*(continued)*

understand the benefits that come from trusting a firm you may quickly realize what a great teammate they could become.

During the collegiate basketball season a sports information director for a top 25 Division I school probably doesn't have time to focus on that great story about the walk-on to the tennis team who is juggling school, work, tennis, married life, and being a new parent—all while getting straight As and making the dean's list. And with everything else going on in the world of sport at that time, there may not be a place for it in the sport section either. But it's a great story, and you think it can really help garner attention for the tennis program. A firm can take that story and create a media pitch, contacting individual reporters whom the firm already knows loves these story angles.

When deciding whether or not to use a public relations firm there are a few factors to consider—money, time, and compatibility. Sports departments must first look within budgets to see whether hiring a firm is an option. Public relations firms vary in pricing and normally work on hourly rates. A firm can be placed on a monthly retainer whereby the company pays for a predetermined number of hours worked each month and the firm strives to accomplish all goals within that time frame. Another option is to hire a firm for project work. A proposal is given to the sports department from the firm listing the number of hours that they believe will be needed to complete the project, and the client in turn pays only for that project. The sports department must look at their internal goals for promotion and decide which option is best.

Time is a huge factor in deciding whether hiring a firm is best for your organization. Does your sport manager and his or her staff have the time to devote to this project to see the desired results? Could this project be handled by an intern or lower-level staff member? Some projects may need more than 50 hours of time to see success, and in-house personnel may not be available.

It may seem silly to think of compatibility as a factor when considering public relations firms, but these individuals will be representing your organization to the press and public. You have to make sure that you feel comfortable working with them, that you trust their vision and instinct, and that you are willing to let them become another voice for your organization.

In 2009 the Bowl Championship Series (BCS) and the Western Athletic Conference (WAC) each hired public relations firms to help with their in-house efforts. The BCS hoped to highlight the positive aspects of the title game and the overall bowl system amid widespread questions concerning the legitimacy of college football's postseason. The WAC used a firm over the summer months to promote conference participant Boise State as a BCS title contender, regardless of the conference's nonqualifying status.

Whether these two organizations represent the beginning of a trend or simply an experiment, the benefits of turning to a public relations firm to assist with sports information is no longer unfamiliar territory.

Allowing someone else to become a voice for your endeavors may be a little scary, but sometimes a fresh perspective can be extremely beneficial for a world that usually operates within itself. Looking outside the athletics bubble and exposing your organization to a new audience, one that just might be curious enough to become further involved, can assist in spreading your message. Allowing a public relations firm to help you in your efforts just might be the missing piece to your puzzle.

*Janae Melvin is a former public relations specialist with The Firm Public Relations and Marketing in Las Vegas. In 2010 she was hired by MGM Resorts International as a public relations specialist.*

banners and signage, hosting skating demonstrations and clinics, staging celebrity appearances, and partnering with other entities such as the World Figure Skating Museum.

### *Evaluation*

The campaign successfully attained its goals (PRSA, 2008a). Planners secured strong evidence in support of their awareness goal by tracking 284 stories placed in the local media and 32 million impressions overall. Attendance totaled 104,000, and the local organizing committee reported high levels of satisfaction from the U.S. Figure Skating Association regarding the role of the campaign in ticket sales. The economic impact of the event was estimated at $30 million.

## Case 2: Rawlings "Summer of the Glove"

Sporting goods manufacturer Rawlings secured public relations firm Fleishman-Hillard (FH) to develop a program that would reenergize the Rawlings brand (PRSA, 2008b). One of the central components of the program was the Rawlings Gold Glove, an award given annually to the top defensive players in Major League Baseball (MLB) and approaching its 50th anniversary in 2007.

### Research

FH conducted primary research by conducting surveys and interviews at MLB ballparks and administering a media audit of Gold Glove Award coverage (PRSA, 2008b). The findings were discouraging. Unaided recall data indicated that 81% of people did not know that Rawlings was the creator and sponsor of the award. The media audit revealed that 90% of media mentions excluded the Rawlings name in mentions of the award.

### Planning

The "Summer of the Glove" campaign was a significant part of FH's larger brand program for Rawlings (PRSA, 2008b). Details of the campaign follow.

- *Goals and objectives*: Three program objectives related directly to the campaign. The first was to reclaim the brand's ownership of the Gold Glove Award. The second was to engage sporting goods retailers. The third was to secure investor relations benefits for Rawlings' parent company, K2.
- *Audiences*: As the objectives indicate, the campaign targeted a range of audiences ranging from MLB fans to sporting goods dealers to investors and members of the financial media.
- *Strategies:* To celebrate the 50th anniversary of the award, Rawlings staged an All-Time Rawlings Gold Glove Award promotion (PRSA, 2008b). A panel of baseball experts identified a list of candidates for the award, and fans voted on the final selections by accessing the organization's website, visiting a sporting goods retailer, or sending phone or text messages. Rawlings secured ESPN as its media partner for the promotion and several high-profile former players to serve as representatives. Rawlings and FH did not disclose their campaign budget.

### Execution

In November 2006 ESPN aired a 30-minute program featuring Ozzie Smith and dedicated to promoting the next year's promotion (PRSA, 2008b). The ballot was released in February 2007 at a media event at the ESPN SportZone in New York. Several players from the first Gold Glove team in 1957, including Willie Mays, joined ESPN host Chris Berman for the event. Voting and debate about the candidates ensued over the next five months.

### Evaluation

Rawlings and FH realized success in regard to each of their goals (PRSA, 2008b). Consumer research documented a 33% increase in unaided awareness of Rawlings' ownership of the Gold Glove Award. Thirteen of Rawlings' top 14 retailers participated in the promotion and devoted increased shelf space to Rawlings' products. The overall brand program produced 500 million media impressions, and Rawlings' parent company, K2, was acquired for $1.2 billion by the Jarden Corporation in August 2007.

## Case 3: McDonald's 2008 Beijing Olympic Games Sponsorship

This final case example demonstrates how a non-sport company, McDonald's, used a sport platform as the basis for its communication campaign. As a sponsor of the 2008 Beijing Olympic Games, McDonald's wanted to realize a variety of benefits pertaining to media coverage, franchise involvement, and consumer response. It employed the public relations firm GolinHarris (GH) to help it address the challenges associated with the Beijing Games (PRSA, 2009). These included competing with other sponsors for media coverage, communicating in ways that would reach diverse audiences around the world, and navigating the political and security challenges set forth by the International Olympic Committee (IOC) and the Beijing Organizing Committee.

### Research

A media audit of coverage leading up to the Games indicated that the majority of media attention was being devoted to either the political dimensions of the event or the athletes striving to qualify for and compete at the Games (PRSA, 2009). Olympic sponsorships were not deemed newsworthy.

### Planning

Fully aware of the challenges, McDonald's and GH structured a media relations campaign designed to attain lofty goals (PRSA, 2009).

- *Goals and objectives*: The campaign had two objectives: secure significant media coverage that placed McDonald's among the top three most covered sponsors and increase McDonald's involvement at the local level by 25% from previous years.

- *Publics*: The campaign was directed toward three audiences. The first was the international media covering the Beijing Games and related issues. The second was McDonald's consumers on a global scale. The third was McDonald's representatives at franchises around the world.

- *Strategies*: The theme of the campaign was "Bringing People Together Like Never Before" (PRSA, 2009), and it developed a series of special events to attract desired media coverage. McDonald's engaged franchise employees with a Champions Crew development program advocated by spokesperson Carl Lewis, a former employee and Olympic champion. The campaign plan called for consumers to be involved through a special promotion for children and an online game developed in partnership with the IOC featuring former Olympian Edwin Moses as one of the gamers. The public relations budget, including GH's fees, was $1 million.

## Execution

The special media events began one year before the Games and included a one-of-its-kind, on-site news conference featuring Lewis just one day before the Games began (PRSA, 2009). Champions Crew members from 36 countries were sent to Beijing to staff the four McDonald's Olympics restaurants. More than 200 children from 40 countries were selected to travel to Beijing for the Games, and the kids filed reports on their experiences with their local media. The online game, "The Lost Ring," involved 2.7 million people from 100 countries.

## Evaluation

McDonald's and GH successfully exceeded each of their goals (PRSA, 2009). Media coverage resulted in 825 million impressions, 90% of which were positive, and research indicated that McDonald's received more coverage with more impact than any other Olympic sponsor. As for involvement at the local level among McDonald's representatives, the company and GH saw an increase in participation of 85%, far exceeding that of previous years.

Although each of the three cases described in this section focused on campaigns with large budgets, the campaign planning process fits all budget sizes. Regardless of whether a campaign budget is several million dollars or a few hundred, the basic considerations are the same. Sport public relations professionals who can systematically think through the planning process place themselves in a much stronger position to achieve desirable public relations outcomes.

## SUMMARY

Sport public relations professionals use campaigns to achieve specific purposes with particular publics over a limited time. As such, campaigns stand in contrast to public relations programs, which are sustained efforts to develop desirable relationships with broader stakeholder groups. Research regarding the nature of the issue or opportunity and affected publics serves as the foundation of the campaign planning process. Although public relations professionals may use a vast array of research approaches to gain campaign-related knowledge, three of the more common methods are interviews and observations, focus groups, and surveys. The campaign planning process involves setting goals and objectives, specifying publics to be targeted, and defining strategies to be employed. Three concerns that must be addressed while formulating strategy are key messages, channels, and budget. Although the best-planned campaigns have carefully defined schedules and responsibilities regarding execution, many require some adaptation to a dynamic environment. Campaigns may be evaluated along numerous dimensions, ranging from process-related considerations to placement rates, but the best assessments are linked to the goals and objectives that were dictated when the campaign was first planned. Some sport managers contract with public relations firms to plan and execute campaigns. These firms typically possess considerable public relations expertise, but they can be costly.

1. Assume that you are a sport public relations professional in one of the following three situations:

   - A college sports information director touting a student–athlete for a high-profile honor
   - A nonprofit service provider seeking to improve corporate donor renewal rates
   - A sporting goods manufacturer seeking to enhance employee communication channels

   What sort of secondary research sources could you use as a starting point for the campaign planning process? Based on that information, what sort of primary research initiatives would you recommend?

2. Based on the information that you gained through activity 1, outline a campaign that will allow your organization to attain its general goal. Take care to address each of the key considerations in the strategy formulation stage.

3. Based on the campaign plan that you outlined in activity 2, how would you recommend assessing it following its execution? What types of assessments (i.e., process, placement, impact) have you recommended?

4. Access the PRSA's Silver Anvil Award website (www.silveranvil.org). Search the site for a campaign profile relating to a sport organization of interest to you. Can you identify the key strategic decisions that led to the success of the campaign?

# 4

# Using the Internet in Sport Public Relations

After reading this chapter, students should be able to

articulate the purposes and capabilities of websites in the context of public relations;

describe general approaches to website design, development, and management;

identify ways in which websites can advance relationships with various stakeholders;

illustrate how social networking media can be used in public relations efforts; and

characterize Internet-related challenges for sport public relations professionals.

Key terms discussed in this chapter include

- e-commerce,
- social media,
- Internet service provider (ISP),
- domain name,
- persistent navigation,
- search engine optimization (SEO),
- stickiness,

- click path analysis,
- bounce rates,
- intranet,
- spam,
- viral marketing, and
- blogging.

# Computer technology has

had an extraordinary influence on society in numerous ways. One particular advancement that has had a profound effect on organizations of all types is the Internet. This technology provides obvious advantages for many organizational functions, including public relations, and the benefits grow as access becomes more common and technologies progress. Internet World Stats (2010) reported that 77.4% of the population of North America use the Internet and that over 1.95 billion people worldwide use the Internet. Internet access has become a routine part of our existence, and wireless technology and mobile device technology now allow for virtually constant Internet access anytime, anywhere. Technology has also created the capacity for a nearly permanent state of connection to each other. The relentless and rapid changes in technology have created unique opportunities and daunting challenges for public relations. The Internet has created an entirely new communication alternative and accelerated the communications process dramatically. Because it has become a platform for disseminating and accessing information quickly and expansively, the Internet offers tremendous potential as a tool for public relations practitioners.

Most sport organizations have an Internet presence and maintain websites for a variety of purposes. Organizational websites are important platforms for the distribution of controlled messages to the organization's community. Given the potential of a website to deliver controlled messages to a mass audience and solicit feedback from large numbers of people, its value as a public relations tool is unmistakable.

In previous chapters, the focus has been on public relation's role in building relationships with the different publics of sport organizations. This chapter will address how technology can be used to enhance these relationships. The emphasis will be on the website as a tool for advancing public relations efforts, although other aspects of technology will be addressed as well. Public relations professionals must be constantly alert to technological advancements that alter the tools and subsequently the practice of public relations. Websites are used for a variety of purposes and can play different marketing and public relations roles for sport organizations. They have become organizational assets, and care must be taken to construct them well and utilize them to their fullest potential.

The opening section of this chapter discusses the capabilities of the Internet as they relate to public relations and outlines the purposes of organizational websites. The second section considers general approaches to website development. The third section addresses the ways that sport organizations can use the Internet to communicate effectively with various stakeholder groups. These groups include members of the media, sponsors, employees, investors, customers, and donors. The final section describes Internet-related developments and challenges for sport public relations professionals.

# Evaluating Web Use in Sport Public Relations

The Internet has become an increasingly important link between sport organizations and their constituencies. Organizations must respond to technological developments by understanding the capabilities of the Internet and the manner in which they can be employed in public relations activities. This section addresses the Internet's capabilities and the ways in which sport organizations can use those capabilities as part of their public relations arsenal.

## Website Capabilities

As a communication medium, the Internet has potential as an important tool for public relations. The capacity of the Internet makes it a valuable instrument for a variety of public relations functions as organizations attempt to establish and expand relationships with their publics. Farkas and Farkas (2002) cited seven capabilities that make the website such an appealing vehicle, including

- global reach,
- speed and user choice,
- support of multiple content types,
- support of transactions,
- computational functions,
- interactive capability, and
- adaptability and customizability.

Each of these capabilities may have implications for public relations.

The extraordinary scope of access to the web may expand the size of various publics or provide constituents much easier access to information about the organization. The scope of content included on a typical professional team's website will accommodate even the most demanding site visitor. A sporting goods firm may experience quantum leaps in its customer base with an Internet presence. The speed with which information can be disseminated and accessed is another attractive aspect of the Internet. In the context of public relations, this speed is particularly appealing because stakeholder satisfaction is often related to timeliness and convenience.

The ability to support different types of content allows organizations to build sites with information that goes beyond text to include audio and video along with graphics and animation. Virtual views allow ticket buyers to select a seat based on desired sightlines, and webcams can be used to show construction progress on a new stadium. Streaming audio and video turn computers and various mobile communication devices into radios or televisions and provide access to games that are simply not available through traditional media in real time. For example, a grandmother can hear her grandson's high school basketball game on the Internet even though she lives in a small town 1,200 miles (2,000 kilometers) away. College athletics programs may be able to persuade recruits to move farther from home because all their games are streamed on the school website for their parents to follow.

Websites also provide a platform for transactional activity. The extraordinary growth of **e-commerce** is demonstrable evidence of the capability of the Internet in this regard. Online consumer spending was reported to be $227.6 billion in 2010 (comScore, 2011), more than four times what it was in 2003. Everything from purchasing an authentic jersey to ordering a new set of golf clubs to submitting a bid for an appealing piece of memorabilia is part of the transactional capability of the Internet. This capacity extends to recording and processing information. One example is the fantasy leagues that are popular in many sports. Online fantasy sites provide computational services to manipulate salary data, statistical information, and player transactions in determining fantasy winners and losers.

But perhaps the most significant influence from a public relations perspective is the prolific growth in interactive capability that not only connects organizations with their constituents in many new ways but also connects constituents with each other. Social networking sites and file-sharing sites (e.g., digg.com, reddit.com, delicious.com), Twitter, YouTube, and Flickr have created extraordinary opportunities for connecting with various publics and sharing information with them on a scale that was unimaginable only a few years ago. The connections established through these sites have the potential to create bonds and engage the most actively involved constituents. Funk (2009) referred to social networking as the new public square and suggested that active and responsible involvement is an increasingly important activity in brand management and control. Monitoring the communication that is taking place may lead to quicker and more effective public relations responses. The conversation prism developed by Solis and Thomas (2008) provided a powerful visual map of the nature of the social web. The authors suggested that "monitoring and in some cases participating in online conversations is critical in competing for the future." (See figure 4.1.) The sidebar titled Using Social Media to Reach Stakeholders, written by sport public relations consultant John Halpin, offers a number of examples of effective **social media** usage within the field.

Finally, websites can be tailored to the needs of specific users. They can be programmed to greet users by name, direct them to parts of the site that their history suggests they might be most interested in, and personalize the presentation of information that they have requested. For example, sites such as CBS' Sportsline.com and pgatour.com allow users to customize scoreboard tracking information to include only those games or players specified by the user.

As websites continue to evolve, new and expanded services for site visitors will enhance the speed and convenience with which interaction occurs. These user benefits can create opportunities for developing and enhancing relationships with an organization's publics.

## Website Purposes

Websites provide a continuous link with organizational stakeholders, and that link offers an opportunity for interactive exchange. For public relations, websites provide a platform for building and sustaining relationships.

Websites have evolved from being primarily information repositories to being interactive centers of information and commerce. They serve a variety of audiences and perform a variety of functions. Farkas and Farkas (2002) identified eight broad categories of website content grouped by purpose:

- Education
- Entertainment
- Provision of news and information
- e-commerce
- Web portals
- Persuasion
- Community building
- Personal and artistic expression

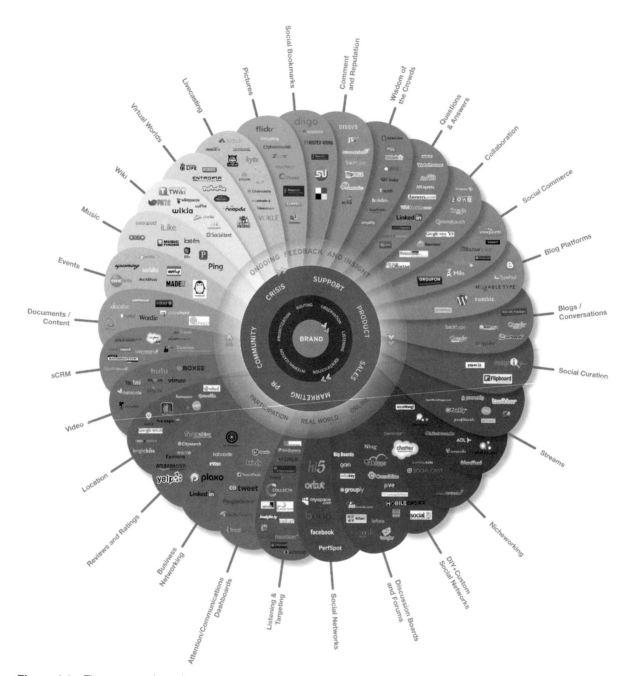

**Figure 4.1** The conversation prism.

© JESS3

These categories are not mutually exclusive, and many sport websites incorporate several of these purposes into their sites. As an example, many professional sport team sites are composed primarily of e-commerce (purchase of tickets and merchandise), information (statistics, rosters, directions to the stadium), and entertainment (video and audio clips, pictures, games). Although these purposes have the highest priority, the site content is likely to reflect other purposes as well. Sites often include an explanation of the rules of the game (education),

links to other sites (web portals), and community service events and activities (community building). Websites for other types of sport organizations contain content that reflects different priorities. A local golf or tennis club may use its website primarily as an electronic newsletter to inform its members or other site viewers of upcoming events, take online reservations, describe the facility's amenities, and provide directions to the club.

From a public relations perspective, most of the publics of any organization can be served by

# Using Social Media to Reach Stakeholders

### John Halpin

Photo courtesy of John Halpin.

Since Internet usage became widespread in the mid-1990s, sport organizations have engaged in a digital arms race to make their websites more attractive to fans. More information, and faster. Flashier design. Enhanced community elements. Live audio and video. With every added feature, these online properties gave fans more reasons to visit.

Now, things are different. Robust websites are important, but with the advent of social media platforms, notably Facebook and Twitter, giving people reasons to come to you is no longer enough. You need to go to them.

According to PCMag.com, as of May 2011 Facebook had approximately 157 million U.S. users, and Twitter claimed 26.9 million. With those kinds of numbers, leagues, teams, and athletes are eagerly devoting time to reaching fans on these platforms in a variety of ways. Although the leagues get huge reach on every media platform, teams and individual athletes are using social media in more interesting, helpful, and personal ways to strengthen relationships with fans.

- Portuguese soccer star Cristiano Ronaldo is a social media superstar as well, having more than 30 million Facebook fans and 3.3 million Twitter followers. Ronaldo, not a public relations person or ghostwriter, uses social media to offer prizes, request fan photos and videos, and refute alleged media falsehoods. He even released the first photo of his newborn son exclusively on Facebook in July 2010. When you have such a huge following, you don't need to court the media as much as you used to. You can just talk to fans yourself, and that's a powerful shift in the communications paradigm.

- The New York Yankees have more than 4 million fans on Facebook and 393,000 Twitter followers. No surprises there. But they also have a Twitter account named "@YankeesWeather" that focuses solely on weather updates for ticket holders. Here's an example of a tweet from one hour before the scheduled start of a rain-threatened June 2011 game:

  *We do not expect to start the game on time but do not anticipate a long delay.*

  That may sound simple, but if you were on your way to a Yankees game, would you rather follow that account or wait for someone on the radio to give you a delayed report? This valuable and free service for fans requires little manpower from the team.

- NASCAR driver Ryan Newman has nearly 100,000 fans that "like" his Facebook page and approximately 43,000 Twitter followers. Many of Newman's competitors use social media mainly for race news and sponsor activities, and that's fine. Newman takes things further by regularly engaging his fans in charitable efforts that promote animal shelter adoption and environmental conservation. In addition to raising awareness and money for good causes, fans are able to see—on feeds delivered directly to them, mixed in with news from friends—what Newman is like outside the racecar. If people come to Facebook as Ryan Newman fans, how can they not become even bigger fans when they see him helping orphaned dogs and endangered forests?

- New York Football Giants VP of public relations Pat Hanlon has more than 20,000 Twitter followers. He parries with beat writers, offers breaking player news, and answers fan

> **Robust websites are important, but with the advent of social media platforms, notably Facebook and Twitter, giving people reasons to come to you is no longer enough. You need to go to them.**

*(continued)*

(continued)

questions about everything from parking to where to find the best concession food in the team's stadium. Hanlon's efforts give the organization a person, not a faceless e-mail account, who will help fans if necessary.

- Fantasy sports and Twitter are a match made in heaven because hardcore fantasy players can ask questions of their favorite analysts. The 140-character brevity that Twitter requires helps both sides be efficient. In this case, fans use social media for rapid-response assistance with their favorite hobby. Fifteen years ago, this exchange would have required an 800 number that charged a fee. You were basically on your own.

The preceding examples use social media in different ways, but they have one thing in common: The athletes and organizations use social platforms to strengthen existing bonds with fans. Traditional advertising, marketing, and communications are mainly about reach: How many new people can we get to buy our tickets or watch our teams? Social media isn't about money or numbers, at least not directly. It's more about deepening existing relationships than creating new ones.

Ronaldo has an exponentially larger social media audience than Newman does, but both are mainly using these relatively new platforms to conduct conversations, almost becoming friends, with existing fans. America's most storied sport franchise is sending 140-character weather reports to provide better customer service. Fantasy football owners can get instant, personalized help from their favorite writers. And it's all free, by computer or smartphone.

Sport leagues, teams, and athletes will always be in the business of making money. Because of the advent of social media, however, they need to be more helpful and accessible than ever before to reach their financial goals. Keeping fans at arm's length is no longer acceptable. In fact, it's a distinct disadvantage.

*John Halpin is a veteran sport public relations consultant who has worked with the U.S. Olympic Committee, the National Hockey League, and the Charlotte Bobcats in the areas of broadcast and media relations. He also writes on fantasy sports for FOXsports.com.*

websites in some way, and most of the purposes of a website are useful in public relations efforts. As sport organizations identify their relevant publics, they should also consider ways in which their websites can serve their constituencies.

# Developing a Website

The development of a website involves a range of considerations that determine the effectiveness and usefulness of the site. Such considerations include goals and objectives, site provider and management, content, site design, site promotion, and site evaluation. These site planning and maintenance issues are addressed in the sections that follow. An effective website essentially is the connection of business goals with the needs of the target audiences (Ryan & Jones, 2009).

## Goals and Objectives

As with any planning, website development involves establishing goals and objectives. Smith (2000) suggested that this step is an essential part of producing a website that engenders loyalty and

serves organizational needs. The goals of a website are going to be related to the purposes of the website and to the audiences that are targeted. If the primary purpose of the site is e-commerce, identifying the targeted consumers and developing goals relevant to that primary purpose will be necessary. Such goals would likely include desired revenue production, profitability, sales volume, market share, customer retention, and customer satisfaction. If the primary purpose is to provide entertainment, the target audience of that entertainment must be determined, and goals will be related to the frequency of use, length of use, and user satisfaction with the entertainment. Investing effort at this stage of website development will prove beneficial when it comes to evaluation because the foundation for assessment will already be in place. Ron Ratner's sidebar provides insight into the strategic development of a website from the perspective of a collegiate athletics conference.

## Website Provider and Management

The first decisions required in website development are to choose who will develop it and how it will

# Strategic Development of a Website

Ron Ratner

Photo courtesy of Ron Ratner.

The face of intercollegiate athletics has been transformed immeasurably over the course of the last decade, most notably in the progression toward a model that more closely resembles a commercial enterprise. Although the trend toward college athletics as a business garners the bulk of the headlines, perhaps the most striking development in the field has been the explosion of new media technologies. Accepting, and more important, embracing this evolution within the industry has enabled the Northeast Conference (NEC) to build its fan base and remain at the forefront of the new media movement.

The NEC, a Division I member of the National Collegiate Athletic Association (NCAA), provides services for 12 colleges and universities located in its Mid-Atlantic footprint. In addition to affording its member institutions and student–athletes the opportunity to conduct intercollegiate athletics as an integral component of their academic programs, the NEC conducts championships, assists members in complying with NCAA and NEC rules and regulations, and helps publicize their athletics programs. Under the public relations and marketing umbrella, the revolution in technology has enabled extraordinary changes in both the presentation and dissemination of information within the conference.

Just 10 years ago print-based media was still thriving, having yet to cede ground to the on-line platforms still in their infancy. Centered in the crowded New York media market, the NEC struggled to tell its success stories and forge a true connection not only with its fans but also within the campus community at each of its institutions. When the NEC first launched its official website in the mid-1990s, few in the conference realized just how powerful and vital the Internet would eventually become as a communication channel. The site was originally conceived to update fans on a weekly basis with news and notes from around the league. Only a short time passed, however, before the conference realized how much they had underestimated the public's appetite for information and their ability to adapt to new technology. The Internet was a game changer, and for the NEC to remain competitive within the industry, the stakes needed to be raised.

The arms race to build content-rich websites was on, and the NEC adapted its public relations strategy to take advantage of the now-flourishing medium. With one carefully planned re-design, the conference website established itself as the league's primary information source. The site initially featured press releases, schedules, standings, statistics, and press clippings, all managed in-house on a daily basis. Lauded by its fan base, media, and membership for its easily navigable structure, timely updates, and a growing database of archived content, the meta-morphosis of NortheastConference.org was far from complete. After Amazon and big-box retailers helped jump-start the online shopping craze, the NEC added an e-commerce site to its list of offerings. Similarly, the league was able to add to its inventory of marketable elements by targeting sponsors who saw value in the growing number of visitors logging onto the site.

> **For all the groundbreaking technological changes of the late 20th century, it wasn't until the broadband revolution took shape and the phrase *new media* became entrenched in the lexicon that the Northeast Conference was able to take the next step in branding the conference and reaching its goal of building an interactive community.**

For all the groundbreaking technological changes of the late 20th century, it wasn't until the broadband revolution took shape and the phrase *new media* became entrenched in the lexicon that the Northeast Conference was able to take the next step in branding the conference and reaching

*(continued)*

*(continued)*

its goal of building an interactive community. The means by which audiences were accessing, consuming, and sharing information had again shifted dramatically with the proliferation of online video content, audio, podcasts, and blogs. Likewise, mobile phone units had become indispensable to the younger, wireless generation, a demographic coveted by the conference. The NEC's need to evolve along with its fan base was evident, and it began with digitizing its own media content. With an annual 25-game television package and tapes of hundreds of games sitting in storage, the league set out to give these games a second life. The decision to repurpose television content through highlight reels on the NEC's new YouTube channel proved popular and led to the similar dual concept of live webcasting of championships and then posting of clips of the events to the channel. Soon thereafter, the league created "NEC on the Run" podcasts, easily downloadable to portable media players, and began streaming one-minute NEC Notebook spots, which provided fans with a rapid-fire rundown of the latest football and basketball news.

The reaction from the fan base was immediate and not entirely unexpected. The public wanted even more content, and desired it in short, quick doses that were easily digestible in a fast-paced world cluttered with entertainment choices. The social media realm had arrived, and again the game changed. Unlike traditional websites, social media platforms presented the opportunity for immediate two-way dialogue with the NEC's audience. Within 24 hours of launching both Facebook and Twitter pages, word began to spread virally throughout the conference and fans began signing on. NEC student–athletes in particular jumped on board, and the goal to create an online community and rich social environment was realized.

In any rapidly transforming field there is no time to rest on one's laurels. An organization must remain nimble and proactive in its strategic approach to achieve long-term sustainability. Technology, in particular, can be humbling as expectations rise, but when harnessed correctly, technology can be utilized, at little or no cost, to promote, or in some cases, monetize a product. In the NEC's case, what began as a simple website has evolved into much more over the course of a decade. Changes in the media landscape and advances in the online world helped build the NEC's brand, but more work remains to be done. The harsh reality is that technology never stands still, and that is a good thing as long as you can keep pace.

*Ron Ratner is the associate commission for communications and television for the Northeast Conference.*

be managed. The selection of an **Internet service provider (ISP)** among the thousands of options is another important initial consideration (Delpy & Bosetti, 1998; Bruno & Whitlock, 2000). Site providers vary in the services that they offer and the fees that they charge. Perry (2003) recommended that several issues be addressed when selecting a service provider. First, sport managers should consider the amount of technical assistance that they will need from the service provider. Some providers offer little more than site hosting, whereas others offer services that may range up to complete site management. Companies can provide anything from a cookie-cutter web page template to a unique design created just for a specific organization. The primary advantage of using substantial external assistance is that these professional developers have extensive experience in designing websites, expertise that may not be readily available in house. Of course, the more services the sport organization needs, the higher the fees will be. Outsourcing maintenance may result in significant costs to the organization

(Bruno & Whitlock, 2000). Some sport organizations are outsourcing the design of their web pages to professional developers who may have more insight into the complexities of a multipurpose site. Many college athletics programs contract with website developers such as Sidearm Sports or PrestoSports to construct their sites. Among the major football and basketball conferences, CBS Interactive (CBSSports.com college network) is one of the prominent service providers. Many sites also partner with companies such as NeuLion and College Sports Direct to provide live video and statistics services. The major professional sport leagues in North America maintain their own in-house website development. As an example, Major League Baseball controls league and franchise websites through MLB Advanced Media, and the National Basketball Association does the same through NBA Media Ventures. The National Football League (NFL) and the National Hockey League (NHL) also have centralized much of the website operations of their franchises. These leagues have an array of websites that can include their network site, special event sites, and geographically targeted sites such as NFL China and NFL.com en Espanol.

Outsourcing has potential cost and control concerns that must be weighed in the development decision. A study of college athletic administrators indicated that those who managed their websites in house reported enjoying greater control over the information posted on their sites and the speed at which it was posted (Stoldt et al., 2001). Those who outsourced the management of their sites reported that the primary advantages of such an arrangement were the technical expertise offered by the service providers and the freeing up of department personnel because of the service. When selecting a service provider, sport managers should consider how effective the service's current sites are in terms of loading time and visual appeal as well as the currency of the information on those sites. A portfolio of strong sites currently in operation may be predictive of satisfactory service. Sport managers are encouraged to contact a service provider's references regarding prices, technical support, and service that those site providers offer (Perry, 2003).

One additional development decision that bears careful attention is the **domain name** or website address. Generally, the simpler the name is, the easier it will be to find the site (Bruno & Whitlock, 2000). The site name should reflect a common reference or logical connection to the organization to be most effective. Assuming that a desired address has not already been purchased, the cost of securing an address is minimal. Registry of the name is important to prevent poachers who register names and then sell the rights to a logical user.

## Website Content

Website content is a function of the site's purpose and audience. It is a reasonable assumption that a website visitor is likely to have a specific purpose in mind. Without substantive and useful content, other aspects of website construction and design will have little meaning. Sport managers planning or managing websites have an array of content options from which to choose. Farkas and Farkas (2002) suggested that brainstorming a content list should be the starting point in choosing the content elements that will be included in the site. This list can be refined when the material is organized and site constraints are considered. The process can be combined with envisioning how the content might best be presented using several categories of content type, including text, graphics, video, audio, animation, multimedia, and interactive tools (e.g., information requests, purchase tools). Some examples of the type of content that might be included on the websites of various sport organizations are summarized in table 4.1.

Content should be offered that can quickly meet the minimum expectations of potential visitors (Hess & Kean, 2000). As technological capability has progressed, the limitations to what can efficiently be included have been reduced. Material that once required too much computer power to make it

## Table 4.1 Potential Website Content

| College athletics sites | Pro team sites | Fitness club sites | Retail sites |
|---|---|---|---|
| Team rosters | Team rosters | Membership information | Merchandise |
| Schedules and results | Schedules and results | Programs | Prices |
| Statistics | Statistics | Facility location | Store locations |
| Historical records | Historical records | Directions | Special sales |
| Ticket information | Ticket information | Hours of operation | Gift cards |
| Facility information | Facility information | Newsletter | Loyalty programs |
| Booster club | Fan clubs | Services and amenities | Prominent brands |
| Directory | Charity partners | Staff directory | Return policies |
| Links to other sites | Merchandise | Special events | Employment |
| Camps | Fantasy camps and games | Community programs | Community programs |
| Photos and video | Photos and video | Facility photos | Investor information |

viable (e.g., video clips) now is routinely available and allows for much more extensive and creative website content.

Although many websites contain primarily marketing- and commerce-related information, much of the content can have a public relations orientation as well. A well-constructed website provides constituents with a broad range of information that creates opportunities to connect with the organization in a variety of ways—not just as a consumer.

A key advantage of the web over other information sources is the capability of modifying and updating in near real time. Providing site users with current and regularly updated content serves as incentive for more frequent visits to the site and enhances user loyalty. Credibility of a website often hinges on the accuracy and currency of the information presented (Migala, 2000a; Baehr, 2007).

## Website Design

Identifying the content to be included on a website is one step, and determining how it should be organized and presented is another. Website design is part art and part science, and several general guidelines should be considered in the site construction process. Kentie (2002) provided suggestions that can assist in designing a successful site.

- Create a structure first.
- Put valuable content on every page.
- Make a good first impression.
- Design with restraint and common sense.
- Make navigation clear and consistent.
- Continually review design and content.
- Always keep the user in mind.

Developing a sound structure is an important first step and allows a logical arrangement of content that makes it easy for users to search, browse, and navigate. For example, a site may be composed of a series of layers that provide users with related information for those who want it. A headline and paragraph about game results may lead someone to a second layer with a more extensive game description. From there another layer may include the box score and statistics for the game, and a further layer could contain video highlights or postgame interviews. Three common structures are linear, hierarchical, and hypertextual, and some sites blend characteristics of multiple forms depending on the complexity of the site (Baehr, 2007). The importance of the home page cannot be overemphasized because it is usually the first contact that the user has with the site. It must have a positive impact and provide the platform for efficient navigation. The home page is also where the aesthetic quality of the site is likely to have an important influence on user behavior because this is likely to be where first impressions are formed.

Site navigation involves helping users know where they are and find what they want. Well-designed website navigation reveals content (Krug, 2006). A variety of tools can help users steer their way through the site, including toolbar menus and buttons, hyperlinks, search utilities, and site maps. The complexity of the site determines the extent to which these tools are employed (Baehr, 2007). Tracking user navigation patterns is an important assessment tool in evaluating site content and design. Continual site evaluation will keep the information current and the structure consistent with user needs.

Several other design issues are involved in constructing a website. Some of these include the following:

- The term **persistent navigation** refers to information that should be part of virtually all pages of a website. Among the numerous possibilities, items such as "About Us," "Frequently Asked Questions (FAQ)," "Directory," "Contact Us," and "Privacy Policy" have particular relevance from a public relations perspective. All web pages should contain a link that sends the user back to the home page (Krug, 2006).
- Sullivan (2003) and Krug (2006) both noted that text must be used judiciously because viewers scan text rather than read it. This requires getting to the point quickly, providing good leads and headings, creating a clear visual hierarchy, and avoiding large blocks of text that require scrolling.
- Sites that include graphics and pictures are much more appealing than those that have just text. One recommendation is to have each web page contain one large action photo and a limited number of smaller graphic elements (Bruno & Whitlock, 2000).

Design has important implications for both initial visitor impression and ease of use. If users can find the information and services that they are looking for quickly and easily, they are more likely to return to the site in the future. Keeping the user in mind during the design process will enhance the chances of effectively meeting user expectations for the site.

# Website Promotion

Getting users to the website is certainly an important consideration because a great website with no visitors is of little use. The purposes and goals of the site have a significant bearing on how much effort is put into promoting it as well as how it will be promoted. Some sport organizations provide websites primarily as a service or a convenience to their stakeholders. The incentive is largely to serve existing stakeholders rather than to attract new visitors. Other organizations, however, are much more interested in expanding their reach. Some sites generate significant revenue by selling advertising space, and the value of that space is a function of how many visitors use the site. For organizations that have e-commerce as a primary purpose, promoting the site becomes a key element in its success.

Given the importance of the sport organization's website to its public relations and marketing efforts, it only makes sense for sport managers to seek effective avenues to promote the site. Migala (2000b) recommended including the site's address in all organizational media, including promotional items that may be distributed to the public. Schedules, posters, business cards, and even sales receipts can be promotional devices. It is now common for receipts to solicit online feedback by offering an incentive for completing a satisfaction survey. On-site signage should also be allocated for promoting the website. Finally, Migala recommended staging offline promotions to drive traffic to the website. For example, fans attending an event may consent to having their picture taken in front of some sort of promotional backdrop. They can later view the photo by visiting the organization's website.

Smith (2000) suggested a variety of methods that can be used to attract site visitors, including advertising on other sites frequented by target customers, using online promotions and sweepstakes to encourage trials, and collaborating with other organizations to gain access to their site users. After contact with a user has been established, persuading her or him to complete a registration or profile will allow additional interaction opportunities. This personalized information can then be used to tailor promotional activity in specific ways, and the user can identify contact preferences. A website visitor who uses a site primarily for fantasy games may be directly alerted to new features or opportunities to participate. Any promotional efforts should be designed to extend the relationship with the site users. For example, the NFL's site, www.NFL.com, introduced free partial-season fantasy leagues designed to rekindle interest for fantasy participants who fared poorly in the full-season games (Adams, 2004).

Another strategy that has become important in designing sites is **search engine optimization (SEO)**. This tool is important because the most common route to a website is likely to be one of the major search engines (e.g., Google, Yahoo, Bing). Those whose sport sites rely on viewers to come to the site via a search engine should understand how search engines evaluate websites. Ryan and Jones (2009) suggested a variety of strategies for optimizing search engine attractiveness. Content is more important than aesthetics in website rankings, and content is evaluated based on key words and phrases. Knowing the target audiences and the types of search phrases that they are likely to use is fundamental to improving the ranking of a site. Using the websites of successful competitors as a benchmark for key words may also be useful. Interior links that connect pages within the site and the quality of other sites that link to a site are all important in moving up the ratings scale. RSS (Really Simple Syndication) feeds may also be helpful in improving SEO. This tool allows a website to provide subscribers with automatic updates directly so that they don't have to visit the site to receive newly posted information. Using blogs and site directories may also be useful in creating exposure for a website. Another promotional strategy involves paid search marketing whereby an organization pays a search engine to have its website appear when various search words are entered.

# Website Evaluation

Because the website is an important interface between organization and constituent, evaluating and subsequently improving the user experience are important. As with any evaluation, website assessment should be tied to identified purposes, goals, and objectives. If the site is primarily commerce oriented, business-focused metrics are likely to be central to evaluation. From a public relations perspective, however, user-focused measures are essential to determining the effectiveness of a website. Among the factors that List (2005) identified as indicators of effectiveness were awareness, popularity, accessibility, usability, and trust. The attempt to measure these factors is likely to involve a variety of web metrics or web analytics including the number of site visitors, time spent on a site (**stickiness**), page views (assessing visit depth), **click path analysis** (navigation assessment), return visits, **bounce rates** (single page visit only), and behaviors produced by site visits such as purchases or donations. Several commercial enterprises offer software and services to analyze many aspects of website operations and provide a clearer sense of the strengths and weaknesses of a site. (See topseos.com for examples of such enterprises.)

# Structuring Websites for Specific Stakeholders

In the course of this book several stakeholder groups are identified as primary targets for sport organizations in their public relations efforts. These publics are also important audiences for organizational websites. Constructing a website that accommodates the needs of constituents such as the media, community, consumers and fans, members, donors, and business partners and sponsors will help enhance these relationships.

## Websites and Media Relations

One of the most important relationships that many sport organizations have is with the media, particularly high-profile spectator sport at the professional and college levels. Websites can help accommodate the needs of the media, especially through the provision of news and information. Members of the media rely on information in many forms, and spectator sport counts on the media for the exposure crucial to financial success. Teams, leagues, conferences, and governing bodies all maintain websites that are at least partially devoted to the kinds of information that the media require. In some cases team and league websites provide distinct sections accessible only to credentialed media. Major League Baseball serves the media with access to a centralized bank of reference information through MLBpressbox.com. Although much of the information could be accessed from a variety of sources, this centralized repository includes nearly everything that the league can provide for the media including links to a "press box" for each team. This material includes game schedules and game notes, lineups, statistics, press releases, media advisories, special events, rules, record books, league executive information, and downloadable audio, video, and photos of players. It offers one-stop shopping for information that the media need to do their job.

News releases that were once mailed in hard copy are now routinely transmitted and stored electronically. The same is true of media guides. The advantages of this technology are obvious and go well beyond the financial savings associated with reduced printing and mailing costs. Speed of communication, convenience of access, timeliness of information, and ease of updating provide added value. Even when the information is not actually sent to the media, it can be stored in a website that media members can access when they need it. The best way to serve the media relationship is to find out what information they want and in what form they want it. The more convenient and usable the information is, the more likely it is that media members will view the organization as a reliable partner.

A broad range of information is desired by the media, and the type of information varies by medium. As an example, the visual media will have more need of photos and video clips, whereas print media may want more statistical information, historical background, and feature material. Some media will want information that ties an organization to the media's market area, such as the success of local athletes. Websites are capable of providing a wide range of material, and electronic transmission of this material to the media can be done efficiently when necessary. Modern sports are oriented toward statistics, and the current and historic statistical detail available is often extraordinary. Technology and the Internet have greatly simplified the media's ability to access and manipulate statistical data and incorporate it into their work.

Most team sites have a wide range of information, including team rosters and individual player biographies, game schedules and results, coaching staff information, game and cumulative individual and team statistics, archived historical records, personnel updates (recruiting, trades, injuries, roster moves), facility information, staff directories, and visitor information.

Other content that may be beneficial to the media as well as other constituents involves links to other information sources such as league, conference, and opponent websites. Virtually all college and professional league websites contain links to the sites of each league member as well as links to a variety of other sources. Individual team websites often have links to the various leagues of which they are members, media outlets, sport-specific sites, booster groups, and relevant governing bodies. Some organizations have sites capable of providing live updates of games or events through services such as Gametracker and NeuLion. The NCAA typically has ongoing updates of championship events on its website. In some cases the sites also include access to live broadcasts (both audio and video) of games, and the distributing media become website partners in some respects. Information may also be available on the process used for distributing press credentials and the protocol for visiting teams who desire to broadcast events. Organizations such as the PGA provide the same types of content but also serve as the conduit to the individual tournaments that serve as the components for the PGA Tour.

## Websites and Community Relations

Sport organizations commonly use their websites for community relations in several ways. The first and probably most common way is as a platform to promote the organization's good works in the community. In some cases this information is among the more prominent elements of the site. Each of the teams in the four major professional sport leagues in the United States has a "Community" section on its website, and other major professional sport operations around the world often have some form of community connection such as a foundation. Photos and video clips are frequently used to display these community efforts. Organizations are likely to use their websites to promote and solicit support for their own (or their foundation's) charitable initiatives or the good works of their affiliated coaches and athletes. A recent examination of the Pittsburgh Steelers website revealed 33 community outreach programs that included affiliations with established charitable organizations (e.g., Toys for Tots, Make-a-Wish) as well as internally developed programs (e.g., Heroes at Heinz Field, Art Rooney Scholarship Fund) (Pittsburgh Steelers, 2010).

Some sport organizations, particularly those in the high-profile entertainment segment, use their sites as tools for managing charitable requests. They provide information regarding the organization's policies for donation requests and sometimes provide interactive tools that enable web users to submit their requests online.

The second way that sport organizations use their websites as a community relations tool is by promoting direct-contact initiatives. Organizational websites may promote speaking and other public appearances by the organization's personnel, mascots, and cheerleaders, and special events such as caravans, open houses, exhibitions, and conferences. Organizations with personnel in high demand for public appearances may also use their sites to dis-seminate information regarding appearance policies and to provide mechanisms for submitting requests for personal appearances.

The third way that websites may be used to improve community relations is by offering services specifically designed to maintain or enhance a sense of community among stakeholders. For example, organizations that may not be prominent enough to secure broadcast distribution outlets may choose to webcast audio or video coverage of their events. This tool enables fans, alumni, and family and friends of competitors to enjoy events even if they are not able to attend.

Other organizations have taken community-building efforts to another level. For example, the NFL's New York Giants have established a fan registry on their website (Migala, 2000a). Users enter their names and contact information into a database that other members of the registry may then view. Users can thus contact other Giants fans. The registry is of particular value to displaced Giants fans who are looking for other fans in their areas with whom they can watch Giants games. In addition, the registry provides the Giants with a database of people they can contact with other public relations and marketing messages. Social networking is a particularly valuable tool for community relations efforts. Sites such as Facebook and MySpace have profoundly altered the community-building landscape. Launched in 2004, Facebook reports 500 million active users with more than 25 billion pieces of content shared each month. More than 250,000 websites have integrated with the Facebook platform, and sport websites are no exception (Facebook, 2010). Most sport organizations of any kind (teams, leagues, retailers, health and fitness clubs, and so on) have a social networking presence that allows fans and patrons to connect with the organization and each other. Monmouth University's athletics department has developed a social media hub on its website that provides a social media directory for each of the teams (Monmouth University Athletics, 2011). This tool does pose some interesting issues as organizations develop and manage these social web platforms. Dellarocas (2010) suggested that successfully harnessing these social communities depends on establishing a reputation built on attracting the right people and content that fits the organization's vision for the site. Sport organizations are only beginning to tap into the potential these tools have to nurture the relationships fundamental to the practice of public relations.

As noted, sport organizations handle the community relations aspects of their websites in different ways. The following material briefly profiles the community relations content found on the sites of three prominent but diverse sport organizations. (Because the organizations update their websites frequently, the exact content of the current sites may be slightly different from the descriptions that follow.)

- *San Antonio Spurs (www.nba.com/spurs)*: The Spurs list a community section among the seven menu options along the top banner of their website. The community section of the site contains eight parts. The first is a news section that provides information regarding the charitable activities that the organization and its members support, including information about civic awards given to Spurs' players. The second is a section about the foundation that profiles the organization's affiliated 501(c)(3) charitable activities. It includes a description of the foundation's mission, its most prominent activities, and its significant accomplishments. Also included is information regarding the team's donation and appearance policies. The third section is a grants page that provides details of the money that the Spurs Foundation contributes to Texas charities. The fourth is a teacher and parent zone that details the organization's initiatives in support of educational achievement and character development. Other segments deal with basketball camps, events, and fund-raisers and a "How can I help?" section.

- *24-Hour Fitness (www.24hourfitness.com)*: One of the eight menu options at the top of the organization's home page is a community component that contains a people section in which customers tell their fitness stories and a section on resource links that serves as an educational service. Information regarding the organization's charitable initiatives can be found through descriptions of support for programs dealing with building playgrounds, low-income school fitness activities, and the V Foundation. It also provides healthy recipes and documents affiliations with the *Biggest Loser* television program and Weight Watchers.

- *Nike (www.nike.com)*: Armed with a diverse array of web pages that showcase its products in multiple languages, Nike also features a section that details aspects of its business operation. A section of the site titled "Nike Responsibility" includes information regarding environmental and sustainability practices, profiles of community investment programs such as the Nike School Innovation Fund, information on diversity initiatives through the Nike Foundation, facts regarding labor practices, reports about community involvement and corporate responsibility, and information regarding

Nike's corporate governance practices. The site also contains a link to ninemillion.org, an agency of the United Nations Refugee Agency that is supported by Nike.

## Websites and Consumer Relations

The web has become a hub for e-commerce, and sport organizations have certainly capitalized on this capability. Most team and league websites contain numerous opportunities to purchase anything from tickets to team merchandise. Subscription options on many sites have additional premium material such as "insider information" or opportunities to purchase broadcast packages. The sidebar titled Websites Lay Foundation for Revenue Generation written by Mike Ross discusses the importance of the Internet as a mechanism for increasing exposure, interaction, and a sense of community.

Just as public relations can supplement marketing to the traditional consumer, it can play a role in developing relationships with e-consumers. Many of the elements that help produce satisfied customers in conventional markets also apply to the electronic marketplace. Customers want convenience, reliable service, and good value, and any vendor who can deliver that is off to a good start.

But that is only the beginning. In e-commerce, finding and evaluating alternatives is only a click away, and the hassle of fighting traffic to get to another store to compare products and prices has been eliminated. This aspect adds to the challenge of developing customer loyalty. Although e-shopping removes many of the inconveniences of traditional shopping, it faces many of the same challenges as catalog shopping, including speed of delivery, order accuracy, return policies, and convenience of return. Commonly employed service strategies include free shipping for orders greater than a certain amount, expedited shipping options, package tracking, gift service, responsive complaint services, fair return policies, and promptly processed returns. A complete explanation of product features can also help customers make decisions. Professional teams and leagues and some college athletics programs now offer a web-based ticket exchange or ticket resale service for fans who may want to buy or sell tickets in the secondary market. Although such a service will produce some revenue, its main purpose may be to ensure a level of security and confidence among consumers that may not exist in the scalper's market. Another concern is the level of security and privacy of personal information that is necessary in

# Websites Lay Foundation for Revenue Generation

## Mike Ross

Photo courtesy of Mike Ross.

The Internet, as an element of a digital media revolution, has changed the way that we function on a daily basis. It's changed how we work, how we shop, and even how we order pizza! But the biggest difference, of course, is that the Internet has changed the way we communicate.

But what if you were to think of it in another way? Can the Internet change the way that a sport organization makes money? Looking at this from a marketer's perspective of exchange is easy, but let's look at it from a public relations standpoint.

**Point 1: The Internet is a great source of publicity**. You learned in chapter 1 that publicity is product information conveyed free of charge by a media source. Although that can involve the mass media, we've seen a shift in the field in recent years as sport organizations move to become their own in-house media sources. In other words, instead of going to the newspaper or relying on the nightly news to spread the word, organizations are using the Internet and social media to do it on their own. Although this tactic offers advantages and disadvantages, the use of social media in its most basic form is free.

Imagine waking up on a Saturday morning with nothing on your schedule. You log on to your Facebook page and see that your favorite team is having a two-for-one ticket promotion or an autographed bat night. It wouldn't take many people to act on this for the team to see a revenue spike because the channel used for its message was basically free.

**Point 2: The Internet is a great source of feedback**. When we communicate we get signs from the receiver that the message was not only received but also understood. We can use that feedback to tell us what worked and what didn't. This information allows us to craft a better message to build an even stronger relationship with our publics. Many websites use Google Analytics to track the number of people who visit the site, the pages that they visit, the links that they click on, and even the amount of time that they spend on the site. The online magazine company ZMags, with whom many organizations build online media guides, can give administrators a graphic highlighting what pictures and other elements within the document the viewer zoomed in on.

One of my favorite examples comes from an NFL franchise. Each week during the season, this team used its Facebook page to introduce a member of the franchise's cheerleading squad. After an excruciating late-season loss, the club continued its weekly tradition, but this time it was met with comments such as "Can she play safety?" "She isn't going to block Ray Lewis either, so why do we care?" and "Maybe we can trade her to Carolina for the #1 pick." Now, although this feedback wasn't positive, the organization used it and quickly responded with interviews and videos about upcoming events and games. Comments turned positive again.

**Point 3: The Internet is a great source of community**. One of the reasons that many of us follow our favorite teams on the Internet or through social media is the sense of connection that we feel when we do so. We feel informed, engaged, and almost as if we are part of the organization when we see behind-the-scenes footage and other items. In a form of direct revenue, we can purchase official items online at the team store. We can even buy game-worn jerseys, helmets, and other game-used items to decorate our homes and offices. Why do we do this? As a way to express our identity and connect to other fans, sometimes even fans of other teams. Rivalries can be fun to talk about with friends who may be fans of other organizations, and that aspect can add to the sense of connection. We applaud and "like" items when our organization succeeds,

> One of the reasons that many of us follow our favorite teams on the Internet or through social media is the sense of connection that we feel when we do so.

*(continued)*

*(continued)*

and we complain and console one another when our organizations fail to live up to expectations.

The organization can also benefit from this sense of community when the team or the community itself goes through a crisis. Social media has become one of the easiest and best ways to communicate during crisis, largely because of the fact that it is mobile. Not everyone will have access to a computer during a time of distress, but many of us have access to social media on our phones, allowing us to provide timely updates and first-hand knowledge of the situation. In late April and May of 2011, social media use took off when a series of violent tornadoes ripped through the Southeast and Midwest. Facebook pages were created to help search for the missing. YouTube and UStream became our nightly news by providing videos and live footage of storm chasers on the ground watching storms as they moved through.

Public relations officials can help organizations not only avoid costly mistakes but also recover quickly from a crisis by minimizing the cost. Whether it is an NCAA violation, a coach in legal trouble, or a natural disaster, the sense of community built in the days before the crisis may well be what helps the organization through the episode. If your connection to the team is strong and deep to begin with, you are much more likely to stick with that organization through tough times as well.

There are countless ways to enhance revenue using websites, social media, and online publications. Getting caught up in the revenue possibilities is easy, but don't lose sight of the fact that building a strong public relations foundation, using feedback from publics, and enhancing the sense of community can make a good digital media plan a great one.

*Mike Ross is a former college athletics communications professional who now serves as a sport management faculty member at Wichita State University.*

the exchange process. Customers need to be reassured that the information they are providing (e.g., credit card number, contact information) will be protected and used only as authorized. The efforts to develop loyalty among online shoppers should be continuous and focus on the highest value customers. Soliciting customer feedback is a standard part of most websites and is the very least that should be done in seeking customer input. The better the relationship is with the consumer, the more the consumer will want to provide information that can be used to enhance satisfaction (Smith, 2000).

## Websites and Employee Relations

As will be discussed in chapter 13, employees make up an important internal public that is at times overlooked in public relations efforts. One method for communicating with and fostering interaction among employees is through an internal website, commonly referred to as the intranet. An **intranet** is a private network accessible only to employees that facilitates the dissemination and exchange of information (Stoddart, 2001). An intranet can provide a variety of benefits to an organization, its employees, and other constituencies that may be given access. The intranet is an information-sharing tool that can be used to enhance productivity by allowing information to be exchanged more quickly and efficiently. Many segments of the organization have specific uses for the intranet, particularly as it relates to sharing information and data across departments. An athletics department might need to share facility scheduling information among various units within the program. Sales and marketing can access market research information, customer service can gain entry into a client information database, and accounting and finance can quickly access payroll information. Although one driving force for intranet use is logistical efficiency, public relations applications are present as well. Human resources can use the intranet in a variety of ways to enhance and expedite intraorganizational communications. Possible examples include newsletters, directories, job listings, personalized employee web pages, benefits information, employee handbooks, events calendars, and employee surveys (Intranet Roadmap, 2005). Effective intranet use may help the organization become less compartmentalized and promote a more open operational environment that can enhance communication and create a more collaborative atmosphere.

The key to a successful intranet is its content. It must be relevant, accessible, available in a timely manner, and updated regularly. Content should be user driven, which means that the design of an intranet site must consider the priorities, needs, and preferences of the users (Garrett, 1996).

## Websites and Donor Relations

The importance of fund-raising for many sport organizations is addressed in chapter 14. For now, suffice it to say that technological advances have provided valuable tools to assist in development efforts. Hart (2002) suggested that in addition to raising money, the Internet can be used to improve donor relationships, fund-raising efficiency, and communication with constituents. The sidebar titled 10 Rules of ePhilanthropy Every Nonprofit Must Know summarizes some basic considerations for using the Internet in fund-raising.

## The 10 Rules of ePhilanthropy Every Nonprofit Must Know

### Rule 1: Don't be invisible.

If you build it, they won't just come. Building an online brand is just as important and difficult as building an offline brand.

### Rule 2: It takes know-how and vision.

Your organization's website is a marketing and fund-raising tool, not a technology tool. Fund-raisers and marketers need to drive the content, not the site developer.

### Rule 3: It's all about the donor.

Put the donor first! Know your contributors and let them get to know you.

### Rule 4: Keep savvy donors; stay fresh and current.

Make online giving enjoyable and easy. Give the donor options. Use the latest technology. Show your donors how their funds are being used.

### Rule 5: Integrate your site into everything you do.

Your website alone will do nothing. Every activity that you have should drive traffic to your site.

### Rule 6: Don't trade your mission for a shopping mall.

Many nonprofit websites fail to emphasize mission, instead turning themselves into online shopping malls.

### Rule 7: Ethics, privacy, and security are not buzzwords.

Many donors will be making their first online contribution. They will expect your organization to maintain the highest standards of ethics, privacy, and security.

### Rule 8: It takes the Internet to build a community.

Many nonprofits, particularly smaller groups, lack the resources to communicate effectively. The Internet offers the opportunity to build a community of supporters.

### Rule 9: Success online requires targeting.

The website alone is not enough. You must target your audience and drive their attention to the wealth of information and services that your website offers. Permission must be sought before you begin direct communication through the Internet.

### Rule 10: ePhilanthropy is more than just e-money.

ePhilanthropy is a tool to be used in your fund-raising strategy. It should not be viewed as quick money. There are no shortcuts to building effective relationships, but the Internet will enhance your efforts.

ePhilanthropy.org © 2005

Although a website may serve as a center for information and the host for online donations, donor relationships can be nurtured through a variety of electronic communications options. E-mail can be used in direct solicitation, but its real public relations value is its contribution to maintaining a communication link with donors. E-mail allows efficient and inexpensive communication with large groups of constituents. It provides an opportunity for dialogue rather than one-way communication and can direct a tailored and targeted message to supporters (Olsen, Keevers, Paul, & Covington, 2001). These contacts should be made only with permission to avoid their being perceived as **spam**, which will impair effectiveness. E-mail can also be passed from initial recipients to many others. This practice, known as **viral marketing**, can be effective in expanding the donor base because it uses existing donors as promoters of the cause (Hart, 2002).

Although the term *viral* may have a negative connotation, it is simply the electronic version of word-of-mouth marketing. Wilson (2000) defined viral marketing as "any strategy that encourages individuals to pass on a marketing message to others, creating the potential for exponential growth in the message's exposure and influence." In the context of fund-raising, viral marketing attempts to capitalize on existing networks of donors to grow the donor base. Having a good cause, presenting it in the right way, and providing attractive incentives will encourage existing donors to pass along the fund-raising appeal to potential donors. Having donors forward the funding-raising appeal personalizes the message for recipients and makes it appear less like spam, which allows organizations to reach prospects to which they have little direct access in a way that has considerable influence.

The Network for Good (www.fundraising123.org) has compiled an extensive list of resources that discuss various aspects of fund-raising, including how to develop websites and integrate social networking as part of an integrated communication and fund-raising strategy. A website can serve as an information hub and be a communication link for a much wider audience. A website can also keep donors and prospective donors informed about an organization's mission and needs, the status of fund-raising efforts, and the way in which the money raised is being used.

Most college athletics websites contain a link to their booster or support organizations. The content includes justification for considering making a contribution, an outline of rewards associated with certain donation levels, and an opportunity to join the booster group. In some cases it allows direct online donations or provides links to the institutional fund-raising arm. Often the site provides information about support group events and photos of past booster group occasions.

## Blogging

One Internet trend gaining popularity is **blogging**. Technorati, a blog search engine, indexes thousands of sport-related blogs. What began as the posting of unedited journals or diaries has evolved into a sophisticated and involved process. Blogs have become more interactive, frequently including the opportunity for comment and discussion and embedding links to related sites and information.

The blogging trend presents opportunities and concerns for sport organizations. One type of blogging involves pieces written by members of the organization or its constituents that provide behind-the-scenes or personal insights about various aspects of the operation. This internal form of blogging housed on organizational websites gives the organization tight editorial control over content. As an example, the NBA's website features nearly 20 blogs from players, league insiders, and coaches. Mark Cuban, owner of the Dallas Mavericks, uses a blog to voice opinions on a variety of issues and to solicit feedback from fans (King, 2005).

Another form of blogging involves blog sites developed by people outside the organization. Sport fuels passion that fans like to share. Blogs have become a frequent outlet for these exchanges. In some respects they have become the Internet version of sports talk radio. A 2011 check on SportsBlogs.org revealed over 2,500 blogs related to major league baseball alone. One obvious concern about these sites is that they are largely outside the control of the sport organizations. They are normally written from the viewpoint of the fan, which brings with it bias that may raise issues of accuracy and credibility (Terdiman, 2005).

Monitoring the information and discourse on these sites can be useful in gauging consumer attitudes and opinions. Sport organizations may also be able to capitalize on the interactive nature of blogs to enhance relationships. But they will also need to confront the problems that sometimes come with rapid and uncontrolled information dissemination. Both personal blogs and topical blogs can pose problems. Employees who write in their personal blogs about their jobs may say more than is appropriate about the workplace environment. Topical blogs are often editorial in nature, and entries are typically quite opinionated. The desire to advance personal agendas or biases may result in spreading damaging rumors that can gather momentum when ignored.

# Identifying New Media Limitations and Problems

The Internet can be an important asset to sport organizations, but it poses some public relations problems. Coombs (2002) noted that the reach and speed of the Internet are both a blessing and a curse for public relations professionals. Although the Internet makes connecting with stakeholders much quicker and easier, it also has the potential to give issues such as personnel changes, disciplinary actions, or controversial policy decisions a contagious quality that can rapidly energize publics. Given this potential, sport organizations that operate on a public stage must monitor the Internet closely and evaluate issues on the potency of the threat posed to the organization. If the mainstream media are monitoring the Internet for news tips and gauging public sentiment, as Layden (2003) reported, sport organizations themselves should be doing nothing less.

Many sport organizations have experienced the problems that come with uncontrolled dissemination of information. Most major college athletics programs are the focus of websites that are developed by people who are not employed by the schools. Some of these sites may give the appearance of being sponsored by the athletics program, when in fact they are usually administered by fans, who often manage the content loosely. Layden (2003) reported that some of these sites have several thousand subscribers. In peak times, notably during recruiting season, these sites may have hundreds of thousands of views and as many as 10,000 postings on message boards. Although these message boards often contain discussion about the previous week's game strategies, they can deteriorate into name calling and rumor spreading. What may begin as a chance to vent, celebrate, or gossip may damage individuals and entire programs when left unchecked (Steinbach, 2003).

Often these websites and blogs are a mix of boosterism and journalism, so questions arise about whether they operate as media or as an arm of the athletics program. In at least one case, the University of Kentucky's athletics program banned a site operator from contact with the program after he reportedly asked subscribers to contact recruits and posted stories and pictures of recruits online (Harmonson, 2004).

Because of the prevalence of small digital cameras and cell phone cameras, coaches have become wary of conducting open practices and cautious about how they behave in social situations. Although these new media sites enjoy First Amendment freedom (see chapter 15), they can create significant problems for managing organizational image. In some cases, schools are limiting access or refusing to provide media credentials to website providers who don't have a newspaper or television affiliation (Matuszewski, 2000). Social networking sites such as Facebook have been the source of embarrassing content posted by athletes that has caused many athletics programs to develop policies and guidelines about how athletes may use such sites. Such policies have now been extended to the use of Twitter in some cases as sport organizations try to control these newer forms of electronic communication. In 2011 Rashard Mendenhall, a running back for the Pittsburgh Steelers, decided to use Twitter to express his views on Osama bin Laden and the 9/11 attacks. His controversial statements resulted in the loss of endorsement with Champion, the sports apparel company. His statements also created a dilemma for his employer as they tried to distance themselves from his comments. Twitter does not lend itself to in-depth discussion of complex issues, and the unfiltered nature of the communication can produce public relations headaches when the emotion of the moment fuels comments (Brown, 2011).

Other considerations must also be addressed when employing Internet technology. Websites require user-initiated contact, which can reduce the control that organizations would like in establishing a connection with constituents. Additionally, many older people may be uncomfortable with some of the new media technology, thus limiting its effectiveness in reaching some important target audiences. A new mobile device application may seem wonderful, but it is useful only if the targeted constituents have an up-to-date mobile device.

One final comment regarding technology: Technological capability changes rapidly. What is commonplace today may be outdated within a short time. This rapid obsolescence has implications for public relations professionals, who must be constantly alert to the technological advances and innovations that alter some of the tools and subsequently the practices of the public relations practitioner.

## SUMMARY

The Internet and related new media present a host of public relations opportunities and challenges to sport public relations professionals. New media enables them to communicate directly with and receive feedback from large numbers of people quickly. Sport organization websites are diverse in purpose and complexity. In some instances, sport organizations offer relatively simple sites to provide critical information to fans, customers, and members of the media. In other cases, sites may be highly complex and offer numerous commerce options such as ticket and merchandise sales. Given the importance of websites as public relations and marketing platforms, careful planning is imperative. Some sport organizations manage their sites entirely in house, whereas others outsource at least some site development and management responsibilities. Most sport organizations evaluate the effectiveness of their sites using a variety of metrics that involve how many visitors come to the site, how long they stay, and how they navigate the site. A sport organization's website may be designed to facilitate communication with diverse stakeholder groups such as members of the media, the community at large, customers, and donors. Site content varies based on the particular interests of each stakeholder group. The Internet also has resulted in several challenges for sport public relations professionals. Blogging, Twitter, YouTube, and social networking sites have created many new opportunities to connect with various constituencies but can also create public relations concerns. The lack of control over information that exists for many of these new media options poses public relations challenges. Irresponsible content posted on fan-based websites and social networking sites, security concerns, and unfiltered Twitter posts have created a number of Internet-related policy concerns. Finally, this rapidly changing area requires both attention and imagination. Creative use of technological innovation can greatly enhance the way that organizations nurture relationships with their stakeholders.

## LEARNING ACTIVITIES

1. Compare the content of a variety of sport organization websites (e.g., NFL franchise, MLB franchise, NCAA Division I institution, NAIA institution, fitness center, sporting goods manufacturer). Based on the content, what appear to be the goals and priorities of the websites?

2. Compare the design of a variety of sport organization websites (e.g., NFL franchise, MLB franchise, NCAA Division I institution, NAIA institution, fitness center, sporting goods manufacturer). How do they rate based on the basic design principles offered in this chapter?

3. Select a sport organization and develop a content list of plausible material that might be included in a website. After you establish a content list, identify the elements that require regular updating to increase the potential for repeat site visits.

4. Select a sport organization website and identify the content related to the organization's community relations efforts.

5. Contrast an internal sport blog with an external sports blog dealing with the same organization. What are the similarities and differences in content?

6. Link to a social networking site for a sport organization and review some of its recent postings. What content on the site poses potential public relations problems or presents public relations opportunities?

# Developing Organizational Media

## After reading this chapter, students should be able to

- describe the purpose and nature of media guides in professional and collegiate sport,
- specify other types of print media that sport public relations professionals may be required to produce,
- address forms of electronic media that sport public relations professionals may be required to produce, and
- discuss the corporate communications function within sport organizations.

## Key terms discussed in this chapter include

- organizational media,
- media guides,
- programs,
- schedule card, and
- corporate communications.

# Most sport organizations

employ a variety of tactics to communicate with their publics, many of which do not rely on the involvement of mass media. Smith (2005) classified these tactics as **organizational media** and emphasized their value as a "middle ground between high-impact, small-audience interpersonal tactics and lower-impact, large-audience news and advertising tactics" (p. 171).

The advantage of organizational media is that they can be tailored to specific publics and are often used by information-seeking publics. A notable downside to organizational media is the potential cost associated with their development and distribution (Smith, 2005). Accordingly, sport public relations professionals should weigh the use of each form of media carefully and consider how a particular tactic might be used in combination with other communication tools.

The most prominent of these organizational media tactics may be the media guide, although the importance and presence of printed media guides are declining. The first section of this chapter describes media guides that are commonly produced by professional, collegiate, and elite amateur sport organizations. This section includes an examination of their purposes, their components, other planning considerations, and current media guide challenges.

Sport public relations professionals have many options beyond media guides for organizational media tactics. The second part of the chapter explores additional print tactics including programs, brochures, newsletters, annual reports, and more. The third part examines electronic tactics such as video and audio recordings. Finally, the chapter concludes with a discussion of the corporate communications function, which often includes production of organizational media.

## Media Guides

One of the primary tasks assigned to many sport public relations professionals is the development of **media guides** (Davis, 1998; Hall, Nichols, Moynahan, & Taylor, 2007; Helitzer, 2000). These guides, designed for the media as well as other constituents, provide detailed information regarding the sport organization and its teams and are generally produced annually. In collegiate settings, a sports information office often produces a separate media guide for each varsity sport and separate publications for men's and women's teams. A single office may produce a dozen or more guides in a single academic year, particularly in higher divisions of competition.

Media guides vary in size and level of detail. Typically, they are 8.5 × 11 inches (21 × 28 cm) at the college level and 5.5 × 8.5 (14 × 22 cm) or 6 × 9 inches (15 × 23 cm) at the professional level. But there are exceptions to those standards. Sport public relations professionals at smaller colleges in particular may opt for smaller publications that are less expensive to print. In some instances, even quad- and trifold brochures function as guides.

Years ago professional guides were produced in sizes that would allow them to fit into the pockets of sports journalists, but the size of most guides today precludes that sort of convenience. Before 2005 no regulations governed the size of college media guides. The 2004 University of Missouri football media guide had 614 pages and weighed 2.2 pounds (1 kg). Effective in fall 2005 the NCAA mandated that universities not exceed 208 pages as a cost-cutting measure. Missouri realized a savings of $20,000 in that first year (Cherner et al., 2005). Subsequent revisions to NCAA bylaws have addressed the amount of color that can be used as well as who can receive a media guide. The most recent legislation, Bylaw 13.4.1.1.2.1 adopted in April 2010 and effective in August 2010, states that a "printed media guide may have only one color of print inside the cover and may not exceed 8 1/2 by 11 inches in size and 208 pages in length" (National Collegiate Athletic Association, 2010).

In addition to their concern with cosmetic issues, several universities expressed unease about the environmental impact of printed media guides. Guides were often distributed to prospective student–athletes, many of whom were conditioned to consult the Internet for information. These recruits often did not look at the guide and subsequently threw it away. In response, two things occurred. First, the NCAA adopted additional legislation in April 2010 (Bylaw 13.4.1.1.2), which states that an "institution shall not provide a printed media guide . . . to a prospective student–athlete" (National Collegiate Athletic Association, 2010).

Second, several universities, led by Big Ten institutions Michigan and Ohio State, agreed to stop printing media guides. A news release distributed by the University of Michigan indicated the cost savings from this initiative to be approximately $250,000. Bill Martin, director of athletics for Michigan at the time, said, "With the new media environment and current economic climate, the decision to cut back in this area was prudent" (Madej, 2009).

Despite these trends, many sport organizations, professional and collegiate, continue to develop media guides. The following sections describe the purposes of media guides, content that should be included in the guides, other relevant considerations, and several related challenges that are currently confronting professionals in the field.

## Purposes

Media guides have grown large and complex to produce because they commonly serve multiple purposes. Although members of the media remain the primary audience of the guides, they are not the exclusive audience. As stated, media guides have become important tools in the recruiting of student–athletes at the collegiate level, and they are also a source of revenue for professional and collegiate sport organizations.

### Media

The information that media guides contain serves as a valuable resource to members of the media who cover the sport organization's teams and events and can generate favorable publicity as a result. Sport organizations typically go to great lengths to make sure that media guides are in the hands of influential media members several weeks in advance of a season, and many journalists rely heavily on those publications throughout the year. Beat reporters may wear out their copies of a media guide, but they are often reluctant to ask for a new copy because they may have made notations and earmarked sections that are especially useful to them throughout the year.

### Revenue

Media guides possess the potential to generate significant revenue for sport organizations through sales to the public, advertisers, and boosters and sponsors. Professional and collegiate organizations frequently produce enough copies of these guides to sell them to members of the general public. Priced anywhere up to $30, guides draw significant fan interest. For example, officials at the University of Tennessee reported generating $70,000 in media guide sales revenue in 2003 (Brown, 2004).

Some sport organizations, particularly professional teams, sell advertising that may be placed within media guides. These advertisements may be particularly marketable when the sport organization uses the guide as both a media tool and a fan publication (e.g., game program with special inserts). For smaller colleges, the entire media guide printing budget may be funded through advertising sales.

Whereas sales to the public and advertisers directly contribute to the sport organization's revenue, media guides may also be a source of indirect revenue when used as incentives. Some sport organizations may use media guides as perks to reward season-ticket holders and boosters. Media guides may also be included in proposed sponsorship packages as a way of adding value to the deal. The inclusion of media guides in ticket, booster, and sponsor packages may not cinch the deal, but every element that adds value to sales inventory boosts the potential for closing the sale.

## Content

The following sections summarize the major components that should be included in most media guides. This listing is based on media guides that the authors have procured and judging forms from College Sports Information Directors of America (CoSIDA) media guide contests. Table 5.1 summarizes the content found in three media guides based on the general categories presented in the following sections. The table contrasts how content may vary based on the nature of the sport organization—professional versus collegiate, team versus league, and

## CoSIDA Media Guide Contests

Competition in collegiate sport extends beyond the realm of athletics. Sports information professionals compete for awards each year in CoSIDA's publications contests. Media guide contests have 19 categories, and most have several divisions (CoSIDA, 2004). Categories are based on the type of media guide (e.g., lacrosse, women's soccer), and divisions are based on level of competition (e.g., NCAA Division I, NCAA Division II). CoSIDA members volunteer to serve as judges, and they evaluate guides submitted for review based on inclusion of required information, thoroughness of presentation, editorial quality, and other design elements.

The purpose of the competition is twofold. First, the competition allows the association to recognize excellence among its members. Second, those who submit their guides for peer review receive feedback from the judges' evaluations that may be helpful as they endeavor to produce higher quality guides each year.

major league versus minor league. Appendix A (pages 317-325) also provides selected pages from a sample media guide.

### General Information

The material included in the general information category varies, but some of this information is among the most-used sections of many media guides. General information includes the following:

- A table of contents that assists readers in navigating these large and frequently complex publications
- A staff directory listing phone numbers, fax numbers, and e-mail addresses

## Table 5.1 Media Guide Content

| General category | Green Bay Packers | University of Oklahoma Women's Basketball | Wichita Wingnuts | World Team Tennis |
|---|---|---|---|---|
| General information | • Table of contents<br>• 2010 Packers schedule<br>• Club information<br>• Packers in the community<br>• Lambeau Field information<br>• Media information<br>• Mission statement | • Table of contents<br>• Why Oklahoma?<br>• Media outlets<br>• Sooner fans<br>• Facility info<br>• Strength and conditioning<br>• Sooner success<br>• Life after basketball<br>• University<br>• Endowment program<br>• Norman, Oklahoma<br>• In the community<br>• Maps and directions<br>• Media policies<br>• Broadcast information | • Table of contents<br>• Wichita Wingnuts contact information<br>• About WIB, LLC<br>• National Baseball Congress World Series<br>• About Wichita, Kansas<br>• Lawrence-Dumont Stadium<br>• Media information<br>• Schedule | • Table of contents<br>• World Team Tennis<br>• WTT recreational league<br>• Glossary<br>• Bonus incentives<br>• Coaches Challenge<br>• TV schedule<br>• Match starting times and team sites<br>• Pro league schedule<br>• Sponsors |
| Team and event information | • Staff directory<br>• Player and coach bios<br>• Executive committee | • Roster and schedule<br>• Season preview<br>• Player bios<br>• Coaches and staff<br>• Offense in motion<br>• Dominating defense<br>• Photo roster | • Coaches and staff<br>• Player bios<br>• Opponent capsules | • World Team Tennis teams<br>• Team contact information |
| Season review | • Results<br>• Regular-season and playoff statistics<br>• Game-by-game results<br>• Participation chart<br>• Transactions<br>• NFL final standings | • A year in photos<br>• Season review<br>• Results<br>• Individual statistics<br>• Game-by-game statistics<br>• Superlatives comparison<br>• Box scores | • Individual and season records<br>• Game-by-game results<br>• Final statistics<br>• Postseason statistics<br>• Will Savage no-hitter | • 2009 season recap |

| General category | Green Bay Packers | University of Oklahoma Women's Basketball | Wichita Wingnuts | World Team Tennis |
|---|---|---|---|---|
| History | • Packers origins<br>• Individual and team records<br>• All-time scoring<br>• Annual team statistics<br>• Career passing, rushing, and receiving leaders<br>• Super Bowl history<br>• Playoff history<br>• All-time coaching records<br>• Attendance records<br>• Hall of Fame<br>• All-Pro selections<br>• NFL awards<br>• Pro Bowl selections<br>• Packers' all-time teams<br>• Retired Packers numbers | • Final Four traditions<br>• Big 12 dominance<br>• Career records<br>• Season records<br>• Individual records<br>• Team records<br>• Miscellaneous records<br>• 1,000-point scorers<br>• Honors and awards<br>• Postseason records<br>• Year-by-year results<br>• Year-by-year team statistics<br>• Year-by-year rosters<br>• Letter winners<br>• Poll history<br>• Series records<br>• All-time results | • Wingnuts name and logo<br>• Wingnuts firsts<br>• Yearly team statistics<br>• All-time largest crowds<br>• Team awards<br>• Wingnuts signed by Major League Baseball organizations<br>• Former MLB draft picks<br>• All-time numerical and alphabetical roster<br>• Tracking the Wingnuts | • WTT Finals recap<br>• Recap of awards<br>• WTT pro league records<br>• WTT history and highlights<br>• 35 seasons of tennis' best |
| Governing body information | • National Football League<br>• 2010 schedule<br>• Nationally televised games<br>• Important dates | • Big 12 Conference<br>• Conference composite schedule<br>• Opponent contact information | • History of the American Association<br>• Commissioner<br>• Administration<br>• All-time American Association cities<br>• Roster rules<br>• 2010 composite schedule<br>• American Association playoffs, schedule, and results<br>• Mileage chart<br>• 2008 and 2009 American Association final standings, leaders, and playoffs<br>• Honors and awards | • Cofounders bio<br>• Commissioner's bio |

Compiled from sources: Green Bay Packers 2010; University of Oklahoma 2009; Wichita Wingnuts 2010; World Team Tennis 2010.

- Media-specific information such as how to apply for event credentials and make interview requests
- Profiles of the organization and the organization's leadership (e.g., team owner, league commissioner, university president, athletic director)
- Recruiting information (in college guides) that describes academic services, student quality of life, and community features
- Travel information that details how media members can contact representatives of the organization at road contests

## Team and Event Information

Information specific to the team or event should include the following:

- Season schedule (placed prominently, often on the back cover)
- Rosters of athletes (preferably with separate alphabetical and numerical rosters)
- Profiles of the coaching staff (if applicable), including relevant coaching records
- Profiles of the athletes, including individual statistical profiles and personal bests
- A thorough preview of the upcoming season or event
- Opponent information (for team guides) that provide overviews of the teams on the upcoming season's schedule
- Facility information that profiles the site at which the sport organization competes

## Season Review

Although historical documentation should not be limited to the most recently completed season, the past year is arguably the most relevant historical information in a media guide because current coaches and athletes are likely to have participated. The season review should include the following:

- Game or event results
- A season-in-review story and individual stories on each game or event
- Complete team and individual statistics

## History

Information regarding the history of the sport organization should extend well beyond the most recent

year. Other historical information should include the following:

- Records, both team and individual for the organization and its opponents
- Coaching history and records
- Complete list of honors and awards received by members of the sport organization
- Complete list of significant team achievement (e.g., championships)
- All-time results, commonly displayed as year-by-year listings of contests and outcomes

## Governing Body Information

Finally, team and event media guides should include information regarding the sport organization's governing bodies. Media guides of professional organizations should include profiles and historical information regarding their leagues and the leaders of those leagues, such as commissioners. College media guides should profile both their conferences and their national organizations, such as the NCAA and National Association of Intercollegiate Athletics (NAIA).

# Other Considerations

As detailed as content decisions may be, they are not the only considerations when planning and producing media guides. The following sections discuss other media guide concerns.

## Planning

Media guide production is a complex process and one of the more challenging aspects of media relations work. Accordingly, sport public relations professionals must create plans to guide them through the process in a timely manner.

Chris Anderson (1997), associate athletic director of communications at the University of Nebraska at Lincoln, recommended that media guide planners establish time lines by working backward from the date when the printed guide must be received by the sport organization. Key steps along the way include the following:

- Conducting interviews with coaching staff and other key individuals
- Gathering information to be used in development of player, coach, and staff profiles
- Tracking down information regarding key events and opponents

- Updating historical records
- Securing copyright permissions for the use of photographs and the reproduction of any editorial content originated outside the sport organization

Anderson also recommended that media guide content be reviewed by several individuals to ensure its accuracy before going to press. Capable proofreaders can usually be found among other public relations staff members. In smaller operations, sport public relations professionals may need to work a bit harder at identifying someone with a good eye for editing. Direct supervisors should also be given the opportunity to proof the guide. In addition, head coaches or their designated representatives should review the information for factual accuracy. Anderson also noted that guide covers likely need to be readied for the printer several weeks earlier than the rest of the publication because they are almost always four color (full color) and they sometimes feature special design elements.

Not surprisingly, some media guides evolve into year-round projects—as soon as one year's guide is complete, work on the next year's guide begins. Most of the work on any guide occurs in the off-season, but some public relations professionals recommend that some work on the upcoming season's guide be done within the current season, particularly as it relates to writing game summaries for that season (Abicht, 2004).

## Design Elements

Design elements are arguably more important for college media guides, which sometimes double as recruiting publications, than they are for professional sport publications. Even so, all sport public relations professionals should strive to make their publications as attractive to readers as possible. Special attention should be paid to cover design, selection of type fonts, graphic elements that may be incorporated throughout the publication, color that may be incorporated into the layout, and the photos that are included in the publication.

The list of layout and design principles relevant to these considerations is too lengthy to detail in this text. Table 5.2 offers some guidelines, but it serves only to alert readers to the most critical questions that professionals must consider. Specific training in desktop publishing and layout and design is highly valuable to sport public relations professionals. Even those with some training in publication design may be wise to collaborate with graphic arts specialists throughout the production process.

## Editorial Quality

As with any other type of organizational publication, media guides must be written with the highest level of editorial quality to achieve credibility with their audiences. At a minimum, media guides should be free of grammatical and syntactical errors. Factual errors are also highly problematic because

## Table 5.2 Media Guide Design Considerations

| Design element | Key questions |
| --- | --- |
| Cover | • Is it attractive?<br>• Does it incorporate key elements (e.g., organization name, logo, year)?<br>• Does it possess a unique look? |
| Type font | • Is the body copy easy to read?<br>• Is the use of fonts consistent throughout the guide? |
| Graphics | • What visual tools are used to make the presentation attractive?<br>  • Screens (shaded areas)?<br>  • Text boxes?<br>  • Logos and symbols?<br>• Is the use of these visual tools consistent? |
| Color | • How may it best be used to enhance the presentation?<br>• Is it allowed (Note: NCAA Division I rules prohibit the use of color on internal pages)? |
| Photos | • Are they clear (i.e., focus, contrast)?<br>• Action photos: Is the ball in the photo?<br>• Action photos: Do they capture the moment? |

members of the media are extremely concerned with accuracy. If media members convey inaccurate information from a media guide in one of their stories, the sport organization's mistake has cost them credibility with their audience. And because media guides are produced primarily for media members, they should conform to Associated Press (AP) style guidelines.

Although much of the material within media guides is presented in a straightforward fashion, other elements may allow more creativity. In an effort to provide members of the media with as many potential story ideas as possible, some media guides include unusual facts about the organization's coaches and players, such as favorite foods, favorite entertainment options, and so forth. Some writers have even included reverse hype elements, such as controversial comments others have made regarding the organization or its representatives (Helitzer, 2000). The rationale for including these comments is that they may serve as story fodder for members of the media, especially when the organization's or individual's performance disproves past criticism.

## Distribution

Multiple methods may be employed to distribute media guides. Public relations personnel often personally deliver guides to members of the media who cover the sport organization on a regular basis. Media guides may also be made available at preseason media days or in less formal settings, such as when a reporter stops by the office for casual conversation.

Guides may be mailed to members of the media who cover the team on occasion but not on a frequent basis (e.g., a writer for a national magazine) as well as to public relations representatives of the opponents that the organization will be facing in the upcoming season. These opponents are likely profiled in the guide, and the publication will serve as an important resource as the opponent's public relations representatives provide relevant information to their own media constituents.

Some sport organizations make media guide content available to the general public as PDF files that may be downloaded through the sport organization's website. This service provides the information to any interested party in a way that does not bring additional cost to the sport organization (i.e., shipping). In spite of those services, most public relations units receive requests from collectors who want a hard copy. Because significant costs are involved in printing media guides and mailing

them, some sport organizations sell the publications to those who are not going to use them for professional purposes.

## Postseason Guides

Successful seasons often lead to postseason competition. Although most sport public relations professionals enjoy those winning campaigns, they present an additional challenge in that information in media guides is usually at least three months old when postseason play arrives. As a result, many sport public relations professionals create special postseason media guides.

Postseason publications are usually less comprehensive than regular media guides and less complex in design and production. They serve as updates, because through the course of a successful season player and coach statistics have changed, awards have been received, and records have been broken. The postseason media guide documents these changes. A typical postseason guide includes the following:

- Updated rosters and depth charts
- Complete regular-season game results
- Complete team and individual statistical reports for the regular season
- Final regular-season standings
- Updated biographies for players and coaches
- Chronology of how the team was built (at professional levels)
- Team postseason records

Most postseason guides are compiled quickly, so time is not available to dress them up with design elements or color or have them printed on glossy paper. Many are simply copied in house and bound with staples or spirals.

# Current Challenges

As noted, the NCAA has adopted legislation that places restriction on the size and distribution of media guides, and some schools have eliminated the production of hard copy media guides altogether in favor of alternative electronic formats. These changes pose problems for sports information directors.

## Alternative Formats

As mentioned, one tactic that sport public relations professionals are employing is publishing the media guide document in a PDF format and placing it on the organization's website or on a compact disc. Some sport organizations are doing so in lieu of printing hard copies of the document. Such a move can result in considerable cost savings and still enable members of the media and other constituents to access the content. Oakland University in Michigan was among the first institutions to distribute media guide content exclusively online (Liberman, 2000). The move, first made in 2000–01, resulted in $31,000 in savings for the program, money that was used to purchase computer equipment and hire a public relations assistant. Cost savings aside, sports information officials express concern that if guides are available only online or on CDs, they will not reach their full potential as publicity tools (Brown, 2004). Media members are accustomed to having organizational information at their fingertips, and they may not be as willing to go online or to a CD to access it.

Public relations professionals at smaller institutions have resorted to printing a limited number of guides on desktop printers for distribution to members of the media who cover a program closely (Smolik, 2004). This approach may achieve the goal of getting a hard copy in the hands of sports journalists, but it is impractical in settings where many media members may be covering a team. Much time is required to print each issue, collate the pages, and bind the guides together.

More recently, college athletics departments have resorted to creating dynamic, online, interactive media guides, aimed mainly at recruits but containing much of the information that appears in a traditional static media guide. Pursuant Sports has created virtual media guides for several Division I universities including Southern Methodist University. Pursuant described the advantages that SMU realized from this technology: "(By) maximizing coaches' and facilities videos to spotlight the heart and soul of their program, this experience links to the traditional media content on their athletics site" (Pursuant Sports, n.d.).

### Time Commitments

Regardless of the final delivery form of a media guide, the amount of time that a sports information department spends working on its production likely remains the same, and not all schools have the spare resources to transition from print to digital.

April Emory, sports information director at Elizabeth City State University, addressed this issue in an October 2009 article in *Athletic Management*.

An added consideration in our decision is the reality that we don't have the resources to make our website the end-all for our teams. As a one-woman sports information operation, adding a lot of bells and whistles to the website is just not feasible. And without that extra attention to the website, it cannot easily replace the media guide as a comprehensive source of information. (Emory, 2009)

# Other Organizational Media

Although the media guide may be a sport organization's largest and most visible organizational media tactic, many other print methods exist, each with its own attributes and objectives. These include, but are not limited to, newsletters, programs, posters, schedule cards, brochures, reprints, and annual reports. Publishing these items is somewhat challenging for the sport public relations practitioner. As Wilcox (2001) pointed out, the public relations professional needs to produce media that promotes management's organizational objectives, serves the interests of constituents, and incorporates journalistic standards. These standards are especially important when producing newsletters, which carry a high degree of credibility because of their design.

## Newsletters

Newsletters combine the look and feel of a legitimate publication such as a magazine or newspaper with organizational publicity information. Newsletters serve a variety of purposes and may be customized for specific publics such as employees, alumni, vendors, donors, and customers. As such, large organizations may choose to produce more than one newsletter, depending on the public that they are targeting. Smith (2005) estimated that the total number of organizational newsletters in the United States may be as high as 1 million.

Traditionally, newsletters were distributed in printed form, often on glossy paper with color photographs, through the mail. But computers are changing that model. More newsletters are considered e-news, or electronic news, that is frequently delivered directly from the organization to the subscriber in an e-mail. Migala (2001) observed that e-mail newsletters not only create a new vehicle to communicate with the public but also strengthen the organization's database for marketing efforts. The distribution of newsletters varies anywhere from daily to quarterly depending on the targeted audience.

One of the main advantages of a newsletter is that it allows organizations to communicate certain information to a large public all at once. The organization has complete control of the message, and because of its design a newsletter may have more credibility with readers because it is not a traditional form of advertising.

Smith (2005) cautioned organizations to follow the principles of newsworthiness (see chapter 8) when writing newsletters. Information in newsletters should be of interest to the readers and not simply information that the organization wishes to disclose. For example, a sport organization's newsletter targeting alumni may include current information about the performance of the organization's teams as well as updates on the whereabouts of former athletes. Alumni will appreciate learning where former teammates are currently living and what they are doing.

The newsletter's focus will help determine whether it will be an internal or external newsletter. Internal newsletters are primarily for people who are or have been part of the organization, including alumni, employees, and volunteers. A university athletics department may produce an alumni newsletter that focuses exclusively on news and information related to student–athletes. This newsletter would be separate from the university's general alumni newsletter that focuses on all former students. Alumni newsletters often play on the sentiment of former athletes and their ties to the university. As such, messages regarding donations and fund-raising are common.

Employee newsletters might focus on human resource information such as benefits and insurance changes. Large organizations with employees in many locations might use a newsletter to update their employees regarding product development as well. For example, a sporting goods company might have its corporate headquarters in a major city, but it might also have distribution centers and manufacturing plants throughout the world. Information that allows employees a measure of pride in the company is common in these newsletters. The sporting goods company may wish to recognize employees for longevity with the company or a specific plant that has set a record for consecutive work days without a lost-time injury. More information on employee newsletters is presented in chapter 13.

Volunteer newsletters are effective at motivating people who donate their time and energy to the organization. Before the 2002 Olympic and Paralympic Winter Games, the Salt Lake Organizing Committee regularly updated its base of nearly 20,000 volunteers on topics ranging from uniform distribution to job-specific training. In addition, the newsletters presented information on the Olympic and Paralympic Games that was designed to make the volunteers more knowledgeable and thus more helpful during the competitions.

External newsletters generally focus on persuading readers about a particular issue or communicating directly with an influential group of people such as investors, customers, and community leaders. Chapter 13 provides additional information on investor relations.

Newsletters that target customers of the organization are frequently tied into the organization's marketing efforts and can be highly measurable. For example, the Los Angeles Dodgers deliver their *Citizens of Dodgertown* newsletter directly to subscribers through e-mail. The newsletter contains exclusive information on ticket deals and merchandise discounts (Los Angeles Dodgers, n.d.). By supplying the subscriber with a discount code or coupon, organizations can track the success of their newsletter in reaching their customers. Many sport organizations connect e-mail newsletters to their affinity marketing programs—programs designed to leverage the strong sense of connectedness that people may feel to a team or organization—and provide these newsletters as a benefit of membership in a fan program (Mullin, Hardy, & Sutton, 2000). For instance, the San Diego Padres provide members of their Frequent Friar Rewards Club program with a newsletter only for program members (San Diego Padres, n.d.).

External newsletters may also target community leaders or advocate a specific position on an impending issue. In the months leading up to the International Olympic Committee's announcement of the host city for the 2012 Olympic Games, the New York 2012 Bid Committee sent its newsletter subscribers regular updates about the committee's progress in submitting its proposal and encouraged supporters to get involved in the community on behalf of the organization.

## Programs

**Programs**, sometimes called scorecards, are typically sold on the day of an event and are written, assembled, and distributed by the organization that is hosting the event. They are sold to the general public and provide lineup information for the event along with feature stories and other information about the host organization. Programs can be a revenue source for an organization in two ways. First, the organization can sell the program directly to spectators attending the event, and second, the organization can sell advertising space in the program to local businesses. The marketing department often handles the advertising sales, and many of the ads are provided through trade with sponsors and other businesses.

The public relations staff usually writes, edits, and designs the program. Occasionally the host organization receives publishing support from a league or governing body or from a national sport publisher who will edit and print the cover and several pages of general information along with national advertisements. In such cases, the host organization adds specific stories about the organization and local advertisements.

The typical program is a four-color, high-gloss magazine with color photographs, although some

sport organizations publish a scorecard featuring only the rosters and lineups of the event participants. Memorabilia enthusiasts often collect programs and scorecards, and many spectators view them as keepsakes to remember attending special events. Sport public relations practitioners thus have an obligation to develop programs that are professional and memorable.

The more elaborate the program is, the more it will cost to produce it. Organizations may charge between $10 and $20 for programs at premier events such as the Super Bowl or Final Four. For example, Major League Baseball sold copies of the 2009 World Series program featuring the Philadelphia Phillies and the New York Yankees for $15. Sport organizations typically charge between $3 and $10 for programs at regularly scheduled events.

## Posters

Like programs, posters often involve both the marketing and public relations departments. Posters, like in figure 5.1, are common at the

**Figure 5.1** 2010 Wichita State University volleyball promotional poster.
Photo courtesy of ICAA Wichita State University.

university level and are generally specific to the sport. Posters that are prominently displayed in businesses and storefronts close to the organization provide visibility to the organization (Smith, 2005).

Most posters have a corporate sponsor who helps to underwrite the production costs of the poster—hence the marketing tie-in. Posters usually feature prominent athletes as well as the season's schedule. If the marketing department has developed an advertising theme for the team, the poster often serves as an extension of those efforts. An additional distribution of posters might be to present them to children before a certain game and allow the children to get player autographs after the game, thus combining a direct-contact community relations activity with marketing objectives.

## Schedule Cards

Somewhat unique to the sport industry is the **schedule card**, a pocket-sized publication that features the organization's schedule. Schedule cards are intended to be both an information and advertising vehicle (Helitzer, 2000). They are typically considered a marketing tactic and often involve a corporate sponsor or advertiser. Schedule cards may be printed with a prominent athlete on one side and the schedule on the other side. Programs that have lengthy schedules such as baseball may opt to create a schedule card with several panels that fold into pocket size. Figure 5.2 displays the schedule card of a minor league hockey team that used the fold-out format, as well as other examples. Cards also may include ticket prices and maps of stadium seating sections that may be priced differently.

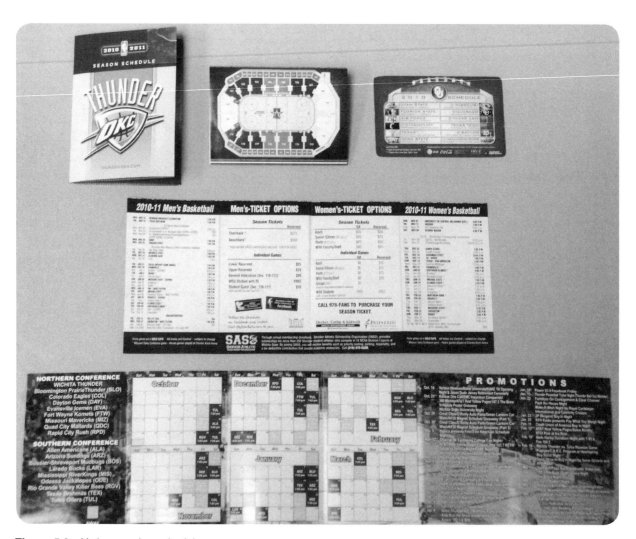

**Figure 5.2** Various pocket schedules.

## Brochures

Sometimes called leaflets or pamphlets, brochures provide basic information about an organization, product, or service. Brochures are distributed through the mail, in information racks, or electronically as PDF files that may be downloaded or sent by e-mail. Sport organizations commonly use brochures in support of marketing initiatives. Prospective season-ticket buyers might receive a brochure that includes specific information regarding schedules, ticket locations, ticket prices, and ordering procedures.

Brochures are often printed on glossy paper and folded. A standard brochure is often folded into thirds, creating six panels. A ticket brochure might be formatted so that one of the panels is an order form and can be detached and mailed to the organization along with payment for tickets.

## Reprints

Because the news media have a higher degree of credibility, an article about a sport organization that appears in print may be of significant value to the organization. A reprint is a copy of an article published in a newspaper or magazine that may support the public relations objectives (Smith, 2005). In an attempt to maximize positive publicity, organizations may choose to distribute reprints of a positive article to publics that did not see the original article. Because most printed articles are copyrighted, organizations must receive reprint permission from the publication before distributing the article.

## Annual Reports

A final organizational media print form is the annual report. The annual report as a function of investor relations is discussed in chapter 13. Increasingly, however, sport organizations issue a season summary as a type of annual report. The season summary is a retrospective of the organization's season complete with a narrative review of the season as well as final statistics and records. Reprints of news articles may also be included as a way to provide historical context. Season summaries are especially helpful for beat reporters and other media that cover the organization. It is, in some respects, a media guide for after the season.

One of the key considerations for sport organizations is unity of message across different forms of organizational media. Dr. Bill Smith, director of marketing and branding at Northwestern State University, addresses the growing importance of convergence for sport properties in the sidebar titled Consistency in Branding.

# Electronic Organizational Media

Smith (2005) noted that electronic forms of organizational media are growing in popularity and can enhance the audiovisual aspects of public relations. He differentiates among video media, audio media, and computer-based media.

## Video

Videos have significant public relations value and can be extremely versatile (Harris, 1998). Sporting goods manufacturers use videos to demonstrate new products. Teams use highlight videos of a successful season as a revenue stream for the organization. Coaches use instructional videos to reach out to aspiring athletes. Organizations use training videos for new employees or volunteers.

Organizations may consider a variety of distribution methods for video such as DVDs, podcasts, and streaming video (e.g., YouTube). Regardless of the distribution platform, Helitzer (2000) advised organizations to consider two things when producing a highlight video for public distribution: professional production and editing and sponsor interest. Specifically, videos should have the look and feel of a professional broadcast. Several broadcast-quality cameras should be used rather than camcorders to capture the action. Approximately 10 minutes of video should be shot for every minute of highlight video. The sport organization should use an editing studio for postproduction of the highlight video, which may prove to be expensive, depending on the amount of video that needs to be edited. Organizations may want to offer existing sponsors an opportunity to underwrite the production in exchange for advertising or sponsorship presentation associated with the video.

Public relations professionals should view their job in the production of a video as that of project manager. Public relations professionals often conceptualize the video and create a storyboard that includes determining which video to use and writing the script that will be recorded over the video (Wilcox, 2001).

## Consistency in Branding

### Dr. Bill Smith

Photo courtesy of Dr. Bill Smith.

"Gee, their stuff always looks good."

That's the ultimate compliment for a sport organization's media relations team. Each generation comes up with its own label for that indescribable quality. In early 21st century marketing speak, it's branding; in the past, it was style, image, or identity. Regardless of what it is called, the ability to project a look that evokes a positive response starts with consistency of the message.

What appears to the outside world as a clean, seamless visual branding requires complex and rigorous internal discipline and operation. The view from 30,000 feet (9,000 m) is possible only after mechanics and pilots have performed a series of checklists and tasks to ensure that the engines will start and take the plane from the ground up to altitude. This process begins by having visual branding guidelines based on the organization's registered trademarks, word marks, identity fonts, and official color schemes. Style books to ensure consistency for both written copy and elements of design are equally important. Finally, the process ends with established policies for internal vetting of material and well-defined systems for external distribution.

Convergence isn't a buzz word for legacy media attempting to combine skills in a digital media world. As the primary content generator within any athletics department, the media relations office is the hub of branding. As the experts in both creation of messages and monitoring of external media, the modern sports information staff is best equipped to lead the public relations efforts for teams.

To get the look, start with the basics. The athletics department's visual branding guidelines are more than the logo slick. An example of how a small detail can become a problem is school colors. With a shift from the printed media guide as the primary document of college athletics media relations, knowing your PMS Pantone numbers is not sufficient. Determine the acceptable conversions into CMYK and RGB percentage as well as the web-safe hex number colors. Guidelines should also define the givens that are always present in a branded item—whether it is a business card or letterhead template of a press release. As an example, at the University of Arkansas these include our trademark Razorback logo, the use of the word marks "Arkansas" and "Razorbacks" typeset in our custom font, and color schemes that include our signature Cardinal.

Creating policies and procedure manuals is time consuming, and constant updating is required as standards change and media coverage evolves. Along with the obvious benefits of being a single place for emergency communication plans, yearly task schedules for sports, and guidelines for students to understand individual sports, a well-constructed media relations manual brings together the quirks that every organization has, such as differences from the *Associated Press Stylebook*, data required in rosters or schedules, and philosophical approaches to visual messaging. With the details of colors, logos, fonts, and wording defined, the process of determining the visual branding becomes focused on the creative message.

**Achievement of a single identity across the wide spectrum starts with similar detail work. The first step is investing time to get the input of all key stakeholders at the beginning to prevent fracturing at the end.**

Achievement of a single identity across the wide spectrum starts with similar detail work. The first step is investing time to get the input of all key stakeholders at the beginning to prevent fracturing at the end. Meetings with coaching staff members help identify which players or themes are important to the upcoming season. They also provide knowledge of the technical needs of the rights holders in the various items to be produced. This task may appear more marketing than media relations, but lack of integration between these two important areas of collegiate athletics results in more mixed visual messaging to the fan base than any other issue. In a networked communications world that encourages scattering of message, creating a single voice ensures accurate transmission of the message. Regardless of whether the item is a traditional mailer from the marketing office, an online advertisement from web communications, a graphic provided to fans as computer wallpaper from new media, the splash screen of a mobile application, or the backdrop of a postgame press conference, the team appears consistent and displays "that look." This identity is best originated by the area within the department that generates the most content—media relations.

Well-designed items appear costly at the outset of the process, but the money and time spent in planning reap dividends later in resources saved in the creation of additional collateral items. A central theme that begins with a promotional poster generally is repurposed to yearbook or media guide covers and to the official schedule items—calendars, posters, schedule cards, magnets, and promotional giveaways. If care is taken with the primary elements, the repurposing to other mediums becomes more about changing resolutions or aspect ratios of designs—for example, changing from a vertical poster to a $16 \times 9$ video board still frame—than restarting with new ideas.

The visuals must translate from the multiple flat printed items to the multiple screens employed by the organization: the coach's television show using a screen capture graphic; wallpapers produced for the team's second screen, the static computer; the third screen, the mobile device; the fourth screen, the in-venue video board production; and even to the digital signage throughout a venue, the fifth screen.

Why is the investment in detail necessary? At the close of the 20th century, the path between a brand and its base was the distribution network of the legacy media. The creation of networked communication fundamentally changed the dissemination of information. In the whole of human history, the barriers to communication among large groups of individuals have never been lower. A vital component of harnessing the networks of information that reach both influencers and followers is preparing materials that convey the context of messages, paying special attention to the visual element and the branding words.

To take advantage of both the media and the social networking of fans to spread the message, effective athletics departments and teams generate memes. Defined as a unit of cultural ideas, the core meme is used across all types of institutional publications. A quick glance at the primary and collateral material produced for a team reveals the level of dedication to branding. The cover of the media guide, the official schedule poster, the official schedule card, the team magnet, trading cards, and the team calendar reflect the same visual image. Executing the original plan requires discipline, but the result is a fan who is not confused about what team and which season is portrayed. Staying with the memes also strengthens the branding of the organization against third parties who seek to associate themselves with the team. Only the official products of the team display the official branding look, another benefit for the team and its sponsors and supporters.

*Dr. Bill Smith is the director of marketing and branding at Northwestern State University. Previously he served as the assistant athletic director for new media at the University of Arkansas, where he worked for 22 years.*

## Audio

Although less popular than video media, audio media represents a publicity opportunity for organizational public relations (Smith, 2005). Common tactics that can be employed in audio media include podcasts, recorded telephone information, and voice mail. Podcasts have been defined as "a music or talk program made available in digital format for automatic download over the Internet to a personal mp3 or digital device" (U.S. Environmental Protection Agency, n.d.). Podcasts may feature audio only or video as well and may be played on traditional computers or mobile devices such as smartphones or iPods. Users may subscribe to podcasts through RSS feeds or iTunes and receive frequent updates from an organization's key messengers.

The use of automated telephone messages has become commonplace in today's business environment. These recorded messages are an opportunity to promote organizational objectives to audiences who are seeking information. After all, the people who call an organization are doing so because they wish to obtain information about the organization.

Sport managers should strive to keep their recorded messages current. Updates regarding ticket availability for an upcoming event or a rebroadcast of positive moments from the previous event are ways that an organization can build on its message distribution.

## Computer-Based Media

A final area of electronic media is computer-based media such as CD-ROMs, presentation software, and e-mail. Harris (1998) noted that CD-ROMs are replacing traditional forms of printed publicity material. The benefits of this type of distribution are attributable to how "the combination of text, graphics, video, and sound adds dimension and excitement to the kinds of material traditionally used in press kits, booklets and brochures" (p. 253).

Presentation software such as PowerPoint has become universally accepted in today's business environment, and organizations may wish to use this format to deliver information about a product or program that it is promoting. Audience members can download the file from the organization's website, or the organization can e-mail it directly to them. In addition, PowerPoint presentations allow people to print the slides for later reference.

Smith (2005) noted the advantages of e-mail distribution for communicating instantaneously with large groups: "Using electronic mailing lists called listservs, PR practitioners can communicate with information-seeking publics" (p. 173). One potential downside to using e-mail distribution, however, could stem from unclear messages. The time necessary to respond to each individual request for clarification or more information may be prohibitive.

Sport public relations professionals are advised to use a cross-section of organizational media tactics in their public relations campaigns (Harris, 1998; Wilcox, 2001; Smith, 2005). Table 5.3 summarizes the various organizational media tactics available to sport public relations professionals, their uses, and their advantages and disadvantages.

Regardless of the tactic, consistency is vital to integrating organizational messages and achieving organizational objectives. For example, sport managers who want to communicate information about an upcoming season's schedule should not rely on schedule cards alone. Instead, an integrated communication plan might involve a news release as discussed in chapter 6 supplemented by the production and distribution of schedule cards, posters, newsletters, and direct e-mails to the organization's listserv.

## Table 5.3 Organizational Media Uses and Advantages

| Organizational media tactic | Target public | Common platforms | Advantages | Disadvantages |
|---|---|---|---|---|
| Media guide | Primarily members of the media and potential student–athletes (for college publications); also may be of interest to fans of the team or event | Print publication, PDF file for download, electronic media guide | Can yield positive publicity from media members who use the guide as a resource; can help persuade recruits to select a particular institution; can generate revenue | High production costs; significant time required to plan, develop, and produce |
| Newsletter | Customizable to a variety of publics including alumni, employees, customers, and community leaders | Print publication, PDF file for download, e-newsletter | Can communicate similar messages across a variety of publics | Potential costs for production and distribution; timeliness |
| Program | Customers attending organizational events | Print publication | Potential revenue stream through direct sales and advertising sales | High production costs; changes for every event |

| Organizational media tactic | Target public | Common platforms | Advantages | Disadvantages |
|---|---|---|---|---|
| Poster | Several but primarily customers (fans) of the organization and community businesses | Print publication | Potential revenue stream through sponsorship; broad publicity | Establishing a distribution network |
| Schedule card | Existing customers of the organization as well as potential new customers | Print publication | Potential revenue stream through sponsorship | Establishing a distribution network; frequent schedule changes |
| Brochure | Several but primarily targeted to customers of the organization and others seeking information | Print publication, PDF file for download or e-mail attachment | Can be used for revenue generation | High production costs; information may become out of date |
| Annual report | Primarily geared toward shareholders for annual reports but also targeted toward media for season summaries | Print publication, PDF file for download, electronic annual report | Positive publicity; targeted to important publics | High production costs |
| Video | Suitable for all publics | DVDs, podcasts, streaming videos | Can be used for a variety of purposes including potential revenue generation | High production costs |
| Audio | Suitable for all information-seeking publics | Podcasts, streaming audio, telephone messaging | Can be updated frequently to ensure timely content | Limited to information-seeking publics |
| Computer based | Suitable for all publics but often targeted to media and customers of the organization | CDs, presentation software, e-mail | Can be timely; wide distribution | Message needs to be explicit |

# Corporate Communications

Sport organizations are structured in diverse ways, so considerable variance is present within the field in terms of which unit assumes functional responsibility for organizational media. Media guides are almost always produced by public relations units within collegiate athletics departments. Professional organizations may be structured in such a way that media relations falls to a communications department that also includes community relations and other public relations programs. Other sport organizations, such as NASCAR, have **corporate communications** units that oversee public relations activities, including the production of organizational media.

Corporate communications departments vary in size and scope of responsibility. For instance, NHL director of corporate communications Michael Dilorenzo stated, "One of the many goals of the NHL's corporate communications unit is to reinforce key league messages with its corporate partners and other influential stakeholders in the business-to-business marketplace" (Dilorenzo, personal communication, Sept. 17, 2010). The goal of Nike's corporate communications unit is to "help the company manage its reputation both internally and externally via the media, (its) community involvement, environmental policy, stakeholder outreach and issues management" (Nike, 2004). The corporate communications department of the U.S. Olympic Committee (USOC) assumes responsibility for communications at USOC events and for the

U.S. Olympic Hall of Fame (USOC, 2004). It also provides media training to U.S. Olympic and Paralympic representatives. In addition, the department operates the organization's National Anti-Doping Education Program. Finally, the unit offers communication services to other USOC departments such as development and entertainment properties.

As with USOC, corporate communications departments often assume both public relations and marketing responsibilities. One of the advantages of this approach is that it may result in more coordinated efforts to integrate organizational media in a consistent manner.

## SUMMARY

Most sport organizations employ some type of organizational media in support of their public relations objectives. Organizational media tactics available to sport public relations professionals are almost as numerous as the number of stakeholder groups that they serve. Media guides produced by professional and collegiate sport organizations may represent the most complex form of organizational media in the field. These guides are resources for members of the mass media, promotional materials that may be sent to prospective student–athletes, and products that are sold to the public and included as incentives for donors or sponsors. Media guides contain in-depth information about the sport organization, its representatives, the current season or event, and the history of the organization. Other forms of organizational print media include newsletters, programs, posters, schedule cards, brochures, reprints, and annual reports. Electronic organizational media include video, audio, and computer-based communication. Each form of media may be customized for specific publics and purposes, but sport public relations professionals should make every effort to achieve some level of consistency in their communication tactics. Responsibility for the planning, design, and production of organizational media is sometimes assigned to a corporate communications department that may assume both public relations and marketing responsibilities.

1. Secure a copy of a media guide from a local professional or collegiate sport organization. Analyze it in terms of type of information provided, likely purposes, editorial quality, and design elements. What recommendations would you make regarding how the publication could be enhanced?

2. Develop a small media guide for a local high school team. Begin by outlining a plan that will guide you through the planning and production phases in a timely manner. Then work through the plan, being careful to involve all the other interested parties (e.g., coaches, administrators) as necessary to ensure the production of a thorough, accurate product.

3. Develop a newsletter for your academic program. Again, start by developing a production plan. As you move to content decisions, be sure to consider the publics who would receive such a document and what their interests may be. Plan to provide information that accommodates those interests while also incorporating elements that will present the program in a favorable light. After developing the newsletter, distribute it to the appropriate publics and solicit informal feedback from them.

4. Secure several types of organizational media produced by a single local sport organization (e.g., team, fitness center). Analyze them to assess their degree of consistency. What elements of consistency can you identify? What recommendations would you make that might enable the organization to achieve greater consistency?

# Focusing on the Sport Organization– Media Relationship

**After reading this chapter, students should be able to**

- define mass media,
- describe the media's influence in society,
- denote the significance of rights fees in the success of sport organizations,
- describe the adaptations that sport organizations have made to accommodate television, and
- identify historical methods of public relations in sport.

**Key terms discussed in this chapter include**

- mass media,
- rights fee,
- gatekeeper,
- Sports Broadcasting Act, and
- College Sports Information Directors of America (CoSIDA).

**As mentioned throughout** the text, sport public relations is a communication-based function that endeavors to develop desirable relationships with the organization's key publics. Those publics may include employees, donors, customers, and many others. The public that perhaps has the greatest potential effect on a sport organization, however, may be the **mass media**.

Few segments of the business world receive more media attention than sport. Most newspapers devote an entire section to sport. Most local television newscasts allocate an entire segment to sport. All-sports television stations, radio stations, weekly news magazines, and websites exist to satisfy the demands of our sport-crazed society.

Sport organizations do not view the mass media merely as a channel through which they can distribute messages. A much closer relationship exists between the media and sport organizations. In essence, the two are partners in delivering sport content to consumers. Organizations stage events, and mass media outlets distribute information about those events. Advertisers use the mass media's distribution channels to gain access to targeted consumer markets, and consumers buy products sold by those advertisers. Bernstein and Blain (2002, p. 3) noted that "sport and the media have become associated to such an extent that it is often difficult to discuss sport in modern society without acknowledging its relationship with media."

Wenner (1989, 1998, 2006) has written extensively about the subject of what he called MediaSport, which he observed is "widely seen as a harmless party providing important social release and cohesion in chaotic and harried postmodern times" (1998, p. 6). He differentiated among MediaSport institutions, or how market dynamics shape sport; MediaSport texts, or how the media influences the reality of heroism, nation, race, and gender; and MediaSport audiences, or how most spectators consume sport.

Indeed, it is impossible to distinguish the mass media from today's sport consumption experience, but that relationship has not always been this close. Many sport organizations initially viewed the media as a threat to profitability rather than a revenue stream. This chapter explores the history of that relationship, tracing the evolution from print coverage in the 1800s to the growth of television during the latter half of the 1900s. Emphasis is placed on sport as entertainment by addressing adaptations that sport organizations have made for the benefit of the media as well as sport created solely for television.

This chapter also discusses the role of public relations throughout the history of the sport organization–media relationship and addresses current challenges that the public relations field is facing. First, however, it is necessary to establish what the term *mass media* means and how media organizations are structured.

# Defining Mass Media

Traditionally, scholars have divided mass media forms into print and electronic (Black & Bryant, 1995; Sage, 1998). Print media include newspapers, magazines, and books, whereas electronic media include radio, television, and film. Some sport governing bodies, such as the International Olympic Committee (IOC), treat each group differently. The IOC refers to non-rights-holding media, such as writers and photographers, covering the Olympic Games as press, and it refers to rights-holding media, such as television and radio personnel, as broadcast (Samaranch, 1996). Most sport managers refer to print and electronic media simply as the media.

That approach fails to consider emerging forms of electronic communication. To that end, Pedersen, Miloch, and Laucella (2007) conceived a strategic sport communication model in which one of three components focused on sport mass media (refer to figure 1.1, on page 4). In it, they distinguish among three segments of sport mass media: publishing and print communication, electronic and visual communication, and new media. Suggesting that the mass media include emerging new media such as Internet-only journalists and bloggers presents some challenges to the traditional view of the mass media and the privileges and protections that come with being a member of the media.

Sage (1998) suggested that the media's power comes from four areas: constitutional protection, universal access to the public, corporate organization, and ability to construct ideology (p. 160). It is possible to break down these areas further to demonstrate the implications that they have for sport public relations professionals.

## Constitutional Protection

In the United States, the media are granted freedom by the First Amendment of the U.S. Constitution, which means that neither the government nor any other organization controls the media. For a sport organization, this means that the media can report whatever they wish, even if it is critical of the organization. A key responsibility for the sport public relations professional is to maintain positive relationships with members of the media to achieve positive influence on news stories and publicity.

Constitutional and media law attorney Scott Gant (2007) argued that the privileges afforded members of traditional mass media outlets under the First Amendment should be extended to Internet-only journalists. He commented (p. 165), "From the standpoint of the Constitution, anyone engaged in disseminating information and ideas is exercising freedom of the press."

Gant distinguished between the profession of journalism and the activity of journalism. The profession involves payment and a licensure system. The activity involves the ability to disseminate information to the public. Access to the public represents the second of Sage's (1998) four areas of media power.

## Access to the Public

Before the development of the Internet, sport organizations had to rely on traditional media to reach the public with their messages. Now organizations can bypass the traditional media altogether to deliver their messages. Statistics confirm that many people have access to some form of mass media. As Stoldt, Dittmore, and Pedersen (2011) noted, in the United States 99% of homes have radios and 98% have television sets, and 74% of the North American population uses the Internet.

Nearly every sport organization has its own website capable of distributing information, video, audio, and other content directly to interested fans. Further, an increasing number of leagues, conferences, and teams have created their own television networks for the purpose of content distribution. This trend has allowed organizations to bypass the traditional communication process in which they relied on the mass media to deliver organizational messages.

Although the ability of a sport organization to access the public directly has changed, the importance of the media is unlikely to diminish. Sport public relations professionals need to balance the needs of the mass media with their own organizational media to ensure the most comprehensive publicity.

## Corporate Organization

Two issues are at play in corporate ownership of media when it comes to sport organizations. First, many news organizations are owned by the same company, creating giant media conglomerates. Second, many of those conglomerates also own sport franchises. Bagdikian (2004) noted that in 1983, 50 media corporations dominated media, but by 2004 the number was down to 5.

The development of large media companies, especially in the newspaper industry, has affected the media on a variety of levels, including consolidation and content, both of which relate to economics. With respect to consolidation, Solomon (1997, p. 75) observed that after a newspaper is bought by a media conglomerate, "its policies and priorities reflect the parent firm's needs, more than the needs of the community in which the newspaper is situated." For the public relations professional, the change in ownership might mean that the newspaper devotes less attention to local or community organizations. For example, persuading the newspaper to cover a local women's volleyball team may be more difficult because the newspaper may be more focused on covering national sports like NASCAR that attract more advertisers and readers, creating more revenue.

Consolidation has also reduced the overall number of newspapers, creating a less competitive marketplace. Media organizations do not seek exclusive stories as frequently in markets that lack competition. Consolidation has reduced the number of outlets that a public relations professional can use to reach the public at large.

As for content, economics again plays a major role. Because many media conglomerates are publicly owned and need to answer to shareholders, each media outlet must operate as a business. Most newspapers determine their size based on the number of advertisements sold—the more ads that are sold, the greater the space that is available for editorial copy. The ability of a public relations professional to place a story in a newspaper promoting an organization may be completely beyond the professional's control.

The second issue, the ownership of sport franchises by media conglomerates, is not new. The Tribune Company, which owns the *Chicago Tribune* and WGN television and radio, owned the Chicago Cubs from 1981 until the Ricketts family purchased the club in October 2009. Throughout the past decade, however, consolidation in sport media has increased alongside the nonsport media. Today, three major players exist in sport media—Comcast, Disney, and News Corporation—together owning more than 40 television networks. The number of networks owned by these companies increased further with regulatory approval of Comcast's purchase of NBC Universal.

McChesney (2000, 2004, 2008) has studied the problems of media ownership in general from a political economy perspective and has identified two scholarly dimensions to the issue. The first considers how media and communication reinforce or challenge existing social and class relationships. The second, which has greater application to sport media, examines "how ownership, support mechanisms (e.g., advertising) and government policies influence media behavior and content" (2000, p. 110).

Ownership of sport teams by media companies creates an avenue for vertical integration within the corporation (Gomery, 2000), allowing media conglomerations to promote their sport franchises at little cost to the organization and permitting them to control all advertising revenue during broadcasts by eliminating the need to pay a broadcast **rights fee**. A downfall to this concept, which led several conglomerates to sell their franchises in the early 2000s, is that a franchise that does poorly and loses money causes the conglomerate to lose money as well. Because many media conglomerates are publicly traded companies, shareholders may voice dissatisfaction with the investment.

## Construct Ideology

Journalists often refer to their role as that of **gatekeeper**. They alone decide what to report and when. The *New York Times* states boldly on its masthead that it reports "All the news that is fit to print." Sage (1998) observed that "the media determine what we think, how we feel, and what we do about our social and political environment" (p. 164). Accordingly, the media strongly influences the ideologies commonly accepted in most cultures. They accomplish this as gatekeepers, deciding which stories to cover, where to place stories in a newscast or newspaper, what quotes to use, and which images to accompany the story. If something newsworthy happens, the media's job is to report it. Ultimately, the media decide what is newsworthy through their allocation of resources. The media's choice not to cover a high school volleyball game does not necessarily mean the game is not newsworthy. Rather, it may mean that the media have decided to dedicate resources to other events that they feel are more newsworthy. The core of a public relations professional's job is convincing a journalist that news about an organization is worthy and fit to print or broadcast.

## Mass Media Structures

Traditionally, members of the mass media could be categorized as either print media or electronic media. Sport public relations professionals were cognizant of the needs and deadlines of each form of media and were able to assist the media in crafting their stories.

But in today's mass media environment, more print and electronic journalists are having their stories published on the Internet (Stoldt, Pratt, & Jackson, 2003). Further, many journalists are crossing over. Traditional print reporters are appearing on television. This evolution has blurred the distinction between print and electronic media and created an environment where the sport public relations professional must understand the needs of all media forms.

## Print Media

Hall, Nichols, Moynahan, and Taylor (2007) found that despite the growth of televised sporting events, "the print media still play a significant role in the delivery of sports information, particularly on the local level" (p. 23). They pointed to the depth of game coverage and variety of sports covered as advantages of print media over traditional electronic forms of media. Print media primarily report on events after they have occurred, whereas the electronic media are able to cover events as they occur. Thus, print media can be categorized as the media of depth and interpretation and electronic media as the media of immediacy.

Pitts and Stotlar (2007) noted one additional distinction between print and electronic media. Because traditional print media such as newspapers and magazines are purchased by people who want to read them, there is some assurance that the reader is willing to accept the information. Although a person may seek out a specific broadcast, the electronic media are essentially free after the viewer has purchased a television set or radio. Sport public relations professionals can use this distinction to their advantage by targeting one of the many specialty print publications that exist to disseminate their information because those readers are more inclined to accept the information.

### Newspapers

As mentioned earlier, the amount of a space that a given newspaper devotes to sport coverage may be directly tied to the amount of advertising that the newspaper has sold. In an attempt to maintain objectivity, newspapers divide into separate business and editorial, or content, departments. The business department sells advertisements and manages circulation. The editorial department produces the content of the newspaper. Because space for content is determined by advertisements sold, the two departments share a working but separate agreement. A newspaper cannot ethically accept a paid advertisement from a sport organization in exchange for increased coverage. Sport organizations wishing to place an ad in a newspaper will likely work with someone other than a reporter who covers the organization.

Further complicating the structure of a newspaper is the difference between editorial writers and the rest of the newspaper staff. Most newspapers have writers, called beat writers, assigned to specific teams and organizations. This staff of writers works independently of the editorial staff, which writes for the opinion page. Sport public relations professionals should be aware that a negative editorial in a local newspaper is not cause to shut out the organization's beat writer. In all likelihood, the beat writer had no idea what the editorial writer was going to say.

The complex structure of a newspaper is not the only concern that a sport public relations professional should have with respect to newspapers. The overall number of daily newspapers in the United States has decreased dramatically during the last 40 years, and the number of advertising dollars directed to newspapers has dropped as well. But the amount of advertising sold and the existence of fewer daily newspapers are just two aspects of traditional media that work against public relations professionals. Another factor that has shaped the way that newspapers cover sport is the number of professional and amateur sports.

Consider how expansion and relocation has affected a city like Phoenix throughout the late 1990s and early 2000s. When the St. Louis Cardinals football team relocated to Phoenix in 1988, the only other professional team in town competing for space was the National Basketball Association's (NBA's) Phoenix Suns. Today, those franchises also compete against the National Hockey League's (NHL's) Phoenix Coyotes, Major League Baseball's (MLB's) Arizona Diamondbacks, and the Women's National Basketball Association's (WNBA's) Phoenix Mercury. In addition, a major National Collegiate Athletic Association (NCAA) institution plays in the Phoenix area, as do a number of high schools and other community-based organizations.

Most newspapers have a sports editor, who may or may not also be a reporter. The larger the circulation of the newspaper is, the less likely it is that the editor also reports. Sports departments usually have beat reporters, who cover a specific organization on an ongoing basis, and columnists, who write about the day's biggest story. More information on specific types of reporters is presented in chapter 7.

Sport public relations professionals often do well to focus on smaller daily and weekly newspapers that may be more community based and do not focus on larger stories for which they lack the necessary resources. Chapter 8 provides tactics such as hometown news releases for reaching smaller newspaper outlets.

## Magazines

Although most newspapers are local, focusing on news and events happening in a given community, most magazines have a national scope and cover a variety of sports on a weekly, biweekly, or monthly basis. Some, such as *Sports Illustrated* and *ESPN: The Magazine*, are general, whereas many others, such as *Runner's World* and *Baseball Digest*, focus on a specific sport or segment of the sport industry.

Another segment of the magazine industry is published annually and offers previews of upcoming seasons like college football. These magazines usually seek information directly from sport organizations for their publications. As mentioned, because these magazines focus on one particular segment, readers are likely to be avid fans and may have a high degree of interest in organizations profiled in the publication.

## Wire Services

The role of a wire service is to provide news and photos of events throughout the world to subscriber organizations. What that means for the sport public relations professional is that a wire service can deliver organizational information about news and events to media who do not have the resources to devote a staff member to cover the news or event. Most wire services have an office, called a bureau, in larger cities. The bureaus frequently employ part-time reporters and photographers, known as stringers, to assist their operations.

The Associated Press, the most recognized U.S. wire service, has many regional bureaus throughout the country as well as internationally. Reuters, a British wire service, is one of the leading international wire services but also has agreements with many of the large daily newspapers in the United States.

Other wire services primarily provide information to areas outside the United States, including the European service Agence France-Presse (AFP), which delivers worldwide news stories in six languages (About AFP, n.d.). AFP maintains large operations in Washington, D.C., and Montreal, Canada, as well. In addition, two large wire services operate in Asia, Kyodo News Service in Japan and Xinhua News Agency in China.

Finally, many U.S. newspapers owned by a single corporation routinely share stories with other newspapers in their chains. Examples of these include the 31 daily newspapers that are part of the McClatchy Company (n.d.), the 90 daily newspapers, including *USA Today*, owned by the Gannett Corporation (n.d.), and the 10 daily newspapers owned by the Tribune Company (n.d.).

Sport public relations professionals can use wire services to help disseminate news, game results, and features about their organizations by cultivating relationships with local wire service staff or stringers. The importance of getting a wire service to cover an event has diminished somewhat with the advent of the Internet, but its coverage still lends credibility to an event.

# Electronic Media

Because the electronic, or broadcast, media have the advantage of covering events as they occur, their structures are somewhat different from those of print media. A distinction exists between electronic media that are broadcasting an event live and electronic media that are reporting as a part of newscast, such as the local evening news. Broadcast media include radio and television as well as Internet journalism.

## Radio

Sport radio broadcasting has remained largely unchanged during the last 70 years. During the 1930s nearly 500 million radio receivers were in use in the United States and all 16 MLB teams broadcast their games to hometown audiences (Hall et al., 2007). Today, most professional and college sporting events in the United States are broadcast on radio to local listeners as well as nationwide audiences.

Most sports radio is local, although there are several national radio networks. Many local stations have found success combining live sport programming with call-in shows that allow fans to voice their opinions about local teams. This talk radio format has revolutionized the industry, growing from just 121 stations nationwide in 1995 to more than 400 in 2004 (Adams, 2004). Much of the success of sports talk radio is because of the ability of the format to draw listeners, which is attractive to advertisers. More than a dozen of those 400 stations generate

in excess of $10 million in advertising revenue each year (Adams, 2004).

Radio stations bid for broadcast rights in the same way that television networks do. Many universities contract radio rights to all their sports teams to one radio station, creating an "official radio station" of the university.

## Television

Long gone are the days when only four television stations were available. Viewers now have hundreds of television stations and hours of programming to choose from. Those stations are delivered to consumers in three ways: broadcast, cable, and satellite.

### Broadcast Television

Broadcast stations are available over public airways to anyone who owns a television set with an antenna. Major networks such as ABC, CBS, and NBC are considered broadcast networks. These networks supply a limited number of hours of programming each day to local affiliates throughout the country. The affiliates fill the hours of nonnetwork programming as they see fit. Many purchase the rights to syndicated television shows, and some purchase the rights to broadcast live sporting events of local interest.

Both national networks and local affiliates have evening news programs that are broadcast live. Local news programs generally run 30 minutes and include a sport segment toward the end of the broadcast. Because the sport segment takes place at the end of the broadcast, local sport often receives limited coverage, especially if breaking or major news must be covered. Local sports anchors may have only two to five minutes into which they must squeeze a summary of a full day of sporting news.

As a result, local sports reporters often face difficult decisions about what to cover. Most focus only on local sporting events and major national or international events. Many local affiliates air more in-depth coverage of local sport on weekends, when there is too much news to cover in the regular newscast.

### Cable and Satellite Television

Before the 1970s the only way to watch television was through broadcast stations. That began to change as cable and satellite television grew in popularity, led by stations such as HBO and ESPN. Cable delivery of television grew from 19.9% of U.S. television households in 1980 to 56.4% in 1990 to approximately 90% today (TV Basics, n.d.a).

The importance of cable and satellite to sport has developed as rapidly as the saturation of the networks. Because not every television household subscribes to cable or satellite, leagues and governing bodies were reluctant to have their programming bid for by those networks. That circumstance has changed during the last 10 to 15 years as television networks only available through cable and satellite have successfully bid for rights fees from all major professional sport leagues.

Marquee events such as the NFL's Pro Bowl and some of MLB's playoff games have been available only to cable or satellite subscribers in recent years. The 2011 BCS Championship Game between Auburn and Oregon, broadcast on cable-only ESPN, drew a 16.1 rating, giving it the highest rating ever for any cable television show (Hiestand, 2011).

A number of broadcast networks have sister networks on cable and satellite systems, providing an opportunity to package rights fees. NBC, a broadcast network, owns U.S. rights to televise the Olympic Games through 2012 but also uses its cable and satellite networks such as CNBC, MSNBC, USA Network, and Bravo to televise coverage of the Games. The increased importance of cable and satellite networks to sport organizations will continue to be a factor as governing bodies seek to gain the greatest exposure for programming.

### Ratings and Shares

The numbers that television programs draw are central to any study of the success of television programming. Television executives concern themselves with a program's rating and share, both of which measure how many households watch a given program at a given time.

A program's rating is the percentage of the overall population (represented by households with televisions) who watches a particular program. A share represents the percentage of the population watching television who tuned into a particular program. Those figures, however, do not measure actual viewers, just households. Further complicating matters is that the U.S. population has grown as has the number of television viewing options. Therefore, comparing one event to another is difficult.

For example, the 2010 Super Bowl between the New Orleans Saints and Indianapolis Colts was watched by a record 106.5 million people, making it the most-watched TV program in history. The game drew a 45.0 rating and a 68 share (Zulgad, 2010), meaning that 45% of overall television households watched the Super Bowl and that 68% of households with a television on during that time, more than two out of every three televisions turned on in the country, were watching the Super Bowl. Still, those numbers do not exceed the 60.2 rating that the final episode of *M*A*S*H* received in 1983.

Of the 20 most watched sporting telecasts of all time, 18 are NFL games. Only the 1994 Olympic Winter Games, which featured the Nancy Kerrigan–Tonya Harding controversy, dented the top 20. Table 6.1 shows the top five most watched sporting events of all time.

## Internet

The newest entry into electronic media is the Internet. Although most print and broadcast journalists contribute to their organization's website, the number of Internet-only journalists is growing. Sport public relations professionals should exercise caution in dealing with people who purport to be journalists. Many may be affiliated with fan-based websites managed by private individuals on their free time. Others may be tied to illegal sports gambling.

### Table 6.1  Top Five Sport Telecasts of All Time

| Show | Date aired | Rating |
| --- | --- | --- |
| Super Bowl XVI (San Francisco vs. Cincinnati) | 1/24/1982 | 49.1 |
| Super Bowl XVII (Washington vs. Miami) | 1/30/1983 | 48.6 |
| XVII Olympic Winter Games | 2/23/1994 | 48.5 |
| Super Bowl XX (Chicago vs. New England) | 1/26/1986 | 48.3 |
| Super Bowl XII (Dallas vs. Denver) | 1/15/1978 | 47.2 |

Data from TV Basics 2004.

One way to evaluate the legitimacy of a website is by measuring the amount of unique content that the site generates, or how much of the content on the site is written exclusively for the site and how much is provided by a wire service. Other ways to evaluate websites include whether any of the content is subscription based and whether the site travels to events. More information about websites is presented in chapter 4.

# Relationship Between Mass Media and Sport

The advent of the telegraph in the mid-1800s began the marriage of mass media and sport. Betts (1953) found that the new technology led to immediate reporting of baseball, boxing, horse racing, and regattas throughout the United States. The symbiotic relationship between the mass media and sport began to play a prominent role in American society in the 1920s, when sport emerged as a social institution (McChesney, 1989). But in the present era of rising player salaries and facility costs, sport organizations depend more than ever on the rights fees paid by broadcasters and on the free publicity that the media provide.

Occasionally, mass media organizations create their own programming, thereby eliminating the need to pay rights fees for a product. Still other media have tried to expand their brand across multiple platforms of mass media. Pitts and Stotlar (2007, p. 30) observed that companies "can link promotional activities and fan participation activities, thus enticing the fan (consumer) to use products all produced by the same company." The success of ESPN since its inception in 1979 is a good example of how this has been accomplished. The network created a number of brand extensions, including additional cable channels such as ESPN2 and ESPN News, an awards show called the ESPYs, a theme restaurant called the ESPN Zone, as well as other mass media outlets like magazines, radio stations, and websites (Croteau & Hoynes, 2001).

ESPN also benefits from a sister relationship with ABC. Both networks are owned by the Walt Disney Company, enabling them to promote programming across a variety of telecommunication platforms and share resources such as announcers and advertising opportunities (Stotlar, 2000). ESPN regularly extends its brand through its promotion of ESPN: The Weekend at Walt Disney World in Orlando, Florida. The Disney Company combined its traditional forms of entertainment, its resorts and theme parks, with the popularity of ESPN programming and shows, billing it as "unique entertainment and interactive experiences for sports fans and sports families" (ESPN, n.d.). Several ESPN shows broadcast live from the various theme parks at Walt Disney World.

ESPN is not the first television network to combine sport, media, and entertainment into a single product. The blending of sport and media as entertainment had its roots in the 1970s and is discussed in more detail later in this chapter.

To understand the complex relationship between sport organizations and the media, it is necessary to discuss the history of that relationship while considering how sport leagues have adapted their product for the benefit of the media as well as how the media has been able to create sport programming.

# Mass Media and Sport History

The beginnings of organized sport in North America can be traced back to the early 1800s, but as Rader (1999) observed, the growth of sport was aided by "improvements in communication and transportation, plus the growth of cities" (p. 20). Communication improvements included both the telegraph and the print media. From there, communication grew to include radio broadcasts and then television broadcasts. The role played by broadcast rights fees is central to today's relationship between sport organizations and the media. The following sections discuss how the relationship has evolved.

## Print Media

William Trotter Porter started the United States' first weekly sport publication in 1831, the *Spirit of the Times*. At its height in 1856, 40,000 subscribers were reportedly reading it each week (Rader, 1999). Twenty-five years would pass before Joseph Pulitzer established the first sports department in a daily newspaper in his *New York Herald* in 1883, and another 12 years passed before the first sport section appeared, developed by William Randolph Hearst in the *New York Journal* in 1895 (McChesney, 1989).

The prominence of the sportswriter grew immensely in the first quarter of the 20th century. Grantland Rice was the most recognized writer during this period. Known for his poetic prose, Rice inspired a new wave of writers who saw "their task to be the construction of an interesting story of what had happened or what was likely to happen" (Rader, 1984, p. 21). Following a Notre

Dame–Army football game in 1924, Rice wrote for the *New York Tribune* what may be the most famous lead sentence of any sport story written in the 20th century: "Outlined against a blue-gray October sky, the Four Horsemen rode again" (Rice, 1954, p. 177). Only after that story did the Notre Dame backfield become known as the Four Horsemen.

Rice and his contemporaries created heroes out of athletes and social drama out of athletic competition. Fans of sport had only two ways to gain a visual image of their athletic heroes at the time—go to a game in person or draw a mental picture in their minds based on the words of sportswriters. In effect, the print media legitimized organized sport in the United States and created a rabid spectator following.

## Electronic Media

Unique to the sport industry is the notion of rights fees. Although most sporting events take place in a public forum, leagues and teams charge members of the electronic media rights fees to broadcast the event. But that was not always the case. For example, during the early days of radio and television in the 1930s and 1940s, Chicago Cubs owner William Wrigley charged nothing for broadcasts. As a result, "as many as seven Chicago radio stations sometimes carried Cubs games" (Rader, 1984, p. 26).

Eventually, owners and leagues realized that the ability of sport programming to draw large audiences meant that many broadcast entities were willing to pay large sums for exclusive rights to carry events. The first league to benefit from a surge in rights fees was Major League Baseball, which saw radio and television broadcasting revenues increase from 3% of total revenues in 1946 to 16.8% in 1956. That percentage would increase to 50% of total revenues in 1990. Local team revenues grew as well, and an imbalance quickly developed. Teams in larger media markets, especially successful teams, reaped greater revenues than did teams in smaller markets. During the 1950s, for instance, the Brooklyn Dodgers garnered $580,000 in broadcasting revenues whereas the St. Louis Cardinals brought in only $9,000 (Zimbalist, 1994).

Most major North American professional sport leagues, including MLB, negotiate national television rights on behalf of all teams and distribute the revenue equitably among clubs. The NFL, however, does not allow its clubs to solicit local television contracts in part because of the scarcity of games (16 regular-season contests per team compared with 162 per team in baseball). Table 6.2 provides a snapshot of current television rights fees for major professional sports in the United States.

Because of the substantial financial contribution that television rights fees make to leagues and individual teams, Pitts and Stotlar (2007) observed that "if television ever stopped its sport coverage, many sport systems would collapse" (p. 267). But signs are appearing that the meteoric rise of television rights fees is slowing. When the NHL's contract with ABC and ESPN expired at the end of the 2003–04 season, the league was facing declining ratings and a labor dispute with its players' association. The current rights deal struck by the NHL was with ESPN for an estimated $65 million per year, or approximately half of the previous agreement with ABC. The NHL also struck a deal with NBC for 0 dollars; instead, the network shared advertising revenue with the league, an agreement that existed through the 2010–11 season (Ourand, 2009).

## Radio Broadcasts

If the print media brought the stories of sports heroes into homes, it was radio that brought sounds to those stories, enhancing the spectator experience. Fueled by technology from World War I, radio broadcasts began to transform consumption of sport. Spectators could experience an event as it was happening instead of waiting for the next day's newspaper story (Rader, 1984).

Early technology did not permit radio announcers to broadcast road games live in their local markets. As a result, announcers relied on Western Union tapes for play-by-play action and augmented the broadcast with in-studio sound effects to create the impression of a live broadcast (Hall et al., 2007).

Owners initially feared that free radio broadcasts would cause a decrease in attendance at games, and many were hesitant to embrace the media. This reluctance disappeared as corporate advertisers became willing to pay for sponsorships of marquee events. The Ford Motor Company paid $100,000 to advertise during the 1934 World Series, and Gillette Safety Razor Company sponsored the World Series for 32 consecutive years beginning in 1939 (Rader, 1984). Owners' fears eased as they welcomed the additional exposure and revenue that radio delivered. Thus began a relationship between the electronic media and sport that continues today. Media want the opportunity to broadcast sporting events because of the large amount of money that advertisers are willing to pay to reach the audience.

## Television Broadcasts

While radio broadcasts of sporting events dominated the period between the 1920s and the late 1950s, televised sporting events did not catch on

## Table 6.2 Current Major Professional and College Sport Television Rights Deals

| League | Network | Amount (length) |
|---|---|---|
| NFL | Fox<br>CBS<br>NBC<br>ESPN<br>DirecTV | $5.76 billion (2006–2013)<br>$4.96 billion (2006–2013)<br>$4.82 billion (2006–2013)<br>$8.8 billion (2006–2013)<br>$4.0 billion (2011–2014) |
| MLB | Fox<br>ESPN<br>Turner | $1.8 billion (2007–2013)<br>$2.37 billion (2006–2013)<br>$700 million (2007–2013) |
| NBA | ABC<br>ESPN & TNT (combined deal) | $7.44 billion (2008–2016)<br>$7.44 billion (2008–2016) |
| NHL | NBC<br>Versus | $0; share revenue (through 2010–11 season)<br>$232.5 million (through 2010–11 season) |
| NASCAR | Fox<br>ESPN & ABC<br>TNT | $1.76 billion (2007–2014)<br>$2.16 billion (2007–2014)<br>$640 million (2007–2014) |
| NCAA Men's Basketball Tournament | CBS & Turner | $771 million (2011–2024) |
| BCS | ESPN | $495 million (2011–2014) |

Data compiled from Fisher, 2006; Ourand, 2006; Ourand, 2009; Ourand & Smith, 2010; Smith & Ourand, 2008.

as quickly. First, the technology at the time allowed the viewer to focus on only one thing at a time. Television was not effective in conveying the experience of a baseball game to viewers. Subtleties such as the positioning of the fielders and the lead of base runners were lost (Roberts & Olson, 1989). As technology improved, innovations such as instant replay and slow motion attracted greater numbers of viewers (McChesney, 1989).

Second, just as with radio, owners feared that fans would stop paying money to attend games in person if the contests were televised. Indeed, attendance at professional football and professional baseball games declined as television became more prevalent. Out of respect for their concerns, television executives blocked home games from being broadcast in local markets (Fielding & Pitts, 2003). Attendance increased as a result.

A factor that contributed directly to the growth of televised sport was the **Sports Broadcasting Act**, passed by Congress in 1961. Before the act was passed, each team was free to negotiate television contracts with national networks. The Justice Department advised league governing bodies that

federal antitrust laws would prohibit them from negotiating national television contracts on behalf of all member teams. As a result, prominent and large-market teams attracted the interest of networks, and clubs in smaller markets suffered from declining attendance and reduction in potential broadcasting revenues (Rader, 1999).

The belief in the 1950s was that "the right to broadcast a game over the air belonged to and thus could be sold by the teams playing in the game" (Weiler & Roberts, 1998, p. 549). The Sports Broadcasting Act took away that right from the individual teams and gave it to governing bodies, such as MLB and the NFL. By representing all member clubs, leagues were able to command a greater rights fee in their negotiations with networks than an individual club could. Leagues subsequently developed a system to distribute rights fees equally among member clubs.

The first league to reap the benefits of this antitrust exemption was the NFL, whose commissioner Pete Rozelle ignited the first bidding war among television networks. CBS had signed a two-year deal with the NFL in 1962 at $4.5 million per year.

As ratings increased dramatically in the early 1960s, all three national networks—CBS, NBC, and ABC—decided to bid in 1964. CBS ultimately submitted a final bid of $14 million per year for two years, so each NFL franchise received more than $1 million (Rader, 1984).

After CBS signed its 1964 deal with the NFL, NBC quickly signed a deal with the rival American Football League (AFL) for $42 million over five years (Rader, 1984). Networks were in a position to up the ante for professional football rights because they had found that companies were willing to pay a premium to advertise during broadcasts. As McChesney (1989) observed, sport "provided access to a very desirable market—not only for 'blue-collar' products like beer and razor blades, but for big-ticket items like automobiles and business equipment" (p. 62).

With his networked blocked from the lucrative professional product, ABC Sports president Roone Arledge approached NCAA president Walter Byers with a proposal to broadcast college football. The NCAA had shuttled among the three major networks from 1960 to 1965. Arledge promised that ABC would not seek professional football if it was awarded exclusive rights to college games (Rader, 1984).

Despite that pledge, ABC entered an agreement with the pros when it signed a contract for *Monday Night Football* in 1970. Even so, ABC also held its exclusive deal with the NCAA until 1982 (Rader, 1984).

Arledge is acknowledged by most as having done more than any other person to cement the marriage between television and sport. Roberts and Olson (1989, p. 114) called him the "most important single individual in modern sports." He is credited with building ABC from a third-place network in the early 1960s to the top-rated network by the mid-1970s through sport programming such as the Olympics, college football, *Wide World of Sports*, and *Monday Night Football*. The sidebar titled ABC Television Changes the Olympic Games summarizes how ABC coverage of the Olympic Games in the 1970s made an indelible mark on the sport organization–media relationship.

Although both broadcasters and sport organizations have clear economic motivation to cooperate, Ashwell (1998) observed that both sides need to look beyond the bottom line and consider benefits that are not as easily measured. For example, NBC has positioned itself in the marketplace as the network of the Olympic Games by locking up television rights for the Games through 2012. This agreement gives NBC a clear advantage over rival networks when competing for advertisers wishing to gain access to the huge audiences the Olympics draw. NBC has used this advantage to promote much of its own programming during Olympic coverage.

For sport organizations, exposure on television may lead to greater promotional opportunities and favorable publicity toward the organization (Ashwell, 1998). Many scholars have attempted to gauge the effect of postseason television exposure on freshman applications to a university. One way to guarantee that an organization will appear on television is to sell the rights to broadcast the organization's events.

# Sport Adaptations for Television

As television networks became more aware of how vital rights fees were to the continued success of sport, the networks began to request changes to the sport product. These modifications were embraced by sport governing bodies that saw the changes as a small price to pay for increased television rights fees and larger fan bases.

To a certain degree, each sport that is broadcast on television has permitted the media to alter its core product in some capacity. Video cameras are placed inside automobiles in NASCAR to provide unique viewer angles, shot clocks and three-point lines were introduced in basketball to create more scoring, and ice hockey adopted a brief overtime period to reduce the number of ties in its games. Additionally, baseball and football both have made well-documented adaptations to their products for the sake of television.

## *Baseball*

Throughout the 1960s MLB suffered through a decline in offensive production because of the rise of dominant pitchers. In 1968 Carl Yastrzemski won the American League batting title with an average of .301, Bob Gibson won the 1968 Cy Young Award with a microscopic 1.12 earned run average and 13 shutouts, and Don Drysdale hurled 58 consecutive scoreless innings. To ignite more offense, baseball lowered the height of the pitching mound in 1969 and the American League adopted the designated hitter in 1973 (Rader, 1984).

Bowie Kuhn became commissioner in 1969 and presided over a variety of changes to the league structure, all of which benefited television in some fashion. Baseball expanded from 20 to 26 teams, creating more markets; each league was split into

# ABC Television Changes the Olympic Games

No televised sporting events did more to alter the landscape of the sport organization–media relationship than the 1972 Munich and 1976 Montreal Olympic Games broadcast by ABC. The human drama played out in and around the sporting arenas riveted the American television audience and forever changed the way that Americans approached the Olympic Games. These Games altered not only the financial viability of the Olympics but also the structure of amateur sport in the United States.

As Rader (1999) observed, ABC's coverage of the Games "contributed immensely to the Games' 'coming of age' as television extravaganzas" (p. 283). Indeed, the percentage increase in American television rights fees from 1972 to 1980 was greater than that in any other period in history. ABC paid $7.5 million for the rights for the 1972 Munich Games and $25 million for the 1976 Montreal Games—a 333% increase. But that dollar amount paled in comparison to the leap that NBC made for the 1980 Moscow Games when it paid $87 million (Senn, 1999). That figure was more than the previous 20 years of U.S. rights fees combined and was a 348% increase over 1976. Through an insurance policy, NBC recovered 90% of the $70 million it had already paid to the Moscow organizers when the United States boycotted the Games (Senn, 1999).

During the 1970s the IOC was on the verge of financial disaster. The increase in rights fees led to a series of changes in the management of the Olympic Games. Sponsors took a more active role when they realized that the Games could attract large television audiences. The IOC brought rights fees negotiations inside its organization and out of the hands of individual organizing committees, allowing the IOC to control the process. By the 1990s the IOC was negotiating long-term television deals rather than one Games at a time. The end result was a more financially stable IOC.

Besides paying escalating rights fees, ABC's Olympics coverage created heroes, magnified the struggle between the United States and Communist nations, and legitimized sport on television as both entertainment and news.

**ABC's coverage of the terrorist incident at the 1972 Olympic Games won the network critical acclaim.**

AP Photo/Kurt Strumpf

Roone Arledge, president of ABC Sports, made a conscious decision in 1972 to focus on a teenage gymnast from the Soviet Union who was a last-minute addition to her nation's roster. For three days Arledge and ABC followed the moves of Olga Korbut as she won three gold medals and, as Arledge (2003) himself wrote, "made a previously obscure sport a television obsession and launched the gymnastics craze among teenage girls in America" (p. 125).

While Americans were becoming fixated on teenage gymnasts like Korbut and, in 1976, Romania's Nadia Comaneci, both from Communist nations, the nationalistic tones of politics took to the Olympic Games as well. American viewers were shocked as television magnified the successes of the Communist bloc nations and the disappointments of American athletes. The United States, tops in the medal count in 1968, finished only four medals ahead of East Germany in 1976 and 31 medals behind the Soviet Union (Rader, 1999).

To address the U.S. decline, President Gerald Ford established a commission to study amateur sport governance (Rader, 1999). This commission eventually passed the Amateur Sports Act in 1978, known now as the Ted Stevens Olympic and Paralympic Amateur Sports Act in honor of the senator from Alaska who chaired the commission. This legislation allowed the U.S. Olympic Committee to govern, manage, and promote all activities of the Olympic and Paralympic teams within and outside the United States (Hums & MacLean, 2004).

Unfortunately, the 1972 Olympic Games were forever scarred by the events of September 5, when members of the Palestinian terrorist group known as Black September stormed into the Olympic Village. The terrorists killed two members of the Israeli delegation in the village and took nine members hostage. All of the hostages were killed in a botched German police ambush attempt at an airport in Munich (Reeve, 2000).

Arledge was producing ABC's coverage of the Games, and as soon as he heard of the takeover in the village, he immediately made plans for ABC to broadcast live, even though it was still the middle of the night in the United States. The network broadcast for 14 hours that day as negotiations between police & the terrorists dragged on for nearly 24 hours.

Americans watched the coverage with an intensity that had not been seen since the 1963 assassination of President John F. Kennedy and the murder of his accused killer, Lee Harvey Oswald (Rader, 1999). ABC's coverage was anchored in its studio by Jim McKay and Chris Shenkel, with reports from Peter Jennings, who had holed up in the village. The network won 29 Emmy awards for its coverage of the tragedy and, by selling commercial spots during the Games, posted the first profit in its history. More than 50% of American households watched some of the 1972 Olympic telecast (Arledge, 2003).

In its coverage of the Olympic Games, ABC, led by Arledge's production, took a sporting event that had previously received little media attention and turned it into a financial success for organizers, advertisers, and the network. By weaving human drama into the competitions, ABC legitimized the Olympic Games as a sporting event. The Games became a television ratings giant to the extent that a little more than 30 years after ABC's broadcast of the 1972 Munich Games, when it paid $7.5 million for the rights, NBC paid $2.201 billion to be the U.S. rights holder for the 2010 and 2012 Olympic Games (Martzke, 2003).

two divisions, creating additional postseason competition; and part of the World Series was scheduled at night, allowing more viewers to watch the games.

## Football

Rader (1999) observed that "no other team sport was quite as responsive to the needs of television as pro football" (p. 255). Beyond the obvious creation of a special night for its product (Monday night), the NFL embarked on a series of rule changes throughout the 1970s designed to bring more offense and scoring to the game that theoretically would make it more attractive to television viewers. The NFL moved hash marks closer together, moved the goalposts back to the end line, changed the yard line for kickoffs, reduced the penalty for offensive holding from 15 to 10 yards, and permitted offensive linemen to extend their arms and open their hands to protect the quarterback (Rader, 1984).

Even before the boom of television, NFL commissioner Bert Bell allowed "television time-outs" as a means to increase advertising opportunities for the network (McChesney, 1989). Other accommodations by the NFL for the benefit of television included sudden-death overtime, two-minute warnings, and wildcard playoff berths.

# Made-for-Television Sport

While many sports were changing rules to make their products more television friendly, television networks were busy creating their own sport products suitable for broadcast. ABC and Arledge led the way by packaging 87 different sports into *Wide World of Sports* between 1960 and 1966. Daredevil Evel Knievel appeared 16 times on *Wide World of Sports*, beginning in 1967 when he attempted to jump the fountains in front of Caesar's Palace in Las Vegas (Roberts & Olson, 1989).

Subsequent made-for-television sport included competitions between athletes from various sports and between Hollywood personalities, as well as competition between world-class athletes during the Cold War and the creation of an Olympic-style event for the developing extreme sport market.

## The Superstars

In the 1970s ABC developed a program called *The Superstars*, which pitted athletes from all sports in events like obstacle courses, bowling, and rowing (Rader, 1984). The contest sought to identify the world's best overall athlete. The success of *The Superstars* led to a variety of spinoffs on all three networks, including ABC's *Battle of the Network Stars*, which featured the stars of popular primetime television shows competing against one another in athletic contests.

Lending continuity to these programs during the 1970s was ABC sportscaster Howard Cosell. A lawyer by trade, Cosell was the dominant presence on all these shows. He served as a color commentator on *Monday Night Football*, as a reporter on *Wide World of Sports*, and as a host on *The Superstars* and *Battle of the Network Stars*. Cosell's presence on a show meant an instant ratings boost. Viewers tuned in just to hear what Cosell would say next. As Jim Spence (1988), former senior vice president of ABC Sports, reflected in his memoir, "We would have been very successful without Howard Cosell; we were a whole lot more successful because of him" (p. 20).

## Goodwill Games

Following the boycott of the 1980 Moscow Olympic Games by the United States and the retaliatory boycott of the 1984 Los Angeles Olympic Games by the Soviet Union, Ted Turner created an international competition to air on his cable television networks. Turner's vision was to create an event that would "ease tensions during the Cold War through friendly athletic competition between nations" (Goodwill Games, n.d.).

The first Goodwill Games took place in Moscow in 1986. The event marked the first time that the United States and the Soviet Union had competed against one another in a multination, multisport format since the 1976 Montreal Olympic Games. Subsequent Goodwill Games would take place in Seattle, Washington; St. Petersburg, Russia; New York; and Brisbane, Australia. After the Cold War ended, the Games' focus shifted toward young people.

The Games' initial success was because of the level of competition, not the television coverage. As Taaffe (1986) reported, Turner encountered a conflict of interest between the creation of the Games and objective reporting: "Is he selling or reporting? How objective can someone be when he's reporting on his own pet project? Is television in this case serving the sport, or vice versa?" (p. 55).

Many world records were set during the 16-year run of the Goodwill Games, which also included one Winter Goodwill Games. Turner generated worldwide interest from members of the Olympic movement in his event without having to pay the astronomical rights fees that the IOC charges to broadcast the Olympic Games. The Goodwill Games officially ceased operations after 2001.

## X Games

ESPN successfully capitalized on the growing segment of the sport industry known as extreme sports when it created the Extreme Games in 1994 as a way to fill programming hours on its new network, ESPN2 (Semiao, 2004). The event, since renamed the X Games, has spawned a winter version, fostered worldwide interest, and developed a loyal following among a segment of the sport industry previously ignored by mainstream media. The rise in popularity of extreme sports has led to sports such as snowboarding being accepted into the Olympic Games.

Similar to Turner's Goodwill Games, the X Games have allowed their creator and owner, ESPN, to control the details of the Games and provide the ideal programming for the network while pocketing all the advertising revenue without having to pay rights fees to broadcast the event (Pitts & Stotlar, 2007).

**ESPN's X Games capitalized on the popularity of extreme sports and allowed the network to fill programming hours while pocketing all advertising revenue without paying rights fees to broadcast the event.**

AP Photo/Jae C. Hong

# Evolution of Sport Public Relations

Organized sport in the United States has employed publicity tactics since the 1800s. Professional and collegiate organizations recognized the value of the media in advancing a particular cause that the organizations might be facing. On the professional level, publicity aided both sides of the early management–labor disputes of baseball's National League (NL), while on the collegiate level publicity played a major role in the growth of football.

## History of Professional Sport Public Relations

One of the first uses of public relations in professional sport occurred during a baseball management–labor dispute in the 1800s. In response to

baseball owners' policies regarding limitations on salaries and the reserve clause, professional baseball players staged a revolt known as the Brotherhood War. Players formed the Brotherhood of Professional Base Ball Players on October 22, 1895, the first players' association in professional sport (Seymour, 1989).

In 1890 the players formed the Players League for one season. More than 80 players left the NL to compete for the upstart league. As league began play, leadership in the Brotherhood used the media to sway public opinion. Popular newspapers *The Sporting News* and *Sporting Life* both endorsed the Players League in articles (Anderson, 2001a). Despite the efforts of both sides to use the media in their favor, Anderson (2006) concluded that neither side was particularly successful. The Players League did not enjoy long-term success—it disbanded after one season—but public opinion of owners definitely turned because of the media attention paid to the league. "Newspapers chose to support either the players or the owners, but after the war all agreed that the owners should manage the game and the players should play the game," Anderson (2006, p. 79) wrote. Seymour (1989, p. 240) noted another consequence: "(Both) the fans and the press were disgusted with baseball after the debacle of 1890."

One of the earliest professional sport public relations practitioners was Steve Hannagan, who relied on the press agentry model throughout the 1920s and 1930s to popularize the Memorial Day Auto Race on the Indianapolis Speedway and help MLB commemorate the centennial celebration of baseball in 1939 (Anderson, 2001b). Cutlip (1994, p. 251) called Hannagan "America's great press agent of the first half century."

Anderson (2001b) found that Hannagan's 1930s public relations practices were "not the two-way street that its practitioners often claimed, because no attempts were made to ascertain public needs or desires, only to send information." Instead, Hannagan's success came as a result of media relations campaigns and grassroots initiatives aimed at reaching a broader public spectrum, not just baseball fans.

## History of College Sport Public Relations

Walter C. Camp is acknowledged by many historians as the Father of Football and the most influential person in the development of the college game (Smith, 1988; Thelin, 1996; Rader, 1999). As head coach at Yale University, Camp installed a system that dominated college football. From 1872 to 1909, Yale recorded 324 wins, 17 losses, and 18 ties (Rader, 1999).

But Camp was not content with growing the sport locally at Yale; he had his sights set on the rest of the country. To increase the exposure of college football, Camp edited an annual college football guide and selected players for the first All-America teams (Thelin, 1996). Camp's tireless promotion of the sport led to the early prominence of college football in the United States.

If Camp was responsible for creating college football, then Notre Dame head coach Knute Rockne was responsible for creating a formula for success in which winning football programs make money for their institutions. As Fielding & Pitts (2003) observed, Rockne advanced the mystique of the Notre Dame football program through the creation of brand equity. Under Rockne, "Notre Dame football became a highly recognizable and distinguished name that consumers and fans associated with value" (p. 55).

Rockne achieved this value in three ways: by creating a winning tradition, by creating brand awareness, and by developing perceived quality (Fielding & Pitts, 2003). The winning tradition was created on the field with star players, but the brand awareness and perceived quality were created off the field, often by student press agents.

Rockne recruited a young Iowa student named Archie Ward to be his sport publicity director in 1919. Ward received no compensation for his work other than the same tuition waiver and room and board provided to athletes. In return, Ward's job was to "see to it that the football news from Notre Dame was what Knute Rockne wanted it to be—no more, no less" (Littlewood, 1990, p. 25).

Ward traveled with the team, writing pregame and postgame stories for out-of-town media outlets. Rockne routinely approved the text of these stories before Ward submitted them, creating a style of writing that "had as its chief objective the glorification of a man and an institution" (Littlewood, 1990, p. 25).

One of Ward's predecessors, George Strickler, was indirectly responsible for the Four Horsemen moniker given to the 1924 Notre Dame backfield. As Rockne's press agent, Strickler traveled with the team to New York for a game against Army. Days before the game, Strickler and the rest of the team had gone to a showing of the *The Four Horsemen of the Apocalypse,* a silent movie starring Rudolph Valentino. During halftime of the game, Strickler mentioned in the press box to sportswriters Grantland Rice and Damon Runyan that the Notre Dame backfield was rolling through Army just as the Four Horsemen had done (Maraniss, 1999).

As mentioned previously, that casual mention in the press box led to the most famous lead sentence in all of sports journalism. Strickler capitalized on the momentum created by the story and arranged for four horses to be brought onto the practice field in South Bend, Indiana, after the team returned from New York. Photographers captured the now famous photo of four Notre Dame players holding footballs while sitting atop horses (Maraniss, 1999; *Four Horsemen*, n.d.).

Camp's use of awards and honors to recognize individual players helped promote college football nationwide. Rockne's employment of full-time public relations personnel created perhaps the most famous brand in college football. Neither would have been as successful without the publicity created through the media.

College sport public relations has evolved considerably over the years. The sidebar Taking Sport Public Relations Back a Generation by Bob Condron, a member of the College Sports Information Direc-

**The legendary Four Horsemen of the 1924 Notre Dame football team.**
AP Photo

tors of America (CoSIDA) Hall of Fame, discusses these changes.

## Development of CoSIDA

Before 1957 university sport public relations professionals belonged to the American College public relations Association. But college football grew quickly in scope and prominence. Radio broadcasts began to enhance the popularity of the sport, and universities began to realize increased publicity and income from football programs (Thelin, 1996). As schools struggled with how best to promote their programs, sport public relations practitioners developed an organization solely for advancing professionalism in the sports information field. With more than 2,400 members today, the **College Sports Information Directors of America (CoSIDA)** is one of the largest professional organizations of sport public relations professionals in the world (CoSIDA, n.d.a). The association bills itself as a

group of "strategic communicators for college athletics."

CoSIDA stages a number of professional development opportunities for its members, including an annual workshop, newsletter, contests, and scholarships. Membership in the organization is available at three levels (student, active, and associate) and is open to all levels of intercollegiate athletics in both the United States and Canada. In addition, members vote on regional and national academic All-America awards for student–athletes (CoSIDA, n.d.b).

## Future of Sport Public Relations

Interaction among sport organizations, the media, and the public continues to evolve at a rapid pace. In the few short years that elapsed between the

## Taking Sport Public Relations Back a Generation

**Bob Condron**

Photo courtesy of Bob Condron.

Pick a nice fall day. The colors are bursting with gold and red. It's college football season. It's game day.

You're the student assistant in the sports information office. Your main goal about four hours before the big game is to get the ditto machine to the press box. Get those stat forms ready to go. Plenty of fluid, ready to crank out those quarterly stats by hand.

On the way up in the elevator, you notice a sign that reads, "No Women or Children Allowed in the Press Box." Must mean wives or girlfriends of the pro scouts. They gotta go.

The small darkroom in the press box is all set up for UPI and AP. The Western Union guy is there, ready to transmit copy from a page pounded out on a Royal typewriter with the big round keys. The typewriters are humming with the staccato sounds of furiously slung carriage releases.

Then the announcement comes from the inside PA: "Gentlemen, there will be no cheering in the press box. Again a reminder that women and children are not allowed in the working area of the press box." Only working folks allowed here.

After the game, the dressing rooms are open 10 minutes after the final gun. Hot steamy showers, little room to move for all the guys. Real life quotes . . . and smells.

It's life at a college football game on a Saturday afternoon in fall.

Fast forward to today's game. Same colors, same excitement. Same number of yards for a first down. He who has the most points wins.

But the sign in the elevator is gone. Women are everywhere. They're working. They're in the locker room. It's still steamy, but there are more towels now. More robes. Interview rooms. Same smells.

There's not an 11 p.m. deadline. It's in five minutes, and the sun is still shining. There's no darkroom. In fact, there is no film. The UPI guy is not there. The photographers all have computers only steps from the field. They can upload photos within seconds because someone changed the world with a lot of little 1s and 0s that formed the digital revolution.

The Western Union guy is gone. There are no telecopiers . . . anywhere. No carbon paper. Damn.

The journalists have spent the day tweeting, posting info on Facebook, blogging. It used to be called writing a column. The guys used to be able to watch the football game. But now they're sending out 140-character notes to people they don't know. For three hours. Soon they will need some video and audio for the website. They shoot interviews in the hot, steamy locker room. They edit it down into a segment and then transmit back to the home office. In a minute or two fans are enjoying it. It is backpack journalism.

The technology has changed. The access has changed. The pressure has changed to a race to get it up, online and first. Not a lot of time for chitchat anymore.

But has the business changed?

Yes and no.

Journalism still has its standards. There are excellent people in the field. Professionals with ethics, with honor. You'd name your kid after them.

> There's not an 11 p.m. deadline. It's in five minutes, and the sun is still shining. There's no darkroom. In fact, there is no film. The UPI guy is not there. The photographers all have computers only steps from the field. They can upload photos within seconds because someone changed the world with a lot of little 1s and 0s that formed the digital revolution.

The way we communicate is different. Back in the day, you either mailed a letter, called on the phone, or sat down and talked. Face to face.

Now it's mainly e-mail. Or text messages while you're driving down the freeway or in a school zone. Or putting everything on a site—Facebook—and having the world go there. You could even Skype. Then there's the rather mundane way of calling from your cell phone, in a loud voice in a crowded place. And in dire circumstances . . . talking in person.

Journalists still want stories. It's not about who wins these days. It's more about the stories. It's about the peg. You gotta know the peg. Blind mother, father a medal of honor winner, sister a ballerina. Dog named Cronkite.

Athletes are media trained. They're schooled in the ways of various media. The sports talk show host. The Internet blogger. The guy on deadline. The press conferences. In many instances journalists will never get a quote with one degree of soul. Or meaning.

But check out the athlete's Twitter and you can get times, names, and video (by way of link to Facebook). It's galactic.

Do relationships still count?

Absolutely. But having a beer and laughing at the guy wearing the weird Hog Hat is probably not part of that relationship. It could be an e-mail relationship, a phone relationship, a press conference relationship. A Facebook relationship. It still matters in today's public relations.

Honesty and integrity are still in there, near the lead. Being available in the good times as well as the bad times is at least in the second graf. And being prepared wafts throughout the entire scene.

A lot has changed. The signs are different in the elevators. The UPI and Western Union guys are now sports talk show hosts. Veins stick out of their necks as they yell into the mike and at each other. But the soul of the business is still strong.

It's like the first time you saw a college football game. That green grass just sparkled when you walked out of the tunnel into the stands. The band was playing. Cheerleaders were jumping around with number one signs on both hands. Great outfits. It was like you just got plugged into an electric socket. You'll never forget it.

The busy intersection that combines public relations and journalism is still good and strong. It gets tested every hour, but it has formed a flexible yet solid partnership.

Tomorrow we may reach a technology where life can be rewound . . . or fast forwarded. Speeded up, slowed down. Or deleted in certain cases.

But today it's fine. It's fall, it's magic, and the words are flowing.

*Bob Condron is the director of media services for the U.S. Olympic Committee and a member of the College Sports Information Directors of America Hall of Fame.*

first edition of this text and the current edition, the ways and the speed with which an organization can communicate messages exploded. Organizations today regularly break news on their own websites without the need for the mass media. Athletes communicate directly with fans through their Twitter accounts. Fans of a particular Major League Baseball team can, for a fee, have out-of-market games streamed directly to their computers. And fans can sign up to receive text message alerts when sports news breaks. No one could have foreseen these developments six years ago, and predicting the next six years is equally as difficult.

What is not likely to change is the ability of fans to receive information almost instantly on their phones or mobile devices. The golden age of sports-writing when sports reporters had hours to craft a game story for the next day's newspaper is long in the past. Fans expect information to be available as it happens. And they want to participate in the development of that information through Twitter, Facebook, blogs, and chat rooms.

That immediacy can create problems for sport public relations professionals. Correcting misinformation, rumor, or miscommunication can be a full-time job. Because poor information may have a negative effect on sales of an organization's product or service, public relations professionals will have to be even more diligent in not only correcting erroneous information but also proactively disseminating information. Strategies for disseminating information will be the focus of many of the chapters forthcoming in the text.

## SUMMARY

The media are a significant enterprise in society, often influencing what the public sees and hears. Today's mass media include traditional forms such as print and electronic but have also grown to include the Internet. The current relationship between sport and the media is symbiotic, meaning that each needs the other to survive. This circumstance represents a shift from earlier thinking when many sport organizations resisted television and radio for fear that they would decrease revenue. As sport on television flourished, many sport organizations made concessions to their rules to maximize publicity. The media have developed the relationship further by creating sport as entertainment and programming. As sport has grown more comfortable in its relationship with the mass media, the need for public relations personnel has emerged.

## LEARNING ACTIVITIES

1. Research the role of the mass media in a sport not discussed in this chapter such as golf, tennis, or auto racing. What sort of financial benefits does the sport receive from television exposure? Has the sport altered its core product to accommodate the media?

2. Watch a sport segment of a local television station's evening newscast with a stopwatch. How much time was devoted to the entire segment? To each story in the segment? How many stories were reported?

3. Visit the websites of two newspapers in the same city, such as Chicago or Salt Lake City. Compare the coverage emphasis of each paper in terms of national versus local sport and professional versus amateur sport. What, if any, recommendations would you make to sport public relations professionals in those markets to increase the amount of coverage that they receive for their organizations?

# Managing the Sport Organization–Media Relationship

**After reading this chapter, students should be able to**

- distinguish among influential sport media,
- describe basic services expected by members of the media at organizational events,
- outline guidelines for media accreditation,
- identify key organizational policies related to spokespersons, and
- illustrate tactics used to generate positive publicity.

**Key terms discussed in this chapter include**

- beat reporter,
- credential,
- statistics,
- media rooms,

- media policy,
- human interest story, and
- media tour.

**Chapter 6 defined** mass media and described the unique relationship between the media and sport organizations. Managing that relationship is a critical part of any public relations professional's daily responsibilities. Because the focus of most sport organizations is the events in which they participate, it is tempting to think that the relationship between media and organizations is based solely on those events. Increasingly, however, media cover organizations throughout the year, so public relations professionals must nurture relationships with the media on a regular basis.

This chapter addresses four main topics relating to the sport organization–media relationship. The first deals with identifying influential members of the sport media who frequently cover the organization and understanding their agendas. After public relations practitioners have cultivated relationships with influential members of the media, organizations can provide a high level of service to those media members that will ideally increase the positive publicity garnered by the organization. Providing facilities and services for members of the media who are covering organizational events enables them to focus on reporting. This subject makes up the second section of the chapter. The third section deals with establishing and communicating organizational policies regarding event management and spokesperson availability. Finally, the goal of these strategies is to maximize positive publicity for an organization. The fourth section of the chapter offers suggestions for maximizing positive publicity.

## Identifying Influential Media

Chapter 6 addressed the idea that media are gatekeepers who decide which stories they will cover. This decision is based on several factors, including a determination of the newsworthiness of a story (see chapter 8), and is sometimes referred to as agenda setting, meaning that the media raise issues that both they and their audience consider important. A public relations professional's job involves analyzing the relationship among the organization's activities, the media agenda, and the interests of key publics (Smith, 2005).

One way that public relations professionals can monitor the media agenda is through developing relationships with the media, particularly those who cover the organization on a regular basis. Most print media outlets have various employees, such as beat reporters and columnists, who have a regular interest in the organization's activities. Electronic media tend to have generalists, such as anchors and reporters, who cover a variety of sport organizations.

The very definition of who is, and who is not, media is evolving. Today's media can include Internet-only journalists such as those whose work is published on mainstream websites such as Yahoo and ESPN.com. But the definition of media may include bloggers, those who write and publish content on nonaffiliated websites.

As mentioned in chapter 6, Pedersen, Miloch, and Laucella (2007) conceived of new media, including bloggers, as one of three segments of sport mass media, and Gant (2007) advocated that bloggers acting in the activity of journalism be afforded the same privileges as traditional mass media.

Considerable recent discussion and attention has focused on whether sport organizations should embrace bloggers as mainstream media and provide them similar access or shut them out from the press box altogether (e.g., Dittmore, 2006; Hardin & Zhong, 2009; Mickle, 2006).

The following sections discuss how to identify and work with beat reporters, columnists, electronic media, and bloggers.

## Beat Reporters

The print reporter who sport public relations professionals interact with most frequently is the **beat reporter**. These reporters are assigned to cover a specific geographical or topical beat on an ongoing basis (Hall, Nichols, Moynahan, & Taylor, 2007). The job of beat reporters is to cover their beat for their readers and report newsworthy information that other media outlets have not presented. As Wilstein (2002) stated, a good beat reporter "knows every trade, every move, and the dollar amount of every deal—before it happens" (p. 12).

Beat reporters must frequently write stories when little news exists, such as on noncompetition days. Good public relations professionals should use these opportunities to pitch positive organizational stories to beat reporters. More information on the tactic of pitching will be discussed later in this chapter. Beat reporters are often receptive to these stories if they receive an exclusive, but they must walk a fine line between being an objective reporter and being a friend of the source. Associated Press (AP) sports editor Terry Taylor warned beat reporters against being too friendly with members of the organizations that they cover. She noted, "You're not put on a beat to be anybody's buddy. You're there to report. . . . We would be fairly worthless if we went in and wrote just love letters" (Wilstein, 2002, p. 25).

Public relations professionals should approach relationships with beat reporters cautiously. On the one hand, beat reporters provide regular publicity through their reporting, and because they attend all organizational events they are easy to befriend. On the other hand, beat reporters are taught to remain objective. Their job is to report what they see and hear, even if that does not place the organization in a positive light.

## Columnists

Columnists tend to live slightly more charmed lives than do beat reporters. Whereas beat reporters are supposed to be objective, columnists are meant to be opinionated and sometimes controversial. Beat reporters cover a regular topic day in and day out. Columnists have the freedom to cover whatever is deemed the big story of the day (Hall et al., 2007). Columnists are frequently the best reporters at a given media outlet, often having spent years working as beat reporters (Wilstein, 2002).

What a columnist writes may be disparaging to an organization, resulting in negative publicity. A common saying is that bad publicity is better than no publicity. If that is true, public relations professionals need to exercise caution if they choose to confront a columnist about a negative column. If something is factually incorrect, the public relations person certainly needs to address it with the columnist, but if the column merely states an opinion, such as "The baseball manager is doing a horrible job of leading his team," then the public relations person should usually leave it alone.

Hall, Nichols, Moynahan, and Taylor (2007) reminded public relations professionals that negative news does not necessarily reflect negatively on them. They advised trying to turn a negative column into a positive news story, stating that columnists who write negatively about an organization or individual "give the subjects of their criticism an opportunity to state a position or to take a written or verbal counterpunch at the journalist" (p. 220).

## Electronic Media

Reporters at most local television and radio stations do not function as beat reporters or columnists. More often, reporters at electronic media outlets are generalists, covering many beats simultaneously. The sport public relations professional's job thus becomes somewhat more challenging. Pitching a story to a beat reporter on a nonevent day is easy because the reporter needs to file a story. On the other hand, electronic media, especially in large markets, may choose not to cover an organization on a nonevent day, focusing instead on other organizations in its market.

One way to increase the likelihood of media coverage from the electronic media, particularly television, is to have something visually exciting to cover. Television is a visual medium that requires video to legitimize a story. Although beat reporters or columnists at a newspaper can write an entire story without ever leaving the office, a television reporter needs video interviews and cover video to report a story.

For example, a professional baseball team has a day off in the middle of the week. Several players decide to spend the day visiting sick children in a hospital. The beat reporter can write a story about this event by talking to the players and a hospital spokesperson over the phone. A television station must have video to show with its story, so the station must be present at the hospital. Using visual story ideas such as action and motion is a good way to attract media attention from broadcast media.

## Bloggers

A critique of independent bloggers is that the content they distribute is not subject to editorial review, they lack professionalism, and, in some instances, they can remain anonymous. All these points are in opposition to the role of traditional media. But research by the Curley Center for Sports Journalism at Penn State University suggests otherwise. Their study of sports bloggers indicated that about 80% believed that bloggers should be held to high ethical standards (as compared with greater than 90% believing that mainstream journalists should be held to high standards) and 81% of sports bloggers believed that they should verify information before reporting it (as compared with 96% believing that mainstream journalists should do likewise) (*From Outside the Press Box*, 2009).

Cultivating bloggers does have several public relations advantages for organizations. As Solis and Breakenridge (2009) suggested, "citizen journalists," or bloggers, first encouraged readers to participate through comments and links, creating online conversations. Many of these features are now commonplace on mainstream media sites.

For example, the Atlantic Coast Conference relied on student bloggers to assist in promoting the conference's 2009 Dr. Pepper ACC Championship Game in Tampa, Florida, through links to "campus correspondents reporting on their respective teams throughout the season through their 'Road to Tampa Bay' blogs, Twitter accounts and Flickr photo pages" (Muret, 2009, p. 5).

In addition, the ACC maintains the website representacc.com where the conference hosts a section for campus correspondent blogs, allowing a blogger from each school to post content on an official conference website.

A discussion of whether bloggers should receive credentials similar to mainstream media will be presented later in this chapter.

# Serving Media at Organizational Events

Chapter 1 defined media relations programs as programs designed to generate favorable publicity and minimize unfavorable publicity by fostering desirable relationships with members of the mass media. Many members of the media attend organizational events to report firsthand on what transpired. Although sporting goods manufacturers, fitness centers, and health clubs do not have games or events, they may hold open houses or other functions that may attract media attention.

Working with media at these organizational events is a key part of any public relations person's job. A survey of college sports information directors by Stoldt and Dittmore (2003) found that coordinating media coverage of events was one of the top three areas of expertise within the profession, along with conducting evaluation research and writing news releases and feature stories.

Sport public relations professionals must understand the needs of media members who cover organizational events and provide services for them. This aspect of the organization–media relationship is unique to the sport industry. At any given sporting event, media members covering the event need a place to observe the event, a place to work on their stories, access to statistics and other related information, and access to the participants after the event for news and opinions. In addition, representatives of the different types of mass media have different needs, much of the media are in competition with each other, and some of the media in attendance have likely never been to the facility in which the event is taking place.

## Credential Policies

At most sporting events, people can enter the facility in two ways, with a ticket or with a credential. A credential is a pass that allows the bearer access to the facility without paying for a ticket. Credential holders have the additional expectation of having access to areas of the facility that the ticket-buying public does not.

Because media members need access to athletes and coaches for interviews, providing them with credentials is appropriate. But the organization should exercise some caution when distributing credentials. Accordingly, many organizations develop credential policies that address eligibility requirements and set limits for media outlets. Other concerns relating to credentials include distribution, application forms, and supplementals.

### Eligibility and Limits

Because a credential permits access to an event for free, the first thing that the organization should address when forming a credential policy is deciding who is eligible to receive one. Typically, organizations focus on local media because they are likely the ones who cover the organization closely. Being familiar with the reach and circulation of local media is a critical first step to determining eligibility. Is a local weekly community paper that focuses primarily on high school sport eligible for a credential to cover a professional football team? What about the writers for an Internet-only fan site?

Those questions can be difficult to answer. On the one hand, the organization is seeking to maximize exposure for its programs and should welcome all forms of media. On the other hand, the space available in the facility for media seating is probably finite. What will happen if a national news outlet requests a credential just before the event? Surely the sport public relations person would welcome the national exposure for the organization, but accommodating the national outlet might be a challenge if space is limited because several smaller media outlets have credentials.

When determining eligibility requirements, organizations should consider what benefits they might derive from the media's presence. Hall, Nichols, Moynahan, and Taylor (2007) observed that a university may wish to exclude representatives from gambling-related publications and media outlets that do not regularly offer sports coverage. In the case of gaming publications, including fantasy sports publications, league or governing body policy may already address their exclusion.

Consider hypothetical media outlet eligibility for an Iowa State University basketball game. The university is located in Ames, Iowa, just north of Des Moines. Both Ames and Des Moines have daily newspapers, and the market has three television stations and several radio stations. In addition, the sports information office at Iowa State will likely get requests from the university's student paper and television or radio station. Because the university is a large state institution, it may also receive requests from television stations in the Cedar Rapids, Sioux City, and Mason City markets, as well as requests from daily newspapers in Cedar Rapids, Waterloo, Iowa City, and many other towns. Iowa State will want to consider how frequently those organizations cover Iowa State athletics and whether their audiences and circulations reach important publics such as alumni. From that information, the university can develop some sort of internal pecking order for determining eligibility. For example, if the only time that the Iowa City *Press-Citizen* covers Iowa State is when it is playing the University of Iowa, which is located in Iowa City, then the *Press-Citizen* might be lower in the pecking order for a contest not involving both Iowa State and Iowa than the Mason City *Globe Gazette,* which is closer to Ames.

Like eligibility, limits are somewhat subjective and vary among organizations. One factor may be physical space. If an organization's press row for a basketball game has 15 seats and one newspaper is requesting 5 of them, the public relations staff needs to decide whether providing one-third of available media seating to one news outlet is appropriate. If the organization issues more credentials than it can accommodate, it may need to find alternative seating for the media or perhaps squeeze them into existing space. One option would be to assign the media specific seats in the seating bowl, which may not have a view as good as that on press row. This option should be the last one, however, because it eliminates potential revenue (i.e., foregone ticket sales) for the organization.

Developing a pecking order for media outlets with respect to eligibility and limits of credentials carries some risk. Media outlets may feel slighted if they are considered a low-priority outlet, and regular media may resent being forced to compete with low-priority media for space and access. Hall, Nichols, Moynahan, and Taylor (2007) advised sport organizations to stick to a policy rather than try to accommodate everyone. Trying to squeeze in extra reporters "may cause greater relationship problems with those media organizations that regularly cover the team. Better to deny access to low-priority journalists at the outset than to provide substandard work space and assistance to all" (p. 157).

Many writers and photographers work as freelancers, meaning that they contract their services to various media outlets. Freelance photographers may ask for credentials to shoot a sporting event without an affiliation. Their hope is that they can sell their photos to media outlets after the event is over or on an as-requested basis. Sport organizations need to address freelance requests in their credential policy. Ultimately, each organization needs to evaluate credentials for freelancers as appropriate. One common tactic is to grant a credential to a freelance journalist only if she or he can produce a letter from a legitimate media outlet indicating that a contract exists between the individual and the media outlet. This letter should be forwarded to the public relations person on the media's letterhead to ensure authenticity.

## Bloggers and Content Restriction

As with freelance journalists, organizations need to consider whether to credential bloggers and decide what type of access they are willing to provide to them. Although individual sport organizations have credentialed bloggers on a case-by-case basis, research has revealed that most organizations have yet to formalize policies regarding bloggers and those who do have policies rely on leagues or conferences to provide guidance (Dittmore, Stoldt, Bass, & Biery, 2009).

Some of the considerations for organizations when establishing credential policies for bloggers include the interests of existing rights holders and the ways in which bloggers might impinge on the value of those rights through frequent updates and live blogging. To address this issue, the Southeastern Conference attempted to enforce a policy before the 2009 football season that would have prohibited not just media but also ticketed fans from producing or disseminating "any material or information about the Event, including, but not limited to, any account, description, picture, video, audio, reproduction or other information concerning the Event" (Ostrow, 2009). The SEC quickly relented and changed its policy before the season began to permit "personal messages and updates of scores or other brief descriptions of competition throughout the Event" (Ostrow, 2009).

Research into the legality of such restrictions is inconclusive. Although facts from sporting events are available in the public domain and are not protected under the Copyright Act of 1976, sports broadcasts are protected because each game is a unique script, the result is unknown, and the camera angles represent original interpretations of the game (Garmire, 2000).

In several high-profile incidents, bloggers and accredited journalists have been denied access or have been kicked out of sporting events because of violations of blogging policies. In 2007 the NCAA removed Louisville *Courier-Journal* writer Brian Bennett from a NCAA Super Regional baseball game for live blogging, which it considered a live representation of the game (Bozich, 2007). Similarly, the Edmonton Oilers of the NHL removed a writer from the press box in October 2008 for live blogging for the Oilers fan site coveredinoil.blogspot.com.

Dallas Mavericks owner Mark Cuban created a controversy in March 2008 when he banned all full-time bloggers from the team's locker room. At the time of the ban, the only person who blogged full time about the Mavericks was a reporter for the *Dallas Morning News*. The NBA league office stepped in, stating that bloggers from credentialed news organizations must be admitted (Arango, 2008).

At the heart of these incidents are restrictions placed on individuals who are granted official credentials to cover an event. Dittmore, Stoldt, Bass, and Biery (2009) explored the common types of restrictions employed by sport organizations. These included parameters on the number of updates and photographs that a person may post, the amount and length of video that may be posted, and the use of statistical information, among several other restrictions.

This evolving topic illustrates the importance of developing an organizational policy for bloggers and blogging, particularly as it relates to media relations. Research by Dittmore, Crow, and Fields (2010) concluded that although organizations appreciate the exposure generated from social media, sport media relations professionals are not aware of case law to guide policy development. Those professionals do understand that protecting the interests of rights holders is a focal point for policy development.

## Creation and Distribution

Sport organizations customarily distribute credentials to their regular media and beat reporters in advance, often creating a pass that is good for the whole season. The public relations professional should also create a number of event-specific credentials that can be distributed to opposing media and any nonregular media. Credentials are best displayed on a lanyard and worn around the neck. The credential should be laminated to prevent falsification. Credentials of different colors are often given to different groups of people. For example, media may wear red credentials, whereas coaches may wear blue credentials. This system helps event security personnel identify who has access to specific areas.

Another method involves printing a new pass for each game, perhaps in a different color than the previous game. This method helps event personnel recognize proper credentials for any given game, although it may be problematic for sports like baseball and basketball that have many games and therefore require many colors.

Regardless of which method is employed, the credential must be both person specific, that is, have the individual's name and organization on it, and event specific. Some high-profile events such as the Olympic Games require the person's photo as well as name. This system prevents the transfer of the credential to an unapproved individual. Sport organizations may wish to print the person's name on the credential with a computer program or simply write the name in permanent marker. A credential should also include the date and time of the event for which it is valid.

Distributing credentials before the season to beat reporters is often accomplished in person, perhaps at the organization's offices or at a media day. For opposing media and game-specific media, the organization should create a media will call window near the media entrance to the facility. Credentials should be available for pickup by the media no later than three hours before the event begins. The will call window should remain open throughout the event because some media may not arrive until after the event begins. Media should be required to show some form of photo identification when picking up their credentials. Condron (2001) cautioned against underestimating this aspect of the process, stating, "A good media will call system is the key to an overall media operation."

For high-profile events, such as the National Collegiate Athletic Association (NCAA) men's and women's basketball championships, advance planning time may be limited. Organizations hosting an event similar to these championships may choose to create a credential pickup area at the official media hotel for the event, although the organization should still arrange for a will call pickup site at the facility on the day of the event.

## Application Forms

Sport public relations professionals should require all media outlets, even beat reporters with whom they are familiar, to submit some form of credential application. Figure 7.1 shows a sample event credential application form for the ING New York City Marathon. Typically these forms are filled out by a sport or photo editor at a print media outlet and by

## Credential Management System

<u>**Welcome to the ING New York City Marathon Credential Application**</u>

Thank you for your interest in covering the 42nd running of the ING New York City Marathon on Sunday, November 6.

This form is intended for journalists, photographers, broadcast or webcast companies, sponsor photographers, or filmmakers. **If you are completing an application for more than one person associated with your organization, please click** <u>here</u> **for the group form.** New York Road Runners recommends that applicants fill out the application completely and include as much information as possible so we can provide you with the appropriate access.

PLEASE NOTE:  IN ORDER TO PROCESS YOUR APPLICATION YOU MUST CLICK THE SUBMIT BUTTON AT THE BOTTOM OF THE APPLICATION.

You will receive a confirmation email if you application was successfully received. If you did not receive an email please contact <u>credentials@nyrr.org</u>.

If you see the message "There are errors with your submission." Please return to your application by accepting the terms and conditions again and correct the missing fields.

For more information on the race, visit <u>www.ingnycmarathon.org</u>

I have read and agree to all the contents of the <u>Terms and Conditions</u>. I also confirm that I am authorized to agree to the ING New York City Marathon's 2011 Terms and Conditions on behalf of my media organization and its employees.

**NOTICE:** In consideration of the grant to me of these credentials, I hereby, for myself, my heirs, executors and administrators, and anyone else entitled to act on my behalf, **WAIVE AND RELEASE** New York Road Runners, Inc., Road Runners Club of America, The City of New York and its agencies and departments, USA Track and Field, USATF-Metropolitan, and all Sponsors (including, but not limited to, ING), and their respective agents and representatives, from any and all present and future claims and liabilities of any kind, known or unknown, for any personal injury or property damage that I may incur in connection with the ING New York City Marathon 2011 or any related events/activites, even though any such claim or liability may arise out of negligence or fault on the part of any of the foregoing persons or entities.

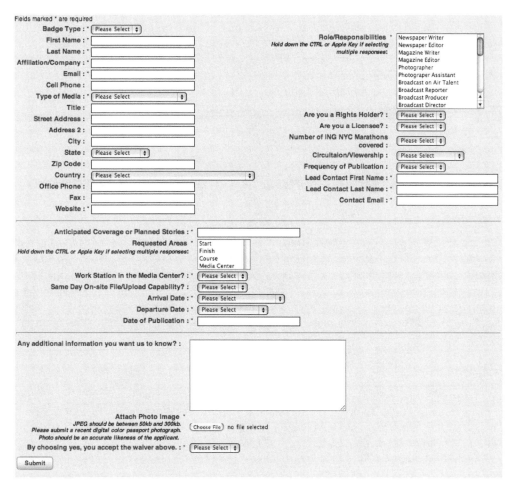

**Figure 7.1**  Media credential application form.

Reprinted, by permission, from ING New York City Marathon.

a sport director at an electronic outlet. These forms are relatively standard and should ask for basic information such as name of the media outlet, contact information, individual names, and type of media (print, photo, or broadcast). The latter information will be helpful in budgeting for supplementals, which are explained in the next section.

As a part of the organization's media credential policy, public relations professionals need to determine whether they will accept credential requests through e-mail, fax, in person, and over the phone. Although media members expect to fill out a credential application form for most events, many believe that sending an e-mail or picking up the phone to request a credential is more efficient. In addition, the organization's policy commonly indicates a specific time after which it will not accept applications for a given event.

### Supplementals

Most sport event managers place restrictions on who can access areas close to the field of play such as the sidelines at football games and the baselines at basketball games. These locations are desirable for photographers and television broadcasters, who need to be as close to the action as possible to capture the best images. Many organizations require some form of additional credential, called a supplemental, to access these areas.

Common supplementals include wristbands, stickers, or sleeves that members of the media are required to wear at all times to gain access to those areas. Supplementals along with a valid media credential should provide access to field-of-play areas. Sport public relations professionals should closely regulate who receives supplementals and should develop event-specific supplementals similar to event-specific credentials. This system prevents people from attempting to use one supplemental for several events.

Figure 7.2 outlines typical credential policies adopted by professional sport organizations.

## Press Box

The late Leonard Koppett, a legendary sportswriter for the *New York Times*, titled his memoir *The Rise and Fall of the Press Box* (2003). The book is a collection of stories from his career combined with lamentations regarding the current state of the sport organization–media relationship. Koppett began by stating that once upon a time, the press box was a "special place where millions of Americans of all ages and all segments of society yearned to be" (p. 3). It was, he said, restricted to working press. Koppett was referring to a period from the 1930s to the 1970s when the importance of newspaper coverage of sporting events was at its height. The press box in baseball

---

## Miami Dolphins Media Credential Policies

### Credentials

Media representatives who do not have press credentials for the entire season (but will be working for an accredited media outlet on an immediate deadline) may request them on a single-game basis. Written credential requests must be made at least one week in advance. Reserved credentials can be picked up at the press gate, located outside Gate G of Pro Player Stadium, on the day of the game. ALL members of the media picking up credentials at the will call window must present a valid photo identification. In addition, all media members must show a valid photo identification upon entering the stadium.

### Photographers

Photographers with accredited media outlets on an immediate deadline may request credentials on a single-game basis from the Dolphins' media relations department. Credentials **WILL NOT** be issued to freelance photographers unless granted special approval by the Dolphins. Field photographers are reminded to remain outside of the bench area. ALL photographers and runners are required to wear wristbands that must be obtained before the game in the Gate G lobby.

---

**Figure 7.2** Miami Dolphins credential policies.

From Greene, Gulkis, and Levit 2004.

was controlled not by the organization, but by the local chapter of the Baseball Writers Association of America.

The press box in today's sport environment is still used by working media, but access is no longer exclusive to that constituency and its management rests squarely with the sport organization. The press box has become a gathering place for sponsors, scouts, agents, team officials and their guests, and many other groups invited into the space by the organization governing the press box. Koppett (2003) blamed this change on television broadcasters, who closely protect access to their broadcast booths, and on sport organizations, which concentrate their efforts on servicing the broadcasters who reach the public more quickly than newspapers and pay the organization for that privilege.

Given the premier location of the press box in most stadiums and arenas, it is not surprising that groups other than the media want access. Sight lines from the press box are among the best in the building, and sport organizations give those seats to members of the media for free. Imagine how much revenue the organization could generate by selling the 50-yard-line seats given to the media at football games. The idea is that the publicity generated by media coverage of its events is worth more than the revenue produced by selling those seats to the public. Sport organizations provide a variety of services to members of the media in the press box as a way of promoting positive publicity. Many of these services have become so commonplace that media members frequently take them for granted. These services include workspace, technology, hospitality, and statistics.

## Workspace

The primary purpose of a press box is to provide accredited, working members of the media with a place to sit and record the actions of the event. The location of this space varies from sport to sport. In baseball, the press box is typically located halfway up the stands behind home plate, whereas in basketball the press box may consist of a row of tables and chairs along the side of the court. Regardless of the location, certain fundamental and often unstated rules govern the workspace.

First, the press box is intended for the media who are covering the event. Public relations professionals should make every attempt to remove people who do not meet this criterion. Second, the workspace should be free of cheering on the part of the occupants. Most members of the media understand the need to remain objective and adhere to this code. public relations professionals and other organizational employees must subscribe to this policy as well.

A third assumed policy of the press box is that some level of hierarchy will be evident through the assignment of seat locations. Separate booths or rooms are generally provided for broadcast media, including television, the home organization's radio broadcasters, and the visiting organization's radio team. Within the main press box workspace, public relations professionals should assign space to specific media organizations. There is no set formula or protocol for this. Helitzer (1996) suggested using a seniority hierarchy for assigning seats. Hall, Nichols, Moynahan, and Taylor (2007) advised providing beat reporters and other regulars the same seat locations each week. Public relations professionals may wish to group visiting media together in one section.

Regardless of how the space is assigned, public relations professionals should place name tags on each seat to eliminate confusion. They may also wish to post a seating diagram on the wall throughout the press box to help members of the media identify their assigned seats.

## Technology

Another service provided by sport organizations to accredited, working members of the sport media is technology to assist with their work. Technology includes a variety of services such as telecommunication and televisions.

### Telecommunication

Most writers and photographers submit stories and pictures over a wireless or broadband connection. Sport organizations are expected to provide access to telephones throughout the workspace. The ratio of phones to seats can vary, but one phone for every two seats is not uncommon. The organization may wish to limit these phones to local and toll-free calls only and require members of the media to pay for any long-distance charges that they might incur, however most media will bring a mobile phone for personal calls.

Wireless broadband connections have become commonplace in press areas. Often these wireless networks are password protected and members of the media need to obtain a password from a public relations staff member. Media outlets may wish to install their own broadband connections or phone lines in the press box at their expense. Sport public relations professionals should assist the media in setting up this service and should monitor use of that connection to ensure that only the correct media organization is using the service. Sport organizations should also provide a fax machine for media use and apply similar restrictions on long-distance dialing as with telephones.

## Televisions

If a sport organization's event is being televised, members of the media working in the press box expect a feed of the telecast to be available on television monitors in the press box or on tables along a basketball press row. Media members use this service to view replays of controversial or important plays as a way of formulating story ideas and angles. If millions of people are watching an event in their living rooms on television, journalists covering the event in person must be able to see what they are watching as well.

## *Hospitality*

Condron (2001) stated that a hospitality area for the media "doesn't help the writers write a better story or the radio play-by-play men do a better broadcast, but it is usually appreciated by the various media." Because event times often overlap with normal meal times, having some type of food service will assist the media who are covering the event. Food may also encourage them to arrive earlier or stay later, affording the organization a greater opportunity to discuss story ideas in person.

The downside to providing food and beverage is the cost incurred. Because of the cost, hospitality varies from soft drinks and cookies to a full buffet. By working with the organization's marketing department, the public relations department may be able to secure donated sandwiches or pizza from one of the organization's sponsors, reducing out-of-pocket hospitality expenses.

## *Statistics*

**Statistics** have evolved in sport as a way of comparing performances over history. Barry Bonds' pursuit of the all-time baseball home-run record was important because it compared his ability with that of Babe Ruth and Hank Aaron. If no one had kept statistics when Ruth played in the 1920s there would be no way of measuring Bonds' ability compared to that of his predecessors. The Base Ball Reporters Association of America invented a standard method for keeping score and statistics in baseball in 1887 (Seymour, 1960). This standardization led to the regular inclusion of box scores with game stories.

Keeping and tracking statistics has evolved into a large part of the sport public relations professional's job. Archival statistics and historical records can be found in every organization's media guide. Story ideas emerge from players' or teams' pursuit of statistical records, many of which are documented in the public relations office. Recording and distributing these statistics in a timely fashion is a critical component of a sport organization's public relations.

Professional sport leagues typically use standard statistical programs to record an event's action, but the NCAA does not mandate use of specific statistical programs by member institutions. Certain programs, however, are widely used and are available from several vendors. According to James Wright of the NCAA's statistics division, to avoid compatibility problems, the NCAA has created its own program that is universally compatible with any statistical programs used by conferences and member institutions (J. Wright, personal communication, June 4, 2004). Thus, the NCAA is able to avoid the problems that can arise when information is shared among various statistical programs.

Among the vendors offering statistical programs for various sports are StatCrew, Daktronics, and Hy-Tek. The most widely used programs are those offered by StatCrew, which claims to have more than 2,000 colleges as well as conferences, high schools, and minor league teams as customers (StatCrew, n.d.). StatCrew produces statistical software programs for basketball, baseball, softball, football, volleyball, ice hockey, soccer, field hockey, lacrosse, and tennis.

Statistical software programs can be used to track cumulative season statistics as well as individual events, and they offer a variety of output options. During an event, frequently generated reports include play by play, scoring summary, team and individual statistics, drive charts, and quickie stats, which are brief statistical synopses that may be generated during time-outs.

Organizations purchase statistic software programs directly from vendors. After the program is installed, the organization must train people on data-entry operations for the software. Procedures, equipment, and individuals needed to operate statistic programs will vary based on the budgets and practices of the organization. No set policies exist for the number of staff required to work an event.

For basketball, most statistical programs require six or seven people. One person is needed to enter data into the program, and one or two people function as spotters, dictating the event action to the data-entry person. One or two people are needed to map the shot chart manually, and at least three people should be conducting simultaneous manual statistical calculations in the event that the data on the computer is lost.

Statistics should be available at regular intervals, such as between quarters or halves, to the media in attendance at events. The public relations professional should oversee staff whose job is to secure a printout of the statistical summary from those running the statistical program. That summary should be photocopied and literally run to the media in attendance. Priority should be given to members of the electronic media who are covering the event live. Writers and other media members not on urgent deadlines should be next. In some cases, the public relations staff may also be responsible for delivering statistics to the coaching staffs of both teams. At the end of a contest, copies of the summaries should be taken to the interview room where reporters gather to ask questions of coaches and players.

### Blogging Areas

The New York Islanders and the Los Angeles Dodgers are two organizations that have embraced blogger access, although in distinctly different fashions. In 2007 the Islanders created the NYI Blog Box, which accommodates several fan blogs in an official media capacity. Participants in the Blog Box watch the game in the press box and are granted access to players and coaches to conduct interviews afterward. According to Islanders director of communications Kimber Auerbach, the Islanders hope "to become a leader in how teams embrace the blogosphere" (Eisenberg, 2010).

The Dodgers have regularly held Blogger Nights at Dodger Stadium when several fan bloggers are invited to watch a game from a suite in Dodger Stadium and are given access to executives in the organization such as general manager Ned Colletti and retired Hall of Fame manager Tommy Lasorda. In addition, the Dodgers have granted media credentials from time to time to bloggers to cover the game from the Vin Scully Press Box, participate in the manager's pre- and postgame talks, and gain access to the team clubhouse.

Although both examples present professionalism challenges to the organizations, they have helped create stronger relationships between the clubs and their primary constituents, their fan bases. Bloggers who write about the experience generally present positive images of the organization to their readership and share photos and behind-the-scene details of the organization.

## Media Operations Checklist

Sport public relations professionals may find it helpful to develop a generic checklist for each event that their organization is running. This checklist can be used to track milestone completion dates as well as delegation of responsibilities. The following items are essential for a successful media operation.

### Credentials

- Application form
- Will call distribution
- Design of pass
- Supplemental for on-field access

### Press Box

- Seating chart
- Name tags for assigned seats
- Telephones
- Internet access
- Power
- Television monitors
- Fax machine
- Photocopier
- Statistics crew with computer and software
- Hospitality

### Media Room

- Publicity materials
- Telephones
- Internet access
- Television monitors
- Power
- Fax machine
- Photocopier
- Hospitality
- Coat racks
- Designated storage areas

### Parking

- Location
- Design of pass

143

## Media Rooms

In contrast to press boxes, which are places to work, **media rooms** are "fundamentally a hospitality suite to serve management's varied interests" (Koppett, 2003, p. 16). That differentiation is fairly accurate, although media rooms serve a work function as well, especially at events that do not have a large press box such as basketball. Media rooms may offer many of the same amenities and services as a press box does, including technology, hospitality, workspace, and statistics. In addition, the sport organization should provide a photocopier for media use and to photocopy statistics and other publicity materials.

Media rooms also function as a base from which public relations staff may distribute publicity materials to the media such as game notes, media guides, and schedules. Each of these items is discussed in more detail in later chapters. The media expect visiting organizations to have similar materials available in the media room. If an organization has a separate media room, it should plan to have a staff member present in the room before, during, and after an event. Journalists frequently use media rooms to store belongings.

## Parking

In addition to the press box and media room, journalists expect the organization to provide free onsite parking in proximity to the media entrance. The organization's marketing department may protest, arguing that those close-in parking spots could be sold to groups who actually pay the organization money, such as season-ticket holders or sponsors. Sport managers may choose to combine the media parking lot with other VIP or reserved parking at the facility.

The media's expectation of parking is based on a couple of factors. First, media members generally bring bags of heavy equipment with them to cover an event, whether they are writers, photographers, or broadcasters. A close-in parking space minimizes the distance that they have to walk from their vehicles to the facility. Second, media members often stay at the facility to file stories long after the ticket-buying public has left. The proximity of media parking may alleviate any concerns about leaving a facility late at night.

A final concern for sport public relations professionals at an event is a formal interview area. Chapter 9 presents more information on formal interview rooms, and the media operations checklist in this chapter provides an inventory of items and issues that sport public relations professionals should consider before hosting an event.

# Developing a Media Policy

Sport organizations command a high level of media attention, so sport managers should consider developing a media policy. Mathews (2004) defined a **media policy** as "a set of guiding principles and behaviors to help ensure consistent, fair and ethical communication with all of your constituents" (p.46). Those principles and behaviors should include identifying who within the organization speaks to the media, what employees should do if they are contacted by the media, and when coaches and players are available to the media. These policies should apply when individuals are being interviewed for a media story and are not just playing an information services role. Chapter 8 details the information services roles played by the sport public relations professional, and chapter 9 focuses on specific interview concerns.

## Identifying the Organizational Spokesperson

The organizational spokesperson is the voice of the organization and answers the media's questions. The spokesperson may be a senior member of the organization, such as a president or general manager, or may be one of the organization's public relations professionals, such as a sports information director.

Some sport organizations develop a hierarchical approach to the spokesperson role based on the information that the media are seeking. Senior management may speak on topics of importance, and the public relations professional may address routine operations. For example, in the case of an announcement about a coach's dismissal, the organization's general manager or athletic director would be the best person to act as spokesperson because he or she is likely the person who decided to dismiss the coach. But if a media member is looking to confirm when tickets will go on sale for an organization's postseason game, the public relations professional would usually handle the request. Chapter 9 discusses the advantages and disadvantages of using senior management as organizational spokespeople.

At the college level, Stoldt, Miller, and Comfort (2001) found that athletic directors considered a sports information staff member to be their department's top public relations official. But the same survey revealed that although athletic directors were highly confident regarding their sports information staff members' ability to complete technical tasks such as maintaining media contacts, they were less confident in their ability to complete managerial tasks such as mediating conflicts, which may require the sports information director to act as a spokesperson.

A final rule of thumb for identifying an organizational spokesperson is to allow the person who has the greatest knowledge, and thus the highest degree of credibility, about a given subject to speak on behalf of the organization. As an example, let's say that a university is building a new on-campus natatorium. A reporter may be interested in knowing precisely how much dirt needs to be moved to grade the land or how much concrete needs to be poured. In this case, the project manager is likely to have the most intimate knowledge of such details and would be the most credible spokesperson.

## Developing an Employee Media Policy

Journalists are taught to be creative and enterprising when it comes to gathering information for a story. Occasionally, a reporter will bypass organizational protocol and contact an employee directly. Organizations should therefore have an employee media policy stating that only the organization's public relations office will speak to the media.

If employees in another department such as accounting receive a call from a reporter, they should refer the reporter to the public relations office. In certain situations, the public relations person, after learning the nature of the reporter's inquiry, may have the accounting employee talk to the reporter because that employee may be the best person to answer the question.

## Determining Coach and Athlete Availability

Unique to sport organizations is coach and athlete availability. Coaches and athletes devote a great deal of time to competition and training and may view media interviews as a disruption to their preparation for an upcoming event. To minimize these intrusions, many sport organizations adopt media policies that set aside specific times when coaches and athletes will be available to speak with the media. Media understand that requests that fall outside those times may not be honored. Limitations might be considered for practice days as well as competition days.

Most policies on coach and athlete availability are communicated to the media either in the organization's media guide or a news release. Media are usually required to contact the organization's sports information or public relations office to arrange the interview ahead of time.

Rutgers University has adopted a policy regarding player interview availability for its football program that precludes player interviews after Wednesday on game weeks. Rutgers allows in-person interviews with players on Tuesdays and Wednesdays, and additional availability is offered at times that are mutually convenient for the player and media. Similarly, Rutgers limits interviews with its head football coach to Mondays on the Big East conference call, Tuesdays at the stadium, and Wednesdays following practice. All other times must be coordinated in advance (Rutgers, n.d.).

Adopting a policy such as the one used at Rutgers allows better planning on the part of the media, coaches, and athletes. Members of the media know that if they wish to speak with someone, they should plan on being at a certain location at a certain time. Coaches and athletes know that they will not be continually distracted by interviews as they prepare for an upcoming competition.

Following an event, an organization may choose to open its locker room to the media following a cooling-off period of around 10 minutes. Most professional sport leagues mandate that coaches and athletes be available for interviews following a game. For example, the National Basketball Association (NBA) mandates that each team have an open locker room before and after a competition. Media representatives are allowed in the locker room for 45 minutes before a game, beginning 90 minutes before tip-off. They are allowed back into the locker room 10 minutes after the conclusion of the game. On nongame days, players and coaches must be available for 30 minutes (Fortunato, 2000). Failure to adhere to these guidelines may result in sanctions against the team or individual. LeBron James, then of the Cleveland Cavaliers, was fined $25,000 by the NBA after he failed to make himself available to the media following the final game of the NBA's 2009 Eastern Conference finals (*LeBron Apologizes*, 2009).

## Being Prepared to Take Advantage of Athletic Success

**Tom Kelly**

Photo courtesy of U.S. Ski and Snowboard Association.

There's no greater thrill in sport than being at the finish of an athletic competition, sharing in the revelry with an athlete who has just achieved victory. Victory comes in many shapes and sizes. As a public relations professional responsible for integrating athletes with the media, the frenzied excitement of working the postevent victory is exhilarating.

But just how prepared are you to manage that victory for your athletes?

The Winter Olympics in Lillehammer, Norway, in 1994 were memorable for U.S. skiing. Tommy Moe opened with a gold medal in the men's downhill. Picabo Street burst onto the scene with a silver in the women's downhill, and Diann Roffe added a surprise gold in the super G. Another silver from Tommy in super G and a mogul silver from Liz McIntyre gave the U.S. ski team an unprecedented five medals.

The team's work on-site garnered enormous media attention, including a *Sports Illustrated* cover. But when the Games concluded, our athletes headed to remote locations and were hardly heard from again. The thrill of victory evaporated. Our medalists enjoyed zero television appearances after the Olympics. That experience opened our eyes to how difficult managing victory can be.

The Lillehammer experience led to the development of the U.S. Ski and Snowboard Association's (USSA's) Managing Victory plan. There was no rocket science to the plan—it was simple and straightforward, designed to seize the window of opportunity in the 7 to 10 days after a major athletic victory. Today's news is tomorrow's history. For athletes to achieve the public recognition they deserve, you have to strike while the iron is hot.

USSA's Managing Victory plan is a turnkey process adaptable to any sport program. It can be applied to a known major event, or, better yet, it can be in place in anticipation of unexpected athletic success. The plan consists of five basic elements:

1. Identify key athletes in advance.
2. Develop media training programs for both athletes and coaches.
3. Develop advance public relations awareness with media.
4. Capitalize on the athletic success both during the event and in the period immediately following it.
5. Return to athletic competition.

## Identify Key Athletes

Identification of key athletes is critical. Although team environments require a balance of fairness to all athletes, the individual identification and support of top athletes will help the entire program. Identify not only those athletes with the best chance of victory but also their story angles and personalities. Winning isn't everything; you have to have a human interest story to go with it.

## Use Media Training

Media training has become relatively common, and athletes at all levels learn how to give basic interviews. But a couple key factors can make this training truly successful. First, make the coaching staff a key part of the training process. Your success in taking advantage of an athlete's success depends on how well you have included the coaches. Your ability to educate the coaches about the benefits of having the athlete spend time with media will be paramount to your success.

Second, although developing interview skills is important, even more important for both the athlete and the coach is understanding why interaction with the media is important. How will it help the athletics program? How will it help the individual athlete? How can it be integrated with sensitivity into the athletics program?

My personal experience is that the most successful public relations professionals are those who take the time to understand the athlete–coach and competition–training relationships. Don't be a bull in a china shop—walk delicately to ensure that you have full buy-in from the coaching staff and therefore the athletes.

## Develop Public Awareness

After you've identified the athletes and have buy-in through media training, get to work telling the story. Telling the story in advance is critical to having media poised for athletic success. But this task requires walking a fine line. Be careful not to create unrealistic expectations or place undue pressure on the athlete. That line varies from athlete to athlete. Some are comfortable talking about expectations, and some are not. Just remember that each athlete is different.

The goal here is twofold: First, create awareness among the media so that the athlete is at least somewhat recognized, and second, be prepared so that when victory occurs, you are ready with background, statistics, and a media plan.

## Capitalize

A good athlete is prepared at the start of every competition and expects to win. As a public relations professional, you need to do the same. It's easy to give in to the temptation to relax or to make plans with friends after the event. If you want to do your job in managing victory for your athlete or team, you have to be as poised, focused, and prepared as the athletes are! It's game day, and you need to come into each competition with your game face on and ready to go. Treat every event as if it were the Super Bowl.

I've found that most public relations professionals are prepared on game day for managing the finish or immediate postgame but lack the planning and focus for the long-term push. That push might be getting next-tier national media exposure after the event or a long-term media tour in the next days or weeks.

The success of follow-up comes down to two factors:

1. Have you done a good job planning for the media push?
2. Do you truly have buy-in from your coaches and therefore your athletes?

Let's think back to our media training program. Did you do a good enough job educating the coaches? Do the coaches understand the importance of having their athletes take time to capitalize on their victory? Have they bought in sufficiently to let athletes take that time in the midst of an athletic training and competition period?

> My personal experience is that the most successful public relations professionals are those who take the time to understand the athlete–coach and competition–training relationships. Don't be a bull in a china shop—walk delicately to ensure that you have full buy-in from the coaching staff and therefore the athletes.

## Return to Athletic Competition

With any luck you've been successful in managing victory for your athlete or team—you've gained the buy-in of coaches and athletes and have conducted a successful postvictory period of media exposure that will benefit the athletes and program for years to come.

One of the keys to success is making sure that everyone understands that in even the biggest of sports, the window of opportunity closes quickly. A victory in the biggest event of the season in February will be old news when the season ends in April.

*(continued)*

*(continued)*

Assuming that your campaign for managing victory is successful, you have only two additional responsibilities. First, return the athletes to their athletics program according to your plan with the coaches. Second, take time to evaluate your program for managing victory and share that evaluation with the athletes and coaches.

At the 1994 Olympics we had no meaningful post-Olympic national television appearances. By managing victory, in 1998 we increased that to about 35 appearances. Our coach and athlete buy-in that year was so strong that coaches actually allowed their athletes to skip international competitions. Four years later, at the 2002 Salt Lake City Olympics, we increased the total national television appearances to about 150.

Managing victory is not rocket science. There's no magic wand. And there are really no requisite skills, except one: planning. It's a simple process that only requires you to take the time to plan and to build relationships. As a public relations professional, you hold the key to public manifestation of athletic success. Take the time to ensure that your athletes get the credit they deserve by managing victory!

*Tom Kelly is the vice president of marketing communications for the USSA. He manages athlete public relations programs across six different ski and snowboard sports, including 14 different national teams.*

# Maximizing Media Exposure

The goal for most sport organizations is to achieve the pinnacle of athletic success. But there can be only one World Series or Stanley Cup champion each year, so approximately 30 organizations in MLB or the NHL did not realize their goal. When that singular moment comes along and the organization finds itself on top of the athletics world, it enjoys a unique public relations opportunity. This opportunity requires the public relations professional to act quickly to help the organization achieve as much exposure as possible. Without the support of organizational management, however, gaining maximum exposure can be difficult. It is easy to get caught up in the excitement of winning a world championship or an Olympic medal. Athletes want to share these moments with teammates, friends, and family. The public relations professional needs to convince management and the athletes that using the media is a positive way to capitalize on that excitement.

The key to maximizing exposure in such situations is for the public relations person to know the organization's product. In this sense, the job is similar to marketing. The public relations professional must know what makes the product unique, how to package and position the product, and how to sell it to the media.

As an example, consider the Olympic Games. No sporting event in the world receives as much media exposure as the Olympics. It is hard to imagine the Olympics without swimming, diving, gymnastics, basketball, volleyball, and the other major sports, and media members actively seek stories on those sports because the public is interested in them. But what about the other 20 or more sports in the Games? How do the public relations for archery and synchronized swimming compete for media coverage? Here the public relations professional needs to think like a marketer. The U.S. Ski and Snowboard Association (USSA) aggressively employs this strategy in its Managing Victory plan after medal-winning performances by its athletes. Tom Kelly, vice president of marketing communications for the association, shares the vision for maximizing this type of exposure in the sidebar titled Being Prepared to Take Advantage of Athletic Success (p. 146).

# What Makes the Product Unique?

Some professional and intercollegiate sports sell themselves. The media pay close attention to them. As a result, the jobs of public relations professionals for those organizations are frequently reactive rather than proactive. But what does the public relations professional do if the media do not know the sport well? Understanding what makes that sport different from others can help sell the story to the media, creating valuable publicity for the organization.

Synchronized swimming is a good example of a nonmainstream sport that garners attention every four years during the Olympics. Despite being physically demanding, the sport has a somewhat negative image. *Saturday Night Live*'s lampoon created an unforgettable image in the minds of the public. In addition, its athletes are female, making it less appealing to males. Understanding those stereotypes was the first step to understanding what is unique about the sport.

U.S. Synchronized Swimming routinely focuses on media outlets that are female friendly and challenges misconceptions about the difficulty of the sport by offering members of the media an opportunity to "synch or sink" in the pool with the U.S. National Team (Eaton, 2001). Rather than fight the stereotypes, the organization recognizes the associations that make its sport unique.

# Packaging and Positioning the Product

Marketers want to use physically attractive packaging for their products to appeal to consumers. Public relations professionals, on the other hand, need to package their products in ways that are appealing to members of the media in the hopes that they will deliver it to the consumer. This is where public relations professionals can distinguish themselves as valuable members of their organizations. Public relations professionals have many tactics at their disposal in packaging the product. Chapter 8 addresses the most common tactic, the news release, as well as other information services, and chapter 9 focuses on news conferences and interviews.

Before choosing which tactic to employ, public relations professionals must first identify how to position the product. In many cases, positioning involves identifying something of interest regarding the organization or athlete, usually related to individual or athletic achievement. Helitzer (1996) stated that good sport stories "keep the self-interest of individuals in mind—their involvement, their benefit and their caring" (p. 207). These story ideas are typically categorized as human interest stories, whereas recognition stories focus on awards or athletic achievement.

## Human Interest Stories

Having an athlete who has overcome some type of obstacle to achieve athletic success is a surefire **human interest story**, as are uncommon athletic achievements. Consider the case of Tim Frisby, a member of the 2004 University of South Carolina football team. Most college football players are 18 to 23 years old. A retired member of the U.S. Army, Frisby was 39 when he walked on to the Gamecocks

football team, making him the oldest college football player. Although he did not make a lasting impact on the field, the media storm surrounding the human interest aspect of Frisby's story landed him on the *Late Show With David Letterman* (*Gamecocks WR Interviewed*, 2004). An appearance on the *Late Show* was probably not the level of publicity initially sought by the University of South Carolina sports information staff when it issued a news release announcing that Frisby had received eligibility clearance from the NCAA. But the story was unique, and in a time of military action it warranted national attention.

## Recognition and Award Stories

Because the focus of sporting events is the athletic competitions themselves, an athlete's accomplishments during the event frequently become a story. Often these stories will be readily obvious to a reporter, but occasionally public relations must proactively promote athletes' performance so that they receive greater recognition.

Awards are frequent in sport on organizational, local, and national levels, and at varying frequencies, such as once a week, month, or year. As Helitzer (1996) observed, awards are a "good way to give recognition and get recognition at the same time" (p. 216). Athletes who win awards are recognized for outstanding accomplishments, and the organization that gives the award is also recognized. Consider a college football team that names offensive, defensive, and special teams players of the week after reviewing game film. The athletes are recognized for their performances, but the team, by giving the award, has created a story that is an opportunity for increased publicity.

Nominating an athlete for an award can bring nearly as much publicity as the athlete's actually winning the award. On the national level, the promotion of an athlete for an award, such as college football's Heisman Trophy, can be expensive. In 2001 the University of Oregon spent $250,000 on a billboard in New York City to promote Joey Harrington for the Heisman. Harrington finished fourth. On a smaller scale, Marshall University spent $25,000 to promote Randy Moss in 1997, Chad Pennington in 1999, and Byron Leftwich in 2002 for the Heisman (Rovell, 2002). None of the three players won the Heisman, but they enjoyed high-profile careers while at Marshall.

Awards are frequently given by conferences, leagues, and other governing bodies on a weekly or monthly basis to recognize athletic achievement.

Typically the organization that presents the award establishes deadlines for nominations. Sport public relations professionals must identify worthy nominees and submit their names by the deadlines. After a winner is chosen, the governing body announces the outcome to the media. Because that release will likely be written for a broad audience, public relations for sport organizations that have an award-winning athlete should supplement the release with additional information that may be of interest to their local media.

## Selling the Product

After the public relations professional has decided what tactics will be used to position the product to the media, attention shifts to selling the product to them. Here the public relations professional actually presents information to the media. Common methods used to sell stories to the media include pitching and media tours.

### Pitching

The nature of big-time sport guarantees media coverage. Daily newspapers cover a Major League Baseball team whether the team is in first place or last place. Therefore, some sport public relations professionals do not need to pitch story ideas to reporters, but practitioners with less-prominent sport organizations do have to pitch stories on a regular basis.

The actual sales process for the public relations professional is a pitch to the media that something is newsworthy enough for them to cover. The pitch is often, but not always, accompanied by some sort of tactic like a news release. Public relations professionals should never just send a news release without following up with a journalist, and that follow-up is the pitch.

Pitching the media is common practice in the sport organization–media relationship, and journalists expect stories to be pitched to them. Frequently done through a personal phone call, the pitch should include some content of the news release. But the pitch is also an opportunity to divulge new or updated information. For example, if a sporting goods manufacturer is unveiling a new line of shoes, its public relations staff may offer claims that the new shoes are lighter than the competition's sneakers. After public relations has distributed a news release or media advisory announcing the unveiling, a public relations professional might want to call reporters, remind them of the unveiling, and ask for their shoe size. When the reporters show up to cover the event, they can try on a shoe that fits properly and judge firsthand how light the shoe really is. See the sidebar titled Pitching a Story Effectively for additional insights.

### Media Tours

Traveling from one media outlet to another may be necessary, in a sort of **media tour**. Harris (1998) defined media tours as "tours of major markets for the purpose of obtaining publicity in local media" (p. 257). Media tours are popular in mainstream business, and although this tactic sounds simple, it may be difficult and time consuming to execute. The goal of a media tour is to maximize media publicity for the organization while minimizing cost and demands on representatives. For example, a U.S. figure skating athlete who wins an Olympic gold medal overseas will be in media demand when he returns to the United States. To minimize the effects on his schedule, the national governing body may

## Pitching a Story Effectively

Public relations professionals working for lesser-known sport or minor league organizations cannot automatically assume that the media will report on their organizations. The practitioner must have some tactics in mind when pitching a story to the media. Several strategies can be effective:

- *Know your sport inside and out.* Be in a position to explain to a reporter the intricacies of the sport, including scoring system, rules, and judging, and seek to identify unique aspects of your sport that the reporter might find interesting.
- *Know your athletes and coaches.* Understanding the off-field interests of athletes and coaches can lead to additional publicity opportunities.
- *Develop your own sources.* Suggesting to reporters where they may turn for another perspective may lead to favorable mentions in the media or additional stories. Be certain, however, that the source will speak favorably about your organization before directing a reporter there.

organize a media tour in an area with a significant media presence such as New York City. This tour may include stops on morning talk shows as well as a publicity stop at an ice rink. The organization may invite sponsors and vendors to attend, further strengthening organizational relationships with those partners.

An alternative form of media tour is a satellite media tour (SMT). An SMT is similar to a teleconference, as described in chapter 8, but it is done with satellite video technology and is used almost exclusively by television reporters. SMTs allow journalists anywhere in the world the opportunity for a live one-on-one individual interview, usually of five minutes or less (Smith, 2005). SMTs allow local television stations to ask specific questions of an interviewee that may be of interest to a local media audience.

## SUMMARY

Managing the sport organization–media relationship is a demanding but critical responsibility assigned to many sport public relations professionals. Sport public relations practitioners must first identify the influential media members with whom they will interact, and they must understand the differing ways in which those media members work. For instance, a newspaper columnist has different needs than a television reporter. After media relationships have been identified, significant planning is necessary to serve the diverse members of the media, particularly at games and other events. Defining media accreditation policies, providing adequate workspace, and offering critical services such as technology support and statistical reports are important aspects of service planning. Because media interest in many sport organizations extends beyond game days, other organizational media policies may be necessary, ranging from defining appropriate organizational spokespersons to specifying interview policies. Finally, because the goal of media relations is to generate maximum positive publicity for the sport organization, sport public relations professionals must be able to define the unique aspects of their product, position the product in ways that make it attractive to members of the media, and pitch those members on the newsworthiness of the product.

## LEARNING ACTIVITIES

1. Having watched local television stations, listened to local radio stations, and read local newspapers in the community where you are attending college, who would you identify as influential members of the sport media? If you were a sport public relations professional in the community, how would you attend to the different needs of each group within the sport media?

2. Interview a sport public relations professional in your community regarding her or his organization's accreditation procedures. Who is eligible for media credentials from the organization? What sort of application process is required? Does media demand for game credentials and media services ever exceed supply? If so, how does the organization address that concern?

3. Place yourself in the position of a sport public relations practitioner working in a Division I college. Your school is holding a celebration of 100 years of basketball, which is a matter of great interest to local media as well as alumni. Many former university greats will be honored. Develop a media services plan for this event, being sure to consider event-day staff concerns and assignments, facility requirements, equipment needs, and hospitality services. What strategies would you employ to maximize your university's exposure in the media?

4. Secure copies of your local newspaper's sport section for the past three days. How many human interest stories can you identify within those sections? How many stories are related to teams, athletes, or coaches who received awards? Can you identify other stories that may have resulted from pitches made by sport public relations professionals?

# Employing News Media Tactics

**8**

**After reading this chapter, students should be able to**

- understand the role of the sport public relations professional in distributing content to publics,
- appreciate the value of news and its effect on media coverage,
- become proficient in standard news release formatting,
- identify the best distribution methods for releasing information, and
- become familiar with the benefits of social media releases.

**Key terms discussed in this chapter include**

- media relations,
- news value,
- lead,
- inverted pyramid,

- AP style,
- social media releases (SMRs), and
- B-Roll.

**It has been** said that information is the currency of a public relations person. The exchange of that information, often to the media, ideally results in favorable publicity for the professional's organization. In turn, the favorable publicity might lead to increased awareness about the organization and ultimately increased revenue. Recently, the role of a public relations person has moved beyond generating favorable publicity into developing a variety of positive content about the organization.

As discussed in chapter 1, two models are commonly used to turn information currency into organizational revenue (see pages 9 and 11). The model most commonly employed by sport public relations professionals is the press agentry and publicity model in which practitioners seek to cultivate as much publicity as possible for their organizations (Grunig & Hunt, 1984). This goal is frequently achieved by disseminating newsworthy information to the media.

A variety of communication tactics are available for distributing information, each with its own relative strengths and weaknesses. Traditionally these tactics can be divided into four categories: advertising and promotional media, news media, organizational media, and interpersonal communi-

nication (Smith, 2005). Table 8.1 illustrates some advantages and disadvantages of the various communication tactics.

Advertising and promotional media are generally reserved for the marketing department and will not be addressed here. Organizational media, which include specific tactics such as media guides and programs, was addressed in chapter 5. Interpersonal communication, or face-to-face personal involvement, is addressed in chapter 11.

Some scholars (e.g., Solis & Breakenridge, 2009) argue that a fifth tactic, the use of social media such as blogs, Facebook, and Twitter, should not only be incorporated into public relations plans but also may even take the place of the more traditional tactics.

This chapter focuses on news media tactics, which Smith (2005) defined as "opportunities for the credible presentation of organizational messages to large audiences" (p. 159), as well as the dissemination of organizational messages through news media channels.

Tactics that involve direct contact between the sport organization's public relations person and the news media are frequently referred to as **media relations**. The news release, the most frequently

## Table 8.1 Communication Tactics—Advantages and Disadvantages

| Tactic | Public reach | Public impact | Sport examples | Advantages and disadvantages |
|---|---|---|---|---|
| Advertising and promotional media | High | Low | Newspaper advertisements that promote an upcoming event | Reach large numbers for low cost; dismissed by the public as a paid message |
| News media | Medium to high | Medium to low | Press conferences; news releases | Reach large numbers for free and are highly credible; rely on a third party (media) to deliver the message |
| Organizational media | Medium to low | Medium to high | Programs; media guides | Reach publics interested in the organization; often require an additional purchase by the consumer |
| Interpersonal communication | Low | High | Community open houses; facility tours | Use highly persuasive face-to-face involvement; reach only those in attendance |

Based on Smith 2005.

used news media tactic, is commonplace in the sport industry (Helitzer, 1996; Davis, 1998; Hall, Nichols, Moynahan, & Taylor, 2007). A public relations professional must know the proper writing style and format of news releases. This chapter examines not just style and format but also types and distribution methods for news releases. Other common news media tactics include media kits, fact sheets, and audiovisual techniques such as graphics and actualities. In all these tactics, information is presented from the organization more or less ready for use (Smith, 2005). Collectively, these news media tactics may also be referred to as organizational content.

# News Releases

Although sometimes called a press release, a news release is a more descriptive term for the intent of the communication tactic. The goal is, in effect, to release newsworthy information to the media in as positive a light as possible. The media usually determines what is and what is not newsworthy. A public relations person's job is to get information into the hands of the media and persuade them to use it because it is newsworthy to some segment of the media's audience.

Sports news releases are written about anything relative to the organization. They may include a preview of a competition or the result of a competition, even if the organization's team lost. They also include announcements regarding personnel, schedules, product launches, event sponsorships, event time changes, and more. Note that not all news releases communicate positive messages. Although distributing a news release that announces the hiring of a new women's volleyball coach is appropriate, it is equally appropriate to distribute one announcing the firing of the previous coach.

Often the public relations person will be placed in the unenviable position of writing a news release following an event in which the organization's team has performed poorly. The public relations person's role is to provide positive messages about the performance. Suggestions for doing this are provided later in the chapter.

A sport public relations person may write a news release that is not picked up by any media outlet. To increase the likelihood that a news release will draw the attention of the media and generate publicity for the organization, attention should be paid to several aspects of the release. The first is the news value of the information. What information does the release contain that may be of interest to the media and the broader public?

Second is the standard news release format and elements. Adhering to an accepted format will make it easier for the media to recognize that the information they are receiving is from an organization and has certain news value. Closely related to format is the third important aspect of a news release—the type and function of the news release. The sport industry includes a diverse population of media that have varying interest levels. As such, several types of news releases are acceptable.

Finally, the distribution method of the news release is important. In today's age of instantaneous media coverage, knowing how to distribute the information quickly and in a manner preferred by the media is critical.

# News Value

Although a given sport organization may think that a piece of information is newsworthy, the news media may not. For example, a sporting goods manufacturer may think that the launch of a new line of tennis rackets is newsworthy. The news media may not because the production of tennis rackets is the core business of the manufacturer; rackets are what the company is supposed to make. But if the production of this new line of rackets will take place completely in Fargo, North Dakota, and will create 50 new jobs in the community, the news media in that area will be interested. The information has the news values of proximity and impact.

The determination of **news value** is somewhat subjective, based on the audience, location, and focus of the individual news media. In the aforementioned example, it is easy to see how media that cover tennis, North Dakota and surrounding states, or the sporting goods industry would be interested in the story. It probably does not have nationwide appeal because it lacks value for most of the news media.

William Thompson (1996, p. 133) developed an easy-to-remember information analysis filter around six basic news values called TIPCUP, or timeliness, impact, prominence, conflict, unusualness, and proximity, that can help the sport public relations professional determine whether or not to write a news release.

## Timeliness

Information that is new, and therefore "news," is always timely. A good public relations person, however, can devise ways to make old information timely depending on what is happening in the world or within the organization (Treadwell & Treadwell,

2000). A 25-year reunion of a championship basketball team is timely and newsworthy, although the reason for the reunion occurred 25 years ago.

Another consideration regarding timeliness concerns news from other industries that may compete for the media's attention. The first week of April is a good time for organizations involved in baseball-related news to seek publicity because the Major League Baseball season is beginning and the sport media is focused on baseball and the optimism surrounding a new season. That period would probably not be timely for a university to announce the hiring of a new basketball coach because the story might not receive much attention.

## Impact

When a public relations person is evaluating the impact of a particular piece of information, the focus should not be the impact on members of the news media, but the impact on their readers and viewers. If members of the news media can see potential relevance to their audiences, they will likely cover the story (Treadwell & Treadwell, 2000). A public relations professional for a health club might demonstrate impact by showing how giving away free blood pressure evaluations to senior citizens can improve the health care system in the community.

## Prominence

Using prominent organizational spokespersons or VIPs to attract the attention of news media is a common public relations strategy (Treadwell & Treadwell, 2000). Because senior managers in an organization are generally more credible than mid-level managers, they generally garner greater media attention. If a soft-drink company is announcing a new athlete endorsement, using the company's CEO as spokesperson will lend greater prominence to the news than would using the company's marketing manager.

## Conflict

The nature of sport is rooted in conflict and battles. Successful organizations win more battles, or competitions, than they lose. Conflict, however, goes beyond the physical confrontation (Thompson, 1996). Each year the NCAA issues a news release placing individuals who may be selling unlicensed Final Four merchandise on alert that it will prosecute them for trademark infringement. This battle to protect unauthorized use of a protected mark represents a conflict for the NCAA. Information

regarding this conflict would likely be considered newsworthy.

## Unusualness

Certainly the announcement of the 68 teams that qualify for the NCAA Men's Basketball Tournament is timely and has considerable local news value for the institutions chosen. But consider the 2004 tournament, for which the Air Force Academy qualified. The news value was easy for the local Colorado Springs media to recognize, but adding the fact that no Air Force team had reached the NCAA tournament since 1962 created a story that had nationwide appeal because of the unusualness of the news.

## Proximity

Although sport organizations love the glamour of being featured on national media outlets such as ESPN and *USA Today*, the reality is that news must be extremely relevant to warrant national attention. Most public relations persons do well to focus on local connections, even for national news. When USA Basketball announced its 20-player USA Men's Select Team in July 2010, Northwestern forward John Shurna was among those selected. Northwestern University's athletics media relations department issued its own news release focusing on Shurna as a team member and providing additional information about him beyond what USA Basketball had released (*Shurna Selected*, 2010).

# Formats and Elements

After a sport organization has decided to release newsworthy information, attention turns to writing the news release. By adhering to a universally accepted format, a public relations person can increase the likelihood that the media will use the information (Treadwell & Treadwell, 2000). Central elements of this format make the release easy to identify, easy to read, and easy to edit (Lorenz & Vivian, 1996).

Those elements include a header with key contact information, a lead paragraph that summarizes the newsworthy elements of the release, text that provides additional details of the newsworthy elements presented in an inverted pyramid style, a tag that identifies the organization, and a symbol to let the reader know that the release has ended. All of this should be written in accordance with the journalistic standards identified in the *Associated Press Stylebook and Briefing on Media Law*.

## Header

The most important element of a news release is a header placed at the top of the page that should contain, at minimum, the organization's name, address, and telephone number; the name of a media contact with phone number; the release date and time; and a headline (Simon & Zappala, 1996). It is acceptable to preprint a news release form with the organization's information as a means to verify that the news is coming from an official source (Helitzer, 1996).

The name of the media contact should include a phone number that will be answered, either a work, home, or mobile number, along with an e-mail address. Because the news media do not work a conventional eight-hour work day, the public relations person must be accessible should a question arise about the information (Helitzer, 1996; Lorenz & Vivian, 1996; Treadwell & Treadwell, 2000).

Generally, the media contact will be the organization's public relations person, although the organization may wish to identify a different organizational spokesperson as discussed in chapter 9.

All news releases should carry the date and time to indicate to the media when the information can be used and where it originated (Treadwell & Treadwell, 2000). Most releases will be available "for immediate release" (Helitzer, 1996; Lorenz & Vivian, 1996; Simon & Zappala, 1996). Occasionally, an organization updates a developing news story by issuing a second news release on the same day. In those cases including the actual time of day when the news release was written is essential so that journalists can identify the most recent information.

Because sport-related news is frequently reported on as it happens, an organization may need to disclose sensitive information before it wishes it to be in the public domain. In that case, the news release should be "embargoed" for a later time (Lorenz & Vivian, 1996). For example, two days before the NCAA released to the public its annual report on academic progress rates (APR) for Division I athletics programs in June 2010, it sent a memo to college sports information directors with links to the data. This approach allowed individual universities to see the data for their programs and prepare organizational messages before their local media received it. The NCAA's memo stated, "The APR data are confidential until Wednesday, June 9, at 2 p.m. Eastern."

Disclosing information under an embargo is risky business for the organization. What guarantees does it have that the media will not violate the embargo? Generally the organization is engaging in a good-faith gesture with the media when it embargos information. Treadwell and Treadwell (2000, p. 231) identified two reasons why news media will honor embargos. First, no professional wants to disclose information in advance that may be subject to change, and second, news media that leak embargoed material may find it difficult to gather information from the organization in the future. But the NFL found out that even those reasons may not be enough to prevent information from leaking. It had planned an exclusive release of its 2004 schedule on the NFL Network for 5 p.m. ET on April 14, 2004, yet the schedule appeared before the announcement in the *New York Daily News* ("False Start for NFL?" 2004).

Given the challenges, the best advice for sport public relations professionals is to avoid embargoing information unless absolutely necessary.

The release location, called a dateline, identifies the city in which the release originates and is usually typed in all capital letters, followed by a hyphen, just before the beginning of the first sentence of the release. Newspaper stories almost always include the location if the news originates outside the local newspaper market (Hall et al., 2007).

The final element of the header is some sort of headline as a means to catch the attention of the release's recipient (Helitzer, 1996; Simon & Zappala, 1996; Treadwell & Treadwell, 2000). Journalists are in no way obligated to use this headline, and most will not. But there is always a chance that the headline will be used verbatim, so it should put the organization in the best possible light. Notice the differences between the following possible headlines for the Seattle Storm of the WNBA.

> Dream flattens Storm, 75-62, to win WNBA title
>
> Storm falls to Dream in WNBA championship game

The first headline places the emphasis on the opposition, the Atlanta Dream, and connotes negativity through the verb "flatten" and the stating of the score. The second headline places the emphasis on the organization releasing the information, the Seattle Storm, and provides a more positive image of the game through the verb "fall" and mention of the championship.

Figure 8.1 demonstrates a properly written and formatted news release.

GATORADE™

Contact: Jen Schmit
312.821.1335
jennifer.schmit@gatorade.com

Josh Holland
312.932.2823
josh.holland@fleishman.com

## GATORADE UNVEILS G SERIES TO MEET MORE ATHLETE NEEDS
### *New product line based in science and tested with elite athletes nationwide*

CHICAGO (January 4, 2010) – To help all athletes get the most out of their performance, scientists from The Gatorade Company, a division of PepsiCo (PEP), have created the G Series – a new line of products supported by the latest science and developed in collaboration with the world's greatest athletes to provide fuel, fluid and nutrients before, during and after activity.

"The G Series highlights Gatorade's longtime commitment to science and is a major step on our journey from a sports drink company to a sports performance innovator," said Sarah Robb O'Hagan, chief marketing officer for Gatorade. "With the G Series, Gatorade has gone beyond hydration to provide sports nutrition solutions that are specifically tailored to meet the different needs of a broad range of athletes before, during, and after practice or competition."

While developing the G Series, Gatorade scientists collaborated with some of the world's top athletes, including Usain Bolt, Serena Williams, Peyton Manning, and Dwyane Wade, and solicited feedback from a comprehensive study of over 10,000 athletes nationwide. The study included 400 one-on-one interviews in 14 states with elite high school athletes and a wide-array of sports health professionals to ensure the G Series meets athlete needs.

"Building on the insight from these athletes, we applied the institute's 20 years of expertise in sports nutrition and developed functional products that address the athlete's needs for performance," said Dr. Craig Horswill, senior research fellow, Gatorade Sports Science Institute.

Each product of the G Series is designed to meet the distinct nutrition and hydration needs around workout or competition usage – pre (1), during (2), and post (3).

- **Gatorade Prime 01:** According to Gatorade research, athletes are looking for energy to kick-start their activity, but don't want to feel too full. Gatorade Prime 01 is pre-game fuel in a convenient and functional 4-oz. pouch that provides real carbohydrate energy, not the perceived energy that comes from highly caffeinated beverages. Designed for use within 15 minutes before a workout or competition, Gatorade Prime 01 provides fuel by facilitating the availability of carbohydrate energy to muscles. The product contains 25 g of carbohydrates (100 calories) to help prime the muscles, as well as 110 mg sodium and 35 mg potassium. Gatorade Prime also provides a good source (10% Daily Value) of the B vitamins – Niacin (B3), Pantothenic Acid (B5) and B6 that aid in energy metabolism as part of a daily diet.

-more-

**Figure 8.1** A properly written and formatted news release.

- **Gatorade Perform 02: Gatorade Thirst Quencher:** In the moment of activity, athletes turn to the most thoroughly researched sports beverage in the world that offers a scientifically backed blend of fluids to help rehydrate, electrolytes to promote replacement of what athletes lose in sweat, and carbohydrate energy to fuel working muscles and enhance athletic performance.

- **Gatorade Perform 02: G2:** A low-calorie sports drink that delivers functional hydration during exercise, with less than half the calories of Gatorade Thirst Quencher.

- **Gatorade Recover 03:** Athletes know it's critical to promote muscle recovery to get ready for their next workout or competition, and Gatorade Recover 03 is the first protein recovery beverage with the consistency and great taste people expect from Gatorade. Formulated for use within 30-60 minutes after activity, a 16.9-oz. bottle contains 16 g of protein to help promote muscle recovery, as well as 14 g of carbohydrate (130 calories), 250 mg of sodium, and 95 mg of potassium to help athletes fully replace electrolytes lost during training and competition.

Sports health professionals have responded positively to the new G Series. After a briefing on the science behind the products, Jamie Reed, head certified athletic trainer for the Texas Rangers commented, "Thanks for caring for my athletes as much as I do."

The G-Series will start shipping in late March to grocery, convenience, mass, and drug stores nationwide, and will be supported by a fully integrated marketing campaign. Gatorade Prime 01 will retail for $1.29-$1.99 for a single 4-oz. pouch; Gatorade and G2 Perform 02 will retail for $1.29 for a single 20-oz. bottle and $1.39-$2.19 for a single 32-oz. bottle; and Gatorade Recover 03 will retail for $1.79-$2.99 for a single 16.9-oz. bottle.

**About Gatorade**
The Gatorade Company, a division of PepsiCo (NYSE: PEP), provides sports performance innovations designed to meet the needs of athletes at all competitive levels and across a broad range of sports. Gatorade Thirst Quencher® is backed by more than 40 years of research and is scientifically formulated and athletically proven to quench thirst, replace fluids and electrolytes, and provide carbohydrate energy to enhance athletic performance. The company's product portfolio is built around the G Series™, a 1-2-3 approach to athlete nutrition and hydration before (Gatorade Prime 01™), during (Gatorade® Perform 02 and G2® Perform 02), and after (Gatorade Recover 03™) training or competition. For more information, please visit www.gatorade.com.

PepsiCo offers the world's largest portfolio of billion-dollar food and beverage brands, including 18 different product lines that each generate more than $1 billion in annual retail sales. Our main businesses – Frito-Lay, Quaker, Pepsi-Cola, Tropicana and Gatorade – also make hundreds of other nourishing, tasty foods and drinks that bring joy to our consumers in over 200 countries. With more than $43 billion in 2008 revenues, PepsiCo employs 198,000 people who are united by our unique commitment to sustainable growth, called Performance with Purpose. By dedicating ourselves to offering a broad array of choices for healthy, convenient and fun nourishment, reducing our environmental impact, and fostering a diverse and inclusive workplace culture, PepsiCo balances strong financial returns with giving back to our communities worldwide. For more information, please visit www.pepsico.com.

###

**Figure 8.1** (*continued*)

Reprinted, by permission, from Gatorade.

## Lead

The opening one or two paragraphs of a news release is called the **lead** and should contain a summary of the most newsworthy elements to the release. A widely accepted practice is to include the who, what, where, when, why, and how (five Ws and one H) within the lead paragraphs (Hall et al., 2007; Helitzer, 1996; Lorenz & Vivian, 1996; Treadwell & Treadwell, 2000). But in sport it is frequently difficult to summarize the why or how elements of an event in a concise manner.

Various approaches can help the sport public relations professional write an effective lead. Thompson (1996, p. 144) advocated a 10-word approach: "In the first 10 words of the lead, define an audience and provide a benefit for that audience." Treadwell and Treadwell (2000, p. 232) suggested the 20-second rule for writing effective leads: "If you had only 20 seconds to tell a friend about your story, what would you say?" Either approach may be effective in any given situation.

Consider the following lead paragraph of a news release from the University of South Carolina following the 2010 NCAA Baseball Championship:

> Omaha, Neb.—Whit Merrifield singled home Scott Wingo in the bottom of the 11th inning, lifting South Carolina to a 2-1 win over UCLA, clinching the National Championship for the Gamecocks. (*Gamecocks Win National Championship!* 2010)

The paragraph probably does not measure up well in Thompson's theory because the reader won't know the most significant element, the winning of a championship, until the end of the lead. But the reader can easily identify many of the five Ws and one H within 20 seconds of reading the paragraph, making it effective in the Treadwell and Treadwell approach. If the writer wanted to follow Thompson's 10-word approach, he or she might have begun the paragraph as follows: "The University of South Carolina won its first NCAA Baseball Championship." This lead succinctly states which audience would be interested in the release, likely anyone interested in the University of South Carolina or the NCAA Baseball Championship. Note that the most newsworthy information, that South Carolina won, is placed first.

Consider how the five Ws and one H apply in that example.

- Who = University of South Carolina
- What = won the NCAA Baseball Championship
- Where = Omaha, Nebraska
- When = June 29, 2010 (listed in header)
- Why = Merrifield's single scored Wingo
- How = 2-1 victory over UCLA

Accepted practice in sports news releases is to provide additional details that enhance the basic news elements of an event news release. The inclusion of the leading scorers tells the reader that two players had good games. The inclusion of the game's attendance helps the reader develop a mental picture of the atmosphere inside the arena where the game was played.

Table 8.2 identifies the five Ws and one H contained in the news release depicted in figure 8.1. Note how much easier it is to identify all the elements in a news release that is a straight news release and not a competition story. More about the various types of news releases frequently used by sport public relations professionals is presented later in this chapter.

## Body

Following the lead paragraphs of a news release, the body of the release should follow the journalistic standard of the **inverted pyramid**, so named because it places the most important information first in the release and the least important information last, thus resembling an inverted pyramid of importance. This style works well for straight news releases and competition stories because the infor-

### Table 8.2 Who, What, Where, When, Why, and How of Figure 8.1

| Who | Gatorade |
| --- | --- |
| What | Created G Series, a new line of products |
| Where | Chicago |
| When | January 4, 2010 |
| Why | To help all athletes get the most out of their performance |
| How | Scientific development |

mation being disseminated is likely new information that the readers do not already know.

Hall and his colleagues (2007) found that the inverted pyramid approach is effective in sport for two reasons. First, it provides the most critical information first. This first piece of information may be all that the journalist reads. Second, it is easily trimmed to fit a particular space on a newspaper page or electronic broadcast. The journalist can merely eliminate the last few paragraphs, or the least important information, without altering the substance of the release.

Following the lead of a news release written in the inverted pyramid style, subsequent sections also have specific functions. Thompson (1996) suggested that the second section should explain the lead, often completing omitted information, and that the third section should present information in support of the lead by offering evidence to back up the lead.

A fourth section provides background to place the news in perspective, and a fifth section includes any specific call to action that the readers might want to take (Thompson, 1996). For example, a news release announcing the beginning of season-ticket sales for a minor league baseball team might close with information about the price per ticket and a phone number that will accept orders.

Unlike some other forms of writing, news release writing should involve short, succinct paragraphs, many of which do not exceed one sentence or one new idea (Thompson, 1996).

## Ending

The ending of a news release is just as important as its header, or beginning. Certain stylistic elements are accepted and expected, including a boilerplate and a notation indicating that the release is complete.

### Boilerplate

Many organizations develop a standard boilerplate paragraph that provides basic information about the organization (Treadwell & Treadwell, 2000). Organizations may wish to use the boilerplate to position themselves within the sport industry in their own terms by identifying key elements of their business strategy and by including information about the organization that a reporter might want to incorporate into an article. For example, Gatorade ends its corporate news releases as follows:

> The Gatorade Company, a division of PepsiCo (NYSE: PEP), provides sports performance innovations designed to meet the needs of athletes at all competitive levels and across a broad range of sports. Gatorade Thirst Quencher® is backed by more than 40 years of research and is scientifically formulated and athletically proven to quench thirst, replace fluids and electrolytes, and provide carbohydrate energy to enhance athletic performance. The company's product portfolio is built around the G Series™ and G Series Pro—a 1-2-3 approach to athlete nutrition and hydration before, during, and after training or competition. For more information, please visit www.gatorade.com. (*Gatorade's New G Series Pro*, 2010)

The inclusion of Gatorade's various products positions the company as being a diverse worldwide sporting goods manufacturer, despite the focus of the news release, which was about tennis. In addition, it provides context as to the longevity of Gatorade by including information about its history.

D.C. United of Major League Soccer chooses to end its news releases by informing journalists of the preferred way to refer to the organization: "Broadcasting and P.A. Request: When speaking of the organization, please refer to the team as either 'D.C. United' or 'United' but not 'the D.C. United' or 'the United.' We appreciate your cooperation" (*Tim Lawson Agrees to Contract*, 2004).

### 30

The journalistic standard for ending a news story is to center the number "30" at the end of the story. The same applies to news releases, although many sport organizations use a variation on that as a means to demonstrate enthusiasm for the team. For example, Ohio State University ends its news releases with "Go Bucks!" and D.C. United ends its releases with a reference to the organization's website, "www.dcunited.com."

Without some sort of ending to a news release, the reader will be inclined to think that more information is contained on a separate page. Given that, if a news release exceeds one page, it is common to center the word "MORE" at the bottom of the page, indicating that more is to come (Lorenz & Vivian, 1996). If a second page is used, it should be identified with a header in the upper right-hand corner indicating the subject of the release and the page number.

Table 8.3 provides a summary of the basic news release elements and their purposes.

## Table 8.3 Basic News Release Elements and Their Purposes

| Element | Purpose | Example from figure 8.1 |
|---|---|---|
| Header | Contains contact information for the organization's public relations person as well as the date and time when the media can use the information | For immediate release—January 4, 2010 Contact: Jen Schmit or Josh Holland |
| Lead | Summary of the most newsworthy elements of the release | Gatorade developed G Series to assist athletes with their performance |
| Body | Follows the lead with supporting information in the inverted pyramid style | Quote from chief marketing officer for Gatorade and senior research fellow at the Gatorade Sports Science Institute followed by description of each product in the G Series |
| Boilerplate | Standard information that communicates an organizational position | Corporate information about Gatorade and its parent company, PepsiCo |
| Ending or 30 | Indicates to the reader that no more information is available | ### |

## Associated Press Style

Many stylebooks exist, but the most commonly accepted guide in the sport industry is the *Associated Press Stylebook and Briefing on Media Law*. Updated almost every two years, the *AP Stylebook* provides essential guidelines for sport public relations professionals in a variety of areas. Although some newspapers such as the *New York Times* and *Wall Street Journal* subscribe to their own style, the *AP Stylebook* dominates most newsrooms. As such, news releases written following **AP style** stand a greater chance of being picked up by newspapers (Newsom & Carrell, 1991; Lorenz & Vivian, 1996).

A key section in the *AP Stylebook* is the chapter "Sports Guidelines and Style." Here, sport public relations professionals can find proper style for sport-specific items such as reporting event scores, deciding between "face off" and "faceoff" in hockey news releases, and measuring distances for track and field events (Goldstein, 2000). The *AP Stylebook* also provides guidance for commonly used words and phrases such as state names, numbers, and personnel titles. All sport public relations practitioners should own a copy.

## Types and Functions of Releases

Sport public relations professionals must differentiate among several types of news releases depending on the nature of the information being released. These types are unique to the sport industry and likely differ from corporate public relations, in which most practitioners write straight news releases.

A sport organization commonly produces straight news releases to announce new information, notes to preview an upcoming competition, stories to summarize a competition, and hometown releases to highlight an individual member of the organization.

## Straight News

A straight news release is the most common type of news release written by public relations professionals, but it is not frequently employed in the sport world because much of what transpires in a sport organization revolves around competition. These basic news releases provide information in a straightforward, timely manner. Many announce an item such as a player trade, the hiring or firing of a new coach, a player injury update, the launch of a new product or service, or a facility groundbreaking event.

Evaluation of the news value discussed earlier in this chapter is useful in determining what information qualifies for a straight news release and what information may be better distributed in another manner. Straight news releases should be brief, no more than two pages, and written in the inverted pyramid style.

Announcement releases frequently contain relevant information such as quotes from key managers within the organization, as well as influential persons outside the organization.

For example, if a minor league baseball team announces that it will sponsor a clinic with the local Boys and Girls Club, it would be newsworthy to include quotes from the team's general manager addressing the positive community ties that the clinic brings to the team as well as a statement from the director of the Boys and Girls Club about the positive effect that the clinic will have on children. These quotes may be used verbatim by a reporter within his or her story, so the quotes provided in news releases should be positive for the sport organization.

### Competition Previews

The basic objective of competition previews is to release information about the participants that will help a reporter craft a story. Competition previews should be written with the assumption that the reader knows nothing about the organization. These releases are sometimes called game advances (Hall et al., 2007) or pregame notes (Davis, 1998).

Most sport organizations either engage in some form of direct competition or are affiliated with a competition that is newsworthy to its key publics. Consider a national governing body such as USA Field Hockey, which does both. It organizes competitive teams to represent the United States in prominent international competitions such as the Pan American Cup, and it provides development programs for members through events such as the National Indoor Tournament for club teams from across the United States and the Grassroots Development programs with local parks and recreation organizations (*About USA Field Hockey*, 2010).

Competition previews are, obviously, distributed before a competition, although the lead time varies by sport industry. For example, a college sports information director working with a football team customarily writes a preview on Sunday for the school's game the following Saturday. An NBA public relations director, however, may have only one day to write a preview of the team's next game if it plays on consecutive nights. Before World Cup qualifying matches, USA Field Hockey distributed a news release previewing the competition, which included basic information such as nations competing, quotes from team members, importance of competition, and tournament dates (*USA Women Ready for World Cup Qualifier*, 2010).

Many sport public relations professionals modify competition previews so that they can be used as game notes. These are then distributed to members of the media before the beginning of the competition. Because they serve many functions, competition previews are often written in a style different from that of straight news releases. Rather than working in a straight inverted pyramid style on a word processor, many organizations customize previews in a desktop publishing program with pictures and fact boxes that provide basic summary information similar to the five Ws and one H mentioned earlier (Hall et al., 2007).

Figure 8.2 identifies common pieces of information that should be included in competition previews. Note the broad range of information beyond the competition itself.

## Information for a Competition Preview

- Teams playing and respective win–loss records
- Date, time, and location of event
- Name of facility and attendance capacity
- Live media coverage on radio or television
- Results of previous meetings between teams
- Probable starting lineups including name, position, height, weight, and current statistics
- Player injury updates
- Game officials
- Late-breaking news

**Figure 8.2** Common pieces of information included in competition previews.

Adapted from Davis 1998.

## Competition Stories

Because most sport organizations participate in some form of competition, the public frequently seeks information regarding the results of those events. Competition stories provide the avenue for the sport public relations professional to deliver the results of competitions in the most positive manner possible. Unlike stories written by journalists who may be critical of the organization, the sport public relations person's competition story should always emphasize positive aspects of the competition. Finding a positive story angle in negative news is not easy, but it is part of the job of a public relations professional. This practice is commonly referred to as spin.

Compare the following lead sentences from news releases following an Arkansas–Arizona State NCAA Super Regional baseball game on June 12, 2010, won by Arizona State 7-6 in 12 innings.

> Bo Bigham had four hits to lead the No. 15 Arkansas Razorbacks baseball team, but after 11-plus innings, the Razorbacks would fall to No. 1 Arizona State in the first game of the Tempe Super Regional at Jim Brock Ballpark, 7-6. (*Razorbacks Fall in Opener*, 2010)

> Deven Marrero's walkoff single in the 12th inning gave the No. 1 Arizona State University baseball team a dramatic 7-6 victory over Arkansas in Game One of the Tempe Super Regional. A sellout crowd of 4,371 at Winkles Field–Packard Stadium at Brock Ballpark saw the Sun Devils move ahead 1-0 in the best-of-three series and improve to 51-8 overall on the season. (*Deven Marrero's Walkoff Single*, 2010)

Both lead sentences describe the new information in the release, that Arizona State beat Arkansas by the score of 7-6 in extra innings. The latter lead, from the Arizona State University release, reveals how the school defeated Arkansas. The former lead, from the University of Arkansas news release, stresses the positive performance by one of the school's team members before mentioning the result of the competition.

Competition stories do not need to be lengthy, but they should be long enough to explain the facts of what happened in the competition, provide some detail of key moments or plays, and quote key participants or coaches. A good idea is to update any records which may have been set along with individual team win–loss records. An effective way to close a competition story is by previewing what is ahead for the organization.

Because this organizational release may be used verbatim by the media, quotes from players or coaches should be positive, even in negative news. If a team is defeated 10-1 in baseball, people associated with the team will already be feeling disenchanted. The sport public relations person need not include a quote from the coach that further exacerbates the situation.

Whereas competition previews may be written as much as a week in advance, competition stories must be written immediately after the competition before the news becomes old. Remember that timeliness is one of the key news values. A newspaper reporter often works under a tight deadline following a competition. So, too, should the sport public relations person.

## Hometown Releases

Hometown news releases are unique to the sport industry and are employed primarily by universities and national governing bodies. The objective of a hometown news release is to spotlight one athlete regardless of ability or prominence and distribute the release to media outlets in the athlete's hometown (Hall et al., 2007).

As such, the headline and lead paragraph of the news release should focus on the individual and the hometown connection. For example, a hometown release about a college football player might begin, "Former Smithville High standout Tommy Jones scored his first touchdown for Big State University last Saturday." Note the emphasis is not on whether Big State won or lost the football game but on how the local player is doing.

Most communities, large and small, have some type of weekly or community newspaper that focuses on, among other subjects, high school athletics. Those papers frequently do not have the resources necessary to staff events outside their region, but their readers enjoy following former local standouts (Hall et al., 2007).

In the era of media consolidation, declining newspaper readership, and reduced television news viewership, many news organizations are repositioning themselves by focusing on stories of interest to local residents. This switch to local news emphasis, termed *hyperlocal*, should not be ignored by sport public relations professionals seeking publicity.

The 2010 annual report on American journalism by the Pew Project for Excellence in Journalism noted that despite the prevalence of alternative and new media, traditional mainstream media outlets continue to be the primary source of information (*The State of the News Media*, 2010). To that end, an April 2010 study of more than 1,000 community newspaper editors and reporters by readMedia of Albany, New York, found that 97.52% of newspapers had published hometown news from targeted news releases in the past 60 days (*Hyperlocal News Connects Communities*, 2010).

# Distribution

Before the advent of the Internet, public relations professionals were frequently left to the "spray and pray" method of distributing news releases—spray the release around a number of media outlets and pray that someone passes the release on to the appropriate person. Public relations professionals can now direct a news release to a specific reporter's e-mail box or post the release on the sport organization's website and direct interested persons to the site. Of course, traditional methods of distribution such as faxing, mailing, and personal delivery are still used, but they lack the immediacy of electronic forms of distribution (Smith, 2005).

A 2010 Oriella PR Network survey of 750 journalists in 15 countries suggested that 75% of journalists still found targeted news releases distributed through e-mail useful, but that number was down from 94% in 2009. The survey question was phrased so that respondents were to assume that the content of the news release was "high quality and well targeted" (Ciarallo, 2010).

An additional concern beyond the method of distribution is the day of distribution. According to Porter (2010), writing on the Journalistics blog, the best time varies depending on the nature and target of the news. Porter cited representatives from PR Newswire and Business Wire, who recommend avoiding Mondays and Fridays but otherwise focusing on earlier in the week.

The public relations professional should identify the preferences of influential reporters who cover the organization. Chapter 6 addressed the notion of beat reporters and managing the media–organization relationship. Regardless of the method of distribution, Harvey Greene, vice president of media relations for the Miami Dolphins, advised that any truly important release be followed up with a phone call (H. Greene, personal communication, July 23, 2003).

## Printed Distribution

Several advantages and disadvantages are prevalent for printed, or "hard copy," distribution of news releases. Printed distribution through the mail allows the organization to authenticate the news release by placing it on some form of letterhead or by providing additional material in the form of media kits, which are discussed later in the chapter. Distribution through the mail also tends to be reliable because material can be sent with return receipt or tracking numbers.

Downsides to printed distribution through the mail include slow delivery and the inability of the public relations person to answer media questions (Treadwell & Treadwell, 2000). One way to expedite delivery to a reporter who may not be able to attend a news conference is to send the printed release through a courier or messenger service. This approach usually guarantees delivery within an hour or less, but it carries a high cost (Helitzer, 1996).

Personal delivery of information is frequently employed when reporters are attending an organizational event such as a news conference or competition. Organizations often place news releases or media kits on a table for the media to pick up on their own (Helitzer, 1996).

## Electronic Distribution

E-mailing news releases directly to reporters has become increasingly common (Treadwell & Treadwell, 2000; Smith, 2005). This form of distribution offers many advantages including immediate dissemination to any reporter anywhere in the world and the ability of reporters to copy and paste information directly from the release into their news stories. The disadvantages are equally important and include compatibility issues from one software program to another and assurance of receipt.

One way to combat the compatibility problem is to send the document as a portable document format, or PDF, invented by Adobe Systems, which allows users to "capture and view robust information—from almost any application, on any computer system—and share it with virtually anyone, anywhere" (Adobe Systems, n.d.). The software necessary to read PDF documents is free, but to create PDF files an organization must purchase the required software. Obviously, for this method of distribution to be effective the recipient must have the required software.

An additional form of electronic distribution is posting news releases on the organization's website. These posts should be shared on the organization's official social media sites such as Facebook and Twitter. Chapter 4 discusses the use of websites for organizational information distribution in more detail.

### RSS Feeds

RSS, which stands for really simple syndication, is a series of standardized web feed formats used to publish frequently updated works such as blogs and news sites. Subscribers can read RSS feeds through software known as RSS readers, feed readers, or aggregators. One popular reader is Google Reader, which also allows users to share interesting updates with other users.

As a website is updated with a new story, such as a sport organization's news release, the RSS feed automatically brings the update into a user's reader. In this way, a reader can subscribe to feeds from sites that he or she finds useful and read them in the reader rather than visit the website multiple times each day.

### Newswires

Newswires are a good method of ensuring distribution of organizational information to all major national news outlets. They are frequently used to supplement the aforementioned distribution methods. The most recognized newswire is PR Newswire, founded in 1954, which provides distribution of information through satellite, e-mail, and fax to thousands of media worldwide. Organizations pay a membership fee to transmit their news releases, digital photos, and other materials electronically to journalists across various newslines based on geography or subject (*Important Facts*, n.d.).

Business Wire is a similar organization that provides a variety of public relations services to its clients including distribution, measurement, search engine optimization, clipping services, and more. It bills itself as having the "most comprehensive news and disclosure network in the world" (Business Wire, n.d.).

A final word regarding print news releases comes from a member of the media. The sidebar, written by Murray Evans of Oklahoma Christian University, discusses what journalists look for in news releases.

## Media Kits

Sometimes referred to as press kits or press packets, media kits contain a variety of publicity information about an organization and are usually assembled to support an event such as a news conference, media day, or new product launch. One advantage of a media kit is its usefulness as a take-home piece to support one of the aforementioned events (Treadwell & Treadwell, 2000). Media kits generally contain a news release corresponding with the event, as well as biographies, fact sheets, and other information.

## Biographies

Events such as a news conference typically feature a speech or presentation by a key person within the organization. Biographies on those individuals will help journalists put together a story about the event. Common information contained in a biography includes correct spelling of the person's name and title, years with the organization, previous employment experience, educational background, and family information.

## Fact Sheets

Fact sheets are brief one-page bulleted outlines of information about the event that is taking place (Smith, 2005). Information is usually presented in a standard who, what, where, when, why, and how format, although providing some context for the announcement may be necessary, such as organizational background and history (frequently called a "backgrounder") as well as the significance of the event.

## Other Items

Other elements of a media kit will vary depending on the nature of the event. If a formal presentation with visual elements like graphs and charts is used, including copies in the media kit or distributing them immediately afterward will aid the journalists' reporting. Photos in either printed or electronic form may also be appropriate. For example, if the event involves a new product launch or logo unveiling, providing an electronic image of the product or logo may increase the likelihood that it will appear on that evening's newscast.

## Social Media Releases

Public relations professionals have begun to harness the power and influence of social networking for promotional purposes through the use of **social media releases (SMRs)**. This new way of conceiving a news release provides organizations an oppor-

Courtesy of Oklahoma Christian University

# A Media Member's Perspective on News Releases

**Murray Evans**

Less than two decades ago, the transmission time for press releases was much slower than it is today. I can recall a time in the late 1980s, while working for a major metropolitan daily newspaper, when that newspaper only had one fax machine in its office building. When you received a fax, it was important.

During the intervening years, technology has completely changed the way that news operations do business. Reporters who used to rely on regular mail (or overnight delivery if something was particularly urgent) now look to e-mail and cell phones, and because of round-the-clock competition, stories that 20 years ago might have not been seen until the next day's newspaper now are immediately published on blogs or media websites.

The basic job of a reporter—gather the news, impartially analyze it, and disseminate it—hasn't changed, but the methods used to accomplish that goal certainly have. As a result, the demands on reporters have increased significantly. Through technology, more and more people have the ability to promote to the media what they believe to be newsworthy events and subjects.

Now, faxes are mostly a thing of the past, and those that do come in usually end up in the trash can because of clutter and overkill.

How do public relations professionals avoid being lost in the shuffle? They must be flexible, creative, and sometimes aggressive in promoting their news releases to the media.

From a reporter's standpoint, a news release should have several characteristics.

- Timely. We don't want to know about old news, unless there is a compelling new angle. We also don't want to learn about potential news at the last minute, if at all possible. If you want to promote an upcoming event that you know will be of interest to a reporter, give the reporter as much lead time as possible to prepare and schedule for the event. If a particular release is more important than usual, it's OK to call and let the reporter know that. It might even be wise. One large university that I used to cover sent me dozens of releases weekly, but its public relations workers made it a point to contact me before (or immediately after) any exceptionally important release to make sure that I was aware of it. For a reporter who covers several beats—and in these days of frequent media layoffs, most reporters fall into that category—that service was invaluable.

- Concise. News releases should be long enough to explain the subject matter and offer pertinent background, but no more than that. As a basic rule, anything longer than two pages often won't be read. A reporter interested in doing a story about the subject matter can call the contact person listed on the news release for more information and background.

- Newsworthy. This point would seem to go without saying—you wouldn't put out a release unless it had some news value in your eyes—but sometimes public relations professionals make the mistake of overkill. Not every detail of your organization or program is of interest to the public at large, which is who the media purport to represent. One small school that I have covered sends as many as 20 athletics-related releases each week during the school year. Were it a major college, that number might be acceptable, but because of the school's size, more often than not the releases are thrown away or deleted from e-mail without being read. Remember to whom you're sending the releases. Although a minor detail about your program might be of interest to local and regional media, larger media outlets that don't cover you on a regular basis might not be interested. Don't overwhelm them.

- Honest. Reporters understand that a public relations professional's job is to put the best picture on any given situation. Inevitably, however, negative situations will arise concerning your organization upon which the media must report. When such a situation occurs,

*(continued)*

*(continued)*

ignoring it or glossing it over will only damage your credibility with the media. For example, if a player from your organization is arrested and charged with a crime, and then dismissed from the team as a result, you shouldn't hide behind catch phrases such as "The player broke team rules." Arrest reports and court documents are public record anyway, and a good reporter will uncover the real reason for the player's dismissal or punishment.

- Convenient. In many cases, a reporter might not have time to follow up sufficiently on the subject of a news release, especially in this era when reduced staffing levels mean that reporters often must juggle numerous stories simultaneously. If the release concisely explains the subject and offers comments from people connected with the story, the reporter's job is much easier. If a reporter cannot cover a press conference held in conjunction with the news release because of time constraints, having quotes in the news release helps immensely. Be flexible, too. If you really want coverage from a particular news organization but a reporter can't make it at the time you've scheduled for your release and press conference, offer them the story early. If it needs to be embargoed until a certain time, most reporters are willing to do so.

More often than not, reporters appreciate the assistance offered by public relations professionals, and many have grown to depend on that assistance in the day-to-day grind of doing their jobs. The best reporters view the work done by public relations professionals as a useful tool and want to have a good relationship. How can you promote that?

**The basic job of a reporter—gather the news, impartially analyze it, and disseminate it—hasn't changed, but the methods used to accomplish that goal certainly have.**

First, be available. News doesn't always happen at convenient hours, so a reporter should have numerous ways to reach you, especially if you're the main contact person for your organization. A work phone number no longer suffices. Give reporters who cover your organization your home and cell numbers. Frequently check your e-mail, voicemail, and text inbox for requests. If you will be unavailable, let your beat reporters know and give them other contact options in case something happens while you're out.

It's also a good idea to contact your beat reporters every so often to see whether you're meeting their needs. Visiting with reporters during nondeadline situations is a good way to build relationships and learn how each reporter does his or her job. Do they prefer releases through e-mail, text, or another method, or do they just want you to call when you have news to share? What is their particular work schedule like?

Finally, be realistic. At times you'll think that a reporter has overlooked something newsworthy, or you'll be irritated about how a story that a reporter has written turned out. Remember, it works both ways—reporters can sometimes be upset with public relations professionals. When that happens, it's good for both parties to remember that burning professional bridges is counterproductive.

*Based in Oklahoma City, Murray Evans is assistant athletic director of Media Relations at Oklahoma Christian University. He has worked as a sports journalist for more than 23 years.*

tunity to share news in a way that reaches publics with information that matters to them, who, in turn, share with others through text, links, bookmarks, tags, and other forms (Solis & Breakenridge, 2009). As Scott (2009) put it, an organization's primary audience is no longer a handful of journalists, but the whole world.

Because content from SMRs is shared among users with similar interests, SMRs represent a tacit third-party endorsement for an organization's products or services. Solis and Breakenridge (2009, p. 117) suggested that the difference made by SMRs "lies in how people interact with it and discover it, and also the tools they use to share and rebroadcast it."

The toolkit for creating effective SMRs includes actualities and podcasts, B-Roll, video news releases, tags, bookmarks, and compelling photos.

## Actualities and Podcasts

An actuality is merely the recording of a quote or speech from an organizational spokesperson made available to the media by the organization (Treadwell & Treadwell, 2000; Smith, 2005). Actualities are generally recorded in advance of their distribution and are an effective way of ensuring that the organizational point of view is presented to radio media, even if the media cannot physically interview the individual. Actualities can be provided on audio CD or made available to download through a computer as an MP3 file. Treadwell and Treadwell (2000) advised providing an accompanying transcript and background information to help journalists present the information.

Some confusion exists about what constitutes a podcast. According to Scott (2009, p. 70), "a podcast is simply audio content connected to an RSS feed." Although the word was derived from Apple's iPod, podcasts can be listened to on an iPod, MP3 player, or directly through a computer. Podcasts vary in length and format. Some, like the Baseball History Podcast, which is produced by fans as a hobby, are less than 10 minutes long. Others, such as the Sports Business Radio podcast, which includes interviews with industry executives, are nearly an hour long.

Scott (2009) noted that the benefits of podcasting from a marketing perspective include developing and regularly updating content that is directed at specific types of buyers. From a public relations perspective, organizations may find it useful to create podcasts of important news conferences or one-on-one interviews with coaches, players, or administrators.

## B-Roll

Organizations frequently provide video B-Roll to television media as a means to deliver quoted statements or other visual information. A video **B-Roll** is a taped series of unedited video shots and sound bites related to a news story (Smith, 2005). A B-Roll is also sometimes referred to as cover video (Cremer, Keirstead, & Yoakam, 1996). Typical video shots may include behind-the-scenes video that a sport organization would like to release to the media. But the organization may not want to allow the media unfettered access to shoot. For safety reasons, a university that is building a new arena may shoot B-Roll of the progress inside the construction zone rather than have the media shoot it themselves.

An obvious consideration for the sport organization is performing a cost–benefit analysis of shooting B-Roll. An organization will incur a significant expense to hire a freelance videographer to shoot B-Roll. Additional cost is associated with editing the B-Roll into logical sequences and producing individual tapes to present to television stations. All this expense will be wasted if no station airs the video, which they are not obligated to do.

## Video News Releases

Although similar to B-Roll, a video news release (VNR) has a slightly different objective. B-Roll contains unedited video that the sport organization provides to the television station in hopes that the station will edit it into a story. A VNR is a ready-for-broadcast package that the organization offers to the television station in hopes that the station will "plug and play" (Treadwell & Treadwell, 2000, p. 263). Lorenz and Vivian (1996) advised keeping a VNR to between 60 and 90 seconds and preparing it to have the feel of a news story.

Organizations often have similar reservations about the costs and benefit of a VNR as they do about B-Roll. VNRs carry increased expenses because of the time necessary to edit B-Roll into video that matches the audio script. In addition, the organization may need to hire someone to record the voice-over for the VNR if no one within the organization is available to record it. VNRs frequently have a lower usage rate by television stations than does B-Roll (Treadwell & Treadwell, 2000).

The popularity of social media and video sharing sites has created an additional avenue for organizations to post their video news releases. By creating an official YouTube channel, organizations can easily share their VNRs with fans of the organization. Similar to standard news releases, these VNR postings should be shared across the organization's other social media sites. Solis and Breakenridge (2009, p. 126) suggested that "online video is the next frontier for PR professionals, adding a new layer of engagement to any existing PR, marketing, and web initiative."

## Tags

An easy way to conceive of a tag in social media releases is to think of a filing cabinet that has several file folders. A tag represents an individual file folder on a specific topic that can be easily searched at an organization's website or at a social media site such as a YouTube channel. As an organization's content is published, several one- or two-word tags should be applied to "file" the SMR in a certain folder. As new readers discover the content, they can easily seek additional, related content.

The concept of geotagging uses latitude and longitude coordinates to add geographical identification to content such as RSS feeds, Twitter status updates, videos, and photographs. This feature can be useful for sport organizations that want to show the sight line of a particular seat in a stadium or along a race course such as the Tour de France.

## Bookmarks

Social bookmarking sites such as Delicious, Digg, and StumbleUpon permit registered users to bookmark the URL of a particular website and tag it for later use. These sites also allow users to share and rate individual stories and URLs. Ostensibly,

higher-rated stories generate greater buzz for their organizations.

## Photography

A sport public relations professional must have access to a reliable photographer who can capture the organization's successes to be forever reproduced. The old saying that a picture is worth a thousand words is definitely true in sport. Lechner (1996, p. 157) called photography the "best medium to convey positive information in a story-telling manner with memorable impact."

Sport public relations professionals use photography on a daily basis as a means to promote the organization. Photos are an essential component to the forms of organizational media discussed in

**Engaging, dynamic action shots are useful tools in promoting your organization.**

AP Photo/Mike Segar, Pool

chapter 5, such as media guides, programs, and posters. In addition, photography is a key component of the organization's website, and social media sharing sites such as Flickr, Picasa, and Facebook allow users to upload and share photos with other users or with no restrictions.

Two types of photos frequently used by public relations professionals are head shots and action shots. Head shots, or mug shots, are basic portrait photos of an individual commonly used in organizational media. The sport public relations person should organize a day before the beginning of the season to shoot photos of team members and coaches. Individuals should dress similarly to one another, perhaps in dress clothes or a team uniform (Lechner, 1996).

Action shots, as the name implies, are photos made during an event of some kind, such as an athletic competition or a press conference that the organization intends to use for publicity purposes in the future. A good rule of thumb for the organization is to have a photographer present at all official functions to capture the spirit of the event.

Because photos shot by photojournalists are copyrighted by the photojournalist's news organization or the individual photographer, an organization may not use them for publicity purposes without consent. Therefore, a sport organization must either hire a permanent photographer to serve on its staff or contract with local freelance photographers. An organization that chooses the freelance route must consider several points when contracting with a photographer.

First, the parties must be certain to agree in advance on the pay rate. Some photographers charge by the hour, whereas others charge per day or half day. The organization must clarify whether the rate includes expenses such as travel and special equipment (Lechner, 1996). Often those expenses are in addition to the hourly or day rate.

Second, the organization must pay attention to the terms of the contract with the photographer. Of particular importance to the organization are the usage rights and ownership of the photos. The organization should strive for usage rights as broad as possible that permit the organization to use pictures made by the photographer in media guides, programs, websites, posters, and other organizational media without paying a royalty to the photographer. This stipulation may increase the hourly or daily rate charged by the photographer, but it will save the organization headaches and money in the future.

Usage rights should also clarify whether the organization can provide the photos to news organizations for publicity purposes. Finally, the contract should specify the byline to be used in conjunction with the published photos. Organizations typically provide credit to the photographer in the front of media guides or program, but doing so is less common in other forms of organizational media such as posters. Frequently, a byline will include both the organization's name and the name of the photographer.

Third, an organization should get subject permission when using photos for commercial purposes. This point is generally not a problem for people associated with the organization such as coaches and team members, but it might be an issue for a prominent guest speaker or alumni who may want compensation for the use of his or her likeness. Photos made exclusively for editorial usage in programs, websites, and media guides are protected under the First Amendment's freedom of speech clause (Lechner, 1996).

## SUMMARY

Because a sport public relations professional functions as a conduit between the mass media and the organization, the distribution of organizational information becomes one of the profession's key aspects. Understanding the methods accepted in the industry for identifying newsworthy information and distributing it can increase the likelihood that the organization will receive favorable coverage. Many tactics are employed to deliver information to the media. Public relations professionals should recognize that the preferred tactic will vary among media types. Incorporating a variety of tactics, such as news releases, media kits, and SMRs, will enhance publicity for the organization.

1. Write a news release about yourself being hired at your first job.

2. Research a current professional athlete and write a news release as if she or he is retiring.

3. Visit your university's athletics website and print off game notes for an upcoming basketball game. Watch the game and write a news release after the game summarizing what occurred. Try to complete your news release within 60 minutes of the end of the game.

4. Attend a university-sponsored news conference. Are media kits being distributed at the event? If so, what sort of information is included in them?

9

# Staging Interviews, News Conferences, and Media Events

**After reading this chapter, students should be able to**

- describe how to use an interview to communicate organizational messages;
- illustrate the steps necessary to prepare someone for a media interview;
- determine what makes an announcement worthy of a news conference;
- identify the key elements of a news conference; and
- distinguish among news conference formats such as teleconferences, media days, and postevent opportunities.

**Key terms discussed in this chapter include**

- interview,
- message development,
- news conference,
- teleconference,

- backdrop,
- moderator, and
- multibox.

**In a memorable** moment from the movie *Bull Durham*, the character of Crash Davis, a veteran catcher, advises hotshot rookie pitcher Nuke LaLoosh to commit a series of cliches to memory for use whenever he's interviewed. LaLoosh responds that the cliches are boring, but that is Davis' point. Sport media have an insatiable appetite for quotes, regardless of how substantive the quote may be. Sayings such as "They need to step up and make plays," "She plays within herself," and "He's coming into his own" dominate today's sport pages.

Representatives of sport organizations must recognize that interview opportunities are just that, opportunities for the organization to communicate messages to its targeted publics. This chapter focuses on the responsibilities of public relations professionals in managing an organization's message through interviews and news conferences. It examines how to prepare individuals to be interviewed by encouraging responses that are consistent with organizational goals and objectives. This chapter also provides a basic checklist for staging a successful news conference as well as a formula for identifying the best timing and location to hold a news conference. Finally, the chapter explores how sport organizations can benefit from hosting a day for the media to interact with players and coaches.

## Interviews

One of the most basic ways in which a journalist gathers information for a story is through interviews. Smith (2005) defined the basic **interview** as a session in which journalists ask questions and someone from the organization responds.

Although that sounds simple, sport interviews are much more complicated. Many interviews are conducted following an event in which the team lost on a last-second play, an occurrence that could adversely affect an interviewee's mind-set before he or she addresses the media. In one memorable moment after Kansas lost the 2003 National Collegiate Athletic Association (NCAA) championship to Syracuse, Jayhawks head coach Roy Williams was asked by CBS' Bonnie Bernstein about rumors that he was going to leave Kansas for North Carolina. Williams responded with an expletive on live national television. He subsequently went to North Carolina.

Hall, Nichols, Moynahan, and Taylor (2007) identified specific characteristics of a sport interview: It is an interchange of information between two or more parties who ask and answer questions, and it

has a specific purpose. Examining those characteristics provides insight into how a sport organization can use an interview situation to its advantage.

By viewing the interview as more than a response to a question, a sport organization can use the exchange as a vehicle to deliver its message about a given subject. Rather than simply respond to a reporter's questions, interviewees should think of the interview as a two-way street by which the organization uses the media to reach a wide audience (Hall et al., 2007; Hessert, 2002).

In all likelihood, the reporter's purpose is to report a story that will inform readers, viewers, or listeners. The organization's purpose may be to explain a critical moment of the game or reinforce positive images of the organization (Hall et al., 2007). A sport interview is thus an opportunity for organizational representatives to respond to media questions with organizational messages.

Public relations professionals who recognize that interviews can be used to the organization's benefit can assist the process from the moment when a member of the media calls to request an interview by fielding the request professionally, selecting an appropriate interviewee, and preparing the interviewee.

## Fielding Media Requests

Often a sport organization reacts to inquiries from the media for interviews as opposed to proactively seeking interview opportunities. The public relations person is usually the first contact between the media and the organization. As such, when fielding media requests, the public relations person should seek to gain information that will help prepare the best response possible.

Specifically, public relations professionals should attempt to determine the reporter's deadline and the story angles that the reporter is working on, including any specific technical information that the reporter might be seeking. Many reporters will comply with these questions because they recognize that they will likely receive better responses from prepared interviewees. Some may be reluctant, however, for fear that the information might hold up the interview process or eliminate the element of surprise (Lorenz & Vivian, 1996).

Early identification of the reporter's time line allows the organization to gauge how long it has to develop a response before the reporter's story will hit the newspaper or airwaves. Understanding what story angles the reporter is working on will help public relations involve the best spokesperson.

For example, if the reporter wants to know why the team is not interested in offering a contract to its free-agent pitcher, the organization may want the owner or general manager to respond because the decision may involve complicated financial issues.

## Preparing the Interviewee

Gauging a public relations professional's direct value to a sport organization is often difficult, but astute public relations practitioners recognize their contribution in preparing interviewees. Harvey Greene, vice president of media relations for the Miami Dolphins, views his role in the interview process as one of helping the team focus by limiting off-field distractions (H. Greene, personal communication, July 23, 2003). He never wants coaches or athletes to be surprised by what they are asked.

Hessert (2000) advised public relations professionals to have a strategy in place that anticipates questions from the media and determines specific goals and messages to be communicated. In many instances, professionals can coach interview subjects regarding those central messages. The sidebar titled Tools for Controlling the Interview describes three techniques for getting to central messages.

Public relations professionals can contribute positively to the interview process in several ways. First, as stated, public relations professionals are usually the first line of communication between the media and the organization. They can exploit this power by gaining as much knowledge as possible of the reporter's topic, story angles, and sources, which will aid in developing and shaping a response (Rowe, Alexander, Earl, & Esser, 2001).

Second, a fundamental responsibility is to understand the media and the external environment of the organization. By trying to think like a reporter, the public relations professional is better able to anticipate what questions might be asked before the interview begins and develop a possible response.

If a member of the university football team is placed on academic suspension, the public relations professional should outline information that will be helpful to the head coach when he is interviewed. A reporter is likely to want to know if the player is the only one suspended or if others might follow. The reporter may also ask how the player's absence will affect the lineup and game preparations. Arming the coach with specifics such as team grade point average can help emphasize a positive rather than dwell on the negative.

Not all anticipated questions relate directly to the organization. Lisa Mushett, assistant sports information director at Notre Dame when Tyrone Willingham was hired as head football coach, recalls that Willingham, the most prominent Division I-A African American head coach, was frequently asked

## Tools for Controlling the Interview

Although the interviewer is the one asking the questions, the interviewee may exert considerable influence on the direction of the conversation. The following list offers three tools for exerting some level of control.

- *Bridging:* Deal with the question honestly and briefly and then move logically to your message. Before you bridge, you must answer the question. Examples include the following:
  - Yes, and in addition . . .
  - No. Let me explain . . .
  - I don't know. I do know that . . .
  - That's the way it used to be. Now . . .

- *Flagging:* Emphasize to reporters what you want them to highlight—what one piece of information you want them to print or broadcast. Examples include the following:
  - The most important thing is . . .
  - This is the bottom line . . .
  - If you remember one thing about our organization . . .

- *Hooking:* You can prompt the next question you want asked by ending your response with a hook. If the interviewer doesn't respond to hooks, then bridge. Examples include the following:
  - And that's just one possibility . . .
  - We've done something no other organization has done . . .

to comment on the National Football League's (NFL's) attempts to increase minority hiring of head coaches. Although these questions had nothing to do with Fighting Irish football, the media still sought Willingham's thoughts on the situation (personal communication, July 28, 2003).

Similarly, the 2010 Southeastern Conference football media days in Alabama occurred at a time when news stories began surfacing about illegal agent contact with a college football student–athlete at the University of North Carolina. Although the alleged incident took place at a non-SEC school, most of the coaches interviewed at media days were asked to discuss the role of agents and their potential contact with student–athletes.

Additionally, public relations professionals may assist organization representatives in preparing interviewees by offering coaching in the areas of **message development**, presentation skills, and the notion of information that is "off the record" or "not for attribution." In the sidebar titled Preparing for a Successful Interview, veteran sport publicist Frank Zang offers suggestions for proper preparation and conduct during an interview.

## Message Development

The media use various tactics to elicit responses from an interviewee. The mere phrasing of a question can affect how a person responds to a given question. Reporters often use open-ended questions, which don't limit answers (Wilstein, 2002). Consider the following questions from a reporter to a coach:

1. Have you ever been more frustrated by your team's play?
2. You must be frustrated. Describe your thoughts on your team's play.

In the first question, the reporter is asking a simple yes-or-no question in a negative tone. If the coach were to answer no to that question, it is easy to imagine a headline the next morning that reads, "Coach Frustrated by Team's Play." In the second question, however, the reporter is leaving the door open for the coach to influence the interview by falling back on one or two organizational messages.

As Hessert (2000) pointed out, the average audience remembers one major point from any given speaker. Deciding on several key messages in advance and sticking to them allows the public relations professional and interviewee to influence the direction of the interview.

One method of identifying messages and repeating them throughout an interview involves keeping in mind the rule of 3s (Rowe et al., 2001). Write down the three message points that the organization deems the most important. State each of the three messages three different times during the interview, bearing in mind that you may be able to convey the same message in different ways (Rowe et al., 2001). Although the organization may not have three different message points that it wants to convey in the interview, the concept of repeating key points multiple times throughout the interview is fundamental to the organization's ability to communicate.

When Mike Mularkey was hired as head coach of the Buffalo Bills in January 2004, he met the local media in a news conference in which a number of questions were thrown at him. In his introductory comments, Mularkey stated that the Super Bowl was "my objective and it's been my objective. I'm a big goal setter." Later during the news conference when asked about the team's direction, Mularkey responded, "You have to set goals and the Super Bowl is the goal" (*Bills Introduce*, 2004).

By repeating that message more than once, Mularkey helped shaped the story written in the *Buffalo News* the next day. The article summarizing the news conference ended with four paragraphs that discussed Mularkey's goal of reaching the Super Bowl, including the quote, "You have to set goals and the Super Bowl is the goal" (Gaughan, 2004).

## Presentation

Interviewees should consider the form of mass media in choosing their approach to each interview because each form is seeking something different. In the event that more than one form of media is present, interviewees should generally use the approach with the widest appeal.

An old saying in business is that "Image is everything." Image plays a vital role in sport as well, especially in interviews. Athletes and coaches can use media exposure to alter or reinforce their public image. In addition, interviewees who put extra effort into their dress, composure, and mannerisms present a better image of themselves than those who don't. Weisman (2002) quoted Cleveland Browns wide receiver Andre Davis as saying, "Anytime you have the opportunity to speak to the media and get on TV, I think you want to let people know what kind of person you are" (p. 1c).

Appearance is important not only for television but for all media. Each of the three major media types has unique qualities that, if the interviewee recognizes them, can facilitate positive impressions of the organization. Further, athletes and administrators are advised to consider their social media status updates as a form of interview.

# Preparing for a Successful Interview

## Frank Zang

Photo courtesy of Boise State University. Photographer John Kelly.

In an interview, only you are responsible for what comes out of your mouth. It is the reporter's job to ask questions. The inquiry may be inappropriate, ill-founded, accusatory, simplistic, or the best question you ever heard. Your job is to answer the question in the most appropriate manner. You are in control.

Before the first question is ever asked, you should already have an answer. What information do you want to deliver? What do you want to say about the topic? Most reporters need your help when they ask questions. They are seeking comment or information that puts their story in context. Without you, they may not have a story. Sometimes they just need an answer—any answer. This is the opportunity to tell your story.

The interview is not always a gut-wrenching experience, but neither is it a conversation between long-lost friends. Remember, you are talking to the public through a reporter. Because you are dealing with the mass media, your side of the dialogue can be heard in much larger circles. Some are masters at this game, and practice matters. You need to remember the purpose of the interview and keep these points in mind.

### Do's

- Be simple, clear, and direct in your answers. Know your message. Make a significant statement.
- Be yourself and show your personality. Be friendly and conversational but remember that there is no such thing as "off the record."
- Repeat your key points.
- Know your audience and develop your answers from their point of view.
- Correct inaccuracies in a reporter's statement or question.
- Use adjectives, headlines, facts, and examples.
- Respect the deadlines of the reporter.
- Practice modesty in victory and self-control in defeat.

### Don'ts

- Don't lie or mislead. You must be truthful to be credible.
- Don't be compelled to say more than you need to. After you answer the question, stop talking.
- Don't speculate on hypothetical questions. Talk only about what you know. Don't guess.
- Don't say, "No comment." It raises the red flag that you have something to hide. If you cannot answer, explain why.
- Don't use jargon that is too technical for the public to understand.
- Don't repeat negative questions in a response.
- Don't allow yourself to be provoked or to argue with a reporter.
- Don't trash your competitor or blame someone.

When conducting an interview, the TV lights and microphone may be in your face, but you have rights as the interviewee. Before the first question is asked, you have the right to know who

*(continued)*

*(continued)*

is conducting the interview, the subject matter, the setting, and the approximate length, including time limits. When fielding questions, you do not have to answer every one. You can defer questions to a third party when appropriate. Finally, you have the right to use your own words by not repeating the reporter's question in your answer.

There are different types of interviews, and your answers need to match the medium. For television, interviewees should speak in 10- to 15-second sound bites. You want to give a concise, straightforward answer. The length of the average sound bite is 8 seconds. Make yourself presentable—pretend that your mother is watching. Don't fall for an interviewer's pause at the end of your answer. That moment of silence is when the most ill-prepared answers are given. Answer your question and then stop (Condron, 2001).

For radio, your answers can be 20- to 30-second responses that provide a little more explanation. Your answers do not need to be as short as those for television. This medium is more relaxed, and you do not need to pause as you do in newspaper interviews. Give good, solid answers and do not ramble.

For print, you have the opportunity to provide background, perspective, and detail around your quote. But remember that what you say will be in black and white for everyone to read (Condron, 2001). If reporters are taking notes, give them time to write. If you talk too fast, they will accurately jot down only the first, third, and fifth statements.

In this age of streaming video and live coverage, you need to be aware that your every word and movement is public. There is no editing. You must be in the zone with your interview game face on.

Preparation is the key to a good interview. Ask in advance what the interview is about, how long it will be, and what materials you need. If the interview comes as a surprise, ask whether you can call the reporter back. Being an expert in your field does not ensure that you will give an expert interview. You can anticipate the most newsworthy questions and have key talking points in your head or on paper. You should know your agenda in advance and bend the response in that direction so that your message is heard. If a question does not make sense, come up with an answer that does (Condron, 2001). If a question stumps you, do not blurt out the first thought that comes to your mind.

> Although the reporter is asking questions, you have equal control of the interview. Prepare in advance, bridge to your message, repeat your key points, and be yourself, and you will conduct a successful interview.

If you simply do not know the answer to a question, say, "I don't know," but offer to find the information or identify the appropriate person, if possible. If a question catches you off guard, pause before you answer to collect your thoughts. If the interview is live, you may need to redirect. It is as simple as ABC: "I can't *answer* that *because* of our policy on pending litigations, but what I *can* tell you is that our organization is working hard . . ." (Kirby, 1995).

Perception is reality. Your appearance is sometimes more important than your words. Your clothes, posture, eye contact, and gestures all communicate a message.

At the end of an interview, as you are shaking hands and thanking the reporter, remember that the interview is not over until the reporter walks out the door. That last off-the-cuff statement could be the next day's headline. If you were uneasy about the interview, offer to provide additional information or clarifications. Asking a reporter to see the story in advance is not appropriate. If inaccuracies appear in a story, call the reporter and politely provide corrections. If the story is well done, drop a quick thank-you note to the journalist.

Most interviews are friendly encounters and not nerve-racking interrogations. You have an opportunity to promote yourself, your team, or your organization. Although the reporter is asking questions, you have equal control of the interview. Prepare in advance, bridge to your message, repeat your key points, and be yourself, and you will conduct a successful interview.

*Frank Zang is the director of university communications at Boise State University. Zang has worked in the media relations office at Georgia Tech, the U.S. Olympic Committee, the Salt Lake Organizing Committee, and the Utah Athletic Foundation.*

## Television

Most television news stories run approximately 60 seconds, and most clips during those stories are 10 to 20 seconds in length, hence the term *sound bite*, which effectively describes what television provides, a bite of sound.

How can interviewees get their message across in 10 to 20 seconds? Several pointers can help them improve their organization's image and deliver their key message on television.

First, interviewees should keep answers concise and try to avoid rambling. Hessert (2002) equated good interviewing to good driving: "It's awfully hard to crash and burn at 30 mph" (p. 24). She advised interviewees to pause a few seconds to collect their thoughts before answering, even in broadcast interviews. Unless the interview is live, the broadcaster will likely edit out the silence.

Second, interviewees should repeat messages. Because television journalists are likely to use only 20 seconds of an interview, interviewees increase the odds that key messages will make it into those 20 seconds by going back to the message frequently.

Third, interviewees should look at the reporter, not the camera. Typically, a television reporter stands to one side of the camera or the other, and because the reporter, not the camera, is asking the question, the interviewee should focus on the reporter.

Finally, interviewees should practice posture, appearance, and nonverbal gestures. Most newspaper writers do not incorporate gestures like slouching or lip licking into their stories, and they generally eliminate "ums" and "uhs" from quotes. Broadcast, however, amplifies those images and sounds (Weisman, 2002).

Many organizations employ professional media trainers to improve the image and effectiveness of interviewees. Media trainers frequently videotape potential interviewees and use the videotape as a training tool.

## Radio

Radio is similar to television in that interviewees should seek to limit the length of their answers and not provide rambling responses. But unlike television, radio interviews do not need to be face to face. Through the use of telephones, sound can be recorded anywhere, allowing a radio reporter to conduct an interview from halfway around the world. That flexibility means that radio is an informal medium. Interviews tend to be more conversational than in other media. Because of that informality, interview-

ees should be wary of not becoming too relaxed and deviating from the predetermined messages.

## Print

Although both television and radio interviews can be conducted live, print interviews are typed, edited, and reproduced. This process can be both an advantage and a disadvantage for the interviewee.

Because print reporters are not limited by time constraints, interviewees can provide more in-depth answers to questions, improving the odds that the organizational message will be conveyed in the story. On the flip side, the likelihood is greater that the interviewee's statements will be misquoted or taken out of context because they are not recorded and played. Many reporters tape-record interviews, but others do not. As Wilstein (2002) stated, using tape recorders has several drawbacks, including speed and convenience. Transcribing an interview generally takes up to four times longer than conducting the interview.

Even the best reporters find it difficult to listen to an audiotape of an interview and type at the same time. Most play a portion of the tape, stop the tape, and type what they just heard. They repeat the process until they have typed the entire quote.

## Social Media Status Updates

People are continually cautioned about how they represent themselves when updating popular social networking sites such as Facebook and Twitter. Journalists consider those comments and updates as being on the record, and they frequently report those details. Increasingly, athletes are being reprimanded by team, league, and other organizational authorities about inappropriate status updates.

Running back Larry Johnson, playing for the Kansas City Chiefs at the time, updated his Twitter account in October 2009 following a 37-7 loss to the San Diego Chargers with language critical of head coach Todd Haley: "My father played for the coach from 'rememeber the titans.' Our coach played golf. My father played for redskins briefley. Our coach. Nuthn" (Rosenthal, 2009). Johnson's comments were widely reported in the media as if Johnson had spoken them directly. Shortly thereafter, Johnson was released by the Chiefs. Although other factors may have contributed to his release, the organization was clearly frustrated with his actions.

Texas Tech University banned its football players from using Twitter in September 2009 after linebacker Marlon Williams Tweeted that the team was waiting on head coach Mike Leach, who was late to a mandatory team meeting (*Texas Tech*, 2009).

### Off the Record and Not for Attribution

The notion of presenting information in an interview off the record poses a problem for journalists. Reporters add credibility to their stories when they identify sources (Lorenz & Vivian, 1996). When interviewees say that something is off the record, journalists are placed in a difficult position. Should they report the information, which is likely newsworthy, or not?

Lorenz and Vivian (1996) defined *off the record* as information given "so that a reporter will better understand a confusing or potentially harmful situation. . . . The information is not to be disseminated, even in conversation" (pp. 374–375). Hall and colleagues (2007) similarly defined *off the record* as "an agreement prohibiting the reporter from using the information in any way in pursuit of the story. . . . He or she also pledges not to repeat it to other sources" (p. 216). Note the emphasis in both of those definitions is not repeating the information.

Understanding the definition of *off the record* and deciding whether to make a statement that is off the record are two different things. After an organization has disclosed sensitive information, it can no longer control it (Hall et al., 2007). The organization should probably not disclose information that it does not wish to see publicized in the media, even if it is off the record.

Information that is off the record differs somewhat from information that is not for attribution, a tactic commonly employed in politics to release information to the media on the record, but without identifying the speaker. "A White House spokesperson confirmed" is a frequently heard statement around Washington, D.C. The practice is becoming more commonplace in sport. Organizations often disclose information, such as a pending news conference, to stimulate interest by the media.

## Controlling Postevent Interviews

Immediately following any sporting event, participants and coaches face a number of demands. Depending on the type of competition, these demands can include live television interviews, radio shows, team meetings, award ceremonies, drug testing, and media interviews.

As mentioned in chapter 5, every organization should develop a media policy that clearly communicates postevent interview procedures to the media. Public relations professionals also have several responsibilities as the event draws to a conclusion, including polling the media to find out who they wish to interview and arranging for live television and radio interviews.

### Polling the Media

The advantage of an open locker room, which is mandated by most professional leagues, is that media members can interview anyone they wish. For organizations with a closed locker room, the public relations professional is responsible for asking media representatives who they wish to interview (Davis, 1998). This task should be done toward the end of the contest, although the public relations person should understand that the media will want to talk to anyone who scores a game-winning goal or makes a last-second basket.

More often than not, most media members will request the same interviewees. Requested interviewees should be brought to the news conference room for the benefit of all media in attendance. Occasionally, a reporter may ask to interview someone that no one else wishes to talk to. In that case, the public relations professional should arrange for the reporter and the individual to meet, perhaps in the hallway outside the interview area.

### Arranging Postevent Interviews

Organizations love the publicity generated by live television broadcasts of their athletic events. For public relations professionals, live events mean increased responsibilities. Television production groups usually meet with the organization at least a day in advance. Any in-game or postgame interview possibilities should be discussed at this meeting. Assuming that both sides agree to in-game or postgame interviews, the public relations person will need to escort the coach or athlete to the area where the interview will take place (Davis, 1998). Taking the organizational representative to the television camera is much easier than vice versa. Rights-holding media such as television and radio networks are frequently given preferential treatment regarding live postevent interviews because they have paid for the right to cover the event and other media outlets, such as newspapers, have not.

Many organizations have a postgame radio show during which the coach and a player of the game are interviewed. The challenge for the public relations person is to balance the needs of the radio affiliate doing a live broadcast and the other media seeking to interview the same coach and athlete in the interview room.

One strategy is to have the coach conduct a news conference first and then do the radio show. This approach allows the coach to limit time in the news conference and conduct a more relaxed interview with the affiliated radio announcers, who are likely to be less confrontational than the media representatives in a news conference in which multiple people ask questions.

# News Conferences

As with news releases and other forms of information services discussed in chapter 6, the goal of a **news conference** is to disseminate noteworthy information from an organization to its targeted publics. Smith (2005) stated simply that "a news conference is a contrived media happening in which an organizational spokesperson makes a newsworthy statement" (p. 197). After the spokesperson finishes the statement, reporters usually have the opportunity to ask questions.

This definition addresses two key aspects to consider when calling a news conference, namely a newsworthy statement and an organizational spokesperson. In other words, what is the organization saying and who is saying it?

A wise first step by an organization is to address why it is considering holding the news conference before going to the trouble of actually doing it (Condron, 2001). An organization should always consider whether holding a news conference will achieve its intended goals. Many organizations wrongly believe that staging an elaborate news conference to impress the team owner automatically results in positive news stories.

As discussed in chapter 8, members of the media generally use six criteria to determine the news value of a story: timeliness, impact, prominence, conflict, unusualness, and proximity (Thompson, 1996). The same criteria should be used to determine whether a sport organization should hold a news conference (Hall et al., 2007).

Although the announcement of a new head coach or a trade involving a star player almost always warrants a news conference, the announcement of a new

footwear sponsor for an athletic team may not. All the aforementioned may be considered timely and important to the operation of a sport organization, but media often prefer not to cover sponsorship agreements because they view such announcements as free advertisement for the sponsor.

Condron (2001) suggested that if an organization does not have a newsworthy reason for staging a news conference, it should not expect a return audience. Merely holding the news conference may not be enough to garner media attention. An organization that calls unnecessary news conferences may get a reputation similar to that of the boy who cried wolf. If and when something deserving of a news conference occurs, the media may be reluctant to attend based on previous experience.

Opinions differ as to what kinds of statements deserve a news conference. Smith (2005) provided three justifications for holding a news conference:

1. To announce news or give a response of major importance
2. To serve the media's interests when a prominent spokesperson is available only for a short time
3. To avoid accusations of playing favorites among reporters

Baus and Lesly (1998) outlined two instances when an organization should hold a news conference:

1. If it will provide the media with something that they could not get in simpler ways such as a news release
2. In the case of a major news event, such as a violent disruption, major accident, sudden death of a top official, or some other emergency

The common element of these definitions is that the event is significant. In sport, major events may include coach firings, player trades, free-agent signings, and facility construction, to name a few. Table 9.1 uses the criteria outlined by Smith (2005) and Baus and Lesly (1998) to illustrate how a sport organization may classify newsworthy announcements. Note that an organization should hold a news conference only to announce major news or to make it easier for the media to report about the organization.

Each sport organization must also consider other factors when assessing the newsworthiness of any given event, such as personnel changes. Assessing

## Table 9.1  Sport Organization News Conference Opportunities

| Reasons to hold a news conference | | |
| --- | --- | --- |
| Smith (2005) | Baus and Lesly (1998) | Examples of newsworthy events |
| Announce news or give a response of major importance | Discuss a major news event or emergency | • Player trades<br>• Personnel changes<br>• Free-agent signings<br>• Facility construction |
| Serve media's interests when a prominent spokesperson is available for a short time | Provide media with something that they could not get in simpler ways | • Interviews with athletic director, CEO, or owner<br>• Visits by prominent alumni or hall of famer<br>• Banquet speakers<br>• New product launches |
| Avoid accusations of playing favorites | | • Postevent news conferences<br>• Media days |

Adapted from Baus and Lesly 1998; Smith 2005.

the news value of the firing of a head college football coach is relatively easy, but how important is the hiring of a running-backs coach for the same team? Both events are personnel changes, but are both newsworthy? Certainly the new running-backs coach thinks his hiring is newsworthy, but will the organization's publics, especially members of the media, agree? The decision about whether to hold a news conference should consider organizational objectives. It may be the goal of the football team to be competitive and increase attendance. The new running-backs coach may help accomplish the former, but it is safe to assume few consumers will be motivated to attend games merely because of a new running-backs coach.

After the organization has determined that it has an announcement worthy of a news conference, it should carefully consider who will speak on behalf of the organization and where and when it will take place.

## Identifying Spokespersons

The *who* of a news conference is as important as the *what* of the news conference. But regardless of who speaks the words, the organization should speak with a single voice, meaning that the message should be consistent from one person to the next (Smith, 2005).

Senior executives such as the owner, general manager, university athletic director, or university president usually speak on behalf of the organization at a news conference. But an organization should not automatically assume that senior executives are the best spokespersons. Often they are not. The best spokesperson will likely vary depending in the subject. For example, a university that is announcing plans to build a new stadium may want to have the architect and construction planner on hand, in addition to the athletic director, to answer questions regarding design and project planning.

Smith (2005) identified several reasons not to presume that the CEO or someone else from senior management is the best organizational spokesperson in every case. First, the organization should save the CEO for big announcements. Second, the CEO may not be as prepared to respond to all the details of a project. Third, the CEO may not have the personality or charisma necessary to make a positive impression in public.

Many organizations use their public relations professional as their spokesperson, but much debate surrounds this practice. Helitzer (1996) argued that because public relations persons are professional communicators and usually have the best relationship with the media, they are best suited to speak for the organization. On the other hand, public relations persons are often viewed with less credibility because of the perception that they are simply mouthpieces of the organization. Whether functioning as the spokesperson or preparing the spokesperson, the job of the public relations person is vital to successful news conferences.

## Location

Given that an objective of a news conference may be to generate publicity, an organization should go out of its way to maximize attendance at news conferences by holding them in a location that is convenient for both the media and the organization. Sport organizations generally have two options for location: on site and off site.

### On Site

The most likely place for an organization to hold a news conference is on site at one of the sport organization's facilities. Obviously, an organization must first estimate the size of the audience that is likely to attend the news conference and then determine whether an on-site facility could accommodate that crowd. When the New York Yankees held a news conference to introduce Alex Rodriguez to the New York media in February 2004, 300 people attended, more than were present for similar news conferences for Jason Giambi, Mike Mussina, and Gary Sheffield (McCarron, 2004). As a result, not everyone in attendance was able to see and hear what was transpiring.

Because most organizations already have an area designated in their stadium or arena for postevent interviews, holding news conferences in that same space, commonly referred to as an interview room, is advantageous for a variety of reasons. First, the organization likely owns or leases the facility, ensuring flexibility in timing and setup. Sport organizations frequently call news conferences about breaking news such as a coach firing or a player trade. As discussed later in this chapter, the organization may be unable to notify media more than an hour or two before the news conference takes place. Locating a venue for a news conference on such short notice may be difficult unless the organization already has control of the facility.

Second, the facility is likely familiar to members of the media who often cover the organization's events. They know where to park, how to enter the facility, and where the room is located, making it convenient for them to cover the event.

Third, having the news conference in the organization's home facility minimizes time demands on participating organizational personnel by eliminating the need for travel to a different location.

Of course, this advantage applies only if the news conference is held in a stadium or arena that also houses the organization's offices.

Finally, staging the news conference on the organization's home turf allows the organization to have greater control over the message and the atmosphere, such as backdrops and organizational banners, of the news conference. Public relations professionals should consider having visual items such as diagrams, trophies, or awards to supplement the verbal information. These visuals may be used by television stations to break up a long sound bite from one of the participants or by still photographers to help frame the person who is talking. For example, it is hard to imagine a news conference to announce the Heisman Trophy winner without the trophy present.

### Off Site

Many sport organizations such as sporting goods manufacturers and governing bodies may not have a home turf advantage because they have no permanent facility where events take place. If the organization does not have a meeting or conference room large enough to host the event, it may have to hold its news conference off site.

The same considerations for news conferences on site should be afforded to choosing an off-site venue. Specifically, the organization should consider size, parking, and convenience for the media. A hotel ballroom or conference room often makes a good news conference location (Baus & Lesly, 1998; Helitzer, 1996). Hotels often have the flexibility to change the size of a ballroom or conference room to accommodate varying crowd sizes. This feature is helpful for an organization that may have small media attendance for its news conference. A large room with few people may present the image that the news conference is not important enough to fill a room.

A hotel probably also has ample parking near the front door, an important and often overlooked consideration for a number of reasons (Condron, 2001). First, members of the media, especially television and still photographers, carry heavy equipment. Having abundant parking near the front entrance to the facility makes the media's job easier. Second, if the news conference is important enough that local television stations will want to carry it live, adequate space must be available for large uplink trucks to park.

An organization usually chooses a hotel that is centrally located in its region, perhaps downtown

(Helitzer, 1996). The news conference is then as convenient as possible for the media to attend. Most newspaper offices are located in the downtown area of a city, whereas television stations are frequently spread throughout a city. Choosing someplace in the middle minimizes the travel time for everyone involved.

Another advantage to using a hotel is the ability to capitalize on many of the services that it can provide. The hotel will likely have a podium and sound system, along with multimedia tools that might be needed. In addition, most hotels offer some form of beverage service for purchase as well as other touches such as coat racks and signage.

Two primary disadvantages associated with using a hotel for a news conference are cost and not having a home turf advantage. Most hotels charge a fee that varies with the size of the room. That fee generally includes basic microphone, podium, sound system, and room setup. Other services such as beverages and projectors can be added at additional cost.

Not using a facility owned or leased by the organization increases the time commitment required of participants. The organization will have less flexibility in arranging the room, displaying atmospherics, and creating an environment favorable to the organization.

# Making the Announcement

After the organization has determined where the news conference will take place, planning for the announcement begins in earnest. Two of the most critical planning elements are timing and notifying the media.

## Timing

For some announcements, such as the firing of a professional basketball coach, the timing of the news conference is irrelevant; the media will show up because of the magnitude of the announcement. For other announcements, especially those involving a crisis, the timing of the news conference is irrelevant because the media representatives will be aggressively seeking organizational comment.

In today's competitive media environment where rumors surface on websites long before an official announcement is made, an organization cannot sit on an announcement for a long time. Keeping the name of a coach secret has become extremely difficult. Most news conferences should be held as

quickly as possible after a decision has been made, often after just a couple of hours, to prevent inaccurate information from being reported (Davis, 1998). But if timing is less critical, certain considerations will help maximize media attendance.

First, know the media's schedule. Early mornings are not generally the best time for a news conference because most sporting events take place at night and on weekends. Reporters are often up late filing stories after an event has ended. The earliest that an organization should consider holding a news conference is late morning to noon. To maximize publicity for the announcement, a news conference should conclude by early to mid-afternoon, providing enough time for television stations to edit stories for the early newscast, usually at 5 p.m., as well as for radio stations to ensure that the story receives coverage during the evening drive time.

Second, know the competition. If, for example, the Kansas City Royals want to hold a news conference in November to announce a free-agent signing during the off-season, they should probably not schedule the announcement for a Monday morning after a Kansas City Chiefs game when the team's head coach is holding his mandated news conference. As mentioned in chapter 7, most newspapers have beat writers, so the Royals beat writer won't be inconvenienced by having to choose which event to cover, but television stations may have to make a choice about which news conference to attend because their staffs are smaller.

Last, know the news cycle, or which days are best to release information to the media. As Baus and Lesly (1998) suggested, "Tuesday, Wednesday and Thursday are generally the best days of the week, with Monday slightly behind" (p. 339). Because most television stations have scaled-back staffs on weekends made up of different anchors, reporters, and producers, weekends should be avoided.

## Notifying the Media

Organizations typically notify the media of a news conference by distributing a media advisory. A media advisory is similar to a news release, except that its goal is to give the media enough information to get their attention but not so much information that they don't need to attend the news conference. Unlike a news release, which is written in ready-to-use form, a media advisory simply presents the basic who, what, where, when, why, and how of the announcement. Figure 9.1 illustrates how a well-written advisory provides the necessary details of a news conference to announce the hiring of a new basketball coach at Ohio State University.

**ATHLETICS COMMUNICATIONS**

Rm. 124, St. John Arena
410 Woody Hayes Drive
Columbus, OH 43210-1166

Phone (614) 292-6861
Fax (614) 292-8547

TRADITION   PEOPLE   EXCELLENCE

July 8, 2004

## MEDIA ADVISORY- Matta Press Conference

*COLUMBUS, Ohio* - Andy Geiger, Ohio State director of athletics, will formally introduce Thad Matta as the Buckeye men's basketball coach at a 3 p.m. press conference Friday. The event will be held in the practice facility on the west side of Value City Arena.

Media should enter the Southwest Rotunda near the corner of Fred Taylor Drive and Lane Avenue.

Because setup for a concert will be underway, parking will be in the lots surrounding Bill Davis Stadium, the Ohio State baseball facility, just north of Value City Arena.

Dr. Karen Holbrook, The Ohio State University president, Geiger, Matta and Ohio State student-athletes will be available.

##GO BUCKS!##

**Figure 9.1**   Ohio State media advisory.

Reprinted, by permission, from Ohio State Athletic Communications.

Because the advisory does not contain any quotes from news conference participants, members of the media know that they need to attend if they wish to complete their stories.

When notifying the media of a news conference, an organization should avoid playing favorites and notify all media representatives who may have an interest in the organization or the announcement (Smith, 2005). Such representatives may include media who do not normally cover the organization. For example, assume that a professional football team is announcing a partnership with the local United Way organization. This story may be more interesting to the local business media than it is to the team's beat writer. The public relations person should know who the business media are and ensure that they are invited.

For a breaking news conference, the general rule is to give the media as much notice as possible, perhaps a couple of hours or more. The key is to give the media enough time to alter their plans so that they can attend the news conference, but not so much time they will be able to announce the story before the announcement.

Occasionally it works in the best interest of the organization to release the information as much as a day in advance of the announcement. Doing so can help prolong the news cycle of the story. When the Buffalo Bills chose Mike Mularkey as their new head coach in January 2004, the information was widely reported one day and Mularkey was introduced as the new coach the next day. This approach allowed the Bills to dominate the news cycle over two days as stories focused on Mularkey's hiring one day and his comments from the news conference the next day. The *Buffalo News* ran 12 stories about the Buffalo Bills during a three-day period before, during, and immediately after the announcement.

## Benefits and Detractions of News Conferences

Besides releasing messages to targeted publics, news conferences have other benefits, including eliminating perceived favoritism by the media, assisting the public relations staff in executing its job, and complying with league or governing-body rules.

As mentioned in chapter 8, an organization may occasionally want to leak news to a media outlet in hopes of generating favorable coverage in exchange for exclusivity. A news conference is just the opposite—it releases information to all media at one time in one place (Helitzer, 1996). The nature of a news conference is such that all persons in attendance hear the same comments at the same time and in the same context, thus eliminating the possibility of perceived favoritism among journalists.

Because a news conference is designed to disseminate information to audiences simultaneously, the staging of a news conference, despite all the planning it requires, may make the public relations person's job easier. For example, most of the media at an event will want to interview an athlete who scores a winning touchdown or hits a game-winning home run. Having that athlete attend a postevent news conference will help the public relations person by eliminating the need to arrange a series of one-on-one interviews with the media and the athlete. The athlete also benefits by not having to answer the same media questions repeatedly.

Finally, many organizations are mandated to hold a news conference by their league or governing body. For example, member organizations of the NFL are required to hold a news conference with the club's head coach on the Monday following a Sunday game (H. Greene, personal communication, July 23, 2003).

In a case study of the National Basketball Association (NBA), Fortunato (2000) pointed out the league's philosophy that the head coach is an integral part of the game and is therefore required to meet with the media following every game. A postgame news conference is the perfect opportunity for that coach to meet with the media.

Whether they are required or not, news conferences in sport are so commonplace that members of the media expect one to be held following an event at nearly every level of athletic competition. At the very least, the public relations person should arrange for one-on-one interviews between the media and athletes following the event. Postevent interviews are discussed earlier in the chapter.

One reason for the proliferation of news conferences in sport is the increased number of media members covering sport. Wilstein (2002) called news conferences a "necessary evil of modern sport" (p. 127) because of the plethora of reporters who need quotes following an event.

Although news conferences offer numerous benefits, detractions are present as well. In reality, most journalists view news conferences as cold, impersonal places to gather information. The basic format of a news conference is awkward and uncomfortable (Smith, 2005; Wilstein, 2002). Interviewees usually sit on a raised dais, above the interviewers, with bright lights focused on them, making it difficult for them to see the person asking the question.

Wilstein (2002) wrote, "The interview room, despite its name, is probably the worst place in sports to interview anyone. It is a concept that thwarts spontaneity and usually produces the most vapid quotes" (p. 127).

One reason for this lack of spontaneity may be the competitive nature of today's media. Most mass media outlets, like most businesses, exist to make money. A magazine such as *Sports Illustrated* can maximize profits by having access to information that its competitors do not. The news conference format of disseminating information to a large audience at the same time negates competition. A newspaper has no opportunity to get exclusive information at a news conference when its competitors get the information at the same time (Smith, 2005).

Given the number of reporters covering any one event and the competitive media environment, it is not surprising that many reporters wait to ask specific questions of interviewees until they are in a one-on-one interview.

## Teleconferences

A sport organization may consider adding a teleconference service to its news conference. A **teleconference** is a news conference using telecommunications to connect the interviewee with interviewers who are not physically present at the news conference. By dialing a predetermined phone number with a password or code, members of the media who cannot be present for a news conference may still listen to, and perhaps even participate in, the news conference.

The Washington Nationals employed a teleconference to announce that its top pitcher and former number one draft pick, Stephen Strasburg, had a torn ligament in his elbow and that surgery was likely. This approach was effective because of Strasburg's success and the media attention that he had been receiving, and it allowed the organization to break the news to a national audience simultaneously, controlling the message.

Using a teleconference offers many benefits. From the organization's perspective, it allows maximum media exposure without the repetition of doing several individual interviews. From the media's perspective, it allows a reporter anywhere to dial into the news conference (Miller & Zang, 2001). For example, if an international sporting goods organization on the West Coast is holding a news conference to release an earnings statement, it may arrange a teleconference with writers on the East Coast, where most business and magazine writers are located. If the CEO is delivering the statement, certainly business writers will be interested, especially if the company is publicly traded.

Perhaps during the teleconference, the CEO also announces plans for a new line of golf shoes to be unveiled in the next few months, along with a new endorsement agreement with a top golfer. This announcement is now certainly of interest to media that specialize in golf coverage, but it may also be of interest to media that cover sport business and marketing. A teleconference will make it easy for these diverse media groups to get information that they need for their stories. At the same time, the CEO, whose time is extremely valuable, is spared from having to schedule multiple interviews about the same topic.

A critical factor regarding teleconferences that cannot be overlooked is geography. In the case of the sporting goods company, the CEO may want the news conference at 9 a.m. on the West Coast where the company is located. But this time falls during the middle of the business day on the East Coast. Thus, a teleconference such as this one may be better timed earlier in the day to make it easier for the media to participate.

## The Big Event

For a public relations professional, a news conference is equivalent to an athlete's game day. It provides an opportunity for public relations professionals to showcase their abilities and skills on behalf of the organization. Therefore, the public relations professional must attend to every detail well in advance to ensure smooth operation of the event.

Public relations professionals must have several reliable people to assist them with the duties outlined in the following section. One person cannot be everywhere at the same time, so having trustworthy assistants can enhance the efficiency of the news conference.

Five critical areas determine the success of a news conference: atmospherics, or the visual elements that can enhance the value of the news conference; press kits that can provide additional information for the media; adherence to a strict format; room setup and equipment, such as microphones and tape recorders; and a quote service, which provides members of the media excerpts of what is said.

### Atmospherics

Atmospherics, a concept addressed by Irwin, Sutton, and McCarthy (2008) as a key marketing consideration, also apply to news conferences. The atmosphere at a news conference can be a positive promotional tool for the sport organization. Prominent placement of the organization's logo on the podium, a backdrop, and even clothing can help maximize media exposure. The sum of these elements affects the physical setting, resulting in additional promotional value for the organization.

One common atmospheric element at news conferences is some sort of **backdrop**. This backdrop is frequently a pattern of the organization's logo and perhaps a corporate sponsor. Given the intense media coverage of news conferences on cable television, organizations may be able to generate significant revenue by selling sponsorship of the backdrop to a corporation.

Attention should be paid to the color of the backdrop so that it presents the right image on television. A backdrop that is predominantly white will wash out on camera. Also, the backdrop should be portable enough that it can be erected in any location, even if the organization is playing a road game. The public relations person must ensure that the backdrop is set up in time for postevent news conferences.

If a backdrop is unavailable, the news conference should be held against a solid wall if indoors, or if outdoors the participants should be positioned at such an angle so as not to cast shadows on their faces. Another alternative is to use some standard exposition-grade pipe and drape, preferably 8 feet (2.5 m) high. Most hotels and convention centers have a supply of these materials on site.

Other items that may enhance the setting of a news conference include anything that is visual and may make for a good picture, adding to the value of the news conference. Championship team trophies such as the National Hockey League's (NHL's) Stanley Cup or individual trophies such as the Heisman Trophy offer a reminder of past accomplishments. Banners or framed jerseys and photos hung on the walls may provide additional exposure for the organization's logo. As Hall and colleagues (2007) noted, the public relations person's job is get the organization into the public eye: "One of the simplest and most effective ways to do so is to display the institution's name and logo in such a manner that

**Sport organizations frequently use backdrops that feature both their logo and a key sponsor's logo.**
Jerome Davis/Icon SMI

they appear prominently in photographs or video clips from the news conference" (p. 108).

## Press Kits

An organization often distributes a press kit to the media upon their arrival at the news conference. Press kits were discussed in detail in chapter 8, but the value of a press kit at a news conference is more pronounced because it includes a schedule of events and biographies of spokespersons (Lorenz & Vivian, 1996).

The schedule of events should include a detailed listing of what time the news conference will start and when certain spokespersons will speak. The schedule assists photographers and television camera crews with their preparation because they need to have cameras trained at a certain spot at a certain time. Biographies should include correct titles for all spokespersons as well as past accomplishments, which helps ensure proper spelling of individuals' names.

Press kits, minus information critical to the announcement, may be distributed ahead of time along with the media advisory. More commonly, they are given to the media on site at the news conference. Public relations persons should ensure that all interested media representatives receive a press kit. An organization may consider hiring a local courier service to deliver the press kits to any media outlet that cannot send representatives to the news conference.

## Format

News conferences should be well organized and stick to the schedule of events distributed to the media in press kits. A **moderator** is often present at a news conference. This master of ceremonies, frequently the public relations person, should be familiar with all participants as well as the media.

Moderators should welcome the media to the news conference and thank them for attending. They should introduce the primary spokesperson and clearly state the person's title. After the initial statements are concluded, it is appropriate for the media to ask questions. The moderator may facilitate this process by calling on individuals to voice their questions.

Some spokespersons may ask the moderator to repeat the question for the benefit of everyone in attendance. Doing so accomplishes two things. First, it allows everyone in the room to hear the question, and second, it allows the spokesperson time to formulate an answer before speaking. The length of the question-and-answer session will vary depending on the nature of the news conference, but it should not exceed 30 minutes. The length of time allowed should be specified in advance.

As the time for questions winds down, the moderator can signal the end of the news conference by calling for the last question. Media members expect some time for one-on-one interviews afterward, which should be budgeted into the overall schedule.

These one-on-one interviews are important to electronic and print media alike. For electronic media, such interviews allow them to use their own microphones with station flags for the interview. This visual cue enhances the television station's credibility because it proves to viewers that the station was in attendance. In addition, it adds to the station's own promotional efforts. For print media, one-on-one interviews allow reporters to ask detailed questions that they do not want their competitors to hear. The business of mass media is to make money, and one way to accomplish that is through exclusive stories. Don't expect the media to ask all their questions in a news conference setting when competitors are present.

The public relations person has the job of escorting the spokesperson from one interview to the next as well as monitoring the interviews to know what is being asked and to ensure that no media outlet gets a longer interview than another.

## Room Setup and Equipment

An often-overlooked element in the basic room setup for a news conference is some sort of check-in procedure. Check-in should take place outside the room in which the news conference will be held to minimize distractions caused by late arrivals. Organizations should request contact information such as name, affiliation, e-mail address, and phone number of all media in attendance to enhance their media list (Irwin, Sutton, & McCarthy, 2002). The check-in area is a good place to distribute press kits, and it should always be staffed by someone in the organization's public relations office who is familiar with the schedule of events.

The basic setup of a news conference requires a podium where participants will stand or a head table where participants can sit in addition to ample chairs arranged in even rows for the media to sit and ask questions. A microphone and sound system must be in place for participants to speak into. In addition, chairs should be placed in a manner that creates adequate circulation space on either side and an aisle down the middle to allow smooth traffic flow (Condron, 2001).This setup also allows space for photographers and camera operators to move closer to the interview participants. Public relations staff members should develop protocols for movement of journalists during a formal news conference. Too much commotion in the middle of the room may distract the participants; therefore, the public relations professional may consider restricting movement to the sides only.

If a head table is employed, it should be on a raised platform, called a dais. The dais should be about 18 inches (45 cm) off the ground and carpeted and draped to reduce noise (Condron, 2001). In addition, the table should be skirted in a color complementary to the backdrop and dais draping. A sufficient number of microphones, two at a minimum, should be located on the head table for the participants. One microphone should be reserved for the moderator, if there is one, and the other microphone can be shared. If the news conference involves more than two participants, an additional microphone should be added for every two persons.

The sound system into which the microphone is tied should include a **multibox** in the back of the room near where television cameras will be positioned. A multibox is a multiple outlet output device that allows media to patch directly into the audio from the sound system (Condron, 2001). Multiboxes are beneficial for both the media and the organization. From the media's standpoint, a multibox produces clear audio without the worry that the speaker will not talk directly into their microphone. From the organization's perspective, a multibox eliminates the need for multiple microphones with different media flags on the head table or podium. This setup presents a much cleaner visual image and may permit additional promotional exposure if the organization uses its logo on the main microphone.

The multibox may be placed on a camera platform, if one is available. If the news conference room has a dais for the head table, a similar dais that is the same height may be provided for cameras in the back. This second dais permits television crews to set up their tripods where people will not bump into them and where the cameras will not block the view of the head table.

Although it may add significantly to expenses, the organization should use its own lighting system.

Optimal broadcast lighting is measured in terms of temperature, usually in degrees Kelvin. Standard indoor lighting for TV news shooting is 3,200 degrees Kelvin. Daylight and sunlight, considered natural light, measure up to 13,000 degrees Kelvin. Artificial light provided by overhead lighting and lamps is considerably darker than natural light, around 2,000 degrees Kelvin. Therefore, an organization must often provide supplemental lighting for news conferences to enhance the artificial light already present in the room. Most electronic news gathering (ENG) crews carry their own battery-powered light kits, which provide an additional 600 to 1,000 watts of artificial light at exactly 3,200 degrees Kelvin. Although those kits are sufficient for one ENG crew, if the news conference has multiple crews with multiple lights, participants in the news conference may find it difficult to see. Therefore, the organization should invest in key and fill lights. As the main light, the key light should be well above the cameras, about 7 feet (2 m) off the ground, and aimed at the subject. The fill lights fill in shadows caused by the key light and should be about 30 degrees to either side of the cameras (Cremer, Kierstead, & Yoakam, 1996).

### Quote Service

The organization holding the news conference customarily provides written excerpts or even transcripts of the conference to the media. The service has become so reliable that many journalists skip postevent interviews altogether and rely on the quote service (Wilstein, 2002).

Obviously, having reporters bypass news conferences should not be the organization's objective, but providing typed quotes for distribution is helpful for several reasons. First, it ensures accurate reporting of the organization's message. Public relations professionals only choose quotes for distribution that support the original messages. Second, it increases the likelihood that the media will pick up those messages. And third, it allows journalists not in attendance to incorporate some form of attribution into their story, although those who do not attend the news conference and rely solely on the quote service may miss the meaning and context of the quote. As Wilstein (2002) pointed out, "Sometimes meaning is conveyed by a facial expression, a gesture or the tone of what was said" (p. 128).

Producing the quotes for distribution is another critical job that should be handled by an assistant or volunteer for the public relations professional (Davis, 1998). One objective of the quote service is timely distribution of the quotes. Typically, a public

relations staff member takes notes just as a reporter does, types them, prints them, and distributes them to the media. Someone other than the author should edit the quote for punctuation errors and typos before copying and distributing it.

### Streaming

Organizations now have the ability to have news conferences streamed live on either their official website or through a third-party site such as Ustream.tv, which claims that its service "enables anyone with an Internet connection and a camera to engage their audience in a meaningful way" (*About Us > Media Kit*, n.d.).

Although the benefits of streaming are still not well documented, the ability to stream live news conferences, or even sporting events, potentially eliminates geographic barriers to the organization's audience. Fans of an organization would be able to watch, live, the news conference of a new player or coach regardless of where they are located, so long as they have an Internet connection.

## Checklist

Many public relations professionals find it helpful to use a checklist when planning a news conference because many details are involved (see figure 9.2). The public relations person must monitor location, timing, notification, and equipment, and may choose to assign each task to a staff member or volunteer to ensure timely completion.

## Media Days

Many sport organizations, particularly professional teams and NCAA Division I universities and conferences, hold media days before the beginning of the competitive season to maximize the team's or league's exposure and minimize demands on the organization. Media days are accomplished by inviting all members of the media interested in the organization to attend one session and by blocking out that day on the team's calendar to facilitate many interviews rather than initiating several interviews each day. In the case of major NCAA conferences, media days may be spread out over several days.

The Southeastern Conference held its 2010 football media days from July 21 through 23. Each of the 12 member schools was required to make its head coach and three players available to the media for nearly three hours. Approximately 900 media credentials were issued for the SEC media days in 2009,

# News Conference Checklist

Date: September 19, 2011
Time: 1:00 p.m.
Subject: Athletic Director Hiring News Conference
Location: Champions Club in Basketball Arena

| Item | Person responsible | Notes |
|------|-------------------|-------|
| Meet with sports information staff and students<br>• Assign specific responsibilities | | Morning of Sept. 18 |
| Set up room<br>• Set up backdrop<br>• Test sound system<br>• Arrange chairs<br>• Skirt table<br>• Set up podium or skirted table for speakers<br>• Set up additional lighting | | Complete by 12:30 p.m., Sept. 19 |
| Write and send media advisory<br>• Include parking instructions<br>• Include fax and e-mail info | | Send at 3:00 p.m., Sept. 18 |
| Phone-call reminders to media | | Morning of Sept. 19 |
| Assemble media kit<br>• Write news release<br>• Write biography of athletic director (AD)<br>• Write biography of university president<br>• Include athletics schedules | | Morning of Sept. 19 |
| Make name cards for AD and university president (if using a table) | | Morning of Sept. 19 |
| Place bottled water on table for speakers and in back for media | | Complete by 12:30 p.m., Sept. 19 |
| Create media sign-in table<br>• Create sign-in sheet<br>• Include media kits<br>• Include miscellaneous athletics posters, schedules | | Complete by 12:30 p.m., Sept. 19 |
| Postevent activities<br>• Distribute quote sheets<br>• Deliver media kits to news outlets not in attendance<br>• Write story for organization website<br>• Post photos on organization website | | As soon as possible after news conference |

**Figure 9.2** Sample checklist for planning a news conference.

including national media as well as local university media and Internet-based media (Paschal, 2009).

Media days have been defined as "an elaborate news conference with a more social atmosphere" (Hall et al., 2007, p. 116). The basic goal of a media day is to provide media representatives with access to members of the organization, such as players and coaches, in a casual atmosphere. Media days at the beginning of a season should be upbeat. After all, each team begins the season without a loss and with lots of optimism. The organization has the opportunity to showcase its product, possibly producing favorable publicity and perhaps even additional revenue through tickets sales or sponsorships.

The distribution of materials at a media day will generally mirror that at a news conference. A press kit containing a schedule of events, biographies, and perhaps a media guide is expected.

A typical media day may begin with a lunch for members of the media and select organizational personnel, followed by a news conference with the team's coach and general manager or athletic director. The media then usually have access to players for interviews. Those interviews may be followed by a light scrimmage or practice that the media are able to watch. Figure 9.3 shows how a university might wish to schedule a media day for its women's basketball team.

The organization's public relations staff may wish to consider several tactics to enhance media coverage. First, they should anticipate that most media members will want to interview the same two or three players and prepare those players in advance. But more players should be made available, particularly seniors who may be graduating. Public relations staff members should be sure to brief all players in advance regarding possible questions.

The public relations staff should also encourage the athletes to wear uniforms with numbers to aid members of the media in identifying players whom they may wish to interview. In addition, because the uniform likely carries the organization's name and logo, the team receives additional publicity.

During the practice, the public relations person should encourage the coach to run plays that are visually exciting such as long passes or two-on-one basketball drills. Broadcast media will shoot the practice and use the video in their stories. Having positive images of players making baskets or catching passes may lead to positive publicity.

One final consideration relates to photographers who wish to make a creative image of media day. A photographer may stage a photo of a group of players, perhaps sitting on the basketball court around the team logo.

## Schedule for Media Day

| Time | |
|------|---|
| 12:00 p.m. | Welcome to media conducted by university sports information director |
| 12:05 p.m. | Sit-down lunch for media |
| 12:35 p.m. | Presentation by team's head coach, including introduction of assistant coaches |
| 12:50 p.m. | Formal question-and-answer period |
| 1:00 p.m. | One-on-one interviews with coaches and media |
| 1:30 p.m. | Sports information director escorts media to practice gym |
| 1:45 p.m. | One-on-one interviews with team players and media |
| 2:15 p.m. | Practice open to media |
| 3:00 p.m. | Media depart |

**Figure 9.3** Sample media day schedule for a university's women's basketball team.

# SUMMARY

Interviews allow sport organizations the opportunity to communicate positive messages to targeted publics. The public relations person for the organization should endeavor to make it as easy as possible for those messages to be communicated. Responding to media inquiries in a professional manner, preparing interviewees, and selecting appropriate spokespersons are essential to influencing the delivery of messages. Sport organizations may use controlled events such as news conferences and media days to assist media members in covering the organization. News conferences should be carefully planned by devoting attention to the timing, location, and setup of the conference. Media days are the organization's opportunity to showcase positive images about a team and cultivate favorable publicity.

# LEARNING ACTIVITIES

1. You are the public relations person for an NHL team. During a home game, a puck flies into the crowd and strikes a spectator, sending her to the hospital in serious condition. Play continues, and at the end of the game the media on site are seeking a reaction from the organization. What would you say and who would say it?

2. As the sports information director for a Division I-A university, you are approached by your athletic director about scheduling a news conference later that day to announce the firing of the head football coach. Detail a plan to notify the media and prepare a location for the news conference.

3. Write a media advisory for the scenario in activity 2. What information would you want to include? How would you distribute it?

4. Ask your university's sports information office for a credential to a home athletic event. Attend the postevent news conference and critique the behavior of the interviewees. Pay attention to their response to questions and their mannerisms during the interview.

5. Working in small groups in class, role-play a news conference. Have one person act as the interviewee (as, say, the head women's basketball coach following a close home win) and have the other group members ask questions. Rotate so that each person has the opportunity to be the interviewee. Provide constructive feedback to your classmates.

# Communicating in Times of Crisis

**After reading this chapter, students should be able to**

- define crisis and crisis communications,
- recognize the importance of crisis readiness,
- understand how to prepare for crises,
- identify the key elements of a crisis communications plan,
- distinguish among various crisis response strategies, and
- understand how crisis responses may be assessed.

**Key terms discussed in this chapter include**

- crisis,
- crisis communications plans,
- call tree,
- crisis response strategy, and
- one-move chess.

**In July 2007** *USA Today* ran a story noting that each of the top three U.S. professional sport leagues faced credibility problems because of major crises (Brady, 2007). The National Basketball Association (NBA) was dealing with a gambling scandal centering on Tim Donaghy, a referee who subsequently went to prison after betting on games, influencing the results of those games, and providing insider information to other gamblers. Major League Baseball (MLB) was facing the prospect that Barry Bonds, widely believed to be a steroid user, would break Hank Aaron's record for career home runs. The National Football League (NFL) was confronting the public relations implications related to the Michael Vick dog-fighting accusations that would ultimately lead to his conviction and imprisonment. The article summarized the magnitude of the problems facing the leagues by stating, "What's left to believe in? Not the results, if it's true an NBA ref fixed games. Not the records, if it's true Bonds took steroids. Not the heroes, if it's true Michael Vick drowned dogs" (Brady, 2007).

Readers are likely familiar with other prominent crises that have occurred, including the following:

- The 2008 Olympic Summer Games in Beijing faced what the head of the International Olympic Committee (IOC) deemed a crisis when protestors in several nations criticized the host nation and disrupted the Olympic torch relay (BBC, 2008). The subjects of the protests were China's human rights record and its treatment of protestors in Tibet.

- NASCAR suffered tragedy in 2001 when star driver Dale Earnhardt was killed in an accident during the final lap of its marquee event, the Daytona 500. Earnhardt was one of four drivers who lost their lives in accidents during racing events or practices during a 10-month period (AP, 2001).

- Indiana University endured several crises pertaining to its men's basketball program over a series of years. Several incidents occurred during the stormy tenure of head coach Bob Knight that ended with Knight's firing in 2000. Knight's successor, Mike Davis, resigned in 2006 after problems with the media and a modest performance record (Clavio, Eagleman, Miloch, & Pedersen, 2007). Kelvin Sampson, who succeeded Davis, resigned in the midst of a NCAA investigation in 2008 and was subsequently the subject of harsh NCAA penalties (Katz, 2008).

- The YMCA in Oklahoma City encountered a crisis in 1995 when its downtown branch was severely damaged by a terrorist's bomb that destroyed a nearby government building. Although no one in the YMCA building was killed, 168 people died in the attack and the YMCA building was a total loss (Bitsche, 1998).

- Nike suffered a lengthy crisis starting in the 1990s when critics charged that Nike's subcontractors paid their employees less than minimum wages, placed employees in unsafe working conditions, and allowed employees to be physically abused (Bernstein, 2004a).

As evident from the preceding, sport organizations are susceptible to a variety of crisis scenarios, and even the most comprehensive risk management plans cannot protect against all potential crises. After a crisis occurs, the manner in which the sport organization's staff responds often has enormous public relations implications. All sport public relations professionals need to recognize the importance of preparing for crises and making sound decisions during crises.

This chapter features four main sections on crisis communications. The first section discusses the nature of crises and their prevalence within sport. The second section describes how sport public relations professionals may prepare themselves for crisis episodes. It includes

- ways to anticipate the crises an organization is likely to face,
- the nature of crisis communications plans and the process of developing them, and
- key elements within a crisis communications plan.

The third section addresses considerations for sport public relations practitioners during crises, including strategies that may be employed to protect or repair the organization's reputation. The fourth section considers how professionals can assess the effectiveness of a crisis response, and it offers a number of examples of both successful and unsuccessful crisis strategies.

# Nature of Crises and the Need to Plan for Them

Not all negative incidents qualify as crises. Some are just that—incidents. Others may be severe enough to qualify as emergencies, but even emergencies are not necessarily crises. For instance, if a spectator who suffers a medical emergency receives prompt attention, the matter likely will not escalate into a crisis because it will have been resolved and probably not deemed newsworthy. Furthermore, not all crises are incident driven; some result from longstanding problems that have never been adequately resolved. For example, it does not take a lawsuit to plunge a sport organization that neglects gender equity into a crisis. A simple media report noting the organization's failure to comply with the law could serve as the impetus for a hailstorm of public criticism.

All organizations are susceptible to crises. When a crisis occurs, it interrupts normal operations, and in extreme cases it can threaten the survival of the organization (Fearn-Banks, 2007).

Crises are often thought of as serious threats to an organization's financial well-being, but their impact extends well beyond monetary considerations. Crises directly affect reputations. Sometimes the impact comes from the crisis itself, but more often it results from the organization managers' response or lack thereof to the crisis. For example, in the aftermath of Dale Earnhardt's accident, NASCAR was widely criticized for its reluctance to adopt additional safety regulations (Poole, 2001). The effect of such negative media coverage on reputation typically outweighs the effect of positive publicity before the crisis (Grunig, Grunig, & Dozier, 2002).

A **crisis** is defined as "a situation or occurrence possessing the potential to significantly damage a sport organization's financial stability and/or credibility with constituents" (Stoldt, Miller, Ayres, & Comfort, 2000, pp. 253–254). This definition takes into account both the diverse nature of crises as well as their potential to affect financial well-being and reputation.

## Purpose of Crisis Plans

Given the potential of crises to cause significant damage to an organization, some sport organizations have developed plans to guide them when crises occur. Sport managers sometimes confuse crisis plans with emergency plans. Although the two are clearly related, they are not identical. Emergency plans guide responses as an emergency occurs. They delineate responses to situations such as a patron having a heart attack, a packed facility being placed under a tornado warning, or a fire occurring at a manufacturing facility. Effectively employed, emergency plans can protect customers and employees and sometimes save lives, thus averting a crisis.

Crisis management or **crisis communications plans** offer guidance on how to proceed after a crisis has occurred. They specify what roles people will play in managing a crisis and address contact procedures (Fearn-Banks, 2007). Because processing and sharing information are critical to managing crises, communication—both internal and external—is usually the primary focus of the plan (Davis & Gilman, 2002):

> The purpose of a crisis communications plan is to ensure that all management and staff are in a position to contain and manage a given crisis as well as provided with the information they require for a swift and effective resolution of that crisis, and that all other affected people are provided with factual information about the crisis as quickly as possible. (Matera & Artigue, 2000, p. 224)

Effective internal communication is critical in ensuring that the management team is equipped with complete information regarding the situation and that other employees know how to proceed during the crisis. Effective external communication is critical in making sure that publics such as the mass media, donors, and customers understand the nature of the organization's response.

## Need for Crisis Plans

Crisis planning is necessary for most sport organizations. Even organizations that do not usually face the glare of the media spotlight may find themselves under public scrutiny as a crisis evolves. For example, one interscholastic athletics program found itself in the midst of a crisis when a gender discrimination complaint was filed with the Office of Civil Rights (Ulrich, 2008). When mediation with the person issuing the complaint failed and an investigation ensued, so did media attention and negative publicity.

Although saying precisely how many sport organizations are faced with crises is impossible, past studies (e.g., Hessert, 1998a) indicated that the number is probably high. A study of NCAA member institutions determined that those with crisis communications plans used the plans an average of 1.15 times per year (Stoldt, Miller, & Comfort, 2001). The investigators queried athletic directors whose programs had developed written crisis management plans about how often they had activated those plans in the past year. Results indicated that 29.2% answered "none," 37.5% answered "once," 22.9% answered "twice," and 10.4% answered "three or more times."

These programs had at least a fighting chance because they had crisis plans to guide them. Research has indicated that most sport organizations do not have such plans. In 2001 Andy McGowan, a sport management instructor and former National Hockey League (NHL) executive, noted that although the National Football League (NFL) and National Basketball Association (NBA) league offices had crisis plans, the NHL did not (McGowan, 2001). Within the NHL, he knew of only two teams—the Dallas Stars and the Minnesota Wild—that had a crisis plan.

We can only wonder about the extent of crisis readiness among other sport organizations. If the majority of organizations at the highest levels of sport—such as the major professional leagues and teams—are ill equipped for crises, the situation is likely even worse in minor league and smaller collegiate sport organizations in which staff members commonly assume multiple jobs. And that speculation does not even begin to take into account crisis readiness within other sectors of the industry.

Working with the media is often the most important task of a sport public relations professional in a crisis. The assignment is challenging because of the proliferation of media organizations and the evolution of media technology. Because numerous media organizations have devoted themselves to 24-hour sport news coverage, sport organizations have found themselves under greater media scrutiny. Furthermore, the immediacy of the broadcast media and the prevalence of social media such as YouTube mean that sport public relations professionals must stand ready to respond more quickly than ever. As one public relations expert noted, "The time to 'think' has been reduced to minutes from hours" (Samansky, 2002, p. 27).

As noted earlier, the potential damage to sport organizations as a result of not responding appropriately to a crisis is significant. Reputations that have been carefully built through years of strong public relations can be irreparably harmed because of a single crisis. Crisis communication plans empower sport organizations to limit the damage and, in some cases, make positive impressions. Although the list of sport organizations that have deftly handled crises may be a short one, nonsport businesses have shown that reputations can be enhanced through crises. The most commonly cited example of this is Johnson and Johnson, which aggressively and effectively responded to a product-tampering crisis involving Tylenol in 1982 (Broom, 2009; Carter & Rovell, 2003). That company responded to the crisis by recalling $100 million worth of its products, offering consumers exchanges for products that they may have already purchased, and developing tamper-resistant packaging for subsequent product distribution.

# Preparing for a Crisis

Coombs (2007a, 2007b) contended that crisis management occurs in three stages—precrisis, crisis response, and postcrisis. Using that description, figure 10.1 presents a recommended approach to crisis communications. The cyclical model starts with preparing for crises by developing and maintaining a crisis communications plan. As noted earlier, the plan prescribes procedures for managing internal and external communication during a time of crisis. The onset of a crisis leads to the second stage in the model—managing the crisis. This phase includes both the activation of the crisis communications plan and additional strategic considerations as the crisis management team defines strategies to protect or repair the organization's reputation. The conclusion of the crisis episode marks the transition to the third stage of the model—assessment of the effectiveness of the plan. Postcrisis evaluation may help organizational management prepare for and manage future crises.

The following sections address each stage of the model in detail.

## Forecasting Crises

The first step that sport public relations professionals should take in moving toward crisis readiness is to anticipate the types of crises that their organizations may face. This job is not pleasant, but it does offer two benefits. First, by identifying potential problems, sport public relations professionals enable their organizations to take preemptive measures and prevent crises from occurring. The second benefit is that the crisis forecast can provide a practical foundation for the development of the crisis communications plan.

As with any important public relations initiative, crisis forecasting should not be left to only the public relations staff. It should include managers from throughout the sport organization including those specializing in human resources, finance, law, and security. Two sources of information that the forecasting team should tap are the sport organization's internal reports and external data regarding similar organizations and the industry in general (Connaughton, Spengler, & Bennett, 2001; Matera & Artigue, 2000). For example, if a minor league franchise has received a number of complaints

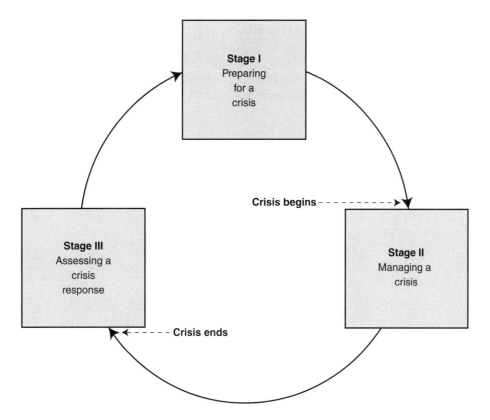

**Figure 10.1** An approach to crisis communications.

about drunken fans, then it should consider fan misbehavior in its forecasting process. Similarly, if the public relations staff for a fitness center notices that several similar businesses around the country have endured crises because of being unprepared for medical emergencies, that concern should be included in their forecast.

Some sport organizations have found it beneficial to hire external consultants to help forecast and plan for crises. For example, the University of Arizona hired the Inocon Group, a company specializing in crisis management, to assist it in moving toward crisis readiness (Lee, 2003). Such companies offer services ranging from forecasting to developing plans to staging crisis simulations. Besides possessing expertise in crisis communications, these external consultants frequently bring fresh perspectives to the table and may enable an organization's sport managers to identify issues that would have been missed had all planning been conducted internally. Although the cost of hiring external consultants can sometime extend to six figures, the investment may prove to be money well spent given the potential for financial damage because of mismanaged crises.

The list of potential crises that a sport organization can face often seems limitless. Managers for one

major sport facility identified 48 crisis scenarios that they could potentially face (Matera & Artigue, 2000).

Favorito (2007) identified five types of crises that sport organizations may commonly encounter:

- Physical plant crises—terrorism and other security threats, natural disasters, construction problems

- On-field crisis—event-related incidents such as competitor death or major injury, fan injuries, and on-field or in-stand violence

- Family crisis—after-hours or offseason incidents including legal infractions and celebrity scandals

- Corporate crisis—financial failure, layoffs, compliance issues, and actions that result in political protests

- Player personnel crisis—trading or releasing prominent players or coaches

Table 10.1 summarizes this crisis typology and offers an example of each that has occurred in recent years.

As noted in the physical plant category, many sport organizations have been forced to consider terrorism a relevant crisis consideration. Terrorism,

## Table 10.1 Types of Sport Crises

| Crisis type | Example |
| --- | --- |
| Physical plant | Tornado strikes the Georgia Dome during the 2008 Southeastern Conference Men's Basketball Championships |
| On field | Spectator killed when hit by a police motor bike at the 2009 Tour de France |
| Family | NFL quarterback Vick imprisoned in 2007 after conviction on dog-fighting charges |
| Corporate | Ladies Professional Golf Association commissioner Carolyn Bivens resigns in 2009 amid pressure from top tour players |
| Player personnel | Serie A soccer club AC Milan sells star player Kaka to Real Madrid in 2009, resulting in fan protests |

Based on Favorito 2007.

however, is not a new reality in sport. The sidebar titled Terrorist Threats to Sport addresses this important issue.

Because a crisis communications plan cannot address every conceivable crisis that an organization may face, public relations experts have recommended prioritizing potential crises based on two dimensions: likelihood and impact (Coombs, 2007b; Fearn-Banks, 2007; Hessert & Gillette, 2002; Sports Media Challenge, 1997). If a particular type of crisis seems highly likely to occur, the organization should plan for it. Similarly, if a crisis possesses the potential to devastate the organization, it too should be addressed, even if it is deemed less probable to occur than others. For instance, many crisis plans address scenarios pertaining to both the arrest of a prominent player and coach and a transportation accident resulting in deaths or serious injuries.

## Terrorist Threats to Sport

The visibility of many sport events and the density of the crowds attending such events make sport venues a possible target for terrorist attacks. That assessment has important implications for sport public relations professionals.

The world of sport has already seen two high-profile terrorist attacks. The first, and arguably most infamous, came in 1972 at the Summer Olympic Games in Munich, Germany (Carter & Rovell, 2003; Coakley, 2007). Eight terrorists slipped into the Olympic village, killed two members of the Israeli team, and took nine others hostage in the hopes of forcing a prisoner exchange for Palestinian inmates. A day later, all the hostages and five terrorists were killed in a firefight at the Munich airport. The second terrorist incident came at the 1996 Olympic Summer Games in Atlanta, Georgia, where a bomb was detonated in the Centennial Olympic Park. One person was killed and more than 100 others were injured. After both the 1972 and 1996 attacks, the Games continued, but with a considerable sense of sadness.

On other occasions, terrorist attacks in nonsport settings have affected the sport industry. In the wake of the September 11, 2001, attacks in New York City, Washington, and Pennsylvania, numerous sport organizations, including the NFL, Major League Baseball, and many college athletics programs, postponed scheduled contests and reevaluated their readiness for future attacks (Brady, 2002; Muret, 2006).

Although recommendations aimed at preventing terrorist attacks were once resisted by sport executives, they were embraced in the climate following the September 11 attacks (Hessert & Gillette, 2002). Major sport properties adopted a series of best practices, including the placement of physical barriers to prevent explosive-laden vehicles from penetrating facilities and the screening of spectators to prevent people from carrying weapons into venues.

Some sport managers and government officials have made specific plans for responding to such a scenario should it occur. A number of communities and sport organizations have staged terrorism drills such as a mock bombing at Shea Stadium, then home of the Mets franchise in 2004 ("NYC Rescue Workers," 2004), and a mock series of attacks in and near PNC Park, home of the Pittsburgh Pirates franchise (Muret, 2006).

The first crisis is one that most professional and college sport organizations are likely to encounter, even in programs that make every effort to recruit upstanding players and coaches. The latter crisis is one that programs are less likely to face, but as administrators at places like Bluffton University can attest, the effects of such an event are overwhelming. That program saw four student–athletes and two other people die in a 2007 bus accident (Bluffton University, n.d.).

Finally, sport managers engaged in crisis forecasting should be aware that two types of crises occur (Carter & Rovell, 2003). The first happens suddenly and with no warning. Examples include an airplane crash or an explosion at a sport facility. The second type of crisis is one for which there is warning. The University of Colorado athletics department endured a crisis relating to criminal activity and sexual misconduct by several members of its football program in 2004. But university officials should not have been surprised by the situation because numerous reports, some dating back several years, indicated that problems existed within the program before 2004 (Anderson & Dohrmann, 2004). Proactive measures may have prevented the problem from reaching critical mass later. At minimum, use of a well-developed crisis communications plan would have prevented some of the unfortunate responses made by athletics department staff members as the crisis unfolded.

## Developing a Crisis Communications Plan

Crises are by nature disruptive and difficult to manage, but by developing a crisis communications plan, sport managers can take a proactive approach. A crisis communications plan provides a framework for responding to crisis situations. It empowers sport managers by specifying the responsibilities in a crisis, the way in which information is to be shared internally during a crisis, and the way in which information is to be shared with other publics in a timely manner (Coombs, 2007a; Matera & Artigue, 2000). By defining such considerations in advance of a crisis, the sport organization may be better positioned to respond in a manner that best protects its reputation and financial interests.

Crisis communications plans are not designed to prescribe responses for every conceivable crisis, nor are they detailed enough to specify every action that must be taken throughout a crisis episode. They are designed to provide general guidelines for the management team (Coombs, 2007a, 2007b), particularly early on. Traditionally, public relations experts have emphasized the importance of the first 24 hours after the onset of a crisis. But 24 hours may be too long in today's age of instant information. Mark Fabiani, a public relations consultant for the NHL, Big East Conference, and San Diego Chargers, has stated that the goal is to "get ahead of the story"

**A memorial at Bluffton University stands in remembrance of those who died in a 2007 accident.**

AP Photo/The Lima NewsMatthew Hasinguchi

(Mullen, 2004, p. 24). Getting ahead now means making an initial response within an hour or two of the onset of the crisis.

To prepare for crises in such a manner, sport managers must follow a number of steps in the process and then develop a plan containing certain key elements. The following sections address both topics. Appendix B (pages 327–338) also provides a sample crisis communication plan.

## Building a Crisis Communications Plan

Five steps are involved in developing a crisis communications plan. The first step is to ensure that senior management supports the development of the plan. Without such support, people who should be involved in the planning process will not view it as a priority, and any plan that is developed will not likely be used after a crisis occurs.

A second step is to maintain the involvement of key personnel on the planning committee. The same staff members who were critical in the crisis forecasting process will likely have important insights in planning for crisis communications. Clearly, the public relations staff is integral in this process, but they are not the only ones.

One of the most important contributors to the plan is the sport organization's legal counsel. Many crises lead to legal action against the sport organization. Therefore, the sport organization's attorneys need to offer insight regarding which actions may be legally defensible and which actions may not. Unfortunately, some attorneys may advise sport organizations to say and do little when crises occur. After all, a statement never made cannot be held against the organization. Such advice is short sighted, however, and fails to recognize the importance of the organization's reputation among key publics besides potential litigants. The sidebar titled Balancing Legal and Public Relations Concerns, written by Ted Ayres, vice president and general counsel at Wichita State University, describes how a sport organization can balance legal and public relations concerns.

A third critical step in preparing a crisis communications plan is to ensure that all employees recognize the existence of the plan and the importance of using it when a crisis occurs. Although not all employees need to have a copy of the complete plan, each member of the organization must understand that they have at least two important responsibilities. First, they must contact an appropriate crisis team member if they recognize a crisis developing. This means that all staff members should keep contact information for the crisis communications

team at hand at all times (e.g., wallet cards). Second, they must refer crisis-related inquires to the appropriate crisis communications official. This means that the crisis communications team must specify the nature of those contacts immediately after the onset of the crisis.

Hessert (1998b) recognized that commitment from coaches may be particularly important in crisis communications plans. Coaches who wish to define their own course of action in a crisis may make statements or take actions that are damaging in the court of public opinion and maybe even in a court of law. A coach who takes a position contrary to that of the coach's organization may be setting the stage for an inevitable parting of ways.

A fourth step is to test the plan. These tests can range from complete mock drills to more limited forms such as call-back exercises in which members of the crisis communications team go through the sequence of mandated contacts to see how quickly important connections may be made (Davis & Gilman, 2002). Written or oral exams may be administered to gauge employees' familiarity with their responsibilities (Matera & Artigue, 2000; Poole, 1999).

The fifth and final step may seem obvious: Sport managers must remain committed to their plan and use it when a crisis occurs. The authors have spoken with a handful of public relations professionals who privately express frustration regarding this step. A crisis communications plan is developed but then left to gather dust on the shelf because senior managers think that they can better manage the crisis by "winging it." If senior managers do not intend to use a plan, there is no reason to develop one.

## Key Elements of the Plan

Crisis communications plans can vary in structure. But given that they are designed to prescribe general communication procedures upon the onset of a crisis, most contain a number of common elements, as discussed in the following sections.

### Crisis Scenarios

Although some crisis communications plans are generic enough that they do not specify crisis scenarios, many experts recommend that the plans list the most likely scenarios and responses to each (Beal, 2003; Connaughton, Spengler, & Bennett, 2001; Helitzer, 2000). The rationale for such a recommendation is that responses vary based on the nature of the crisis. For example, the crisis communications plan for one NCAA Football Bowl Subdivision program specifies responses to the following crises:

# Balancing Legal and Public Relations Concerns

**Ted Ayres**

Anticipating and planning for a crisis is mandatory in today's world of sport (Dorn, 2004). Anticipation and planning, however, will be of little value if an organization's management does not work together cohesively when an event occurs. This cohesiveness, of course, means that there must be coordination, cooperation, and communication between the public relations professional and legal counsel.

Although they will come from different perspectives, the public relations professional and the organization's legal counsel both have the best interests of the organization in mind as they seek to respond to a crisis. Each must understand the role, concerns, objectives, and perspectives of the other.

Whether legal counsel is provided by an in-house attorney or by a lawyer or firm retained by the organization (or some combination thereof), I encourage public relations professionals to engage counsel and develop a relationship of trust and understanding before a problem or crisis develops. This process, of course, benefits the organization and all individuals generally, not only in responding to a crisis. In fact, most attorneys would welcome the opportunity to work with the public relations professional in an effort to practice preventative law (i.e., working to help the organization and its employees avoid litigation and legal jeopardy). A sense of confidence based on previous interaction and understanding between the public relations professional and legal counsel will pay significant dividends in a crisis.

Although lawyers may differ in style or manner, all are concerned with protecting the legal interests of their clients. Ethically and professionally, lawyers must be devoted to their clients, and within the boundaries of the law and the legal system, lawyers must provide advice, support, and guidance that either avoid or, when required, minimize the financial exposure, embarrassment, and disruption that naturally arise from a poor decision.

Clearly, a lawyer would prefer to defend a case without dealing with ambiguous or worse statements made by the client or the client's representatives. In fact, unguarded statements made in the heat of the moment in an effort to "protect" an athlete or colleague may be a significant catalyst in causing a lawsuit to be filed. Nevertheless, most attorneys recognize that an abrupt and defensive position of "no comment" is generally not advisable. As proved time after time, allowing the media to proceed from a "What are they hiding?" approach can be disastrous, particularly when the news becomes the media's efforts to learn the real story and bits and pieces of the situation are trumpeted daily on the front page of the newspaper or as the lead story of the evening television news.

Of course, in some situations an organization may be clearly and undeniably at fault and legally responsible for a crisis and the consequences thereof. In this situation, the public relations professional; the organization's management, owners, and decision makers; legal counsel; and insurers should collaborate on a plan of strategic admission and acceptance. I have found that honesty is always a valuable foundational platform for decision making.

The public relations professional and legal counsel should communicate frequently and work together in responding to a crisis. They should work together to control what information is provided, when it is provided, and by whom. In my experience, being as forthcoming as possible is the best approach, particularly if done in a manner that avoids legally inadvisable statements or comments. In other words, the public relations professional and counsel must work together to provide a flow of information that informs but also avoids misunderstandings and doesn't create legal landmines. This can be done!

> **I encourage public relations professionals to engage counsel and develop a relationship of trust and understanding before a problem or crisis develops.**

*Ted Ayres is vice president and general counsel at Wichita State University. He has coauthored two projects relating to crisis management in sport settings.*

- Death or catastrophic injury to a student–athlete
- Major brawl or riot
- Violence directed at an official
- Incidents involving law enforcement outside of competition
- Incidents involving NCAA rules violations
- Death of a staff member
- Death or catastrophic injury of a spectator
- Terrorist activity
- Transportation accidents

The makeup of the crisis management team and the types of initial responses vary within the plan based on the specific scenario.

### Initiation of the Plan

When a crisis occurs, someone with the sport organization, usually the senior manager, is responsible for initiating the plan and activating the management team. Complete contact information (e.g., office, home, and cell phone numbers) for each members of the crisis team should be included in the plan. Given the importance of this information in activating the crisis team, someone—likely the sport organization's top public relations person—should be charged with ensuring that all contact information remains current. Further, team members should have easy access to others' contact information, whether they have the full plan in hand or not.

### Definition of Response Teams

Definition of response teams is one of the most important elements of a crisis communications plan. Although some managers, such as those from public relations, legal, finance, and human resources will be involved in responding to most crises, other team members may vary depending on the situation.

Delineating the general responsibilities of each team member on the crisis team may also be advisable. Figure 10.2 displays the responsibilities of

---

# Responsibilities of Select Crisis Team Members

## Director of Athletics

The director of athletics will lead the emergency response team and act as the final decision maker in any emergency situation. The director of athletics will be responsible for contacting the university president, the university's general counsel, the vice president for student life, the vice president for university advancement, and the vice president for administration and finance. All athletics staff, as directed by the director of athletics, will work cooperatively with the appropriate law enforcement and medical officials as the situation warrants. The director of athletics will be responsible for coordinating with the university emergency response plan and will oversee communications with student–athletes, their families, the conference office, the NCAA, the media, and the general public.

## Senior Associate Athletic Director/Senior Woman Administrator

The first priority of the senior associate athletic director/senior woman administrator in the event of an emergency is to inform and brief the director of athletics on the situation. After the situation is defined the senior associate athletic director/senior woman administrator will be responsible for coordinating all communications with student–athletes, their families, and the university if the emergency directly or indirectly affects student–athletes. In the event that the director of athletics is not available, the senior associate athletic director/SWA will assume leadership of the emergency response team.

## Senior Associate Athletic Director/External Operations

The senior associate athletic director/external operations will be the designated spokesperson for the athletics department regarding any emergency situation. She or he will oversee all media-related functions for the athletics department in any emergency situation.

## Assistant Athletic Director/Media Relations

The assistant athletic director/media relations will be the designated media contact for the athletics department regarding any emergency situation. This individual will coordinate the release of information to the public with the director of athletics, senior associate AD/external operations, and the emergency response team. This person will be responsible for writing any press releases concerning the emergency situation. The assistant athletic director/media relations will also be responsible for the handling of all media requests, from interview requests to requests for information.

---

**Figure 10.2** Responsibilities of select crisis team members.

select members of the crisis management team for a college athletics department.

## Internal Communication Plan

In the heat of a crisis episode, it is easy to overlook one of the sport organization's most important publics—its own employees. Internal communication during a crisis event involves at least two distinct tasks. The first is informing important internal publics of what has happened and what they should be doing because of the crisis. Many organizations employ a **call tree** whereby the responsibilities for notifying employees of the situation is delegated to multiple parties, each of whom has specific contacts to make. Figure 10.3 displays the call tree used by the crisis management team for Wichita State University athletics (Wichita State University, 2009).

The second task involves internal communication designed to secure additional information relevant to managing the crisis (PRSA, 2000). Such information may include contact information in personnel

records, documentation of existing organizational policies, and records regarding how past incidents were been handled.

## External Communication Plan

Members of the media are not the only external public with whom the sport public relations staff must communicate during a crisis, but they are often the most important because the mass media are usually the conduit through which the sport organization communicates with other external publics. Figure 10.4 illustrates this concept. As indicated, the sport organization may use several methods (i.e., personal contact, news releases, website) to communicate with key publics (family members, the media, fans). In turn, the media will communicate with those external publics, including some who will not receive information from any other source. To the degree that sport managers can successfully manage communications with media representatives, they can also successfully share critical information with those other publics.

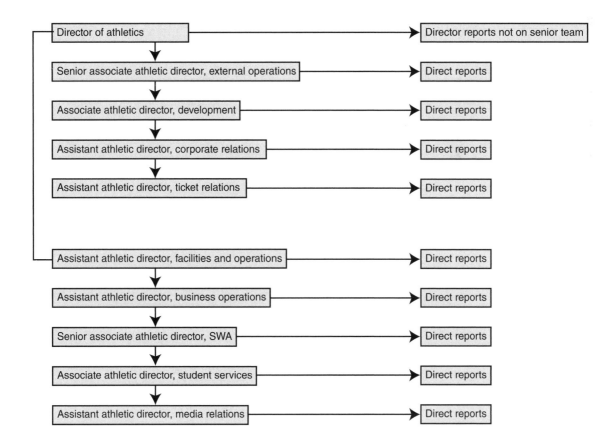

**Figure 10.3** Crisis communications call tree. If conditions warrant it, a calling tree may be activated. The decision to activate the calling tree will be made by the director of athletics. All department heads and supervisors will be responsible for contacting their direct reports. If you are unable to contact your person on the flow chart, skip to the next person and then contact the immediate supervisor of the person you could not reach so that he or she can make contact with direct reports.

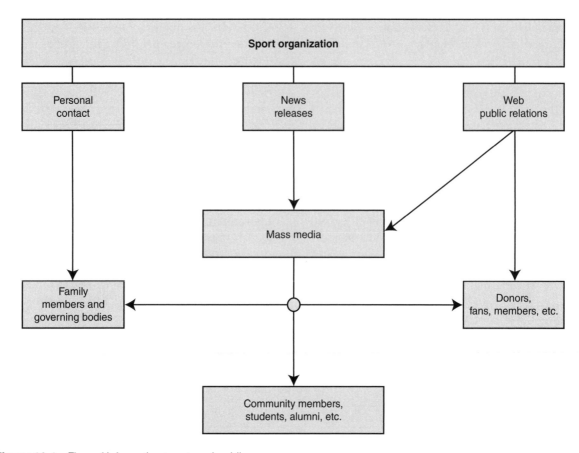

**Figure 10.4** Flow of information to external publics.

Crisis communications experts recommend that organizations plan to make themselves the best source of information regarding the crisis for the media (Carter & Rovell, 2003; Broom, 2009; Poole, 1999). If the sport organization can successfully position itself in this manner, it may be able to reduce the degree to which members of the media look to other sources, some of them possibly adversarial, for information. If a sport organization learns about a negative story brewing in the media, it may be in the organization's best interest to announce the negative news itself. As stated by communications consultant Kathleen Hessert in her sidebar in chapter 2, "Go for the quick hemorrhage, not the slow bleed."

Crisis plans should delineate procedures for communicating with the media as quickly as possible. Two key considerations are the preparation of initial statements for the media and the identification of the organization's spokesperson.

### Initial Media Statements

One tactic commonly employed is to prepare generic templates that can be customized given the circumstances of the crisis and quickly released to

the media (Coombs, 2007a, 2007b). Those initial statements serve to acknowledge the situation and promise additional communication. For instance, when Manny Ramirez of the Los Angeles Dodgers was suspended for 50 games in 2009 for use of a banned substance, the team issued the following statement:

> Los Angeles Dodgers CEO Jamie Mc-Court issued the following statement in reaction to today's statements from Major League Baseball, the Major League Baseball Players Association, and Manny Ramirez.
>
> "We share the disappointment felt by our fans, our players, and every member of our organization. We support the policies of Major League Baseball, and we will welcome Manny back upon his return."
>
> This statement will constitute the comment of the Los Angeles Dodgers organization until Joe Torre meets with the

media at approximately 4:30 p.m. today at Dodger Stadium. (Los Angeles Dodgers, 2009)

### Spokesperson Identification

One of the most important elements of the crisis communications plan is the identification of the sport organization's primary spokesperson during the crisis. Although public relations professionals are involved in preparing spokespersons for their tasks, they usually do not play the spokesperson role themselves. Instead, spokespersons tend to be prominent individuals within the organization.

The designated spokesperson may vary depending on the crisis scenario. The most serious crises demand a senior-level spokesperson such as a CEO, general manager, or director of athletics. Less serious episodes such as a player running afoul of the law may be effectively addressed by a head coach. Whatever the situation, the spokesperson must possess excellent public speaking and media relations skills. A prudent measure is to identify backup spokespersons in the event that the primary spokesperson is unavailable because of the crisis ("Tips and Techniques," 2000).

# Managing a Crisis

When a crisis occurs, a well-prepared sport organization implements its crisis communications plan according to the specified procedures. As a result, the crisis communications team is activated, preliminary information regarding the situation is shared internally, and an initial statement is made available to members of the media. These actions position the crisis team to respond in a timely and appropriate fashion, but they represent only the initial steps in successfully managing the situation. When the crisis team gathers, it assembles as much information as possible, begins to formulate a strategy that will protect or repair the organization's reputation, and delineates subsequent communication tactics. The nature of the crisis determines not only the strategies and tactics employed in managing the episode but also the length and frequency of the crisis team meetings. Some crises, such as the trading of a star player, are fairly short lived; others, such as a protracted labor dispute, are more enduring. Either way, the crisis management team must determine when the crisis has ended, and sometimes they must publicly state that to be the case.

# Selecting a Strategy

Perhaps the single most important decision that the crisis communications team will make is what the organization's posture toward the crisis will be. Will the organization accept responsibility for the crisis? Will it counterattack those making accusations? Will it take steps to improve the situation? What else might be involved in its response?

Coombs (2007b) noted that the selection of an appropriate **crisis response strategy** is based on an accurate appraisal of three issues. First, the type of crisis fundamentally affects how key publics are likely to perceive the organization. When a crisis is caused by something beyond the control of the organization, such as when a tornado struck the Georgia Dome in 2008 during the Southeastern Conference basketball tournament, key publics generally do not hold the organization responsible. When a crisis results from an accident, like the one that occurred at the 2009 Tour de France when a woman crossing the road was hit and killed by a police motorbike, key publics tend to hold the organization only minimally responsible. But when human misdeeds or negligence result in a crisis, such as the 2004 "Malice at the Palace" episode when NBA players and fans brawled in Detroit, key publics hold the sport organization highly responsible. A second consideration in selecting the appropriate crisis strategy is the sport organization's crisis history. Organizations that frequently suffer crises, such as college athletics programs that have repeatedly incurred major NCAA sanctions, face greater challenges in dealing with crises than those with cleaner records. Finally, the overall reputation of the sport organization will affect the situation. Key publics tend to assign lower thresholds of responsibility to organizations with poor reputations.

Having assessed the situation and the organization's standing in regard to the crisis, the crisis communications team is well positioned to select a response that will either protect the organization's reputation or begin to repair it. A number of scholars have identified and described image repair strategies (see, e.g., Allen & Caillouet, 1994; Benoit 1995). Coombs (2006) compiled a number of these strategies, condensed them, and then categorized them into four general postures.

## *Denial Posture*

Denial strategies are recommended when the organization is facing false rumors or unwarranted challenges (Coombs, 2007b). Three specific strategies fall within this general posture (Coombs, 2006). The first, attacking the accuser, involves challenging those making claims against the organization. This strategy occasionally involves the threat of a lawsuit against the accuser. A second strategy is straightforward denial in which the organization denies that a crisis exists and offers explanations about why there is no crisis. A third strategy is scapegoating. When scapegoating, the organization blames people or groups outside the organization for the crisis.

### Diminishment Posture

Diminishment strategies are recommended when a crisis is an accident or is caused by something beyond the control of the organization (e.g., workplace violence), especially when an organization has an unfavorable crisis history or poor reputation (Coombs, 2007b). Two specific strategies fall under this category (Coombs, 2006). The excusing strategy is employed when the organization wants to emphasize that it had minimal, if any, responsibility for the crisis. The justification strategy attempts to minimize the amount of perceived damage resulting from the crisis. Justification can be accomplished when the crisis produces minimal injuries or damage, or when victims bear significant responsibility for their injuries because of their own actions.

### Rebuilding Posture

Rebuilding strategies are recommended whenever a preventable crisis occurs or when an organization with a weak crisis history and a poor reputation suffers an accident (Coombs, 2007b). The two rebuilding strategies are apology and compensation (Coombs, 2006). Apology includes both accepting full responsibility for the crisis and apologizing to victims. Compensation involves offering money or other gifts to those harmed in an effort to offset their suffering.

### Bolstering Posture

Bolstering strategies are recommended as complements to the other postures (Coombs, 2007b). They are not designed to stand alone. Coombs (2006) identified three bolstering strategies. The first is reminding, in which the organization reminds key publics of the many positive things that it has done in the past. The second is ingratiation, in which the organization heaps praise on its stakeholders for their support. The third is victimage, in which the organization emphasizes how it too has suffered because of the crisis.

Bruce and Tini (2008) suggested a related strategy that was not included in Coombs' typology (2006) and that may be unique to sport organizations. In their analysis of a salary cap scandal in Australasian men's rugby, Bruce and Tini observed a strategy that they described as diversion, in which the sport organization redirects attention away from itself to players and fans who suffer because of the crisis. The rugby club that they studied successfully garnered public sympathy by emphasizing how their own players had been harmed by the misdeeds of management. Diversion may sometimes be a successful strategy for sport organizations because of the emotional attachment between players and fans, but it should be employed only when the players or fans bear no responsibility for the consequences that they suffer (Bruce & Tini, 2008).

## Communicating Effectively

As crisis management teams select protection and repair strategies, they will also have to consider how to communicate the organization's position and share additional information with relevant publics. Accordingly, they must determine key messages and employ appropriate channels of communication to share those messages. One key platform will likely be messages conveyed by the mass media.

### Determining Key Messages

One of the key responsibilities of public relations professionals serving on crisis management teams is to facilitate the crafting of key messages to be emphasized in communications. Key messages are often brief statements that are easily replayed in sound bites and may appear as succinct quotes in text. Of course, they are delivered to multiple publics, not just the media, and the organization must be consistent in emphasizing its selected key messages. Common key messages include expressions of concern for those negatively affected by the crisis and statements of commitment to improving the situation, even if the sport organization was not responsible for the crisis.

### Choosing Communication Channels

As noted in chapter 1, messages are delivered through channels of communication. Sport managers frequently use numerous channels during crisis episodes, but the channels should be carefully selected. Some channels are more influential than others. Face-to-face interaction is the most persuasive, so personal contact with those most affected is highly recommended. In addition, having the designated spokesperson personally interact with members of the media through news conferences and interviews is highly advisable. Live interviews may be particularly effective ways to share key messages, because they are not subject to editing ("Q&A: The Interview," 2001).

The Internet can also play a key role. Information posted on a sport organization's website is not subject to filtering through the mass media, so sport organizations should use their websites to distribute crisis-related information. Usually, this information will be housed within the sport organization's regular website, but on some occasions, special sites may be set up to deal with the crisis (Coombs, 2007a). For instance, when the National Hockey League implemented a lockout before the 2004 season, the league set up a standalone website to convey its story to members of the media, fans, and other constituents (Bernstein, 2004b). The site contained information ranging from consumer research supporting the league's stance to economic reports emphasizing the need for changes in the labor agreement. Beyond organizational websites, sport organizations may also use e-mail distribution lists to share information with members of key publics.

## Dealing With Media

As mentioned earlier, dealing with the media is often the most important and most difficult aspect of the crisis communications process. Crises are by definition newsworthy, and members of the media will attempt to generate as much information as possible about the story. Accordingly, sport public relations professionals must take painstaking steps to establish themselves and their organizations as credible sources of information.

Frequent updates to the media are necessary to maintain the organization's position as the leading source of information. In some cases, the organization may need to provide an information center from which the media may work (Broom, 2009; Matera & Artigue, 2000). Media centers are best set up in sites that are located some distance from the actual scene of the crisis (Davis & Gilman, 2002) and that may facilitate the delivery of media services such as news conferences, interviews, media advisories, and news releases.

Of course, several other principles should guide effective communication with members of the media during a crisis. The section that follows contains a list of 10 recommendations that can guide sport public relations professionals as they interact with the media and as they prepare other individuals to serve as spokespersons.

1. Organizational spokespersons must be truthful. Attempts to mislead members of the media are almost always discovered, and the resultant damage is even greater than what would have occurred had the truth been told in the beginning.

2. Public relations officials should anticipate difficult questions that the organizational spokesperson may face when talking with the media. This approach allows the public relations staff to assist the spokesperson in formulating responses that include key messages.

3. Organizational spokespersons should avoid the phrase "No comment." Even if they are not willing to answer a question, they must find more polite and informative responses.

4. Organizational spokespersons should not speculate when talking with the media. Speculation only fuels additional what-if questions and may limit response options at a later date.

5. Organizational spokespersons should avoid making statements off the record. Off-the-record comments are discussed in chapter 9.

6. Organizational spokespersons should not attempt to promote their organization's products or services during a crisis (Broom, 2009; Matera & Artigue, 2000). By attempting to use the crisis as a sales platform, they will likely be perceived as mercenary and unethical.

7. Sport public relations professionals should not ask media members to withhold damaging information. If members of the media are reporting stories that will present the sport organization in an unfavorable light, the best the public relations staff can ask for is that the organization's side of the story be included in the news coverage.

8. Both the public relations staff and the organizational spokesperson should remain calm and professional, even in emotionally charged settings. Maintaining composure can be extremely challenging given the stress caused by crisis situations.

9. The public relations staff should anticipate that at least some of the media members

assigned to cover a crisis will be different from those who may otherwise cover the sport organization (Helitzer, 2000). Some media organizations may replace their regular beat writers with other reporters who are perceived as stronger in dealing with hard news coverage. Additionally, a crisis will likely attract attention from media outlets that do not normally cover the sport organization.

10. Public relations officials should track media coverage and Internet chatter during a crisis. By monitoring media coverage, they can gauge how their organization is faring in the court of public opinion and whether they are being effective in disseminating key messages.

## Declaring the End of a Crisis

Sometimes, determining when a crisis is over is easy. For example, the NCAA issues a final report regarding its investigation. Charges are dropped. A problem coach is terminated.

In other situations, assessing when a crisis ends is more difficult. If people are killed in an accident, when does the crisis end? When does a sport organization put to rest a reputation-related crisis? The effects of such episodes can linger for years.

Regardless, some crisis experts believe that sport organizations should publicly state when they believe that a crisis is over (PRSA, 2000). Such a declaration may bring public closure to the event. Practically speaking, it may also signal to the media that the special services the sport organization has provided during the course of the crisis are coming to an end.

The difficulty with such pronouncements is that they must be based on an accurate assessment of the crisis event and its news life cycle. Just as the sport organization cannot control whether a crisis unfolds, it cannot mandate its ending. Attempts to declare an end to a crisis prematurely usually backfire and reignite simmering controversy. Arrogant athletes who commit misdeeds and then declare that it's all behind them fail to recognize that mistakes are not fully set aside until members of key publics are willing to do so. The Tiger Woods crisis illustrates this point. Recall that the crisis began with an automobile accident on November 27, 2009. Almost two months later on February 19, Woods finally made his first public statement in a tightly controlled setting that did not include a questions-

and-answers session. He then conducted two brief interviews on March 21 with representatives from ESPN and the Golf Channel. Despite Woods' apologies in both the statement and the interviews, he was subject to harsh questioning in his first true news conference April 5 (Busbee, 2010). One year later, at the 2011 Masters, Woods was still dealing with ramifications of the crisis. A *USA Today* column by Christine Brennan (2011) stated,

> It has been 17 months since Woods won a golf tournament, going all the way past his run-in with that fire hydrant Thanksgiving weekend 2009, and the unraveling of his personal life. He has gone 11 consecutive majors without winning (he missed 2 of them because of knee surgery). For nearly three years now, he has been stuck on 14 majors. As each major comes and goes, the refrain will get louder, and it will be something along the lines of this: Is Tiger Woods still Tiger Woods?

## Assessing a Crisis Response

Regardless of whether a crisis is short term or sustained, when the management team decides to shift from crisis mode back to normal operations, it must assess the effectiveness of its crisis communications plan. The best way to do this is by convening the same group of managers to review available data such as media coverage of the event, consumer comments, sales records, and other indicators of the performance of the plan. They should also debrief managers who served on the crisis communications committee but who were not included in formulating crisis communications plans to get their insights into the effectiveness of the plan.

Key questions that the crisis communications team should address include, but are not limited to, the following:

- Was the plan activated in a timely and efficient manner?
- Were initial communication procedures executed as assigned?
- Were initial communication procedures adequate given the situation?
- How quickly was the crisis communications team able to assess the situation and select a crisis response strategy?

- In retrospect, was the crisis response strategy appropriate?
- Were all important publics identified and served effectively?
- How effective were the key messages specified by the crisis communications team?
- How effective were the channels of communication used to carry those key messages?
- How effective was the organization's spokesperson in dealing with those key publics, particularly the media?
- How well did the public relations staff prepare the organization's spokesperson for interaction with members of the media or other key publics?
- Was the organization able to position itself as the best source of information regarding the crisis?
- Were all important services needed by members of the media or other key publics provided?
- How well did the plan perform in protecting the financial interests of the organization?
- How well did the plan perform in protecting the reputation of the organization?
- Most important, how can the plan be improved before the next crisis that the organization may face?

By addressing such questions, the crisis management team may better position their organization to navigate future crises successfully.

# Successful Crisis Responses

Although rarely will a sport organization endure a crisis unscathed, analyses of several high-profile crisis cases in sport indicate that some organizations effectively managed the crises that they faced and, as a result, recovered rather quickly. Two such organizations are MLB's Houston Astros and NCAA Division I institution Montana State University.

## *Houston Astros*

The Astros' organization faced a major crisis in December 2001 when stadium naming-rights partner Enron filed for bankruptcy amid allegations of corporate scandal (Jensen & Butler, 2007). The team moved promptly to seek a release from the naming-rights contract so that they could remove the Enron brand from their stadium. When that failed, the Astros bought back from Enron the naming rights to the ballpark and renamed the facility Astros Field before the start of the 2002 season. Months later, they resold the naming rights to Minute Maid.

Jensen and Butler (2007) lauded the Astros' aggressive efforts to dissociate themselves from Enron. They also noted that the franchise committed itself to finding a subsequent naming-rights partner with both deep connections to the Houston community and a pristine reputation. As a result, the Astros avoided serious financial and reputational damage to their franchise.

## *Montana State University*

Montana State University's (MSU) athletics program suffered a major crisis in 2006 and 2007 after the murdered body of a drug dealer was found on campus (Ulrich, 2008). The ensuing police investigation revealed that a number of MSU student–athletes were involved in trafficking narcotics and that MSU scholarship money had been used in several drug transactions. Ultimately, two former student–athletes were arrested for the murder, one of whom ultimately confessed (Ulrich, 2008). The university responded by firing the head football coach, and it faced the challenge of repairing its image in the midst of a capital campaign.

Peter Fields, athletic director at MSU, formed a crisis management team to lead the crisis response (Ulrich, 2008). The team's first priority was to conduct a thorough evaluation of the situation. That assessment resulted in a two-pronged communications strategy. The first part of the strategy was to promote the many positive stories associated with MSU student–athletes, most of whom were admirable. The second part of the strategy was to disclose as much information as possible regarding the crisis episode. The crisis management team also prioritized stakeholders. Donors, boosters, and the campus community received top priority. The department also secured an independent evaluation of its recruiting practices and has since established a crisis communications plan.

Ulrich (2008) reported that MSU's response was effective, as evidenced by the success of its capital campaign and positive publicity in the media. Fields noted that although the crisis posed a significant challenge, "There is no doubt that MSU athletics is stronger because of the turmoil we went through. It forced us to redefine our core mission and come together as a staff like never before" (Fields as quoted in Ulrich, 2008, p. 32).

# Unsuccessful Crisis Responses

Just as successful responses may serve as educational tools regarding how to communicate effectively during a crisis, case study of unsuccessful responses also yields insights, especially mistakes to avoid. The examples of unsuccessful crisis responses come from NCAA Division I institution Duke University, MLB's Rogers Clemens, and the NFL's Terrell Owens.

## Duke University

Duke University suffered one on the most prominent crises in the recent history of college athletics when three members of its men's lacrosse team were accused of rape and other crimes in 2006. The charge was made by an exotic dancer hired by members of the team to perform at an off-campus party (Associated Press, 2007). In the course of a controversial investigation, the district attorney indicated that as many as 46 members of the team were under suspicion of having violated the law (Associated Press, 2007).

Twelve days after the party, Duke officials forfeited two upcoming men's lacrosse games in response to team members' hiring exotic dancers and engaging in underage drinking at the party (Associated Press, 2007).Three days later, university officials suspended the program while awaiting "clearer resolution of the legal situation" (Associated Press, 2007). Less than 10 days later, Duke's men's lacrosse coach resigned, and the school president canceled the remainder of the team's season. The move followed the revelation of a vulgar e-mail from a lacrosse player about killing strippers (Associated Press, 2007). Two months after suspending the program, the university president reinstated the program with stricter monitoring (Associated Press, 2007). Months later, charges against all three players were dropped, and ultimately the district attorney resigned after a state bar panel concluded that he acted improperly during the course of the investigation (Wilson & Holusha, 2007).

Analysis of how Duke administrators managed the lacrosse incident revealed four key mistakes (Yaeger & Henry, 2009). First, Duke erred in that it did not use an established internal communications plan, as evidenced by the fact that the school president learned of the incident by reading the school newspaper (ABC News, 2007; Yaeger & Henry, 2009; Yaeger & Pressler, 2007). Second, Duke administrators failed to maintain consistent communication with the media throughout the crisis, thereby in-creasing the need for reporters to find other sources for their stories. Third, Duke administrators unsuccessfully attempted to reduce the news value of the story when they canceled the season. Fourth, and foremost, Duke administrators failed to wait on all relevant facts before acting. Yaeger and Henry (2009) likened the approach to **one-move chess**—that is, "making decisions with no respect for strategy."

## Roger Clemens

Roger Clemens, who enjoyed a long and successful career in MLB, faced a crisis when he was named in the 2007 Mitchell Report as someone who took both steroids and human growth hormone at times during his career (Sanderson, 2008). Days after the release of the report, Clemens issued a written denial that he used performance-enhancing drugs (PEDs) on his foundation's website. In a video he denied the charges on both the foundation's website and YouTube. Weeks later, he repeated the denial in an interview that aired on CBS' *60 Minutes*. The day following the airing of that interview, Clemens and his attorney held a news conference to respond to other questions from the media.

Sanderson's (2008) analysis of the news conference indicated that Clemens employed four image repair strategies in the news conference. Denial was employed when Clemens' attorney accepted the blame for having Clemens wait nearly a month before facing the media. The attorney indicated that he had advised Clemens to refrain from using such a tactic. Attacking the accuser was the second strategy employed. Clemens and his attorney attempted to discredit the witness cited in the Mitchell Report and accused the authors of the report of leading the witness to make false or inaccurate statements. Suffering was the third strategy used because Clemens portrayed himself as a victim of presumed guilt. Minimization was the fourth strategy, evident when Clemens refused to condemn another player who had admitted to using PEDs. Clemens also pleaded ignorance regarding the seriousness of the charges being leveled against him as the reason that he refused to be interviewed as part of the Mitchell investigation.

Sanderson (2008) observed that the press conference was a series of contradictions in which Clemens and his attorney would promise not to do something, such as attack the accuser, and then they would proceed to do that very thing. Accordingly, "Clemens's image-repair strategies . . . were ineffective and raised more questions than they answered" (Sanderson, 2008, p. 258). The confounding strategy was duplicated little more than a month later when

Roger Clemens testifies before a U.S. Congressional panel, an appearance that one communication expert described as "disastrous."

Zuma Press/Icon SMI

Clemens testified before a U.S. Congressional panel with similarly "disastrous results" (Sanderson, 2008, p. 258).

## Terrell Owens

Star NFL wide receiver Terrell Owens faced a crisis because of a contract dispute with the Philadelphia Eagles in 2005 (Brazeal, 2008). While attempting to force the Eagles to renegotiate his contract, Owens criticized the organization, his coaches, and quarterback Donovan McNabb. When Owens refused to offer a team-mandated apology to McNabb, he was suspended midseason.

To address the situation, Owens and his controversial agent Drew Rosenhaus held a news conference days after Owens' suspension. An analysis of the news conference indicated that Owens used two image repair strategies and Rosenhaus employed five such strategies (Brazeal, 2008). Owens bolstered his image by emphasizing his fierce competitiveness, and he offered an apology to those who may have taken offense. He did not, however, admit

that he was wrong or indicate that he planned to change his behavior. Rosenhaus also bolstered Owens' image by praising the athlete's sincerity. He emphasized that Owens was sorry about the situation and argued that Owens' most controversial statements had come about because of his good intentions in attempting to accommodate the media. Rosenhaus also strongly accused Owens' attackers, particularly the media, for their mistreatment of his client.

Brazeal (2008) concluded that Owens and Rosenhaus faced a significant challenge in attempting to repair the damage that Owens' reputation had already suffered. They failed and arguably made a bad situation worse. "In the end, Owens and Rosenhaus needed to sincerely apologize, offer corrective action, and demonstrate humility if they hoped to repair Owens' image. Instead, they offered half-hearted apologies and lashed out against the media" (Brazeal, 2008, p. 149). Owens did not return to the Eagles in 2005 and was released the following spring.

## SUMMARY

Crises are events or controversies that may damage a sport organization's financial standing and credibility. Despite the widespread occurrence of crises within sport, many sport organizations are unprepared for them. Crisis communication plans specify the public relations responsibilities of various staff members during a crisis, and most focus on how information is shared both internally and externally. Effective crisis communication plans may address crises that are deemed likely to occur or are of significant potential impact. Such plans include details regarding how they are to be activated, who should be involved in the crisis management process, who should be contacted regarding the crisis, and what should be said, at least initially. Perhaps the most important decision that a crisis response team will make is which strategy to employ in responding to the crisis. Such decisions are usually based on the type of crisis and the organization's history and reputation. By adhering to a number of crisis communications principles, sport public relations professionals and organizational spokespersons can effectively engage the media, perhaps the single most difficult aspect of a crisis. After a crisis ends, the public relations staff and other managers should thoroughly review the performance of the crisis plan and make revisions to improve it.

## LEARNING ACTIVITIES

1. Scan sports news sources on the Internet to gain a sense of the major sport stories of the day. Which sport organizations are dealing with crisis episodes? What types of crises are they facing? What strategies are they employing in response to the crisis?

2. Conduct an interview with a sport public relations professional. Ask the public relations official about what her or his organization has done to prepare for crises. Do they have a written plan? If so, what things are specified in that plan? Have they ever used the plan? How well did it work? If they do not have a written plan, what would they do in the event of a crisis?

3. Search the Internet for a sport organization website that is being used as a communications channel during a crisis. What kind of information is included on the site? Does the site employ blogs as a communication tool? What recommendations might you make regarding other information or features that would make the site more effective?

4. Develop a case study regarding a sport organization that has faced a crisis. Be sure to specify how the crisis unfolded, how quickly and in what ways the sport organization responded to the crisis, and what crisis response strategies appear to have been employed. Given the gift of hindsight, what would you have advised the organization to do differently and what might have been the effects of your recommendations?

# Exploring Unmediated Communication Tactics

## After reading this chapter, students should be able to

- describe how unmediated communication tactics relate to community relations,
- specify the advantages of unmediated communication tactics as public relations tools,
- identify the benefits that unmediated communication tactics bring to the sport organization,
- recognize the types of unmediated communication tactics commonly used in sport,
- discuss key considerations when planning unmediated communication tactics, and
- note how unmediated communication tactics may be leveraged to generate revenue for the sport organization.

## Key terms discussed in this chapter include

- community relations,
- unmediated communication,
- speakers bureaus,

- exclusive and nonexclusive representation,
- OTSM, and
- caravan.

**Discussions of sport** public relations often focus only on media relations. This emphasis is understandable given the intense media interest in sport, the power of publicity to promote sport, and the number of media relations jobs in the field. But this approach does not adequately recognize the value of other public relations activities (Jackowski, 2001), particularly **community relations**. Many sport managers have found that although favorable publicity in the mass media can be powerful, there is no substitute for communicating and interacting directly with constituents in the community.

The first chapter of this text described community relations as organizational activity designed to foster desirable relationships between the sport organization and the communities in which it is either located or has strategic interests. Community relations are the second most common form of public relations practice (Stoldt, Pratt, & Dittmore, 2007). In some sport settings, community relations may be even more important than media relations. For instance, a for-profit fitness center may be able to gain occasional media attention for its products and services, but it will likely be able to use community relations more consistently to promote itself and enhance its reputation within the community.

Although most sport organizations engage in community relations at some level, the function is housed differently depending on the setting. Most major league professional sport entertainment franchises have community relations departments. Minor league franchises commonly amalgamate media and community relations or marketing and community relations within the responsibility of a single department and staff member. In college athletics, community relations initiatives may be managed by one or more departments—student services or life skills, marketing and promotions, or media relations. The sidebar Athletic Student Services and Community Relations written by Chandra Andrews discusses the various community relations programs in the Wichita State University athletic department.

The following two chapters address programs and practices that allow sport organizations to build relationships with members of their communities. This chapter focuses on unmediated communication tactics such as giving speeches, making public appearances, and staging open houses and other special events. Chapter 12 addresses corporate social responsibility (CSR) as a public relations function designed to enhance both the organization and its community.

The starting point for this discussion of community relations is unmediated communication tactics. **Unmediated communication** has been defined as "two-way contact that does not pass through a channel or medium" (Fawkes, 2008, p. 19). Many sport organizations have found unmediated communication initiatives to be effective tools for establishing and enhancing relationships with various publics. Unmediated communication seems to be particularly effective for professional and collegiate sport organizations, whose players and coaches enjoy high public profiles because of publicity generated through the mass media.

Unmediated communication as a public relations tactic comes in many forms. These forms include

- public speeches,
- personal appearances,
- promotional tours,
- clinics, and
- open houses.

This chapter explores the nature of unmediated communication ventures. It opens by detailing the advantages and benefits that sport organizations may enjoy as a result of unmediated communication activities. It then examines the most common types of unmediated communication tactics employed within sport and addresses key considerations in planning and executing each type. Finally, the chapter wraps with a brief discussion of how unmediated communication activities may help generate revenue for the sport organization.

# Advantages of Unmediated Communication Tactics

Unmediated communication tactics offer three distinct advantages as public relations tools. The first is that the interaction is face to face and sometimes even person to person. When a sport organization's representatives make public speeches, they stand before their audiences. When they make personal appearances in other settings, they frequently talk one to one with those in attendance. When they host a special event, they are looking to make personal contact with their constituents. These are far more personal forms of contact than other public relations tactics such as news releases or even social

# Athletic Student Services and Community Relations

## Chandra Andrews

Photo courtesy of Chandra Andrews.

Many people do not think of an athletic student services department as relating to public relations. But at Wichita State University and many other colleges and universities, the athletic student services department relates to the athletic department's public relations function in a number of ways, including engaging in community service efforts, supporting development functions, promoting positive relationships on campus, and building relationships with recruits and high schools.

Our athletic student services department organizes most of the community service activities in which our student–athletes partici- pate. When we are contacted about participating in a community service event, we take many factors into consideration as we work to make a good decision about the opportunity. We look at who the key publics are, which team might be a good fit for the opportunity, and which people would be the most effective in building a relationship with those publics. For instance, our pen pal program is a way to have a positive influence on the youth in our community. It involves a number of our student–athletes corresponding with sixth-graders in a local school on a monthly basis. The program shows that our athletes are not too busy to give back as they write letters throughout the year and then host the sixth-graders when they visit our campus in the spring. The pen pal program is a positive influence for the kids, and it shows the kids' families and friends that our student–athletes are good people. This in turn may increase the likelihood that a family will attend a sporting event or support one of our teams that they would not normally support.

Some of the other community service activities that our student–ath- letes participate in include reading to elementary school students and hosting young people who visit our campus for a safety program. Each year we have approximately 45 student–athletes visit local schools to read to grade school kids. We also host 140 middle school kids for the Shocks, Cops, and Kids program, which stresses personal and Internet safety. We also make an effort to raise money during the holidays to as- sist a family in need as another way to give back and show others that we want to contribute to the community. We get positive coverage from media sources, which helps us promote a positive image.

> **Our athletic student services department organizes most of the community service activities in which our student–athletes participate.**

At WSU, the Shocker Athletic Scholarship Organization (SASO) funds our student–athletes' scholarships, and although SASO has the resources it needs to perform its major tasks, our department assists by getting student–athletes to participate in a number of functions. SASO exists because donors contribute funds to the organization, and SASO members love to watch the student–athletes whom they support with their gifts. They also enjoy meeting the athletes whose scholarships they help fund. Our department aids in this process by involving coaches and student–athletes in several SASO events. Something as simple as encouraging student–athletes to attend a SASO ice cream social can be important because we show our donors how much we appreciate them and how important their SASO contributions are.

Another way the athletic student services department contributes to our public relations function is by enhancing relationships with faculty and staff. We always try to send positive messages on campus regarding our student–athletes' commitment to academic success, and we want faculty and staff to know that we value what they do for our student–athletes. On occasion, however, problems occur between student–athletes and their instructors. That is when our staff does its best to maintain or repair relationships, and we typically do that by expressing support for the faculty

*(continued)*

*(continued)*

or staff member. We do not want the actions of a single student–athlete to ruin a relationship that may affect others taking a class with that faculty member the following semester.

The last way the athletic student services department has an opportunity to build relationships with others is by working with recruits. When we meet with a prospective student–athlete, we are one more face that can influence that person's decision to attend WSU. If someone has a positive experience with our staff, he or she is more likely to consider a visit to our school and to sign a letter of intent to come to Wichita State.

*Chandra Andrews is an academic coordinator in the athletic department at Wichita State University.*

media updates. They also allow the representatives to respond to specific questions asked by their constituents.

The second major advantage of unmediated communication events staged by sport organizations is that audience members who attend are usually predisposed to be interested in and favorable toward the representatives and their organizations. Because most people are inclined to embrace messages that support existing interests, attitudes, and opinions, the potential is great for the sport organizations' representatives to communicate intended messages successfully. For instance, a room full of boosters will likely respond favorably to coaches who talk about the exciting future of their programs.

The third distinct advantage is that the sport organization can exert a high degree of control over the messages that are communicated in these settings (Helitzer, 2002). Person-to-person interaction is dynamic and occasionally unpredictable. But the people who represent the sport organization in unmediated communication activities are almost always employees or advocates. The sport organization therefore has greater control of the message than it does in situations in which it attempts to communicate with the public through the mass media. Ideally, public relations staff members will coach those representatives regarding what messages are most important to emphasize and how to respond if faced with difficult questions.

Figure 11.1 illustrates these concepts. The horizontal axis represents a continuum ranging from mediated to unmediated communication. The vertical axis represents a continuum ranging from no message control to absolute message control. Various public relations tactics are located on the grid based on the degree to which they are personal in nature and the degree to which they offer message control. As indicated, publicity-generating media relations practices are characterized as low in both personal nature and message control. Publicity is valuable, but it is impersonal because it is deliv-

ered through mass communication channels and ultimately through third parties (i.e., media outlets rather than the sport organization). Publicity is low in message control because although the sport organization controls the messages that it sends to the media, it has no control over how the media convey (or choose not to convey) those messages to the public. Communication through organizational websites, blogs, and social media updates (all topics addressed in chapter 4) is more direct in that its source is the sport organization itself, but it is impersonal in that it is delivered through a mass communication medium. On the other hand, it is highly controlled because the sport organization dictates what information is placed on the site or in the messages. Unmediated communication tactics are the most personal form of public relations practice, and they offer a relatively high degree of message control. The level of this control is less than that offered by websites, blogs, and social media updates but greater than that present in publicity-generating activities.

# Results of Unmediated Communication Tactics

Sport organizations stand to receive a number of benefits as a result of unmediated communication community relations tactics. These include but are not limited to the following:

1. The development of personal connections with members of key publics
2. The production of goodwill and favorable attitudes among numerous publics
3. The generation of publicity
4. The ability to generate revenue, at least indirectly

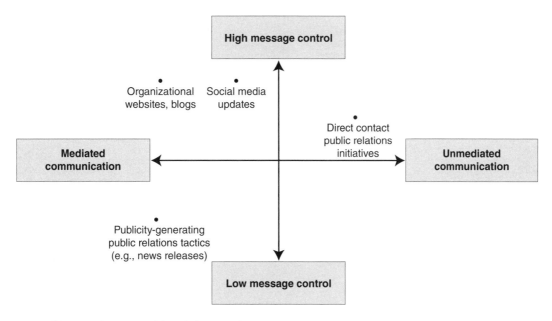

**Figure 11.1**   Characteristics of public relations tactics.

Each of these benefits is briefly examined in the sections that follow.

# Developing Personal Connections

Community relations programs, specifically those that result in access to coaches and athletes, are effective in developing connections between the organization and members of its publics. As stated by one group of sport marketing experts, "The gift that fans want more than any other is accessibility . . . Accessibility of the team and its players will lead to greater attraction for the team among fans" (Sutton, McDonald, Milne, & Cimperman, 1997, p. 20). Specific outcomes of this enhanced connection include decreased sensitivity to price changes and decreased sensitivity to disappointing performance. In other words, if members of the public feel personally connected to the sport organization and its members, they are more likely to tolerate price increases and losses.

# Producing Goodwill and Favorable Attitudes

As stated in chapter 1, community relations activities have traditionally been viewed as long-term investments in public goodwill (Mullin, Hardy, & Sutton, 2007). Positive feelings among members of the public are generated among three groups:

- *Group 1*: People who personally interact with the representatives of the sport organization.
- *Group 2*: People who hear of the personal contact from those who were there. This communication may be through word of mouth or social media.
- *Group 3*: People who learn of the positive gesture on the part of the sport organization through resultant mediated communication (i.e., mass media coverage).

Figure 11.2 illustrates the magnitude of impact that unmediated communication ventures are likely to have on each front. As indicated, group 1 is likely to be the most affected because they are present at the unmediated communication venture. Those in group 2 are likely to be more affected than those in group 3 because of the power of interpersonal communication, particularly with friends and family, but that is not to say that the impact on group 3 is insignificant. Figure 11.2 also illustrates that group 1 is likely to be the smallest of the three groups. Group 2 is likely to be larger because many people will share the personal interaction with more than one person. Group 3 is the largest because of the sizable audience served by mass media outlets.

# Generating Publicity

Unmediated communication tactics such as public speeches, special events, and personal appearances

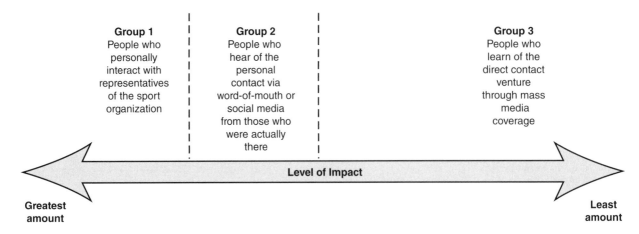

**Figure 11.2** Impact of unmediated communication tactics.

are, as mentioned, often newsworthy and may result in considerable publicity. And because the messages that are delivered tend be controlled by the sport organization, most of the resultant publicity is likely to be favorable. This feature is important for two reasons. First, many sport entertainment organizations (i.e., professional teams and college athletics programs) have difficulty generating positive publicity because of poor team performance, frequent roster changes, and inappropriate behavior by players or coaches. In such cases, publicity from community relations ventures may be the only way to generate positive publicity for the team (Irwin, Sutton, & McCarthy, 2008). Second, sport organizations such as fitness providers and equipment manufacturers may find gaining frequent news coverage to be challenging. Speeches, demonstrations, and open houses offer specific and positive story ideas that public relations professionals can pitch to members of the mass media.

## Generating Revenue

Because many unmediated communication tactics provide opportunities for members of the sport organization to interact with current and potential customers, they fit into the marketing equation for most sport organizations. An organizational representative making a speech may tout a new product offering, a caravan tour may result in advance ticket orders, and an open house may generate new memberships. Some unmediated communication ventures are more sales focused than others, but even those without an explicit sales pitch have been described as indirect sales activities (Irwin, Sutton, & McCarthy, 2008).

# Types of Unmediated Communication Activities

The most common forms of unmediated communication activities within sport include public speaking, personal appearances, promotional events such as off-season caravans and customer appreciation days, clinics and informational seminars, and open houses and other special events. Although the precise nature of these activities varies somewhat based on the specific setting, most are not unique to any one sector. Table 11.1 lists the major sectors of the sport industry and forms of direct contact commonly used within each sector.

The sections that follow describe the more common types of direct contact found in sport and address key considerations in planning and executing each initiative. This list is not comprehensive; a multitude of options are available to sport public relations professionals. Creative thinking can uncover additional innovative and effective approaches.

## Public Speaking Opportunities

Sport figures have delivered some of the most memorable speeches of our time. In spring 2009 *USA Today* posted an online poll asking readers to select the greatest speech (Cherner & Weir, 2009). The top vote getters were basketball coach Jim Valvano's "Don't ever give up" speech at the 1993 ESPY awards and baseball star Lou Gehrig's "Luckiest man" speech to New York Yankees fans in 1939.

## Table 11.1 Unmediated Communication Tactics in the Sport Industry

| Sport industry sector | Common tactics |
|---|---|
| Entertainment (organizations whose primary purpose is to provide entertainment to sports fans)<br>Includes professional, college, and high school athletics programs | Public speaking<br>Personal appearances<br>Promotional caravans<br>Fan appreciation days<br>Draft day parties<br>Clinics<br>Open houses<br>Community events |
| Participation services (organizations whose primary purpose is to provide sport participation opportunities)<br>Includes for-profit and nonprofit fitness centers, tennis, and golf clubs | Public speaking<br>Customer appreciation days<br>Clinics<br>Open houses<br>Community events |
| Sporting goods companies (organizations whose primary purpose is to supply sports equipment and apparel to individuals and sport organizations)<br>Includes manufacturers, wholesalers, and retailers | Public speaking<br>Personal appearances<br>Demonstrations<br>Open houses<br>Community events |
| Service providers (organizations whose primary purpose is to supply special services within sport)<br>Includes sport commissions, special event companies, and special service providers (e.g., agencies, sport travel services) | Public speaking<br>Personal appearances<br>Customer and fan appreciation days<br>Clinics<br>Demonstrations<br>Open houses<br>Community events |

Adapted from Miller, Stoldt, and Comfort 2005.

Given their prominence, sport figures are frequently in high demand as public speakers. For example, the 2010 spring commencement season saw NFL Commissioner Roger Goodell speak at the University of Massachusetts Lowell and New Orleans Saints quarterback Drew Brees talk at Loyola University New Orleans. Sheila Johnson, president and managing partner of the WNBA's Washington Mystics, spoke at the graduation ceremony for the school of business at Georgetown University. And Curt Menefee, now of *Fox NFL Sunday*, was the speaker at Coe College ("To the Class of 2010," 2010).

To satisfy public demand for sport figures as speakers and to leverage opportunities to interact with members of the public, some sport organizations have established **speakers bureaus**. These bureaus respond to requests for speakers. Many sport organizations have speakers bureaus within

their public relations units. Figure 11.3 displays the speakers bureau section of a professional baseball team's community relations plan. The complete community relations plan can be found in appendix C.

Not all sport organizations have speakers bureaus, and sport figures sometimes work with service providers outside their own organizations to manage public speaking requests. On one hand, an organization wanting to book an executive from Spalding simply needs to contact that company to make arrangements. On the other hand, a group hoping to land Olympic gymnast Mary Lou Retton would need to contact the Washington Speakers Bureau, her **exclusive representative** for public speaking appearances. Other sport figures, such as Miami Heat president Pat Riley, have **nonexclusive representation** and may be secured through a variety of speakers bureaus.

# Speakers Bureau

The Community Relations Department will continue to build and coordinate a Speakers Bureau for (team). Our goal is to be proactive in providing speakers and presentations to community groups, charities, service organizations, schools, and corporations in the community. The Community Relations Department, with help from the Sales Department, has obtained a list of all area organizations that may be interested in a speaker for their functions. The Community Relations Department will contact each of those organizations in an effort to place speakers at events.

The Community Relations Department will maintain a calendar of upcoming events. Any interested organization would simply need to write (the team) a letter on their stationery to request a speaker. All reasonable requests for speakers will be honored. When scheduling a speaking appearance, the Speakers Bureau will complete an information sheet detailing the purpose of the gathering, the number of people involved, the name of the principals organizing the group, and specific topics that they would like the speaker to address in the presentation.

A standard presentation may include opening remarks by a (team) associate, comments from a player or coach, a Q & A session, and an appearance by (the mascot). The presentation will be adjusted to meet the specific needs of the host group.

The Community Relations Department will make the Group Sales Department aware of all presentations by turning in a Community Appearance Form to Group Sales for recruiting purposes. (The team) will distribute pocket schedules, season ticket and miniplan information, and group outing flyers at all events. A drawing will also be held to gather the names of the individuals in attendance for future reference. Tickets to a game will be the standard prize.

**Figure 11.3**  Speakers bureau plan.

Adapted from Wichita Baseball, Inc.

Regardless of where the speakers bureau is housed, its basic functions are the same. They include identifying individuals who are effective public speakers, securing opportunities for those speakers, and preparing speakers to make positive impressions when they go before the public.

## Identifying Speakers

Standout athletes, coaches, and senior executives are the people within sport organizations who are most in demand as speakers, but they are not the only sport figures who can effectively represent their organizations. Professional and collegiate organizations may also use team broadcasters, members of their public relations departments, and former players and coaches. Fitness and recreational service providers may use employees with specific expertise in fitness and sport participation opportunities. Advocacy organizations within sport may employ high-profile supporters. Sporting goods manufacturers may use endorsers.

Sometimes, the most high-profile sport figures are not the most polished and effective representatives of a sport organization. Although circumstances may dictate that those representatives frequently go before the public, other qualities should be considered when identifying representatives that the speakers bureau may actively seek to place as public speakers. Three characteristics make for effective representation—the ability to speak well, the ability to interact with others effectively, and the knowledge to affect audiences (Baus & Lesly, 1998).

## Securing Opportunities

The amount of work involved in securing speaking opportunities depends on the sport organization. Big league professional programs, Division I-A college athletics programs, and major sporting good manufacturers frequently operate in a reactive mode, simply processing requests for speakers from their organizations. Sport public relations professionals in less high-profile settings frequently must be proactive in seeking public speaking opportunities. In such settings, the public relations staff provides information regarding the availability of their representatives to groups who use speakers. This approach is the one used by the baseball franchise whose plan is displayed in figure 11.3. Although the proactive approach can be time consuming, the benefits of public speaking usually make the investment worthwhile.

Opportunities for speaker placement are diverse. A variety of organizations seek speakers for regularly scheduled meetings; special breakfasts, luncheons, or dinners; conferences; and awards ceremonies. Such organizations include

- civic organizations,
- professional associations,
- business groups,
- service organizations,
- educational institutions,
- youth organizations,
- charitable groups, and
- religious organizations.

Helitzer (2002) advised that before agreeing to fill speaker requests, sport public relations professionals should be able to identify a specific benefit such as a fee for the speaker, on-site product sales or promotional opportunities, or the chance to affect a key public. Declining requests that do not offer such opportunities is part of the job.

Sometimes, appealing requests must be denied simply because the requested speaker cannot squeeze another commitment into her or his schedule. For example, University of Tennessee women's basketball coach Pat Summitt accepted only about 4% of the requests made of her in 2010–11 (D. Jennings, personal communication, May 23, 2011). In many such instances, however, alternatives such as other dates and speakers can be explored before turning down a request.

Speaker fees are an especially important point to negotiate. Some sport organizations are willing to provide speakers free of charge in exchange for the opportunity to interact with members of important publics. In other instances, fees are substantive. The fee to secure cycling great Lance Armstrong is at least $100,000 (W Business Speakers, n.d.), and that figure is just the amount of the honorarium. The client is also generally responsible for the cost of travel, food, lodging, and other expenses. Fees are especially important negotiating points when external speakers bureaus are involved, because the bureau's commission is based on the honorarium.

Another point that needs to be carefully negotiated is the publicity element. Although some groups expect the right to hold a private event, others hope that having a sport figure as the featured speaker will help them build a crowd. These groups devote considerable effort to publicizing the speaker's appearance. In such instances, the sport organization's public relations staff plays a supporting role, perhaps by providing a bio and photos of the speaker.

On other occasions, the sport organization may need to take a more central role in publicizing the speech. Advance publicity efforts may help increase the number of people in group 1 of the impact model (figure 11.2 on page 220), those in the group that is directly contacted. Publicity efforts following the speech may result in a greater impact on group 3, those who will hear of the event only through the mass media.

## Preparing Speakers

Even those who are naturals in front of crowds will be more effective if they receive some assistance in preparing for public speaking. Others require more intensive preparation. Preparing speakers to represent the sport organization typically involves one or more of the following five activities.

### General Coaching

The first thing that organizational representatives need to understand about speeches is that success is not just about what is said. As important as message development is, other factors may be more important in determining the ultimate impact of the speaker. Researchers have determined that when people receive information, 55% of what they get comes from the facial cues of the speaker, 38% comes from the speaker's tone of voice, and 7% comes from the speaker's words (Mehrabian, 1972). Therefore, fully integrated presentation skills are critical to speakers who want to be effective. The sidebar titled Tips for Delivering an Effective Speech offers additional coaching insights.

### Audience Analysis and Objective Identification

Before developing a speech, speakers should have a clear sense of who their audience is, how they are likely to react, and what they want (Eisenmann & Paine, 2007; Hessert, 1998). For example, one of the authors of this text was enlisted by a local business group to deliver a speech on the business of sport. In conversations with the group's contact before the speech, he learned that the group wanted only a relatively brief overview of the sport industry. Perhaps fearing a dry, extended treatise, the group's representative admitted, "What we really want is a bunch of funny stories."

Speakers must understand not only the makeup of the audience and its interests but also the way in which the speech relates to their own organization's goals and objectives (Eisenmann & Paine, 2007). Accordingly, the purpose of a speech may be to enhance the organization's reputation. It may be to position the speaker, as an organizational representative, as an authority in the field. The purpose could be to achieve a marketing outcome, such as ticket sales or trial service usage. The purpose of the speech drives the key message that will be delivered to the audience. The rest of the speech should be developed with that focus in mind. By emphasizing the central point in a variety of ways throughout the presentation, the speaker is more likely to impart the key message to the audience.

Sandy Hatfield Clubb, athletic director at Drake University, conveys her department's brand identity in each of her public speeches (Ulrich, 2009). "The Drake Way," as she describes, differentiates her program from other nearby NCAA Division I institutions such as the University of Iowa and Iowa State University. According to Clubb, "We fit a different niche, and my job is to help the community see that it's a special and unique niche" (as quoted in Ulrich, 2009).

### Question-and-Answer Preparation

Frequently, speeches conclude with a question-and-answer session with the audience. This period is an important opportunity for the speaker and the audience because it involves direct interaction, but it can be problematic if the speaker encounters hostility or is surprised by a difficult question.

Two strategies are commonly employed in preparing speakers for question-and-answer sessions, and both call on the expertise of sport public relations professionals. The first strategy is for speakers and their public relations liaisons to anticipate questions, particularly difficult ones, and formulate appropriate responses in advance. This strategy is doubly beneficial because it not only allows speakers to offer an appropriate answer but also empowers them to avoid the embarrassment of being knocked off balance by a surprise question. The second strategy is to coach speakers on the art of bridging (Helitzer, 2002; Hessert, 1998). In this technique, speakers briefly respond to the question but then transition to a subject that they are more comfortable talking about. Tools for Controlling the Interview in chapter 9 (page 175) offers additional insight into question-and-answer preparation.

### Speech Development

In most situations, speakers write their own speeches or at least an outline. In some instances, however, public relations professionals are called on to write speeches or outlines for other organizational representatives to deliver. This process usually involves some give and take between the writer and the speaker, although the speaker has the final authority to alter the speech as she or he sees fit. The sidebar

## Tips for Delivering an Effective Speech

Public speaking experts offer numerous tips for effective public speaking (Henry, 1995; Hessert, 1998; Jefkins, 1993). Speakers should

1. not yell, but should project their voice to be heard;
2. enunciate clearly enough to be understood;
3. not rush their speech;
4. vary the pace of their delivery and the inflection of their voice;
5. stand up straight, but not appear wooden;
6. not fidget (e.g., by playing with loose change in pockets, rocking on their heels, continually removing and replacing their eyeglasses);
7. avoid other nervous habits, including the use of "um" and "like" to fill gaps in the speech;
8. not stay locked in place behind the lectern unless microphone placement necessitates it;
9. move with intent, but not pace or violate the audience's comfort zone;
10. look at members of the audience, not above or below them;
11. not allow their eyes to dart from person to person;
12. gesture intentionally, but not wildly and nonstop; and
13. match their facial expressions and gestures to the message.

Sport public relations professionals should be aware of these guidelines and should be ready to offer positive reinforcement and constructive criticism to organizational representatives when possible.

titled Tips for Writing an Effective Speech focuses on speech writing, specifically the components that should be included in most speeches.

Another tool sometimes used to help prepare speakers is the speaker's kit. The typical speaker's kit includes copies of standardized speeches or speech outlines, literature regarding frequently asked questions and recommended responses, coaching tips, support materials, and information on how to contact the organization's public relations representatives in the event of problems (Henry, 1995). For example, the Salt Lake Organizing Committee's speakers bureau prepared its representatives for speaking engagements in several ways. They provided speakers with a list of general talking points that could be customized to specific audiences. They also armed speakers with video and takeaway items such as brochures (F. Zang, personal communication, December 10, 2003).

## Supporting Materials

Visual aids and other supporting materials usually enhance public speeches, and the sport organization's public relations staff members are often responsible for developing or at least securing those aids. Common supporting materials include electronic presentations (e.g., PowerPoint, Prezi), overhead transparencies, flip charts, handouts, and video presentations.

Speakers should not only possess appropriate supporting materials but also be well versed in using them. The following guidelines for speakers may help (Henry, 1995):

1. Practice using supporting materials before incorporating them into the speech.

2. Arrive early enough to confirm that any equipment related to supporting materials (e.g., computers, projectors) is functioning properly.

3. Don't display or hand out the supporting materials before being ready to talk about them and do not display them after discussing them.

4. Make sure that the supporting materials are easily understood.

5. Don't block the audience's view of visual aids.

6. Talk to the audience, not the visual aids.

## *Assessing Effectiveness*

Eisenmann and Paine (2007) contended that a variety of measures can be employed to evaluate the effectiveness of a speaker or a speaking program. The selection of an appropriate assessment generally depends on the objective of the speech. For instance, if the objective of the speech is to achieve revenue-related outcomes such as donations, sponsorship inquiries, or trial usage, then steps should be taken to capture data about the audience members (i.e., prospects) in attendance. The organization can then use this data to track the long-term purchase or donation behavior of these prospects and then evaluate the financial impact of the speaking opportunity. In some instances, the calculated value of the speech can be compared with the impact value of other organizational communication tactics (Eisenmann & Paine, 2007).

Another approach recommended by Eisenmann and Paine (2007) is to track the opportunity to see or hear a key message (**OTSM**) numbers. By noting the key messages included in speeches and the number of audience members receiving those key messages, an organization can calculate OTSM results over time. If the speakers' program receives budget support, a cost per OTSM figure can be calculated and used as justification for continued budget support or as a benchmark against which to assess future performance.

# Personal Appearances

Players and coaches affiliated with professional and college sport organizations have the potential to draw large audiences when making public appearances, even when they are not making speeches. Instead, these representatives may meet and greet people, sign autographs, display a product (e.g., licensed merchandise), conduct demonstrations, and engage in other activities related to the appearance (e.g., serve meals). In some cases, representatives make appearances at partners' events to fulfill sponsorship agreements.

Autograph sessions are particularly powerful draws, but the dynamics involved in autograph sessions have grown increasingly complex in recent years. The sidebar titled The Autograph Controversy highlights why parties on both ends of the pen are becoming increasingly frustrated.

Coaches and athletes are not the only individuals who can effectively represent sport organizations in public settings. Team mascots, front-office personnel, broadcasters, and spirit squads may also draw public interest. In the case of some minor league sport franchises that have high turnover of players and coaches, the team mascot may be the most enduring and recognizable representative of the team.

# Tips for Writing an Effective Speech

Some public relations experts have observed that although a multitude of speeches are delivered each year, only a few significantly affect their audiences (Baus & Lesly, 1998). Sport public relations professionals who are capable of writing effective speeches significantly enhance the potential for their organization's representatives to have an effect as speakers.

Most well-crafted speeches contain three components—an introduction, a main body, and a conclusion. Each element should be carefully designed to facilitate delivery of the central message that the speaker wishes to deliver (Henry; 1995; Hessert, 1998). The elements must also be tailored to the attitudes and interests of the audience.

## Introduction

The old saying about never getting a second chance to make a good first impression certainly applies to public speakers. The introduction is the speaker's best opportunity to win the attention of the audience. It should also set the stage for what is to follow in the main body of the speech.

Common tactics for opening a speech include humorous anecdotes, personal stories, insightful questions, and powerful statements of fact. The tactics should match the personality of the speaker. Not everyone can tell a joke, and not everyone can pull off dramatic stories. Taking speakers outside their comfort zone in the introduction usually sets the stage for a disastrous speech.

## Main Body

After capturing the attention of the audience and introducing the subject, the speech must fully develop the theme in the main body. Organizing the body of the speech may be the most difficult task for the writer. There is no single way to organize the body, but several guidelines may be of assistance:

1. Organize key points and specify them in the speech (e.g., "There are four keys to our upcoming season"). Then help the audience track progress through those points (e.g., "The first key is . . . The second key is . . .").

2. Use examples, humor, statistics (in limited amounts), and personal stories to develop those key points.

3. If technical words are necessary, make sure to define them (Henry, 1995). Otherwise, avoid jargon and other terminology outside the audience's scope of experience.

Writers must be careful to integrate the key message into each element within the main body of the speech. Thinking of the speech as a journey may be helpful. The speaker and the audience must know both where they are going (i.e., the key message) and how they are getting there (i.e., the organization of the main body).

## Conclusion

As the speech comes to a close, restating the key message and summarizing the major points offered in support of that message are usually appropriate. Referring back to the material from the introduction may be a good way to wrap the presentation into a well-organized package. Finally, if the speaker is asking the audience to do something, this call to action must be specified in the conclusion.

Several other key points should be kept in mind as well:

1. Short speeches tend to be better received than long speeches; 10 to 20 minutes is a good length.

2. Common words are better than uncommon ones.

3. Short sentences tend to be better than long ones. Helitzer (2002) contended that the average sentence length in speeches should be 14 words.

4. Keep the style informal (Henry, 1995). The speech may be written, but its content will ultimately be spoken.

Once written, the speech should be read aloud by the writer and then revised for easier delivery if necessary. The speaker should rehearse the revised speech, too. And the speaker has the right of final revision.

Of course, public appearances are good public relations tools for other types of sport organizations, too. Fitness advocates may find that public demonstrations are particularly effective promotional tools (Horine & Stotlar, 2004). If these demonstrations are held in a shopping mall or other high-traffic setting, sizable audiences may attend. Well-promoted demonstrations may even draw additional people to the scene, resulting in a win–win situation for the fitness organization and its host.

## Booking Considerations

In many respects, booking organizational representatives for public appearances is similar to securing them for speaking engagements. High-profile sport organizations typically function in a reactive mode, fielding more requests than they can fulfill. Less-prominent organizations need to be proactive if they desire such opportunities. Appearance opportunities should be evaluated based on their potential to benefit the sport organization in terms of making favorable impressions on those attending, generating publicity, and producing revenue. Some appearances must be coordinated among the group seeking the appearance, the athlete's or coach's sport organization, and the individual's representatives. Compensation for appearances is also important, especially when professional athletes or coaches are involved.

But sport managers are finding it increasingly difficult to persuade athletes to make such appearances (Schoenfeld, 2007). High-profile athletes are more time pressed than ever, and many are compensated highly enough that the additional incentives offered for an appearance do not offer much motivation. Athletes with sponsorships often obligate themselves to a number of appearances on behalf of their sponsors, so getting them to make additional appearances on behalf of their teams can be challenging (Schoenfeld, 2007). To clarify expectations and mandate compliance, the NBA has included appearances as part of its collective bargaining agreement with the NBA Players Association. Select franchises in other leagues, such as the NFL's New England Patriots and NHL's Colorado Avalanche, include appearance clauses in players' contracts (Schoenfeld, 2007). Other sport organizations attempt to motivate athletes to make appearances by synergizing charitable interests or by crafting public events that are fun for the athletes involved.

# The Autograph Controversy

The classic image of the young fan approaching a sports hero for an autograph is part of American sport mythology. Sport figures who accommodate autograph requests make positive impressions of both themselves and their organizations with autograph seekers and their families and friends. Although sport figures who shun autograph seekers have always been around, the issue has grown more complicated in recent years.

As sport has continued to grow in popularity, the volume of autograph requests has become unmanageable, especially for superstar athletes. Even sport figures who frequently accommodate autograph requests express frustration at being criticized for sometimes having to say no (Reilly, 1999). Making matters still more difficult is a perception among sport figures that autograph seekers are ill mannered and too demanding (Hawkins, 2001). Fans and collectors have become so aggressive that some sport figures fear personal injury.

Athletes also question the motives of many autograph seekers. A thriving memorabilia market means that many people seek autographs that they can sell rather than keep in their personal collections. Even children are suspect, because dealers may hire them to secure autographs for sale (Reilly, 1999).

How large is the market? One visit to auction site Ebay (www.ebay.com) in 2009 yielded a listing of nearly 130,000 autographed sport items up for sale at prices ranging all the way up to $179,000. Unfortunately, many of these items are not authentic. Experts indicate that as much as 80% of the memorabilia in the marketplace are forgeries (Morones, 2004).

Fans seeking authentic signed memorabilia have two choices. They can seek opportunities to secure autographs themselves. Resources such as the subscription website Signings Hotline may be of assistance in that task because the site catalogs thousands of signing opportunities. Another choice is to pay a premium for autographed memorabilia purchased directly from companies with contracts for the autograph rights from particular coaches and athletes (Morones, 2004). For example, Upper Deck has deals in place with many high-profile athletes, including Kobe Bryant, Peyton Manning, and Tiger Woods (Upper Deck Company, n.d.).

## Conduct of Representatives

Perhaps the worst possible outcome of a public appearance occurs when the sport organization's representatives embarrass the organization and produce unfavorable impressions among members of the attending public. A 2002 *Sports Illustrated* article on the behavior of members of the NBA's Portland Trail Blazers related one such instance in which team members behaved poorly at a team-sponsored holiday event (Wertheim, 2001). Rather than participate in serving a holiday breakfast and distributing Christmas trees to families in need, team members remained aloof and disengaged. The article quoted one team member as saying, "We're not really going to worry about what the hell [the fans] think about us. They really don't matter to us" (p. 43).

Public relations professionals can minimize the chances that such episodes will occur by taking the following steps:

1. Make sure that the organizational representatives are aware of the incentives for the public appearance (i.e., appearance fee, contractual obligation).

2. Make sure that the organizational representatives are fully briefed on what the purpose of the event is, how it will unfold, and what they will be asked to do. Concerns should be addressed in advance, not in the midst of the event.

3. Seek opportunities to match appearance opportunities with existing interests of organizational representatives (S. Tate, personal communication, February 13, 2001).

4. Cultivate a public relations orientation among all members of the sport organization.

## Promotional Events

Promotional tours allow sport organizations to make direct contact with numerous publics, some of whom may not reside in the community in which the sport organization is located. A common example of such tours is the **caravan**, which is a popular tactic for many college athletics programs and big league professional sport franchises.

One professional organization that has long used the caravan to reach publics in far-flung markets is the Cincinnati Reds. As a franchise with regional appeal, the Reds' annual winter caravan visits communities in Ohio, Kentucky, Indiana, Tennessee, and West Virginia. In 2010 the Reds' caravan plan called for several groups of representatives—current play-

ers, former players, team executives, broadcasters, and mascots—to make stops in 16 communities (Cincinnati Reds, n.d.). Caravan events are free for fans, and they typically include a presentation regarding the upcoming season and opportunities for fans to get autographs from and take photos with team representatives. Some caravan stops include visits to local children's hospitals.

Major college athletics programs stage promotional tours during the spring and summer to connect with fans before the start of the new athletic year. For example, North Carolina State University's tour includes more than 20 stops ("On the Road," 2008). These college promotional tours are usually coordinated by either the school's booster club or its alumni affairs office.

Planning for caravan tours begins at least two months before the tour takes place. Key considerations include the following:

1. Identifying communities that are most likely to generate big crowds (M. Gifford, personal communication, December 11, 2003)

2. Securing dates that do not conflict with other major sport or entertainment events in the community

3. Finding accommodations for representatives if they will stay overnight

4. Planning promotional stops so that they include a major event for the public, another event specifically for members of the media, and a little time so that the touring players and other caravan members can relax

5. Promoting caravan events to maximize attendance by members of the public and the mass media

Of course, sport organizations also recognize the importance of their home markets, and they often stage special events in those markets, too. For example, many MLB teams host winter promotional events to generate excitement about the upcoming season. The St. Louis Cardinals hold a three-day event in January at a large hotel in downtown St. Louis. The event features numerous appearances by players and coaches, question-and-answer forums, and autograph sessions, and it typically attracts more than 10,000 guests. Proceeds from the event benefit the team's charitable foundation.

Team officials report that although the caravan and winter warm-up events generate advance tickets sales, their primary value is to achieve public relations gains such as media coverage during the off-season and to please happy fans who get to interact with the players and coaches for whom they cheer throughout the season (M. Gifford, personal communication, December 11, 2003). The most difficult aspect of such events is persuading players to participate. Those who participate in caravan events tend to be lower-salaried players or athletes who simply feel a sense of obligation to the organization and the fans.

Although winter promotional events are common in MLB, draft parties are a popular tactic employed by many NFL teams (Williams, 2007). More than 100,000 fans attend the various draft parties staged by NFL teams each spring. Some teams sell tickets or game-used equipment at draft parties, but the primary goal is simply to connect with fans during the off-season. Draft parties may include autograph sessions with players, performances by team cheerleaders, and even ancillary events such as the 5K run staged by the New York Giants (Williams, 2007). Some teams are finding draft parties popular enough to attract event sponsors.

Customer appreciation days are another common promotional event. A variety of sport organizations from professional and collegiate organizations to sport fitness facilities and sport retail businesses use customer appreciation days. This subject is addressed in detail in chapter 14.

## Clinics

Clinics are highly effective forms of unmediated communication for many sport organizations because they are set within the realm of sport participation. Most public speaking occurs off the field or court, but clinics may be held on the front line of competition. Given the setting and the interactive nature of clinics, they hold significant potential to generate positive responses among those in attendance.

Professional sport teams and college athletics programs often host clinics to provide coaching instruction to children and young people. These clinics may be held in conjunction with a home event as part of a special game promotion (i.e., all kids with tickets may attend a pregame clinic with players or coaches), or they may be held in other community settings as part of the teams' charitable programs (see chapter 12). Fitness providers and sporting goods retailers may hold clinics to educate consumers regarding products and services. Either way, clinics provide opportunities for sport organizations to strengthen their relationships with members of select publics and to deepen people's commitment to various forms of sport participation.

Even high school athletics programs have found clinics to be effective unmediated communication tactics. Female student–athletes at Hartford High School in Vermont frequently spend portions of their weekends teaching children in their community how to play sports such as basketball, field hockey, golf, ice hockey, soccer, softball, and tennis (J. James, personal communication, December 11, 2009; Read, 1999). Coaches and administrators at the school cite numerous benefits of the program:

1. Children benefit from the presence of the student–athletes as role models.

2. Children have more access to instruction and coaching in their chosen sport.

3. Children develop interest in following the high school teams as fans.

4. Student–athletes learn how to live out their responsibilities as role models.

5. Student–athletes develop greater appreciation for coaches.

6. The reputation of the athletics program is enhanced.

7. School athletics programs benefit when children who were once taught by student–athletes enter high school as more skilled athletes.

Many of the considerations in planning clinics are common to all forms of direct contact: careful scheduling, advance promotion, coordination among all parties involved, and delineation of key messages. Clinics also call for at least one other planning component: risk management. Administrators involved in planning clinics must make sure that every precaution is taken to protect those participating and should make sure that existing insurance policies cover potential liabilities.

## Open Houses

Open houses offer community members the opportunity to tour sport facilities and catch a behind-the-scenes look at operations. Open houses are commonly employed by fitness centers as they seek to attract new members. Often these events are promoted through direct marketing efforts, publicity tactics, and social media. Current members are often given incentives to invite guests, and prospects are enticed with incentives such as trial memberships and prize giveaways. When guests attend, club representatives capture their contact information, and following the event, club representatives engage in follow-up sales activities. Cuocci (2006) recommended the club party as an energetic form of open-house event that employees, members, and prospects can enjoy even as it generates new revenue for the business.

Open houses can be designed for a variety of constituents, including members of the community, employees, investors, and business partners. For example, when construction was complete on the new Hartman Arena in Wichita, Kansas, the arena played host to an open-house event so that members of the community could see the new facility. The event featured a ribbon-cutting ceremony, a rock band, a children's fun fair, and the monster truck Bigfoot on display. More than 3,500 people attended (Hartman Arena, 2009).

Sport public relations professionals involved in planning and executing open houses should keep in mind several factors that will determine the success of the initiative, including the following:

1. Ensure that the site is in pristine condition for the event.

2. Promote the event heavily in advance to attract a sufficient number of guests.

3. Provide specific incentives for guests to attend, such as free food and drink, prizes to be given away, and notable special guests.

4. Make every effort to exceed the guests' expectations regarding incentives after they arrive.

5. Use appropriate organizational representatives to greet and chat personally with guests. Be sure to communicate appreciation for their attendance.

6. If guided tours are planned for guests, avoid overkill. Emphasize the facility's top features but do not feel compelled to cover every part of the facility ("Seven Secrets," 2001).

7. Look for opportunities to secure contact information from guests. This information will be invaluable in future communication and marketing efforts.

Careful attention to these considerations will likely lead to successful outcomes.

## Other Unmediated Communication Forms

Opportunities for public relations benefits through unmediated communication with important publics are not limited to the categories described previously. Numerous other ventures are available to sport managers. Two that warrant discussion are professional or academic conferences and exhibitor fairs.

Numerous sport organizations host conferences or special meetings designed to provide professional development services for current members and to attract new members. These conferences range from large-scale events such as the annual NCAA convention, which has attracted more than 3,000 delegates, to smaller events such as a promoters' conference staged by the National Championship Racing Association that attracted 30 or so members. Regardless of scope, such conferences and meetings offer valuable opportunities for sport managers to meet constituents, engage in informal conversations, receive feedback, and even attend social events.

Horine and Stotlar (2004) described fitness fairs as events that include exhibitions from health service providers. Exhibitors may include fitness equipment and supplement manufacturers, wholesalers and retailers, food and nutrition specialists, and community health service providers. Sometimes, sports celebrities serve as attendance draws. These events may be held in conjunction with professional conferences and meetings, special events (e.g., running competitions, walk-a-thons), and other community events, and they offer numerous unmediated communication opportunities. Special displays combined with promotional materials available for attendees to pick up and personal interactions can serve as effective communication tools.

## Leveraging for Revenue

As indicated in many of the examples provided, unmediated communication ventures can be used to generate revenue. In most cases, they can be used as platforms in which sales materials such as ticket brochures, membership information packets, and other promotional materials (e.g., free tickets, coupons, schedule magnets) are distributed.

On other occasions, sport organizations can conduct sales efforts on site. When professional and collegiate sport organizations stage special events, tickets may be sold on site. When fitness businesses play host to open houses, sales representatives may use the opportunity to sign up interested prospects. And when other sport organizations stage fitness fairs or conferences, they can use those events to sell products, services, and memberships.

The opportunities for such transactions mean that unmediated communication ventures offer both public relations and marketing opportunities.

Accordingly, careful coordination between those units and others within the sport organization such as operations and ticket sales is imperative if these events are to be leveraged to full benefit. Given the power of personal contact to foster desirable relationships between the sport organization and its publics, sport managers must be fully attentive to all relevant planning and execution considerations.

## SUMMARY

Unmediated communication programs provide sport organizations with opportunities to communicate with important publics. They offer many advantages to sport public relations, including opportunities for face-to-face interaction and a high level of message control. Sport organizations that develop unmediated communication programs can expect to develop personal connections with members of their publics, receive publicity because of their efforts, and generate revenue based on their promotion of products and services. Many sport organizations find that they have representatives in high demand as public speakers, and they have developed speakers bureaus to identify organizational spokespersons, secure speaking opportunities, prepare speakers to be effective representatives, and provide other support services. Other forms of unmediated communication include personal appearances, caravans and promotional tours, and clinics. Regardless of type, unmediated communication activities require careful scheduling, advance promotion, coordination among all parties involved, identification of key messages that the organization wishes to convey, and definition of the incentives for the sport organization and its representatives to participate.

## LEARNING ACTIVITIES

1. Attend an event at which a sport figure is the featured speaker and take a few notes on the speech. Was it well organized, and were you able to identify its key messages? Overall, how effective was the speaker? What qualities contributed to that effectiveness?

2. Visit the website of a Major League Baseball team. Does it include information regarding an off-season caravan or winter fan festival staged by the team? What cities and towns are involved? Which organizational representatives are part of the caravan group? Are charitable partners involved in the event?

3. Read the sport section of your daily newspaper over the span of a week. Clip and save any stories relating to unmediated communication events staged by sport organizations. Would you evaluate the stories as being primarily favorable or unfavorable? What sort of impressions would you say that those stories made on people who did not attend the event but read about it in the newspaper?

4. Visit a local fitness center and inquire about whether the facility hosts open houses on occasion. If so, how often? What do they hope to achieve through such events? What things do they do at the open house? To whom do they promote the event, and how do they do so?

5. Contact your institution's athletics department to inquire about the tactics that it uses to connect directly with its fans. Seek out an opportunity to observe one of these events or, better yet, volunteer to assist with it. Take note of the key planning considerations and the way in which those plans are activated at the event.

# Demonstrating Social Responsibility

**After reading this chapter, students should be able to**

- discuss the nature of corporate social responsibility,
- describe the various dimensions of corporate social responsibility,
- describe the nature of charitable programs common in sport,
- discuss how sport organizations are advocating environmental responsibility,
- characterize the different approaches to corporate social responsibility program planning, and
- identify the benefits of demonstrating corporate social responsibility.

**Key terms discussed in this chapter include**

- social responsibility,
- philanthropy,
- foundations,

- strategic philanthropy,
- carbon neutrality, and
- cause-related marketing.

The sports industry has turned its attention to social responsibility. Sadly not everyone, but enough people in very high places. They are answering the call to make the world a better place, and that gives new status to sports and new hope for the industry and to the world in which it prospers.

## So wrote John Genzale, founding editor of *Street & Smith's SportsBusiness Journal*, in a 2006 opinion piece. **Social responsibility** is often referred to as corporate social responsibility (CSR) even though many organizations that embrace the notion are not corporations. In sport, issues of social responsibility are being embraced at most levels, ranging from multinational corporations such as Nike, which has taken steps to address concerns regarding workers in overseas manufacturing facilities, to interscholastic athletics programs such as Hartford High School, which as described in the previous chapter offers weekend sport clinics for children.

No commonly accepted definition exists for CSR, as evidenced by one scholar's identification of 37 different definitions of the term (Dahlsrud, 2008). But according to Bradish and Cronin (2009), "CSR can be broadly understood as the responsibility of organizations to be ethical and accountable to the needs of their society as well as their stakeholders" (p. 692). In other words, organizations embracing CSR are not exclusively focused on their own financial interests. They also consider and respond to broader social needs and expectations. CSR often involves philanthropy, but it is much more than charitable giving. It may be described as "a holistic business mind-set, much like a corporate culture, where the 'socially responsible' obligations of the firm could and indeed, should incorporate both social and economic interests" (Bradish & Cronin, 2009, p. 692).

Although recognizing the lack of a commonly accepted definition for CSR, Heath and Ni (2009) observed that three themes characterize the various ways that CSR is perceived. The first is that organizations practicing CSR receive "positive associations" from their strategic philanthropy when key publics know about it. The second theme is that when attempting to embrace CSR, organizational managers make decisions that they deem to be in alignment with the expectations of their stakeholders. The third theme, as the term would imply, is that

social problems such as poverty or the environment are commonly the focus of CSR efforts.

CSR involves managerial decision making, but it is also a communication-based function (Heath & Ni, 2009). For example, how are managers to determine the expectations of key stakeholders without communicating with them? And how are important stakeholders to know about an organization's philanthropic activities without communication? Clearly, organizational communication, or public relations, is foundational to effective CSR. In fact, public relations practitioners are uniquely qualified to lead CSR efforts given their experiences managing stakeholder relationships and the processes involved in maintaining those relationships (Freitag, 2008). Practically speaking, public relations practitioners sometimes lead the efforts, but not always. Kim and Reber (2008), in a non-sport-specific study of public relations professionals, found a range of roles that public relations practitioners played relating to CSR. These ranged from a significant managerial role, in which public relations professionals advised senior managers on CSR-related issues, to no role in CSR efforts whatsoever. The authors of this text believe that if a similar sport-specific study were conducted, the findings would be similar, although the former role is far preferable to the latter for the reasons previously discussed.

Within sport, the relationship between public relations and CSR was alluded to more than 10 years ago when sport public relations scholar Mick Jackowski advocated a strategic shift in primacy from media relations to community relations. Noting the problem that sport fans are becoming alienated from increasingly commercialized sport properties, Jackowski (2000) encouraged sport managers to focus on relationship development within their communities: "To accomplish this, you not only have to be seen in the community, but you have to get involved and meet people, get their feedback and show that you care about the issues they feel are important" (p. 40).

This chapter addresses social responsibility in sport from a public relations perspective. First, it describes the unique aspects of CSR in sport. Second, it examines several commonly employed CSR initiatives within the field. Charitable programs and environmental initiatives are included in that discussion. Third, it characterizes the various approaches to CSR program planning and describes the qualities associated with the most effective philanthropic programs. Fourth, it describes the benefits that sport organizations and their communities may realize because of CSR efforts.

# Unique Aspects of CSR in Sport

The practice of CSR is different in sport than it is in most other industries. One of the ways that it is unique is that many of the people involved in CSR activities, particularly athletes, possess "star power," so they are highly visible (Walker & Kent, 2009). Similarly, the actions of many sport organizations, whether they are competitive accomplishments, personnel transactions, or CSR activities, are reported and known in the community (Babiak & Wolfe, 2009). In many cases, particularly with high-profile sport entities, powerful connections exist between teams and their communities (Babiak & Wolfe, 2009; Walker & Kent, 2009). As stated by Smith and Westerbeek (2007), "Sport organisations are already implicitly woven into society, an integrative characteristic limited in commercial business organisations" (p. 48). Given those connections, it is not surprising that sport consumers are deeply passionate about their teams and athletes (Babiak & Wolfe, 2009; Walker & Kent, 2009).

In addition, many in the community perceive sport organizations as being the beneficiaries of public subsidies (e.g., tax money for new stadia and arenas) and special protections (e.g., antitrust exemptions) (Babiak & Wolfe, 2009). The resultant expectations regarding how sport organizations should give back to the community are often high, exceeding the expectations of businesses that either have not enjoyed similar advantages or have not had their advantages publicized as heavily.

Given the combination of visibility, strong community connections, and high expectations among the public, CSR is probably more important for sport organizations than it is for other entities. Many sport entities seem to understand this situation and are responding accordingly. The section that follows describes some of the primary ways in which sport organizations are activating CSR.

# CSR Dimensions in Sport

Sheth and Babiak (2010) surveyed team owners and community relations directors for MLB, the NBA, the NFL, and the NHL, presenting them with a list of business-related practices and asking them which of those practices were a part of their CSR efforts. Seventy percent or more of the respondents identified five practices as relating to CSR:

- Donating funds to nonprofit organizations and charities
- Supporting social causes
- Conserving resources, materials, and minimizing waste
- Treating all employees fairly
- Complying with Equal Employment Opportunity Commission policies

The authors of this text recognize the importance of all five practices at the top of the survey respondents' list. This section, however, focuses on the three practices that seem to pertain most to sport public relations professionals—donating funds to charities, supporting good causes, and being environmentally responsible.

## Donating to Charities

Charities often seek the support of sport entities not only because the sport entities have resources that they need, but also because those sport organizations and representatives can serve as highly visible supporters. The involvement of prominent sport figures can generate additional awareness about a good cause. For instance, cyclist Lance Armstrong has become a leading figure in the fight against cancer. A cancer survivor himself, Armstrong has raised more than $250 million through his foundation in support of people affected by cancer (Lance Armstrong Foundation, n.d.). Armstrong has also increased public support of the cause, as evidenced by the more than 60 million people wearing Live Strong wristbands.

Charitable support within sport occurs in a variety of settings. Both sporting goods manufacturers and retailers may offer cash and in-kind donations. Within college athletics, national organizations, conferences, member institutions, programs within those institutions, and even their booster clubs may contribute to charitable causes. At the professional level, charitable giving occurs at three levels—the individual player or coach, the team, and the league. Table 12.1 presents a few examples of giving at the team level within the Women's National Basketball Association.

The nature of charitable programs varies depending on the type, size, and mission of the sport entity, but most sport organizations engage in charitable activities of some kind. Such activities are sometimes referred to as **philanthropy**, a term that has been described as "an act of trust on the part of the donor towards the organization that will receive

**Cyclist Lance Armstrong is perhaps the world's most prominent figure in the fight against cancer.**

Anan Sesa/Imago/Icon SMI

## Table 12.1  Donating to Good Causes

| Type of support | Franchise | Description |
|---|---|---|
| Product or in-kind donations | San Antonio Silver Stars | Community ticket donation program to benefit underprivileged children and their families |
| | Seattle Storm | Autographed memorabilia donations to nonprofits that serve girls and women, promote youth education or health and fitness |
| Cash donations | Indiana Fever | Grants in support of organizations that promote positive self-image and life skills for young women in Indiana |
| | New York Liberty | Portion of game ticket revenue and fund-raising proceeds donated to Kay Yow/WBCA Cancer Fund |

Adapted from WNBA 2009.

and use the donation" (Brayley & McLean, 2001, p. 101). The donor is placing faith in the recipient to use the gift responsibly and serve the community by its actions.

The practice of philanthropy by publicly owned businesses has been the subject of some debate over the years. Friedman argued that the "statement that 'corporate philanthropy is a good thing' is flat wrong" ("Rethinking the Social Responsibility," 1995). His rationale was that money devoted to charitable causes comes off the bottom line, diminishing the profits paid to stockholders who should have control over where those monies are spent after receiving their dividends. If individual shareholders choose to donate their money to a worthy cause, that is their prerogative, but the company should not be spending that money for them.

This argument, however, fails to recognize both the social *and* business value of charitable initiatives. Public relations programs are founded on the understanding that organizations within a community are interdependent. Regardless of the nature of the organization—professional or college team, fitness service provider, retailer, or sporting goods manufacturer—it is in the organization's best interest for its community to thrive. Similarly, it is in the community's best interest for its institutions, including sport organizations, to prosper. Philanthropic initiatives, often administered by community relations professionals, facilitate healthy communities that in turn nurture sport organizations. These benefits are discussed at greater length later in this chapter.

The following sections address the two kinds of donations—in-kind and cash—common in the sport industry and the mechanism that many sport entities use to support charities, the not-for-profit foundation.

## In-Kind Donations

Donations of products to charitable causes are common within sport. The nature of the gift varies based on the type of sport organization. Professional teams and college athletics programs frequently donate autographed memorabilia and tickets. Service providers such as fitness centers and golf courses donate memberships, free play, merchandise, or other services. Sporting goods manufacturers and retailers frequently make product donations.

Such in-kind donations offer two advantages. First, they are often valuable assets that can be auctioned or raffled off for significant amounts of money by the charity. For example, a local fitness center may donate a year-long membership valued at $1,000 to a nonprofit that will in turn leverage the donation for a cash contribution through a fund-raising event. The donor who purchases the membership earns a tax deduction on any money paid beyond $1,000 and receives a valuable service in exchange, and the charity keeps the money. The second advantage is that for the sport organization, the true cost of in-kind gifts is relatively low. A sporting goods retailer who donates a set a golf

clubs paid the wholesale price rather than the retail price to obtain them. A college athletics program may forego a potential sale when it donates tickets, but those donations rarely mean that significant costs are incurred. Usually, ticket donations come from inventory that the sport organization does not expect to sell anyway.

Used equipment may even support charitable causes. Game-used jerseys, balls, and bats are frequently of value, and used fitness equipment may sometimes be useful to charitable groups. But public relations professionals should exercise some caution when donating used materials. A sport organization that donates outdated computers may not be making much of a contribution. The resultant perception that the sport organization offers only leftovers may even damage its reputation (Garrett, 2001).

Sport organizations can sometimes exercise creativity in the way that they make in-kind donations. MLB's Oakland Athletics supported a local high school student's efforts to get baseball equipment to underprivileged children in the Dominican Republic by shipping the equipment that she had collected to their training facility in the Dominican Republic and then distributing it from that location (Francis, 2003). The A's already supported a Little League program in the Dominican Republic, so they were well equipped to support the student's initiative.

## Cash Donations

Although in-kind donations are probably more common in sport than cash contributions, many sport organizations and individuals, particularly those with considerable resources, do make cash gifts to charitable causes. The methods in which those donations are made vary considerably within the field. In many instances, the organization or individual simply donates directly to a charitable cause. Such contributions offer tax advantages because private contributions are deductible for the amount of the contribution less the value of any significant premiums received in consideration for the donation. Altruistic motives, however, typically outweigh tax benefits when people give (Pollick, 2009).

Some sport organizations may support their employees' charitable giving by offering matching programs. For example, Nike matches the gifts that its U.S. and European employees make to charitable organizations (Nike, 2005). In 2004 its U.S. employees gave $2.5 million to various charities. Nike recognized that the program resulted in company funds going to some causes that the organization would not otherwise support, but they "trust that, on the whole, encouraging our employees to be active will lead to positive ends for communities and for Nike" (Nike, 2005, p. 76).

## Foundations

Sometimes, sport entities—leagues, teams, and individuals--establish charitable organizations that in turn donate to good causes. At times, these efforts may be mutually supportive, such as when MLB's St. Louis Cardinals make donations in support of charitable events staged by Albert Pujols' foundation. The incentive for leagues and teams to support the charitable activities of individual members seems clear. Practically speaking, the distinctions between league, team, and player initiatives may blur when members of the public hear about such activities. Pujols' initiatives reflect well on both the team and the league. In the same way, distasteful behavior by an organizational representative (i.e., player or coach) in a community relations setting can reflect negatively on the player, team, and league. The example cited in chapter 11 regarding inappropriate conduct by members of an NBA team at a charitable holiday event (page 228) is an excellent example of this reality.

Table 12.2 presents data regarding a select group of league charities, and table 12.3 offers information on several charities affiliated with players' associations. Other notable examples include the Red Sox Foundation, the official team charity of the MLB's Boston franchise, which donated more than $28 million over a seven-year period to worthy organizations in New England (Sports Philanthropy Project, 2009a). And in Cincinnati, where Marvin Lewis serves as head coach of the NFL's Bengals, the Marvin Lewis Community Fund has given more than $5 million to good causes (Sports Philanthropy Project, 2009b). Both the Red Sox Foundation and Marvin Lewis Community Fund were recognized with national awards in 2009 from the Sports Philanthropy Project, an organization dedicated to advancing the potential of the sport industry to affect communities in positive ways (Sports Philanthropy Project, 2010).

The U.S. Internal Revenue Service (IRS) classifies private **foundations** and public charities as 501(c)(3) organizations, meaning that they are not-for-profit organizations that may be supported through tax-deductible contributions (IRS, 2009). Private foundations and public charities differ in

## Table 12.2  Select League Charities

| Charity | 2008 revenue | 2008 expenses | Top beneficiaries |
|---|---|---|---|
| NFL Charities | $11.8 million | $8.07 million | NFL Youth Education Town, American Heart Association, Player Assistance Trust |
| PGA Tour Charities | $4.76 million | $4.09 million | Intrepid Fallen Heroes Fund, Homes for Our Troops, Wounded Warrior Project |
| NASCAR Foundation | $3.62 million | $3.19 million | Victory Junction Gang Camp, Halifax Medical Center Foundation, Baptist Health South Florida |
| MLB Charities | $3.22 million | $2.06 million | Boys & Girls Clubs of America, Jackie Robinson Foundation, Little League Baseball |
| LPGA Foundation | $2.18 million | $1.13 million | Scleroderma Research Foundation, World Golf Foundation Golf 20/20, Pro Kids Golf Academy |
| NTRA Charities | $1.62 million | $1.57 million | Permanently Disabled Jockeys Fund/Barbaro Fund, Jockeys' Guild/ Permanently Disabled Jockeys Fund, University of Pennsylvania School of Veterinary Medicine |
| NHL Foundation | $528,457 | $577,216 | All Stars Helping Kids, Children's Hospital Foundation, Shaka Franklin Foundation |
| ATP Tour Charities | $144,766 | $127,452 | Andre Agassi Foundation, MaliVai Washington Kids Foundation |

Based on *Street & Smith's SportsBusiness Journal* 2009.

## Table 12.3　Select Players' Association Charities

| Charity | 2008 revenue | 2008 expenses | Top beneficiaries |
|---|---|---|---|
| NBA Players Association Foundation | $2.70 million | $1.04 million | NBA Retired Players Association, Dikembe Mutombo Foundation Hospital, Feed the Children |
| Professional Athletes Foundation (NFL Players Association) | $2.56 million | $1.53 million | Former players and their families, Living Heart Foundation, Center for the Study of Retired Athletes (University of North Carolina) |
| Major League Baseball Players Trust | $2.25 million | $1.59 million | Volunteers of America, Medicines for Humanity, Negro Leagues Baseball Museum |

Based on *Street & Smith's SportsBusiness Journal* 2009.

several ways. A key difference is that the primary activity of foundations is to make grants to other charitable organizations, whereas public charities directly operate their own charitable programs (IRS, 2009). Foundations are more common in sport, and sport entities that establish their own foundations also commonly engage in fund-raising to generate support for the foundation.

Babiak and Wolfe (2009) reported a dramatic rise in the number of major professional sport franchises with team-related foundations over the last 20 years. A report in the *Salt Lake Tribune* indicated that in the NBA alone, more than 100 athletes had established their own charitable organizations (Siler, Semerad, & Lewis, 2008). The sidebar titled United for D.C.: Making a Difference by Aprile Pritchet discusses the effect that one team is making through its charitable foundation and its other community relations activities.

Some foundations are highly successful; others are not. As previously noted, foundations such as those operated by Lance Armstrong and Marvin Lewis have had significant impact. In many other instances, athlete and coach foundations are fraught with problems. An analysis of 89 NBA player charities reported some troubling findings (Siler, Semerad, & Lewis, 2008):

- Roughly 25% did not have the most basic documentation required by the IRS.
- Players commonly put family members on their foundation's board, despite IRS rules requiring that the majority of a board's members be nonrelatives.

- Of the $31 million generated over three years by those organizations, only 44% actually reached good causes.
- Extravagant fund-raising events commonly operated at a net loss.

Such findings stand in stark contrast to industry standards. Well-run foundations typically operate at 4:1 or 5:1 ratio of money going to charities versus overhead expenses (Pollick, 2008a). Some of the best foundations tout 9:1 ratios.

One NBA executive stated that the league encourages player participation in programs like NBA Cares as an alternative to setting up their own foundations (Babiak, 2009). The executive observed that many players and agents do not understand how challenging it is to set up and operate foundations successfully. Pollick (2008b) estimated that most athlete foundations are relatively small, having annual budgets of $25,000 or less. If so, they may lack sufficient support to be successful given that start-up costs can reach $20,000 and that a minimum of $50,000 is needed for annual operations (Pollick, 2008c). A common recommendation is that in anticipation of at least $100,000 in operating expenses, foundations should start with a minimum of $500,000 in assets (Pollick, 2008a).

Pollick (2008b, 2008c) advocated that athletes should establish foundations in instances when the cause that they plan to support is not being served by other nonprofits. If other services exist to serve the cause, athletes may be able to leverage their celebrity and resources just as effectively by collaborating with existing nonprofits. "Sports

# United for D.C.: Making a Difference

**Aprile Pritchet**

Photo courtesy of Aprile Pritchet.

The single most important reason that I can do my job is that I have support from the top down. D.C. United's president and CEO understand the importance of giving back to the community. The team's mission statement is simply to win championships and serve the community. It is great to know that D.C. United understands the responsibility it has to its community.

My current position is director of community relations, but I am lucky in that I have had the opportunity to work on both the community relations side of the business and the charity side. Although the two are often confused, they are very different. The team's charity, United for D.C., is a 501(c)(3) founded in 2002 and has its own mission, separate from the team. The work done on the charity side benefits youth in economically disadvantaged areas of the city. United for D.C. is a charity committed to supporting programs and organizations that help D.C. United achieve its mission of serving the community.

Born from the request of parents throughout Southeast Washington, D.C., for opportunities for their children to play organized soccer, United for D.C. created its own after-school soccer program, United Soccer Club (USC). The overall goal of USC is to partner with community-based organizations to invest in the athletic, emotional, and social welfare of children. The primary focus is to teach the joy of the game, help youth players develop soccer skills, and emphasize the character that team sports produce in athletes. Launched at the Barry Farm Recreation Center in March 2006, USC has now expanded to 12 sites in D.C., Maryland, and Virginia. It has been exciting to see how this program has grown. I am particularly proud that our organization established this program in response to a request from a community that knows little about soccer but didn't want its children to fall victim to gangs, violence, and drugs.

> **My position as community relations director and my involvement with the team's charity give me an excellent opportunity to give back to the community and help disadvantaged youth. Our work gives young people opportunities that they might otherwise not have.**

In addition to promoting physical activity through soccer, United for D.C. promotes literacy among children and their families through the United Reads program. Watching students fall in love with reading is a real joy. Southeast D.C., where many of our programs take place, has some of the worst educational statistics in the country. We want to do our part to combat those deficiencies. Besides distributing new children's books three times per school year, United for D.C. operates a reading challenge at these schools and encourages reading comprehension through guest readings performed by D.C. United players and front office staff. These individuals also speak on the importance and fun of reading on a daily basis. United Reads donates over 15,000 books throughout the school year and has more than 9,000 students enrolled in the program.

Community relations (CR) is much broader in its reach by dealing with the community as a whole. The CR department coordinates player appearances in the community, works with cause-related organizations, and provides volunteers for nonprofit organizations. The CR department operates five signature programs, in addition to managing a number of events such as Meet the Team Day and an alumni weekend in which former D.C. United players are invited back to celebrate the success of the team.

Social responsibility is becoming increasingly important for businesses. I think a growing trend will be employers allowing their employees to volunteer their time during the workday. One of our most successful CR programs is called United Builds. United Builds serves as the team's employee volunteer program and gives our fans and players a way to work together on community projects that benefit a variety of nonprofit organizations. Over the past couple of years, we have logged over 500 volunteer hours working in partnership with Habitat for Humanity, *Extreme Makeover: Home Edition*, local soup kitchens, and area hospitals, to name a few. All this work occurs during the workweek. Obviously, support from senior management was needed to make a program such as this a success.

Another CR program that has proven to be extremely successful is United Drives. During the course of each MLS regular season, D.C. United collects and distributes between 4,000 and 5,000 items to local nonprofit organizations. Each game, a collection booth is set up in front of the stadium where our staff, players, and fans donate a variety items. These items include but are not limited to soccer equipment, food, children's books, and school supplies. A new component has been added to increase community involvement with the United Drives program. Youth soccer teams throughout metropolitan D.C. have been invited to participate in "The Challenge." The Challenge rewards the team that collects the most items on a monthly basis with an exclusive dinner with a D.C. United player. Youth are encouraged not only to give back to the community but also to work together as a team, both on and off the field.

Both the CR department and the United for D.C. foundation programs are extremely important to the overall business. Being involved in both aspects of community outreach is great. I am extremely grateful that I work for an organization that "gets it." It's not uncommon for organizations, especially professional sport teams, to neglect this area of the business because it is not a revenue-generating department. Organizations that have a strong commitment to the community encourage high morale among their employees and realize a higher retention rate.

My position as community relations director and my involvement with the team's charity give me an excellent opportunity to give back to the community and help disadvantaged youth. Our work gives young people opportunities that they might otherwise not have.

*Aprile Pritchet is the director of community relations for D.C. United.*

philanthropy is no different from general philanthropy in that . . . more will be achieved, with far greater efficiency, if opportunities to join forces and pool resources are viewed as paramount" (Pollick, 2008b, p. 13).

## Fund-Raising Activities

The foundations established by sport organizations and figures are often supported not only by contributions by affiliated teams or individuals but also by fund-raising events. In the big leagues the most common fund-raising activities are golf tournaments, theme nights, auctions, and special luncheons (Berkhouse & Gabert, 1999; Rollins, 2003). Although the primary purpose of these events is to raise money for good causes, community relations professionals indicate that they hope to achieve other outcomes as well. They aim to assist a number of individuals and organizations, provide an enjoyable event for their fans, and do something that provides personal satisfaction for members of the organization (Rollins, 2003).

The revenue generated at such events can be significant. For example, the NFL and Super Bowl XL Host Committee held a charity bowling tournament in connection with the 2005 Super Bowl in Detroit (Babiak & Wolfe, 2006). The event, staged in lieu of the usual Super Bowl golf tournament because the site was a northern city, featured 75 celebrities and generated more than $200,000 benefitting Detroit Youth Education Town. Similarly, the 2009 Celebrity Soccer Challenge featuring Mia Hamm and Nomar Garciaparra yielded nearly $200,000 in revenue for Children's Hospital Los Angeles and the Mia Hamm Foundation (Bollinger, 2009).

Despite the examples cited, fund-raisers are not automatic money makers. In fact, many fund-raising events lose money (Pollick, 2007), especially large, celebrity-driven events in which the expectations of high-profile participants can quickly drive up costs. Elmore (2002) observed that in some cases the ultimate purpose of charitable events is lost in the midst of ego-driven issues. Some people may be more concerned with how the number and caliber of guest celebrities will affect their own reputations rather than how much the charity is benefiting from the event. And unfortunately, some of those who participate in such tournaments are not even

**Mia Hamm's foundation was one of the beneficiaries of the Celebrity Soccer Challenge in which she played.**

Tony Quinn/Icon SMI

aware of the real purpose of the event. It is difficult to imagine that under such circumstances the host individual or organization is gaining the personal satisfaction that comes from engaging in worthy endeavors or is receiving the maximum public relations benefit from the event. Pollick (2007) noted the importance of maintaining a focus on the charitable cause behind the event and allowing that focus to drive difficult decisions that may be necessary in terms of cost containment and ego management.

## Support Options

A number of organizations are working to assist athletes and other sport figures in managing the challenges facing them as they seek to identify and support good causes. Three such organizations are particularly prominent. One is Athletes for Hope, an organization founded in 2006 by a who's who of sport philanthropists—Andre Agassi, Muhammad Ali, Lance Armstrong, Warren Dunn, Jeff Gordon, Mia Hamm, Tony Hawk, Andrea Jaeger, Jackie

Joyner-Kersee, Mario Lemieux, Alonzo Mourning, and Cal Ripken Jr. Its purpose is to educate athletes about charitable initiatives, assist them in connecting with others (e.g., sport organizations, charitable programs) with similar interests, and recognize philanthropic efforts with the goal of inspiring others (Athletes for Hope, n.d.). Hundreds of current and former athletes have since joined the organization.

A second notable support organization is the Giving Back Fund, which provides consulting and managing services to a number of high-profile sport figures, such as the NFL's Ben Roethlisberger and the NBA's Yao Ming. Its services include providing and maintaining donor-advised funds and other financial tools for philanthropic activities. A public charity itself, the Giving Back Fund also promotes top celebrity donors and offers educational programs highlighting best practices in the field (Giving Back Fund, n.d.).

A third support organization is the aforementioned Sports Philanthropy Project (SPP). Besides its own charitable mission of reducing childhood obesity, the SPP recognized a number of the most effective charitable initiatives in sport with the Steve Patterson Award for Excellence in Sports Philanthropy. While the SPP continues operations, the Patterson Award is now administered by the Robert Wood Johnson Foundation (Robert Wood Johnson Foundation, n.d.). The honor is named for Patterson, a basketball star and coach who died of cancer in 2004 and who was involved with the SPP and other charitable ventures. Besides the Red Sox and Marvin Lewis, other Patterson Award winners have included the San Francisco Giants Community Fund and the Steve Nash Foundation.

## Supporting Good Causes

Cash or in-kind donations are powerful ways to support good causes, but many sport organizations find other ways to give back. Supplying volunteers to worthy organizations, sharing facilities with the community, and offering sport outreach programs are all common tactics that sport organizations employ to support good causes. Such efforts allow sport organizations to interact with groups that they do not reach through other public relations and marketing programs. Professional and collegiate teams develop public relations programs to serve the mass media and marketing programs to target ticket purchasers and sponsors. Fitness and health providers frequently build marketing programs aimed at individuals and groups who may become members. Sporting goods manufacturers and retailers design programs to reach customers. However well structured these programs may be, they connect with limited numbers of people in the community, many of whom are relatively homogenous. Charitable initiatives allow sport organizations to connect with a wider variety of people in terms of age, race, and socioeconomic background (Berkhouse & Gabert, 1999).

### Volunteerism

Avid fans of the National Football League (NFL) know that public service announcements (PSAs) for the United Way are as much a part of their television viewing experience as beer commercials and in-game updates. The PSAs highlight the services offered by the United Way and showcase NFL players such as Washington's Santana Moss and Jacksonville's Maurice Jones-Drew, who volunteer through the charity. The partnership between the NFL and the United Way of America dates back more than 35 years and is a prominent example

of a sport organization that engages in charitable activity (United Way, n.d.).

In some ways, volunteerism is the most powerful form of support that sport entities can provide. The personal engagement necessitated by volunteerism communicates a deeper commitment to social responsibility than in-kind or cash contributions (Garrett, 2001). Highly recognizable sport figures may be particularly effective volunteers because they can often rally additional support for the cause. The notoriety that they have gained through sport may also make them more effective in connecting with people served by charitable organizations.

Although players and coaches are likely to be in high demand as volunteers, they are not the only important organizational representatives that teams have at their disposal. The sidebar titled Involving Spouses, Alumni, and Spirit Squads in Charitable Activities describes three other key sets of representatives that sport entertainment organizations often use.

Prominent representatives such as athletes, coaches, and spirit squad members are not the only organizational employees who volunteer. Most any employee can do so, and organizations may encourage such community service in a couple of ways. One is through the use of matching gifts in which, as mentioned earlier, the organization financially supports the charities with which its employees volunteer. Another way to encourage volunteerism is to provide employees with designated amounts of paid time off to volunteer. Organizations that support employees who volunteer may find their employees more satisfied in their work and more productive (Coler, 2011).

### Use of Facilities

Some sport organizations have found that the best way to connect with their communities is to open the doors of their facilities for use by charitable organizations or even by the public. Several high schools in the Boston area have begun offering before- and after-school access to their fitness centers to local residents (Popke, 2001). In some cases, residents are asked to pay low user fees, but many have found that the schools are less expensive alternatives to full-service clubs. Additionally, the user fees either go directly to support the after-hours programs or other school programs. Students are offered free after-hours access.

Other sport organizations are finding ways to share facilities in ways that benefit their communities. Cornell College, a NCAA Division III institution in Iowa, has collaborated with neighboring Mount

Vernon High School to renovate two facilities, a softball field and a football stadium, that the two institutions will share (Ulrich, 2009). They are also collaborating on the development of a new sport complex that will serve both schools' baseball, soccer, and cross country programs. Cornell's athletic director indicated that the partnership has resulted in better facilities than either school could have funded on its own, and it has generated community support and interest in the college's athletics program (Ulrich, 2009).

## Sport Outreach Programs

Growing the game is often an emphasis when sport organizations structure community outreach programs. MLB's Reviving Baseball in Inner Cities (RBI) was established in 1989 to offer young people in economically disadvantaged areas of Los Angeles an organized baseball program (MLB, n.d.). The program has since grown to include more than 200 leagues in 203 cities, including all MLB markets, serving 120,000 male and female participants. The RBI program offers more than just playing opportunities. It also features a life skills program focusing on alcohol and drug abuse prevention, HIV–AIDS prevention, and education advocacy.

Similarly, the United States Tennis Association has established the Big Serve as an outreach and advocacy program (USTA, n.d.). The program is designed to foster the growth of places to play tennis, generate opportunities for young people to play after school, and support varsity and recreational tennis programs at colleges and universities. The Big Serve provides supporters with a wealth of advocacy information, offers grants in support of tennis programs at the community level, and partners

# Involving Spouses, Alumni, and Spirit Squads in Charitable Activities

Besides players and coaches, sport entertainment organizations have at least three other types of representatives who can participate in charitable ventures. Spouses of players, team alumni, and spirit squads are frequently used in charitable programs.

Player spouses and other family members may be key contributors to charitable initiatives at the professional level. In fact, a survey of community relations professionals in MLB, the NBA, and the NFL found 98% of respondents reporting that player spouses were involved in their community relations programs (Berkhouse & Gabert, 1999). Their involvement ranged from producing calendars sold to benefit charities to participating in fund-raising events to making hospital visits. For instance, the wives of MLB Atlanta Braves players were involved in two charitable initiatives in 2009 (Atlanta Braves, n.d.). The first was a toy drive in which fans who donated a toy valued at $10 or more received an autographed item from the team. The second was its Brown Bag Bonanza in which fans purchased brown bags containing autographed balls from Braves' players. Proceeds went to the Atlanta Braves Foundation and a local charity.

A second group that may be involved in charitable programs is alumni. Professional organizations and collegiate programs sometimes use former players in charitable activities. More than 30 former players with the NFL's Kansas City Chiefs volunteer as part of the club's Ambassadors program (Kansas City Ambassadors, n.d.). The Ambassadors assist in generating funds for worthy causes, make personal appearances at team-related events, and support current and former Chiefs players in making career transitions.

A third group that may be involved in volunteerism is spirit squads and mascots. The NFL's Denver Broncos report that their cheerleaders are frequently involved in fund-raising activities that benefit the team's charity fund (Denver Broncos, n.d.). In addition, Broncos cheerleaders volunteered more than 1,000 hours to other charitable activities in 2009.

College and university spirit squads also participate in charitable activities. At the University of California at Los Angeles (UCLA), members of the spirit squad make appearances at local schools to encourage academic achievement and goal setting (UCLA Spirit Squad, n.d.). Their appearances include performances, question-and-answer sessions, and sometimes clinics.

Given the wide array of charitable programs that sport organizations now administer, it only makes sense to involve as many representatives as possible. Organizations that do so expand the number of opportunities they have to make positive contributions to their communities and enhance their image among important publics.

with other organizations that advocate healthy lifestyles.

Programs such as RBI and the Big Serve allow sport organizations to invest in community improvement while also cultivating future participants and followers. As such, they may be considered forms of **strategic philanthropy**. In writing on that subject, Cordova (2006) offered five recommendations, each of which is illustrated by the two examples previously discussed:

1. Embrace the role of community leader
2. Address community health needs
3. Support programs to raise high school graduation rates
4. Help the assimilation process
5. Use relevant themes in advertising (p. 17)

Sport management scholars observed that "this redefinition of philanthropy recognizes that while businesses should be good corporate citizens, they must not forget their fundamental obligation to their shareholders and employees, and to the company's profit-and-loss statement" (Southall, Nagel, & LeGrande, 2005, p. 159).

### Other Initiatives

Sport figures and organizations may initiate many other forms of charitable activity as well. They may make personal appearances at schools, hospitals, or other worthy settings. They may elect to build a program that advocates desirable social goals such as decreasing dropout rates in schools, increasing literacy rates, or reducing violent crime. They may also spearhead programs to garner donations from the public in support of charitable ventures.

The activities described thus far should not be considered discrete categories. Some of the most effective charitable ventures involve a blend of cash support, in-kind donations, volunteerism, personal appearances, and so on. MLB's Texas Rangers have worked in partnership with Habitat for Humanity for a number of years by participating in fundraising events, making donations, and leading volunteer efforts (Texas Rangers, n.d.). Those efforts have resulted in 22 Habitat for Humanity homes. The Rangers' Habitat for Humanity program is an excellent example of a sport organization that is proactively demonstrating social responsibility and addressing a cause with a well-integrated approach.

# Being Environmentally Responsible

"The defining challenge of the 21st century will be to face the reality of energy conservation and protection of the environment" (Giannoulakis, 2008, p. 34). As part of their CSR efforts, many sport organizations are increasingly focusing on environmental issues (Babiak & Trendafilova, in press; Weiss, 2008). A 2008 survey of 1,100 sport executives found that only 17% of respondents indicated that their organizations had not instituted green initiatives (Turnkey Sports Poll, 2008). The survey also reported the top three reasons why companies initiate green programs:

- Seen as having a direct, positive effect on the environment
- Good financial decision for the company
- Customers or employees have asked for it (Turnkey Sports Poll, 2008)

Other research supports that last point. A survey of stakeholders for Hong Kong businesses indicated that the environment was their top CSR issue (Welford, Chan, & Man, 2007).

Broadly speaking, sport organizations can support environmental responsibility in two ways. The first is by taking measures to reduce the negative impact that the organization may have on the environment. The second is by promoting their efforts to be environmentally responsible and encouraging others to follow suit.

### Reducing Impact

Sport is commonly a burden on the environment (Smith & Westerbeek, 2007, p. 47). Major sporting events have been described as "gluttonous consumers of power and prodigious producers of waste" (King, 2008, p. 16) because sport facilities typically require significant amounts of electricity for lighting, heating, and cooling. They also produce a large volume of trash because fans in attendance discard concessions packaging, leftovers, and organizational media. These same fans, and often the competing athletes, travel to the events by airplane, bus, or automobile, all of which consume fuel and release pollutants. As a result, many sport organizations have taken measures to reduce environmental consequences by adopting recycling programs, reducing or offsetting carbon emissions, and taking other steps to operate in a more environmentally friendly fashion.

## Recycling Programs

According to the sport executives surveyed in the aforementioned 2008 poll, the most common way that sport organizations can have a significant green impact is by instituting recycling programs at events (Turnkey Sports Poll, 2008). MLB's Seattle Mariners report that a crowd of 40,000 will produce more than 30,000 pounds (13,000 kg) of trash (King, 2008). The team has enacted a recycling program that allows it to recycle roughly 30% of that waste. The keys to their success have been a compost program that collects food scraps and leftovers, the use of biodegradable cups made of corn, and promotional tactics designed to encourage fans to place recyclable items such as plastic bottles in designated bins.

Some sport managers indicate that the ceiling is high for recycling programs, but several significant challenges impede additional progress (King, 2008). The first challenge is convincing senior managers of both the environmental and economic benefits of recycling programs. Well-structured programs can produce considerable cost savings in waste services. The second challenge is addressing economic limitations that may impede recycling programs from reaching their potential. For instance, the labor costs involved in having cleaning crews manually sort through stadium or arena trash to separate recyclable items from other trash that should go to the landfill is often cost prohibitive. Sport managers often must take a pragmatic approach to their recycling programs, doing what they can until more efficient options are available. The third challenge is activating fans in recycling programs. Even in Seattle where recycling is widely embraced, Mariners' officials estimate that 90% of plastic bottles do not make it into recycling bins (King, 2008).

## Carbon Reductions

When fossil fuels burn, they produce greenhouse gasses, including carbon dioxide, that contribute to global warming. Sport organizations are responsible for high levels of carbon dioxide because the electricity that they use is likely produced by burning fossil fuels, the trash that they discard produces greenhouse gases when decomposing, and the vehicles that they attract mostly run on gasoline. Many are addressing this problem by finding ways to reduce carbon emissions or offsetting them in an attempt to achieve or at least move toward **carbon neutrality**.

Arguably the best way to reduce greenhouse gas emissions is to reduce consumption of power sources generated by burning fossil fuels. Sport organizations are doing this in a variety of ways. Some are finding more efficient ways to heat and cool their facilities, thereby diminishing their demand for electricity. Others are tapping into other

The wind turbine at Wichita's Hartman Arena supports the facility during off-event hours.

forms of power, such as solar or wind energy. The NFL's Philadelphia Eagles, whose Go Green environmental program is recognized as one of the best in the industry, use wind electricity exclusively, even though it typically costs more than other forms of power (King, 2008). Denver's Pepsi Center is considered the first large sport facility to attain carbon neutrality (Popke, 2008). All of its electrical power comes from a clean-energy provider, and it rewards fans who drive hybrid vehicles by providing them with preferred parking.

Because most sport organizations do not rely exclusively on clean energy sources, some attempt to offset the carbon emissions for which they are responsible by planting trees. In 2007 the National Football League learned that Super Bowl XLI would result in 1 million pounds (450,000 kg) of carbon dioxide being released into the air. To compensate, the league planted 3,000 trees around the state of Florida (Wolff, 2007). Similarly, the Canadian Football League manages an environmental program with carbon offset elements in an effort to "Green the Grey Cup" (Grey Cup, n.d.).

### Other Environmental Initiatives

Environmental initiatives in sport extend well beyond recycling programs and carbon reduction efforts. For example, the United States Golf Association's (USGA) Green Section, which publishes information about golf course management, promotes methods that allow golf courses to contribute to the environment rather than damage it (USGA, 2009). The Green Section promotes the use of recycled water as a way for golf courses to conserve water supplies and save money. It also provides information regarding grasses that are tolerant of dryer conditions and require less maintenance. The Green Section also extends its educational efforts to golfers, attempting to convince them that environmentally responsible course management does not necessarily result in a diminished playing experience (USGA, 2009).

Some recreation facilities are using recycled flooring, high-efficiency lights, and toilet and shower fixtures that conserve water (Steinbach, 2008). They are reducing energy demand by having cleaning crews work during regular hours of operation so that the building can close overnight, and those crews are using green cleaning supplies.

A number of sport facilities have pursued certification through the U.S. Green Building Council (USGBC) that they are environmentally responsible in multiple ways, including energy savings, water usage, carbon emissions, and more (USGBC, 2010). Buildings and communities that meet USGBC standards are Leadership in Energy and Environmental Design (LEED) certified. Numerous sport facilities have received LEED certification including the American Airlines arena in Miami, Phillips Arena in Atlanta, the Washington Nationals Ballpark in Washington, D.C., and Medlar Field at Lubrano Park on the Penn State University campus (Barclay, 2009).

## Promoting Responsibility

Many environmental initiatives within sport receive considerable attention. Some sport organizations promote their own efforts, as evidenced by the increase in environment-related content on team websites (Babiak & Trendafilova, in press). In other instances, mass media outlets cover stories relating to teams and the environment, particularly accounts of engaging in environmentally friendly practices over the last 10 years (Babiak & Trendafilova, in press).

To the extent that the promotional communication is accurate, contributes to favorable perceptions of the sport organizations, and possibly encourages others to take steps toward higher levels of environmental responsibility, it should be viewed as a positive. Considerable skepticism exists, however, regarding the substance of much of this promotion. A 2009 poll of sport industry executives found that nearly 50% indicated that they believed green initiatives in sport were "just a marketing gimmick" (Turnkey Sports Poll, 2009). Kevin Donovan, a sport communication expert, cautioned against "greenwashing," described as the "appearance of environmental preservation at the expense of real action" (as quoted in Snow, 2009, p. 19). Sport organizations that tout their green status often open themselves to criticism about environmental problems they have yet to address. Even sport entities with sterling environmental credentials may be subject to opposition and protests if they partner with sponsors who do not share the same level of commitment (Snow, 2009).

An appropriate balance between substantive environmental initiatives and credible promotional communication would seem to be a fair prescription, particularly because sport entities often play the role of opinion leader. As stated by sport journalist Alexander Wolff (2007), "Therein may lie the great value of sports. What happens in an arena so familiar and beloved may sound an alarm we will hear and heed."

# Planning CSR Programs

The preceding discussion illustrates the vast array of CSR-related activity in the sport industry. CSR initiatives in sport range from the simple (e.g., donating tickets to a local nonprofit so that they may be auctioned off at a fund-raising event) to the complex (e.g., developing and funding an ongoing charitable outreach program). Accordingly, the ways that sport organizations approach CSR vary. Further, sport managers who hope to maximize the effectiveness of their organization's CSR activities, particularly their philanthropic endeavors, should be mindful of best practices in the field. Both topics are addressed in the sections that follow.

## Approaches to CSR Programs

Having studied CSR in major professional sport, Babiak and Wolfe (2009) proposed a framework that describes four approaches to managing CSR. Their model, presented in figure 12.1, illustrates that two key factors largely determine the way that professional sport organizations approach CSR. The first determinant is the sport organization's external orientation, specifically, external pressures such as the nature of the organization's key publics and the social needs to which those publics are attuned. The second determinant is the organization's perception of its internal resources, specifically, the organization's inventory of resources (e.g., facility, star athletes).

Figure 12.1 displays how the determinants of external orientation and internal resources intersect to create four approaches to CSR. The four approaches are (1) ad hoc CSR, (2) corporate-centric CSR, (3) stakeholder-centric CSR, and (4) strategic CSR (Babiak & Wolfe, 2009). In settings where the sport organization is not particularly guided by either its evaluation of external pressures or the potential of its internal resources, its CSR activities are likely to be of an ad hoc nature. Ad hoc CSR may have a positive effect, but it is likely to be random in nature rather than reflect some type of systematic approach.

Corporate-centric CSR results when the organization's assessment of its internal resources outweighs its evaluation of external pressures in the planning process. Babiak and Wolfe (2009) cited the NFL's Punt, Pass, and Kick program, which supports youth football and gives youngsters the opportunity to display football skills in competition, as an example of a corporate-centric program. The program

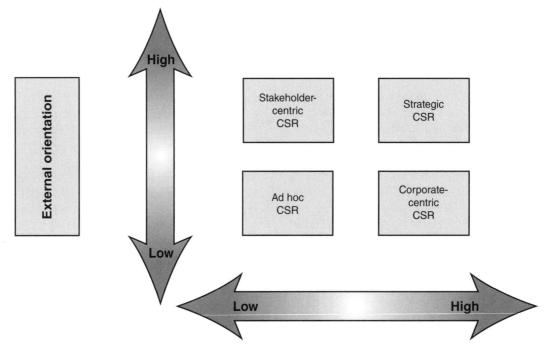

**Figure 12.1.** Approaches to CSR in professional sport.

Reprinted, by permission, from K. Babiak and R. Wolfe, 2009, "Determinants of corporate social responsibility in professional sport: Internal and external factors," *Journal of Sport Management* 23: 717-742.

is designed to generate interest in football among young people, but it is not particularly geared to address societal problems or issues.

Stakeholder-centric CSR is a product of an organization's placing more emphasis on its external orientation than on its internal resources. Babiak and Wolfe (2009) observed that the NBA's Read to Achieve program is an example of a stakeholder-centric CSR program. Read to Achieve is commendable in that it supports literacy and encourages children to develop a passion for reading, but the educational nature of the program does not naturally align with the resources of the league's member franchises.

Strategic CSR results when sport organizations merge high sensitivity to external pressures with a strong evaluation of their internal resources. Babiak and Wolfe (2009) cited the NBA's Fit Kids, Healthy Future program as a good example of a strategic CSR program because it activates resources that the league's franchises already possess, such as athletes and mascots, with a community issue, unfit children and the resultant consequences. Babiak and Wolfe (2009) described strategic CSR as the optimal approach to CSR.

## Characteristics of Effective Programs

Greg Johnson, founder of the Sports Philanthropy Project, contributed to a symposium on CSR at the 2007 North American Society for Sport Management conference. In his presentation, Johnson (2007) characterized best practices as they relate to philanthropy. He used the acronym *FILES* to guide his discussion:

- *Focused*: Programs that are focused on particular social problems in defined areas are likely to be more effective than those that are broader in nature.

- *Impactful*: Programs designed to achieve particular outcomes are more likely to be effective than programs with more general goals.

- *Leveraged*: Program effectiveness can be enhanced by partnering with other organizations or working in collaboration with not-for-profits having similar goals.

- *Evaluated*: Program outcomes are monitored with the goal being to improve effectiveness.

- *Sustained*: Long-term programs are likely to be more effective than short-term ventures.

Arguably, the characteristics Johnson (2007) described could relate to all facets of CSR, not just philanthropy. Whether the focus is supporting a good cause, being environmentally responsible, or treating employees fairly, programs structured to meet the FILES guidelines are better positioned for success than those that are not.

# Benefits of Demonstrating CSR

Organizations and individuals within the sport industry typically possess several motives for committing to CSR. Many of these benefits are accrued by the sport organization itself; others are farther reaching. They can range from building commitment among the organization's employees to earning favor with the organization's regulators to positively affecting the planet's ecosystem. The sections that follow describe four of the primary benefits of CSR.

## Enhance Image

Doing good may be intrinsically rewarding, but many sport managers and communications specialists believe that there is value in being seen doing good. Walker and Kent (2009) conducted a study of NFL fans in two cities to determine how teams' CSR activities related to team reputation. They found that CSR did indeed have a positive effect on perceived reputation, and accordingly they recommended that sport organizations adopt CSR as part of their mission and emphasize communicating their CSR actions to their constituents (Walker & Kent, 2009).

Interviews with major professional sport executives regarding environmental initiatives indicated that those executives were motivated at least in part by the resultant positive publicity (Babiak & Trendafilova, in press). Philanthropy may also contribute to an enhanced image. Dean (2002) conducted a survey in which respondents were asked to assess their perception of a grocery chain before and after being presented with information regarding its support of Special Olympics, a sporting event designed for people with intellectual disabilities. Although the survey subjects did not know it at the time, the support for Special Olympics was merely a hypothetical initiative, a control to negate the effect that any advance knowledge of an actual sponsorship might have on responses. Survey results indicated that respondents had significantly more favorable perceptions of the grocery chain after learning of its supposed support for Special Olympics.

Babiak and Wolfe (2006) observed that mega-events such as the Olympics and the Super Bowl embrace CSR at least in part to protect their image in the face of criticisms relating to public funding in support of their events and environmental impact. Conversely, scholars have observed that CSR may be particularly important for sport organizations that enjoy less competitive success because the publicity generated by their good works may be the primary way in which they gain positive public attention (Irwin, Sutton, & McCarthy, 2008; Sheth & Babiak, 2010; Walker & Kent, 2009).

For a sport organization to enhance its image by supporting charitable causes or being environmentally responsible, it must communicate that activity to the public. Figure 12.2 displays an advertisement that the PGA Tour has used to promote its good works. Promotional communication of this nature can be a tricky proposition because the organization does not want to be perceived as self-serving. For the communication to be positively received, it must be factual and cannot embarrass those receiving its support. Further, it cannot be perceived as a smokescreen designed to divert attention from organizational sins. As stated by Heath and Ni (2009), "Reputation is a key link in the CSR chain.... However, the chain is no stronger than the weakest link's ability to withstand critics' scrutiny."

OVER 2,000 CHARITIES, A MILLION STORIES, ONE GOAL.

The PGA TOUR's leading scorer averaged 68.4. And the biggest hitter routinely drove the ball over 321 yards. But the number that mattered most last year was the $83 million that the PGA TOUR and its tournaments gave to over 2,000 charities, touching countless lives along the way.

**Figure 12.2** PGA Tour advertisement.

PGA Tour, Inc.

# Grow the Game

Sport organizations have long structured their CSR activities in ways that enable them to build interest and participation in the products or services they offer. The aforementioned examples of MLB's RBI and the USTA's Big Serve programs illustrate how two sport entities are working to grow their games. Another illustration is the National Hockey League's (NHL's) Hockey is for Everyone program. Initiated in 1999, the league's program is executed in February each year to coincide with Black History Month (NHL, 2010). Special events staged in a variety of markets and public service messages carried by league communication platforms (e.g., NHL Network) emphasize the NHL's commitment to support nonprofit organizations that promote youth hockey. As of 2010 nearly 50,000 young people had experienced hockey through the program.

Beyond growing the game through youth outreach programs, some sport managers are using CSR as a stimulus for global expansion in other ways. Babiak (2009) interviewed senior executives in four of the major professional sport leagues in North America and found that each indicated that CSR either already was or likely would be one of the keys to international expansion. An NBA executive indicated that league commissioner David Stern had deemed global CSR a league priority (Babiak, 2009). An executive with the NFL noted that the league was in the midst of expanding its CSR efforts internationally and was currently dealing with the challenge of "finding the right ways that are organic and make sense to extend a CSR message that is not just a U.S. message" (Babiak, 2009).

# Improve the Bottom Line

Corporate social responsibility can also enhance the sport organization's bottom line in two ways. One way is through indirect contributions, because customers often tend to favor businesses they view as being socially responsible. For example, a 2006 study of those in the millennial generation (age 13 to 25 at the time) indicated that

- 69% consider a company's social and environmental commitment when deciding where to shop,
- 89% are likely or very likely to switch from one brand to another (price and quality being equal) if the second brand is associated with a good cause, and

- 66% will recommend products or services if the company is socially responsible (Cone Inc., 2006).

Therefore, investments in CSR may also be viewed as investments in customer loyalty and as an impetus for word-of-mouth promotion.

Other studies support this notion. Margolis and Walsh (2003), in compiling more than 100 studies analyzing the financial performance in light of social investment, found indications of "a positive association and certainly very little evidence of a negative association between a company's social performance and its financial performance" (p. 277).

The second way that CSR may contribute to the bottom line is directly as sport organizations employ a variety of strategies to blend good works with generating revenue. Two such approaches are described in the following sections.

## Relating Causes to Marketing Programs

Many sport organizations have found that they can promote their products and services by allowing consumers to support a worthy cause by purchasing from the sport organization. The idea behind **cause-related marketing** is that the sport organization can distinguish itself in the competitive marketplace and add value to its products and services based on its association with a charitable organization. Consumers know that by spending money with the sport organization they are also supporting a good cause. Associations of this sort can cause consumers to develop stronger attachments to a particular sport brand (Sutton & McDonald, 2001). Cause-related marketing benefits publics such as the nonprofits who receive support, the people who are served by those nonprofits, consumers who gain increased satisfaction from their purchases, employees who enjoy increased morale, and investors who reap benefits from the sport organization's increased effectiveness (Won & Park, 2003). A non-sport-specific study of consumer reactions to various affinity-marketing programs indicated that programs linked to a social cause were viewed more positively than other affinity-marketing techniques such as linking a company to a particular sport (Bloom, Hoeffler, Keller, & Basurto Meza, 2006).

Cause-related marketing programs are relatively common within sport. For example, the Alaska Club incorporated a cause-related element in its promotion of a new location (Larson, 2000). One of the incentives offered to new members was the donation of the standard $50 enrollment fee to the American Heart Association (AHA). The linkage between the fitness center and the AHA was evident, and the donation element enhanced the perceived value of a new membership.

The NHL's Tampa Bay Lightning are one of many professional teams to use cause-related marketing by promoting charitable causes to fans who purchase tickets to home games. One such event is the team's Pucks and Paws Night in which fans attending the game were encouraged to bring a bag of dog or cat food to be donated to the local Humane Society (Tampa Bay Lightning, 2010). Fans making a donation were entered in a raffle to win a jersey autographed by former MVP Martin St. Louis. The Humane Society's pet adoption unit was also on hand for the event.

## Developing Strategic Partnerships

Another method for generating revenue through CSR is to develop partnerships with charitable organizations and other local businesses that facilitate

organizational goal achievement for all three parties. A number of sport executives indicated that the development of such partnerships with corporate partners and community organizations is a CSR priority (Sheth & Babiak, 2010).

One NFL executive noted that the league and some of its major partners such as Nike and Gatorade have similar social interests, so they have defined ways to link their CSR efforts (Babiak, 2009). Similarly, the league has been able to attract new partners because of its CSR efforts. For example, Kellogg Company partnered with the NFL because they shared an interest in youth fitness. As a result, Kellogg signed on as a sponsor of the NFL Play 60 program, which encourages children to play actively for an hour each day (Babiak, 2009). This type of arrangement has been described as a triple-win situation (Sutton & McDonald, 2001). Society benefits when children become more physically active. Kellogg significantly enhances its ability to achieve one its key CSR goals and positive brand association because of its partnership with the league. The NFL increases the value of its partnership with

**The NFL's Play 60 program has resulted in good works, support from program sponsors, and enhanced sponsorship value for the league.**

Jason DeCrow/AP Images for NFL Network

Kellogg while taking the lead on an important social outreach program.

Jackowski (2000) advocated a concept that he called the super community as a mechanism for sport franchises to develop such partnerships. Specifically, he recommended that sport entertainment organizations formalize their relationships with the charitable groups seeking their assistance. The super community that consists of the sport organization and its affiliated nonprofit partners can then be marketed to the sport organization's corporate partners, providing sponsors with a platform to advance their own CSR programs. Super communities increase the value of the sport franchise's corporate sponsorships while simultaneously increasing support for the affiliated nonprofit organizations. Furthermore, the corporate sponsors empower their own philanthropic efforts by aligning themselves with the sport organization.

Figure 12.3 portrays the super community concept. The sport franchise's affiliated nonprofits are grouped together based on common missions, and as the lines extending from the sport organization to the charitable groups indicate, a formal linkage exists between the sport franchise and those nonprofit organizations. The model includes three types of charitable groups, but that number is only hypothetical. Similarly, most sport franchises have more than two corporate partners. The point of the model is to illustrate the exchanges that take place among the three parties involved. The nonprofits receive resources (e.g., cash donations, in-kind gifts, volunteers) from both the sport franchise and its corporate partners. In exchange, the sport franchise and its corporate partners attain their philanthropic objectives. Furthermore, exchanges take place between the sport franchise and its corporate partners. The sport franchise receives additional revenue in exchange for the platform that it provides its corporate partners to promote their charitable activity. All three groups achieve their goals because of this relationship (Jackowski, 2000).

The NFL's Baltimore Ravens took the notion of the super community to a new level by agreeing to a 15-year, $75 million naming-rights deal with M&T Bank (Liberman, 2003). The selling points in the deal were the community relations opportunities that the Ravens could provide. The deal allowed M&T not only to gain naming rights to the team's stadium but also to sponsor community relations programs designed to raise money for players' charities, reward children for extraordinary accomplishments, fund the Ravens' marching band, and sponsor a football education program for new fans.

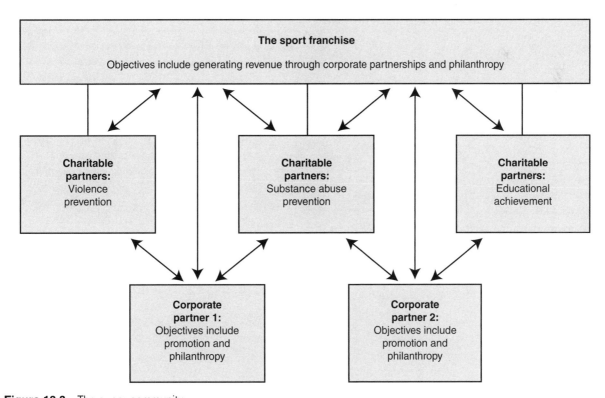

**Figure 12.3** The super community.

Based on Jackowski 2000.

## Enhance the Community

In many instances, sport organizations are motivated to embrace CSR at least in part by their own interests. Another motivating factor is to enhance their communities. A focus on community was one of the priorities cited by major professional sport executives who were interviewed about their CSR activities (Sheth & Babiak, 2010).

The ways in which sport entities can enhance their communities vary considerably, as demonstrated by the breadth of CSR-related actions. In some cases, the benefit is simply the financial or promotional support offered by the sport organization to the charitable cause. The United Way reports that since initiating its partnership with the NFL, its annual donations have grown from $800 million to $4 billion (United Way, n.d.). Although it is impossible to specify the degree to which that growth has resulted directly from the NFL partnership, the organization states that no other factor has been more important in its growth (United Way, n.d.).

In other instances, the sport organization is more directly engaged. Breitbarth and Harris (2008) offered an example of CSR initiatives by Arsenal London Club and London Stadium that support education and antiracism efforts within the community. They observed that such initiatives offer "professional football the chance to integrate the public agenda with its own organizational goals through self-enlightened CSR that brings the modern game back to the English community" (Breitbarth & Harris, 2008, p. 194).

On an even larger scale, Right to Play is an international organization that uses sport as a tool to promote social change in more than 20 countries affected by war, poverty, and disease (Right to Play, n.d.). Top athletes from more than 40 countries support the organization. Its ambassadors include former NFL quarterback Steve Young, softball star Jennie Finch, Canadian skeleton racer Jon Montgomery, and the Chelsea Football Club. Right to Play trains community leaders in each nation to deliver Right to Play's program, which uses sport and play as catalysts for (1) basic education and child development, (2) health promotion and disease prevention, (3) conflict resolution and peace building, and (4) community development and participation. Stressing the inclusion of all children and the sustainability of the programs and their effects, Right to Play was reaching 688,000 children weekly as of 2009, and it had served more than a million children since its founding in 2000 (Right to Play, n.d.).

It is little wonder then that many people tout sport as a catalyst for social improvement. Attorney and sports broadcaster Len Elmore (2002) contended, "As an instrument for positive world change, sports ranks high in potential value and effectiveness" (p. 25). Genzale (2006) took it a step further, asking, "Can a bouncing ball save the globe?" (p. 34). Citing Right to Play and other initiatives, Genzale described how sport is assisting the disadvantaged, breaking down political barriers, and promoting understanding. Whether similar efforts are focused on a community, a nation, or the world, they are to be lauded as substantive contributions to the well-being of all, not just those in sport.

## A Final Word

This chapter illustrates the varied nature of CSR in sport and the multiple benefits that result for sport organizations, their partners, and their communities. Given the prominence that sport commonly enjoys, it is also important to recognize the industry's potential to serve as a role model in regard to CSR. As stated by Godfrey (2009),

> The CSR-sport relationship may work both ways; that is, CSR may be good for sport and sport organizations *and* sport may be good for CSR. Participation in CSR and related activities broadens the base and hence the social legitimacy of the whole CSR notion, that private-sector organizations have at least real interests, if not real obligations, in creating and sustaining a higher quality of life. (p. 712)

If true, sport managers who embrace social responsibility may be positively affecting their world in more ways than they can imagine.

Social responsibility, or CSR as it is referred to in business settings, refers to the obligation of sport organizations to act beyond their own narrow interests for the betterment of their communities and the world. Sport organizations take a variety of approaches to CSR. Some are fairly random in nature, whereas others effectively merge the interests of external constituents with the unique strengths of the organization. Three of the main CSR emphases in sport are (1) donating money to charities; (2) supporting good causes through volunteerism, the sharing of facilities, and sport outreach programs; and (3) being environmentally responsible. Many sport organizations have established charitable foundations to support their philanthropic interests. The environmental programs established by sport organizations range from initiatives designed to reduce waste to campaigns that encourage green practices with communities. Sport organizations may accrue multiple benefits because of their CSR activities, including enhancing their images, growing the games that they play, generating revenue both indirectly and directly, and improving their communities.

# LEARNING ACTIVITIES

1. Contact a public relations official with a local sport franchise and ask several questions regarding the organization's CSR efforts. What does the organization do in this regard? What benefits does the official believe that the organization receives because of its CSR? Based on what you learn, how would you characterize the organization's approach to CSR (see figure 12.1)?

2. Contact a representative of a charitable organization and ask several questions. Does the representative's organization receive support from sport figures or organizations? If so, what kind? Does the representative know of a particularly effective partnership between a sport organization and a nonprofit organization? If so, how was it executed? How did each party benefit?

3. Visit the website of a major professional sport franchise of your choice. You will likely find a link to a page detailing the team's philanthropic initiatives. Has the organization established a charitable foundation? What causes does the team support? What type of support is provided? Does the team involve others (e.g., fans, corporate partners) in its philanthropic efforts?

4. Staying with that team's website, see whether you can locate information pertaining to environmental responsibility. Has the team initiated a waste reduction or recycling program? Is it addressing its carbon footprint? Does it promote green practices among its fan base or within its community?

5. Select a professional or collegiate sport organization of your choice. Using the ideas presented in this chapter, identify three ways in which the organization could generate revenue as a direct result of its CSR activities. Be specific regarding how the program could be structured and who would be involved.

# Communicating With Internal Publics

## After reading this chapter, students should be able to

- describe the nature and importance of employee relations,
- discuss common employee communications activities,
- note unique aspects of employee relations in sport,
- address the importance of organizational culture to the effectiveness of public relations,
- describe the nature and importance of investor relations,
- discuss common investor relations activities, and
- address general public relations orientations as they relate to investor relations.

## Key terms discussed in this chapter include

- employee communications,
- labor relations,
- organizational culture,
- investor relations,
- annual reports,
- shareholder approach, and
- stakeholder approach.

**Thus far, this** book has focused on public relations activities directed at two large stakeholder groups—the mass media and the sport organization's communities. Although these two groups justifiably receive substantial attention, they are not the only stakeholders in sport organizations. This chapter focuses on a sport organization's internal stakeholders, employees and investors, and chapter 14 addresses external stakeholder groups.

The first portion of the chapter deals with employee relations. Specifically, it examines the nature and importance of employee relations. It also describes common employee relations practices as well as unique aspects of employee relations in sport. Finally, it focuses on how organizational culture relates to overall public relations effectiveness. The second portion of the chapter addresses investor relations. It examines the nature of investor relations activities and common responsibilities of investor relations professionals. It concludes with a discussion of a fundamental debate over investor-related philosophies that may drive publicly owned sport organizations.

## Employee Relations

Sport organizations do not commonly have units or departments with *employee relations* in the title. As in nonsport organizations, the function is commonly housed in human resources departments (Grunig, 1992). Employee relations has been conceptualized as one of numerous human resources (HR) practices, including recruitment, performance management, and training and development (Taylor, Doherty, & McGraw, 2008). But employee relations, or **employee communications**, is a public relations function that has the goal of establishing desirable relationships between a sport organization's management and its other employees.

The foundations of effective employee relations are the same as they are for other forms of public relations. They include researching the nature of key publics, carefully planning communication activities that will connect with people within those key publics, and assessing the effectiveness of those activities. Although employee relations activity largely involves channeling messages within the sport organization, it also relates to broader concerns such as employee morale, employee behaviors, and organizational culture (Mogel, 2002). As such, the employee relations function permeates the sport organization.

## Importance of Employee Relations

Simply put, employees are an organization's greatest resource (Miller, 1997), so employee relations may be an organization's most important public relations priority (Broom, 2009). More professionals seem to be recognizing this reality, as evidenced by a non-sport-specific survey of members of the Council of Public Relations. The results indicated that within the last year or two more than half were engaging in more work than ever pertaining to employee relations and involvement (Council of Public Relations Firms, 2008).

Employee relations is usually challenging because employees are often skeptical about management-initiated communications (Guiniven, 2000). Employees often doubt whether their organization's leadership is forthright and fully discloses information that they believe they need to know. In some cases, employees may even be hostile toward management, believing that they have been manipulated or dealt with unfairly on past occasions.

Such suspicions are often justified. *Sports Illustrated* writer Peter King reported in February 2009 that the NFL's Carolina Panthers had laid off 20 employees in response to the global economic crisis (King, 2009). The move was particularly troubling because the team had just that week signed one player to a six-year $60 million contract and another to a one-year $16.5 million deal. King opined:

> I don't like this one bit, and the Panthers are not the only team to do this, obviously. The NFL is a profitable venture, and in times of economic stress, teams need to show loyalty to the people who've worked hard for them—people not at the top of the salary food chain. (King, 2009)

Even when organizational management is transparent and fair in its dealings with employees, the us–them distinction that many employees make concerning management is often present. Effective employee communications are not likely to eliminate that perception, but they can facilitate interaction that fosters employee commitment and satisfaction and enables both senior management and other employees to work more effectively.

Employee relations, in concert with other HR activities, affect organizational performance in general and desirable HR outcomes in particular

(Taylor et al., 2008). Three outcomes in particular merit mention. First, employees who are satisfied with their work environment are easier to retain than are dissatisfied employees. Because the cost of replacing employees is almost always high, sport organizations logically desire to keep the productive employees that they already have. As stated by Carter and Rovell (2003), "Long-term, mutually beneficial, and bargained for relationships minimize the strife between organizations and their employees. Once these ideal working relationships are formed the ability to avoid and overcome conflict is greatly increased" (p. 112).

A second reason why effective employee relations is important is that happy, satisfied employees are likely to be more productive in their jobs than their dissatisfied counterparts. A study of the top 75 publicly owned companies in North Carolina tied employee perceptions of their organization to the organization's financial performance (Bridges, Marcum, & Kline Harrison, 2003). Those firms whose employees indicated that their employers were less committed to them than to their customers and stockholders were characterized by lower sales totals, net income, and market value than competitors whose employees reported a higher commitment. The implication of this study is that although an organizational commitment to customers and investors is highly commendable, employees who feel marginalized respond consciously or otherwise with lower productivity. Spoelstra (2001) went so far as to argue that employees should be valued even more than customers and shareholders because the resultant increase in employee productivity inevitably satisfies customers, whose increased business results in happy shareholders.

This point leads to the third reason why employee relations is critical. Every employee of a sport organization is a public relations representative. Their job titles may not include the term *public relations*, but nearly all of them interact with other people who are part of the sport organization's key stakeholder groups. Employees on the front line of customer service such as ticket representatives, front-desk personnel, ushers, and security staff likely log more hours in direct contact with consumers than members of the public relations staff do. Most employees live in the communities of their sport organizations and interact with people from their neighborhoods, their civic organizations, their religious assemblies, and their children's schools. The messages that those employees communicate about their employers influence how others perceive the sport organization, in ways that may have greater influence than formal organizational communications. It behooves sport organizations to cultivate employees who will advocate their organizations whether on the clock or off.

In light of these considerations, it is not surprising that a survey regarding competencies for sport event managers found that both practitioners and academics rated "Maintains effective communications with staff" as the most important competency that managers can possess (Peng, 2000). Such communications are critical not only to the functioning of the event staff but also to the administration and reputation of the event among its stakeholder groups.

Employee relations, therefore, warrants careful attention from organizational managers, just as any other public relations program does (Grunig, 1992). For most sport organizations, public relations planning should extend well beyond media relations and community relations.

## Nature of Employee Relations Practice

Communication flow within sport organizations may be conceptualized in several ways (Lussier & Kimball, 2009). Vertical communication is formal in nature and may flow downward from senior management to other employees as well as upward from employees to senior management. More will be said about vertical communication in the following sections. Two other forms of communication are also commonplace. Horizontal communication is also formal in nature but takes place among peers who are essentially at the same level within the organization. This communication often takes the form of memorandums and meetings. The third way in which communication occurs within the sport organization is informal, or through the grapevine. This type of communication often fills the gaps left by vertical and horizontal communications, and the existence of the grapevine is not necessarily negative for the sport organization. In fact, employee relations professionals may find the grapevine to be a useful tool if they are able to tap into it (J. Fulgham, personal communication, August 25, 2004). By monitoring the grapevine, employee relations professionals can identify recurrent themes and issues that may warrant managerial attention and formal communication. This activity is not a matter of snooping; it is simply a matter of being attuned to one of the sport organization's key stakeholder groups.

## Downward Communication

Formal communication from the sport organization's leadership to its employees may be classified as downward communication (Lussier & Kimball, 2009). As with horizontal communication, downward communication commonly takes the form of meetings and memorandums. A wide array of channels may carry messages from the organization's leadership, including annual reports, bulletin boards, internal video, organizational publications, online communications (i.e., intranet), and satellite TV (Mogel, 2002).

The messages carried through these channels typically address one or more of three subjects of interest to employees (Mogel, 2002, p. 105). First, they may explain how the organization is faring in the pursuit of its mission and vision. Such status reports have fundamental implications for all members of the organization because personnel and budgetary resources usually hinge on performance. Second, downward communications may describe technological developments that may affect the organization. This subject is of interest because employees may be called on to use those new technologies. Third, downward communication may address plans for the organization and strategies that the organization plans to use in those pursuits. This point is also of keen interest to employees, who are understandably interested to learn how those plans will affect them. Employees of IMG, a global sport and entertainment company, received a memo of this sort when a new CEO wrote to address widespread fears about the company's future (Mullen, 2006). In a letter described as "lengthy and surprisingly candid" (Mullen, 2006, p. 5), Ted Forstmann discussed leadership and strategic changes at IMG. He also committed to subsequent communication with employees, stating, "I believe that you are entitled to know my vision for the company, and I am entitled to your support" (Forstmann as cited in Mullen, 2006).

Clearly, employees want information that directly affects their careers. A survey conducted by the International Association of Business Communicators listed organizational plans for the future, job advancement opportunities, and job-related how-to information as the three subjects that were of greatest interest to employees (Center & Jackson, 1995). The survey also found human interest stories about other employees and personal news such as birthdays and anniversaries to be of the least interest.

Although meetings and memorandums are commonplace, publications remain the primary media for employee communication (Broom, 2009). Organizational newsletters are particularly common, so common that many public relations practitioners may not give them the attention they deserve. If they are to be leveraged for maximum value, however, employee newsletters must be thoroughly planned and carefully crafted. Figure 13.1 displays the first page of an employee newsletter from MLB's Tampa Bay Rays.

Treadwell and Treadwell (2005) offer several pieces of advice about employee newsletters. First, as is the case with most public relations initiatives, practitioners are advised to start by learning about their audience. They must have a thorough understanding of who the employees are and what their interests and attitudes are toward the sport organization. This knowledge will allow newsletter producers to offer editorial content of interest and importance. Second, newsletter producers should understand the purpose of the newsletter. Is its purpose simply to convey information from top management, or is it to be used to solicit feedback from employees? Third, public relations professionals should publish newsletters with regularity, whether that means weekly, monthly, or quarterly. After the schedule is established, they should stick with it so that employees know when to expect communication from their organization's leadership.

As for content, Treadwell and Treadwell (2005) recommended that editorial decisions be based on audience interests and management desires. Including both agendas may seem difficult, but considerable overlap should exist between the two. Management teams who constrain their communications staff from addressing employee interests run the risk of losing their employees' attention. They can also lose support by desperate attempts to spin negative news. As stated by Atkins (2003), "Tell us—your employees—why this company's best days are ahead of it. . . . Tell us what success looks like and the role we can play to achieve it; and please: stop calling layoffs 'career transition opportunities'" (p. 62).

Finally, Treadwell and Treadwell (2005) advised practitioners to use distribution channels that put the information in the hands of those to whom it is directed. Common channels include internal mail, the organization's website or intranet, and e-mail. Some organizations send relatively brief e-mails containing the leads for each newsletter story, providing links that readers may follow for Internet access to the complete stories. Decisions regarding distribution channels should be based on the employees' patterns of media consumption, not what is most convenient or least expensive for the organization.

Week of April 20             Tampa Bay Rays

Volume XXV

# RAYS Monthly

## *Energize Our Community Through the Magic of Baseball*

**Contributors: Geoff McQueen, Matthew Hahn, Valerie Fava, Carey Cox, Dave Haller, Mike Roy**

## Announcements

### CONGRATS RYAN

Kristi and **Ryan Henry** became the proud parents of Elliot Jackson Henry on March 18. Elliot was welcomed into the world at 2:06 p.m. and weighed 8 lbs, 5 oz. Ryan is a former Marketing/Community Relations intern and is currently a member of the Street Team.

### CONGRATULATIONS STEVE

Monika Kurowski and **Steve Dapcic** were united in marriage on Saturday, March 28 at the Don Cesar in St. Petersburg by Rev. Tom Greene. Monika graduated from Illinois State University and is currently a kindergarten teacher at Richey Elementary School in Pasco County. The couple will honeymoon in Puerto Vallarta, Mexico, in April.

## Player Spotlight

### RHP Jason Isringhausen

With over 13 years of major league service (a majority spent as a closer for Oakland and St. Louis), right-handed reliever Jason Isringhausen will add more veteran presence to the Rays bullpen. Even though he will begin the season on the DL, Izzy is expected to join the team before the end of April. When healthy, Izzy throws an 89-90 mph fastball, 87-88 mph cutter with enough break to fool hitters, and a 78-79 mph curveball with above-average 12/6 break. In addition, Izzy is able to throw all of his pitches for strikes.

### OF Ray Sadler

Through the course of Spring Training, outfielder **Ray Sadler** caught the attention of just about everyone. He led the team in home runs and slugging percentage. Sadler has spent the last nine years in the minor leagues with Houston, Pittsburgh, and Chicago (NL), but he has logged a total of four days in the big leagues. Sadler plays all three outfield positions and has an above-average arm. Moreover, he has plus raw power. If he continues his spring performance, Sadler could add more days and years to his major league service.

## Media Guide

Communications completed the media guide in February and publishing wrapped up in March. The guide was actually shortened by 88 pages, to a trim 488, after tipping the scales at 576 last season. This was quite a challenge considering the addition of a postseason section. In addition to the normal distribution to local and national media and internally, this year's guide is being sold to fans in the gift shop for $12 and is being sent to season-ticket holders.

*Inside Pitch*, the official (and free) game program produced internally, has undergone a handful of changes this year. The magazine is being printed on slightly larger, and different stock, paper. The scorecard is now included on the centerfold, after being printed separately in 2008. Pat Burrell is the cover boy for the first issue, which also includes new features in "Johnny Comeback" (a baseball Q&A with a snarky cartoon character inspired by this very newsletter) and "The Dirt on..." (a personality profile on players). The next issue will introduce original prose by Fernando Perez and "On the Road with Dave & Andy."

## New Partnerships

### Stanley Works:

Stanley Works has come on board with a multi-year agreement to be the Official Tools of the Tampa Bay Rays. Their deal includes ballpark signage, radio commercials, and the radio feature "How to Build a Winner." Apologies to Geoff McQueen, who loses his status as "Official Tool of the Tampa Bay Rays."

### MillerCoors:

MillerCoors will sponsor the 6th inning of Rays games, which will be promoted via radio and in-ballpark signage. They will also be hosting watch parties throughout the season which will feature Miller Lite specials. Keep on an eye on the Corporate Sales page on myrays.com for more information.

### Cornerstone Bank:

If the Rays score 10 or more runs in a game at home this season, Cornerstone Bank will donate $1,000 to a local charity and award a lucky fan $1,000.

## Community Fund Grant Update

The Rays Baseball Foundation awarded 29 local organizations nearly $150,000 through the 2009 Community Fund Grant. The average award is $5,000 but the amounts vary based on individual organizational need(s). Recipients will be honored on the field May 2 vs. Boston.

## Teaming Up for the Environment

The Rays "Teaming Up for the Environment" 2009 program initiative will promote six local organizations that support the environment through educational programs. The organizations will receive a $1,000 grant in support of their continuing efforts, in-game partnership and recognition at a select Rays game in addition to being featured in Community Corner and 20 tickets to the game. Partners will be announced on Earth Day (April 22) and recognition nights will begin in May.

## Minor League Spring Training

Port Charlotte lost over 50% of its occupancy by April 5. The big league club moved out on Thursday, April 2, and on the 5th, three full-season minor league clubs packed their bags and headed north. The Durham Bulls and Montgomery Biscuits opened up at their respective homes on April 9, when Durham hosted the Norfolk Tides and Montgomery faced the West Tennessee Diamond Jaxx. The Bowling Green Hot Rods opened up on the 9th as well, but did do so on the road against the Hickory Crawdads. The Charlotte Stone Crabs stayed in Port Charlotte for their home opener on the 9th against the Fort Myers Miracle.

You can still catch future Rays because the Hudson Valley Renegades, Princeton Rays, and Gulf Coast Rays will continue their Spring Training in Port Charlotte until their seasons begin in late June.

**Figure 13.1** First page of a two-page organizational newsletter.

Courtesy of Tampa Bay Rays.

## Upward Communication

Upward communication, which flows from employees to senior management, is another form of vertical communication (Lussier & Kimball, 2009), and it is at least as important as downward communication. Chapters 2 and 3 addressed the strategic nature of public relations and the planning process. Both chapters emphasized that sport managers should know their publics and design communication activities that facilitate feedback from those groups. By establishing two-way communication with employees, sport managers will be more persuasive when their aim is to win consent (i.e., asymmetrical approach as described in chapter 2) and be savvier when their goal is compromise (i.e., symmetrical approach as described in chapter 2). Taylor, Doherty, and McGraw (2008) noted that the two-way interaction resulting from upward communication also enables management to access employees' skills and experience, thus improving organizational processes.

Research is the key to successful two-way communication. All the research methods detailed in chapter 3 may be used to gain information from employees. For example, focus groups could assess employee reactions to new management strategies. Surveys could be used to measure how comfortable employees are with new technologies and to identify subjects meriting additional employee training. In some cases, a tool used for downward communication may also be used to generate upward communication. For instance, employee newsletters may generate feedback by incorporating brief surveys or by featuring question-and-answer columns in which employees can broach topics of interest (Broom, 2009).

One of the challenges facing some sport organizations, particularly larger ones, is the increasingly diverse nature of the employee workforce. Because publics are best characterized as relatively homogenous, some sport organizations are finding more publics within their employee stakeholder groups. Obtaining feedback from the stakeholder group thus becomes more complex. For example, Gear for Sports, a sportswear company, has a large and diverse employee base; nine primary languages are spoken on its production floor. Sending out a written survey in English may not be sufficient for securing feedback from such a diverse group. Multiple tools, and often multiple versions of the same tool, are necessary to give voice to the varied publics. Furthermore, special communication strategies may be necessary to facilitate a cohesive workgroup. The sidebar titled Effectively Communicating With Diverse Employees by Dr. Mark Vermillion offers additional thoughts on this topic.

One other key point bears emphasis here as well. As effective as formal communication practices and structured research programs may be in stimulating two-way communication, basic interpersonal communication between managers and employees is the foundation of effective employee relations (Grunig, 1992). Most employees indicate that their preferred method of communication is direct interaction with their immediate supervisor (Bobo, 2000; Broom, 2009). If organizational managers have been successful in building strong relationships with their staffs, it seems likely that those interpersonal exchanges are the setting in which the most honest opinions and insightful ideas are shared.

## Unique Aspects of Employee Relations in Sport

Unlike media relations and community relations, employee relations in sport shares many elements with the same practice in nonsport settings. The same goals, practices, and challenges may be found in each setting. Nevertheless, employee relations in sport has three unique features that warrant discussion.

The first unique feature is that because of the popularity of sport, employees of sport organizations often enjoy a sense of social prestige because of their organizational affiliation (Acosta Hernandez, 2002; Todd, 2003). For example, Xing and Chalip (2009) reported that lower-level employees with the Beijing Organizing Committee for the Olympic Games understood the high-profile nature of their organization and valued the opportunity to participate in a historic event. Similarly, researchers at ESPN may never see a second of camera time and ticket sellers for a big-league sport franchise may not even see the home games that their team plays, but they may receive personal benefits such as esteem and respect because of their professional associations.

For these reasons, sport organizations are uniquely positioned to build employee commitment by stressing organizational pride. One way to do this is by enabling employees to display their organizational affiliation. Organizations may provide apparel with the organization's logo to employees free or at low cost, recognize employees in organizational publications, and allow lower-profile employees to work with higher-profile employees in public initiatives such as volunteer ventures.

The second unique aspect of employee relations in sport is that for many sport organizations, volunteers are an integral part of the internal work team necessary for the organization to function effectively. Volunteers are particularly critical to sport organizations in countries like Canada and Australia that have club-based sport systems (Cuskelly, Hoye, & Auld, 2006), and communication with volunteers may be particularly challenging because volunteers usually do not work regular hours like paid employees do (Taylor et al., 2008). The sidebar on page 266, Building Relationships With Volunteers by Chris Wyche of Sporting Kansas City, describes how one organization successfully manages volunteer relations.

# Effectively Communicating With Diverse Employees

**Dr. Mark Vermillion**

Courtesy of Wichita State University

Diversity has been on corporate America's radar screen since the social upheaval of the 1960s and 1970s (Gardenswartz & Rowe, 2009). Both traditional businesses and sport organizations have recently acknowledged the need for both an understanding of and participation in diversity-based initiatives. Indeed, McRae and Short (2010) emphasized the importance of racial and ethnic diversity to decision makers and policy decisions. Understanding how communication with increasingly diverse employees or constituents can enhance an organization's social, business, or economic position is crucial for future sport, recreation, and physical activity practitioners. To communicate better with diverse employees, potential sport and recreation managers need to understand how diversity relates to leadership. I will briefly discuss both topics and offer an example of how we incorporated these ideas into our own cultural awareness program for a staff training event within a campus recreation environment.

## What Is Diversity?

Cunningham (2007) differentiated between two types of diversity: surface level and deep level. Surface-level diversity includes attributes such as easily perceived or observed differences (e.g., race or gender), whereas deep-level diversity focuses on differences that are not easily observed, including political or religious ideologies (Cunningham, 2007). Key to establishing diversity initiatives within business and sport organizations is that leadership within these organizations recognizes the practical and social implications of diversity. Practically speaking, having diverse working environments allows leaders to pull from a larger pool of diverse ideas, thereby increasing the chance of establishing more effective protocols. For example, Barrett (2008) related how the Shell Oil Company conducts diversity training sessions in an effort to develop skilled employees within the globalized marketplace.

Sport organizations have been effective in highlighting the social implications of diversity. For example, Branch Rickey's decision to integrate Major League Baseball with Jackie Robinson in 1947 shows the socially relevant nature of diversity and the role that sport plays in this process. More recently, the Laboratory for Diversity in Sport at Texas A&M released a report titled "Diversity in Athletics: An Assessment of Exemplars and Institutional Best Practices" in spring 2009. Within the report, Cunningham and Singer (2009) highlighted the diversity initiatives in specific NCAA-affiliated athletics departments that have successfully addressed diversity or multiculturalism. Additionally, the report highlighted how diversity, exemplified in a variety of ways, is integrated within the collegiate athletics environment, which is important not only to student–athletes but also to coaches, administrators, and fans.

> **Understanding how communication with increasingly diverse employees or constituents can enhance an organization's social, business, or economic position is crucial for future sport, recreation, and physical activity practitioners.**

## Leadership, Diversity, and Training and Education

Leadership plays a crucial role in effectively communicating or implementing diversity initiatives (Barrett, 2008; McRae & Short, 2010). Specifically, leadership is defined as a "process of mutual influence" (Parker, 2005, p. 27). Leadership, then, is intuitively intertwined with communication

*(continued)*

*(continued)*

and the dialectical relationship between leader and subordinate. As previously discussed in this chapter, vertical communication (whether upward or downward) can effectively disseminate vital information to employees within the sport organization.

As a result, an understanding of diversity and ways to communicate that knowledge is crucial for the implementation of diversity-based initiatives (Barrett, 2008). Indeed, Cunningham (2007) identified the most effective means for initiating a diversity training or cultural awareness program within a sport or recreation organization; effective communication strategies are vital to establishing such a program. Recognizing that multiple roles are played in every type of group situation (Carron, Hausenblas, & Eys, 2005), diversity training programs should address a variety of diversity characteristics geared toward both employees and leaders. Each individual plays a role not only in understanding diversity but also in learning how to implement new knowledge. Indeed, one of the most effective forms of leadership in sport organizations is labeled transformational leadership, which incorporates continuing education for both leaders and subordinates (Doherty & Danylchuk, 1996).

## Our Program

I was approached by the department of campus recreation here at my university about putting together a cultural awareness program. I developed a program in consultation with Jessica Varlack, our assistant director of aquatics and risk management, and we made the presentation to the campus recreation staff, which included both student staff and coordinators or directors. The presentation included two activities sandwiched around a short, informational presentation. The first activity involved a "webbing" activity in which respondents completed a written diagram by putting their names in a center circle and filling in the connecting circles with words describing them as individuals. Most people filled in words describing the roles that they play in society. The second activity involved participants selecting an index card, turned over, which had some kind of diversity characteristic written on it. Without looking at the cards, participants held the cards on their foreheads. They then walked around as a group interacting with one another based solely on the characteristics written on the cards. Resulting discussions centered on topics such as (1) how people were treated based solely on one characteristic, which they may or may not know about, and (2) how important surface-level and deep-level characteristics are to effective communication.

## Concluding Remarks

Strong organizational leaders have recognized the importance of not only diversity in general but also the ways in which diverse employees, constituents, and marketplaces affect their organizations' goals, programs, and products. A comprehensive knowledge of communication strategies and theories assists sport and recreation managers by providing them with a roadmap for understanding diverse and complex organizational dynamics. Managers who make decisions or develop protocols must be armed with the latest ideas, theories, strategies, and practices to balance not only the organizational dynamics of sport organizations but also the social environment and implications that sport has for society at large.

*Dr. Mark Vermillion is an assistant professor in sport management at Wichita State University. His specialization is the sociocultural dimensions of sport.*

A third unique aspect of employee relations relates to professional sport, in which **labor relations** with powerful players' unions are not only often difficult but also of intense interest to their fan base (Carter & Rovell, 2003). Contentious negotiations are not unique to sport, but the amount of attention and the intense public interest in the outcome of the negotiations do seem to be unique to sport. Unions represent athletes in five professional leagues in the United States—the National Basketball Association (NBA), the Women's National Basketball Association (WNBA), the National Football League (NFL), the National Hockey League (NHL), and Major League Baseball (MLB). Since these associations began gaining power in the 1970s, negotiations over collective bargaining agreements have often been both public and ugly. In many instances, work stoppages have occurred. As a result, fans have been alienated; media partners, host facilities, sponsors, and related businesses have been damaged; and the reputations of owners, union leaders, and players have been tarnished. Table 13.1 lists the work stoppages that have occurred in U.S. professional sport over the last 50 years.

## Table 13.1 Work Stoppages in U.S. Professional Sport 1960–2010

| Year | Type of work stoppage | Games lost | Notes |
|---|---|---|---|
| **National Basketball Association (NBA)** | | | |
| 1995 | Lockout | 0 | |
| 1996 | Lockout | 0 | Lockout lasted less than one day and did not result in the cancellation of any games. |
| 1998–99 | Lockout | 424 | |
| **National Football League (NFL)** | | | |
| 1968 | Lockout and strike | 0 | Training camps were boycotted, but no regular-season games were lost. |
| 1970 | Lockout and strike | 0 | Training camps were boycotted for 20 days, but no regular-season games were lost. |
| 1982 | Strike | 196 | Season was shortened from 16 games per team to 9. |
| 1987 | Strike | 14 | Games were cancelled only for week 3 of the regular season. Weeks 4, 5, and 6 were played with replacement players, and results counted toward final regular-season standings. |
| **National Hockey League (NHL)** | | | |
| 1992 | Strike | 0 | All postponed games were made up. |
| 1994–95 | Lockout | 468 | |
| 2004–05 | Lockout | 1,230 | Complete season was lost. |
| **Major League Baseball (MLB)** | | | |
| 1972 | Strike | 86 | |
| 1976 | Lockout | 0 | Spring training was postponed for 17 days, but no regular-season games were lost. |
| 1981 | Strike | 713 | |
| 1985 | Lockout | 0 | |
| 1990 | Strike | 0 | |
| 1994–95 | Strike | 669 | Figure does not include additional postseason games that were also cancelled. |

Based on Associated Press 2005; Coates and Humphreys 2001; Staudohar 1996; Staudohar 1999.

# Building Relationships With Volunteers

## Chris Wyche

Photo courtesy of Chris Wyche.

The process of conducting an event must include staffing the event, and usually that means that at least some of the people whom the event relies on for success are volunteers. The challenge is selecting, training, and motivating volunteers so that they can accomplish the tasks necessary to make the event successful and be available to lend a hand again the next time, albeit with some experience under their belt. How you do that can determine the short- and long-term success or failure of the event.

At Sporting Kansas City we rely on volunteers to fill key positions in our management of game-day activities. As a professional sport team, we naturally attract people who have an affinity for our sport and an interest in being involved with the team. This circumstance is no different from that faced by other types of organizations that need to find people who for one reason or another have a desire to make a difference and the goal of helping wherever possible. In truth, this task is many times the easiest part of the equation.

After someone has volunteered to be part of your efforts, you need to make sure that they know what they are doing so that their talents can be maximized. We listen to volunteers' interests so that we can match them up with the best possible area for their efforts. After we understand what motivates them and catches their interest, we search out job assignments that make sense for both the individual and the organization. Doing that accomplishes the obvious goal of matching skills and interests to responsibilities, but it also leaves volunteers feeling as if we truly have their best interests at heart. This approach also opens the door for a positive response when we have a last-minute task that may not fit their priorities. Because they know that we are listening to them, they are willing to help in other areas on a short-term basis.

> I can assure you that many changes in operational plans have been made at the suggestion of a volunteer.

After volunteers are engaged in the project, the focus shifts to three main points—their well-being, their accomplishment of the tasks for which they are responsible, and retaining them for future efforts. I stated them in that order on purpose, because having a happy volunteer sometimes makes issues 2 and 3 much easier to manage. We want to ensure that all volunteers have the tools they need, because when they are properly equipped they will be able to accomplish much more and feel much better about what they are doing. Sometimes it is as simple as having the same apparel as everyone else so that they feel a part of the team. Other times it is about having the right communication devices or equipment to perform their assigned tasks. At all times it is about the volunteers knowing that they have our support and can ask for help when needed. One tactic that I use is checking with volunteers regularly to see how they are doing and, more important, what they are learning and how we might improve. For the volunteers, this is another affirmation of their value. For our organization, the volunteers' feedback can provide valuable input for our future planning. I can assure you that many changes in operational plans have been made at the suggestion of a volunteer.

When you ask volunteers to help, you are expecting them to be able to perform tasks that you have designated them to do. They need to understand those tasks, so we prepare documents that have their schedules and descriptions of their jobs before the event so that they can read up on the plan. In some cases we have further phone contact to see whether they have any questions. Sometimes we even meet with volunteers before the event to review the plan. When volunteers know what their assignments are and feel comfortable with their responsibilities, their production level should skyrocket. We also try to increase their value as volunteers by equipping them with as much information as possible about the event so that they feel confident in answering questions or finding someone who can answer a specific inquiry. In that way, they do not feel as if they have been exposed as not being knowledgeable.

Ultimately, an event is likely to need the services of your volunteers multiple times, and the number of volunteers needed the next time often increases as the scope of the event grows. Happy volunteers who prove themselves valuable at one event can be resources at the next and can help by recruiting other volunteers to the fold. We like the volunteer recruiting system because after someone has experienced what we are about and wants to come back, anyone whom that person recruits is likely to be a quality volunteer who will be a benefit to the event. Through that process we have found some of the best people we have working game days.

Ultimately, you need to debrief the volunteers in some manner to glean the information they have that can make your event better. Besides the value to the event itself, this process shows volunteers that they have value, and this serves as a catalyst for more involvement.

Over the years it has been my privilege to work with thousands of volunteers. Through much trial and error, I have found that when you are honest about the workload and endeavor to make it fun, the volunteers are happy and productive. My experience in this is not only in supervising volunteers but also in serving as one myself, so I understand the importance of placing value on volunteers, as well as the ramifications of not doing so. Treat your volunteers like the gold they are, and the payback to your organization will defy measurement.

*Chris Wyche is the executive vice president for operations of MLS' Sporting Kansas City.*

As the manuscript for this text was being written, all four of the major U.S. professional sport leagues—MLB, NBA, NFL, and NHL—were facing the prospect that their collective bargaining agreements with their respective players' associations would expire in 2011. Each of the leagues was feeling the effects of the global economic crisis that started in 2008. Some were dealing with new leaders representing the players, and most were confronting long-simmering issues of discord. Little wonder one writer described the four agreements expiring in the same year as "disharmonic convergence" (Mullen, 2009, p. 1). Many industry insiders believed that one or more leagues would endure the first work stoppage in major U.S. professional sport since 2004–05 (Mullen, 2009).

The critical nature of player relations has meant that managers have been hired at senior-level positions to work primarily with their players' association. For example, one of MLB's senior executives, Robert Manfred, is specifically assigned to labor relations and human resources (MLB, n.d.). Manfred is an attorney who has an extensive background in labor relations, and his job calls for him to work closely with the MLB Players Association and the World Umpires' Union on an ongoing basis, not just when collective bargaining agreements need to be negotiated.

# Organizational Culture and Public Relations Effectiveness

The subject of internal public relations cannot be adequately addressed without considerable discussion of organizational culture. **Organizational culture** refers to the values, attitudes, and behaviors that characterize the way that an organization operates, and it has been linked to the effectiveness of public relations. The scholars who conducted the Excellence Study (see chapter 1 for a brief description of this project) linked both participative climates and environments that are supportive of women and minority employees to overall excellence in public relations (Dozier, Grunig, & Grunig, 1995; Sriramesh, Grunig, & Buffington, 1992).

The investigators involved in the Excellence Study described two broad categories of organizational culture—authoritarian and participative (Dozier et al., 1995). Authoritarian culture may be characterized by

- centralized power,
- top-down decision making,
- historical processes (i.e., "the way we have always done it"),

- distrust between management and employees,

- refusal to consider new ideas, and

- failure of the organization's units to work in a teamlike manner.

Participative culture, on the other hand, is typified by

- decentralized power,

- collaborative decision making,

- innovative processes,

- basic trust between management and employees,

- openness to new ideas, and

- organizational units that work as teams.

One of the key findings of the Excellence Study was that organizations that scored highly on measurements indicating a participative culture tended to score highly on measurements of overall public relations effectiveness (Dozier et al., 1995; Grunig, 1992). Participative cultures contribute to effective internal public relations because they are characterized by a two-way flow of information. They may also indicate a basic management philosophy that values interaction as opposed to isolation, which has profound implications for the way that management is likely to think of external public relations.

The second major finding of the Excellence Study in terms of organizational culture was that organizations that scored highly on measurements of support for women and minority employees also tended to score highly on measurements of public relations effectiveness (Dozier et al., 1995). This support ranges from basic steps such as the establishment of nondiscrimination and sexual ha-

rassment policies to the development of mentoring and advancement programs. Again, the rationale for such measures is that they deepen and empower employees, contributing to the organization's public relations efforts, and serve as evidence of progressive approaches by management to public relations.

Overall, the public relations profession is one of the few in which women are the majority (Hampson, 2001), but that does not seem to be the case within sport. The *2004 Racial and Gender Report Card* was the last to offer specific data regarding the level at which women and racial and ethnic minorities were represented in top public relations positions at the highest level of professional sport. Table 13.2 summarizes the study's findings about gender. As shown, women held relatively few of the director of public relations positions, particularly in the NFL where no women held such a job. Women were better represented in director of community relations positions, where they were a majority in three of the major leagues and held 50% representation in the NFL and Major League Soccer. A 2008 report on diversity in college athletics indicated that women held just 11% of the sports information director positions at the NCAA Division I and II levels and 14% of those positions at the Division III level (Lapchick, Little, Lerner, & Mathew, 2009). Another study found more equitable gender representation in lower-level positions such as assistant sports information director at NCAA I-A institutions (Stoldt, Miller, & Comfort, 2003). That finding could indicate that more women were entering the field, and it could be that levels of representation at other ranks will equalize as those women advance in the field. But some evidence indicates that the women who have already advanced to senior positions continue to be treated inequitably. Although 44% of men in senior media relations positions (i.e., assistant athletic

## Table 13.2  Gender Representation in Public Relations

| League | Public relations director | | Community relations director | |
| --- | --- | --- | --- | --- |
| | Women (%) | Men (%) | Women (%) | Men (%) |
| MLB | 13 | 87 | 57 | 43 |
| MLS | 20 | 80 | 50 | 50 |
| NBA | 28 | 72 | 55 | 45 |
| NFL | 0 | 100 | 50 | 50 |
| WNBA | 43 | 57 | 88 | 12 |

Adapted, by permission, from R. Lapchick, 2004, *2004 racial and gender report card* (Orlando, FL: University of Central Florida, Institute for Diversity and Ethics in Sports).

director, sports information director) reported that they functioned primarily as managers, only 11% of women in the same jobs reported functioning in a similar manner (Stoldt et al., 2003). The rest were relegated to a technical role.

Public relations theory such as that developed by the Excellence Study calls for organizations to treat female employees fairly and take steps that will empower them to advance their careers in ways that benefit the organization. Women within the field have other resources at their disposal as well. The sidebar titled FAME: An Organization Supporting Women in Athletic Communications describes an important professional association and the way in which it serves women in the field.

Table 13.3 summarizes the findings of the *2004 Racial and Gender Report Card* in terms of racial diversity in top public relations positions in major league sport organizations. As indicated, white people hold the vast majority of public relations director positions for those five leagues (Lapchick, 2004). Greater diversity can be found in the director of community relations position, but even in that position minorities are often underrepresented.

## Table 13.3 Racial Representation in Public Relations

| | Public relations director | | | | | Community relations director | | | | |
|---|---|---|---|---|---|---|---|---|---|---|
| League | White (%) | African American (%) | Latino (%) | Asian American (%) | Other (%) | White (%) | African American (%) | Latino (%) | Asian American (%) | Other (%) |
| MLB | 94 | 6 | 0 | 0 | 0 | 81 | 14 | 5 | 0 | 0 |
| MLS | 90 | 0 | 10 | 0 | 0 | 90 | 10 | 0 | 0 | 0 |
| NBA | 79 | 14 | 3 | 3 | 0 | 52 | 45 | 0 | 3 | 0 |
| NFL | 80 | 20 | 0 | 0 | 0 | 75 | 19 | 6 | 0 | 0 |
| WNBA | 71 | 0 | 14 | 14 | 0 | 38 | 50 | 0 | 13 | 0 |

Adapted, by permission, from R. Lapchick, 2004, *2004 racial and gender report card* (Orlando, FL: University of Central Florida, Institute for Diversity and Ethics in Sports).

## FAME: An Organization Supporting Women in Athletic Communications

The Female Athletics Media Relations Executives (FAME) organization's mission is "to discuss issues facing women in the sports media relations field and to develop appropriate strategies to deal with those issues. FAME members are committed to encouraging and mentoring all women working in athletics media relations as a career" (FAME, 2001). The group was established in St. Louis in 2000 at the annual conference of the College Sports Information Directors of America (CoSIDA). An impetus for the founding of the group was a research project titled "Women in Intercollegiate Sport" that showed a decline in the number of women holding the title of sports publicity director (Haverbeck, 2006).

A core group of 12 CoSIDA members invited all the women at the conference to an impromptu meeting, and they were surprised at the large number of women who attended and at the range of issues that were brought forward for discussion (Haverbeck, 2006). Subsequent dialogue through a listserv resulted in the selection of the organization's name and an invitation for women working in communication positions in a variety of sport-related organizations, not just college athletics, to join (Haverbeck, 2006).

FAME members have engaged in a variety of activities to advance opportunities for women in the field. The organization has provided forums for discussing important issues such as work–life balance, standards of professionalism, and research pertaining to women in the field (Haverbeck, 2006). Members have also advocated for one another in seeking opportunities for professional recognition within CoSIDA. The group has been highly successful, as 30 of its members received various national-level CoSIDA honors between 2001 and 2010.

Diversity issues extend beyond the presence of women and members of racial and ethnic minorities within sport organizations. Representation is critical, however, and how sport organizations respond may have profound implications for their overall public relations effectiveness. As noted by Lapchick and colleagues (2009), "This element of diversity can provide a different perspective, and possibly a competitive advantage for a win in the boardroom as well as on the athletic fields of play" (p. 2).

## Investor Relations

Also referred to as financial relations, **investor relations** is a public relations function that seeks to establish desirable relationships with individual investors, investment firms, and financial analysts. It has been described as "a strategic management responsibility that integrates finance, communications, marketing and securities law compliance to enable the most effective two-way communication between a company, the financial community, and other constituencies, which ultimately contributes to a company's securities achieving fair valuation" (NIRI, 2009a). This portion of the chapter discusses the nature of investor relations programs, three responsibilities that investor relations professionals commonly assume, and the place of investors in the hierarchy of stakeholder groups.

Numerous sport organizations are publicly owned. As such, they must consider investor relations one of their critical public relations functions. Such organizations include Nike, Speedway Motorsports, and Churchill Downs. A strategic communication model developed by Argenti, Howell, and Beck (2005) summarized investor relations practice as having two broad objectives (transparency and meeting financial expectations) and three constituents (investors, analysts, and the media). Often nested within an organization's corporate communications department, investor relations practitioners must be accomplished in both public relations and finance. Accordingly, they tend to be the most highly paid public relations professionals (Broom, 2009). Investor relations professionals need knowledge in the following areas (Miller, 1998):

- Government regulations relating to financial publicity
- Policies of the national stock exchanges
- The nature of financial statements
- Strategies and operations of their companies

The NIRI reported that it has more members with professional or educational backgrounds in finance than in communications (NIRI, 2009d). (See the sidebar titled What Is the National Investor Relations Institute? for information about this organization.) Specifically, 49% of its members reported specializations in finance, whereas 46% listed corporate communications or public relations. Because investor relations professionals must practice in compliance with legal requirements, some companies assign these tasks to accountants and attorneys (Conger, 2004). This approach may be a mistake because it seems unlikely that financial or legal experts have the communications background necessary to maximize public relations benefits for sport organizations.

Mogel (2002, pp. 166–168) listed nine responsibilities typically assumed by investor relations professionals:

- Liaison with executive management
- Financial publicity

## What Is the National Investor Relations Institute?

The National Investor Relations Institute (NIRI) is a professional association of investor relations professionals. It is "dedicated to advancing the practice of investor relations and professional competency and stature of its members" (NIRI, 2009a). Founded in 1969, NIRI has an international membership base of more than 4,000 members.

The NIRI offers membership to a variety of constituents, including current investor relations practitioners, consultants, those who provide support services, and others (NIRI, 2009b). The organization provides its members with educational tools such as an annual conference and seminars addressing specialized topics (NIRI, 2009c). It produces a weekly online update, a monthly newsletter, and a membership directory. The NIRI also conducts regular surveys to identify trends and challenges facing investor relations professionals. For more information, see the organization's website at www.niri.org.

- Stockholder correspondence
- Conducting stockholder surveys
- Preparation of other stockholder publications
- Financial and educational advertising
- Planning the annual meeting of stockholders
- Regional meetings of stockholders
- Working with security analysts

Like other aspects of public relations, investor relations professionals may approach their work from either a reactive or a proactive perspective. Those practicing in a reactive mode limit their activities to complying with government laws, responding to inquiries, and managing traditional organizational activities (e.g., annual reports, stockholder meetings). People practicing in a proactive mode will not only meet those requirements but also structure a program and develop plans designed to advocate the sport organization's financial position to investors.

Investor relations professionals indicate that their work provides value to their organizations in four ways (Laskin, 2006). First, practitioners believe that investor relations activity can positively communicate the information about the drivers of stock prices, resulting in a stronger market for their organization's stock (Laskin, 2006). The more information that is available regarding the sport company and its investment potential, the more likely it is that investors will be attracted to its stock. As stated by Conger (2004), "The more you tell, the more you sell" (p. 30). Higher values for a company's stock mean greater potential for that organization to generate new capital. For instance, a company preparing to issue an additional 100,000 shares of stock can generate an additional 33% in new capital if those shares are valued at $20 each ($2 million total) rather than $15 each ($1.5 million total). The second way that investor relations activity provides value, according to practitioners, is that it can contribute to the trading volume and liquidity of stocks, if the organization so desires (Laskin, 2006). Liquidity is important to some investors, because they may seek to buy and sell for short-term gain. A third way that investor relations can benefit an organization is by positively affecting financial analysts' coverage of the company (Laskin, 2006). Both the amount of coverage and its tone are of interest to investor relations professionals, but they are especially concerned with the quality of coverage, noting the importance of accurate and timely information in the marketplace. The fourth

benefit of investor relations practice is relationship building with analysts and investors (Laskin, 2006). As summarized by Laskin (2006) in a statement with which practitioners agreed,

> The rewards of this relationship can be significant. Value gaps tend to diminish because investors believe management can accomplish what it says. Positive events and development earn higher stock gain rewards. A flat or down quarter isn't an automatic sell signal. Investors look for explanations and, when convinced that fundamentals are still strong and growing, are more likely to hold their shares or even increase their positions. (p. 24)

In the wake of the global economic crisis that began in 2008 and the various corporate scandals accompanying it, investors are understandably wary of business leadership. Frequent and open communication may alleviate some of those suspicions. Investor confidence is often based on variables that are not necessarily addressed in corporate financial statements. These intangibles include the company's leadership, the strategies that it is employing, the value of its brand, the state of its reputation, and the way that it is evolving technologically (Kalafut, 2003). Communicating with investors regarding those intangibles may mean overcoming managerial inclinations toward secrecy. But if investors are ultimately the group to which company leadership and boards of directors answer, then such steps are necessary. Atkins (2003) spoke for the investment community by asking, "With 11,000 individual stocks we could buy, why buy yours? Tell us early, often and over and over the three reasons to buy and hold your stock" (p. 62).

## Investor Relations Activities

Investor relations professionals employ a variety of strategies and tactics in pursuing their objectives, but they commonly engage in three activities that warrant description. Most investor relations practitioners are involved in the development of annual reports and the planning and management of annual shareholder meetings. Interactive technologies are also addressed because of their growing importance as communication channels for investor relations.

## Annual Reports

**Annual reports** are one of the most important aspects of investor relations professionals' jobs. In corporate settings, their primary function is to report financial information to shareholders, investment firms, and the financial media. In the United States, the Securities and Exchange Commission (SEC) mandates that certain financial information be disclosed so that investors can make informed decisions. Most annual reports include the following information (U.S. SEC, 2008):

- Opening letter from the chief executive officer
- Financial data
- Results of continuing operations
- Market segment information
- New product plans
- Subsidiary activities
- Research and development activities on future programs

Publicly owned U.S. companies must also disclose additional financial information as mandated by the SEC. The Form 10-K is an annual report that provides readers with detailed business and financial information (U.S. SEC, 2009). Figure 13.2 lists the primary sections mandated for inclusion in an annual 10-K report. For additional information regarding information to be included in each section, see the SEC website: www.sec.gov/about/forms/form10-k.pdf.

In nonprofit settings the Internal Revenue Service (IRS) requires some level of financial reporting, and many organizations produce complete annual reports. Just as businesses may expand annual reports to address other stakeholders such as suppliers and customers, nonprofit organizations may design their annual reports for use as a development tool (Treadwell & Treadwell, 2005).

Generally speaking, annual reports are 8.5 × 11 inches (21 × 28 centimeters) in size and 16 to more than 100 pages in length. They are almost always at least two-color publications, and they are commonly four color, or full color (Miller, 1998). Most companies make their annual reports available on their websites, either as a file to be downloaded or as a savvy web presentation. Because most annual reports are not read in their entirety, graphic elements and pull-out quotes are particularly useful in helping readers quickly digest key messages.

## Annual Shareholder Meetings

Annual shareholder meetings provide stockholders with the opportunity to hear from the corporation's leadership, learn more about the company, and vote on matters ranging from the election of board members to proposals submitted for shareholder consideration. A company's public relations staff is typically involved in planning and executing annual shareholder meetings in five ways (Broom, 2009):

1. They help plan the physical setup for the meeting.
2. They develop handouts and other materials to be presented to attendees.
3. They provide company tours and secure souvenirs or gifts that may be distributed to attendees.
4. They provide meeting-related information to the mass media and accommodate media requests for the meeting.
5. They assist executives in preparing for presentations to shareholders and for questions that they may face during the meeting.

## Interactive Communications

A third set of activities that warrants attention in this section involves the use of interactive communication channels that are becoming increasingly important to investor relations. Conference calls and webcasts are now long-established tools in providing access to events such as annual meetings (Marshall & Heffes, 2004). Investors and analysts who tune into those meetings indicate that they are better able to determine how open management is regarding the company's finances.

Websites are also critical platforms for investor communications. For instance, Speedway Motorsports provides varied information of interest to investors and analysts on its website (www.speedwaymotorsports.com). This information includes annual reports for the last 10 years, current and historic stock quotes, governance documents, SEC filings, and a sign-up option allowing people to receive e-mail notifications regarding new information.

Social media such as Facebook, Twitter, blogs, and message boards are also becoming increasingly influential communication channels for investor relations professionals. A 2009 survey of investors

# Primary Sections of 10-K Report

## Part I

Item 1.   Business
- Item 1A. Risk Factors
- Item 1B. Unresolved Staff Comments

Item 2.   Properties

Item 3.   Legal Proceedings

Item 4.   Submission of Matters to a Vote of Security Holders

## Part II

Item 5.   Market for Registrant's Common Equity, Related Shareholder Matters and Issuer Purchases of Equity Securities

Item 6.   Selected Financial Data

Item 7.   Management's Discussion and Analysis of Financial Condition and Results of Operations
- Item 7A. Quantitative and Qualitative Disclosures About Market Risk

Item 8.   Financial Statements and Supplementary Data

Item 9.   Changes in and Disagreements With Accountants on Accounting and Financial Disclosure
- Item 9A. Controls and Procedures
- Item 9B. Other Information

## Part III

Item 10.   Directors, Executive Officers and Corporate Governance

Item 11.   Executive Compensation

Item 12.   Security Ownership of Certain Beneficial Owners and Management and Related Shareholder Matters

Item 13.   Certain Relationships, Related Transactions and Director Independence

Item 14.   Principal Accountant Fees and Services

## Part IV

Item 15.   Exhibits and Financial Statement Schedules

**Figure 13.2**   The primary sections to be included in an annual 10-K report.

From United States Securities and Exchange Commission 2009.

and financial analysts in the United States and Europe indicated that the influence of social media was limited but growing (Brunswick Group, 2009). Twelve percent of survey respondents indicated that social media were among the three most influential sources of information that they used, but 58% believed that social media would grow in influence.

Beyond the survey's findings pertaining to new media, the study revealed that 83% of investors and analysts indicated that "information direct from companies" was among their top three sources of information (Brunswick Group, 2009). Such a finding underscores the importance of investor relations practice.

## Balancing Stakeholder Interests

Managers of publicly owned sport companies are clearly concerned with providing returns to their investors and enhancing the value of the organization's stock. The sacrifices that they are willing to make in terms of their relationships with other stakeholder groups may depend on the extent to which they are solely concerned with providing value to investors. Smith (2003) contrasted two basic approaches to this issue. The first is the **shareholder approach**, in which the primary responsibility is to investors. The second is the **stakeholder approach**, in which managers attempt to balance the interests of investors with other constituents such as employees, customers, and the local community: "The fundamental distinction is that the stakeholder theory demands that interests of *all* stakeholders be considered *even if reduces company profitability*" (p. 86).

Smith (2003) offers three recommendations for managers regarding this conflict. The first is to re-move the phrase *maximizing shareholder value* from communications because it implies a willingness to do anything, even violate ethical and legal boundaries, to make a profit. The second is that company executives can operate with their board's blessing from either perspective because the shareholder approach does not call on managers to ignore any concern but profits and the stakeholder approach does not mandate apathy toward investors. The third recommendation is that executives should clearly state in organizational communications which philosophy they have adopted. Whether constituents approve of the choice or not, they will benefit from knowing which approach is taken. The likely reality is that most organizations are not purely in one camp or another; their philosophies are somewhat mixed in that they serve the interests of both shareholders and stakeholders at least to some extent. Therefore, it may be most helpful to view the shareholder–stakeholder dichotomy as a continuum that has few organizations stationed on either extreme.

## SUMMARY

This chapter addressed two forms of internal public relations—employee relations and investor relations. Employee relations, or employee communications, relates to efforts of managers to foster desirable relationships with employees. When strong employee relationships are present, the sport organization is likely to enjoy numerous benefits, including greater employee satisfaction and productivity. Vertical communication tactics such as newsletters are common employee relations tools, but the importance of frequent, open communication between employees and direct supervisors is critical. Employee relations within sport is unique because of the prestige that employees affiliated with a sport organization may enjoy, the prevalence of volunteers as key constituents for many sport organizations, and the high-profile nature of labor relations in professional sport. As in other sectors, however, public relations professionals must be attentive to the notion of organizational culture because it significantly influences overall public relations effectiveness. Publicly owned sport organizations establish investor relations programs to offer transparency and support positive financial outcomes. Although investor relations is a diverse practice, virtually all practitioners are involved in the production of annual reports, the staging of annual shareholder meetings, and the use of web-based technologies to facilitate management–investor communications. Senior managers deal with investors from one of two basic orientations—the shareholder approach, in which investor returns are considered an overriding priority, and the stakeholder approach, in which the interests of investors are balanced with the interests of other stakeholders.

1. Most college campuses have a recreation and fitness center. Visit yours and inquire whether it produces an employee newsletter. If it does, secure a copy and evaluate it using the concepts presented in this chapter. Does it simply convey information, or is it designed to produce reader feedback? How often is it published? How is it distributed? Does the newsletter include a transparent attempt by management to spin negative news? Overall, does it seem to address topics of interest to employees?

2. Assuming that your class has guest speakers from time to time, ask one or more of them to describe their sport organization's culture. Does it seem to be more authoritarian than participative? Have measures been taken to support women and minorities within the organization? If so, are those steps relatively basic (e.g., discrimination policies) or more advanced (e.g., mentoring programs)?

3. Visit the website of a publicly owned sport organization and search to see whether its most recent annual report is available for downloading. If so, download it and evaluate it based on the information presented in this chapter. Besides the mandated financial disclosure data, does it take steps to communicate key messages in an understandable manner? Does the report address any of the intangibles that might be of interest to investors? Based on the information provided, how do you evaluate the investment potential of the organization?

4. Evaluate the annual report from activity 3 to ascertain the basic philosophy of the organization's senior management. Are phrases present that would indicate a shareholder approach (e.g., "maximizing shareholder value")? Does any material provide evidence of a stakeholder approach? What is your overall evaluation of the philosophy being communicated?

# Communicating With External Publics

**After reading this chapter, students should be able to**

- describe the major components of customer relationship management (CRM);
- specify ways that customer satisfaction contributes to organizational success;
- outline the contributions that public relations can make to customer relations;
- articulate the relationship among customer service, customer satisfaction, customer loyalty, and customer retention;
- explain the role that public relations plays in building and maintaining donor relationships; and
- describe how public relations contributes to the development and quality of political relationships.

**Key terms discussed in this chapter include**

- customer relationship management (CRM);
- member relationship management (MRM);
- customer equity;
- recency, frequency, and monetary (RFM) analysis;

- customer loyalty;
- consumer-generated media (CGM);
- relationship fund-raising;
- public affairs; and
- lobbying.

**Previous chapters have** discussed the role of public relations in fostering relationships with the media and the community as well as with internal publics such as employees and investors. Although these publics receive much attention, other external publics must be attended to as well. The consumer public is one group that is beginning to receive more attention as a target for public relations efforts that extend beyond traditional marketing activities. As sport organizations have become increasingly aware of the long-term value of customers, they have increased their focus on building lasting relationships. This trend is occurring in all progressive sport organizations, from baseball teams to sporting goods stores to fitness clubs. Developing a loyal consumer base makes good business sense, and public relations efforts can help produce loyalty. Similarly, donors are an increasingly important public for many sport organizations such as high school and college athletics programs and nonprofit operations such as the YMCA. Public relations efforts directed at these publics also focus on loyalty and have the goal of building devoted and consistent support. Another public that can be influential in the sport world includes government agencies and other regulatory and political groups. A different type of public relations approach is taken with this public because the goal may be less oriented toward revenue generation and more toward gaining influence and support.

This chapter addresses the public relations strategies used to build relationships with an organization's customers and members as well as donor publics. The chapter also looks at associations with government and other political or governing agencies that can influence the operation of sport organizations.

# Customer Relations

The four Ps of marketing—product, price, place, and promotion—are the fundamental tools that marketers use in trying to meet consumer needs and produce an exchange of value between consumer and organization. The relationship between marketing and public relations often centers on the promotional mix—advertising, publicity, personal selling, and sales promotion. These communication-oriented marketing functions, particularly publicity, are typically connected to public relations efforts. Most of the discussion about consumer relationships is found in marketing literature; two large handbooks of public relations devote fewer than 25 of more than 1,500 pages directly to consumer and customer topics (Lesly, 1998; Heath, 2001). Yet public relations plays an increasingly important role in the development of relationships with consumers as sport organizations become more attentive to the value of long-term loyalty.

Customers are referred to in many different ways. Timm (2001) noted that terms such as *clients, members, patrons, associates, guests, buyers, viewers,* and *subscribers* are some of the ways that organizations refer to people with whom they engage in transactions. A single sport organization may often use several of these terms to refer to specific target groups. In recent years many spectator sport operations have moved toward the Disney concept of considering visitors to be guests. Regardless of terminology, the success of any revenue-driven sport organization is determined by how well it can relate to these groups. Normal marketing functions serve as the fundamental connection between producer and consumer. Manipulation of the product, price, place, and promotion is used to elicit consumer action. Each marketing tool has an important role in the effort to influence consumer behavior, and sport marketers have a large arsenal of tactics to employ as they direct the use of these marketing tools. For example, athletic shoes come in a variety of styles and colors. YMCA memberships and season-ticket packages are tailored to individual circumstances. Golf clubs and tennis rackets are available in a wide price range. New fitness club sites match population expansion in a community. Bobblehead dolls, stuffed toys, and fireworks are used to attract fans to the ballpark. Advertisements take myriad forms using numerous distribution platforms. Although some of these marketing efforts may have an enduring effect on consumers, others have a transient effect or none at all. The relationships fostered through many of these marketing activities are transitory, and the temporal quality of many consumer relationships should be a concern for any sport organization. A buyer-beware mentality does little to enhance connections to consumers and is impractical in today's competitive marketplace. Given that the focus of public relations is building and nurturing relationships, it must certainly play a role in managing relationships with customers.

## Customer Relationship Management

In recent years sport organizations have become much more attentive to establishing enduring and personalized relationships. A variety of approaches have been developed to address this added attention to the consumer, from **customer relationship management** (**CRM**) and customer equity management to more emphasis on consumer satisfaction and service management. Swift (2001) defined CRM as the effort to understand and influence customer behavior in order to improve customer acquisition, retention, loyalty, and profitability. Smith went on to describe CRM as the process of

1. finding customers,
2. getting to know them,
3. communicating with them,
4. ensuring their satisfaction, and
5. retaining them.

CRM uses extensive customer information to strengthen an operation's ability to serve its customers. If the only contact with the consumer is transactional, no real relationship exists. If the only interaction with a ticket purchaser is at the ticket booth, the relationship has little substance. CRM engenders two-way communication and relies on the kind of detailed information about customer history, transactions, and communications that technological advances now allow.

Databases can be developed that contain comprehensive records of individual consumer profiles and behaviors. For example, sport organizations can now go well beyond collecting routine demographic information about their clientele. Computerized exercise equipment logs types of activity and frequency of use. Membership cards and access cards can be scanned to record times and days that patrons use facilities. A variety of organizations use loyalty cards to track consumption behavior; professional teams use such cards to monitor the behavior of fans as they purchase tickets, concessions, and merchandise. Retailers also use loyalty cards to track consumption patterns of their customers. These tools can be used to build a consumer data bank. Such information is valuable for a variety of marketing purposes and can serve as the basis for building consumer relationships. Rubio and Laughlin (2002) warned, however, that data should be collected with a plan for how it will be used. If the data have no immediate purpose, they may not be fresh when accessed. The data should be updated systematically to ensure that the information retains its usefulness. Another criticism of some CRM databases is that

they contain only transactional information (e.g., what was purchased, how much was spent, how it was paid for). Rubio and Laughlin (2002) addressed the need for not only the hard data often available within the organization's own records such as basic demographic information (e.g., age, gender, income, address) and transactional activity but also soft data about attitudes, values, and preferences. Raab (2010) went even further in suggesting that traditional outbound marketing driven by this data is becoming outdated. Technology has given consumers powerful new tools that allow them to screen marketing messages and gather information from external sources that they may find more trustworthy (e.g., Facebook, blogs, and so on). He suggested that organizations need to collect information from social media content and web interactions and update databases in near real time so that marketing execution can take place with the requisite speed.

Customer relationship management may result in the blurring of traditional marketing and public relations roles because establishing relationships requires more than the traditional marketing efforts. Although much of the information from a well-designed CRM program will be used in direct marketing (e.g., product offerings and modifications, advertising and pricing strategies), it can also be the basis for public relations communication that can play a role in both the acquisition and retention of customers. For example, many professional baseball teams use winter caravans to keep in touch with fans. In many cases these caravans are designed to build relationships rather than sell tickets. The Minnesota Twins' winter caravan travels to communities up to 400 miles (650 km) from Minneapolis–St. Paul to visit people who are hardly major ticket purchasers. In many cases these markets are composed primarily of media consumers who are often important to financial success. Such activities may support higher media rights fees or add value to sponsorship deals. Open houses, draft parties, preseason "fanfests," and grand openings can also be used to nurture relationships with consumers. Some direct marketing usually occurs during such events, but it is often secondary to the chance to connect with clientele. Such events provide a chance to listen and engage in dialogue, an activity that is frequently overlooked when only transactional relationships exist. In addition, important information can be collected and prospects can be identified. Such activities and events can be the basis for subsequent direct marketing.

## Member Relationship Management

One type of customer designation relevant to many sport organizations is members. Fitness clubs, tennis facilities, YMCAs, and country clubs are just of few of the sport-related organizations that use membership as a significant source of revenue. **Member relationship management** (MRM) is one phrase used to describe efforts to increase member satisfaction and loyalty. Because clubs operate in a competitive environment and face tight economic conditions, member retention is essential. The cost of acquiring a new member is typically five times greater than that of retaining a current member. The sidebar titled Impeccable Service: It Is the Goal Because It Is the Expectation, written by Chris Branvold, describes some of the ways a private golf club retains members. Interaction with members should occur regularly rather than sporadically to be most effective and should solicit feedback about problems and difficulties. A consistent, systematic communication process conditions members to becoming part of the continual evaluation that is geared toward meeting and exceeding member expectations (Gulko, 2003). Nearly all clubs have a web presence that provides one important communication channel, and many organizations now extend that electronic presence to Facebook, Twitter, and other social media. Certainly the nature of the membership is an important consideration in selecting communication channels. Text messaging an over-65 water aerobics classes about upcoming programs may produce disappointing results.

## Customer Equity

Many of the strategies designed to build enduring relationships with customers are based on the idea that the customer is a financial asset. Blattberg, Getz, and Thomas (2001) used the concept of **customer equity** to address the value of a customer relationship over its life cycle, which runs from prospect to early buyer to core customer to defector. Customer equity management involves measuring both the costs of and revenue produced by the activities used to acquire and retain customers as well as efforts to add value to the relationship. For example, as relationships are established with certain customers, the goal is to expand and solidify that relationship by moving them into the core customer category. Core customers are characterized by larger and more repetitive purchase behaviors (e.g., multiple season-ticket holders for several years). Wyner (1996) re-

ferred to these consumers as high-value customers and suggested that they should command more resources because they produce a greater return. The value to the team of the long-term season-ticket holder clearly warrants different consideration from that offered to the occasional consumer who attends a few games a season. Patrons who shop at a sporting goods store several times a month or regularly make sizable purchases should receive treatment that recognizes their loyalty. Organizations must be aware of the lifetime value of these customers and allocate resources accordingly. During the 2011 management–labor impasse in professional football, NFL Commissioner Roger Goodell conducted a series of conference calls with season-ticket holders for many of the franchises. He fielded questions and presented the position of the league in the labor negotiations (Associated Press, 2011a). This action was clearly a public relations strategy focused on high-value customers.

From a strategic standpoint, the Value Equity in Spectator Sports Scale (VESSS) developed by Sweeney (2008) and summarized in figure 14.1 is an exceptionally thorough effort at addressing the factors that drive customer equity. Using a framework of value equity, brand equity, and retention equity as the foundation (Rust, Zeithaml, & Lemon, 2000), Sweeney isolated a variety of elements within each of these categories as key factors contributing to customer equity. Many of these factors are at least partially influenced by both strategic and tactical public relations activities because organizations attempt not only to provide products and services that customers value but also to create strong brand identity and retention strategies that drive customer equity.

Several mechanisms are used to measure customer value. **Recency, frequency, and monetary (RFM) analysis** is one such tool. Data must be collected about the frequency and recency of customer transactions as well as the size of those transactions. These data, often a part of a CRM database, can be of use in segmenting customers based on behavior, volume, and profitability, and ultimately can serve as the supporting rationale for marketing and public relations decisions (Blattberg, Getz, & Thomas, 2001; Weinstein, 2002).

Customer equity management allows organizations to make reasoned decisions about how to apportion resources across the customer life cycle because it offers an idea of the value that each customer brings to the organization. Customer equity management helps answer questions about where resources should be distributed in prospecting for clientele, serving customers at various levels of

# Impeccable Service: It Is the Goal Because It Is the Expectation

## Chris Branvold

Photo courtesy of Chris Branvold.

Sewickley Heights Golf Club, founded in 1961, is a private golf club in western Pennsylvania. It has a membership of between 300 and 400 members. The club is golf only, but it does have a restaurant in the top floor of the clubhouse. The club has 18 holes, a full driving range and practice area, and is a mid- to high-end club as characterized by course quality and amenities offered.

What sets the private golf club sector apart from most other golf course operations is the service that members expect. At a private club all employees should be focused on providing members and their guests an experience that is memorable and unparalleled. That goal should extend to all aspects of the experience at the club from the golf itself to any of the amenities such as the driving range, pro shop, and restaurant.

We expect our staff to know our members by name, so one of the first tasks for new employees is to learn several hundred names. But knowing names is only where the expectations begin. In the private club environment expectations extend to knowing the members' quirks and their expectations every time they step on the property. Many expect us to have everything that they need to play in their cart and waiting for them, which means that clubs are ready, shoes are out and waiting, and a certain golf ball that they play has already been charged to the account and is in their bag. Obviously, an employee cannot learn these things in a day, a week, or a month. Many times employees need years to learn all the little things that raise service to its highest level. The expectations do not stop in the clubhouse. The course is expected to be well maintained and lush, whatever the weather. This expectation is one of the hardest to meet, because we have the least control over it. Mother Nature is largely in control of course conditions, but the members' expectations often do not change, regardless of the weather. Managing expectations can save employees from difficult situations. For example, if we alert members to course conditions before they arrive, they can adjust their expectations. Making sure that members know in advance that special events may disrupt their routine will minimize their frustration and staff aggravation. Often members are using the club and its services to entertain guests or clients. The more thoroughly we do our job in serving our member, the more effectively the member can nurture the relationship with his or her guests. This translates into membership loyalty and commitment.

An employee at a private club must nurture the relationship with members but at the same time maintain a certain professional distance. Friendships will inevitably develop over time, but it is extremely important to be unbiased in decision making when it comes to dealing with issues that come up among members. This task can be difficult because decisions will often affect small pockets of members who will not agree with the outcome. Here we need to remember to make decisions for the club as a whole, not just one subgroup of the club such as women, retirees, or social members.

Private club membership is meant to feel exclusive, and members pay a substantial sum of money for the privileges associated with such exclusivity. Members are seeking a certain atmosphere of comfort that is produced when their expectations are met as a matter of routine. This aspect of private club operation requires a great deal of focus on relationships. As soon as a club stops taking care of the members' needs, the club has lost its fundamental value. If employees act with that thought in mind, the operation will move in a direction that is best for the whole organization.

*Chris Branvold is an assistant golf professional at Sewickley Heights Golf Club in Sewickley, Pennsylvania.*

> **As soon as a club stops taking care of the members' needs, the club has lost its fundamental value.**

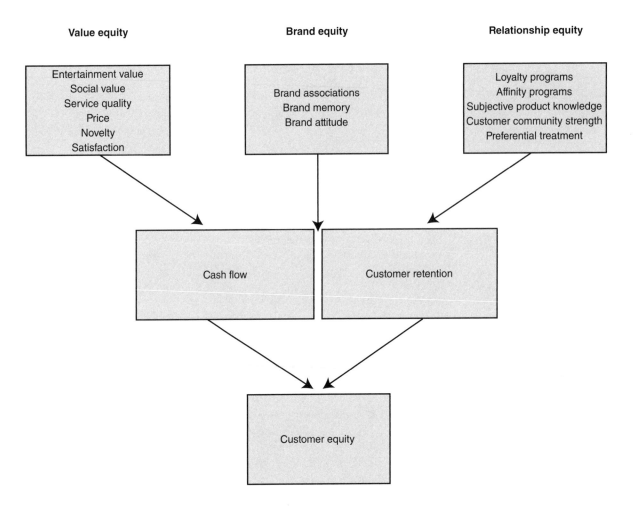

**Figure 14.1** Drivers of customer equity.

consumption, retaining core customers, and reacting to defectors.

## Customer Satisfaction

One of the keys to organizational success is customer satisfaction. It is common knowledge that keeping existing customers is less expensive and more profitable than finding new ones. Customer satisfaction fosters **customer loyalty**, which is reflected in retention rates. Kotler (2000) noted that satisfied customers stay loyal longer, talk favorably about the organization, pay less attention to the competition, are less sensitive to prices, and cost less to serve than new customers.

A key to retention rates is the ability to identify what makes customers happy and what irritates them. Of course, basic customer satisfaction cannot be achieved without a product or service of adequate quality to meet consumer expectations. Meeting consumer needs with an inferior product

is difficult. To have truly loyal customers, an organization must exceed expectations. Timm (2001) identified six areas of opportunity for surpassing consumer expectations and, by extension, six opportunities to build customer relationships. These six areas are value, information, speed, personality, add-ons, and convenience (VISPAC).

Going beyond what the consumer expects in any or all of these areas increases the likelihood of developing loyal customers. Some of these areas are largely within the scope of direct marketing, whereas others are at least partially within the scope of public relations. The ways in which these areas are addressed will influence the consumer's perception of the organization and ultimately shape its reputation.

### Value

Some of Timm's VISPAC opportunities are largely connected to product quality and product service. He defined value as the quality of a product or ser-

Customer satisfaction is a major concern for fitness centers hoping to retain a high percentage of their current members.

vice relative to its price. Although value is, in the final analysis, a personal determination, in some cases it can be measured in more specific terms such as how long a product lasts, or its durability. Many equipment purchases are evaluated on that basis. Most consumers have some sense of how long they expect to wear a pair of golf shoes or use an outdoor basketball. When durability is a priority for the patron, it is only good business to build it into the product and emphasize that attribute in communicating with customers. The golf ball that can withstand the mis-hits of the duffer without falling apart may receive not only repeat consumption but also positive word-of-mouth publicity.

In other cases value is somewhat more subjective, and customers are likely to evaluate their satisfaction based on a more personal set of expectations. When fans spend $100 to attend a professional football exhibition game, the organization must have some idea of what criteria fans will use to evaluate whether they got their money's worth. When customers end their first year as members of a fitness club, retaining their membership will be a function of how well their expectations were met. Their judgments about the value of their experiences will be based on criteria that could include anything from the cleanliness of the facility to the variety of available equipment to the quality of aerobics instruction.

## Add-Ons

Add-ons can enhance customer satisfaction, particularly when the add-on has perceived value. In many cases, these additional benefits are directly associated with public relations efforts to enhance customer relationships. Supplementing the purchase of a tennis racket with a carrying case or a new

fitness club membership with a free fitness assessment can make consumers feel as if their purchase has added value. Satisfaction or quality guarantees are also common add-ons that give the consumer some purchase security as well as instill confidence that the organization stands behind its product.

## Convenience and Speed

Convenience and speed are associated with quality of service. Meeting and exceeding consumer expectations in these areas are particularly important in a culture that is obsessed with immediacy. In some cases these attributes are part of the product or service. For example, personal trainers who come to the client or home exercise equipment are examples of convenience built into the product. Professional teams have made it much more convenient to purchase tickets through multiple distribution options. Technology gives online ticket buyers a virtual view from various locations in the stadium as an added convenience.

Speed of service, delivery, and response to complaints may all influence consumer satisfaction. Anyone who has spent half an hour on the phone trying to reach the right person or even any live person at all can identify with frustration produced by slow service. Long lines at the checkout counter or concession stand will result in annoyed customers. Failure to meet promised delivery dates for tournament T-shirts or deadlines for game programs will cost a supplier future business and damage its reputation.

## Information and Personality

Perhaps the two areas most directly associated with public relations are information and personality. Sport organizations use information in a variety of ways to engage the consumer and add value to their product. Information may be part of a service such as personal instruction on how to use all the computer features on a piece of exercise equipment. It may be a follow-up phone call to see whether the consumer is adjusting well to the new oversized driver. In some cases, information can be delivered in less personal ways through e-mail or even signage. Even the scoreboard can be used as a public relations tool by providing information, such as greetings for groups, birthday and anniversary wishes, candid shots of spectators, and so on, that shows an appreciation for the fans.

Personality is also an opportunity to create satisfied customers, and it provides a clear example of public relations as the responsibility of everyone in the organization. Treating the consumer with courtesy and consideration can make a powerful impression. Many people serve as the "face" of the organization, notably those who make the first direct contact with patrons. Employees such as greeters, ushers, ticket takers, salespeople, front-desk personnel, secretaries, and cashiers are on the public relations frontline. Their influence on consumers should not be undervalued. Being polite, friendly, and sincere conveys the image that most organizations want to transmit to their clientele.

## Evaluation of Customer Satisfaction

One aspect of customer relations that should not be overlooked is measuring customer satisfaction. Regardless of whether this process is viewed as a marketing function or a public relations function, mechanisms must be in place to gauge consumer perceptions on an ongoing basis and apply that feedback throughout the organization. Myers (1999) identified a series of steps that should be taken to develop a meaningful evaluation process. These steps include determining (1) what the assessment objectives are, (2) which customers will be surveyed, (3) what information is needed for assessment, and (4) how that information will be structured. Assessment objectives might address increasing customer retention, improving service, and tracking service quality over time. Sources of information needed to achieve those objectives are current and former customers, competitors' customers, and noncustomers. Selecting the attributes to be measured is perhaps the most important component of this process, and input from customers and employees should be

used in constructing an assessment tool that is both thorough and relevant.

In the effort to assess customer satisfaction, the evaluation framework should start with all the contact points, or touch points, between the customer and the organization. Customers have more contact with the organization beyond the simple act of buying a product or service. They may have contact in a variety of ways from advertising exposure to billing inquiries. All these interactions contribute to customer opinion about the organization ("The Customer is King," 2003). For example, the consumer may interact with a minor league baseball organization on the phone, at the ticket window, at the concession stand, through various facility services and amenities, and on the team website. The organization must then identify the attributes that are most likely to determine satisfaction for each type of interaction. For instance, the concession interaction may be judged on criteria such as price, quality of food, breadth of menu, speed of service, and courtesy of service. Determining the priority of these attributes for the consumer is also important. If consumers are simply asked to evaluate their satisfaction with each of these attributes, the results may not reveal which attributes have the most influence on concession-buying behavior. Dissatisfaction with price may not alter buying behavior, whereas serving a hot dog that tastes like an old army boot may change consumption patterns a great deal. Nicholls, Gilbert, and Roslow (1998) developed a consumer satisfaction survey instrument that identified some common factors that might apply to most organizations in measuring customer satisfaction (see table 14.1). The survey addressed those items in the context of both personal service satisfaction and

### Table 14.1 Basic Customer Satisfaction Factors

| | |
|---|---|
| Courteous | Prompt help |
| Timely service | Reasonable service costs |
| Competent employees | Easy to get help |
| Fair treatment | Easy access to service |
| Helpful personnel | Convenient operating hours |
| Organization backs up its promises | Neat and clean |
| Organization delivers what it promises | Security within the organization |
| Quality of treatment received | Security outside the organization |
| Employees listen | Overall product and service quality |

Adapted from Nicholls, Gilbert, and Roslow 1998.

satisfaction with the setting. This aspect is especially relevant for many sport organizations because the setting is an important component of the customer's overall experience. The 18-factor survey would at least be a good starting point for the assessment of customer satisfaction.

Yoshida and James (2010) also addressed the concept of satisfaction across core product (game) and service quality satisfaction in an attempt to distinguish between the influence of game satisfaction and service satisfaction on subsequent behavior. One interesting finding in this study was that game satisfaction was reported to have an influence on behavioral intentions in both the United States and Japan but that the relationship between service quality satisfaction and behavioral intentions was significant only in Japan.

Measuring customer satisfaction can produce important benefits for any sport organization, but measurements should be tailored to specific organizational circumstances. Beyond obvious information about the likes and dislikes of the consumer, this process provides regular two-way communication between the organization and its patrons, and it can serve as the mechanism for nurturing, maintaining, and even repairing relationships with customers.

# Customer Service and Support

One of the more important contributions of public relations to customer relationships is in the area of service and support. Swift (2001) noted that service is an important differentiator among competitors, adds value to the product, and enhances customer satisfaction. The fundamentals of service are interacting with customers courteously, professionally, and promptly and listening to what they have to say. The consumer should receive this treatment consistently throughout the entire organization. The efforts of a polite customer service representative who helps a patron exchange tickets from one game to another will be undermined when the business office is rude in dealing with that patron's complaint about being double charged for the tickets.

The value of service quality is difficult to measure, but it certainly makes an important contribution to customer satisfaction. Quality customer service is not without cost, but some of the basics of customer service (e.g., courtesy, willingness to listen) can be provided without a large investment. A cost is involved in hiring enough qualified people to provide product support and to ensure a prompt and thorough response to customers, and these costs must obviously be balanced against the value that they provide.

In many cases, the quality of service aspect of the customer relationship focuses on customer problems and complaints. Timm (2001) put problems into three categories: value turnoffs, system turnoffs, and people turnoffs. Value turnoffs involve products or services that fail to meet the consumer's quality expectations. Without product improvements or price manipulation, value turnoffs may be difficult to resolve.

A much clearer public relations component is evident in the response to system turnoffs and people turnoffs. Systems such as facilities, employees, record keeping, sales and return policies, and communications are frequent sources of customer dissatisfaction. The extent to which these turnoffs can be addressed varies a great deal. Basch (2002) saw customer complaints as one of the best opportunities to reinforce the consumer relationship. Solving a problem can win over customers and may enhance the likelihood of a continued affiliation. And just as dissatisfied customers will spread the word of their discontent at a rapid rate, patrons whose problems were solved will become advocates for the competence and responsiveness of the organization. Word-of-mouth support is powerful because it has a credibility that organization-initiated messages do not. Blackshaw (2008) identified six credibility drivers: trust, authenticity (sincerity), transparency, listening, responsiveness, and affirmation (general support). In a world of **consumer-generated media (CGM)**, the ability of angry customers to reach large numbers of people quickly has changed how organizations must approach customer service and monitor customer satisfaction. Problems and incidents that are chronicled in somebody's blog or documented on YouTube can create public relations troubles that can persist and spread rapidly. There are numerous examples of organizational spokespersons or individual athletes making statements that do little to help their cause because they seem insincere and orchestrated. Tiger Woods' first "press conference" addressing his marital infidelity was criticized by many as being stiff and impersonal and probably did little to smooth over his situation.

# Customer Loyalty and Retention

Customer satisfaction ideally creates loyal consumers who continue to patronize the business. Organizations should constantly question what they are doing to merit consumer loyalty. Developing and keeping loyal customers is an increasingly challenging pursuit. McKenna (2002) contended that the ability to maintain loyalty is eroding in the face of technological advances and product innovation that have expanded consumer options. Although the array of choices is apparent in the shoe inventory displayed in a large sporting goods store, e-commerce now allows people to "shop the world" from home, which increases consumer choice exponentially. This array of choices extends to the sport spectator as well. Although a fan might once have attended games of a small-college football team, he or she might find it difficult to pass up multiple top-notch college games viewed from the comfort of the living room. Cable, satellite, and subscription services as well as the Internet provide access to so many games that loyalty in the form of live attendance may diminish. NFL attendance dropped slightly in both 2008 and 2009, and some speculate that the drop is at least partially attributable to improvements in the at-home experience offered by big-screen HD TV and expanded access to more games and information (Leahy, 2010). Fans may contend that they are still loyal to a particular team, but such loyalty has less practical effect if it is no longer attached to attendance-related consumption.

Companies must earn the loyalty of their consumers and will retain them in a competitive market only if they can meet the customer's expectations better than their competitors can. Loyalty comes in several forms, some of which have little to do with consumer allegiance or devotion. They include the following (SaferPak, 2004):

- Monopoly loyalty—No options are available.
- Convenience loyalty—Switching is too inconvenient.
- Habitual loyalty—The routine is comfortable.
- Incentives loyalty—Rewards accompany continued involvement.
- Committed loyalty—The best product or service earns devoted consumers.

Monopoly loyalty is associated with limited consumer choice. Professional sport franchises certainly enjoy this type of loyalty because in a given market few options are available to those who want to see a professional game in person. Loyalty can be simply a product of convenience or habit. The athletics department that goes back to the same uniform supplier year after year to avoid the hassle of looking for a new supplier demonstrates convenience loyalty. Habitual loyalty is a common form of repeat business that, in most cases, reflects

consumption of expedience. A sporting goods store near home or work is likely to receive more business because it is the most convenient option. Many sport operations use incentives loyalty by encouraging repeat consumption through some form of reward. Loyalty cards that record consumption are becoming much more common within the sport industry, from sporting goods stores (e.g., Dick's ScoreCard Rewards Program) to professional teams. Committed loyalty reflects consumers' belief that they are buying the best product or service. This type of commitment resembles what Fullerton (2003) described as affective commitment, which can be closely associated with friendship, rapport, and trust. This type of emotional commitment contrasts with continuance commitment, which is predicated on dependence, lack of choice, and cost of switching. Consumer loyalty may be influenced by both types of commitment, but affective commitment tends to be more effective at producing the kind of dedication that manifests itself in consumers who may accept higher prices, travel farther, resist switching, and more readily recommend the product or service to others.

McAlexander, Kim, and Roberts (2003) contended that the concept of satisfaction leading to loyalty is too simplistic, noting that several studies suggested that overall satisfaction may have little influence on future purchase intentions. They viewed the creation of loyalty as an evolutionary process driven by cumulative experiences that result in trust and commitment. Their research conducted in a casino setting on brand communities (defined as the cumulative connections with the product, other consumers, and the organization) as an important influence on loyalty has great relevance for sport organizations. Rosenbaum, Ostrom, and Kuntze (2005) suggested that communal loyalty programs, organizationally sponsored loyalty programs that provide members a sense of community and belonging, may be effective for certain organizations. (An example is the HOGs, the Harley-Davidson owners group). Such communal groups need to provide a sense of belonging, offer a feeling of influence, meet some need (e.g., status), and create an emotional bond. Because much sport consumption involves a social component with strong emotional connection, sport organizations would be well served to nurture this aspect of consumption. A familiar sport example is tailgating—an experience that for some is as important as the event itself. Creating or facilitating these types of social experiences and connections should be built into the product offerings of many sport operations. Social networking technology has produced additional opportunities for sport operations to embrace this aspect of satisfaction. Digital communities can be enabled by sport organizations through their own websites (sort of a virtual booster club) or supported when constructed outside the organization's direct control. Some examples include FitLink.com, GolfLink.com, InfieldParking.com (for NASCAR fans), and AnglingMasters.com, which touts itself as the world's largest fishing community.

In *The Loyalty Effect* (1996), Reichheld reported that the typical company experiences annual defection rates ranging from 10 to 30%. Even small improvements in preventing defection can have a profound effect on profitability. Loyal customers tend to increase spending over time and often require less service. They also share their satisfaction with others and become less sensitive to price. Effective customer retention also helps control customer acquisition costs. When a large proportion of existing ticket holders renew or expand their ticket packages, fewer resources need to be allocated to recruiting new customers. A few fortunate franchises have even been able to capitalize on excess demand by creating waiting lists to bring prospective customers into closer connection with the organization.

# Sponsor Relationship Management

One of the most important exchange relationships for many sport organizations is the relationship with sponsors. These associations provide sport organizations and events with important financial resources and often other goods and services as well. Professional teams, college athletics programs, sport governing bodies such as the National Collegiate Athletic Association (NCAA), and local youth sport leagues as well as events of all types such as golf and tennis tournaments, bowl games, and sport camps use sponsors as a vital revenue source. Although an element of philanthropy may be motivating some sponsors, most substantive sponsorship arrangements are primarily business deals. Sponsors enter into such agreements expecting to get a return on their investment and are likely to have many options as they look to maximize that return.

Sponsor relationships have many of the same characteristics as customer relationships. The topics of customer equity, satisfaction, service, and retention that were discussed in the previous sections apply to sponsors just as they do to other customers. Teams and athletics programs must develop the same understanding of the companies that they target as sponsors as they have of the individuals whom they target when selling season tickets. Sport organizations must customize their efforts in building and maintaining their affiliations with sponsors. Collecting data about sponsors is essential to building constructive, lasting relationships. Knowing when a company makes sponsorship decisions, what their sponsorship history is, who makes the decisions, what the sponsorship budget is, and what benefits they are looking for in a sponsorship will be invaluable in tailoring a sponsorship proposal and communicating it to the right people in the right way. A number of important dimensions such as these are discussed in the sidebar titled Managing Sponsor Relations.

# Donor Relations

Donors are another public that requires special relationship attention. The donor public has become an increasingly important asset to many sport organizations in recent years. Stier and Schneider (1999) noted that more than ever, sport administrators are expected to generate additional resources through development and fund-raising activities. The fund-raising environment is highly competitive, because donors have many opportunities for giving. A good cause is simply not sufficient to ensure sustained support. College and high school athletics programs as well as nonprofit sport and recreation organizations count on donors to provide funds for many of their operational needs. The role of public relations as a part of the fund-raising process has evolved as well. Annual campaigns require a more relationship-oriented approach than special campaigns do, which means that public relations is likely to play an even more important role today than when most fund-raising was driven by special projects. In some respects donors are much like customers, and development officers may use some traditional marketing techniques to attract donors. This section is not intended to be a blueprint for raising funds; rather, it is designed to identify the role of public relations in building lasting relationships with donors.

## Developing Donor Relationships

Successful fund-raisers have become more adept at recognizing donor motivations and meeting donor

# Managing Sponsor Relations

Sponsorship is ubiquitous in sport these days. Corporate connections are attached to virtually every event and facility. In a highly competitive environment for sponsorship dollars, sport operations must be conscientious in nurturing their relationships with sponsors. The mind-set has become one of developing corporate partnerships rather than mere transactional connections. Four important elements in building and sustaining successful sponsor relationships include sponsor equity, service and support, sponsor satisfaction, and sponsor loyalty and retention.

## Sponsor Equity

Most sport organizations have a tiered system of sponsorship opportunities so that they can offer a variety of sponsorships and levels of commitment. Few firms can afford the financial commitment required to be a title sponsor for a major event or to purchase the naming rights to a major sport facility. Tiered sponsorship broadens the prospect base and provides opportunity for a much wider range of corporate involvement. The commitment required for a major professional sport team sponsorship may range from a few thousand dollars to several million dollars. Although every sponsor is important, it is only logical that certain sponsors will receive extra attention based on the commitment that they have made. Replacing a small-scale sponsor may be inconvenient, but replacing a multimillion-dollar sponsor can take years. Sponsor equity involves prioritizing relationship efforts based on the size and length of sponsorship commitment and is a way of recognizing the differential value of an organization's sponsors.

## Service and Support

Servicing and supporting sponsorship partners will affect the organization's ability to satisfy and retain them. In many respects, basic customer service principles apply to sponsors just as they do in more traditional customer relationships. Perhaps the most important mechanism for sponsor support is an effective communications system. Clear communications can minimize many of the problems that can hinder the organization's relationship with sponsors. A checklist of characteristics that reflect quality service might include the following:

- Timely
- Courteous
- Responsive
- Helpful
- Informative
- Flexible
- Communicative
- Approachable
- Convenient

Helping sponsors solve their problems and achieve their sponsorship objectives will lead to sponsors that want to maintain the relationship.

## Sponsor Satisfaction

Sponsor satisfaction is predicated on how well sponsor needs and expectations are met. Organizations that solicit sponsors need to know what benefits are being sought and how the sport organization might best accommodate sponsor interests. Sport organizations can accomplish this by matching the list of sponsor needs with a list of organizational deliverables. The list of sponsor needs should be developed based on thorough research of prospective sponsors that includes direct interaction so that sponsorship proposals can be constructed specifically for particular clients. Developing a list of deliverables involves conducting a complete assessment of assets that might be of interest to sponsors. The following lists illustrate what sponsors might be looking for and what sport organizations might have to offer.

### Sponsor Needs

| | | |
|---|---|---|
| Exposure, visibility | Increased store traffic | Employee recognition |
| Product distribution and trials | Community involvement | Competitive advantage |
| | Image enhancement | Specialized market reach |
| Goodwill | Corporate entertainment and hospitality | Link to charity |
| Media attention | | Cross-promotion opportunities |
| Increased sales | Corporate networking | |

**Sport Organization Assets**

| | | |
|---|---|---|
| Tickets | Sponsor exclusivity | Sport personalities |
| Signage space | Appealing market segments | Other sponsor partners |
| Media coverage | Advertising space | Organizational prestige |
| Naming rights | Special events | Charity affiliations |
| Logo usage | Mailing lists | Website links and exposure |
| Suites and luxury boxes | | |

A sponsorship relationship is more likely to be formed and sustained when substantial congruity is found between sponsor needs and organizational assets. Satisfaction can be reinforced with postevent or postseason reports that demonstrate how sponsor needs have been met.

## Sponsor Loyalty and Retention

One measure of the quality of the relationship with sponsors is their willingness to continue the relationship. For many sport organizations, sponsorship retention is the final stage of a perpetual process depicted in figure 14.2. Quality service and support produce satisfied, loyal sponsors that are easier to retain and move to higher levels of commitment. This approach is much more cost effective than continually prospecting for new sponsors to replace those who are dissatisfied.

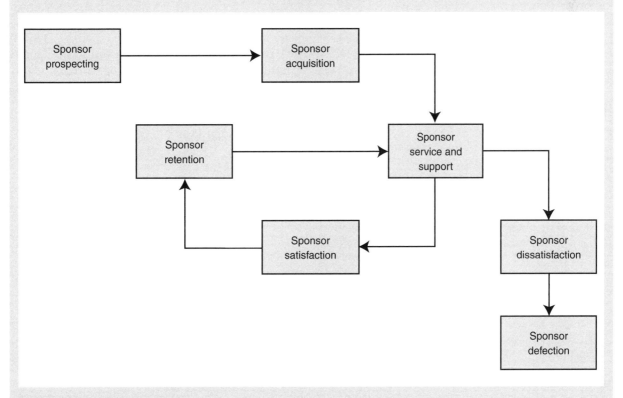

**Figure 14.2**  Overview of the sponsor relations process.

Adapted, by permission, from D. Sweeney, 2008, *An integrated model of value equity in spectator sports: conceptual framework and empirical results.* Doctoral dissertation (Gainesville, FL: Florida State University).

needs. The process of identifying prospects and converting them into advocates requires patience and a combination of effective marketing and relationship-building strategies. Burnett (1992) uses the phrase *relationship fund-raising* to describe the process of developing the special relationship between a cause and its supporters rather than focusing simply on raising money. For nonprofit organizations such as the YMCA, now known as just the Y as it rebrands itself (Strom, 2010), supporters' attachment may be direct membership in the organization or the belief that the Y makes a worthy social contribution. Athletics programs often enjoy a special relationship with their donors because of the passion and enthusiasm of the donors for the program. Alumni and fans often exhibit a loyalty and dedication that can be extremely beneficial in fund-raising efforts.

Attention must be given to what prompts donors to maintain and increase their support as well as what might inhibit an increase in donor involvement. Understanding donor motivation is just as important to successful fund-raising as understanding consumer needs is to successful marketing. And, as with consumers, the goal is loyal contributors. In ongoing fund-raising efforts, the aim is to retain donors and move them to increased levels of contribution. One key difference in this relationship, however, is that although donors provide money, goods, or services, what they get in return is usually much less tangible. Weir and Hibbert (2000) sum-

marized donor motives, which include self-esteem, recognition, habit, peer pressure, concern, guilt, and being asked. They reported that even when contributions are driven primarily by the desire to help, an egotistic dimension is usually present as well. These motives can certainly be applied to those who contribute to sport organizations. Verner, Hecht, and Fansler (1998) studied the motivation of donors to athletics programs and isolated several key influencers of donor behavior. Table 14.2 lists those key motives and offers examples of related incentives.

Addressing these factors is important to accommodating the needs of donors, and public relations can be an important part of the overall fund-raising effort. Because of the intermittent nature of direct interaction between fund-raisers and donors, public relations can assist in developing donor relationships by sustaining the lines of communication. A variety of tactics are employed to keep donors informed about organizational activities. Public relations personnel are well suited for this informational role and can use such tools as newsletters, mailings, personal contacts, thank-you notes and acknowledgments, and event invitations to establish and maintain communication continuity (Weir & Hibbert, 2000). Many college athletics departments employ newsletters and magazines to keep donors informed of activities and events, and they may include material that makes the recipients feel as if they are getting inside information. Several kinds

## Table 14.2 Types of Donor Motives

| Motivational factor | Example |
| --- | --- |
| Participation in secondary events | Attending special donor receptions and luncheons |
| Public recognition | Plaques, lapel pins, or publication acknowledgment |
| Donation of time and energy | Volunteering at department-sponsored events |
| Inside information | Access to special information on recruiting |
| Priority treatment | Access to special seating or parking |
| Philanthropy | Providing money for educational opportunities for athletes |
| Collaboration | Joining others to make a significant purchase |
| Creation | Contributing to a new facility |
| Change | Contributing to upgrades and improvements in the athletics program |
| Curiosity | Attending a pregame strategy session |
| Power | Influencing key athletics department decisions |

Adapted from Verner, Hecht, and Fansler 1998.

**Hall of Fame induction events provide important occasions for sport organizations to host donors.**

AP Photo/Mike Groll

of events may also be employed to strengthen relationships with donors. These events go beyond direct solicitations and other fund-raising activities and are often designed to preserve the association with donors. Alumni reunions during homecoming, meet the team parties, Hall of Fame induction dinners, and so on may involve no direct fund-raising solicitation at all; they are simply opportunities to help donors feel more connected to the program.

## Assessing Donor Satisfaction and Defection

Assessing donor satisfaction is vital to sustaining relationships. Sargeant (2001) identified three factors that should be considered in efforts to retain donors. One factor is responsiveness, the personal attention that the donor receives in response to specific needs and questions. A second factor is feedback quality, the information that donors receive about the way that their money was used and the confidence ex-

pressed that it was used appropriately. The third factor is effectiveness, which is associated with donor perceptions about how well the organization uses donations. For athletics, many donors would want to see tangible results of their contributions such as facility improvements or even on-field success. Organizations must meet or exceed the expectations of their supporters and make them feel important to organizational progress.

Determining the barriers to donor retention is crucial to reducing donor defection rates. Sargeant (2001) reported that only one in five donors defects because of a change in financial circumstances. Donors discontinue their support for many other reasons, such as the following:

1. Other more deserving causes

2. Support provided in other ways

3. Not reminded to give again

4. Failure to acknowledge previous support

5. Asking for inappropriate amounts

6. Failure to accommodate wishes

7. Failure to inform how money was used

8. Perception that support is no longer needed

9. Poor quality of service or communication

Viable responses can be made to many of these retention barriers, and public relations is one of the tools that should be employed. Several causes of defection have roots in poor communication. Not acknowledging gifts, not providing information on how the gifts were used, and poor service quality can be remedied by better public relations efforts. Public relations can also play an important part in altering perceptions about the worthiness of the cause or the need for continued support. Just because the local Y has reached its fund-raising goal for a new expansion does not mean that it has no other needs. Relationship fund-raising concentrates on creating an ongoing connection rather than viewing the link with the donor as purely transactional.

## Annual Campaign Versus Special Project Fund-Raising

Fund-raising in some sport organizations has expanded from activities to support special projects to holding annual fund drives that make up a significant portion of the operational budget for many educational institutions. College and high school athletics programs have become much more reliant on fund-raising as a contributor to daily operations. In 2008 contributions made up about 25% of the generated revenue (revenue produced directly by the athletics department including ticket sales, radio and television receipts, alumni contributions, guarantees, royalties, NCAA distributions, and other sources that do not depend on entities outside the athletics department) of the typical Division I athletics department. The median amount for contributions at Football Bowl Subdivision (FBS) schools was nearly $7.5 million (Fulks, 2009). As high school budgets are squeezed, external fund-raising and booster clubs have become an integral part of the financial landscape at that level as well.

There are some differences between raising money for a single cause and raising money for operational use. Special project fund-raising has a much clearer focus, and the goal and outcome are more easily communicated to donors. Whether the goal is renovating a weight room or building a new stadium, the costs and desired results are relatively clear. Special projects provide a different

set of challenges for fund-raisers than the annual campaign, in which the fund-raising goal may be clearly articulated but the way in which the funds will be used may be more ambiguous.

For special projects, much of the early work involves public relations elements because fund-raising has to do with cultivating relationships with donors who are being targeted for major contributions. Large gifts may take months or even years to arrange, and nurturing the sport organization–donor relationship through the process is vital to closing a deal. These donors may be individuals, corporations, or foundations that contribute to a variety of causes. When requesting large amounts of money, additional complications (e.g., tax consequences, terms of the gift, form of payment) may require an extended period of discussion. Occasional nonlogistical complications can create public relations headaches. For example, a University of Connecticut donor wanted his $3 million back and his name taken off the football practice facility because he felt left out of discussions on the hiring of a new football coach (Schad, 2011).

Although soliciting large gifts is part of many fund-raising efforts, it is especially important for special projects because a few large gifts often encourage others to donate. Organizations typically announce a fund drive only after a substantial portion of the money has already been raised or at least pledged. Delaying public announcement until a sizable portion of the funding has been raised provides the perception that the project is well on its way to meeting its goal and needs just a little more help. Subsequent donors have the sense that their contributions are meaningful in attaining the fund-raising goal.

For annual campaign fund-raising, the sport organization has a more continuous relationship with donors. This type of fund-raising is often termed development. In many respects, building this type of relationship with donors is similar to building relationships with customers. Many of the marketing strategies used to appeal to consumers can be used in attracting donors, and many of the CRM principles are useful in developing and retaining a donor base. Finding and getting to know donors, collecting relevant information, and tailoring communication and fund-raising approaches to the characteristics and needs of each donor are basic to donor development. Gathering demographic and contribution information (frequency of gifts, size of gifts, solicitation preference) on donors provides a valuable tool for evaluating and developing strategies for improving fund-raising efforts. Such information may clarify the effectiveness of certain development tactics, supply data regarding retention and defection rates, and provide insight into the productivity of donors.

The concept of customer valuation certainly has a parallel in fund-raising. Gaffney (1996) reported that it requires 12 to 18 months before a newly acquired donor becomes an asset in terms of net income. The Pareto principle, or 80–20 rule, applies to fund-raising in that 80% of funds come from 20% of donors. Stier (1994) extended that concept even further, calling it the 90–10 rule. He also suggested that a third of an organization's donations may come from its top 10 donors. The obvious response to these concepts is that considerable attention must be focused on the most productive donors.

Effective fund-raising of any type relies on knowing what motivates, satisfies, and inhibits donors. Contributors to sport organizations often have a strong emotional attachment that can be used as an asset in generating donations, but the passion of supporters only goes so far in a competitive fund-raising environment. Public relations can help maintain donor relationships, prevent defection, and improve donor productivity. (Chapter 4 includes some additional information about using new media in donor relations.)

# Government Relations

Managing an organization's interest in political issues and its relationships with government organizations is called **public affairs** (Gruber & Hoewing, 1980). Sport organizations of all types can benefit from healthy relationships with any number of governmental, political, and regulatory entities. Sport operations are likely to profit from having a voice in the political process or the opportunity to wield influence. Sport organizations can be affected by anything from federal legislation such as Title IX and the minimum wage law to local government actions such as zoning and sales and amusement taxes. Political activity can have a significant effect on the operating environment of nearly any sport organization, so it only stands to reason that developing relationships with influential governmental and regulatory units is prudent. As an example, in 2011 a Congressional push to come up with safety standards for children's football helmets prompted Riddell, a major football helmet manufacturer, to sharply increase their lobbying activities. They framed their more aggressive lobbying efforts by saying,

We believe it is only prudent to follow this legislation and to help members (of Congress), and their staffs, better understand the leadership role that Riddell has played in designing the best head protection we can manufacture for athletes who play football. (Associated Press, 2011b)

# Identifying Power Centers

Much of the political relationship building done by organizations falls within the scope of public relations and begins with strategic planning to identify political groups with whom important relationships can or should exist. This process also involves determining key issues that confront the organization and identifying the political and regulatory settings in which the organization will most benefit from having influence and contacts. In other words, where are the external power centers that make rules and regulations that affect organizational operations? Organizations such as the NCAA or the major professional sport leagues may need to forge relationships with Congress and individual legislators or other federal agencies to address such issues as antitrust legislation and tax laws that may affect league operations or the constituents that the organizations represent. For a small local fitness club, relationships may be necessary with the zoning board that controls whether the operation can expand to include a day care. A group desiring to run an event such as a marathon on city streets will certainly benefit from a positive relationship with the city council. College and high school athletics programs must form relationships with regulatory bodies such as the NCAA or the state high school athletics association as they navigate the system of rules to which they must conform.

People charged with helping organizations comply with the rules are not routinely considered part of what might commonly be called public relations, but they have the task of maintaining good relations with the governing body by monitoring their organization's activity and engaging in a regular dialogue that minimizes the likelihood of rules violations.

An effective association with government and regulatory agencies involves establishing connections with people. Identifying who has power within these organizations allows public relations resources to be deployed effectively. In some cases, discerning those who support organizational interests and those who are opposed is important. For example, making a case for funding a new community recreation center requires knowing who can be counted on for support and who may be uncommitted or opposed to the proposal. Public relations efforts may be directed toward convincing those who are not supportive, but they may also be aimed at encouraging influential supporters to sway the opinions of detractors or those who are undecided.

## Formulating Influence Strategies

Public relations planning must include decisions on the strategies of influence. Determining where influence needs to be directed is useful only if the organization can establish relationships that create an environment conducive to influence and persuasion. Holyoke (2003) noted that selecting the appropriate audience is only one component of effective lobbying. Decisions must also be made about the timing and intensity of those influencing efforts as well as the alliances that might be useful in providing additional clout. As an example, influencing a political official in an election year may be much easier if the issue has substantial public support. The politician may see support of the issue as an asset to retaining or gaining office. Conversely, if the issue is controversial, getting an official to make a public statement of support may be difficult unless doing so can deliver some political benefit.

Sport organizations from sporting goods manufacturers to the major professional leagues to outdoor recreation areas are all affected by legislative and regulatory agencies. Regulations such as product safety rules, guidelines for nonprofit status, antitrust laws, and environmental directives can significantly influence the operations of certain sport organizations. For large organizations with a national or international presence, the scope of desired influence may be expansive and include many audiences in high places. **Lobbying** is a common tool used by organizations as they seek to influence government and political activity. In some cases, lobbying efforts may be less structured and involve organizational personnel interacting with a government agency when a situation calls for influencing efforts. For example, the owners of a professional team may seek an audience with city or state officials to discuss what types of support could be provided for the construction of a new arena or stadium. In other cases, lobbying may be more systematic and involve a more consistent presence. Organizations may staff an office, hire lobbyists, or use trade associations to lobby on their behalf. As an example, the NCAA has an office of government relations in Washington, D.C., which was established in 1995 to provide the organization with up-to-date information on federal activities of interest and to advise management on policy decisions related to governmental interaction. This office works closely with other associations of higher education and serves as an information resource for members of Congress, education associations, and the media on issues relevant to the federal government and intercollegiate athletics (NCAA, 2004). The NFL has its own in-house lobbyist and formed a political action committee (PAC), and the NFL Players Association employs a lobbying firm to address the players' interests in Washington, D.C. (Frommer, 2010). The Y is another sport organization that engages in lobbying. The sidebar titled Lobbying Is a YMCA Right and Responsibility, written by George Babish, addresses this subject.

Lobbying efforts have various purposes and can involve direct communication with specific government or political groups, or they may be directed toward activity through a third party or lobbyist. Lobbyists can provide a variety of services that include collecting and interpreting information, serving as an advocate, and functioning as a liaison and communication link (Grunig & Hunt, 1984). Any sport organization that is regularly subject to the actions of political entities should consider the benefits of lobbying as a potential means of shaping its political environment.

# Lobbying Is a YMCA Right and Responsibility

## George Babish

Photo courtesy of George Babish.

Many Ys do not feel comfortable with lobbying. It is not viewed as a priority compared with such activities as board development, philanthropy, or fiscal management. Some Y executives may believe that lobbying is irrelevant, inappropriate, or even illegal. It may be one of the most misunderstood and underused responsibilities of Ys today.

Ys serve more than 18 million members a year in a variety of human development programs such as camping, child care, after-school activities, wellness, and active older adult programs. Half of all Y members are under 18. "We build strong kids, strong families, and strong communities" is more than a catchy slogan for Ys around the country. YMCA staff and board members must speak out to policy makers or risk missing an enormous opportunity to advance their mission further.

Policy makers need to hear directly from organizations that work with people in need. Ys have a unique perspective on community problems that comes from experience. Lobbying can be used not only to change laws but also to educate policy makers on important societal concerns. Lobbying is at the heart of our democratic system, where we seek to influence the writing of laws by policy makers. It is an ethical act when exercised properly. Lobbying is mission advocacy at its highest level.

The 1976 lobbying law breaks lobbying into two categories: direct and grassroots. Direct lobbying refers to communication with a legislator or government official about specific legislation. Grassroots lobbying focuses on communication to the public to influence them to take action. The law clearly defines how much lobbying is permitted and what activities are considered lobbying. IRS Form 5768 needs to be filled out for a not-for-profit agency to apply for coverage under this act. If a Y has a budget of $500,000 or less, it can spend 20% of its budget, or up to $100,000, on lobbying. If its budget is between $1 million and $1.7 million, the limit is $225,000 plus 5% of the budget in excess of $1.5 million. If its budget is over $1.7 million, its limit is $1 million.

Other ways that Ys can influence policy short of official lobbying activity include contacting government officials to change existing regulations, communicating with members about positions on legislation, testifying before a committee, volunteering time for lobbying, and communicating with legislative bodies to clarify a position on a possible decision that could affect the organization.

On a national level, Ys have organized themselves into state alliances to focus their efforts on advocacy and lobbying. To date, 47 states have such alliances. One particular group, the Pennsylvania State Alliance of Ys, represents the 81 corporate Ys in Pennsylvania. The resolution sent out to local boards asking for their support reads as follows:

> **Lobbying is at the heart of our democratic system, where we seek to influence the writing of laws by policy makers. It is an ethical act when exercised properly. Lobbying is mission advocacy at its highest level.**

## Resolution in Support of the Pennsylvania State Alliance of Ys

To foster effective collaboration among the Ys of the Commonwealth of Pennsylvania,

To speak with a united voice on public policies of concern to Ys,

To encourage and support Y programs for Pennsylvania's young people, particularly teenagers,

To develop and present a common message about our Ys' mission and charitable work to the elected officials, media, and general population of Pennsylvania,

Our Y hereby affirms our affiliation with the Pennsylvania State Alliance of Ys.

*(continued)*

*(continued)*

The Massachusetts Alliance provides another example of successful lobbying. Through their efforts, they were able to increase the state child care subsidy rate, resulting in an additional $60 million over the last five years for local Ys while doubling the number of Ys receiving subsidies. They were also able to defeat potentially damaging International Health, Racquet, and Sportsclub Association (IHRSA) legislation through their efforts.

Lobbying clearly is a mission activity. It is a right and responsibility of every Y.

*George Babish is a consultant for Y of the USA and Pennsylvania Alliance of Ys.*

## SUMMARY

Public relations plays a key role in developing and maintaining relationships, and sport organizations must make a concerted effort to nurture their relationships with a variety of external publics, including customers, members, sponsors, donors, and government and regulatory agencies. The quality of the relationship between an organization and its customers or members is likely to determine its success. Public relations can take interaction with consumers and sponsors beyond a transactional relationship and increase the possibility that they are satisfied, loyal, and committed. Learning more about consumer and donor motivation and behavior will help in developing strategies for delivering quality service and in directing marketing and public relations efforts to those consumers and donors who provide the greatest return. Determining reasons for defection is also vital to improving service quality and reducing loyalty barriers.

Public relations plays an important role in political relationships as well. Most sport organizations are affected by political and regulatory actions and must employ strategies to influence those actions. Sport organizations should identify the regulatory agencies that are likely to influence their operating environment and then determine the appropriate methods for influencing political actions and promoting organizational interests.

# LEARNING ACTIVITIES

1. Identify a sport organization and develop the framework for a CRM database. Specify what types of information should be collected and the most effective methods for collecting that information to develop a thorough consumer profile.

2. Many sport organizations have members as their primary clientele. What types of information would you include in a newsletter to members that would assist in maintaining member relationships?

3. Timm's VISPAC model of customer service includes personality. Specify a sport organization, identify positions that routinely interact with the customer in some way, and suggest how the organization can improve the quality of those interactions in the context of personality.

4. Most organizations interact with constituents in a variety of ways. Select a sport organization and identify at least three common points of interaction with constituents or customers. Identify at least three aspects of that interaction that are likely to influence the level of satisfaction that the constituent has with the interaction.

5. You are organizing a local 5K race on campus to raise money for cancer research. Identify some logical sponsor targets. What assets does your event have that are compatible with the likely needs of these potential sponsors?

6. For many college athletics programs, annual campaigns are now common fund-raising practice. What public relations activities might be employed to encourage a high rate of donor retention and higher donation levels?

7. Your organization is pushing for the construction of a new stadium with the help of taxpayers and various levels of government. What centers of power will need to be convinced that this project is worthwhile? Describe the nature of lobbying and other influencing activities that the organization can engage in to help this project come to fruition.

# Legal and Ethical Dimensions of Sport Public Relations

**Dr. Anastasios Kaburakis and Dr. Galen Clavio**

## After reading this chapter, students should be able to

- identify legal issues in sport public relations and the way in which those issues affect teams, leagues, and organizations;
- anticipate emerging legal issues, particularly in relation to the development of digital media content;
- understand the importance of legal analysis in sport public relations;
- evaluate ethical dilemmas present in sport public relations; and
- recognize the need for ethical decision making in sport public relations.

## Key terms discussed in this chapter include

- Family Educational Rights and Privacy Act (FERPA),
- Freedom of Information Act (FOIA),
- intellectual property,
- slander and libel, and
- codes of ethics.

**The legal dimension** of sport public relations grows in importance and influence each year. The process of maintaining favorable relations between a sport organization and its publics often involves balancing the marketing effects of communication with the legal ramifications of both the topic in question and the method of communication itself.

Closely tied to the legal dimension of sport public relations are the ethical ramifications of decision making and the process of relating those decisions to an organization's publics. Not all legally sound decisions are ethical, and not all ethical decisions are legal. Sport organizations must examine their actions from an ethical perspective because of the importance of sport in the larger societal framework.

Consider the following example. NCAA Division I football and men's basketball student–athletes are featured in video games licensed through the NCAA Collegiate Licensing Company and produced by game producer Electronic Arts in recent times, as well as by other companies in the past. This practice has been the object of considerable criticism and analysis, and class action suits were brought against it in the federal courts of California in 2009 and 2010 (Kaburakis et al., 2009).

The most recent and prominent of these lawsuits was filed by Sam Keller, a former quarterback for Nebraska and Arizona State, against the NCAA, the Collegiate Licensing Company (CLC), and Electronic Arts. The suit alleged that the NCAA, in conjunction with EA and the CLC, purposefully circumvented the prohibition on using student–athlete names by allowing users to modify and download rosters from an EA-hosted online server. Those rosters are easily adapted to the real names of the players, and most "real" players have a digital analogue present in the game (Kaburakis et al., 2009).

As with any intellectual property situation, several issues are at work. On the one hand are the fundamental intellectual property rights of student–athletes, which frequently conflict with those of their institutions and the NCAA, and on the other is the constitutionally recognized freedom of expression, including commercial speech, that communication professionals and industry executives need to be aware of and incorporate in their communications and strategic planning.

At the same time, major corporations and athletics associations or governing bodies need to maintain the balancing act between a positive public image measured against practical and mostly financial considerations. Answers to the difficult questions posed by such conflicts often are provided by either black letter law or, in most contemporary situations, by recent case precedent, as well as through policy solutions that governing bodies reach after considerable membership and constituent input leading to consensus (Kaburakis et al., 2009).

## Legal Dimensions of Sport Public Relations

The Duke lacrosse scandal stands as one of the most important and cautionary sport public relations tales of recent times. In 2006 three members of Duke University's lacrosse team were accused of raping an African American stripper at a team party. Both the district attorney's office and large sections of the Duke academic community rushed to judgment on the case, declaring the players guilty before trial. The university even went so far as to cancel the remaining games of the season and fire the head coach.

As the story began to unfold, however, it was found that the accuser had manufactured her claims against the players. Worse still, the district attorney, Mike Nifong, had withheld evidence to win indictments against the players. For that crime, Nifong was disbarred and made to serve a short jail term for lying to a judge. The players were exonerated, and they eventually sued the district attorney and the county. The former head coach, who had been pressured into resignation in the initial wake of the charges, filed suit against the university, as did other lacrosse players who had not been formally charged. The president of Duke University, Richard Brodhead, eventually apologized to the players and team, saying that the university had made the families of the lacrosse players feel abandoned by not reaching out to them during the process.

Furthermore, Brodhead was forced to address comments from faculty members at the university, many of whom were venomously critical and accusatory toward the players and team as a whole. Brodhead and the university were put into a position where in effect they had to disavow those comments, indicating that they did not represent the sentiments of the university as a whole.

The Duke lacrosse scandal highlights many of the pitfalls present when considering the legal and ethical aspects of sport public relations. Practitioners are often expected to respond to stories without knowing the complete story, and the comments and verbiage produced by the public relations

The Duke lacrosse team is a perennial power, but the squad saw its season cancelled midyear in 2006 as a university response to a scandal.

Peyton Williams/Icon SMI

department are ultimately attributed to both the individual and the organization. Numerous actors are often at play in public relations scenarios, and the added complications of technology, federal law, and state statutes can serve to muddy already unclear waters. This section examines some of the major factors facing sport public relations workers in today's digital age.

## Social Networking

Social networking represents a new and potentially perilous frontier in the world of sport public relations. The ability of athletes to maintain their own publicly viewable web pages, filled with pictures, language, and interactive messages to friends, poses quite a challenge for sport public relations workers, because of the potential exposure of damaging information being uncovered by fans and the media.

The most popular social networking sites, such as Facebook and Twitter, allow athletes, coaches, and others to "be themselves" and interact with their friends and acquaintances. The vast majority of athlete and coach actions on social networking sites are innocuous and do not warrant concern. But incidents that occurred early in the development of social media and networking have created a great deal of caution among sport public relations professionals regarding these services.

In 2006 the Northwestern University women's soccer team became embroiled in a hazing controversy after several photos emerged that showed team members engaged in hazing-related activities that the school and media considered embarrassing. Although no one is completely certain where the photos were originally posted on the Internet, they spread like wildfire, ending up on several sport-related blogs. This incident, along with others during the same period, caused sport public relations officials to become increasingly concerned with athletes' ability to post pictures and other material on publicly viewable social media sites such as Facebook.

## Dealing With Issues in Social Networking

Many sports information directors on the college level have taken to putting on special workshops for their athletes to explain the potential pitfalls of social media. Beyond simply the fear of embarrassing materials being published, these institutions are also concerned with potential legal issues, including libel, copyright violations, and other problems that could arise from athletes under scholarship with the school. Furthermore, the potential for liability issues exists, particularly with photographs of student–athletes engaged in behavior that violates local statutes and laws, such as those relating to alcohol consumption. There is no better way to prepare student–athletes in such educational sessions for problems than to review the outcomes of publicized cases in which inappropriate use of social networking led to teams' seasons being forfeited and athletes being charged with violations of student or student–athlete conduct, hazing policies, state statutes, or even federal law. In certain cases, the incidents resulted in dismissal from the school or team and even criminal charges. Besides those outcomes, others can pertain to privacy and the potential risks for students' safety, such as recently documented cases of harassment or cyberbullying that led to suicide in one case, and the stalking of athletes by fans pursuant to social networking updates, which assumed a new level through Twitter updates.

The emergence of Twitter as a communication medium has brought other potential legal issues to the forefront of sport public relations directors' minds. Although public relations methodology tends to favor official team messages coming through a single outlet (such as a media relations official or team website), Twitter and Facebook allow players, coaches, and even team personnel to publicize their thoughts and feelings on all sorts of topics.

Beyond the concerns that athletes and coaches could get themselves into trouble by making ill-advised or ill-conceived statements that are subsequently taken out of context by the media, an additional concern is that these messages could result in a range of legal issues for both athlete and organization. Unmoderated words from athletes and coaches, particularly when written in the aftermath of a heated game, could result in anything

from defamation of character claims, to libel, to breach of contract in relation to sponsors.

To mitigate potential legal issues related to Twitter, sport organizations have taken steps to minimize their players' and coaches' exposure. In the NBA, for example, players are not allowed to tweet from 45 minutes before the start of a game until after they have finished with their official duties. This no-tweeting policy includes halftime. The NBA has shown that they are serious about enforcing this rule by fining Milwaukee Bucks player Brandon Jennings $7,500 during the 2009–10 season for violating the Twitter rule. Other leagues, including the NFL, have instituted similar restrictions. The sidebar titled The Legal Side of Sport Public Relations, written by John Koluder, offers advice on using social media and other legal aspects of sport public relations.

## Monitoring Social Networks

In addition, the expansion of social networking outlets and their patent popularity has led to entrepreneurial ventures by shrewd investors and administrators inside and outside the sport realm. One such service, YouDiligence, provides subscribers the opportunity to monitor the textual content of selected social networking sites. YouDiligence started as a service for higher education administrators and athletics department officials to help monitor the social networking sites of their athletes, and it has now expanded to subscriptions for concerned parents. Although the service does not allow monitoring of images on social networking sites, it does cause certain keywords that might produce concern to trigger an alert that draws monitoring attention. Administrators are thus alerted to potentially questionable online behavior by their athletes, thereby allowing them to take action.

The presence of this system allows athletic administrators to avoid the "nuclear" option of rendering social media sites off limits, an action that would raise major concerns regarding invasion of privacy and abridgement of freedom of expression. The ability to monitor these sites, combined with athletics-department-mandated educational sessions for athletes about the perils of social networking sites, helps make the online sphere a safer place for both the athlete and the administrator. Recommending that athletes keep their profiles and accounts private, counseling them to be sure that they know anyone whom they "friend," and advising them of acceptable content that can be posted online will help sports information practitioners steer their teams and athletes away from inappropriate usage of social networking tools.

# The Legal Side of Sport Public Relations

## John Koluder

Photo courtesy of John Koluder.

Most aspiring public relations professionals looking at sport public relations don't think about the legal aspects of things. But whether it's dealing with social-media-related player issues, intellectual property, or reporting on foreign nationals and the way that their signings and releases are handled, my job has all kinds of legal aspects that require constant vigilance.

I've been working in MLS in various media relations capacities for over a decade, so it wasn't as if I came into the job with a categorical knowledge of these processes. Much of what we run into legally with sport public relations is trial and error. Some of it, particularly the social media issues that have popped up recently, we're seeing for the first time ever, so we're having to use past precedent from other situations as our guideposts for how to act.

Let's take the signing of a foreign-national player as an example. During the visa and immigration process, my department is constantly getting updates on where the team is in the process of signing the player. This includes updates on what we can and cannot say, and what we should confirm or deny. The immigration process itself is not handled by media relations, but we're in the room when the conversations are occurring.

Although certain methods are prescribed for dealing with player immigration issues, the situations are often so fluid that media relations has to address issues without any understanding of how the situation will work out. Visa and immigration issues can be affected by myriad factors beyond the team's control, and what seems like a sure thing one minute can completely change in the next hour.

In many of these cases, you're handling situations on the fly. There's no handbook or manual for these things. The primary thing to keep in mind is to talk to absolutely everyone in your organization who's involved and get to a level of clearance where you feel comfortable before putting out a press release. Ultimately, as the team's public relations person, you're the one who's pressing "send" and putting the information out there. You have to feel confident in what you're putting out there before you do so.

I can't stress enough the importance of following established channels of information clearance before putting anything out, be it a press release, tweet, blog post, or whatever, if it involves an immigration issue. As long as the information being released has been cleared by team or league management, the media relations worker is normally safe from personal liability. But if you decide to tweak something that you think is harmless and it comes back to hurt you, you're going to have to bite that bullet and take responsibility. Always have someone above you in the team hierarchy sign off on information that you think might be sensitive in nature.

When it comes to social media, the best advice that I can give is to try to walk that fine line between caution and innovation. If we've learned anything over the last five years in terms of social media, it's that it works great in the hands of experienced people who know what they're doing. Unfortunately, even experienced users sometimes don't think about the ramifications of posting a picture or tweeting a message. There are the obvious issues of accidentally posting something illegal or immoral. But then there are also situations where sponsors can see something that they don't like in a picture and view it as a breach of contract.

The easiest fix to most of these problems is simply to educate your players, coaches, and front office staff. Make sure they know how to use the technology properly. Be sure they know what kinds of things they can and can't post, give them the reasons why, and advise them about the legal ramifications should something go wrong. Remember, what you think is common sense simply might not occur to someone else.

*John Kulder is the assistant director, soccer media services for Real Salt Lake (MLS).*

> **If we've learned anything over the last five years in terms of social media, it's that it works great in the hands of experienced people who know what they're doing.**

# Safeguarding the Organization, Players, Coaches, and Staff

Various state and federal laws may serve to protect information that would be considered private for players, coaches, and sport organizations. Three key acts pertain to the protection of educational records (and by extension many items that reflect a student–athlete's participation in intercollegiate athletics), medical records, and genetic information:

- Family Educational Rights and Privacy Act
- Health Insurance Portability and Accountability Act
- Genetic Information Nondiscrimination Act

## *FERPA*

The 1974 **Family Educational Rights and Privacy Act (FERPA)** is a federal law that protects the privacy of student education records. The law applies to all schools that receive funds under an applicable program of the U.S. Department of Education (U.S. Department of Education, n.d.a).

Also referred to as the Buckley amendment, after Senator James Buckley, its main sponsor, it has been the most prevalent and extensively summoned federal legislation that sport administrators in educational settings have to abide by and consider while making everyday decisions. It has been frequently criticized for its contentious and hasty passing, many amendments, challenges in enforcement, and interpretational challenges (U.S. Department of Education, n.d.b).

Under FERPA, parents or eligible students can request educational records, but others are restricted in access to those same records, including information pertaining to student status, grades, school attendance, and performance. Institutions are allowed to share such information only through waivers, except in a small number of circumstances. The consent of student–athletes to FERPA releases is embedded in their participation in intercollegiate athletics, and NCAA member institutions use that consent to disseminate certain information about those athletes.

The use of FERPA by college athletics departments has further stretched the boundaries of the original intent of the law, according to some. For instance, an investigation by the *Columbus* (Ohio) *Dispatch* regarding NCAA violations in the Ohio State Buckeyes football program found literally hun-

dreds of so-called secondary violations of NCAA rules. But when asked to reveal the names and incidents related to those violations, the university claimed that FERPA guidelines did not allow them to disclose such information, because the violations involved student–athletes. Critics pointed out that Ohio State was using FERPA as a shield to protect the athletics department's interests and public perception.

Other incidents involving FERPA-related controversies in college athletics have included the question over what types of information should be redacted from official documents when a student–athlete's name is involved. Some universities have claimed that all information should be redacted and that FERPA mandates such behavior. Other universities have taken a more moderate approach.

## *HIPAA and GINA*

The Health Insurance Portability and Accountability Act of 1996 (HIPAA) and its regulations (the "privacy rule" and the "security rule") protect the privacy of an individual's health information and govern the way that certain health care providers collect, maintain, use, and disclose protected health information. Certain terms and practices are prescribed for public relations professionals when dealing with HIPAA, such as language for conditions released to the public, prerequisites for discussing medical information with hospital or medical professionals, and conditions for retrieving the extent of information allowed by HIPAA and institution and league policy.

The application of HIPAA in sport public relations has been uneven (Bell, Ratzlaff, & Murray, n.d.). In many cases on the professional level, sport leagues require the disclosure of injury-related information on players. The primary purpose of disclosing this information relates to gambling and the desire of sport teams to avoid so-called insider information on player health from being circulated among professional gamblers and handicappers. Beyond the realm of gambling, fans and media observers are generally interested in the injury status of players, both in terms of what medical problems they face and in the amount of time and type of rehabilitation that they will require to get better.

An exception to this philosophy occurs in the sport of hockey, in which injury disclosure is considered unwise. Certain minor league hockey teams have even engaged in the practice of not releasing injury information, claiming HIPAA protection for the athletes in question.

A related law, the Genetic Information Nondiscrimination Act of 2008 (GINA), protects individuals, including athletes, from a variety of genetics-related issues (Department of Health and Human Services, 2009). The law renders it unlawful for an employer to deny employment or to discriminate against an employee based on genetic information. It also keeps employers from depriving opportunities to individuals based on genetic information and from requesting that employees submit genetic information for work-related purposes.

The implications of GINA could be wide and far-reaching in the world of sport. One possible area where it could affect a professional organization relates to Major League Baseball and its teams. A major source of talent in MLB is Latin America, and baseball scouts regularly scour the nations of the Caribbean, Central America, and South America for up-and-coming talent. In many cases, record keeping in those countries is apocryphal at best, and items such as birth certificates can be easily forged or purchased to make a player appear younger than he actually is. This deceit can lead to financial loss for a team that signs such a player, particularly if the team has offered a larger salary to the player because it is under the impression that the player is younger than he actually is. Under GINA, teams would not be able to use genetic testing to examine the player's age scientifically.

Another application of GINA is in the testing of players for genetic defects, particularly in relation to cardiovascular issues. College and professional teams are not allowed to test players genetically for those defects in the course of making contract or signing decisions about a player. The landmark incident in sport regarding this sort of issue involved NBA player Eddy Curry, who in 2005 was under contract with the NBA's Chicago Bulls. The Bulls refused to extend Curry's contract unless he took a genetic test to determine whether he had a potentially serious heart issue. Curry refused to take the test and ended up being traded to another team, with whom he signed a contract without having been tested.

Note that GINA extends protection only to players who do not wish to be tested against their will. Players are not prohibited from getting their own tests performed and submitting those results to teams. In some cases, this approach can be beneficial to the player, because the presence of a voluntary genetic test can ease the mind of a general manager or owner who might otherwise have had questions regarding a player's age or genetic health.

## Governmental Protections

Several state and federal laws aim to govern the public's access to information, maintain transparency in state actors' affairs, and protect the public's right to express opinions and criticism. Other than Constitutional protections afforded by the First Amendment in respect to freedom of speech and expression, key legislative means to accomplish these goals include the following:

- Freedom of Information Act
- Sunshine and open door laws
- Anti-strategic lawsuits against public participation regulations

### Freedom of Information Act

The **Freedom of Information Act (FOIA)** is a federal law designed to make available previously unreleased documents and information that are in the domain of the federal government (Department of Justice, n.d.). The FOIA generally provides that any person has the right to request access to federal agency records or information (Blanton, 2006).

All agencies of the U.S. government are required to disclose records upon receiving a written request, except those records that are protected from disclosure pursuant to certain exemptions and exclusions. The FOIA applies only to federal agencies and does not create a right of access to records held by Congress, the courts, or state or local government agencies.

Any requests for state or local government records are directed to the appropriate state or local government agency. With the exception of the U.S. Olympic Committee, other public sport agencies and public institutions would be governed by state open records and sunshine laws, which frequently pose stricter requirements and earlier deadlines. For example, the state of Illinois requires a deadline of 5 days for responses to FOIA requests, compared with the 10-day deadline that the federal FOIA guidelines mandate.

In a recent case, several national and Florida media outlets pursued FOIA requests against the NCAA for access to records that were considered confidential under a Florida State University counsel agreement with the NCAA. It was decided that the NCAA would have to release documents leading to the Committee of Infractions meetings with the university officials—records that were thus far protected under NCAA policy and agreements with the member institutions (Schrimpf, 2009). In a

# A Closer Look: NCAA v. Associated Press et al. (Fla. 1st DCA, October 1, 2009)

This case was an interesting conflict between FOIA and Florida Public Records Laws, and FERPA, as well as the private affairs of the NCAA as a private voluntary membership organization. As the Court of Appeals acknowledged, the Florida courts construe public records laws liberally in favor of the state's policy of open government. If there is any doubt about the application of the law in a particular case, the doubt is resolved in favor of disclosing the documents (p. 8).

The media entities that brought this case wanted access to two documents, the transcript of the Committee of Infractions hearings in the Florida State University case in 2008 and the Infractions Appeals Committee response to the university in 2009. The NCAA countered that disclosing the full documents would violate FERPA and would compromise the NCAA's enforcement process, because informants and private information may be included in the original documents. The trial court sided with the plaintiffs and held that FERPA would not be violated because there was no student-specific educational information and that the NCAA's allegation on the effect on its enforcement process was irrelevant.

An important problem that the Appeals Court handled was whether the state agent or university employee viewing the confidential (and according to the NCAA, private) information would render this a public document. The NCAA vehemently disagreed that the mere review by a public agent of the documents renders them public records. Sensitive and private facts were contained therein, and the NCAA argued that nondisclosure would be imperative to its private enforcement process, frequently residing with self-reporting and whistle blowing by informants and university employees. The court disagreed with the NCAA, remarking that the purpose of those documents was official governmental business, that is, the university's appeal to the NCAA. Had the university lawyers, per the court's rationale, simply viewed an unrelated student's record through the secure website that the NCAA provided, indeed those would be FERPA-protected records, but not in this case, because all the documents in question were part of the university's defense strategy. At the same time, the confidentiality agreement that the university lawyers signed with the NCAA had no effect according to the court, because official public records should always be available, regardless of the fact that a state agent signed a document to protect them.

Because the documents did not "directly" pertain to a student's educational record, the court held that FERPA would not be violated. Intriguingly, the court held that the documents "pertain to allegations of misconduct by the University Athletic Department, and only tangentially relate to the students who benefited from that misconduct" (p. 18). As long as students' identifying information would be redacted, the court held there would not be a FERPA violation issue. It also held that it was in no position to determine whether unredacted versions of the documents should be released to the public.

The court also disagreed with the NCAA's claim that the public records law as applied here would be unconstitutional, under the commerce clause and freedom of association provisions in the U.S. Constitution. The court decided that the public records law as interpreted here had nothing to do with interstate commerce, and it discounted related cases summoned by the NCAA from other jurisdictions, because they pertained to disciplinary proceedings and not open public records.

In fact, the court found that the NCAA's allegation that such an application would "rip the heart out of the NCAA" (p. 21) was overstated, because no individual private informant was identified therein. Rather, the findings were the result of the university's internal self-reporting mechanism. Moreover, the court defended its application of Florida open records laws, citing instances and similar statutes in most states that would not render the Florida application of open records so distinct that the NCAA would not be able to function in that particular state. And in conclusion, the Florida Appeals Court in this case decided that in no way did its application abridge the NCAA's right to freely associate and manage its affairs.

This case, the recent findings from the Indiana University infractions scandal in which private communications were disclosed (and not redacted, containing even private expressions of affection toward spouse or family members) to the *Indianapolis Star*, as well as others call for the attention of public relations and sport communications professionals. Perhaps the most important lesson is that people cannot be too careful about what they put on paper or in an e-mail or official school record, especially when dealing with a public institution, through the means of institutional communications (school e-mail). If the NCAA was not able to seal the enforcement records discussed earlier and protect information contained therein from public letter to the president of Florida State, former NCAA president Myles Brand remarked that if the Florida courts continued to side with the plaintiffs in the case, the association's ability to conduct investigations and enforce bylaws would be greatly affected. Regardless of the NCAA's desire for secrecy and obfuscation, FOIA requests are important tools of the media, so sport public relations officials must learn how to deal with FOIA requests. The sidebar A Closer Look provides more detail regarding the NCAA case.

## Sunshine and Open Door Laws

Open meeting and records laws, also known as sunshine laws, are an important element of governmental oversight on the state level. These laws generally require that state and local government organizations, including school boards and universities, make public their meetings and decision-making processes, although the degree of openness varies from state to state (McDonald, 2001; Missouri Attorney General, n.d.). Similarly, these groups must make available to the public all documentation and other records for the purpose of oversight. Sport public relations workers should be familiar with the sunshine laws of the state in which they are working, for the purposes of both providing legally thorough and accurate information and accurately informing organizational members of what the laws stipulate in terms of openness and access (McDonald, 2001).

One of the more interesting cases involving sunshine laws surrounded the firing of head basketball coach Bob Knight at Indiana University. Following a series of inquiries in the wake of Knight's firing, a lawsuit was filed against the university by a group of fans, claiming that the university's trustees and then-president Myles Brand (who later served as the head of the NCAA) subverted the sunshine laws of the state of Indiana during the decision-making process for the firing. Specifically, the plaintiffs alleged that Brand had purposefully kept the trustees in two separate rooms where neither group formed a quorum of members, thereby avoiding the necessity of calling an official meeting of the trustees, which would have required a public announcement. The court ultimately found in favor of the university, but commentary surrounding the case indicated that the actions of Brand may have violated the spirit of the sunshine laws.

## SLAPP and Anti-SLAPP

The term *strategic lawsuits against public participation* (SLAPP) refers to lawsuits that aim at silencing critics. These suits are usually filed by corporations, associations, or government and public officials. The purpose of SLAPP cases is often to silence critics through threats, entangle defendants in time-consuming litigation, and generally to affect criticism and cause critics to yield, settle, or discontinue their stance toward the organization and its interests (Coleman, 2011; Pring & Canan, 1996).

SLAPPs assume several forms, and defendants can use state legislation to have SLAPP lawsuits struck from the court (Kline, 2009). The primary burden on the defendants is to prove that their conduct was aligned with the right to petition and free speech guaranteed by the First Amendment. As long as the matter is of public interest, the defendants' actions fall within the public's rights, and the court is convinced that the plaintiff would not prevail in the suit, anti-SLAPP statutes allow defendants these special motions to strike SLAPP suits (Brown, 2009). The major issue with SLAPP-related cases is the difficulty in distinguishing between a SLAPP and a bona fide suit. Courts will have to weigh the competing interests carefully and err on the side of public participation and free speech (Society of Professional Journalists, n.d.).

The possibility of SLAPP suits occurring in sport is higher than one might imagine. Any league or team wishing to silence critics and media entities that disagree with their decision making could ostensibly file a SLAPP suit. These suits could focus on legal issues such as defamation, invasion of privacy, or other legal doctrines. Furthermore, SLAPP could be used by educational institutions and associations, such as the NCAA or state high school athletics federations, who wish to shield themselves preemptively against inquiries related to their internal affairs or business practices.

For instance, if a professional sport team attempts to receive public funding for a new stadium through voting initiatives or other public procedures, considerable opposition may arise in the public sphere. The team could choose to pursue critics of such a stadium deal with SLAPP lawsuits to stifle public debate and cast the stadium's opponents in a negative light. An anti-SLAPP statute could allow these critics to organize more effectively without fear of having to defend themselves in court against a well-financed opponent who has a tremendous financial stake in the overall situation (Kling, 2005).

# Emerging Legal Issues in Sport Public Relations

With the advent of new media and technology tools to express opinions and to aim at profiting from the use of innovative digital expression, seemingly countless legal issues have emerged, which state and federal laws and key provisions of existing legislation are attempting to resolve. A crucial point to recognize for anyone studying these issues and working in the field is that the law is evolving as technology advances; it is dynamic, fickle, and sometimes conflicting depending on the jurisdiction. When there is a contradiction among district and federal appeals courts, the U.S. Supreme Court might hear a case to provide resolution. There is also the prospect of federal legislation to resolve such conflicts. The latter is the case with efforts to introduce federal acts on rights of publicity and amendments to existing provisions of the Copyright and Trademark Acts that address contemporary legal problems. The following sections briefly summarize these issues:

- Intellectual property evolution
- Copyright law and commercial misappropriation
- Trademark law
- Rights of publicity
- First Amendment and federal law preemption of intellectual property rights

## Intellectual Property and Right of Publicity

Sport public relations and communications in the 21st century touch a wide variety of **intellectual**

**property** issues. This section focuses on the areas that have the greatest application to the emerging areas of new and social media, along with areas that lack strongly established precedent. Some of these areas include copyright, trademark, and patent law, as well as rights of publicity and speech.

### Copyright Law and Commercial Misappropriation

Contemporary copyright law is rooted in 18th century English law, which attempted to protect intellectual property under several common law principles. Through the intervening years, copyright law has been progressively expanded, adding to the classes of intellectual creations that are protected (Copyright.gov, n.d.).

Copyright protection is currently extended to "original works of authorship fixed in any tangible medium of expression, now known or later developed" (17 U.S. Code § 102 (a)). Although this law provides protection to a wide variety of creative processes, the standard on which originality is based requires independent creation and a minimal degree of creativity. Copyright protection, for example, does not apply to a sporting event, although it does apply to a broadcast of a sporting event.

Copyright law affords the copyright owner specific exclusive rights; for example, the owner holds the right to perform the work publicly. To balance the rights of owners and users, Congress instituted what is known as the Fair Use Doctrine. This doctrine allows non-copyright holders to use copyrighted works for the purposes of criticism, comment, news reporting, teaching, or research.

Individuals and organizations have battled in the past over the application of the Fair Use Doctrine and its possible or real effect on the marketplace for a copyrighted work. Prior case law has established that each situation has a different line over which usage crosses from fair to infringement, such as the case of *Zacchini v. Scripps Howard Broadcasting* (1977), in which the U.S. Supreme Court found that a television station could not broadcast a human cannonball performance in its entirety without the performer's prior consent, because of the possibility that the performer's ability to capitalize financially on his work would be compromised.

In *Monster Communications v. TBS* (1996), the broadcaster's use of copyrighted footage of Muhammad Ali in a documentary of his life constituted fair use because of the "combination of comment, criticism, scholarship, and research involved." The protection granted to factual compilations has been especially difficult for sports news broadcasters, who would claim that reporting only the facts of a sporting event, using excerpts from copied portions of a televised broadcast, should not infringe upon the rights of the copyright holder. The main rule would be that the newscast is obligated to seek permission from the copyright holder before supplementing the report with copied portions of the televised broadcast.

Frequently, elements of commercial misappropriation appear in copyright cases, in which an individual or organization has been found to be "ripping off" the work of someone else, at the expense of the creator of that work. An early precedent in news gathering was set in the case of *International News Service v. Associated Press* (1918), which found that the International News Service, which had been copying the Associated Press' bulletins and reprinting them without permission, needed to stop this practice, because it was unfairly competing with the AP (Magliocca, 2009).

The concept of copyright as it applies to sport and its games has developed over the years. An early case involved the Pittsburgh Pirates baseball team, which had signed an exclusive broadcast rights contract with General Mills Corporation. Another company attempted to broadcast Pirates games on the radio, using paid observers stationed outside the ballpark, on premises leased by the defendant that afforded the observers good views of the action. Although this company did not use the official accounts of the authorized broadcast of the game, the court found that the Pirates maintained a "property or quasi-property" right by way of the creation of their games, the control of the ballpark, and their restriction of the dissemination on news of the games. In other words, the Pirates held a copyright on the reporting of the game as it happened in real time.

The court has ruled, however, that this protection applies only to that real-time relation. Later case law indicated that after a sport event occurred, the details of the event immediately became part of the facts of history. News information itself cannot become the subject of a property right belonging exclusively to any person. Although the content of a broadcast can be copyrighted, the actual events of a game or contest may not.

This finding was upheld by the Federal Appeals Court for the Second Circuit in a case involving the NBA and a lawsuit against Motorola. The communications company had developed a portable device called Sports Trax, which operated as a sort of sport-oriented pager system that provided real-time, continuously updated scores of NBA games.

The NBA sued, claiming that Sports Trax was both causing the loss of ticket sales because of its real-time updates and taking away future opportunities from the NBA in terms of creating their own stats-based update system. The court held that although the product offered by Motorola was a derivative of the NBA's work, it was not so similar that it created a substantial threat to the NBA's existence. Furthermore, the court found that receiving statistical or score updates in real time was not a substitute for attending the game in person and therefore had no competitive effect on the NBA's business because the NBA was capable of creating its own competitor to the Motorola system.

Prior court cases have also considered the legal concept of work for hire as it relates to athletes' performances in games as portrayed through broadcasts. Case law has dictated that, despite the protestations of players, a player's performance in a game is indeed copyrightable by the team or league who broadcasts it, because of the presence of artistic merit and creativity. As a result, the players were unable to claim the right of publicity to the broadcasted renditions of their performances. This issue remains an active concern today because of the proliferation of Internet-based video and the reorganization of media to feature teams and their media relations departments as the primary source of distributed video content and highlights.

## Trademark Law

Another aspect of intellectual property is trademark law, which focuses on the protection of marks, words, names, symbols, designs, and combinations thereof. Ultimately, trademark law helps to protect brands and brand names, as well as logos and other individual and collective marks. Trademark law also protects colors and symbols that have acquired secondary meaning in conjunction with an organization.

Established trademarks are often used by sport public relations professionals, primarily through the creation of media and dissemination of team-related content. This usage can include the distribution of "official" marks and symbols to media outlets, the inclusion of trademarked items on team press releases and video, and the design and maintenance of team websites.

Sport public relations officials are also often the first line of defense when dealing with violations of a team's trademarks. The sport public relations worker must be constantly vigilant on the Internet to ensure that trademarked items are not being used for profit by unofficial websites. Furthermore, observing the actions of commercial entities in the local marketplace is important. Businesses often misappropriate sport team logos and marks without obtaining permission, and it is often the domain of the public relations worker to observe these occurrences in the media.

In sport the protection of trademarks is important because the trademarked items are often used as a proxy for the name of the sport team. In the case of a possible violation of a team's trademark, several prerequisites must be met to sue the violator successfully. The trademark holder must first have established a protectable right. Second, the holder must demonstrate that the violator's actions are causing confusion in the marketplace, which might adversely affect the holder. Third, the holder must establish that the violator is purposefully imitating the trademark to gain a financial advantage.

To sue an entity successfully for violating a trademark, the courts tend to require survey information demonstrating that consumers have indeed been or are likely to be confused by the violator's usage of the trademark. Generally, a plaintiff would want to generate consumer confusion surveys because the court may look more favorably on a claim if it can be proved that consumers are unsure about the nature of a trademark (International Trademark Association, 2008). In some cases, the courts have tried to balance consumer confusion against the public interest in the right of free expression. An earlier case, involving a painting of Tiger Woods winning the Masters, was found to contain sufficient artistic merit to warrant First Amendment protection. A textbook case in trademark law for the sport industry is *Indianapolis Colts v. Metropolitan Baltimore Football Club*. This case was important for the procedural reason of confirming the value of consumer confusion surveys and their weight in court proceedings. The Colts' franchise used evidence from market surveys that arguably proved that the public could have been confused if Baltimore was allowed to continue its use of the Colts nickname and respective marks.

### Right of Publicity

From a legal perspective, the right of publicity has grown out of jurisprudence related to the individual right to privacy. Generally, the right of publicity protects a person from having the commercial value of his or her identity appropriated by someone else without the person's consent. The identity in question includes such items as a person's name, likeness, voice, or other indicia (Kaburakis & McKelvey, 2009).

The landmark case *White v. Samsung Electronics America* (1993), in which Samsung used a robot impersonating Vanna White in *Wheel of Fortune*, is one of the most important lessons for contemporary right of publicity litigation and theory. The majority opinion of the Ninth Circuit held that Samsung had violated White's right of publicity.

There have been several cases related to right of publicity involving sport figures. In *Montana v. San Jose Mercury News*, a court held that posters depicting the past triumphant moments of Joe Montana and the San Francisco 49ers, regardless of whether or not they were made for profit, were protected under the First Amendment simply because Joe Montana was a major player in contemporaneous newsworthy sport events.

Moreover, in *Gionfriddo v. Major League Baseball*, former professional baseball players argued that their common law and statutory rights of publicity were violated by MLB's use of their names, photographs, and video images in websites, media guides, video clips, and game programs. The California court declared that the information posted by MLB was protected speech. MLB's use commanded substantial public interest, MLB did not sell a product, which would render such use commercial, and when determining the balance between competing interests, the players' proprietary rights were deemed negligible compared with the public's enduring fascination with baseball. Therefore, the public interest was served by the free communication of such information. Interestingly, this case would foreshadow the issues of the 2000s relating to the usage of statistics and figures in fantasy sports, specifically whether leagues were unfairly profiting from the statistical production of their players.

Ultimately, the burden of proof for establishing a violation of an athlete's right of publicity is fivefold. First, there must be actual usage of the athlete's identity. Second, that identity must have some intrinsic commercial value. Third, the commercial value of the identity must have been appropriated for the purposes of trade. Fourth, there must be a lack of consent. And finally, there must be a demonstrable commercial injury resulting from the misappropriation of identity.

### First Amendment and Federal Law Preemption of Intellectual Property Rights

Most cases in the field of sport public relations and communication have dealt with First Amendment rights, as well as federal preemption of common law and statutory rights of publicity. Federal preemption is generally based on a patchwork of theoretical grounds because of the wide variety of statutory and common laws on the books.

Important cases illustrate these conflicts. In *Cardtoons v. Major League Baseball Players Association*, the Tenth Circuit held that Cardtoons' First Amendment rights to parody baseball players in a transformative, artistic way preempted the players' Oklahoma-based statutory rights of publicity. Although the statute permitted newsworthy, noncommercial uses, Cardtoons would *prima facie* violate the players' rights; nonetheless, the comic use was deemed "commentary on an important social institution."

One problem exists in several courts' reasoning in attempting to balance athletes' and celebrities' rights against the public interest and First Amendment protections; namely, the argument is that such prominent figures "are already handsomely compensated." Of course, that condition does not apply to amateur athletes, whose intellectual property rights may also be used for promotions of the collective benefit.

In *C.B.C. Distribution and Marketing, Inc. v. Major League Baseball Advanced Media*, the Eighth Circuit held that the combination of names and statistics used in fantasy leagues is protected by the First Amendment as factual data readily available in the public domain. Disagreeing with the district court, the Eighth Circuit nonetheless found that the elements for establishing a violation of the baseball players' rights of publicity had been met under Missouri common law. The First Amendment preemption of the common law rights of publicity was established, even though the use had a commercial nature. The Eighth Circuit balanced competing economic interests with the benefit to the public.

The most difficult challenge in forthcoming litigation will be delineating the new frontiers to this expanded public domain. Would it be prudent, for example, to argue that images, likenesses, and the very identities of both real people and their avatars, virtual depictions, artistic creations, and expressive works would all be within the realm of a borderless, limitless (if not lawless) public domain through the advent of new media interactive worlds, where innovation and creativity are compensated in more than virtual money? Would one be reasonable to assume that because NCAA student–athletes' names, likenesses, and even identities are broadly available for use on the Internet that their images in video games would not be protected under right of publicity theory?

## Legal Ramifications of Crisis Communication

Crisis communication is a major element of sport public relations and one of the most important elements of a media relations director's job. But legal and ethical considerations in crisis communication can severely and negatively affect not just the organization but also the public relations workers themselves.

During a crisis communication situation, comments must often be made about situations despite a lack of solid information. For instance, a sport organization can ill afford to wait to comment on the arrest of a player or the death of a fan in an incident at the team's stadium. Even if the information on a subject has not yet materialized, the team's public relations efforts must include some sort of official comment. The public relations worker must be careful here to avoid making comments to the media that place him- or herself or the team in any legal jeopardy. Making broad, general statements is usually better than commenting specifically on the subject at hand.

Furthermore, public relations workers should ensure that the organization is speaking with one voice during a crisis to avoid the possibility of future legal action because of on-the-record statements from team personnel that do not reflect the agreed-upon opinions of ownership and management. Proper planning and implementation of a crisis communication plan can help protect athletes and organizations from incidents such as these.

One example of a crisis communication situation gone awry occurred with golfer Tiger Woods. During a holiday weekend in November 2009, a story broke in the national press that Woods had been involved in a car accident and had been released from the hospital in good condition. Woods' public relations team did not attempt to get out in front of the story, and after a few days, the tone of the national conversation had been irretrievably altered by rumors that Woods had been involved in a domestic violence situation as a result of an argument with his wife, Elin. The public perception of Tiger went from sympathy to disgust in a short time. Further revelations, including allegations that Woods' handlers had attempted to buy off the press in exchange for keeping previous stories of Woods' sexual dalliances out of print, did nothing to help Woods' image.

**Tiger Woods' then-pristine image suffered serious damage during a scandal in 2009.**

Charles Baus/Icon SMI

## Libel and Slander in the Electronic Realm

The explosion of digital expression opportunities in the 21st century has opened up limitless conditions under which defamation can occur. The Restatement (Second) of Torts (1977) outlined the common law tort of defamation, under which an individual is subject to liability if he or she damages another person's reputation by speaking (slander) or publishing (libel) false statements about that person to a third party. Defamatory statements have the potential to tarnish a person's social standing and even discredit a person's business and economic status. An entity that publishes or disseminates a defamatory statement may also be liable.

Defamation law generally posits that to establish the tort of defamation a plaintiff needs to prove

1. a false and defamatory statement of fact
2. published or communicated to a third party;
3. fault, or at least negligence, of the publisher or communicator; and
4. harm leading to damages.

Defamation torts are divided into two categories: **slander** and **libel**. Slander relates to communication by spoken word, and libel relates to publication or communication through written materials. Other than punitive damages, whereby the U.S. system of jurisprudence attempts to make an example and prevent future torts, the main two categories of damages in defamation are general (i.e., humiliation, degradation, mental suffering) and special, which must be particularly established for each plaintiff and would include items such as lost wages and business income. Unless there is a *per se* slanderous or libelous defamatory statement, the plaintiff has to prove sustaining special damages. In *per se* defamation situations, special damages are not necessary to establish because they pertain to

1. moral turpitude;
2. professional, business, or trade practices and abilities;
3. loathsome diseases; and
4. sexual misconduct.

In the digital era, most communications delivered by the Internet (i.e., social networking, message boards, chat rooms, blogs) would fall under the category of libel. Libel includes comment sections relating to podcasts, YouTube clips, and other audio-based components. The actual audio or video, including communications on VOIP, Skype, and other systems, would fall under slander. In some cases, particularly relating to Skype, Instant Messenger, and other services that offer simultaneous writing and speaking, a person can commit libel and slander simultaneously.

As an example, saying that your former friend is an "STD encyclopedia" in a podcast or videocast would be considered slander, whereas making that same remark in a chat room, a message board, or on Facebook would be considered libel (both *per se* defamatory statements). Note that common carriers (such as a DSL Internet provider) would not be held liable for defamation, and neither would the service distributors (e.g., Amazon, Barnes & Noble, and so on), unless they had prior or active knowledge of the defamatory work.

But the publishers of the defamatory statement, that is, newspapers, editors, and the several online entities involved in publication means, could be held liable for defamation. Facebook, MySpace, YouTube, and even Google have been targets of suits in this realm. This fact should increase the sense of responsibility among direct employees of an athletics department or professional sports information department to check sources, conduct research with due diligence, and ensure that they have established the dependability and credibility of sources.

Note that anonymity on the Internet does not ensure a free ride when it comes to defamation claims. Sufficient ways are available to establish the IP and source of post addresses, so it is definitely prudent to err on the side of caution and not engage in commentary that may arguably be considered defamatory.

If a person is confronted with such claims encompassing posts from his or her IP address, a line of defense could be a claim that the IP address was erroneous. As is usually the case with piracy over the Internet, proxy servers are utilized to that end. The U.S. Department of Justice, in cooperation with state attorneys general offices, engages in a continuous effort to fight cybercrime (Department of Justice, 2002). Anonymity on the Internet will not be assured if a person is not careful with her or his digital conduct, especially when such communications emanate from a PDA or web-enabled cell phone, iPhone, or Blackberry (Seltzer, 2009). People who attempt to circumvent federal and state policies of Internet use could face criminal charges as well. This area is a primary focus for Department of Justice officials in the new digital age (Department of Justice, 2002).

Other than certain privileged circumstances, in most cases the one defense for a defamation suit is the truth of the communicated statement. If the statement is not verifiable, and it is merely an opinion, the defendant may enjoy First Amendment protection for freedom of expression.

Defamation has always been an area of the law in which First Amendment freedom of expression has conflicted with the protection of one's reputation and public image. The journalism law textbook case of *New York Times Co. v. Sullivan* of 1964 and the subsequent decision by the U.S. Supreme Court serve as the example for determining defamation suits. In that case, public officials' access to media and publicity meant that they had to reach a higher standard when attempting to prove defamation than would a normal person. As a result of the case, public officials have to establish actual malice on the part of the defamer; it must be proven that the defendant either intended to harm the plaintiff by making a statement that the person knew to be false or that the defendant had a reckless disregard for the validity of the statement and its subsequent effect.

A case closely related to *Times v. Sullivan* was *Curtis Publishing Co. v. Butts* (1967), in which the athletic director at the University of Georgia was accused of delivering the football game plan to his friend, Alabama head football coach Bear Bryant, before a contest between the two squads. The court found that the standard for actual malice to succeed in a defamation case would extend to public figures who "commanded sufficient continuing public interest." In *Gertz v. Robert Welch* (1974), the U.S. Supreme Court defined an additional legal fiction, that of "limited-purpose public figures." The finding reinforced that a public figure, even if that figure is public in a limited capacity, must meet the actual malice burden of proof to claim defamation.

College and professional sport coaches are generally considered public figures, although there have been exceptions, such as the case of a Louisville assistant baseball coach in *Warford v. Lexington Herald* (1990). In the realm of high school sport, however, there is considerable controversy over the public status of athletes and coaches. In *Wilson v. The Daily Gazette Company* (2003), the West Virginia Supreme Court decided that high school athletes are not public figures, even though the athlete in question had achieved a great deal of notoriety and media attention for his sporting achievements. Given the nationwide popularity that a high school athlete today can potentially accrue, such as that attained by LeBron James during his pre-pro days in Ohio, it begs the question of whether these athletes, despite being high school students, are not actually public figures.

# Ethical Dimensions of Sport Public Relations

The ethical dimension of sport public relations does not receive a great deal of attention, but it can be extremely important for both the individual public relations practitioner and the organization as a whole. The way that a public relations department treats ethical considerations sets the tone for external perception of the organization as a whole.

## Codes of Ethics

Many sport media organizations have their own **codes of ethics**, which act as guidelines for professional behavior among workers in the field. For sport media relations professionals on the collegiate level, the professional organization of the College Sports Information Directors of America (CoSIDA) publishes a code of ethics, which contains behavioral guidelines and parameters.

The CoSIDA code of ethics details the organization's stated preferences for sports information director conduct as it relates to a wide variety of items. Some areas of ethical concern include support of institutional policies, loyalty to the athletic director and coaching staff, respect for athletes, professional interactions with the media, prohibition of criticism of officials, and avoidance of conflict of interest with products or sponsors.

Regardless of the organization, sport public relations officials are expected to conduct themselves professionally while simultaneously acting in the best interests of their organizations. This responsibility includes producing positive content relating to athletes, coaches, and team officials.

## Questions of Fairness in Coverage

Sports information directors and other professional media relations workers are often concerned with equity in coverage of their sports by the media.

The process of dealing with inequities in coverage through external media is a long-standing ethical concern, but the growth of team and organizational websites as a news source has led to ethical issues of fairness in coverage within these organizations.

Newspapers and television stations have long been criticized for giving preferential coverage to more popular sports while ignoring or minimizing others. Several studies have established that mainstream media outlets tend to cover high-revenue sports, such as college football and men's basketball, while minimizing coverage of low-revenue sports, particularly women's sports. This problem has been exposed even at the high school level, where boys' sports receive far greater coverage than girls' sports.

Particularly at the collegiate level, sport public relations workers often find themselves in the ethical dilemma of having to promote coverage of one sport over another. This issue can take many forms, from resource allocation (i.e., assigning personnel to provide coverage to a sport) to money spent on promotion and writing. On the one hand, the sports information director has an ethical responsibility to attract equitable coverage to all sports, particularly those that are traditionally underexposed. On the other hand, the athletics department needs to have greater attention paid to the revenue sports for financial reasons.

Athletics departments must make these decisions in relation to their own websites as well. Does the school provide equal promotion to stories about all varsity sports on its website, or does it focus its coverage on sports such as football and men's basketball, which are liable to attract greater web traffic and therefore generate more revenue?

## Moral Differences in Domestic and International Sport

Although we tend to focus mostly on the legal or political differences between jurisdictions and governing bodies on the international stage, significant moral differences are found domestically as well, colored in large part by the cultural and historical underpinnings of each city, country, and region. The sport experience in the United States features several intense rivalries, on both the professional level (e.g., New York Yankees and Boston Red Sox, Chicago Cubs and St. Louis Cardinals, Green Bay Packers and Minnesota Vikings) and the collegiate level (e.g., Michigan and Ohio State, North Carolina and Duke, Texas and Oklahoma). But the way that people treat sport in other parts of the world is vastly different, and it begins with team affiliation of youth essentially "out of the womb." Socioeconomic, religious, cultural, and demographic differences render certain teams' competitions as classic rivalries, essentially becoming battles in a long-standing war against supporters of the opposite camp or team, often with religious, political, and socioeconomic overtones.

Thus, sport communications professionals need to be aware of the sensitivities of each region. Before a Celtic–Rangers, Barcelona–Real Madrid, Partizan–Red Star Belgrade, or Panathinaikos–Olympiakos game, public relations workers need to attempt a balanced report and try to ease the inherent pressure. Furthermore, public relations professionals need to do the same on the national team stage before classic rivalries with historical underpinnings (i.e., Argentina v. Brazil, Serbia v. Croatia, Russia v. USA). Particularly with the advent of breakaway republics formed out of the former Eastern Bloc, Yugoslavia, and other areas of the world, public relations professionals need to conduct some fundamental research so that they can cover such events and games responsibly and minimize irritation among administrators or fans from either camp. A good example nowadays is when U.S. reporters refer to the Former Yugoslav Republic of Macedonia (FYROM) by only the last component of the U.N.-acknowledged name, which immediately raises fiery protest by Greek audiences because of the history of the Greek region of Macedonia (northern Greece).

At the same time, public relations professionals working in international sport settings need to be familiar with the customs and traditions for each sport and region. Otherwise, they might not know how to handle the presence of SWAT or special forces units deployed in rivalry games in each region and would not know at which stages of the event they would need to keep their distance or protect themselves from foul play.

Of course, the tone, character, and delivery of written pieces are also important to consider in an international context. Entitlements and freedoms upheld in the United States may not be respected in other regions. When a public relations worker is covering an international event, significant research and interaction with local public relations and sport communications staff would assist in forming an educated and well-planned strategy for work in such different settings (Halgreen, 2004; Kaburakis, 2008).

## Ethical Dilemmas for Public Relations Professionals

Sport public relations can have its share of ethical dilemmas. The conflict between what is right for the athlete or coach and what is right for the organization can sometimes lead to uncertainty about how to proceed. Furthermore, the responsibility that public relations workers have to their employers can also be affected by larger societal issues.

When dealing with the firing of a coach or the release of a player, issues often arise between the team and that coach or player. The sport public relations worker should approach every firing situation from a professional and neutral perspective. Although a person's primary obligation is to the team or league of employ, she or he must also consider the ethics of reporting false information to the team's constituent groups, including fans, sponsors, and the media.

Public relations officials must also be careful to balance the needs of the organization with the needs of the fans. Although casting the team and its players in the best possible light is important, the public relations worker risks appearing unrealistic or out of touch if the tone of press releases or content is blindly positive. This point is particularly apt during seasons when a team is losing a large number of games. Balancing the ethical obligation of projecting positivity with the obligation to provide truthful information can be a challenge.

## SUMMARY

The legal and ethical considerations of sport public relations are numerous and ever changing. This area of sport public relations is perhaps the most severely affected by the advent of technology. New issues and problems arise every year for sport public relations professionals in the management of these new tools. Today's sport public relations professionals must remain up to date on emerging communication trends that athletes, fans, and media are using. They must be able to consider not only the benefits of those trends but also the potential drawbacks. Anticipating where possible legal issues may arise can mean the difference between success and trouble in the sport public relations realm. Questions of ethics in sport public relations also change constantly, and sport public relations professionals must be able to adapt to the ethical mores of the generation in cultural command. These changes need not be for the worse, and certain ethical standards may be relaxed as younger and less conservative fans become the majority. Sport public relations professionals need to understand these changes and use them to the benefit of their organizations.

## LEARNING ACTIVITIES

1. Find and examine a recent news article that covers a legal issue relating to sport, such as the arrest of a key player, a lawsuit brought against a governing body, or a court ruling that affects the eligibility of athletes to compete (such as the NBA's one-and-done rule). What are the key elements of the issue? Who stands to benefit from the current rule? What is the background of the rule, and how did it get to where it is today?

2. Organize an in-class debate in which one group of students assumes the position of the NCAA student–athletes' advocates, claiming violations of their rights of publicity because of the NCAA–CLC–EA Sports licensing agreements and use of images and identities in college sport video games. The other groups each defend a defendant, arguing for consent defense, First Amendment preemption of student–athletes' rights, and so on.

3. Examine several areas of sport public relations and communications, focusing especially on innovation and new media. Prepare a presentation and brief paper analyzing how you would test the (nowadays expanding) limits of the public domain, promoting the interests of a sport corporation, institution's athletics department, media outlet, personal blog, or LLC. Ensure that your organization is fully prepared to deal with a suit such as copyright or trademark infringement, right of publicity violation, invasion of privacy, defamation, commercial misappropriation, and so on.

4. Read and evaluate the code of ethics of a nationally known sport entity or governing body. What are the central ethical tenets expressed in the code?

# appendix A

# Selected Pages From a Media Guide

**Media guides provide** detailed information regarding the sport organization and its teams. In collegiate settings, an athletics communication office often produces a separate media guide for each varsity sport and separate publications for men's and women's teams. A single office may produce a dozen or more guides in a single academic year, particularly in higher divisions of competition.

Media guides vary in size and level of detail. Typically, they are 8.5 × 11 inches (21 × 28 cm) at the college level and 5.5 × 8.5 (14 × 22 cm) or 6 × 9 inches (15 × 23 cm) at the professional level. But there are exceptions to those standards. Sport public relations professionals at smaller colleges in particular may opt for smaller publications that are less expensive to print. In some instances, even quad- and trifold brochures function as guides.

This appendix provides selected pages from a media guide.

# Quick Facts

## GENERAL INFORMATION
Institution:............................... University of Oklahoma
Website:.............................SoonerSports.com
Location:............................... Norman, Okla.
Enrollment:.......................................28,582
Colors:.............................Crimson and Cream
Founded:.........................................1890
Nickname:......................................Sooners
Membership:...............................NCAA Division I
Conference:..........................................Big 12

## UNIVERSITY INFORMATION
President:...........................David L. Boren (Yale, 1963)
Faculty Representative: ....... Connie Dillon (Oklahoma State, 1972)
VP for Athletics Programs:.........Joe Castiglione (Maryland, 1979)
Senior Woman Administrator: ......Dr. Nicki Moore (Missouri, 1996)
Athletics Department Phone: ......................(405) 325-8208
Ticket Office Phone: ..............(405) 325-2424/(800) 456-4668

## PROGRAM INFORMATION
First Year of Basketball: ...............................1974-75
All-Time Record: .......................................637-437 (.593)
All-Time Conference Record: ......................240-178 (.574)
All-Time Big 12 Record: ........................... 146-77 (.655)
NCAA Tournament Appearances:................................13
Final Four Appearances:.......................3 (2002, 2009, 2010)
Regular Season Conference Titles: .................................
.....................7 (1986, 2000, 2001, 2002, 2006, 2007, 2009)
Conference Tournament Titles:...........4 (2002, 2004, 2006, 2007)
2009-10 Overall Record:...................................27-11
2009-10 Big 12 Record: ..................... 11-5 (T-Second)
Letterwinners Returning/Lost:..............................8/3
Starters Returning/Lost: ..................................3/3
Newcomers: ...............................................6

## STAFF INFORMATION
Head Coach: ............... Sherri Coale (Oklahoma Christian, 1987)
Overall Record/Years:.....................313-143 (.686)/14
Big 12 Record: .............................. 146-77 (.655)
NCAA Appearances: ........................................11
WNIT Appearances: .........................................1
Assistant Coaches:.............Jan Ross (Oklahoma Christian, 1986),
............................... Stacy Hansmeyer (Connecticut, 2001),
......................Chad Thrailkill (Southern Nazarene, 1993)
Director of Operations:............................. Guy Austin
Athletics Trainer:............... Carolynn Loon (Ohio State, 1999)
Strength & Conditioning Coach:......Tim Overman (Creighton, 2000)
Video Coordinator: ...........Makina Waye (Lynn University, 2006)
Team Manager: ...........Ryan Lawrence (Washington State, 2008)
Administrative Assistants:..............Paula Smalling, Kate Gaines
Women's Basketball Office Phone: .................(405) 325-8322

## MEDIA RELATIONS INFORMATION
Mailing Address: ..... 180 W. Brooks, Suite 2525, Norman, OK 73019
Media Relations Phone: ...........................(405) 325-8231
Media Relations Fax:...............................(405) 325-7623
Sr. Assoc. AD/Communications: Kenny Mossman (kmossman@ou.edu)
Associate Directors:..................Mike Houck, Jared Thompson
Assistant Directors: .........David Bassity, Cassie Gage, Craig Moran
Pubications Coordinator:.............................Debbie Copp
Graphic Designer: ...............................Scott Matthews
Women's Basketball Contact:Jared Thompson (jaredthompson@ou.edu)
Press Row Number: ..............................(405) 325-1024

This publication was printed by OU Printing Services at no cost to the taxpayers of the state of Oklahoma. The University of Oklahoma is an equal opportunity institution. **October 2010**

**Cover**
Scott Matthews

**Writing, Layout and Design**
Jared Thompson and Tiona Bowman

**Photos**
Ty Russell, Candid Color, Stockton Photo, Shannon Ho Photography, Shevaun Williams and Associates, Barry Gossage/ NBAE, Jerry Laizure

# 2010-11 Sooners

# 10

**THE YEAR IN PHOTOS**
Relive the Final Four trek with the top photos of the 2009-10 season.

# 30

**FINAL FOUR TRADITION**
The Sooners have made three national semifinals in eight years, including back-to-back trips in 2009 and 2010.

# 38

### WHY OKLAHOMA?
In their own words, the players describe what made the University of Oklahoma the choice above all others.

# 130

### SHERRI COALE
Profiling the winningest coach in Oklahoma and Big 12 history.

# 172

### 1,000 POINT SCORERS
The wall of honor grew by three as Danielle Robinson, Nyeshia Stevenson and Amanda Thompson crossed the threshold last season.

# Whitney Hand

6-1 | Sophomore (RS) | Guard | Fort Worth, Texas | Liberty Christian

## 25

## COLLEGIATE ACCOLADES
• Big 12 Freshman of the Year (2009)
• All-Big 12 Honorable Mention (2009)
• All-Big 12 Freshman Team (2009)
• NCAA Championship All-Region (2009)
• Big 12 Freshman of the Week (4x, 2009)

**2009-10 - SOPHOMORE**: Made five starts, averaging 13.4 points and 4.4 rebounds, before tearing ACL shortly before halftime of OU's blowout win of San Diego State in the U.S. Virgin Islands Paradise Jam (Nov. 27) ... Scored over 14 points per game in first four contests and had 10 at time of first-half injury ... Made 10 of 26 (.385) 3-pointers, 13 of 28 (.464) 2-pointers and 11 of 14 (.786) free throws.

**2008-09 - FRESHMAN**: Averaged 9.2 points, 2.9 rebounds and 37.3 3-point field goal percentage in 33 games started ... Big 12 Freshman of the Year ... All-Big 12 honorable mention ... Big 12 All-Freshman Team selection ... NCAA Championship All-Oklahoma City Region Team member ... Ranked fourth in Big 12 in 3-point field goal percentage ... Four-time Big 12 Freshman of the Week (Dec. 1, Jan. 12, Jan. 26, Feb. 9) ... Averaged 13.0 points, 4.8 rebounds and 2.0 steals during NCAA Championship ... Scored season-high 22 points versus Purdue in Oklahoma City Regional Semifinal (March 29) ... Led Oklahoma to first win over defending national champions Tennessee with 20-point performance ... Made 8-of-9 field goals, including 4-of-5 3-point attempts, in win over Lady Vols (Feb. 2) ... Also scored 20 points in win versus Marist (Nov. 26) ... Became just seventh true freshman under Sherri Coale to start first career game, netting 11 points versus UC-Riverside (Nov. 15).

## HIGH SCHOOL ACCOLADES
• Nation's No. 14 Overall Player (SLAM Magazine)
• Nation's No. 5 Shooting Guard (SLAM Magazine)
• Texas' No. 1 Shooting Guard (SLAM Magazine)
• Nation's No. 33 Overall Player (Blue Star Report)
• Nation's No. 39 Overall Player (ESPN Hoopgurlz)
• High School All-American (Women's Basketball Coaches Association)
• Texas Player of the Year (Chevrolet's Inside High School Basketball)
• 2008 TAPPS Large Division Player of the Year (Texas Association of Basketball Coaches)
• 2008 TAPPS All-State Class 5A First Team
• 2008 TAPPS All-District 1-5A MVP
• 2008 TAPPS All-District 1-5A First Team
• 2008 TAPPS Academic All-State Basketball
• 2008 TABC All-Star Game Selection
• 2008 TABC Private High School (Large Division) Player of the Year
• 2008 All-Texas First Team (Premier Basketball Report)
• 2008 TAPPS Class 5A Female Athlete of the Year
• Greater Denton Sports Commission Female Athlete of the Year Runner-Up
• 2007 TAPPS All-State Class 5A First Team
• 2007 TAPPS All-District 1-5A Co-MVP
• 2007 All-Area MVP (Denton Record Chronicle)

## CAREER STATISTICS

| SEASON | GP-S | FG | % | 3FG | % | FT | % | REB | RPG | AST | TO | BLK | STL | PTS | PPG |
|---|---|---|---|---|---|---|---|---|---|---|---|---|---|---|---|
| 2008-09 | 33-33 | 106-268 | .396 | 62-166 | .373 | 29-35 | .829 | 97 | 2.9 | 54 | 64 | 17 | 40 | 303 | 9.2 |
| 2009-10 | 5-5 | 23-54 | .426 | 10-26 | .385 | 11-14 | .786 | 22 | 4.4 | 11 | 13 | 2 | 6 | 67 | 13.4 |
| **TOTAL** | **38-38** | **129-322** | **.401** | **72-192** | **.375** | **40-49** | **.816** | **119** | **3.1** | **65** | **77** | **19** | **46** | **370** | **9.7** |

# Jan Ross

ASSISTANT COACH

15th Season

Jan Ross is entering her 15th season as an assistant coach on the Oklahoma basketball staff. Ross has played an instrumental part in rebuilding the Oklahoma program. She has helped head coach Sherri Coale turn the Oklahoma women's basketball program into a nationally recognized name.

Since Ross' arrival, the Sooners have won six Big 12 Conference regular season titles, four Big 12 Postseason Championships, produced nine 20-plus win seasons and advanced to 11 consecutive NCAA Tournaments. Ross also helped OU to the 2002 National Championship game and back-to-back national semifinals in 2009 and 2010.

Ross has been extremely active in all phases of Oklahoma's emergence into the national spotlight. Ross' area of emphasis includes coaching OU's frontcourt, recruiting and scouting opponents. Not only is her expertise with post players essential, but Ross is a mastermind when it comes down to the Xs and Os of the game. She is also one of the top recruiters in the game. Ross' recruiting efforts have ensured that the Sooners will remain one of the top women's basketball programs in the country.

In addition to the Sooners' team accomplishments with Ross on the sideline, OU post players have flourished individually. She has helped Phylesha Whaley, Courtney Paris and Caton Hill develop into three of the top post players in the country. All three players are among the best in Oklahoma history and the records books illustrate it.

In past seasons, Ross monitored the academic progress of each student-athlete. As a team, the Sooners have posted a team GPA of 3.0 or better for 24 of the 28 semesters she has been at OU and have had three student-athletes earn Academic All-America first team honors under Ross' watch. Oklahoma has produced 79 Academic All-Big 12 selections in 14 seasons.

With the Sooners' recent success, Ross has experienced first hand the growing interest in girls basketball within the state and surrounding areas as noted by the rapid attendance increase in OU's Sooner Sessions Camps. OU annually hosts approximately 1,500 campers, which includes more than 100 teams.

As a player at Oklahoma Christian, she collected numerous playing and academic honors including NAIA honorable mention All-America, All-District IV and All-Sooner Athletic Conference selection as a senior. She also was an NAIA Scholar Athlete and was elected to Who's Who. An all-state athlete at Putnam City West, Ross ranks 11th on Oklahoma Christian's career scoring list with 1,348 points. She holds the school record for career steals (300) and completed her career with a .537 field goal percentage and 494 assists.

After ending her collegiate career with Oklahoma Christian, Ross joined the program as an assistant coach for five years and served as assistant athletics director for two years. This Oklahoman was inducted into her alma mater's Athletic Hall of Fame in February 2003.

Ross also gained coaching experience at Broken Arrow (1995-96) and Del City high schools (1991-95) as the head coach.

The Chickasha, Okla. native received her bachelor's degree in mathematics with a minor in physical education from Oklahoma Christian University (1986) and her master's degree in sports administration from the University of Oklahoma (1990).

**COLLEGE COACHING CAREER**
Oklahoma, Assistant Coach, 1996-Present

**PLAYING CAREER**
Oklahoma Christian, 1983-96

**EDUCATION**
Oklahoma Christian, 1986
Oklahoma, 1990

**HOMETOWN**
Born in Chickasha, Okla.

**NCAA TOURNAMENTS COACHED**
2000, 2001, 2002, 2003, 2004, 2005, 2006, 2007, 2008, 2009, 2010

**PROMINENT PUPILS**
LaNeisha Caufield, Utah Starzz
Stacey Dales, Chicago Sky
Dionnah Jackson, Sacramento Monarchs
Abi Olajuwon, Chicago Sky
Ashley Paris, Los Angeles Sparks
Courtney Paris, Sacramento Monarchs
Rosalind Ross, Los Angeles Sparks
Leah Rush, Pheonix Mercury
Nyeshia Stevenson, Phoenix Mercury
Amanda Thompson, Tulsa Shock
Maria Villaroel, Phoenix Mercury
Phylesha Whaley, Minnesota Lynx

# 2009-10 Results

| Date | (S) | Opponent | Result | Score | Att. | High Points | High Rebounds |
|------|-----|----------|--------|-------|------|-------------|---------------|
| 11/13/09 | | MERCER | W | 108-66 | 6732 | (17)Robinson/Thompson | (9)Olajuwon/Thompson |
| 11/15/09 | | at Georgia | L | 51-62 | 4567 | (13)Hand,Whitney | (13)Thompson,Amanda |
| 11/21/09 | | TCU | W | 74-70 | 6679 | (23)Olajuwon,Abi | (11)Thompson,Amanda |
| 11/26/09 | 1 | vs South Carolina | W | 75-67 | 506 | (16)Stevenson,Nyeshia | (9)Thompson,Amanda |
| 11/27/09 | 1 | vs San Diego State | W | 87-48 | 577 | (18)Thompson,Amanda | (9)Thompson,Amanda |
| 11/28/09 | 1 | vs Notre Dame | L | 71-81 | 711 | (26)Robinson,Danielle | (7)Olajuwon,Abi |
| 12/3/09 | | UT-ARLINGTON | W | 100-67 | 6038 | (29)Roethlisberger,C | (10)Thompson,Amanda |
| 12/5/09 | | ARKANSAS | Wot | 87-86 | 6736 | (31)Robinson,Danielle | (14)Thompson,Amanda |
| 12/9/09 | | at Marist | Wot | 80-71 | 2828 | (32)Stevenson,Nyeshia | (11)Thompson,Amanda |
| 12/10/09 | | at Army | W | 59-46 | 721 | (17)Stevenson,Nyeshia | (13)Olajuwon,Abi |
| 12/20/09 | | at Creighton | W | 67-58 | 1453 | (22)Robinson,Danielle | (7)Cloman/Robinson |
| 12/30/09 | | CS-FULLERTON | W | 95-76 | 5586 | (25)Olajuwon,Abi | (9)Thompson,Amanda |
| 1/3/10 | | at TENNESSEE | L | 75-96 | 13332 | (26)Thompson,Amanda | (11)Thompson,Amanda |
| 1/9/10 | * | TEXAS TECH | W | 73-58 | 7018 | (17)Thompson,Amanda | (10)Stevenson,Nyeshia |
| 1/13/10 | * | at Baylor | L | 47-57 | 7718 | (15)Robinson,Danielle | (12)Thompson,Amanda |
| 1/17/10 | * | TEXAS A&M | W | 74-65 | 8159 | (24)Robinson,Danielle | (11)Olajuwon/Thompson |
| 1/20/10 | * | at Missouri | W | 62-61 | 1347 | (23)Stevenson,Nyeshia | (11)Thompson,Amanda |
| 1/23/10 | * | KANSAS | W | 81-69 | 8331 | (22)Stevenson,Nyeshia | (8)McFarland/Thompson |
| 1/27/10 | * | at Iowa State | L | 56-63 | 10121 | (14)Stevenson,Nyeshia | (10)Thompson,Amanda |
| 1/30/10 | * | at Texas Tech | W | 70-66 | 7897 | (26)Robinson,Danielle | (13)Thompson,Amanda |
| 2/3/10 | * | TEXAS | L | 57-75 | 7151 | (19)Thompson,Amanda | (11)Thompson,Amanda |
| 2/6/10 | * | at Oklahoma State | W | 77-66 | 6264 | (36)Robinson,Danielle | (10)Thompson,Amanda |
| 2/10/10 | * | BAYLOR | Wot | 62-60 | 8493 | (19)Thompson/Robinson | (19)Thompson,Amanda |
| 2/13/10 | * | COLORADO | W | 65-55 | 8298 | (16)Thompson,Amanda | (8)Olajuwon,Abi |
| 2/15/10 | | CONNECTICUT | L | 60-76 | 11865 | (18)Robinson,Danielle | (13)Thompson,Amanda |
| 2/21/10 | * | at Kansas State | W | 64-58 | 4523 | (24)Stevenson,Nyeshia | (11)Thompson,Amanda |
| 2/24/10 | * | NEBRASKA | L | 64-80 | 7756 | (16)Olajuwon,Abi | (14)Olajuwon,Abi |
| 2/27/10 | * | at Texas | W | 75-60 | 6579 | (28)Stevenson,Nyeshia | (16)Thompson,Amanda |
| 3/2/10 | * | at Texas A&M | L | 55-78 | 5205 | (16)Robinson,Danielle | (10)Olajuwon,Abi |
| 3/7/10 | * | OKLAHOMA STATE | W | 95-62 | 12387 | (29)Thompson,Amanda | (11)Thompson,Amanda |
| 3/12/10 | 2 | vs Baylor | W | 59-54 | 4239 | (26)Robinson,Danielle | (10)Olajuwon,Abi |
| 3/13/10 | 2 | vs Oklahoma State | W | 74-69 | 4675 | (19)Robinson,Danielle | (18)Thompson,Amanda |
| 03/14/10 | | vs Texas A&M | L | 67-74 | 3120 | (20)Thompson,Amanda | (19)Thompson,Amanda |
| 3/21/10 | 3 | SOUTH DAKOTA ST. | W | 68-57 | 5368 | (17)Stevenson,Nyeshia | (15)Thompson,Amanda |
| 3/23/10 | 3 | UALR | W | 60-44 | 6305 | (19)Olajuwon,Abi | (11)Olajuwon,Abi |
| 3/28/10 | 4 | vs Notre Dame | Wot | 77-72 | 5907 | (21)Stevenson,Nyeshia | (14)Olajuwon,Abi |
| 3/30/10 | 4 | vs Kentucky | W | 88-68 | 4423 | (31)Stevenson,Nyeshia | (14)Thompson,Amanda |
| 4/4/10 | 5 | vs Stanford | L | 66-73 | 25817 | (23)Robinson,Danielle | (9)Olajuwon/Thompson |

**SCHEDULE LEGEND:**
* = Conference game
1 = U.S. Virgin Islands Paradise Jam
2 = Big 12 Championship (Kansas City, Mo.)
3 = NCAA First/Second Rounds (Norman, Okla.)
4 = NCAA Kansas City Regional (Kansas City, Mo.)
5 = NCAA Final Four (San Antonio, Texas)
CAPS - Indicates home game

| RECORD | OVERALL | HOME | AWAY | NEUTRAL | | ATTENDANCE | TOTALS | AVERAGE |
|--------|---------|------|------|---------|--|------------|--------|---------|
| All Games | 27-11 | 13-3 | 8-5 | 6-3 | | Home | 122,902 | 7,681 |
| Big 12 | 11-5 | 6-2 | 5-3 | 0-0 | | Away | 122,530 | 5,581 |
| Non-Conference | 16-6 | 7-1 | 3-2 | 6-3 | | Neutral | - | 5,553 |

## BIG 12 CONFERENCE STANDINGS

| | Conference | | Overall | |
|--|------------|--|---------|--|
| | W-L | Pct. | W-L | Pct. |
| Nebraska | 16-0 | 1.000 | 32-2 | .941 |
| Iowa State | 11-5 | .688 | 25-8 | .758 |
| Oklahoma | 11-5 | .688 | 27-11 | .711 |
| Texas A&M | 10-6 | .625 | 26-8 | .765 |
| Texas | 10-6 | .625 | 22-11 | .667 |
| Baylor | 9-7 | .562 | 27-10 | .730 |
| Oklahoma State | 9-7 | .562 | 24-11 | .686 |
| Texas Tech | 5-11 | .312 | 18-15 | .545 |
| Kansas | 5-11 | .312 | 17-16 | .515 |
| Kansas State | 5-11 | .312 | 14-18 | .438 |
| Colorado | 3-13 | .188 | 13-17 | .433 |
| Missouri | 2-14 | .125 | 12-18 | .400 |

# Individual Statistics

## INDIVIDUAL STATISTICS - ALL GAMES

| ## | Player | GP | GS | Tot | Avg | FG | FGA | Pct | 3FG | FGA | Pct | FT | FTA | Pct | Off | Def | Tot | Avg | PF | FO | A | TO | Blk | Stl | Pts | Avg |
|----|--------|----|----|-----|-----|----|-----|-----|-----|-----|-----|----|-----|-----|-----|-----|-----|-----|----|----|---|----|-----|-----|-----|-----|
| 13 | Robinson,Danielle | 38 | 38 | 1333 | 35.1 | 240 | 516 | .465 | 2 | 15 | .133 | 157 | 179 | .877 | 26 | 101 | 127 | 3.3 | 98 | 4 | 202 | 155 | 3 | 71 | 639 | 16.8 |
| 01 | Stevenson,Nyeshia | 38 | 38 | 1354 | 35.6 | 202 | 474 | .426 | 86 | 259 | .332 | 63 | 90 | .700 | 22 | 120 | 142 | 3.7 | 41 | 0 | 54 | 84 | 4 | 45 | 553 | 14.6 |
| 25 | Hand,Whitney | 5 | 5 | 141 | 28.2 | 23 | 54 | .426 | 10 | 26 | .385 | 11 | 14 | .786 | 9 | 13 | 22 | 4.4 | 9 | 0 | 11 | 13 | 2 | 6 | 67 | 13.4 |
| 21 | Thompson,Amanda | 38 | 38 | 1282 | 33.7 | 199 | 484 | .411 | 24 | 79 | .304 | 74 | 90 | .822 | 141 | 259 | 400 | 10.5 | 116 | 2 | 97 | 103 | 36 | 20 | 496 | 13.1 |
| 34 | Olajuwon,Abi | 38 | 38 | 876 | 23.1 | 161 | 318 | .506 | 0 | 0 | .000 | 79 | 128 | .617 | 105 | 174 | 279 | 7.3 | 117 | 4 | 18 | 86 | 34 | 20 | 401 | 10.6 |
| 10 | Roethlisberger,C | 38 | 18 | 930 | 24.5 | 82 | 232 | .353 | 41 | 140 | .293 | 48 | 63 | .762 | 49 | 106 | 155 | 4.1 | 91 | 1 | 46 | 63 | 10 | 19 | 253 | 6.7 |
| 53 | McFarland,Joanna | 38 | 0 | 577 | 15.2 | 55 | 114 | .482 | 1 | 5 | .200 | 34 | 59 | .576 | 55 | 89 | 144 | 3.8 | 100 | 2 | 11 | 46 | 10 | 12 | 145 | 3.8 |
| 45 | Hartman,Jasmine | 38 | 15 | 765 | 20.1 | 29 | 84 | .345 | 11 | 35 | .314 | 16 | 31 | .516 | 15 | 45 | 60 | 1.6 | 34 | 1 | 63 | 45 | 4 | 12 | 85 | 2.2 |
| 44 | Cloman,Lyndsey | 21 | 0 | 187 | 8.9 | 15 | 40 | .375 | 0 | 0 | .000 | 6 | 9 | .667 | 16 | 27 | 43 | 2.0 | 24 | 0 | 2 | 14 | 5 | 3 | 36 | 1.7 |
| 14 | Willis,Lauren | 28 | 0 | 236 | 8.4 | 13 | 47 | .277 | 11 | 39 | .282 | 6 | 7 | .857 | 4 | 21 | 25 | 0.9 | 14 | 0 | 8 | 13 | 1 | 4 | 43 | 1.5 |
| 31 | Morrison,Kodi | 5 | 0 | 19 | 3.8 | 3 | 9 | .333 | 1 | 5 | .200 | 0 | 0 | .000 | 1 | 2 | 3 | 0.6 | 0 | 0 | 0 | 2 | 0 | 1 | 7 | 1.4 |
| | Team | | | | | | | | | | | | | | 63 | 89 | 152 | | | | | 7 | | | | |
| | Total......... | 38 | | 7700 | | 1022 | 2372 | .431 | 187 | 603 | .310 | 494 | 670 | .737 | 506 | 1046 | 1552 | 40.8 | 644 | 14 | 512 | 631 | 109 | 260 | 2725 | 71.7 |
| | Opponents...... | 38 | | 7701 | | 913 | 2333 | .391 | 187 | 620 | .302 | 501 | 691 | .725 | 461 | 943 | 1404 | 36.9 | 641 | 9 | 417 | 598 | 131 | 286 | 2514 | 66.2 |

| Score By Periods | 1st | 2nd | OT | Total |
|------------------|-----|-----|----|-------|
| Oklahoma | 1256 | 1433 | 36 | 2725 |
| Opponents | 1198 | 1297 | 19 | 2514 |

## INDIVIDUAL STATISTICS - BIG 12 CONFERENCE GAMES

| ## | Player | GP | GS | Tot | Avg | FG | FGA | Pct | 3FG | FGA | Pct | FT | FTA | Pct | Off | Def | Tot | Avg | PF | FO | A | TO | Blk | Stl | Pts | Avg |
|----|--------|----|----|-----|-----|----|-----|-----|-----|-----|-----|----|-----|-----|-----|-----|-----|-----|----|----|---|----|-----|-----|-----|-----|
| 13 | Robinson,Danielle | 16 | 16 | 557 | 34.8 | 89 | 203 | .438 | 1 | 11 | .091 | 91 | 95 | .958 | 10 | 41 | 51 | 3.2 | 43 | 2 | 79 | 57 | 2 | 24 | 270 | 16.9 |
| 01 | Stevenson,Nyeshia | 16 | 16 | 587 | 36.7 | 88 | 218 | .404 | 37 | 114 | .325 | 20 | 27 | .741 | 7 | 58 | 65 | 4.1 | 19 | 0 | 17 | 36 | 1 | 16 | 233 | 14.6 |
| 25 | Hand,Whitney | 0 | 0 | 0 | 0.0 | 0 | 0 | .000 | 0 | 0 | .000 | 0 | 0 | .000 | 0 | 0 | 0 | 0.0 | 0 | 0 | 0 | 0 | 0 | 0 | 0 | 0.0 |
| 21 | Thompson,Amanda | 16 | 16 | 528 | 33.0 | 87 | 203 | .429 | 12 | 27 | .444 | 35 | 42 | .833 | 58 | 108 | 166 | 10.4 | 49 | 0 | 37 | 45 | 13 | 22 | 221 | 13.8 |
| 34 | Olajuwon,Abi | 16 | 16 | 383 | 23.9 | 57 | 124 | .460 | 0 | 0 | .000 | 32 | 49 | .653 | 38 | 89 | 127 | 7.9 | 51 | 4 | 7 | 39 | 9 | 7 | 146 | 9.1 |
| 10 | Roethlisberger,C | 16 | 10 | 390 | 24.4 | 27 | 94 | .287 | 10 | 52 | .192 | 26 | 34 | .765 | 24 | 40 | 64 | 4.0 | 43 | 1 | 16 | 29 | 1 | 5 | 90 | 5.6 |
| 53 | McFarland,Joanna | 16 | 0 | 240 | 15.0 | 20 | 44 | .455 | 1 | 2 | .500 | 7 | 17 | .412 | 27 | 33 | 60 | 3.8 | 47 | 0 | 5 | 25 | 2 | 7 | 48 | 3.0 |
| 45 | Hartman,Jasmine | 16 | 6 | 361 | 22.6 | 12 | 32 | .375 | 6 | 12 | .500 | 8 | 15 | .533 | 4 | 10 | 14 | 0.9 | 14 | 0 | 26 | 20 | 0 | 6 | 38 | 2.4 |
| 44 | Cloman,Lyndsey | 10 | 0 | 81 | 8.1 | 5 | 14 | .357 | 0 | 0 | .000 | 4 | 7 | .571 | 4 | 8 | 12 | 1.2 | 9 | 0 | 1 | 4 | 2 | 2 | 14 | 1.4 |
| 14 | Willis,Lauren | 12 | 0 | 81 | 6.8 | 4 | 14 | .286 | 4 | 11 | .364 | 0 | 3 | 1.000 | 2 | 5 | 7 | 0.6 | 3 | 0 | 2 | 7 | 0 | 1 | 15 | 1.3 |
| 31 | Morrison,Kodi | 3 | 0 | 17 | 5.7 | 1 | 7 | .143 | 0 | 4 | .000 | 0 | 0 | .000 | 1 | 2 | 3 | 1.0 | 0 | 0 | 0 | 2 | 0 | 1 | 2 | 0.7 |
| | Team | | | | | | | | | | | | | | 32 | 36 | 68 | | | | | 3 | | | | |
| | Total......... | 16 | | 3225 | | 390 | 953 | .409 | 71 | 233 | .305 | 226 | 289 | .782 | 207 | 430 | 637 | 39.8 | 278 | 7 | 190 | 267 | 30 | 91 | 1077 | 67.3 |
| | Opponents...... | 16 | | 3226 | | 372 | 941 | .395 | 71 | 251 | .283 | 218 | 303 | .719 | 174 | 386 | 560 | 35.0 | 272 | 4 | 170 | 240 | 64 | 123 | 1033 | 64.6 |

| Score By Periods | 1st | 2nd | OT | Total |
|------------------|-----|-----|----|-------|
| Oklahoma | 490 | 582 | 5 | 1077 |
| Opponents | 470 | 560 | 3 | 1033 |

# Media Policies

**ATHLETICS COMMUNCIATIONS OFFICE**
The department is housed in suite 2525 of the Gaylord Family-Oklahoma Memorial Stadium, nearly two miles north of the basketball arena. The office can be accessed by using Gate 7 on the north side of the stadium.

**CREDENTIALS**
All members of the media covering the game in a working capacity must seek appropriate credentials at least 24 hours in advance. Please e-mail associate director Jared Thompson with your request on company letterhead. Credentials will be mailed if courier information is provided. Credential requests will be accepted beginning Oct. 1.

**INTERVIEW POLICIES**
Oklahoma players and coaches are available for interviews throughout the season. Arrangements must be made through Jared Thompson in the Media Relations office at least 24 hours in advance. Home and cellular phone numbers of players and coaches will not be released.

**PRESS ROW**
Media seating is located in the southwest corner of Lloyd Noble Center. The press row phone number is (405) 325-1024.

**MEDIA SERVICES**
Pregame notes, flipcards, media guides, programs and statistics will be provided to working media prior to each game. At halftime, a box score and play-by-play will also be distributed in the media work room. A complete postgame packet, consisting of game notes, halftime and final box scores, shot charts and play-by-play, will be handed out approximately 20 minutes after the conclusion of the game.

**MEDIA WILL CALL/LLOYD NOBLE CENTER**
The media entrance and the media will call is located at the south tunnel (check map on right) of the Lloyd Noble Center. Those picking up credentials will be required to furnish photo identification to the attendant. Credentials will be ready one hour prior to tipoff and are available at media will call. Media representatives are strongly encouraged to park on the south end of the arena and enter through the lower south entrance.

**MEDIA WORK ROOM**
The media work room is located at the top of the south tunnel, west of the ramp. Game programs, flip cards, media guides and pregame information sheets will be provided to the working media members in this area. Halftime and final box scores, postgame notes and coaches and players quotes will also be available at this location.

**PARKING**
There is reserved parking for working media in the south parking lot at the Lloyd Noble Center. No parking pass is required.

**PRACTICE SCHEDULE**
The OU women's basketball team begins practice on Friday, Oct. 17. Regular season practices are irregularly scheduled on weekday afternoons at the Lloyd Noble Center. The team will generally practice on the main floor at LNC. Please contact Jared Thompson at the OU Athletics Media Relations office for practice times. Practices are open to the media and public. If you plan to attend practice, advance notice is required.

**PHOTOGRAPHY**
During regular season games, the photographers work area includes the floor area at both ends of the court, on the side opposite the team benches. Special arrangements for strobes or catwalk access must be made through both the Media Relations and Lloyd Noble Center offices. In the event of heavy requests for photo credentials for a particular game, shooting locations will be assigned. All photographs are to be used in editorial coverage and cannot be sold for any commercial enterprise benefiting the photographer. The University of Oklahoma follows NCAA and Big 12 Conference photography guidelines.

**PREGAME MEALS**
Pregame meals are furnished for all credentialed media. The meal is served across the hall from the media work room.

**POSTGAME INTERVIEWS**
After a 15-minute cooling-off period, OU head coach Sherri Coale and requested players will attend a postgame media conference. The visiting team, unless they do not request a formal media conference, will always go first in the press conference room.

The media conference will be held in the same room that the pregame meal is served, across from the media work room. Jared Thompson will take player interview requests prior to the conclusion of the game. Oklahoma and opponent locker rooms are closed to the media.

**ROAD GAME CREDENTIALS**
Media credentials for OU road games can either be requested through OU or the opponent media relations contact. Please be specific when requesting the type of credentials needed.

**RADIO LINES**
Phone lines will be available and provided to Big 12 Conference opponents. In addition, Big 12 opponents will be provided with an ISDN line and Ethernet access. Please contact OU Telecommunications at (405) 325-1873 a week prior to the contest to ensure a working line if you are not a member of the Big 12 Conference.

**TELEPHONE LINES**
A limited number of telephone lines are available in the Lloyd Noble Center media work room. Any media representative desiring a private line to be installed court side or in the media work room should contact the OU Telecommunications office at (405) 325-1873 at least five working days prior to the requested game.

**TRAVEL INFORMATION**
For media travel information, contact Jared Thompson by e-mail, jaredthompson@ou.edu, or by phone at (405) 325-3671.

**The Lloyd Noble Center**

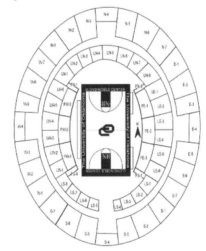

Media Entrance Through South Tunnel

# Sample Crisis Communication Plan

**A crisis communications** plan provides a framework for responding to crisis situations. It empowers sport managers by specifying the responsibilities in a crisis, the way in which information is to be shared internally during a crisis, and the way in which information is to be shared with other publics in a timely manner. By defining such considerations in advance of a crisis, the sport organization may be better positioned to respond in a manner that best protects its reputation and financial interests.

Crisis communications plans are not designed to prescribe responses for every conceivable crisis, nor are they detailed enough to specify every action that must be taken throughout a crisis episode. They are designed to provide general guidelines for the management team, particularly early on. To prepare for crises in such a manner, sport managers must follow a number of steps in the process and then develop a plan containing certain key elements.

Appendix B provides a sample crisis communication plan.

# University Athletic Department Crisis Communications Plan

A crisis is defined as a situation or occurrence possessing the potential to significantly damage the university's and athletic department's reputation. This document describes the steps that are to be taken to (a) identify emerging crises and (b) respond appropriately to such crises.

All athletic department staff members should be familiar with their responsibilities when a crisis occurs. This will enable the department to respond in an appropriate and coordinated manner. It is critical that all potential crises be addressed only within the framework of this plan. While not comprehensive, the following is a brief list of some crises that may be encountered:

1. Accusations of criminal activity against a staff member or student-athlete
2. Accidents involving student-athletes and staff members resulting in serious injury or death
3. Accusations of NCAA rules violations
4. Fan-related incidents involving serious injuries or criminal activity at an athletic event

Athletic department staff members encountering these or other potentially damaging incidents should quickly gather as much information as possible and then immediately contact a member of the crisis assessment committee (CAC). The CAC consists of four members—the senior associate AD/SWA, associate AD for business affairs, assistant AD for media relations, and assistant AD for operations. They may be contacted as follows.

| Position and name | Office # | Home # | Cell # |
|---|---|---|---|
| Sr. Associate AD/SWA/Chair of the CAC<br>Kathy Reaves | 555-0002 | 555-1547 | 555-8729 |
| Associate AD-Business Affairs<br>Christopher Jones | 555-0015 | 555-0042 | 555-9496 |
| Assistant AD-Media Relations<br>Terri Cox | 555-0003 | 555-3514 | 555-7894 |
| Assistant AD-Operations<br>Andrew Easterling | 555-0016 | 555-4069 | 555-5441 |

Upon being notified of the situation, the CAC, in consultation with appropriate parties (i.e., director of athletics, university counsel, university president), will determine whether to fully implement the crisis communication plan. If the situation involves student-athletes or staff members specific to a program, that program's head coach will also be contacted.

The following sections summarize initial CAC response plans. They address the four crisis scenarios previously listed and also provide a generic response plan that may be used for crises that do not fall in the first four categories.

## Scenario 1 Accusation of criminal activity against a staff member or student-athlete

### Objectives

1. Ensure that all parties involved—the accused, the accuser, and others—are treated fairly and in accordance with existing legislation and university policy.
2. Communicate to key publics that the athletic department holds its members to high standards of behavior and upholds its obligation to treat its members with fairness.
3. Take action as quickly as circumstances will permit given objectives 1 and 2.

## Procedures

1. The CAC chair will contact other personnel who serve as members of the crisis communications committee (CCC) for the duration of the crisis episode. They include the following:
   - Director of athletics
   - Senior associate AD
   - Assistant AD for media relations
   - Assistant AD for compliance and student services
   - University general counsel
   - Head coach (if student-athlete is accused)
   - Campus security chief (if incident took place on campus)
   - University director of news and media relations

   Complete contact information is available in appendix A.

2. AD informs university president of the situation.

3. If a student-athlete is involved, head coach contacts the student-athlete's parent or legal guardian.

4. AD approves use of planned response to media inquiries. The planned response, to be attributed to the AD and released by the sports information office, is as follows: "We are obviously very concerned about any and all allegations concerning our (student-athletes or staff members). However, we are still in the early stages of gathering relevant information. As we gather more information and determine how best to proceed, we will make every effort to be fair to all parties involved, while also holding our (student-athletes or staff members) to the highest standards. We will provide additional information as soon as it is available."

5. AD informs athletic department personnel that all media inquiries are to be referred to the office of media relations.

6. Assistant AD for media relations makes initial statement available to media officials who are making inquiries. Assistant AD for media relations informs media members that subsequent inquiries should be directed to, and additional information will be released from, the media relations office. The assistant AD for media relations will also maintain a record of all media inquiries, responses, and follow-up actions.

7. AD's office updates the following individuals: vice president for student affairs, dean of students, faculty athletic representative, and other senior members of the athletic department. Contact information may be found in appendix B.

8. Assistant AD for media relations informs appropriate staff members (e.g., media relations officers assigned to the program involved).

9. Senior associate AD gathers as much information as possible regarding who is involved in the incident, what happened, when and where it happened, and how it unfolded.

10. CCC meets to plan subsequent actions. Key issues to address include the following:
    - Who will serve as primary spokesperson?
    - What will be department's response regarding the accused (e.g., no action until trial, suspension, dismissal)?
    - How may the department best communicate that information to the mass media?
    - How quickly can the department make additional public comment regarding the situation?
    - Who else needs to be contacted regarding the situation and who should make those contacts?

11. As quickly as possible, take those actions deemed important in the crisis committee meeting.

12. As quickly as possible, release additional information regarding the department's response to members of the mass media. A complete list of media contacts is provided in appendix C.

The previous 12 steps provide a framework for how to proceed. Additional CCC meetings may be necessary given the circumstances.

*(continued)*

*(continued)*

## Scenario 2 Accident involving student-athletes and staff members resulting in serious injury or death

### Objectives

1. Ensure that the privacy of those directly and indirectly involved is protected.
2. Release information to key publics as quickly as possible in accordance with objective 1.
3. Communicate the athletic department's
   - sincere concern and sadness regarding the accident,
   - commitment to fully investigate what happened, and
   - commitment to minimize the possibility of such an event occurring again.
4. Minimize exposure to possible legal action.

### Procedures

1. The CAC chair will contact other personnel who will serve as members of the CCC for the duration of the crisis episode. They include the following:
   - Director of athletics
   - Senior associate AD
   - Assistant AD for media relations
   - Assistant AD for compliance and student services
   - University general counsel
   - Head coach (if student-athletes or staff members of specific programs are involved)
   - Campus security chief (if accident took place on campus)
   - University director of news and media relations
   - Student-athlete counselor
2. AD informs university president of the situation. Contact information is located in appendix B.
3. AD and senior associate AD make preliminary contact with family of parties involved in the accident. Contact information is available in student-athlete personnel records.
4. AD approves use of planned response to media inquiries. The planned response, attributed to the AD and released by the media relations office, is as follows: "We are deeply concerned about this incident. We are still in the early stages of gathering pertinent information and will release relevant information as soon as it is available to us, while protecting the privacy of the parties involved and their families."
5. Assistant AD of media relations makes the prepared response available to media officials who are making inquiries. Assistant AD of media relations informs media members that subsequent inquiries should be directed to the media relations office. All additional information will be released from the media relations office as well. Media relations director will maintain a record of all inquiries, responses, and follow-up actions as needed.
6. Media relations director informs all media relations personnel of the situation. If necessary, all media relations personnel will be asked to report to the athletic department to assist with media services.
7. AD's office informs the following people: vice president of student affairs, dean of students, faculty athletic representative, and other senior members of the athletic department. Contact information is located in appendix B.
8. Senior associate AD gathers as much information as possible regarding the accident including who was injured and to what extent, who else was involved, when and where the accident occurred, and what may have caused the accident.
9. The communication crisis team meets to plan the following actions:
   - Who will serve as primary spokesperson?
   - How will the department communicate the information?

- How quickly can the department release additional information?
- What other university personnel need to be contacted and who is going to do this?
- How will senior staff liaisons be assigned to each affected family?

10. AD and senior associate AD contact family units of those involved to update them regarding the situation and to introduce the senior staff liaison assigned to each family, who will arrange for their transportation to the city if warranted.

11. As quickly as possible, take other actions deemed important in the CCC meeting.

12. The athletic department holds a news conference. Update the media, providing as much information as possible while keeping regard for the families and parties involved. Work with law enforcement to ensure only facts are released and not speculative information.

13. Release additional information to the mass media as quickly as possible regarding the department's response. Have a media update at least every 48 hours. All additional information will be given to families before it is released to media. A list of media contacts is provided in appendix C.

The previous 13 steps provide a framework for how to proceed. Additional CCC meetings may be necessary given the circumstances.

## Scenario 3  Accusation of NCAA rules violations

### Objectives

1. Ensure that all parties involved—the accused, the accuser, and others—are treated fairly and in accordance with existing legislation and university policy.

2. Communicate to key publics that the athletic department holds its members to high standards of behavior and upholds its obligation to treat its members with fairness.

3. Take actions as quickly as circumstances will permit given objectives 1 and 2.

### Procedures

1. The CAC chair will contact other personnel who will serve as members of the CCC committee for the duration of the crisis episode. They include the following:
   - Director of athletics
   - Senior associate AD
   - Assistant AD for media relations
   - Assistant AD for compliance and student services
   - University general counsel
   - Head coach (if student-athlete is accused)
   - University director of news and media relations

   Contact information is available in appendix A.

2. AD informs university president of the situation. Contact information is located in appendix B.

3. AD approves use of planned response to media inquiries. The planned response, attributed to the AD and released by the media relations office, is as follows: "We are very concerned about the reports regarding NCAA violations involving our program. However, we are still in the early stages of gathering pertinent information. As we inquire more deeply into the situation at hand, we will make every effort to be fair to all parties involved while holding members of our program to the highest standards. We will provide additional information as soon as it is available."

4. Assistant AD for media relations makes the prepared response available to media officials who are making inquiries. Assistant AD for media relations informs media members that subsequent inquiries should be directed to the media relations office. All additional information will be released from the media relations office as well. Media relations office will maintain a record of all inquiries, responses, and follow-up actions.

*(continued)*

*(continued)*

5. AD's office informs the faculty athletic representative.

6. Assistant AD for compliance gathers as much information as possible regarding who is involved, what has happened, and how it happened.

7. Assistant AD for compliance contacts the NCAA.

8. CCC meets to plan subsequent actions. Key issues to address include the following:

   - Who will serve as primary spokesperson?
   - What will be the department's response to the accusations?
   - How may the department best communicate that information to the mass media?
   - How quickly can the department make additional public comment regarding the situation?
   - Who else needs to be contacted regarding the situation and who should make those contacts?
   - What additional steps need be taken to facilitate the internal investigation of what has been reported?

9. As quickly as possible, take all actions specified in the CCC meeting.

10. As quickly as possible, release additional information regarding the department's response to members of the mass media. A list of media contacts is provided in appendix C.

The previous 10 steps provide a framework for how to initially proceed. Additional CCC meetings may be necessary given the circumstances.

## Scenario 4  Fan-related incident involving serious injuries or criminal activity at an athletic event

### Objectives

1. Ensure that the privacy of those directly and indirectly involved is protected.

2. Release information to key publics as quickly as possible in accordance with objective 1.

3. Communicate the athletic department's
   - sincere concern and sadness regarding the accident,
   - commitment to fully investigate what happened, and
   - commitment to minimize the possibility of such an event occurring again.

4. Minimize exposure to possible legal action.

### Procedures

1. The CAC chair will contact other personnel who will serve as members of the CCC for the duration of the crisis episode. They include the following:
   - Director of athletics
   - Senior associate AD
   - Assistant AD for media relations
   - Assistant AD for compliance and student services
   - University general counsel
   - Head coach (if student-athletes or staff members are involved)
   - Campus security chief (if incident took place on campus)
   - University director of news and media relations
   - Director for environmental control (determined by incident)
   - City law enforcement liaison (determined by incident)

   Contact information is available in appendix A.

2. AD informs the university president of the situation. Contact information is in appendix B.

3. AD and senior associate AD make preliminary contact with the injured parties and their families to express concern.

4. If a student is involved, the AD will work in conjunction with the dean of students to contact the parent or legal guardian. If a student-athlete is involved, the head coach will contact the parent or legal guardian.

5. AD approves use of the planned response to media inquiries regarding the incident. The planned response to be released on behalf of the AD by the media relations office is as follows: "We are deeply concerned about this incident. However, we are still in the early stages of gathering relevant information. We will release information as soon as it is available while protecting the privacy of the individuals involved."

6. AD informs athletic department personnel that all media inquiries are to be referred to the office of media relations.

7. Assistant AD for media relations makes the prepared response available to those media officials who are making inquiries. Assistant AD for media relations informs media members that subsequent inquiries should be directed to the media relations office and that all additional information will be released from the media relations office. Media relations office will maintain a record of all inquiries, responses, and follow-up actions as needed.

8. Media relations director informs all media relations personnel of the situation. If necessary, all media relations personnel report to the athletic department to assist with media services.

9. Senior associate AD gathers as much information as possible regarding the incident.

10. CCC meets to discuss subsequent action for the following issues:
    - Are any immediate public safety issues at athletic facilities needing to be addressed?
    - Who will serve as the primary contact for the individuals who were involved and their families?
    - Who will serve as the primary spokesperson for media inquiries?
    - How will the process be coordinated so that public comment never precedes the sharing of information with the individuals who were involved and their families?
    - How will information be shared with the media?
    - What will be the department's position regarding the accused?
    - What messages will the department attempt to communicate to fans regarding their safety at athletic events?
    - Who else needs to be contacted regarding the situation and who should make those contacts?

11. Promptly take actions deemed important in the CCC meeting.

12. Release additional information to the media as it becomes available, ensuring the privacy of the patrons and families involved. All additional information will be given to families before it is released to media. Media contact information is available in appendix C.

The previous 12 steps provide a framework for how to initially proceed. Additional CCC meetings may be necessary given the circumstances.

## Scenario 5  Other crises

### Objectives

1. Fulfill the athletic department's obligations to its various constituents while protecting its reputation.

2. Adhere to existing department and university policies that may be relevant to the situation.

3. Communicate effectively with the mass media and other key publics regarding the crisis.

*(continued)*

*(continued)*

## Procedures

1. The CAC chair contacts the director of athletics. Together, they identify other department and university personnel who may need to be temporarily added to the CCC. Contact information for those most likely to be needed may be found in appendix A.
2. AD informs university president of the situation.
3. If a student-athlete is involved, head coach contacts the student-athlete's parent or legal guardian.
4. AD and assistant AD for media relations consult regarding an initial response to media inquiries regarding the situation.
5. AD informs athletic department personnel that all media inquiries are to be referred to the office of media relations.
6. Assistant AD for media relations makes initial response available to media officials who are making inquiries. Assistant AD for media relations informs media members that subsequent inquiries should be directed to and additional information will be released from the media relations office. The assistant AD for media relations will also maintain a record of all media inquiries, responses, and follow-up actions.
7. Assistant AD for media relations informs appropriate staff members (e.g., media relations officers assigned to any programs involved).
8. Senior associate AD gathers as much information as possible regarding what has happened.
9. CCC meets to assess the situation and determine responses. Key issues to address include the following:
   - Who will serve as primary spokesperson?
   - How quickly can the department make additional public comment regarding the situation?
   - How may the department best communicate with the mass media?
   - What messages should be communicated?
   - Who else needs to be contacted regarding the situation and who should make those contacts?
10. As quickly as possible, take actions as specified in CCC meeting.
11. As quickly as possible, release additional information regarding the department's response to members of the mass media. A list of media contacts is provided in appendix C.

The previous 11 steps provide a framework for how to proceed. Additional CCC meetings may be necessary given the circumstances.

## Appendix A

The following list contains the names and phone numbers of individuals who may be added to the CCC at the request of the AD or CAC chair.

| Position and name | Office # | Home # | Cell # |
| --- | --- | --- | --- |
| Director of Athletics<br>Gary McClane | 555-0001 | 555-1111 | 555-2222 |
| Sr. Associate AD/SWA<br>Kathy Reaves | 555-0002 | 555-1547 | 555-8729 |
| Assistant AD for Media Relations<br>Terri Cox | 555-0003 | 555-3514 | 555-7894 |
| Baseball<br>Jeff Williams | 555-0004 | 555-1234 | 555-9876 |

| Position and name | Office # | Home # | Cell # |
|---|---|---|---|
| Cross country<br>Leigh McCarty | 555-0005 | 555-4321 | 555-3258 |
| Men's basketball<br>Mike Baker | 555-0006 | 555-9148 | 555-3594 |
| Men's golf<br>Corey Harris | 555-0007 | 555-8252 | 555-0739 |
| Men's tennis<br>Andre Mills | 555-0008 | 555-1010 | 555-1011 |
| Men's and women's track<br>Fred Horn | 555-0009 | 555-4545 | 555-8889 |
| Softball<br>Angela Iles | 555-0010 | 555-7474 | 555-9369 |
| Volleyball<br>Jessica Dees | 555-0011 | 555-7139 | 555-1828 |
| Women's basketball<br>Holly Scott | 555-0012 | 555-2270 | 555-8055 |
| Women's golf<br>Patricia Miller | 555-0013 | 555-0781 | 555-1244 |
| Women's tennis<br>Jennifer Caldwell | 555-0014 | 555-3254 | 555-1355 |
| Vice President and General Counsel<br>John Smith | 555-0020 | 555-4194 | 555-9812 |
| Associate AD for Development<br>Brian Jones | 555-0021 | 555-9080 | 555-7030 |
| Faculty Athletic Representative<br>Jane Mathew | 555-0022 | 555-3461 | 555-8257 |
| Assistant AD for Marketing and Promotions<br>Scott Anderson | 555-0023 | 555-9997 | 555-2013 |
| Assistant AD for Facilities and Events<br>Richard King | 555-0024 | 555-5521 | 555-6663 |
| Assistant AD for Compliance and Student Services<br>Jenny Walton | 555-0025 | 555-1147 | 555-7733 |
| Chief of Campus Security<br>Larry Shirley | 555-0026 | 555-2352 | 555-9293 |
| Dean of Students<br>Mary Jackson | 555-0027 | 555-8147 | 555-8391 |
| VP Student Affairs<br>Jason Williams | 555-0028 | 555-3160 | 555-3338 |
| University Director of News and Media Relations<br>Ronald Bailey | 555-0029 | 555-1115 | 555-5111 |
| Director of Environmental Control<br>Josh Foster | 555-0030 | 555-8459 | 555-6540 |

*(continued)*

*(continued)*

## Appendix B

The following list includes the names and phone numbers of key individuals who may need to be contacted regarding crisis situations.

| Position and name | Office # | Home # | Cell # |
|---|---|---|---|
| University President<br>Kirk Hebert | 555-0035 | 555-0336 | 555-0337 |
| Vice President and General Counsel<br>John Smith | 555-0020 | 555-4194 | 555-9812 |
| VP Academic Affairs<br>Paula Johnson | 555-0036 | 555-0149 | 555-9432 |
| Associate AD for Development<br>Brian Jones | 555-0021 | 555-9080 | 555-7030 |
| Faculty Athletic Representative<br>Jane Mathew | 555-0022 | 555-3461 | 555-8257 |
| Assistant AD for Marketing and Promotions<br>Scott Anderson | 555-0023 | 555-9997 | 555-2013 |
| Assistant AD for Facilities and Events<br>Richard King | 555-0024 | 555-5521 | 555-6663 |
| Assistant AD for Compliance and Student Services<br>Jenny Walton | 555-0025 | 555-1147 | 555-7733 |
| Chief of Campus Security<br>Larry Shirley | 555-0026 | 555-2352 | 555-9293 |
| Dean of Students<br>Mary Jackson | 555-0027 | 555-8147 | 555-8391 |
| VP Student Affairs<br>Jason Williams | 555-0028 | 555-3160 | 555-3338 |
| Director of Multicultural Affairs<br>Sallie Day | 555-0037 | 555-5371 | 555-5376 |
| Environmental Health and Safety Director<br>Andy Smith | 555-0038 | 555-4646 | 555-6267 |
| Physical Plant<br>Trent Temple | 555-0039 | 555-8686 | 555-4767 |

## Appendix C

The following list includes media outlets and specific contacts that cover university athletics on a frequent basis. Each outlet should be included when releasing information regarding a crisis situation. Media members inquiring about the crisis situation will likely need to be added to this list as the crisis unfolds. Detailed records regarding those inquiries and relevant contact information should be maintained throughout the episode.

| Company name | First name | Last name | Address | Work phone | Fax number | E-mail address |
|---|---|---|---|---|---|---|
| AP | Carol | Ambler | 825 Main St. City1, State1, 77777 | 123-555-0813 | 123-555-0814 | writer@ap.org |
| City Chronicle | Clark | Kent | PO Box 7120 City1, State1, 77777 | 123-555-2020 | 123-555-7079 | kkent@citychronicle.com |
| KAAA-TV | Alan | Thomas | PO Box 1010 City1, State1, 77777 | 123-555-2121 | 123-555-2122 | athomas@kaaa.com |
| City Gazette | Bob | Hart | PO Box 91700 City1, State1, 77777 | 123-555-2222 | 123-555-2223 | sports@citygazette.com |
| KBBB-TV | George | LeRay | 111 Elm St. City1, State1, 77777 | 123-555-3333 | 123-555-3334 | gleray@kbbb.com |
| The Daily University | Melvin | Branch | 1845 Maple St. City1, State1, 77777 | 123-555-4444 | 123-555-4445 | mbranch@dailyuniversity.com |
| City Courier | Ramon | Perez | 201 First St. City1, State1, 77777 | 123-555-5555 | 123-555-5556 | perez@citycourier.com |
| Town News | Travis | Lee | 555 Pine St. City1, State1, 77777 | 123-555-6666 | 123-555-6667 | tlee@townnews.com |
| City Times | Jake | Royer | PO Box 41207 City1, State1, 77777 | 123-555-7777 | 123-555-7778 | jroyer@citytimes.com |
| KCCC-TV | Greg | Kerr | 5050 North St. City2, State1, 77777 | 123-555-8888 | 123-555-8889 | gkerr@kccc.com |
| Daily Sun | Jack | Nichols | PO Box 2881 City2, State1, 77777 | 123-555-9999 | 123-555-9990 | jnichols@dailysun.com |
| KDDD-TV | Jeff | Love | PO Box 1044 City2, State1, 77777 | 123-555-2131 | 123-555-2132 | jlove@kddd.com |
| KEEE-TV | Jim | Fox | 7121 Central St. City2, State1, 77777 | 123-555-2231 | 123-555-2232 | jfox@keee.com |
| KFFF Radio | John | Dotel | 4211 High School Drive City3, State1, 77777 | 123-555-2331 | 123-555-2332 | jdotel@kfff.com |
| Town Journal | Trent | Tucker | 616 Kirby St. City3, State1, 77777 | 123-555-8486 | 123-555-6568 | ttucker@townjournal.com |

*(continued)*

| Company name | First name | Last name | Address | Work phone | Fax number | E-mail address |
|---|---|---|---|---|---|---|
| *Town Daily* | Melissa | Hooks | PO Box 977 City4, State2, 77777 | 123-555-8412 | 123-555-8445 | mhooks@towndaily.net |
| *Town Star* | Mike | Harris | 5446 Texas Ave. City5, State2, 77777 | 123-555-8515 | 123-555-8444 | mharris@tstar.com |
| KGGG | Anne | Roach | 9772 Country Club Circle City6, State1, 77777 | 123-555-7171 | 123-555-7393 | newsdirector@kggg.com |
| *Town Gazette* | Joe | Weldon | PO Box 888 City7, State1, 77777 | 123-555-4580 | 123-555-0704 | chief@tgaz.com |
| *City Daily* | Mark | Smith | PO Box 1478 City8, State2, 77777 | 123-555-6551 | 123-555-7255 | msmith@citydaily.com |
| *City Eagle* | Ryan | Presley | PO Box 1888 City9, State2, 77777 | 123-555-8788 | 123-555-9304 | rpresley@cityeagle.com |
| *City Journal* | Eric | Woodard | PO Box 7179 City10, State3, 77777 | 123-555-0098 | 123-555-8894 | ewoodard@cityjournal.com |

| Additional Media | | | | | |
|---|---|---|---|---|---|
| The City Reporter | Gary Barbee | 100 Crawford | 123-555-2835 | 123-555-0854 | gbarbee@cityreporter.com |
| *East City News* | Paula Hebert | 3789 Main St. | 123-555-2655 | 123-555-3993 | phebert@eastcitynews.com |
| KHHH-TV | Ted Joshlin | 1234 Fifth St. | 123-555-2129 | 123-555-3314 | tedjoshlin@khhh.com |

# Community Relations Plan for a Minor League Baseball Franchise

**Community relations are** the second most common form of public relations practice. In some sport settings, community relations may be even more important than media relations. Favorable attitudes among community members may be fostered by positive interactions between representatives of the sport organization and the public and by the charitable contributions, financial and otherwise, that a sport organization makes to its community.

Because of their community relations programs, sport organizations may realize such outcomes as demonstrating social responsibility, building public awareness, generating favor with customers, increasing employee morale, contributing to their community's well-being, and gaining tax advantages. They may also be able to reach publics who are not targeted by the organization's other marketing and public relations activities.

Community relations may be particularly important for sport organizations that have difficulty attracting positive media attention for being successful in other areas.

Appendix C provides a sample community relations plan.

# Wichita Baseball, Inc., Community Relations Plan

## Community Relations Department Mission

The community relations department of Wichita Baseball, Inc., (WBI) strives to increase the company's profit margin through educational, charitable, and social appearances and donations, while placing the organization among the city's community leaders.

## Community Relations Department Goals

1. Convert community and school appearances into future group outings by implementing a process in which all requests are evaluated on the basis of the likelihood of a group outing at the ballpark to enhance their overall experience with WBI, Wranglers players, and associates. Success will be measured by the booking of at least 100 group outings generated by community appearances.

2. Maintain high usage rate of donated tickets by having 90% or more of donated tickets distributed to charitable groups. We will accomplish this by using the tickets for donations as door prizes, auction items, and so on. Continued contact with charitable organizations to increase awareness of the availability of tickets is essential. Mailings and follow-up phone calls are a must.

3. Increase involvement of players in Wichita and surrounding communities by organizing at least five player appearances per month during the season. Achievement of this goal would be aided by continuing baseball and softball clinics and the Corporate Buddy program, and through charity programs in which a few players focus their attention on one organization, like Big Brothers and Big Sisters Big for a Day program.

4. Continue to develop our Corporate Buddy Program with distribution of 3,000 tickets to charitable organizations for use on two Corporate Buddy nights (1,500 each night). At least two-thirds of these tickets should be purchased by corporate sponsors. The other third will come from tickets donated by existing season-ticket holders. Corporations will be asked to provide a general admission ticket, program, soda, and hot dog for $5.00 per child (a $10.00 value), in blocks of 20 ($100 donation).

5. Assist in planning and executing the Kansas City Royals caravan during the off-season. Success will be measured by the staging of four to five appearances during a one-day stop in Wichita and booking at least three group outings with participating agencies for the season.

6. Remain proactive in traveling to surrounding communities of Wichita. Devote one day per community with a Wranglers associate, Wilbur the mascot, and a coach or player during the off-season, visiting different groups in the community. This would need to be prearranged between the community relations coordinator and representatives from the community. If sponsored again by same organization, this program will be incorporated with the Achievers Program. If not, it will be titled the *Wranglers Caravan* and the goal will be to hit 10 outlying communities.

## Community Relations Plan

### Contents

1. Objectives
2. Player Involvement
3. Wilbur T. Wrangler
4. Speakers Bureau
5. Community Events
6. Achievers Program and School Appearances
7. Sponsor and Client Appearances
8. Charitable Requests
9. Big Buddy Program

10. Adopt a School Program
11. Guest Coach Program
12. Hispanic Outreach Program

### Section 1: Objectives

Objectives for developing and coordinating a comprehensive community relations program for WBI include the following:

- To help cultivate greater personal and emotional involvement between Wranglers players and the community, helping develop new fans and increasing ties with existing fans
- To secure positive publicity for WBI through involvement in charitable events and nonprofit organizations, thus helping increase attendance and sponsorship revenue
- To develop goodwill within the community by displaying WBI's commitment to area organizations and events, thus supporting other sales and marketing efforts
- To increase interest among potential fans in attending Wranglers and National Baseball Congress events through proactive involvement in Wichita and surrounding communities

### Section 2. Appearance Procedures

The community relations department will work to maximize the involvement of Wranglers players in the community. Beginning during spring training, the community relations department will establish relationships with all new and returning Wranglers players and coaches to determine their level of interest in becoming involved in local events.

A standard procedure for player, coach, mascot, and management appearances will be established using a community appearances book that will be maintained by the community relations department. The book will feature several ways of tracking appearances:

1. A ledger to record who booked the appearance, where it was, who was used, the number of miles traveled, and the number of people in the audience
2. Monthly calendars to track all appearances
3. Appearance forms that outline all pertinent information (including the group contact for future sales opportunities) for each appearance
4. A results sheet recording any attendance generated from the appearance during the season to be used to measure the return of the investment in the future

To book the appearance of players, coaches, Wilbur, or staff members, an appearance form needs to be completed with all the required information and turned in to the community relations director at least two weeks before the required time. The staff member will be responsible for immediately notifying the requested parties and scheduling the appearance. In the event of a request for mascot, the community relations director will find someone to play Wilbur and return the name and number of the individual to the staff member who will be handling the appearance.

The stadium operations manager will be responsible for working with the Wranglers' team manager in scheduling appearances. The manager will be notified of all player appearances. Compensation for player appearances at charity and nonprofit organizations will be provided by WBI in the form of food certificates and cash when appropriate. Complete details are provided in the community appearances book.

Compensation for appearances at for-profit businesses will be provided by the business in the form of a preapproved amount of cash or gift certificates. It will be the responsibility of the WBI account executive for the business to provide details on compensation. Compensation for Wilbur appearances is detailed in the community appearances book. Compensation for front-office personnel (such as vice president of WBI, general manager, marketing director) appearances will not be provided by Wichita Baseball, Inc., but may be negotiated independently by the appropriate sales associate.

All attempts will be made to avoid scheduling players and coaches on the first day of a home stand, get-away day, or off day. In the event an appearance is needed on one of those days, permission will

*(continued)*

*(continued)*

need to be granted by the manager. Wilbur and front-office personnel appearances are not limited to any particular days.

All players will be asked to participate in at least seven (7) full team appearances during the season. These events include but are not limited to the following:

- Koch Industries Youth Clinic
- Stampede Booster Club picnic
- Camera Day
- Autograph Day for Fans
- Stampede Booster Club end-of-season lunch
- Autograph party for season-ticket holders
- Knothole Gang autograph

Further, those players identified as having a good rapport with the public will be asked to handle other requests. It will be the goal of the program to have each player develop a local relationship with a charity with which they have been involved in the past or assist with current team community relations programs. Any player who makes a paid appearance will also be required to make a "free" appearance for a charity or nonprofit organization, as asked by the stadium operations manager.

### Section 3. Wilbur T. Wrangler

The community relations department will work to maximize promotional appearance opportunities for Wilbur both in the off-season and during the season. Sales associates should promote Wilbur as the most identifiable individual within WBI. Associates should look into booking mascot appearances for their clients for promotion of upcoming events and promote Wilbur appearances as an additional benefit for successful partnerships. An informational brochure has been created by the community relations department to promote Wilbur and create a rate schedule for commercial and charitable appearances of $50 per two-hour appearance (includes travel time and a 15-minute break for each 30 minutes in the costume). This will help in screening mascot appearances, and in the end, produce some revenue.

WBI will also continue to use the Wilbur character during all games. WBI will seek a sponsor to produce Wilbur photos to give to kids during autograph sessions and during home games. WBI will work with the marketing director in coming up with a sponsorship for Wilbur products, like photo cards to use as giveaways.

WBI will retain [person's name] to appear as Wilbur for all home games and, when available, for off-site personal appearances. For times when [name] is not available, WBI will hire a backup Wilbur or secure an interested staff member to make the appearance for a wage of $40.00 for a two-hour appearance with the same in costume—break ratio previously specified.

### Section 4. Speakers Bureau

The community relations department will continue to build and coordinate a speakers bureau for Wichita Baseball. Our goal is to be proactive in providing speakers and presentations to community groups, charities, service organizations, schools, and corporations in the Wichita community. The community relations department, with help from the sales department, has obtained a list of all area organizations that may be interested in speakers for their functions. The community relations department will contact each of those organizations in an effort to place speakers at events.

The community relations department will maintain a calendar of upcoming events. Any interested organization simply needs to write WBI a letter on their stationery to request a speaker. All reasonable requests for speakers will be honored. When scheduling a speaking appearance, the speakers bureau will complete an information sheet detailing the purpose of the gathering, the number of people involved, the name of the principals organizing the group, and specific topics they would like the speaker to address in the presentation.

A standard presentation may include opening remarks by a Wranglers associate, comments from a Wrangler player or coach, a question-and-answer session, and an appearance by Wilbur T. Wrangler. The presentation will be adjusted to meet the specific needs of the host group.

The community relations department will make the group sales department aware of all presentations by turning in a community appearance form to group sales for recruiting purposes. WBI will distribute pocket schedules, season ticket and miniplan information, and group outing flyers at all events. A drawing will also be held to gather the names of the individuals in attendance for future reference with tickets to a Wranglers game as the standard prize.

### Section 5. Community Events

The community relations department will contact the Wichita Chamber of Commerce and the Wichita Visitors and Convention Bureau to secure a calendar of upcoming community events for possible involvement by WBI. The community relations department will work closely with both organizations and will offer to coordinate personal appearances by players, coaches, or Wilbur or to provide promotional materials for any appropriate event.

The community relations department will also work with the general manager and other associates to create and coordinate our own off-season events and activities to bring together fans, potential fans, Wranglers players and coaches, and WBI associates. These events will include a holiday tour, preseason fan party, sponsor and player golf tournament, kids' clinics, coaches' clinics, picnics, Wranglers Caravan, and other events.

### Section 6. Achievers Program and School Appearances

The Kansas Farm Bureau Life Insurance and Wranglers Achievers program teaches fifth-grade students about goal setting and goal achievement in a fun, entertaining, and informative atmosphere. Students who successfully reach their goal will receive a card that serves as a ticket to specified Achiever's Days during the summer. The Achievers' coordinator will work with the group department to tie School Kids Days and Nights with Achievers schools.

The community relations department will also look to participate in any school assembly or antidrug program that time permits. All appearances will be coordinated with the group sales department. WBI will make Wilbur available to any interested school for their presentations, and when possible, arrange an appearance by a Wranglers player or coach. One way to be proactive in arranging appearances is by participating in the Reading Is Fun program. School appearances will be tied into School Kids Days and Nights at Wrangler games.

### Section 7. Sponsor and Client Appearances

The community relations department will assist the WBI sales staff in coordinating personal appearances and autograph sessions by players, coaches, or Wilbur at places of business for WBI clients and sponsors. The community relations department will assist the staff member as they work directly with the client or sponsor and promote the event to local media.

### Section 8. Charitable Requests

The community relations department will respond in writing to all donation requests from charitable organizations and will coordinate the Wranglers honorary bat boy and bat girl program with the account representative whose client has the bat boy or girl program. Donation requests must come in writing by the organization at least two weeks in advance. The community relations department will use tickets as WBI's primary form of donation.

### Section 9. Big Buddy Program

The community relations department will work with the group sales department to ensure a minimum 90% usage rate of all tickets for donations to the Dream Team, Bat Brigade, and season ticket donations. Last season, more than 500 donated tickets were used by schools, Big Brothers and Big Sisters, the Wichita Public Library Summer Reading Program, the Wichita Police Department at-risk clinics, and the United Way.

### Section 10. Adopt a School Program

The community relations department will contact a school in the vicinity of L-D Stadium that tends to be attended by at-risk children and offer to adopt the school. This would entail arranging appearances by players, Wilbur, and so on whenever possible and in response to the school's requests.

*(continued)*

*(continued)*

Some possible candidates for this school would be Franklin Elementary, Allison Middle School, and West High School.

### Section 11. Guest Coach Program

The community relations department will contact the area Boys and Girls Club or Planeview Area leagues to see if Wrangler players would be able to assist in their league development. The community relations coordinator will be responsible for contacting these league leaders and seeing how players could be of assistance throughout the season.

### Section 12. Hispanic Outreach Program

The community relations department will facilitate player appearances at events in the Hispanic community through contacts focused on the Horace Mann Elementary School. Special effort will be devoted to using players with Hispanic backgrounds in making connections with Hispanic audiences.

Reprinted, by permission, from Wichita State Baseball, Inc.

# references

## Chapter 1

Battenfield, F.L., & Kent, A. (2007). The culture of communication among intercollegiate sport information professionals. *International Journal of Sport Management and Marketing, 2*(3), 236–251.

Berkhouse, J., & Gabert, T. (1999, June). *Community relations within Major League Baseball, National Basketball Association, National Football League, and the National Hockey League.* Paper presented at the meeting of the North American Society for Sport Management, Vancouver, British Columbia, Canada.

Britten, B.R. (2001). Brian R. Britten, manager, public relations. In M.J. Robinson, M.A. Hums, R.B. Crow, & D.R. Phillips (Eds.), *Profiles of sport industry professionals* (pp. 221–228). Gaithersburg, MD: Aspen.

Broom, G. (2009). *Cutlip and Center's effective public relations* (10th ed.). Upper Saddle, NJ: Pearson.

Burt, M., Kelly, M., Shatek, C., & Shields, C. (2002). *Nike global community affairs.* Unpublished manuscript.

Caple, J. (2002, July 10). *Feeling cheated? Get used to it.* Retrieved July 17, 2003, from http://espn.go.com/mlb/allstar02/s/2002/0710/1403880.html

Carter, D.M. (1996). *Keeping score: An inside look at sports marketing.* Green Pass, OR: Oasis Press.

Clark, M.S., & Mills, J. (1979). Interpersonal attraction in exchange and communal relationships. *Journal of Personality and Social Psychology, 37,* 12–24.

Douglas, P.S. (2001). P. Scott Douglas, promoter/director of media. In M.J. Robinson, M.A. Hums, R.B. Crow, & D.R. Phillips (Eds.), *Profiles of sport industry professionals* (pp. 213–220). Gaithersburg, MD: Aspen.

Dozier, D.M., Grunig, L.A., & Grunig, J.E. (1995). *Manager's guide to excellence in public relations and communication management.* Hillsdale, NJ: Erlbaum.

Favorito, J. (2007). *Sports publicity: A practical approach.* Burlington, MA: Elsevier.

Freitag, A. (2008). Staking claim: Public relations leaders need to shape CSR policy. *Public Relations Quarterly.* Retrieved June 24, 2009, from www.allbusiness.com/company-activities-management/business-ethics/10635842-1.html

Funk, D.C., & Pritchard, M.P. (2006). Sport publicity: Commitment's moderation of message effects. *Journal of Business Research, 59,* 613–621.

Greenstein, T. (2009, June 19). After U.S. Open rainout, USGA gets out of the rough by offering mulligan. *Chicago Tribune.* Retrieved June 23, 2009, from www.chicagotribune.com/sports/golf/chi-090619-us-open-tickets,0,6814807.story

Grunig, J.E. (Ed.). (1992). *Excellence in public relations and communication management.* Hillsdale, NJ: Erlbaum.

Grunig, J.E., & Hunt, T. (1984). *Managing public relations.* New York: Holt, Rinehart, and Winston.

Grunig, J.E., & Repper, F.C. (1992). Strategic management, publics, and issues. In J.E. Grunig (Ed.), *Excellence in public relations and communication management* (pp. 117–157). Hillsdale, NJ: Erlbaum.

Grunig, L.A., Grunig, J.E., & Dozier, D.M. (2002). *Excellent public relations and effective organizations.* Mahwah, NJ: Erlbaum.

Hall, A., Nichols, W., Moynahan, P., & Taylor, J. (2007). *Media relations in sport* (2nd ed.). Morgantown, WV: Fitness Information Technology.

Hallahan, K. (1992, August). *A typology of organizational relationships between public relations and marketing.* Paper presented at the meeting of the Association for Education in Journalism and Mass Communication, Montreal, Quebec, Canada.

Hardin, R., & McClung, S. (2002). Collegiate sports information: A profile of the profession. *Public Relations Quarterly, 47*(2), 35–39.

Hardy, S., & Sutton, W.A. (1999). The SMQ and the sport marketplace: Where we've been and where we're going. *Sport Marketing Quarterly, 8*(4), 9–14.

Helitzer, M. (2000). *The dream job: $port$ publicity, promotion and marketing* (3rd ed.). Athens, OH: University Sports Press.

Helsley, J. (2008, August 23). Behind the scenes, the heart of Bob Stoops revealed. *Daily Oklahoman.* Retrieved June 16, 2009, from http://newsok.com/behind-the-scenes-the-heart-of-bob-stoops-revealed/article/3287620

Henniger, W. (2003, May 5–11). Preakness' wild 2-week ride a challenging piece of reactive PR. *Street & Smith's SportsBusiness Journal, 6,* 12.

Horn, B. (2011, February 1). Entertainment industry makes Super Bowl Media Day a circus. *Dallas Morning News.* Retrieved May 17, 2011, from www.dallasnews.com/sports/super-bowl/the-scene/20110201-entertainment-industry-makes-super-bowl-media-day-a-media-circus.ece

Irwin, R.L., Sutton, W.A., & McCarthy, L.M. (2008). *Sport promotion and sales management* (2nd ed.). Champaign, IL: Human Kinetics.

Lancaster JetHawks. (n.d.). *Front office*. Retrieved June 29, 2009, from www.jethawks.com/team/front-office/

Lasswell, H.D. (1948). The structure and function of communication in society. In L. Bryson (Ed.), *The communication of ideas* (pp. 37–51). New York: Harper.

Laubscher, B.L. (2001). Brian L. Laubscher, sports information director. In M.J. Robinson, M.A. Hums, R.B. Crow, & D.R. Phillips (Eds.), *Profiles of sport industry professionals* (pp. 229–240). Gaithersburg, MD: Aspen.

Li, C., & Bernoff, J. (2008). *Groundswell: Winning in a world transformed by social technologies*. Boston: Forrester Research.

Maple Leaf Sports and Entertainment (MLSE) Inc. (2009). *Report to the community*. Retrieved March 15, 2010, from www.mlseteamupfoundation.org/downloads/MLSE_RTTC_FINAL.pdf

McCarthy, E.J. (1960). *Basic marketing: A managerial approach*. Homewood, IL: Irwin.

McGowan, A., & Bouris, G. (2005). Sport communications. In L.P. Masteralexis, C.A. Barr, & M.A. Hums (Eds.), *Principles and practice of sport management* (2nd ed., pp. 340–359). Gaithersburg, MD: Aspen.

Migala, D. (2000, July 17–23). Remember these 5 C's to make your content shine. *Street & Smith's SportsBusiness Journal, 3,* 17.

Milne, G.R., & McDonald, M.A. (1999). *Sport marketing: Managing the exchange process*. Sudbury, MA: Jones and Bartlett.

Miloch, K.S., & Pedersen, P.M. (2006). Sports information directors and the media: An analysis of a highly symbiotic and professional relationship. *Journal of Contemporary Athletics, 2*(1), 91–103.

MLB Advanced Media. (n.d.). *Front office directory*. Retrieved June 29, 2009, from http://arizona.diamondbacks.mlb.com/team/front_office.jsp?c_id=ari

Mullin, B.J., Hardy, S., & Sutton, W.A. (2007). *Sport marketing* (3rd ed.). Champaign, IL: Human Kinetics.

National Consumers League. (2006, May 31). *Survey: American consumers' definition of the socially responsible company runs counter to established beliefs*. Retrieved June 24, 2009, from www.nclnet.org/news/2006/csr_05312006.htm

Neupauer, N. (1999). A personality traits study of sports information directors at 'big' vs. 'small' programs in the East. *Social Science Journal, 36*(1), 163.

New Balance. (n.d.). *Responsible leadership*. Retrieved June 24, 2009, from www.newbalance.com/corporate/socialresponsibility/index.php

Parent, M. (2008). Evolution and issue patterns for major-sport-event organizing committees and their stakeholders. *Journal of Sport Management, 22,* 135–164.

Pedersen, P.M., Miloch, K.S., & Laucella, P.C. (2007). *Strategic sport communication*. Champaign, IL: Human Kinetics.

Pettinger, R. (1999). *Effective employee relations: A guide to policy and practice in the workplace*. London: Kogan Page.

Ries, A., & Ries, L. (2002). *The fall of advertising and the rise of PR*. New York: HarperCollins.

Rovell, D. (2008, April 4). *Jose Canseco: Best selling athlete (author) of all time?* Retrieved June 17, 2009, from www.cnbc.com/id/23955250/

Schwartz, P.J. (2010, February 3). The world's top sports brands. *Forbes*. Retrieved Aug. 31, 2011, from http://www.forbes.com/2010/02/03/most-powerful-sports-names-tiger-woods-nike-cmo-network-sports-brands.html

Scott, D.M. (2008). *The new rules of marketing and PR: How to use news releases, blogs, podcasting, viral marketing, and online media to reach buyers directly*. New York: Wiley.

Shannon, C.E., & Weaver, W. (1949). *The mathematical theory of communication*. Urbana, IL: University of Illinois Press.

Shilbury, D. (2009). *Strategic sport marketing* (3rd ed.). St. Leonards, New South Wales, Australia: Allen & Unwin.

Sriramesh, K., Grunig, J.E., & Buffington, J. (1992). Corporate culture and public relations. In J.E. Grunig (Ed.), *Excellence in public relations and communication management* (pp. 577–598). Hillsdale, NJ: Lawrence Erlbaum Associates.

Stier, W.F. (2003). *Marketing, fundraising & promotions for sport, recreation and fitness programs*. Boston: American Press.

Stoldt, G.C. (2000). Current and ideal organizational roles of NCAA Division I-A sports information professionals. *Cyber-Journal of Sport Marketing, 4*(1). Retrieved May 24, 2000, from www.cjsm.com/vol4.stoldt41.htm

Stoldt, G.C., Dittmore, S.W., & Branvold, S.E. (2003, May). *Teaching about sport public relations*. Paper presented at the meeting of the North American Society for Sport Management, Ithaca, NY.

Stoldt, G.C., & Narasimhan, V. (2005). Self assessments of collegiate sports information professionals regarding their public relations task expertise. *International Journal of Sport Management, 6*(3), 252–269.

Stoldt, G.C., Pratt, C., & Dittmore, S.W. (2007). Public relations in the sport industry. In J.B. Parks, J. Quarterman, & L. Thibault (Eds.), *Contemporary sport management* (3rd ed., pp. 243–265. Champaign, IL: Human Kinetics.

Strunk, W., Jr., & White, E.B. (2008). *The elements of style* (50th anniversary ed.). New York: Longman.

Trotter, J. (2011, January 23). *Don't question Cutler's toughness*. Retrieved May 17, 2011, from http://sportsillustrated.cnn.com/2011/writers/jim_trotter/01/23/packers.bears/index.html

Value Based Management.net. (n.d.). *Corporate reputation.* Retrieved June 26, 2009, from www.valuebasedmanagement.net/methods_corporate_reputation_quotient.html

Whisenant, W.A., & Mullane, S.P. (2007). Sport information directors and homologous reproduction. *International Journal of Sport Management and Marketing, 2*(3), 252–263.

# Chapter 2

Aaker, D. (1991). *Managing brand equity.* New York: Free Press.

Adams, W.M. (2006). *The future of sustainability: Re-thinking environment and development in the twenty-first century.* Report of the IUCN Renowned Thinkers Meeting, January 29–31, 2006. Retrieved August 29, 2010, from cmsdata.iucn.org/downloads/iucn_future_of_sustainability.pdf

Balfour, F., & Jana, R. (2008, August 4). Sponsors walking away from the Olympics. *Business Week.*

Barnett, M., Jermier, J., & Lafferty, B. (2006). Corporate reputation: The definitional landscape. *Corporate Reputation Review, 9*(1), 26–38.

Cook, W. (1998). Fact-finding for public relations. In P. Lesly (Ed.), *Lesly's handbook of public relations and communications* (pp. 297–304). Chicago: NTC Business Books.

*Corporate reputation quotient.* (n.d.). Retrieved October 20, 2004, from www.valuebasedmanagement.net/methods_corporate_reputation_quotient.html

Dale, M. (2002). Issue-driven strategy formation. *Strategic Change, 11,* 131–142.

David, F. (1996). *Strategic management.* New York: Macmillan.

DiMeglio, S. (2010, February 16). "Down year" has an upside as LPGA season begins. *USA Today.*

Dozier, D., & Ehling, W. (1992). Evaluation of public relations: What the literature tells us about their effects. In J. Grunig (Ed.), *Excellence in public relations and communications management* (pp. 159–184). Hillsdale, NJ: Erlbaum.

Edelman, R. (2010). *2010 trust barometer executive summary.* Retrieved on August 31, 2010, from www.scribd.com/doc/26268655/2010-Trust-Barometer-Executive-Summary

Environmental Leader. (2009). *Sports arenas go green.* Retrieved August 29, 2010, from www.environmentalleader.com/2009/04/08/sports-arenas-go-green

Ettenson, R., & Knowles, J. (2008). Don't confuse reputation and brand. *MIT Sloan Management Review,* Winter, 19–21.

Fombrun, C. (1996). *Reputation: Realizing value from the corporate image.* Boston: Harvard Business School Press.

Fombrun, C., Gardberg, N., & Sever, J. (1999). The reputation quotient: A multi-stakeholder measure of corporate reputation. *Journal of Brand Management, 7*(4), 241–255.

Fryer, J. (2010, July 27). NASCAR fights its perception problem. *Detroit News.*

Grunig, J. (1993). Image and substance: From symbolic to behavioral relationships. *Public Relations Review, 19,* 121–139.

———. (2006). *After 50 years: the value and values of public relations.* Institute for Public Relations: 45th Annual Distinguished Lecture, The Yale Club, New York, November 9, 2006.

Grunig, J., & Hunt, T. (1984). *Managing public relations.* New York: CBS College.

Harris, T. (1998). *Value-added public relations.* Chicago: NTC Business Books.

Heath, R. (1997). *Strategic issues management: Organizations and public policy changes.* Thousand Oaks, CA: Sage.

Hendrix, J. (1998). *Public relations case* (4th ed.). Belmont, CA: Wadsworth.

Hon, L. (1998). Demonstrating effectiveness in public relations: Goals, objectives, and evaluation. *Journal of Public Relations Research, 10*(2), 103–105.

Hon, L., & Grunig, J. (1999). *Guidelines for measuring relationships in public relations.* Institute for Public Relations, Commission on Public Relations Measurement and Evaluation.

Hunsberger, D. (2009, July 18). Can the LPGA tour be fixed? *Daily Commercial.*

Hutton, J. (1996). Integrated marketing communication and the evolution of marketing thought. *Journal of Business Research, 37,* 155–162.

Kelly, K. (2001). Stewardship: The fifth step in the public relations process. In R. Heath (Ed.), *Handbook of public relations* (pp. 279–289). Thousand Oaks, CA: Sage.

Kotler, P. (2000). *Marketing management.* Upper Saddle River, NJ: Prentice Hall

Lesly, P. (1998). *Lesly's handbook of public relations and communications.* Chicago: NTC Business Books.

Lipsey, R. (2010). It's time for LPGA tour to go global. *Sports Illustrated* vault. Retrieved June 9, 2011, from sportsillustrated.cnn.com/vault/article/web/COM1171868/index.htm

Macnamara, J. (2006). *Reputation measurement and management* (research paper). Media Monitors, 2–6.

Martzke, R., & Cherner, R. (2004, August 17). After 25 years, ESPN still channels how to view sports. *USA Today,* p. 1C.

Meyer, N.D. (2005, July 26). *Mission, vision, and values statements.* Retrieved September 7, 2005, from www.cio.com/leadership/buzz/column.html?ID=9311

Millman, C. (2009, July 24). Sports leagues sue to stop betting. *ESPN the Magazine.*

Mullin, B., Hardy, S., & Sutton, W. (2007). *Sport marketing* (3rd ed.). Champaign, IL: Human Kinetics.

National Collegiate Athletic Association (NCAA). (2010a). *2010–11 Revenue distribution plan.* Indianapolis, IN: NCAA.

———. (2010b). *2010–11 NCAA Division I manual.* Indianapolis, IN: NCAA.

Neely, A., Adams, C., & Crowe, P. (2001). The performance prism in practice. *Measuring Business Excellence, 5*(2), 6–12.

Newport, J. (2009, November 27). Fighting for its future, the LPGA goes global—with new hope but some reluctance. *Wall Street Journal*, p. w242.

Ozanian, M., & Schwartz, P. (2007, September 27). The world's top sports brands. *Forbes*.

Pearce, J., & Robinson, R. (2005). *Strategic management* (9th ed.). Boston: McGraw-Hill Irwin.

Penguins' new arena seeks gold LEED status. (2009, March 23). *Pittsburgh Business Times*.

Pentilla, C. (2002, May). Missed mission. *Entrepreneur*, 73–74.

Pepper, D. (2009). *LPGA tour needs to adjust its business model*. Golf.com. Retrieved August 25, 2010, from www.golf.com/golf/tours_news/article/0,28136,1871601,00.html

Pinkham, D. (2004). *Issues management*. Public Affairs Council. Retrieved October 19, 2004, from www.pac.org/public/issues_management.shtml

Poole, M. (2004, March 15). Companies that use PR effectively multiply value of their sponsorships. *Street and Smith's SportsBusiness Journal, 6*, 13.

Rawlins, B. (2006). *Prioritizing stakeholders for public relations*. Institute for Public Relations: Commission on Public Relations Measurement and Evaluation.

Ries, A., & Ries, L. (2002). *The fall of advertising and the rise of PR*. New York: HarperCollins.

## Chapter 3

Ahles, C.B. (2003). Campaign excellence: A survey of Silver Anvil award winners compares current PR practice with planning, campaign theory. *Public Relations Strategist, 9*(3), 46–53.

Austin, E.W., & Pinkleton, B.E. (2006). *Strategic public relations management: Planning and managing effective communication campaigns* (2nd ed.). Hillsdale, NJ: Erlbaum.

Brody, E.W., & Stone, G.C. (1989). *Public relations research*. New York: Praeger.

Broom, G. (2009). *Cutlip and Center's effective public relations* (10th ed.). Upper Saddle, NJ: Pearson.

Collins, E.L., Zoch, L.M., & McDonald, C.S. (2004, May). *A crisis in reputation management: The implications of Kasky v. Nike*. Paper presented at the annual meeting of the International Communication Association, New Orleans, LA. Retrieved July 15, 2009, from www.allacademic.com/meta/p113246_index.html

Council of Public Relations Firms. (2005). *Public relations generally accepted practices study: GAP III*. Retrieved July 23, 2009, from www.prfirms.org/_data/n_0001/resources/live/GAP_2005-08-10.pdf

———. (n.d). *Working with your public relations firm: A guide for clients*. Retrieved July 23, 2009, from www.prfirms.org/_data/n_0001/resources/live/working.pdf

Cuneen, J., Schneider, R., Gliatta, A., & Butler, N. (2006). Where have you Ben? Miami University's 2003 Heisman Trophy campaign challenges. *Sport Marketing Quarterly, 15*, 53–61.

Dillman, D.A., Smyth, J.D., & Christian, L.M. (2009). *Internet, mail and mixed-mode surveys: The tailored design method* (2nd ed.). Hoboken, NJ: Wiley.

Dozier, D.M. (1981, August). *The diffusion of evaluation methods among public relations practitioners*. Paper presented at the meeting of the Public Relations Division, Association for Education in Journalism, East Lansing, MI.

Dozier, D.M., & Ehling, W.P. (1992). Evaluation of public relations programs. In J.E. Grunig (Ed.), *Excellence in public relations and communication management* (pp. 159–184). Hillsdale, NJ: Erlbaum.

Dozier, D.M., Grunig, L.A., & Grunig, J.E. (1995). *Manager's guide to excellence in public relations and communication management*. Hillsdale, NJ: Erlbaum.

Dozier, D.M., & Repper, F.C. (1992). Research firms and public relations practices. In J.E. Grunig (Ed.), *Excellence in public relations and communication management* (pp. 185–215). Hillsdale, NJ: Erlbaum.

Festinger, L. (1957). *A theory of cognitive dissonance*. Evanston, IL: Row, Peterson.

Funk, D.C., Haugtvedt, C.P., & Howard, D.R. (2000). Contemporary attitude theory in sport: Theoretical considerations and implications. *Sport Management Review, 3*, 125–144.

Gratton, C., & Jones, I. (2004). *Research methods for sport studies*. London: Routledge.

Grunig, J.E., & Grunig, L.A. (2001). *Guidelines for formative and evaluative research in public affairs*. Gainesville, FL: Institute for Public Relations. Retrieved July 20, 2009, from www.instituteforpr.org/files/uploads/2001_PA_Research.pdf

Grunig, J.E., & Hunt, T. (1984). *Managing public relations*. New York: Holt, Rinehart, and Winston.

Harris, T.L. (1998). *Value-added public relations*. Chicago: NTC Business Books.

Heath, R.L., & Coombs, T.W. (2005). *Today's public relations: An introduction*. Thousand Oaks, CA: Sage.

Hendrix, J.A. (1998). *Public relations cases* (3rd ed.). Belmont, CA: Wadsworth.

Henninger, W. (2002, March 4–10). Upper Deck regroups behind gizmo after a PR launch that wasn't. *Street & Smith's SportsBusiness Journal, 4*, 10.

Higgins, S.H., & Martin, J.H. (1996). Managing sport innovations: A diffusion theory perspective. *Sport Marketing Quarterly, 5*(1), 43–48.

Hyman, H.H., & Sheatsley, P.B. (1947). Some reasons why information campaigns fail. *Public Opinion Quarterly, 11*, 412–423.

Irwin, R.L., Sutton, W.A., & McCarthy, L.M. (2008). *Sport promotion and sales management* (2nd ed.). Champaign, IL: Human Kinetics.

Jackson, P. (2000). PRoSpeak: Strategy is everything. In F.R. Matera & R.J. Artigue (Eds.), *PR campaigns and techniques: Building bridges into the 21st century* (pp.104–105). Boston: Allyn and Bacon.

Kendall, R. (1996). *Public relations campaign strategies* (2nd ed.). New York: HarperCollins.

Marker, R.K. (1977). The Armstrong/PR data measurement system. *Public Relations Review, 3*(4), 51–59.

Matera, F.R., & Artigue, R.J. (2000). *PR campaigns and techniques: Building bridges into the 21st century.* Boston: Allyn and Bacon.

McCleneghan, J.S. (1995). The sports information director—no attention, no respect and a PR practitioner in trouble. *Public Relations Quarterly, 40*(2), 28–32.

Mehrabian, A. (1972). *Nonverbal communication.* Chicago: Aldine-Atherton.

Migala, D. (2003, January 20–26). Close but no Heisman: E-mail campaign's still a winning strategy. *Street & Smith's SportsBusiness Journal, 5,* 14.

Mitrook, M.A., Parish, N.B., & Seltzer, T. (2008). From advocacy to accommodation: A case study of the Orlando Magic's public relations efforts to secure a new arena. *Public Relations Review, 34,* 161–168.

Mogel, L. (2002). *Making it in public relations* (2nd ed.). Mahwah, NJ: Erlbaum.

Nichols, W., Moynahan, P., Hall, A., & Taylor, J. (2002). *Media relations in sport.* Morgantown, WV: Fitness Information Technology.

Public Relations Society of America (PRSA). (n.d.a). *PRSA strategic overview 2008–10.* Retrieved July 7, 2009, from www.prsa.org/aboutUs/strategicPlanning.html

———. (n.d.b). *Accredited in public relations (APR).* Retrieved July 8, 2009, from www.prsa.org/PD/apr/index.html?WT.ac=PD_APRTopNav

———. (2008a). *Silver Anvil profiles—community relations: Figure Skating Championships.* Retrieved July 7, 2008, from www.prsa.org/jobcenter/community%20relations/Silver%20Anvil%20Figure%20Skating%20Championships

———. (2008b). *Silver Anvil profiles—corporate communications: Rawlings.* Retrieved July 21, 2008, from www.prsa.org/jobcenter/corporate%20communications/Silver%20Anvil%20Rawlings

———. (2009). *McDonald's global 2008 Beijing Olympic Games sponsorship: "Bringing People Together Like Never Before."* Retrieved July 10, 2009, from http://auth.iweb.prsa.org/xmembernet/main/pdfpull.cfm?prcfile=6BW-091011.pdf

Ries, A., & Ries, L. (2002). *The fall of advertising and the rise of PR.* New York: HarperCollins.

Roberts, K. (2002, November). Hold the back page. *SportsBusiness International, 75,* 30–31.

Seltzer, T., & Mitrook, M. (2009). The role of expert opinion in framing media coverage of the Heisman Trophy race. *Journal of Sport Media, 4*(2), 1–29.

Smith, R.D. (2009). *Strategic planning for public relations* (3rd ed.). New York: Routledge.

Spoelstra, J. (1997). *Ice to the Eskimos.* New York: HarperCollins.

Stacks, D.W. (n.d.). *Best practices in public relations research.* Gainesville, FL: Institute for Public Relations. Retrieved July 15, 2009, from www.instituteforpr.org/research_single/best_practices_in_pr_research/

———. (2002). *Primer of public relations research.* New York: Guilford Press.

———. (2006). *Dictionary of public relations measurement and research.* Gainesville, FL: Institute for Public Relations. Retrieved July 15, 2009, from www.instituteforpr.org/research_single/dictionary_public_relations/

Stoldt, G.C., & Ledbetter, E.A. (2005, June). *Characteristics of award-winning sport public relations campaigns.* Paper presented at the North American Society for Sport Management Conference, Regina, Saskatchewan, Canada.

Stoldt, G.C., Ratzlaff, S.E., & Ramolet, A. (2009). The "Vote Yea" campaign: A case study in two-way asymmetrical communication. *International Journal of Sport Management, 10,* 410–428.

# Chapter 4

Adams, R. (2004, November 8–14). Keying on growth, nfl.com rolls out new fantasy game. *Street & Smith's SportsBusiness Journal, 7,* 5.

Baehr, C. (2007). *Web development: A visual-spatial approach.* Upper Saddle River, NJ: Pearson Prentice Hall.

Brown, S. (2011, May 6). Twitter comments cost Mendenhall endorsement deal. *Pittsburgh Tribune-Review.*

Bruno, R., & Whitlock, K. (2000). Nothin' but net. In M. Helitzer, (Ed.), *The dream job: $port$ publicity, promotion and marketing* (3rd ed., pp. 429–441). Athens, OH: University Sports Press.

comScore. (2011). *The 2010 U.S. digital year in review.* ComScore.

Coombs, W. (2002). Assessing online issue threats: Issue contagions and their effect on issue prioritisation. *Journal of Public Affairs, 2*(4), 215–229.

Dellarocas, C. (2010). Online reputation systems: How to design one that does what you need. *Sloan Management Review,* Spring, 33–38.

Delpy, L., & Bosetti, H. (1998). Sport management and marketing via the World Wide Web. *Sport Marketing Quarterly, 7*(1), 21–27.

ePhilanthropy Foundation. (2001). *The ten rules for ephilanthropy.* Retrieved December 8, 2004, from www.ephilanthropy.org/site/PageServer?pagename=tenrules

Facebook. (2010). *Facebook press room*. Retrieved August 26, 2010, from www.facebook.com/press/info.php?statistics

Farkas, D.K., & Farkas, J.B. (2002). *Principles of web design*. New York: Longman.

Funk, T. (2009). *Web 2.0 and beyond*. Westport, CT: Praeger.

Garrett, D. (1996). *Intranets unleashed*. Indianapolis, IN: Sams.net.

Harmonson, T. (2004, February 4). Fans and schools in a tangled web, as sites may violate rules. *Orange County Register*.

Hart, T. (2002). Ephilanthropy: Using the internet to build support. *International Journal of Nonprofit and Voluntary Sector Marketing, 7*, 353–360.

Hess, E., & Kean, J. (2000, June 27). *Basics of keeping Web pages current*. Paper presented at the College Sports Information Directors of America Conference, St. Louis, MO.

Internet World Stats. (2010). *Usage and population statistics*. Retrieved August 26, 2010, from www.internetworldstats.com/stats.htm

Intranet Roadmap. (2005). *Uses of an intranet*. Retrieved June 17, 2005, from www.intranetroadmap.com/uses.cfm

Kentie, P. (2002) *Web design tools and techniques*. Berkeley, CA: Peachpit Press.

King, D. (2005, January). A blog to remember. *Information Today, 22*(1), 27–29.

Krug, S. (2006). *Don't make me think* (2nd ed.). Berkeley, CA: New Riders.

Layden, T. (2003, May 19). Caught in the net. *Sports Illustrated, 98*, 46–50.

List, D. (2005). *Measuring the effectiveness of websites*. Retrieved June 20, 2011, from www.audiencedialogue.net/webmeasure.html

Matuszewski, E. (2000, February). Tangled Web. *CoSIDA Digest, 50*, 7.

Migala, D. (2000a, July 17–23). Remember these 5 C's to make your content shine. *Street & Smith's SportsBusiness Journal, 3*, 17.

———. (2000b, July 31–August 6). As fans take a look at Web sites, so should teams. *Street & Smith's SportsBusiness Journal, 3*, 18.

Monmouth University Athletics. (2011). *Monmouth university athletics social media hub*. Retrieved June 21, 2011, from www.gomuhawks.com/ViewArticle.dbml?

Olsen, M., Keevers, M., Paul, J., & Covington, S. (2001). E-relationship development strategy for the nonprofit fundraising professional. *International Journal of Nonprofit and Voluntary Sector Marketing, 6*(4), 364–373.

Perry, P.M. (2003, May). Server ace. *Athletic Business, 27*(5), 44–47.

Pittsburgh Steelers. (2010). *Pittsburgh Steelers website*. Retrieved August 26, 2010, from www.steelers.com

Ryan, D., & Jones, C. (2009). *Understanding digital marketing*. London & New York: Kogan Page Limited.

Smith, E. (2000). *E-loyalty*. New York: HarperCollins.

Solis, B., & Thomas, J. (2008). *Introducing the conversation prism*. Retrieved June 21, 2011, from www.briansolis.com/2008/08/introducing-conversation-prism/

Steinbach, P. (2003, March). Low posts. *Athletic Business, 27*(3), 26–30.

Stoddart, L. (2001). Managing intranets to encourage knowledge sharing: Opportunities and constraints. *Online Information Review, 25*(1), 19–28.

Stoldt, G.C., Seebohm, B., Booker, J., Kramer, J., & Laird, A.J. (2001). In-house management versus outsourcing: An examination of mid-level NCAA Division I web sites. *National Association of Collegiate Marketers of Athletics Ideas, 8*, 2, 6.

Sullivan, C. (2003, October). Writing for the web. *CoSIDA Digest, 55*(9), 24–25.

Terdiman, D. (2005, April 18). A blog for baseball fans builds a league of sites. *New York Times*, C8.

Wilson, R. (2000, February 1). The six simple principles of viral marketing. *Web Marketing Today*, 70.

# Chapter 5

Abicht, A. (2004, June 28). *Basics of the profession*. Paper presented at the College Sports Information Directors of America Workshop, Calgary, Alberta, Canada.

Anderson, C. (1997, July 1). *Getting your publication to the printer*. Paper presented at the College Sports Information Directors of America Workshop, New Orleans, LA.

Brown, G.T. (2004, February 16). Out of print? Proposal threatens publication of popular media guides. *The NCAA News*. Retrieved November 1, 2004, from www.ncaa.org/news/2004/20040216/active/4104n02.html

Cherner, R., Kushlis, J., Rupp, A., O'Toole, T., & Bennett, C. (2005, July 26). *NCAA reins in hefty college media guides*. Retrieved September 10, 2010, from www.usatoday.com/sports/college/2005-07-26-media-guides_x.htm

College Sports Information Directors of America (CoSIDA). (2004). *2004–05 CoSIDA publications committee handbook*. Retrieved November 1, 2004, from www.cosida.com/contests/default.asp

Davis, H.M. (1998). Media relations. In L.P. Masteralexis, C.A. Barr, & M.A. Hums (Eds.), *Principles and practice of sport management* (pp. 356–379). Gaithersburg, MD: Aspen.

Emory, A. (2009, October/November). Proud to print. *Athletic Management*. Retrieved Sept. 10, 2010, from www.athleticmanagement.com/2009/10/19/print_it/index.php

Green Bay Packers. (2010). *2010 Green Bay Packers media guide*. Green Bay, WI: Author.

Hall, A., Nichols, W., Moynahan, P., & Taylor, J. (2007). *Media relations in sport* (2nd ed.). Morgantown, WV: Fitness Information Technology.

Harris, T.L. (1998). *Value-added public relations: The secret weapon of integrated marketing*. Lincolnwood, IL: NTC Business Books.

Helitzer, M. (2000). *The dream job: $port$ publicity, promotion and marketing* (3rd ed.). Athens, OH: University Sports Press.

Liberman, N. (2000, August 21–27). Oakland University dumps traditional media guides, uses Internet. *Street & Smith's SportsBusiness Journal, 2*, 16.

Los Angeles Dodgers. (n.d.). *Keep in touch with the Dodgers*. Retrieved Sept. 10, 2010, from http://losangeles.dodgers.mlb.com/la/fan_forum/newsletters.jsp

Madej, B. (2009, Sept. 8). *U-M, OSU agree to halt printing sports guides*. Retrieved from www.ur.umich.edu/update/archives/090529/56

Migala, D. (2001, January 29). Imagination, manpower strengthen e-mail newsletters. *Street & Smith's SportsBusiness Journal*. Retrieved November 18, 2004, from www.sportsbusinessjournal.com/index.cfm?fuseaction=search.show_article&articleId=12275&keyword=newsletter,%20email

Mullin, B.J., Hardy, S., & Sutton, W.A. (2000). *Sport marketing* (2nd ed.). Champaign, IL: Human Kinetics.

National Collegiate Athletic Association (2010, July). *2010–11 NCAA Division I Manual*. Indianapolis, IN: Author.

Nike. (2004). *Kirk Stewart*. Retrieved November 9, 2004, from www.nike.com/nikebiz/nikebiz.jhtml?page=7&item=exec&ex=kirk

Pursuant Sports (n.d.). *Portfolio*. Retrieved September 10, 2010, from www.pursuantsports.com/ourwork/

San Diego Padres. (n.d.). *Frequent Friar Rewards Club*. Retrieved September 10, 2010, from http://sandiego.padres.mlb.com/sd/fan_forum/frequent_friar.jsp

Smith, R.D. (2005). *Strategic planning for public relations* (2nd ed.). Mahwah, NJ: Erlbaum.

Smolik, D. (2004, October). "What? I don't have any money for media guides?" or ideas for the budget challenged to produce media guides. *CoSIDA Digest, 56*, 23.

Top 10: Media guide absurdities. (1998, November 2). *Sports Illustrated, 89*, 88.

United States Olympic Committee (USOC). (2004, November 2). *USOC names Jeff Howard as director, corporate communications*. Retrieved November 5, 2004, from http://uscopressbox.org

University of Oklahoma. (2009). *2009–10 Oklahoma women's basketball media guide*. Norman, OK: Author.

U.S. Environmental Protection Agency. (n.d.). *Communications stylebook: Appendix B—glossary*. Retrieved November 28, 2011, from www.epa.gov/stylebook/appb.html

Wichita Wingnuts. (2010). *Wichita Wingnuts baseball—2010 media guide*. Wichita, KS: Author.

Wilcox, D.L. (2001). *Public relations writing and media techniques* (4th ed.). New York: Addison-Wesley.

World Team Tennis. (2010). *2010 WTT media guide*. New York: Author.

# Chapter 6

About AFP. (n.d.). Retrieved July 23, 2010, from www.afp.com/afpcom/en/content/afp/our-services

About Gannett. (n.d.). Gannet. Retrieved August 9, 2004, from www.gannett.com/map/gan007.htm

About Tribune. (n.d.). Chicago Tribune. Retrieved August 9, 2004, from www.tribune.com/about/index.html

Adams, R. (2004, February 16–22). On the air and on a roll. *Street & Smith's SportsBusiness Journal, 6*, 42, 15.

AFP in a nutshell. (n.d.). Retrieved August 9, 2004, from www.afp.com/english/afp/?cat=about

Anderson, D. (1983). Sports coverage in daily newspapers. *Journalism Quarterly, 60*, 498.

Anderson, W.B. (2001a). Creating the national pastime: The antecedents of Major League Baseball PR. *Media History Monographs, 4*(2). Retrieved July 26, 2010, from http://facstaff.elon.edu/dcopeland/mhm/mhmjour4-2.htm

———. (2001b). The 1939 Major Leagues Baseball centennial celebration: How Steve Hannagan & Associates helped tie business to Americana. *Public Relations Review, 27*, 351–366.

———. (2006). The symbiotic relationship between the sport press and Major League Baseball. In G.C. Stoldt, S.W. Dittmore, & S. Branvold. *Sport public relations: Managing organizational communication* (pp. 78–81). Champaign, IL: Human Kinetics.

———. (n.d.) Baseball public relations. *Media History Monographs, 4*(2). Retrieved May 28, 2004, from www.elon.edu/dcopeland/mhm/mhmjour4-2.htm

Arledge, R. (2003). *Roone: A memoir*. New York: Harper Collins.

Ashwell, T. (1998). Sport broadcasting. In L.P. Masteralexis, C.A. Barr, & M.A. Hums (Eds.), *Principles and practice of sport management* (pp. 380–400). Gaithersburg, MD: Aspen.

Bagdikian, B.H. (2004). *The new media monopoly*. Boston: Beacon Press.

Bennett, W.L. (1988). *News: The politics of illusion* (2nd ed.). New York: Longman.

Bernstein, A. (2003a, February 10–16). NBC will put boxing on 2 networks and 2004 Olympics on 5. *Street & Smith's SportsBusiness Journal*. Retrieved August 18, 2004, from www.sportsbusinessjournal.com/index.cfm?fuseaction=search.show_article&articleId=28570&keyword=nbc,%20olympics,%20athens

———. (2003b, June 30–July 6). Yankees at 100: Team charts its own course in broadcast deals. *Street & Smith's SportsBusiness Journal*. Retrieved October 8,

2004, from www.sportsbusinessjournal.com/index.cfm?fuseaction=search.show_article&articleId=31609&keyword=yankees,%20rights,%20fee

———. (2004a, March 29–April 4). NBA ratings up on cable, down on ABC. *Street & Smith's SportsBusiness Journal, 6*, 48, 4.

———. (2004b, May 24–30). NHL touts value of NBC promotion as key to partnership. *Street & Smith's SportsBusiness Journal, 7*, 5, 1.

———. (2004c, September 27–October 3). High-altitude showdown brews. *Street & Smith's SportsBusiness Journal, 7*, 21, 5.

———. (2005, April 25–May 1). NFL restores NBC's clout. *Street & Smith's SportsBusiness Journal, 8*, 2, 1.

Bernstein, A., & Blain, N. (2002). *Sport, media and culture: Global and local dimensions.* London: Frank Cass.

Betts, J.R. (1953). The technological revolution and the rise of sport, 1850–1900. *Mississippi Valley Historical Review, 40*, 230–256.

Black, J., & Bryant, J. (1995). *Introduction to media communication* (4th ed.). Dubuque, IA: Brown & Benchmark.

Bonventre, P. (1976, January 5). Off the reservation. *Newsweek, 87*, 51.

Burgeois, N. (1995). Sports journalists and their sources of information: A conflict of interests and its resolution. *Sociology of Sport Journal, 12*, 195–203.

Caught on the fly. (1890, October 18). *Sporting News*, p. 4.

Chadwick, H. (1890, March 23). Reserve rule benefits. *Chicago Tribune*, p. 7.

Condon, D. (1976, February 10). Greed of players, owners ruining box office. *Chicago Tribune*, sec. 4, p. 3.

*Corporate structure.* (n.d.). Knight Ridder. Retrieved August 9, 2004, from www.knightridder.com/about/structure.html

CoSIDA. (n.d.a). *What is CoSIDA?* Retrieved July 27, 2010, from www.cosida.com/about/general.aspx

———. (n.d.b). *Membership benefits.* Retrieved July 27, 2010, from www.cosida.com/About/memberbenefits.aspx

Croteau, D., & Hoynes, W. (2001). *The business of media: Corporate media and the public interest.* Thousand Oaks, CA: Pine Forge Press.

Cutlip, S. (1994). *The unseen power: Public relations (PR), a history.* Hillsdale, NJ: Erlbaum.

Dworkin, J.B. (1981). *Owners versus players: Baseball and collective bargaining.* Boston: Auburn House.

ESPN. (n.d.). *ESPN: The Weekend.* Retrieved July 23, 2010, from http://espn.go.com/espntheweekend/

Fielding, L.W., & Pitts, B.G. (2003). Historical sketches: The development of the sport business industry. In J.B. Parks & J. Quarterman (Eds.), *Contemporary sport management* (2nd ed., pp. 41–78). Champaign, IL: Human Kinetics.

Fisher, E. (2006, July 17). Fox's call for change pays off. *Sports Business Journal.* Retrieved July 27, 2010, from www.sportsbusinessjournal.com/article/51215

*Four horsemen.* (n.d.). Retrieved August 16, 2004, from http://und.collegesports.com/trads/horse.html

Fullerton, H. (1928, April 21). The fellows who made the game. *Saturday Evening Post, 200*, 184.

Gannett Corporation. (n.d.). *Gannett daily newspapers and TV stations.* Retrieved July 23, 2010, from www.gannett.com/about/map/propmap.htm

Gant, S. (2007). *We're all journalist now: The transformation of the press and reshaping of the law in the internet age.* New York: Free Press.

Garrison, B., and Sabljak, M.J. (1993). *Sports reporting* (2nd ed.) Ames, IA: Iowa State University Press.

Garrison, B., and Salwen, M.B. (1994). Sports journalists assess their place in the profession. *Newspaper Research Journal. 15*, 37–49.

Gomery, D. (2000). The television industries. In B. Compaine & D. Gomery (Eds.), *Who owns the media? Competition and concentration in the mass media industry* (3rd ed., pp. 193–284). Mahwah, NJ: Erlbaum.

Goodwill Games. (n.d.). *Goodwill Games ceases operations.* Retrieved August 6, 2004, from www.goodwillgames.com

Hall, A., Nichols, W., Moynahan, P., & Taylor, J. (2007). *Media relations in sport* (2nd ed.). Morgantown, WV: Fitness Information Technology.

Henderson, J.K. (2001). Public relations. In E.K. Thomas & B.H. Carpenter (Eds.), *Mass media in 2025: Industries, organizations, people, and nations* (pp. 63–74). Westport, CT: Greenwood Press.

Hiestand, M. (2011, January 11). BCS title game TV ratings down. *USA Today.* Retrieved June 12, 2011, from http://content.usatoday.com/communities/gameon/post/2011/01/bcs-title-game-tv-ratings-down/1

History of X. (2004, June 21). Retrieved July 12, 2004, from www.espneventmedia.com/pr.php?p=943&e=554

Huenergard, C. (1979, June 16). No more cheerleading at the sports pages. *Editor & Publisher*, 11.

Hums, M.A., & MacLean, J.C. (2004). *Governance and policy in sport organizations.* Scottsdale, AZ: Holcomb Hathaway.

Lieb, F. (1977). *Baseball as I have known it.* New York: Ace.

Littlewood, T.B. (1990). *Arch, a promoter, not a poet: The story of Arch Ward.* Ames, IA: Iowa State University Press.

Lombardo, J. (2003, May 5–11). Grizzlies, Kings latest in NBA to consider starting RSNs. *Street & Smith's SportsBusiness Journal, 6*, 2, 14.

Maher, C. (1975, December 24). Messersmith ruling imperils the reserve clause. *Los Angeles Times*, p. D1.

Maraniss, D. (1999). *When pride still mattered: A life of Vince Lombardi.* New York: Simon & Schuster.

Markus, R. (1975, December 25). Baseball ruling may mean a strike. *Chicago Tribune*, sec. 6, p. 1.

———. (1976, March 7). Start the season without the club owners? *Chicago Tribune*, sec. 3, p. 3.

Martzke, R. (2003, June 6). NBC keeps rights for Olympic broadcasts through 2012. *USA Today*. Retrieved September 13, 2011 from http://www.usatoday.com/sports/olympics/2003-06-06-nbc_x.htm

McChesney, R.W. (1989). Media made sport: A history of sports coverage in the United States. In L.A. Wenner. (Ed.) *Media, sports and society* (pp. 49–69). Newbury Park, CA: Sage.

———. (2000). The political economy of communication and the future of the field. *Media, Culture, and Society*, 22, 109–116.

———. (2004). *The problem of the media: U.S. communication politics in the 21st century*. New York: Monthly Review Press.

———. (2008). *The political economy of media: Enduring issues, emerging dilemmas*. New York: Monthly Review Press.

McClatchy Company. (n.d.). *Daily newspapers*. Retrieved July 23, 2010, from www.mcclatchy.com/2006/06/09/354/daily.html

McCutcheon, J. (1975, December 25). Baseball faces the inevitable. *Chicago Tribune*, sec. 3, p. 2.

Meyers, J. (1976, February 25). Spring without baseball is . . . um . . . ah . . . unthinkable. *St. Louis Post-Dispatch*, sec. C, p. 2.

Murray, J. (1975, December 25). Ho-ho-ho! Santa leaves baseball holding bags. *Los Angeles Times*, p. 1.

Nielsen weekly sports ranking. (2004, February 16–22). *Street & Smith's SportsBusiness Journal*, 6, 42, 12.

Oakes, J.B. (1975, December 25). Don't kill the umpire. *New York Times*, p. 20.

Ourand, J. (2006, July 17). With deal, Turner steals OLN's buzz. *Sports Business Journal*. Retrieved July 27, 2010, from www.sportsbusinessjournal.com/article/51216

———. (2009, Nov. 9). Big deals, bigger questions: With margins shrinking, how can broadcasters remain in the game and keep buying sports rights? *Sports Business Journal*, 12(28), 1, 16–23.

Ourand, J., & Smith, M. (2010, April 26). NCAA's money-making matchup. *Sports Business Journal*. Retrieved July 27, 2010, from www.sportsbusinessjournal.com/article/65533

Pedersen, P.M., Miloch, K.S., & Laucella, P.C. (2007). *Strategic sport communication*. Champaign, IL: Human Kinetics.

Pitts, B.G., & Stotlar, D.K. (2007). *Fundamentals of sport marketing* (3rd ed.) Morgantown, WV: Fitness Information Technology.

PL and NL negotiations. (1890, October 18). *Sporting Life*, p. 1.

Rader, B.G. (1984). *In its own image: How television has transformed sports*. New York: Free Press.

———. (1999). *American sports: From the age of folk games to the age of televised sports* (4th ed.). Upper Saddle River, NJ: Prentice-Hall.

Recent television rights deals. (2004). *Street & Smith's SportsBusiness Journal*. Retrieved August 11, 2004, from www.sportsbusinessjournal.com/index.cfm?fuseaction=page.feature&featureId=974

Reeve, S. (2000). *One day in September*. New York: Arcade.

Rice, G. (1954). *The tumult and the shouting: My life in sport*. New York: Barnes.

Richter, F. (1889, November 13). The brotherhood's secession—its status and effects. *Sporting Life*, p. 4.

Roberts, R., & Olson, J.S. (1989). *Winning is the only thing: Sports in America since 1945*. Baltimore: Johns Hopkins University Press.

Sage, G.H. (1998). *Power and ideology in American sport: A critical perspective* (2nd ed.). Champaign, IL: Human Kinetics.

Samaranch, J.A. (1996). Introduction. In *The Olympic movement and the mass media* (pp. 9–10). Lausanne, Switzerland: Author.

Semiao, R. (2004, June 21). *The creation of the X Games*. Retrieved July 12, 2004, from www.espneventmedia.com/pr.php?p=942&e=554

Senn, A.E. (1999). *Power, politics and the Olympic Games*. Champaign, IL: Human Kinetics.

Seymour, H. (1989). *Baseball: The early years*. New York: Oxford University Press.

Shaw, D. (1975, February 7). Sports page: Look, ma, no decimal point. *Los Angeles Times*, sec. III, p. 1.

Smith, M., & Ourand, J. (2008, Nov. 24). How ESPN bid bowled over BCS. *Sports Business Journal*. Retrieved July 27, 2010, from www.sportsbusinessjournal.com/article/60652

Smith, R. (1975, December 24). Christmas spirit. *New York Times*, p. 16.

Smith, R.A. (1988). *Sports and freedom: The rise of big-time college athletics*. New York: Oxford University Press.

Solomon, W.S. (1997). The newspaper business. In A. Wells & E.A. Hakanen (Eds.), *Mass media and society* (pp. 71–83). Greenwich, CT: Ablex.

Spalding, A.G. (1911) *America's national game*. New York: American Sports.

Spence, J. (1988). *Up close and personal: The inside story of network television sports*. New York: Atheneum.

Spink, A.H. (1889, September 28). The labor situation. *Sporting News*, p. 4.

Stoldt, G.C., Dittmore, S.W., & Pedersen, P.M. (2011). Communication in the sport industry. In P.M. Pedersen, J.B. Parks, J. Quarterman, & L. Thibault (Eds.). *Contemporary sport management* (4th ed., pp. 270–289). Champaign, IL: Human Kinetics.

Stoldt, C., Pratt, C., & Jackson, J. (2003). Public relations in the sport industry. In J.B. Parks & J. Quarterman (Eds.), *Contemporary sport management* (2nd ed., pp. 211–230). Champaign, IL: Human Kinetics.

Stotlar, D. (2000). Vertical integration in sport. *Journal of Sport Management*, *14*, 1–7.

Surface, B. (1972). The shame of the sports beat. *Columbia Journalism Review*, *10*, 49.

Taaffe, W. (1986, July 21). Goodwill, but not a very good show. *Sports Illustrated*, *65*(3), 55.

Television households. (n.d.). *Television Bureau of Advertising*. Retrieved July 9, 2004, from www.tvb.org/rcentral/index.asp

The reasons for it. (1890, November 8). *Sporting News*, p. 4.

Thelin, J.R. (1996). *Games colleges play: Scandal and reform in intercollegiate athletics*. Baltimore: Johns Hopkins University Press.

Thomas, E.K., & Carpenter, B.H. (Eds.). (2001). *Mass media in 2025: Industries, organizations, people, and nations*. Westport, CT: Greenwood.

Tribune Company. (n.d.). *Tribune Company business units and websites*. Retrieved July 23, 2010, from www.tribune.com/about/webguide/index.html

TV Basics. (2004). *Top 50 sports telecasts of all time*. New York: Television Bureau of Advertising. Retrieved August 11, 2004, from www.tvb.org/nav/build_frameset.asp?url=/rcentral/index.asp

———. (n.d.a). *Alternate delivery systems (national)*. Retrieved August 18, 2004, from www.tvb.org/rcentral/mediatrendstrack/tvbasics/12_ADS-Natl.asp

———. (n.d.b). *Cable and VCR households*. Retrieved August 18, 2004, from www.tvb.org/rcentral/mediatrendstrack/tvbasics/04_Cable_and_VCR_HH.asp

Weiler, P.C., & Roberts, G.R. (1998). *Sports and the law: Text, cases, problems* (2nd ed.). St. Paul, MN: West Group.

Wenner, L.A. (1989). *Media, sports, & society*. Newbury Park, CA: Sage.

———. (1998). *MediaSport*. London: Routledge.

———. (2006). Sports and media through the super glass mirror: Placing blame, breast-beating and a gaze to the future. In A.A. Raney & J. Bryant (Eds.), *Handbook of sports and media* (pp. 45–60). Mahwah, NJ: Erlbaum.

Woodward, S. (2003, June 16–22). GE/NBC Games bid: Overwhelming force. *Street & Smith's SportsBusiness Journal*, *6*, 8, 1.

Zimbalist, A. (1994). *Baseball and billions: A probing look inside the big business of our national pastime*. New York: Basic.

Zulgad, J. (2010, February 8). Super Bowl most watched program ever. *Star Tribune*. Retrieved July 23, 2010, from www.startribune.com/sports/vikings/blogs/83806092.html

# Chapter 7

Arango, T. (2008, April 21). Tension over sports blogging. *New York Times*. Retrieved April 22, 2008 from http://www.nytimes.com/2008/04/21/business/media/21bloggers.html?_r=1&pagewanted=1&ei=5070&en=510354f4eecb5dfd&ex=1209441600&emc=eta1

Bozich, R. (2007, June 11). Courier-Journal reporter ejected from U of L game. *Louisville Courier-Journal*. Retrieved June 12, 2007 from http://www.courier-journal.com/apps/pbcs.dll/article?Date=20070611&Category=SPORTS02&ArtNo=706110450&SectionCat=&Template=printart

Condron, B. (2001). Media operations when hosting an event. In K. Neuendorf (Ed.), *Olympic public relations association handbook*. Colorado Springs, CO: Author.

Dittmore, S. (2006, July 31). Bloggers deserve entry to press box. *Sports Business Journal*, *9*(14), p. 21.

Dittmore, S.W., Crow, C.M., & Fields, T.E. (2010). *Property rights in the age of digital media: Exploring the legal and practical impacts of restricting content usage*. Abstract presented at the Fourth Summit on Communication and Sport, March 18–20, 2010, Cleveland, OH.

Dittmore, S.W., Stoldt, G.C., Bass, J.R., & Biery, L. (2009). *Media policies in the era of new media: An analysis of how sport organizations approach bloggers and blogging*. Abstract presented at the 2009 North American Society for Sport Management Conference, May 27–30, 2009, Columbia, SC.

Eaton, B. (2001). Dealing with the chuckles of your sport. In K. Neuendorf (Ed.), *Olympic public relations association handbook*. Colorado Springs, CO: Author.

Eisenberg, J. (2010, Aug. 17). *The new NYI blog box*. Retrieved December 16, 2010, from http://islanders.nhl.com/club/news.htm?id=536037

Fortunato, J. (2000, Winter). Public relations strategies for creating mass media content: A case study of the National Basketball Association. *Public Relations Review*, *26*(4), 481–497.

*From outside the press box: The identities, attitudes and values of sports bloggers*. (2009, July). John Curley Center for Sports Journalism at Penn State. State College, PA: Author.

*Gamecocks WR interviewed after Travolta*. (2004, September 30). Retrieved October 12, 2004, from http://sports.espn.go.com/ncf/news/story?id=1892507

Gant, S. (2007). *We're all journalists now: The transformation of the press and reshaping of the law in the internet age*. New York: Free Press.

Garmire, C. (2000). The Super Bowl III problem: A review of the development of the property right in live professional sports broadcasts and a practical application of copyright law to an infringement action for the unauthorized reproduction and distribution of a taped broadcast of Super Bowl III. *Chicago-Kent Journal of Intellectual Property, 2*(1). Retrieved from http://jip.kentlaw.edu/jip_archives.asp?vol=2&iss=1

Greene, H., Gulkis, N., & Levit, S. (2004). *Miami Dolphins 2004 media guide.* Miami, FL: Author.

Hall, A., Nichols, W., Moynahan, P., & Taylor, J. (2007). *Media relations in sport* (2nd ed.). Morgantown, WV: Fitness Information Technology.

Hardin, M., & Zhong, B. (2009, Aug. 24). Most bloggers aspire to higher standard. *Sports Business Journal, 12*(17), p. 32.

Harris, T.L. (1998). *Value-added public relations: The secret weapon of integrated marketing.* Lincolnwood, IL: NTC Business Books.

Helitzer, M. (1996). *The dream job: $port$ publicity, promotion and marketing* (2nd ed.). Athens, OH: University Sports Press.

Koppett, L. (2003). *The rise and fall of the press box.* Toronto, Ontario, Canada: Sport Classic.

LaPointe, J. (2007, June 14). Blogger's eject may mean suit for NCAA. *New York Times.* Retrieved June 15, 2007, from www.nytimes.com/2007/06/14/sports/baseball/14blogs.html?_r=2

*LeBron apologizes for behavior.* (2009, June 5). Retrieved December 16, 2010, from http://sports.espn.go.com/nba/playoffs/2009/news/story?id=4232264

Mathews, W. (2004, May–June). What should I tell them? Why every organization should have an official policy for communicating. *Communication World,* pp. 46–60.

Mickle, T. (2006, June 19). Should bloggers get a seat in the press box? *Sports Business Journal, 9*(8), p. 3.

Muret, D. (2009, Aug. 17). ACC turns to social media, student bloggers to promote title game. *Sports Business Journal, 9*(16), p. 5.

Ostrow, A. (2009, Aug. 17). *Social media banned from college stadiums.* Retrieved March 7, 2010, from http://mashable.com/2009/08/17/sec-new-media-policy/

Pedersen, P.M., Miloch, K.S., & Laucella, P.C. (2007). *Strategic sport communication.* Champaign, IL: Human Kinetics.

Pitts, B.G., & Stotlar, D.K. (2007). *Fundamentals of sport marketing* (3rd ed.) Morgantown, WV: Fitness Information Technology.

Rovell, D. (2002, August 12). *A little Heisman hype can go a long way.* Retrieved November 6, 2002, from http://sports.espn.go.com/espn/print?id=1416126&type=story

Rutgers University. (n.d.). *Press information.* Retrieved October 26, 2004, from www.scarletknights.com/football/pressbox/info.htm

Seymour, H. (1960). *Baseball: The early years.* New York: Oxford University Press.

Smith, R.D. (2005). *Strategic planning for public relations* (2nd ed.). Mahwah, NJ: Erlbaum.

Solis, B., & Breakenridge, D. (2009). *Putting the public back in public relations: How social media is reinventing the aging business of PR.* Upper Saddle River, NJ: Pearson Education.

StatCrew. (n.d.). *Customers.* Retrieved September 16, 2004, from www.statcrew.com/html/customers1.shtml

Stoldt, G.C., & Dittmore, S.W. (2003, May). *Competencies and priorities of college sports information directors: Analysis of a national survey.* Paper presented at the North American Society for Sport Management Conference, Ithaca, NY.

Stoldt, G.C., Miller, L.K., & Comfort, P.G. (2001). Through the eyes of athletics directors: Perceptions of sports information directors, and other public relations issues. *Sport Marketing Quarterly, 10,* 164–172.

Wilstein, S. (2002). *Associated Press sports writing handbook.* New York: McGraw-Hill.

# Chapter 8

*About USA Field Hockey.* (2010, March 12). Retrieved July 12, 2010, from www.usfieldhockey.com/usfha/index_new.php

Adobe Systems. (n.d.). *Adobe and PDF.* Retrieved July 12, 2010, from www.adobe.com/products/acrobat/adobepdf.html

Business Wire. (n.d.). *About us.* Retrieved July 12, 2010, from www.businesswire.com/portal/site/home/about/

Ciarallo, J. (2010, July 7). *Survey: 75% of journalists find "targeted" press releases useful.* Retrieved July 12, 2010, from www.mediabistro.com/prnewser/measurement/survey_75_of_journalists_find_targeted_press_releases_useful_166863.asp

Cremer, C.F., Keirstead, P.O., & Yoakam, R.D. (1996). *ENG television news.* New York: McGraw-Hill.

Davis, H.M. (1998). Media relations. In L.P. Masteralexis, C.A. Barr, & M.A. Hums (Eds.), *Principles and practice of sport management* (pp. 356–379). Gaithersburg, MD: Aspen.

*Deven Marrero's walkoff single gives #1 baseball 7-6 extra-inning victory over Arkansas.* (2010, June 12). Retrieved July 12, 2010, from http://thesundevils.cstv.com/sports/m-basebl/recaps/061310aaa.html

False Start for NFL? (2004, April 19–25) *Street & Smith's SportsBusiness Journal, 6,* 51, 10.

*Gamecocks win National Championship!* (2010, June 29). Retrieved July 12, 2010, from http://gamecocksonline.cstv.com/sports/m-basebl/recaps/063010aaa.html

*Gatorade's new G Series Pro line up now available at Dick's Sporting Goods.* (2010, June 1). Retrieved July 12, 2010, from www.prnewswire.com/news-releases/gatorades-new-g-series-pro-line-up-now-available-at-dicks-sporting-goods-95305444.html

Goldstein, N. (2000). *The Associated Press stylebook and briefing on media law*. Cambridge, MA: Perseus.

Grunig, J.E., & Hunt, T. (1984). *Managing public relations*. New York: Holt, Rinehart and Winston.

Hall, A., Nichols, W., Moynahan, P., & Taylor, J. (2007). *Media relations in sport* (2nd ed.). Morgantown, WV: Fitness Information Technology.

Helitzer, M. (1996). *The dream job: $port$ publicity, promotion and marketing* (2nd ed.). Athens, OH: University Sports Press.

*Hyperlocal news connects communities*. (2010). Retrieved July 12, 2010, from www.scribd.com/full/30302135?access_key=key-276d2agg20yjliq7qlcy

*Important facts about PR Newswire*. (n.d.). Retrieved July 12, 2010, from http://prnewswire.mediaroom.com/index.php?s=40

Lechner, T. (1996). Sports photography: A sight for more eyes. In M. Helitzer, *The dream job: $port$ publicity, promotion and marketing* (2nd ed.) (pp. 157–178). Athens, OH: University Sports Press.

Lorenz, A.L., & Vivian, J. (1996). *News reporting and writing*. Needham Heights, MA: Allyn and Bacon.

Migala, D. (2003, Jan. 20–26). Close but no Heisman: E-mail campaign's still a winning strategy. *Street & Smith's SportsBusiness Journal*. Retrieved October 8, 2004, from www.sportsbusinessjournal.com/index.cfm?fuseaction=search.show_article&articleId=27824&keyword=migala

*News distribution & targeting*. (n.d.). New York: Author. Retrieved April 15, 2004, from www.prnewswire.com

Newsom, D., & Carrell, B. (1991). *Public relations writing: Form & style* (3rd ed.). Belmont, CA: Wadsworth.

Paschal, D. (2009, July 21). *SEC media days event to be bigger than ever*. Retrieved August 27, 2010, from www.timesfreepress.com/news/2009/jul/21/sec-media-days-event-to-be-bigger-than-ever/

Porter, J. (2010, July 7). *The best day to send a press release*. Retrieved July 12, 2010, from http://blog.journalistics.com/2010/the-best-day-to-send-a-press-release/

*Razorbacks fall in opener to Arizona St*. (2010, June 13). Retrieved July 12, 2010, from www.arkansasrazorbacks.com/ViewArticle.dbml?SPSID=30667&SPID=2415&ATCLID=204958911&DB_OEM_ID=6100

Rosenthal, G. (2009, Oct. 26). *Larry Johnson continues Twitter meltdown*. Retrieved August 27, 2010, from http://profootballtalk.nbcsports.com/2009/10/26/larry-johnson-continues-twitter-meltdown/

Scott, D.M. (2009). *The new rules of marketing & PR: How to use news releases, blogs, podcasting, viral marketing & online media reach buyers directly*. Hoboken, NJ: Wiley.

*Shurna selected to compete for United States select team*. (2010, July 8). Retrieved July 12, 2010, from http://nusports.cstv.com/sports/m-baskbl/spec-rel/070810aac.html

Simon, R., & Zappala, J.M. (1996). *Public relations workbook: Writing & techniques*. Lincolnwood, IL: NTC Business Books.

Smith, R.D. (2005). *Strategic planning for public relations* (2nd ed.). Mahwah, NJ: Erlbaum.

Solis, B., & Breakenridge, D. (2009). *Putting the public back in public relations: How social media is reinventing the aging business of PR*. Upper Saddle River, NJ: Pearson Education.

*Texas Tech football team bans Twitter pages*. (2009, Sept. 28). Retrieved August 27, 2010, from http://nbcsports.msnbc.com/id/33059550/ns/sports-college_football/

*The state of the news media 2010: An annual report on American journalism*. (2010, March 15). Retrieved July 12, 2010, from www.stateofthemedia.org/2010/index.php

Thompson, W. (1996). *Targeting the message: A receiver-centered process for public relations writing*. White Plains, NY: Longman.

*Tim Lawson agrees to contract terms with D.C. United*. (2004, August 28). D.C. United. [News Release]. Washington, DC: Author.

Treadwell, D., & Treadwell, J.B. (2000). *Public relations writing: Principles in practice*. Needham Heights, MA: Allyn and Bacon.

*USA women ready for World Cup qualifier*. (2010, March 24). Retrieved July 12, 2010, from www.usfieldhockey.com/news/article.php?newsID=167

# Chapter 9

About Us > Media Kit (n.d.). Author. Retrieved Sept. 13, 2011 from http://www.ustream.tv/about/mediakit

Baus, H.M., & Lesly, P. (1998). Preparations for communicating. In P. Lesly (Ed.), *Lesly's handbook of public relations and communications*. Chicago: Contemporary.

*Bills introduce head coach Mike Mularkey*. (2004, January 15). Retrieved January 20, 2004, from www.buffalobills.com/news/index.cfm?cont_id=224442&dsp=press

Condron, B. (2001). The PR operation: Press conferences. In K. Neuendorf, (Ed.), *Olympic public relations association handbook*. Colorado Springs, CO: United States Olympic Committee.

Cremer, C.F., Keirstead, P.O., & Yoakam, R.D. (1996). *ENG television news* (3rd ed.). New York: McGraw-Hill.

Davis, H.M. (1998). Media relations. In L.P. Masteralexis, C.A. Barr, & M.A. Hums (Eds.), *Principles and practice of sport management* (pp. 356–379). Gaithersburg, MD: Aspen.

Fortunato, J.A. (2000, Winter). Public relations strategies for creating mass media content: A case study of the National Basketball Association. *Public Relations Review, 26*(4), 481–497.

Gaughan, M. (2004, January 16). Bills' new man has a plan. *Buffalo News*. Retrieved January 20, 2004, from www.buffalonews.com/editorial/20040116/pdf/1050956.pdf

Hall, A., Nichols, W., Moynahan, P., & Taylor, J. (2007). *Media relations in sport* (2nd ed.). Morgantown, WV: Fitness Information Technology.

Helitzer, M. (1996). *The dream job: $port$ publicity, promotion and marketing* (2nd ed.). Athens, OH: University Sports Press.

Hessert, K. (2000, June/July). Jousting with the press. *Athletic Management, 12*(4), 17.

———. (2002, February/March). Framing the facts. *Athletic Management, 14*(2), 24.

Irwin, R., Sutton, W., & McCarthy, L. (2002). *Sport promotion and sales management.* Champaign, IL: Human Kinetics.

———. (2008). *Sport promotion and sales management* (2nd ed.). Champaign, IL: Human Kinetics.

Kirby, A. (1995, September). *Media training for your athletes.* Presented at the meeting of the Olympic Public Relations Association in Colorado Springs, CO.

Lorenz, A.L., & Vivian, J. (1996). *News reporting and writing.* Needham Heights, MA: Allyn and Bacon.

McCarron, A. (2004, February 18). Wow! A-Rod is the Bronx beamer. *New York Daily News,* p. 56.

Miller, C., & Zang, F. (2001). Teleconference calls: Maximizing interview time. In K. Neuendorf (Ed.), *Olympic public relations association handbook.* Colorado Springs, CO: United States Olympic Committee.

Paschal, D. (2009, July 21). SEC media days event to be bigger than ever. Retrieved August 27, 2010, from www.timesfreepress.com/news/2009/jul/21/sec-media-days-event-to-be-bigger-than-ever/

Rosenthal, G. (2009, Oct. 26). *Larry Johnson continues Twitter meltdown.* Retrieved August 27, 2010, from http://profootballtalk.nbcsports.com/2009/10/26/larry-johnson-continues-twitter-meltdown/

Rowe, S., Alexander, N., Earl, R., & Esser, A. (2001, July). Media interview tips to make the most of your expertise. *Nutrition Today, 36,* 4.

Smith, R.D. (2005). *Strategic planning for public relations* (2nd ed.). Mahwah, NJ: Erlbaum.

*Texas Tech football team bans Twitter pages.* (2009, Sept. 28). Retrieved August 27, 2010, from http://nbcsports.msnbc.com/id/33059550/ns/sports-college_football/

Thompson, W. (1996). *Targeting the message: A receiver-centered process for public relations writing.* White Plains, NY: Longman.

Weisman, L. (2002, December 2). Image follows suit. *USA Today,* 1C.

Wilstein, S. (2002). *Associated Press sports writing handbook.* New York: McGraw-Hill.

# Chapter 10

ABC News. (2007, January 5). *Lacrosse player sues Duke professor who failed him in wake of scandal.* Retrieved September 18, 2009, from http://abclocal.go.com/ktrk/story?section=news/national_world&id=4907958

Allen, M.W., & Caillouet, R.H. (1994). Legitimate endeavors: Impression management strategies used by an organization in crisis. *Communication Monographs, 61,* 44–62.

Anderson, K., & Dohrmann, G. (2004, February 23). Out of control? *Sports Illustrated, 100,* 64–69.

Associated Press (AP). (2001, February 18). *Recent auto racing deaths.* Retrieved February 10, 2004, from http://espn.com/rpm/2001/0218/1093851.html

———. (2007, April 13). *Timeline of Duke lacrosse investigation.* Retrieved August 28, 2009 from http://nbcsports.msnbc.com/id/18041327//

BBC. (2008, April 10). Olympics to 'rebound from crisis.' *BBC News.* Retrieved July 30, 2009, from http://news.bbc.co.uk/2/hi/asia-pacific/7339959.stm

Beal, M. (2003, July). When things go wrong. *SportsTravel, 7,* 9.

Benoit, W.L. (1995). *Accounts, excuses, and apologies: A theory of image restoration.* Albany: State University of New York Press.

Bernstein, A. (2004a, September 20). Nike's new game plan for sweatshops. *Business Week.* Retrieved July 30, 2009, from www.businessweek.com/magazine/content/04_38/b3900011_mz001.htm

———. (2004b, February 23–29). League takes labor stance to Web site. *Street & Smith's SportsBusiness Journal, 6,* 6.

Bitsche, R.E., Jr. (1998, April). Memorializing America's tragedy: Community leaders unite to remember victims of Oklahoma bombing [Electronic version]. *Corrections Today, 60,* 148–149.

Bluffton University. (n.d.). *Bluffton University baseball team in accident in Georgia.* Retrieved August 3, 2009, from www.bluffton.edu/about/news/newsreleases.asp?show=030207_00

Brady, E. (2002, September 11). Continuity of sports helped ease the pain. *USA Today,* p. 1C.

———. (2007, July 24). Three major sports must deal with credibility crisis. *USA Today.* Retrieved July 30, 2009, from www.usatoday.com/sports/2007-07-24-sports-controversy_N.htm

Brazeal, L.M. (2008). The image repair strategies of Terrell Owens. *Public Relations Review, 34,* 145–150.

Brennan, C. (2011, April 11). Tiger Woods' charge fades as questions persist. *USA Today.* Retrieved May 20, 2011, from www.usatoday.com/sports/columnist/brennan/2011-04-10-tiger-woods-masters-charge-fade_N.htm

Broom, G. (2009). *Cutlip and Center's effective public relations* (10th ed.). Upper Saddle, NJ: Pearson.

Bruce, T., & Tini, T. (2008). Unique crisis response strategies in sports public relations: Rugby league and the case for diversion. *Public Relations Review, 34,* 108–115.

Busbee, J. (2010, April 5). *Tiger Woods turns in impressive performance in news conference.* Retrieved May 20, 2011, from http://sports.yahoo.com/golf/blog/

devil_ball_golf/post/Tiger-Woods-turns-in-impressive-performance-in-p?urn=golf-232143

Carter, D., & Rovell, D. (2003). *On the ball*. Upper Saddle River, NJ: Prentice Hall.

Castorino, S., & Minkoff, R. (1998, April). Crisis management: Does your department have a plan? *Athletic Administration, 33*, 17–18.

Clavio, G., Eagleman, A.N., Miloch, K.S., & Pedersen, P.M. (2007). Communicating in crisis. In J. James (Ed.), *Sport marketing across the spectrum: Research from emerging, developing, and established scholars* (pp. 15–27). Morgantown, WV: Fitness Information Technology.

Coakley, J.J. (2007). *Sports in society: Issues and controversies* (9th ed.). New York: McGraw-Hill.

Connaughton, D., Spengler, J.O., & Bennett, G. (2001). Crisis management for physical-activity program. *Journal of Physical Education, Recreation & Dance, 72*(7), 27–29.

Coombs, W.T. (2006). The protective powers of crisis response strategies: Managing reputational assets during a crisis. *Journal of Promotion Management, 12*, 241–259.

———. (2007a). *Crisis management and communications*. Gainesville, FL: Institute for Public Relations. Retrieved July 30, 2009, from www.instituteforpr.org/essential_knowledge/detail/crisis_management_and_communications/

———. (2007b). *Ongoing crisis communication* (2nd ed.). Los Angeles: Sage.

Davis, S.C., & Gilman, A.D. (2002). Communications coordination. *Risk Management, 49*(8), 38–44.

Dorn, M.S. (2004, August). Keys to survival: Crisis media relations. *College Planning & Management, 7*, 16.

Favorito, J. (2007). *Sports publicity: A practical approach*. Burlington, MA: Elsevier.

Fearn-Banks, K. (2007). *Crisis communications: A casebook approach* (3rd ed.). Mahwah, NJ: Erlbaum.

Forde, P. (2004, September 22). Teamwork the key during a crisis. Retrieved September 23, 2004, from http://sports.espn.go.com/ncf/columns/story?columnist=forde_pat&page=program/crisis

Grunig, L.A., Grunig, J.E., & Dozier, D.M. (2002). *Excellent PR and effective organizations*. Mahwah, NJ: Erlbaum.

Hadden, C., & Sattler, T.P. (2003, April). Solid business rules to follow before, during and after a crisis. *Fitness Management, 19*, 27.

Helitzer, M. (2000). *The dream job: $port$ publicity, promotion and marketing* (3rd ed.). Athens, OH: University Sports Press.

Hessert, K. (1998a). *The 1998 Hessert sports crisis survey*. Retrieved March 17, 1999, from www.sports.mediachallenge.com/crisis/0106.htm

———. (1998b, October/November). The management before the crisis. *Athletic Business, 10*, 22–24.

Hessert, K., & Gillette, C. (2002, October/November). Part of the game plan. *Athletic Business, 14*, 22–25.

Jensen, R., & Butler, B. (2007). Is sport becoming too commercialized? The Houston Astros' public relations crisis. *International Journal of Sports Marketing & Sponsorship, 9*(1), 23–32.

Katz, A. (2008, November 25). *Sampson receives NCAA's harshest penalty*. Retrieved July 30, 2009, from http://sports.espn.go.com/ncb/news/story?id=3725832

Koolbeck, T. (2003, January/February). Do you have a media plan when the cameras start rolling. *Facility Manager, 19*, 22–25.

Lee, J. (2003, June 23–29). Arizona brings in Atlanta's Inocon Group for crisis management plan. *Street & Smith's SportsBusiness Journal, 6*, 19.

Los Angeles Dodgers. (2009, May 7). *Statement from the Los Angeles Dodgers*. Retrieved August 5, 2009, from http://mlb.mlb.com/news/press_releases/press_release.jsp?ymd=20090507&content_id=4607172&vkey=pr_la&fext=.jsp&c_id=la

Matera, F.R., & Artigue, R.J. (2000). *PR campaigns and techniques: Building bridges into the 21st century*. Boston: Allyn and Bacon.

McGowan, A. (2001, September 24–30). Don't wait for crisis to write crisis plan. *Street & Smith's SportsBusiness Journal, 4*, 32.

Moberg, D. (1999, June 7). Bringing down Niketown: Consumers can help, but only unions and labor laws will end sweatshops [Electronic version]. *Nation, 268*, 15.

Mullen, L. (2004, January 12–18). Ex-Clinton aide brings political tactics to sports. *Street & Smith's SportsBusiness Journal, 6*, 24.

Muret, D. (2006, March 8–12). Staying on guard. *Street & Smith's SportsBusiness Journal, 8*, 19–25.

NYC rescue workers hold terrorism drill. (2004, March 15). *USA Today*, p. 3A.

Pines, W.L. (2000). Myths of crisis management. *PR Quarterly, 45*(3), 15–17.

Poole, M. (1999, September 20–26). Draft your emergency plan before bad news hits. *Street & Smith's SportsBusiness Journal, 2*, 11.

———. (2001, March 5). Tragedy brings NASCAR to safety-question crossroads. *Street & Smith's SportsBusiness Journal, 3*, 13.

Public Relations Society of America (PRSA). (2000). Tips and techniques: Crisis planning and management. *PPC Online*. Retrieved October 4, 2000, from www.prsa.org/ppc/68001.html

Q&A: The interview—Gail Brown. (2001, November/December). *SportsTravel, 5*, 22–23.

Samansky, A.W. (2002). Run!: That's not the crisis communications plan you need. *PR Quarterly, 47*(3), 25–27.

Sanderson, J. (2008). "How do you prove a negative?" Roger Clemens's image-repair strategies in response to the Mitchell Report. *International Journal of Sport Communication, 1*, 246–262.

Sports Media Challenge. (1997). *Crisis barometer*. Retrieved March 17, 1999, from www.sports.media.challenge.com/crisis/0106.htm

Stoldt, G.C., Miller, L.K., Ayres, T.D., & Comfort, P.G. (2000). Crisis management planning: A necessity for sport managers. *International Journal of Sport Management*, 1, 253–266.

Stoldt, G.C., Miller, L.K., & Comfort, P.G. (2001). Through the eyes of athletic directors: Perceptions of sports information directors, and other PR issues. *Sport Marketing Quarterly*, 10(3), 164–172.

Tips and techniques: Crisis planning and management. (2000). *PPC Online*. Retrieved October 4, 2000 from http://www.prsa.org/ppc/68001.html.

Ulrich, L. (2008, August/September). Turning the corner. *Athletic Management, XX*(5), 32–41.

Wichita State University. (2009, February). *Emergency management plan*. Wichita, KS: Author.

Williams, J. (2000). PR. In H. Appenzeller & G. Lewis (Eds.), *Successful sport management* (2nd ed.). Durham, NC: Carolina Academic Press.

Wilson, D., & Holusha, J. (2007, June 15). Duke prosecutor says he will resign. *New York Times*. Retrieved September 2, 2011 from http://www.nytimes.com/2007/06/15/us/15cnd-duke.html

Wilson, S., & Patterson, B. (1987, November). When the news hits the fan. *Business Marketing*, 72, 92–94.

Yaeger, D., & Henry, J. (2009, July 2). *Institutional reputation management*. Paper presented at the College Sports Information Directors of America Convention, Tampa, FL.

Yaeger, D., & Pressler, M. (2007). *It's not about the truth: The untold story of the Duke lacrosse case and the lives it shattered*. New York: Threshold.

## Chapter 11

Baus, H.M., & Lesly, P. (1998). Direct communications methods. In P. Lesly (Ed.), *Lesly's handbook of public relations and communications* (5th ed., pp. 457–474). Chicago: NTC Business Books.

Cherner, R., & Weir, T. (2009, March). *What's the greatest sports speech ever?* Retrieved November 6, 2009, from http://blogs.usatoday.com/gameon/2009/03/whats-the-gre-1.html

Cincinnati Reds. (n.d.) *Reds winter caravan*. Retrieved December 9, 2009, from http://cincinnati.reds.mlb.com/cin/fan_forum/caravan.jsp

Cuocci, A. (2006, November 10). Hosting events that drive membership sales. *Club Industry's Fitness Business Pro*. Retrieved December 11, 2009, from http://clubindustry.com/stepbystep/sales/driving-club-membership-sales/

Eisenmann, M., & Paine, K.D. (2007, February). *Measuring the effectiveness of speakers programs*. Gainesville, FL: Institute for Public Relations. Retrieved December 28, 2009, from www.instituteforpr.org/research_single/measuring_the_effectiveness_of_speakers_programs/

Fawkes, J. (2008). Public relations and communications. In A. Theaker (Ed.), *The public relations handbook* (3rd ed., pp. 18–32). New York: Routledge.

Hartman Arena. (2009, March 26). *Hartman Arena open house a smashing success*. Retrieved December 11, 2009, from www.hartmanarena.com/news/article28.html

Hawkins, J. (2001, May). Sign of the times: Autographs are becoming more trouble than they're worth. *Golf Digest*, 52, 73.

Helitzer, M. (2002). *The dream job: $port$ publicity, promotion and marketing* (3rd ed.). Athens, OH: University Sports Press.

Henry, R.A., Jr. (1995). *Marketing public relations*. Ames, IA: Iowa State University Press.

Hessert, K. (1998). *The coach's communication playbook*. Charlotte, NC: Sports Media Challenge.

Horine, L., & Stotlar, D. (2004). *Administration of physical education and sport programs* (5th ed.). New York: McGraw-Hill.

Irwin, R.L., Sutton, W.A., & McCarthy, L.M. (2008). *Sport promotion and sales management* (2nd ed.). Champaign, IL: Human Kinetics.

Jackowski, M. (2001, October). Telling advice: Effective public relations is vital to successful public-private partnerships. *Athletic Business*, 25, 42–45.

Jefkins, F. (1993). *Planned press and public relations* (3rd ed.). Glasgow: Blackie Academic & Professional.

Mehrabian, A. (1972). *Nonverbal communication*. Chicago: Aldine-Atherton.

Miller, L.K., Stoldt, G.C., & Comfort, P.G. (2005). Careers in sport management. In S. Hoffman (Ed.), *Introduction to kinesiology: Studying physical activity* (2nd ed., pp. 523–550). Champaign, IL: Human Kinetics

Morones, S. (2004, Spring). Exclusive autograph deals: What value to the athlete and their fans? *Entertainment and Sports Lawyer*, 22(1), 10.

Mullin, B.J., Hardy, S., & Sutton, W.A. (2007). *Sport marketing* (3rd ed.). Champaign, IL: Human Kinetics.

On the road. (August/September, 2008). *Athletic Management, XX*(5), 46.

Read, D. (1999, October/November). Weekend warriors: Hartford High School. *Athletic Management*, 11(6), 24.

Reilly, R. (1999, April 5). The signature moment in sports. *Sports Illustrated*, 90, 120.

Schoenfeld, B. (2007, July 23–29). Getting athletes to give back. *Street & Smith's SportsBusiness Journal*, 50–52.

Seven secrets of open-house success. (2001, April). *Curriculum Review, 40*, 10.

Stoldt, G.C., Pratt, C., & Dittmore, S.W. (2007). Public relations in the sport industry. In J.B. Parks, J. Quarterman, & L. Thibault (Eds.), *Contemporary sport management* (3rd ed., pp. 243–265). Champaign, IL: Human Kinetics.

Sutton, W.A., McDonald, M.A., Milne, G.R., & Cimperman, J. (1997). Creating and fostering fan identification in professional sports. *Sport Marketing Quarterly, 6*(1), 15–22.

To the class of 2010. (2010, June 28). *Street & Smith's SportsBusiness Journal.* Retrieved September 9, 2011 from http://www.sportsbusinessdaily.com/Journal/Issues/2010/06/20100628/Pomp-And-Circumstance-On-Campus/To-The-Class-Of-2010.aspx?hl=%22to%20the%20class%20of%202010%22&sc=0

Ulrich, L. (2009, February/March). In the neighborhood. *Athletic Management, XXI* (2), 28–35.

Upper Deck Company. (n.d.). *Signed memorabilia: Guaranteed authentic.* Retrieved November 27, 2009, from http://sports.upperdeck.com/memorabilia/authenticity.aspx

W Business Speakers. (n.d.). *Celebrity and sports speakers.* Retrieved November 6, 2009, from www.wbusinessspeakers.com/category/Celebrity+and+Sports

Wertheim, J. (2001, December 24–31). Losing their grip. *Sports Illustrated, 97,* 41–45.

Williams, P. (2007, April 16–22). Draft parties keep teams connected. *Street & Smith's SportsBusiness Journal,* 15.

# Chapter 12

Athletes for Hope. (n.d.). *Our mission.* Retrieved January 15, 2010, from www.athletesforhope.org/miandpu.html

Atlanta Braves. (n.d.). *Community.* Retrieved January 15, 2010, from http://atlanta.braves.mlb.com/atl/community/calendar_2009.jsp

Babiak, K. (2009). *The role and relevance of corporate social responsibility: A view from the top.* Manuscript submitted for publication.

Babiak, K., & Trendafilova, S. (in press). Corporate social responsibility in professional sport: Motives to be "green." In P. Rodriguez, S. Kesenne, & J. Garcia (Eds.). *Social responsibility and sustainability in sports.* Oviedo, Spain: Oviedo University Press.

Babiak, K., & Wolfe, R. (2006). More than just a game? Corporate social responsibility and Super Bowl XL. *Sport Marketing Quarterly, 15,* 214–222.

———. (2009). Determinants of corporate social responsibility in professional sport: Internal and external factors. *Journal of Sport Management, 23,* 717–742.

Barclay, E. (2009, May 20). *A greener playing field. National Geographic: Green guide for everyday living.* Retrieved January 30, 2010, from www.thegreenguide.com/travel-transportation/green-sports-stadiums

Berkhouse, J., & Gabert, T. (1999, June). *Community relations within Major League Baseball, National Basketball Association, National Football League, and the National Hockey League.* Paper presented at the meeting of the North American Society for Sport Management, Vancouver, British Columbia, Canada.

Bloom, P.N., Hoeffler, S., Keller, K.L., & Basurto Meza, C.E. (2006). How social cause marketing affects consumer perceptions. *MIT Sloan Management Review, 47* (2), 49–55.

Bollinger, R. (2009, January 18). *Garciaparra, Hamm go to head-to-head.* Retrieved January 15, 2010, from http://web.mlsnet.com/news/mls_news.jsp?ymd=20090118&content_id=212902&vkey=news_mls&fext=.jsp

Bradish, C.L, & Cronin, J.J. (2009). Corporate social responsibility in sport. *Journal of Sport Management, 23,* 691–697.

Brayley, R.E., & McLean, D.D. (2001). *Managing financial resources in sport and leisure service organizations.* Champaign, IL: Sagamore.

Breitbarth, T., & Harris, P. (2008). The role of corporate social responsibility in the football business: Towards the development of a conceptual model. *European Sport Management Quarterly, 8,* 179–206.

Coler, E. (2011, February 2). Employee volunteer opportunities can bring extra job satisfaction. *The Business Monthly.* Retrieved September 9, 2011 from http://www.bizmonthly.com/employee-volunteer-opportunities-can-bring-extra-job-satisfaction/

Cone Inc. (2006). *The 2006 Cone Millennial cause study: The Millennial generation: Pro-social and empowered to change the world.* Retrieved March 5, 2010, from www.coneinc.com/stuff/contentmgr/files/0/b45715685e62ca5c-6ceb3e5a09f25bba/files/2006_cone_millennial_cause_study_executive_summary.pdf

Cordova, T. (2006, May 22–28). Teams can build fan base by building a healthy community. *Street & Smith's SportsBusiness Journal,* 17.

Dahlsrud, A. (2008). How corporate social responsibility is defined: An analysis of 37 definitions. *Corporate Social Responsibility and Environmental Management, 15,* 1–13.

Dean, D.H. (2002). Associating the corporation with a charitable event through sponsorship: Measuring the effects on corporate community relations. *Journal of Advertising, 31*(4), 77–87.

Denver Broncos. (n.d). *Denver Broncos cheerleaders appearances.* Retrieved January 15, 2010, from www.denverbroncos.com/page.php?id=301

Elmore, L. (2002, November 18–24). Sport philanthropy can reach far, wide. *Street & Smith's SportsBusiness Journal, 5,* 25.

Francis, Z. (2003, May 12). Local high school student gives the gift of baseball. *Tri-Valley Herald,* Local, p. 4.

Freitag, A.R. (2008). Staking claim: Public relations leaders needed to shape CSR policy. *Public Relations Quarterly, 52,* 37–40.

Garrett, A. (2001, January). Get on with your community. *Management Today.* Retrieved September 10, 2003, from http://web2.infotrac.galegroup.com/itw/infomark/763/173/40057188w2/purl=rc1_EAIM_0_A69441814&dyn=6!xrn_2_0_A69441814?sw_aep=ksstate_wichita

Genzale, J. (2006, October 16–22). Change the world. *Street & Smith's SportsBusiness Journal*, 34–35.

Giannoulakis, C. (2008, November 10-16). How to make green and cool coexist. *Sports Business Journal*, 34.

Giving Back Fund. (n.d.). *The Giving Back Fund: Integrity and innovation in philanthropy*. Retrieved January 15, 2010, from www.givingback.org/brochure/index.html

Godfrey, P.C. (2009). Corporate social responsibility in sport: An overview and key issues. *Journal of Sport Management*, 23, 698–716.

Grey Cup. (n.d.). *CFL green drive*. Retrieved September 9, 2011 from http://greycup.cfl.ca/page/greendrive

Heath, R.L., & Ni, L. (2009). *Corporate social responsibility: Three R's*. Gainesville, FL:

In-depth: Sports gives back. (2009, September 14–20). *Street & Smith's SportsBusiness Journal*, 13–20.

Institute for Public Relations. Retrieved July 20, 2009, from www.instituteforpr.org/essential_knowledge/detail/corporate_social_responsibility_three_rs/

Internal Revenue Service (IRS). (2009, July 24). *Public charities*. Retrieved January 15, 2010, from www.irs.gov/charities/charitable/article/0,,id=137894,00.html

Irwin, R.L., Sutton, W.A., & McCarthy, L.M. (2008). *Sport promotion and sales management* (2nd ed.). Champaign, IL: Human Kinetics.

Jackowski, M. (2000, October 2–8). Repair, rebuild relationships with your community. *Street & Smith's Sports-Business Journal*, 3, 40–41.

Johnson, G. (2007, June 1). *CSR: The view from the field*. Paper presented at the North American Society for Sport Management Conference, Ft. Lauderdale, FL.

Kansas City Ambassadors. (n.d.). *About us*. Retrieved January 15, 2010, from www.kcambassadors.com/docs/about.asp

Kim, S-Y., & Reber, B.H. (2008). Public relations' place in corporate social responsibility: Practitioners define their role. *Public Relations Review*, 34, 337–342.

King, B. (2008, November 10–16). Finding growth in green. *Street & Smith's SportsBusiness Journal*, 16–23.

Lance Armstrong Foundation. (n.d.). *About us: Financial information*. Retrieved January 7, 2010, from www.livestrong.org/site/c.khLXK1PxHmF/b.2662367/k.5D4A/Financial_Information.htm

Larson, E. (2000, January). The Alaska Club. *Fitness Management*, 16, 45, 49.

Liberman, N. (2003, May 12–18). Bank sponsorship takes turn. *Street & Smith's SportsBusiness Journal*, 6, 6.

Major League Baseball (MLB). (n.d.). *History of RBI presented by KPMG*. Retrieved January 28, 2010, from http://mlb.mlb.com/mlb/official_info/community/rbi_history.jsp

Margolis, J.D., & Walsh, J.P. (2003). Misery loves company: Rethinking social initiatives by business. *Administrative Science Quarterly*, 48(2), 268–289.

National Hockey League. (2010, February 1). *February designated as Hockey is for Everyone Month*. Retrieved from www.nhl.com/ice/news.htm?id=515853

Nike. (2005). *Corporate responsibility report*. Beaverton OR: Author. Retrieved January 7, 2010, from www.nikebiz.com/responsibility/documents/Nike_FY04_CR_report.pdf

Pollick, M. (2007, May 28-June 3). With right approach, Athletes for Hope has much to contribute. *Street & Smith's SportsBusiness Journal*. Retrieved September 9, 2011 from http://www.sportsbusinessdaily.com/Journal/Issues/2007/05/20070528/Opinion.aspx

———. (2008a, October 16–22). Charities offer many opportunities for athletes to give back. *Street & Smith's SportsBusiness Journal*, 15.

———. (2008b, April 7–13). With teamwork much can be accomplished in charitable world. *Street & Smith's SportsBusiness Journal*, 13.

———. (2008c, September 1–7). Charity must complement not diminish an athlete's reputation. *Street & Smith's SportsBusiness Journal*, 15.

———. (2009, December 7–13). Charitable giving shares holiday spirit, improves tax status. *Street & Smith's SportsBusiness Journal*, 18.

Popke, M. (2001, January). Community service. *Athletic Business*, 25, 26–28.

———. (2008, September). Carbon copy. *Athletic Business*, 32, 22–23.

Rethinking the social responsibility of business: A Reason debate featuring Milton Friedman, Whole Foods' John Mackey, and Cypress Semiconductor's T.J. Rodgers. (1995, October). *Reason*. Retrieved January 7, 2010, from http://reason.com/archives/2005/10/01/rethinking-the-social-responsi

Right to Play. (n.d.). *At a glance*. Retrieved March 5, 2010, from www.righttoplay.com/International/about-us/Pages/AtAGlanceCon%27t.aspx

Robert Wood Johnson Foundation. (n.d.) *The Steve Patterson Award of Excellence in Sports Philanthropy*. Retrieved September 9, 2011, from http://www.rwjf.org/patterson/

Rollins, K.J. (2003). *Successful fundraising activities within the National Hockey League*. Unpublished manuscript.

Sheth, H., & Babiak, K.M. (2010). Beyond the game: Perceptions and practices of corporate social responsibility in the professional sport industry. *Journal of Business Ethics*, 91, 433–450.

Siler, R., Semerad, T., & Lewis, M.C. (2008, December 26). NBA player charities often a losing game. *Salt Lake Tribune*. Retrieved September 9, 2011 from http://www.sltrib.com/ci_11314692

Smith, A., & Westerbeek, H. (2007). Sport as a vehicle for deploying corporate social responsibility. *Journal of Corporate Citizenship*, 25, 43–54.

Snow, J. (2009, September 21–27). Green marketing requires caution. *Street & Smith's SportsBusiness Journal*, 19.

Southall, R.M., Nagel, M.S., & LeGrande, D.J. (2005). Build it and they will come? The Women's United Soccer Association: A collision of exchange theory and strategic philanthropy. *Sport Marketing Quarterly*, 14, 158–167.

Sports Philanthropy Project. (2009a, September 9). *Red Sox to receive national philanthropy award*. Retrieved January 15, 2010, from www.sportsphilanthropyproject.com/assets/library/654_pattersonredsoxfinalrelea.pdf

———. (2009b, August 24). *Cincinnati Bengals Marvin Lewis becomes first coach to receive national philanthropy award*. Retrieved January 7, 2010, from www.sportsphilanthropyproject.com/assets/library/651_pattersonawardrelease2009.pdf

———. (2010). *About SPP*. Retrieved January 7, 2010, from www.sportsphilanthropyproject.com/about/index.php

Steinbach, P. (2008, April). Environmental education. *Athletic Business*, 32(4), 39–40.

Sutton, W.A., & McDonald, M.A. (2001, April/May). A triple play. *Athletic Management*, XIII, 18.

Tampa Bay Lightning. (2010, January 14). *Gameday events—Lightning vs. Panthers*. Retrieved March 5, 2010, from http://lightning.nhl.com/club/news.htm?id=513573

Texas Rangers. (n.d.). *Rangers events*. Retrieved January 28, 2010, from http://texas.rangers.mlb.com/tex/community/rangers_events.jsp

Turnkey Sports Poll. (2008, November 10–16). *Street & Smith's SportsBusiness Journal*, 19.

———. (2009, September 21–27). *Street & Smith's SportsBusiness Journal*, 19.

UCLA Spirit Squad. (n.d.). *UCLA Spirit Squad appearance request*. Retrieved January 15, 2010, from www.spirit.ucla.edu/appearance_request/home.aspx

Ulrich, L. (2009). In the neighborhood. *Athletic Management*, XXI(2), 28–35.

United States Golf Association (USGA). (2009, December 14). Water works. *Sports Illustrated*. Promotional insert.

United States Green Building Council (USGBC). (2010). *Intro—what LEED is*. Retrieved January 28, 2010, from www.usgbc.org/DisplayPage.aspx?CMSPageID=1988

United States Tennis Association (USTA). (n.d.). *The Big Serve: About us*. Retrieved January 28, 2010, from http://thebigserve.usta.com/about/

United Way. (n.d.). *Partnership history*. Retrieved January 15, 2010, from www.liveunited.org/nfl/partnership.php

Walker, M., & Kent, A. (2009). Do fans care? Assessing the influence of corporate social responsibility on consumer attitudes in the sport industry. *Journal of Sport Management*, 23, 743–769.

Weiss, R. (2008, November 10–16). Sports is growing green, and you can read about it—and feel it—in these pages. *Street & Smith's SportsBusiness Journal*, 16.

Welford, R., Chan, C., & Man, M. (2007). Priorities for corporate social responsibility: A survey of businesses and their stakeholders. *Corporate Social Responsibility and Environmental Management*, 15, 52–62.

Wolff, A. (2007, July 5). Going, going green. *Sports Illustrated*. Retrieved June 30, 2008, from http://sportsillustrated.cnn.com/2007/writers/alexander_wolff/07/07/eco0312/3.html

Women's National Basketball Association (WNBA) (n.d.a). *San Antonio Silver Stars: Reaching out to make a difference*. Retrieved January 15, 2010, from www.wnba.com/silverstars/community/making_a_difference.html

———. (n.d.b). *Seattle Storm: Auction donation requests*. Retrieved January 15, 2010, from www.wnba.com/storm/community/auction_donation.html

———. (n.d.c). *Indiana Pacers: Be YOUnique Fund of the Pacers Foundation*. Retrieved January 15, 2010, from www.wnba.com/fever/community/community_beyouniquefund.html

———. (2009, August 17). *Liberty to team with Kay Yow/WBCA Cancer Fund for breast health awareness night, presented by the Hallmark Channel*. Retrieved January 15, 2010, from www.wnba.com/liberty/news/bha_night_090817.html

Won, D., & Park, M. (2003, May). *A proposed conceptual framework for cause-related marketing in sports*. Paper presented at the meeting of the North American Society for Sport Management, Ithaca, NY.

# Chapter 13

Acosta Hernandez, R. (2002). *Managing sport organizations*. Champaign, IL: Human Kinetics.

Argenti, P.A., Howell, R.A., & Beck, K.A. (2005). The strategic communication imperative. *MIT Sloan Management Review*, 48(3), 82–89.

Associated Press (AP). (2005, February 16). *Lockout over salary cap shuts down NHL*. Retrieved September 9, 2005, from http://espn.com/nhl/news/story?id=1992793

Atkins, C. (2003, June). We're listening; but nobody's talking: A corporate communications executive calls on today's leaders to lead. *Financial Executive*, 19, 62.

Barrett, D.J. (2008). *Leadership communication* (2nd ed.). Boston: McGraw-Hill Irwin.

Bobo, C. (2000). Gaining support for a strategic emphasis on employee communications. *Tactics*, 7(2), 18.

Bridges, S., Marcum, W., & Kline Harrison, J. (2003). The relation between employee perceptions of stakeholder balance and corporate financial performance. *SAM Advanced Management Journal*, 68(2), 50–56.

Broom, G. (2009). *Cutlip and Center's effective public relations* (10th ed.). Upper Saddle, NJ: Pearson.

Brunswick Group. (2009). *Brunswick Group releases survey findings on new media usage by investment com-*

*munity.* San Francisco: Author. Retrieved October 15, 2009, from http://niri.org/findinfo/Social-Media/Survey-Findings-on-New-Media-Usage-by-Investment-Commmunity.aspx

Carron, A.V., Hausenblas, H.A., and Eys, M.A. (2005). *Group dynamics in sport* (3rd ed.). Morgantown, WV: Fitness Information Technology.

Carter, D., & Rovell, D. (2003). *On the ball.* Upper Saddle River, NJ: Prentice Hall.

Center, A., & Jackson, P. (1995). *Public relations practices* (5th ed.). Englewood Cliffs, NJ: Longman.

Coates, D., & Humphreys, B.R. (2001). The economic consequences of professional sports strikes and lockouts. *Southern Economic Journal, 67*(3), 737–747.

Conger, M. (2004, January–February). How a comprehensive IR program pays off. *Financial Executive, 20,* 30–34.

Council of Public Relations Firms. (2008, May 21). Is internal communications the new media relations? *Firm Voice.* Retrieved July 23, 2009, from www.thefirmvoice.com/ME2/Audiences/dirmod.asp?sid=&nm=T…33970092570045D722&tier=4&id=5FF05B9439B54DCBAE684DF210E01611

Cunningham, G.B. (2007). *Diversity in sport organizations.* Scottsdale, AZ: Holcomb Hathaway.

Cunningham, G.B., & Singer, J.N. (2009). *Diversity in athletics: An assessment of exemplars and institutional best practices.* Indianapolis, IN: National Collegiate Athletic Association.

Cuskelly, G., Hoye, R., & Auld, C. (2006). *Working with volunteers in sport.* London: Routledge.

Doherty, A.J., & Danylchuk, K.E. (1996). Transformational and transactional leadership in interuniversity athletics management. *Journal of Sport Management, 10,* 292–309.

Dozier, D.M., Grunig, L.A., & Grunig, J.E. (1995). *Manager's guide to excellence in public relations and communication management.* Hillsdale, NJ: Erlbaum.

Female Athletic Media Relations Executives (FAME). (2001). *FAME: Supporting women in our profession.* Syracuse, NY: Author.

Gardenswartz, L., & Rowe, A. (2009). The effective management of cultural diversity. In M. A. Moodian (Ed.), *Contemporary leadership and intercultural competence: Exploring the cross-cultural dynamics within organizations* (pp. 35–43). Los Angeles, CA: Sage Publications, Inc.

Grunig, J.E. (1992). Symmetrical systems of internal communication. In J.E. Grunig (Ed.), *Excellence in public relations and communication management* (pp. 531–575). Hillsdale, NJ: Erlbaum.

Guiniven, J. (2000). Suggestion boxes and town hall meetings: Fix 'em or forget 'em. *Public Relations Tactics, 7*(2), 22.

Hampson, R. (2001, April 25). Women dominate PR—is that good? *USA Today,* p. 6B.

Haverbeck, M.J. (2006). FAME and women in sport publicity. In G.C. Stoldt, S.W. Dittmore, & S.E. Branvold (Eds.), *Sport public relations: Managing organizational communication* (pp. 248–249). Champaign, IL: Human Kinetics.

Kalafut, P.C. (2003, July–August). Communicate value to boost investor confidence. *Financial Executive, 19,* 19–20.

King, P. (February 22, 2009). Lewis a Cowboy? Cassell a Chief? Previewing free agency. *Sports Illustrated.* Retrieved February 23, 2009, from http://sportsillustrated.cnn.com/2009/writers/peter_king/02/22/mmqb/3.html

Lapchick, R. (2004). *2004 racial and gender report card.* Orlando, FL: University of Central Florida, Institute for Diversity and Ethics in Sports.

Lapchick, R., Little, E., Lerner, C., & Mathew, R. (2009). *2008 racial and gender report card: College Sport.* Orlando, FL: University of Central Florida, Institute for Diversity and Ethics in Sports.

Laskin, A.V. (2006). *The value of investor relations: A Delphi panel investigation.* Gainesville, FL: Institute for Public Relations. Retrieved October 9, 2009, from www.instituteforpr.org/research_single/value_of_investor_relations/

Lussier, R.N., & Kimball, D. (2009). *Applied sport management skills.* Champaign, IL: Human Kinetics.

Major League Baseball (MLB). (n.d.). *MLB executives.* Retrieved September 18, 2009, from www.mlb.com/mlb/official_info/about_mlb/executives.jsp?bio=manfred_rob

Marshall, J., & Heffes, E.M. (2004, May). Investor relations: Conference call, Web usage grows. *Financial Executive, 20,* 10.

McRae, M.B. & Short, E.L. (2010). *Racial and cultural dynamics in group and organizational life: Crossing boundaries.* Los Angeles, CA: Sage Publications.

Miller, E. (1998). Investor relations. In P. Lesly (Ed.), *Lesly's handbook of public relations and communications* (pp. 161–206). Lincolnwood, IL: NTC Business Books.

Miller, L.K. (1997). *Sport business management.* Gaithersburg, MD: Aspen.

Mogel, L. (2002). *Making it in public relations* (2nd ed.). Mahwah, NJ: Erlbaum.

Mullen, L. (2006, February 13–19). Forstmann addresses worries. *Street & Smith's SportsBusiness Journal,* 5.

———. (2009, August 17–23). Deal or no deal? *Street & Smith's SportsBusiness Journal,* 1, 28–29.

National Investor Relations Institute (NIRI). (2009a). *About us.* Retrieved October 9, 2009, from www.niri.org/FunctionalMenu/About.aspx

———. (2009b). *Membership requirements.* Retrieved October 9, 2009, from www.niri.org/joinniri/MemberJoin.aspx

———. (2009c). *Member benefits.* Retrieved October 9, 2009, from www.niri.org/joinniri/ReviewBenefits.aspx

———. (2009d). *Member profile.* Retrieved October 9, 2009, from www.niri.org/joinniri/memprofilecfm.aspx

Parker, P.S. (2005). *Race, gender, and leadership.* Mahwah, NJ: Lawrence Erlbaum.

Peng, H. (2000). *Competencies of sport event managers in the United States.* Doctoral dissertation, University of Northern Colorado.

Smith, H.J. (2003). The shareholders vs. stakeholders debate. *MIT Sloan Management Review, 44*(4), 85–90.

Spoelstra, J. (2001). *Marketing outrageously.* Marietta, GA: Bard Press.

Sriramesh, K., Grunig, J.E., & Buffington, J. (1992). Corporate culture and public relations. In J.E. Grunig (Ed.), *Excellence in public relations and communication management* (pp. 577–598). Hillsdale, NJ: Erlbaum.

Staudohar, P.D. (1996). *Playing for dollars.* Ithaca, NY: Cornell University.

———. (1999, April). Labor relations in basketball: The lockout of 1998–99. *Monthly Labor Review, 122,* 3–9.

Stoldt, G.C., Miller, L.K., & Comfort, P.G. (2003). The status of women working in NCAA Division I-A sports information departments. *National Association of Girls and Women in Sport Online Journal.* Retrieved from www.aahperd.org/nagws/template.cfm?template=articles.html

Taylor, T., Doherty, A., & McGraw, P. (2008). *Managing people in sport organizations: A strategic human resource management perspective.* Burlington, MA: Butterworth-Heinemann.

Todd, S. (2003, May). *Towards a framework for examining distinct job attitudes in the job industry.* Paper presented at the meeting of the North American Society for Sport Management, Ithaca, NY.

Treadwell, D., & Treadwell, J.B. (2005). *Public relations writing: Principles in practice* (2nd ed.). Thousand Oaks, CA: Sage.

United States Securities and Exchange Commission. (2008). *Annual report.* Retrieved October 15, 2009, from www.sec.gov/answers/annrep.htm

———. (2009). Form 10-K. Retrieved October 15, 2009, from www.sec.gov/answers/form10k.htm

Xing, X., & Chalip, L. (2009). Marching in the glory: Experiences and meaning when working in a sport mega-event. *Journal of Sport Management, 23,* 210–237.

# Chapter 14

Associated Press. (2011a). *NFL commissioner takes message straight to fans.* Retrieved May 18, 2011, from sportsillustrated.cnn.com/2011/football/nfl/05/16/commissioner.roger.goodell.fans.ap/index.html

———. (2011b). *Helmet bill stokes lobbying effort.* Retrieved May 16, 2011, from www.bostonherald.com

Basch, M. (2002). *Customer culture.* Upper Saddle River, NJ: Prentice Hall.

Blackshaw, P. (2008). *Satisfied customers tell 3 friends, angry customers tell 3000.* New York: Doubleday.

Blattberg, R., Getz, G., & Thomas, J. (2001). *Customer equity.* Boston: Harvard Business School Press.

Burnett, K. (1992). *Relationship fundraising.* London: White Lion Press.

Frommer, F. (2010, February 3). *The influence game: Fearing a lockout, NFL players ramp up lobbying effort.* ABC News/ESPN Sports. Retrieved May 24, 2010, from abcnews.go.com/Sports/wireStory?id=9738278

Fulks, D. (2009). *2004–2008 revenues and expenses of Division I intercollegiate athletics program report.* Indianapolis, IN: National Collegiate Athletic Association.

Fullerton, G. (2003, May). When does commitment lead to loyalty? *Journal of Service Research, 5*(4), 333–344.

Gaffney, T. (1996). Advanced techniques of donor recognition. *Journal of Nonprofit and Voluntary Sector Marketing, 1*(1), 41–49.

Gruber, W., & Hoewing, R. (1980). The new management in corporate public affairs. *Public Affairs Review, 1,* 13–23.

Grunig, J., & Hunt, T. (1984). *Managing public relations.* New York: CBS College.

Gulko, L. (2003, November). Managing member relationships. *Fitness Management,* 30–32.

Heath, R. (Ed.). (2001). *Handbook of public relations.* Thousand Oaks, CA: Sage.

Holyoke, T. (2003, September). Choosing battlegrounds: Interest group lobbying across multiple venues. *Political Research Quarterly, 56*(3), 325–336.

Kotler, P. (2000). *Marketing management: Analysis planning, implementation, and control* (10th ed.). Englewood Cliffs, NJ: Prentice-Hall.

Leahy, S. (2010, September 1). HD TV and technology pit NFL stadiums vs. fans' living rooms. *USA Today.*

Lesly, P. (Ed.). (1998). *Lesly's handbook of public relations and communications.* Chicago: NTC/Contemporary.

McAlexander, J., Kim, S., & Roberts, S. (2003, Fall). Loyalty: The influences of satisfaction and brand community integration. *Journal of Marketing Theory and Practice, 11*(4), 1–11.

McKenna, R. (2002). *Total access.* Boston: Harvard Business School Press.

Myers, J. (1999). *Measuring customer satisfaction.* Chicago: American Marketing Association.

National Collegiate Athletic Association (NCAA). (2004). *Government relations.* Retrieved November 1, 2004, from www1.ncaa.org/eprise/main/Public/hr/about.html

Nicholls, J., Gilbert, G., & Roslow, S. (1998). Parsimonious measurement of customer satisfaction with personal service and the service setting. *Journal of Consumer Marketing, 15*(3), 239–253.

Raab, D. (2010). Marketing infrastructure for a customer-driven world; marketers must adjust to changing expectations and communication challenges. *Information Management, 20*(1), 36.

Reichheld, F. (1996). *The loyalty effect.* Boston: Bain & Company.

Rosenbaum, M., Ostrom, A., & Kuntze, R. (2005). Loyalty programs and a sense of community. *Journal of Services Marketing, 19*(4), 222–234.

Rubio, J., & Laughlin, P. (2002). *Planting flowers, pulling weeds.* New York: Wiley.

Rust, R.T., Zeithaml, V.A., & Lemon, K.N. (2000). *Driving customer equity.* New York: Free Press.

SaferPak. (2004). *Customer loyalty: How to measure it, understand it and use it to drive business success. The leadership factor.* Retrieved October 23, 2004, from www.saferpak. com/csm_sat_loyal.htm

Sargeant, A. (2001, Winter). Relationship fundraising: How to keep donors loyal. *Nonprofit Management & Leadership, 12*(2), 177–192.

Schad, J. (2011, January 26). *UConn donor unhappy with AD.* ESPN.com news services.

Stier, W. (1994). *Successful sport fund-raising.* Dubuque, IA: Brown.

Stier, W., & Schneider, R. (1999, June/Sept). Fundraising: An essential competency for the sport manager in the 21st century. *Mid-Atlantic Journal of Business, 35*(2/3), 93–104.

Strom, S. (2010, July 12). YMCA is downsizing to a single letter. *New York Times,* p. A10.

Sweeney, D. (2008). *An integrated model of value equity in spectator sports: Conceptual framework and empirical results.* Doctoral dissertation, Florida State University.

Swift, R. (2001). *Accelerating customer relationships.* Upper Saddle River, NJ: Prentice Hall.

The customer is king: Understanding and measuring customer loyalty. (2003, April). *Materials Management and Distribution, 48*(3), 82.

Timm, P. (2001). *Customer service* (2nd ed.). Upper Saddle River, NJ: Prentice-Hall.

Verner, M., Hecht, J., & Fansler, A. (1998). Validating an instrument to assess the motivation of athletics donors. *Journal of Sport Management, 12*(2), 123–137.

Weinstein, A. (2002). Customer retention: A usage segmentation and customer valuation method. *Journal of Targeting, Measurement and Analysis for Marketing, 10*(3), 259–268.

Weir, L., & Hibbert, S. (2000, April). Building donor relationships: An investigation into the use of relationship and database marketing by charity fundraisers. *Service Industries Journal, 20*(2), 114–132.

Wyner, G. (1996, Summer). Customer valuation: Linking behavior and economics. *Marketing Research, 8*(2), 36–39.

Yoshida, M., & James, J. (2010). Customer satisfaction with game and service experiences: antecedents and consequences. *Journal of Sport Management, 24*(3), 338.

## Chapter 15

Associated Press. (2010). *Legal fees revealed for NCAA probe.* Retrieved June 21, 2011, from http://sports.espn. go.com/ncf/news/story?id=5025440

Bell, R., Ratzlaff, S.E., & Murray, S.R. (n.d.). *The impact of the HIPAA privacy rule on collegiate sport professionals.* Retrieved June 20, 2011, from www.thesportjournal. org/article/impact-hipaa-privacy-rule-collegiate-sport-professionals

Blanton, T. (2006). *Freedom of information at 40.* Retrieved June 20, 2011, from www.gwu.edu/~nsarchiv/ NSAEBB/NSAEBB194/index.htm

Brown, S. (2009). *The need for H.R. 4364.* Retrieved June 20, 2011, from www.anti-slapp.org/?q=node/71

Cardtoons v. Major League Baseball Players Association, 95 F.3d 959 (10th Cir. 1996).

C.B.C. Distribution and Marketing, Inc. v. Major League Baseball Advanced Media, 505 F.3d 818 (8th Cir. 2007).

Coleman, R. (2011). *About that SLAPP thing.* Retrieved June 20, 2011, from www.likelihoodofconfusion.com/ about-that-slapp-thing/

Copyright.gov. (n.d.). *Copyright law of the United States of America and related laws contained in Title 17 of the United States code.* Retrieved June 20, 2011, from www.copy-right.gov/title17/92preface.html

Curtis Publishing Co. v. Butts, 388 U.S. 130 (1967).

Department of Health and Human Services. (2009). *The Genetic Information Nondiscrimination Act of 2008.* Retrieved June 20, 2011, from www.genome.gov/Pages/ PolicyEthics/GeneticDiscrimination/GINAInfoDoc.pdf

Department of Justice. (2002). *Nevada cybercrime task force nets hacker.* Retrieved June 20, 2011, from www.justice. gov/criminal/cybercrime/sanduskyPlea.htm

———. (n.d.). *Department of Justice guide to the Freedom of Information Act.* Retrieved June 20, 2011, from www. justice.gov/oip/foia_guide09/introduction.pdf

Gertz v. Robert Welch, 418 U.S. 323 (1974).

Gionfriddo v. Major League Baseball, 114 Cal.Rptr.2d 307 (2001).

Halgreen, L. (2004). *European sports law—A comparative analysis of the European and American models of sport.* Copenhagen, Denmark: Forlaget Thomson.

Indianapolis Colts v. Metropolitan Baltimore Football Club, 34 F.3d 410 (7th Cir. 1994).

International News Service v. Associated Press, 248 U.S. 215 (1918).

International Trademark Association. (2008). *Adverse inference for failure to conduct likelihood of confusion survey.* Retrieved March 10, 2009, from www.inta.org/index. php?option=com_content&task=view&id=1920&Item id=153&getcontent=3

Kaburakis, A. (2008). International comparative sport law—The US and EU systems of sport governance: Commercialized v. socio-cultural model—competition and labor law. *International Sports Law Journal, 3*(4), 108–127.

Kaburakis, A., & McKelvey, S. (2009). Facenda Jr. vs. NFL Films, Inc.: "Voice of God" case settled after third circuit ruling. *Sport Marketing Quarterly, 18*(2), 107–111.

Kaburakis, A., Pierce, D., Fleming, O., Clavio, G., Lawrence, H., & Dziuba, D. (2009). "It's in the likeness." NCAA Student-Athletes' Rights of Publicity, EA Sports, and the video-game industry. The *Keller* forecast. *Entertainment and Sports Lawyer, 27*(2), 1–39.

Kline, J. (2009). *Anti-SLAPP statutes in the US by state*. Retrieved June 20, 2011, from www.legal-project.org/149/anti-slapp-statutes-in-the-us-by-state

Kling, S.L. (2005). *Missouri's new anti-SLAPP law*. Retrieved June 20, 2011, from www.mobar.org/e9b8133e-9ebe-4c38-809b-fc3cffde6e58.aspx

Magliocca, G. (2009). *Misappropriation and William Randolph Hearst*. Retrieved June 20, 2011, from www.concurringopinions.com/archives/2009/09/misappropriation-and-william-randolph-hearst.html

McDonald, G. (2001). *State sunshine laws under attack*. Retrieved June 20, 2011, from www.stateline.org/live/ViewPage.action?siteNodeId=136&languageId=1&contentId=14356

Missouri Attorney General. (n.d.). *Summary of Missouri sunshine law*. Retrieved June 20, 2011, from http://ago.mo.gov/sunshinelaw/sunshinelaw.htm

Monster Communications v. TBS, 935 F. Supp. 490 (S.D. N.Y. 1996).

Montana v. San Jose Mercury News, 24 Cal. App. 4th 790 (1995). NCAA v. Associated Press et al. (Fla. 1st DCA, October 1, 2009).

New York Times Co. v. Sullivan, 376 U.S. 254 (1964).

Pring, G.W., & Canan, P. (1996). *SLAPPs: Getting sued for speaking out*. Philadelphia: Temple University Press.

Schrimpf, A. (2009). *Florida court orders NCAA to hand over records*. Retrieved June 20, 2011, from www.rcfp.org/newsitems/index.php?i=11051

Seltzer, D.S. (2009). *More on sentencing for online crimes from a Miami cyber crime criminal defense lawyer*. Retrieved June 20, 2011, from www.cybercrimelawyerblog.com/2009/04/

Society of Professional Journalists. (n.d.). *A uniform act limiting strategic litigation against public participation: Getting it passed*. Retrieved June 20, 2011, from www.spj.org/antislapp.asp

U.S. Department of Education. (n.d.a). *Family educational rights and privacy act (FERPA)*. Retrieved June 20, 2011, from www2.ed.gov/policy/gen/guid/fpco/ferpa/index.html

———. (n.d.b). *Legislative history of major FERPA provisions*. Retrieved June 20, 2011, from www2.ed.gov/policy/gen/guid/fpco/ferpa/leg-history.html

Warford v. Lexington Herald, 789 S.W.2d 758 (1990).

White v. Samsung Electronics America, 989 F.2d 1512 (9th Cir. 1993).

Wilson v. The Daily Gazette Company, 588 S.E.2d 197 (2003).

Zacchini v. Scripps Howard Broadcasting, 433 U.S. 562 (1977).

# index

*Note:* The italicized *f* and *t* following page numbers refer to figures and tables, respectively.

Photo courtesy of Ryan Stoldt.

**G. Clayton Stoldt, EdD,** is a professor and chair of sport management at Wichita State University in Kansas. He has taught and conducted research in sport public relations since 1998. He was a college sport information director for 10 years and currently maintains involvement in sport public relations practice through media service roles such as television time-out coordinator and statistician for televised games.

In addition to the first edition of *Sport Public Relations*, Stoldt has published six book chapters and 37 articles in academic and professional publications, and he has made several presentations on the subject of sport public relations at various academic and professional conferences. His work as a sport information director has also been recognized in various state and national competitions. Stoldt is a member of the North American Society for Sport Management (NASSM) and the College Sports Information Directors of America.

Stoldt enjoys spending time with his family and friends, attending sporting events, and reading.

Photo courtesy of University of Arkansas.

**Stephen W. Dittmore, PhD,** is assistant professor of recreation and sport management at the University of Arkansas in Fayetteville. He also teaches a course in sport media and public relations for Instituto de Empresa in Madrid, Spain.

Dittmore worked for 10 years in sport public relations for the Olympic movement in both the 1996 and 2002 Olympic Games as director for the Salt Lake Olympic Organizing Committee, coordinator for the Atlanta Committee for the Olympic Games, and public relations manager for USA Wrestling. He is on the editorial board for the *International Journal of Sport Communication* and is a member of the College Sport Research Institute, North American Society for Sport Management (NASSM), Sport Marketing Association, and Sport and Recreation Law Association. In 2011, he was recognized with the Rising Star Award at the University of Arkansas.

Dittmore enjoys traveling with his wife and family and playing sports with his son.

**Scott E. Branvold, EdD,** is a professor of sport management at Robert Morris University. He has over 20 years of teaching experience in the sport management field and practical experience in sports information and event management. Branvold earned his doctorate in education from the University of Utah. He is the faculty athletics representative at Robert Morris University. He has contributed chapters to two books on sport management, written articles for sport marketing and management journals, and given numerous presentations on topics related to the sports industry.

Photo courtesy of Robert Morris University.